S0-DTD-708

Financial
Markets
and
Institutions

Financial Markets and Institutions

Robert D. Auerbach

MACMILLAN PUBLISHING CO., INC.
NEW YORK

Collier Macmillan Publishers
London

Copyright © 1983, Macmillan Publishing Co., Inc.

Printed in the United States of America

All rights reserved. No part of this book may be reproduced or transmitted in any form or by any means, electronic or mechanical, including photocopying, recording, or any information storage and retrieval system, without permission in writing from the Publisher.

Macmillan Publishing Co., Inc.
866 Third Avenue, New York, New York 10022

Collier Macmillan Canada, Inc.

Library of Congress Cataloging in Publication Data

Auerbach, Robert D.
    Financial markets and institutions.

    Includes bibliographical references and index.
    1. Finance. 2. Financial institutions. I. Title.
HG173.A97 1983   332   82-14891
ISBN 0-02-304610-4

Printing: 2 3 4 5 6 7 8 Year: 3 4 5 6 7 8 9 0

ISBN   0-02-304610-4

In Appreciation

A number of people have assisted me whenever I asked. They include Grasty Crews II, Lewis Gasper, David Meiselman, Kevin Quinn, Chip Price, Jack Rutner, and Robert Weintraub. I benefited greatly from the extensive and excellent suggestions of Morgan J. Lynge (University of Illinois), Hugh McLaughlin (Indiana University), and Richard Zock (University of Houston). I am indebted to Charles M. Place, Jr., who originally suggested that I write this book.

This book also benefited from my experience from 1976 to 1981 as an economic adviser to former Chairman Henry S. Reuss and Chairman Fernand St Germain of the Banking Committee of the U.S. House of Representatives. My understanding of economic policymaking was enriched by the knowledge shared with me by the chairmen and the excellent staff of the Banking Committee, which included Lewis Gasper (again), Robert Feinberg, Jake Lewis, Paul Nelson, Peggie Rayhawk, David Secrest, Robert Weintraub (again), and Gregory Wilson. I also benefited from the conversations and work done with Beryl Sprinkel, Undersecretary for Monetary Affairs of the U.S. Treasury when I served on his staff during the first year of the Reagan administration.

I have also drawn material from some of the individuals under whom I trained: Milton Friedman, Arnold Harberger,

Harry Johnson, Abba Lerner, Lloyd Metzler, Harry V. Roberts, Lester Telser, and Henri Theil (who served on my dissertation committee).

I also wish to thank Hurd Hutchins, production supervisor at Macmillan.

Anna Gessner gave valuable editorial help and supervised the production of the manuscript on a word processor. Michelle Campbell and David Weisblat assisted in the preparation of questions and the index. Carole Palmisani and June Copeland assisted with the typing. My wife Linda was very helpful and together with Donald and Katie made the writing of this book a most enjoyable task.

R.D.A.

Contents

Part II   Loanable Funds and the Rate of Interest

Part V   Financial Intermediaries

Part VI   Financial Markets

Part VII   Government and Financial Markets

Part VIII   Forecasting

1

An Overview

Claims to the present and future income in the nation are traded in financial markets. These claims are called financial assets. They include stocks and bonds. The New York Stock Exchange and the over-the-counter market are familiar names to many people in the United States as well as in countries throughout the free world. On evening television news programs in the United States millions of viewers hear and see the change in the Dow Jones industrial average and the number of shares traded. Whatever their level of understanding, they are faced with these data as well as the prime rate and the Treasury bill rate. Charismatic announcers with dramatic emphasis place great importance on these numbers. Thousands of individuals, actively or intermittently, trade in financial markets. For them, many more aspects of the financial markets may be familiar. Selling short, the options market, and buying a straddle may all be as commonplace as ordering lunch.

Financial asset prices, expected future income, and *interest rates* are all related and vital variables that both influence and are affected by aggregate and individual economic activity. It is in every adults' interest, both for planning his or her economic activities and for understanding the economic conditions with which they live, to know about these variables. Financial asset prices and interest rates are determined largely in financial markets. Financial markets, in turn, bring together and reflect underlying conditions in the economy as they serve to allocate funds in a modern developed economy.

Given all the attention and the importance of financial markets, it might be expected that financial markets are well understood. This is simply not so. Few people are well versed in the functions financial markets perform for the society, the fundamental determinants of the prices on financial markets, or even the important characteristics of the items traded.

There is, instead of a rational understanding of financial markets, a homespun folklore. It is filled with stories of instant millionaires who followed simple, but heretofore purportedly secret techniques. There are imagined conspirators with sorcerers' powers to control financial markets. The conspiratorial theories are occasionally nourished by a relevant episode, which is taken as confirmation for the generality. Gloom, doom, and collapse forecasts, which frequently involve financial markets in which the prices of financial assets are supposed to plummet, are popular versions of the folklore. It is, of course, true that very bad events will occur sometime in the future—sometime from now to infinity. The essential piece of information that is usually lacking or incorrect in the gloom, doom, and collapse folklore is the date.

Graft, corruption, and fraud are found in many parts of the economy. Organized crime has made inroads into sectors of the U.S. economy which have severely threatened free enterprise. Financial markets are not without their share of the blame; their record is certainly not unblemished. However, one of the great virtues of fairly competitive and efficient (terms to be discussed in Chapter 3) financial markets is that they are very difficult to manipulate. Large purchases of stock, block trades by the largest investors, amounting to billions of dollars, may have little effect on the price of the stock traded after an hour on a modern financial market. In fact, the information that such a trade will take place may cause an adjustment in prices beforehand. At the time the trade occurs it is impossible to identify microscopic irregularities even with very sophisticated statistical techniques such as spectral analysis (discussed in Part VIII).

Financial markets have been plagued at times by failure to deliver securities that have been sold. Fraudulent stock and bond certificates, phoney corporations built on paper empires with few or no assets, and the provision of deliberately false information either in a firm's published report or from advisors who profit from buying or selling stock or bonds issued by the firm are all on the record. "Speculative bubbles," sudden huge increases in the price of an item sold in a financial market, induced by little more new information than that the price is rapidly rising, rarely occur. Yet the few such incidents that do occur are spectacular enough to capture the attention of some writers, who then seek to describe financial markets largely in terms of such events.

An example that brought forth allegations of illegal activities and manipulation of trading rules occurred in 1980 in the futures market for silver, where contracts to buy and sell silver in the future are traded. The state of the argument is evidenced by the following media story.

SILVER DEALERS, MARKETS, SUED BY INVESTORS

By Jerry Knight, Washington Post Staff Writer

A group of silver investors filed a $194 million lawsuit yesterday accusing the two big silver markets and major silver dealers of fraud, conspiracy, violating antitrust laws and manipulating the price of the metal when silver prices collapsed two years ago.

The lawsuit was filed in U.S. District Court in New York by 184 members of Free Market Compensation, a Boston-based organization that contends silver market insiders conspired to drive down silver prices in the spring of 1980.

Defendants in the case are the Commodity Exchange Inc. (Comex) of New York and the Comex Clearing Association, the Chicago Board of Trade and its clearing association and five silver dealers—Englehardt [sic] Minerals and Chemicals, Mocotta Metals Corp., Ametalco Inc., Sharps-Pixley Inc. and J. Aron & Co. and one of its affiliates.

The lawsuit is the third legal action filed in the past week charging that federal laws were violated during the dramatic rise and fall of silver prices in 1979 and 1980. A Minnesota investor, David Bishop, sued Comex earlier this week.

Last Friday, a Lichtenstein corporation, Wall Street Establishments, filed an $8 million lawsuit accusing Texas billionaires Nelson Bunker Hunt and W. Herbert Hunt, the Comex and the Chicago Board of Trade of rigging silver prices.

The lawsuits are being filed now to meet a two-year statute of limitations. It was two years ago today that Comex ordered a change in its rules that prohibited new buyers from coming into the silver futures market and forced those already in to sell some holdings.

The price of silver hit a record $50 an ounce on Jan. 21, 1980, then plunged steadily until it bottomed out at $10.85 on March 28, wiping out billions of dollars of paper profits for silver speculators, including the Hunts.

The Comex claimed the change in rules was necessary because the Hunts and a few other speculators had acquired vast numbers of silver futures contracts and were artificially inflating the price.

The Hunts, on the other hand, repeatedly have accused silver market insiders of changing the rules of the game and forcing prices down to further their own interests.

The Hunt brothers are not among the 184 silver investors who filed the $194 million lawsuit yesterday, but the plaintiffs—like the Hunts—all held silver futures contracts at the time the market collapsed. Brian Walsh, president of Free Market Compensation, insists his group is not a front for the Hunts.

The lawsuit repeats arguments made by the Hunts and utilizes a costly study financed by the Hunts that alleges the silver dealers and Comex directors stood to lose $2 billion unless prices went down.

The lawsuit accuses the silver market insiders of violating the Sherman Antitrust Act and the Commodity Exchange Act as well as "common law fraud, conspiracy to manipulate and fix prices, restrain trade and defraud" investors.

The lawsuit seeks $48 million in damages, asks that amount be tripled under antitrust laws and asks $50 million punitive damages.

Changes in silver trading rules on Jan. 7 and Jan. 21, 1980 caused prices to collapse, the petition contends, and permitted "the members of the Comex and its board of governors to reap tremendous profits."

The rules changes were voted by the Comex board, which included representatives of the big metal dealers. The dealers involved did not vote on the rules change and therefore have insisted there was no conflict of interest by the board.

But Walsh's group contends the board was protecting its own members, even if they did not vote on the particular rule change, and even Comex board members who were not in the silver market had a conflict of interest because of their membership in the Comex Clearing Association. The Clearing Association is a separate but related corporation that handles the paperwork.

Contributing to this story was special correspondent John Kennedy.[1]

It should be noted that the price of silver has fluctuated between $7 and $15 an ounce in 1981 and 1982; so it does not appear that the demand and supply of silver justified a long-run silver price of $50 an ounce. It is incorrect to generalize from examples of alleged graft, corruption, and fraud in financial markets that such activities explain the operations of financial markets. Bad apples do not characterize the market for food. Even if bad apples were abundant, they would not prevent the forces behind the demand and supply of apples from converging on equilibrium prices in a manner described by conventional theory. In support of this view, modern statistical tests used by financial market analysts have failed to uncover evidence of continuing manipulation of the prices of items traded in the formal U.S. financial markets. Surveillance is maintained by the Securities and Exchange Commission, a federal government agency, and by personnel employed by some of the markets. Competition is probably the best force preventing the manipulation of prices.

The stories of simple techniques to become rich by trading in financial markets, together with testimonials from those who have drunk the potion and cured their poverty, can usually be found in general bookstores in the section labeled "Business."

These trade books are entirely different from textbooks, which are confined in sale almost entirely to college bookstores, in part because of their lower markup. The instant millionaire books, plus the gloom, doom, and collapse books, strike the public fancy. They promote daydreaming, a projection of frustration on evil conspirators, and require little in the way of mental strain. They are the type of business trade book that sells so well that they sometimes find a position on the best-seller list. Some of these books explain financial markets in terms of generalizations based on anecdotal tidbits of the following variety. A stock was rapidly rising in price. A savvy, affluent trader immediately sold a large block of the stock. "Why did you do this?" he or she is asked. The answer, "If such a large sale doesn't stop the rally, I will know it's not a false start and buy into it."

The anecdote is not wrong. However, such anecdotal stories can lead to unsupported general conclusions and trading techniques that are not profitable. Worst of all, when combined with other anecdotal stories, unconnected by a testable body of theory, they add fuel to incorrect conspiratorial conclusions. These views sometimes hold price changes on financial markets to be contrived by a handful of large traders. Financial markets are, in these views, little more than rigged crap games.

This way of thinking about financial markets is not a benign conclusion of those who follow these trade book exposés. It carries over into government policies. Attempts to intervene in or control financial markets to achieve a social objective often create disorder and fail to meet the intended objective. For example, the intervention in the secondary mortgage market, in part to build up housing in the central cities, diverted funds instead to middle-class suburbs. This intervention consisted of the sponsorship of government and quasi-government entities that borrowed large amounts of funds and then bought residential mortgages in the wholesale mortgage market. (This subject is explained in Chapter 22.) An example of direct control can be found in the financial markets called futures markets. Attempts to make these markets more orderly by placing daily limits on price changes in these markets may well produce greater fluctuations—as well as unfair advantages for some traders—by preventing the markets from achieving equilibrium prices. Attempts to prevent loans from being made for unproductive purposes—which one congressman said were as clearly identified as pornographic pictures—result in costly red tape with little or no evidence of any social benefit.

Not all government intervention in financial markets is misguided nor does it always produce other than the intended result. There is a place for laws that protect against fraud and deception, such as the issuance of worthless securities. Appropriate government efforts to provide a better coordinated nationwide stock information network, and any other efforts to make the markets more competitive and efficient, can be beneficial to the society. Intervention by the government in the financial markets that fails to produce a desired result, such as aid to the cities, does not make that aid undesirable. That is another issue, the selection of the proper targets for policy. Given an appropriate target, policies for government intervention in financial markets should, before being adopted, be subjected to what is known in the fields of study of financial markets.

The purpose of this book is to present a rational view of financial markets based on the immense amount of knowledge that has been gathered on this subject in the fields of finance and economics. Every attempt has been made to be accurate and faithful to the subject matter while making it as simple and interesting as possible.

The book begins with a discussion of the characteristics of financial assets and financial markets. Financial assets include stocks, bonds, and money. Then some important related concepts are described: wealth, income, interest rates, and the flow of funds. Finally, the arithmetic of interest rates is discussed. The reader should have a hand calculator of the type described at the beginning of Chapter 5.

In Part II, a discussion of the demand for and supply of money is followed by a broader view of the demand for and supply of loanable funds. These subjects focus on the determinants of the level of *observed market rates of interest*. The determinants of the basic *real rate of interest*—which is an important part of the observed market rate of interest—are presented in the last chapter of this part of the book.

In Part III, a description of the determinants of the different rates of interest on bonds with different maturities is given. This subject is called "the term structure of interest rates."

Then in Part IV, the general principles for selecting a portfolio of assets are presented. The discussion centers around the risks and the rate of return or yield from individual assets and from the entire portfolio of assets held by an individual or corporation.

Part V presents the important subject of financial intermediaries—firms that buy, sell, and create financial assets. This is followed in Part VI by a further and more complete description of financial markets than was presented in Part I. The role of the government in financial markets is presented in Part VII. Part VIII contains a discussion of statistical forecasting methods. The final part of the book turns to international financial markets. Besides the conventional subjects, such as exchange rates and the balance of payments, special attention is given to the important Eurodollar market and to activities in international financial markets that tie interest rates in different countries to exchange rates.

Each chapter contains study questions for review. In addition, Chapter 5, "The Arithmetic of Interest Rates," contains practice problems and answers throughout the chapter. A glossary of the terms used is given at the end of the book.

NOTE

1. *The Washington Post* (January 21, 1982), pp. G1, G2.

Part I

Some Basics

2

Financial Assets

Introduction

Stocks, bonds, notes, bills, and even money are all *financial assets*. Financial assets are claims against present and future income. They are the assets traded in *financial markets*. They are sometimes distinguished from other assets, such as buildings and machinery, by the material of which they are made. Financial assets are usually made of materials with negligible alternative value. They may be pieces of paper or even a blip in a computer's memory bank.

The material of which they are made has no relation to the powerful, even pervasive, influence of the quantity, price, and yield of financial assets. Changes in the quantity of some financial assets, such as money, are a policy tool that the government uses to influence the general level of prices of goods and services throughout the economy, the nation's real output, and the rates of interest in the economy. In an advanced society, other financial assets, such as stocks and bonds, are the primary vehicles for storing and transferring wealth. Financial assets are, of course, the goods traded in financial markets, the subject of this book.

A basic understanding of what financial assets are is necessary before moving on to the theory, policy applications, structure of financial markets, and more detailed descriptions of particular types of financial assets.

Financial assets can be defined as claims against present or future income from another (or more than one) participant in the economy. The claim may be in a formal agreement in proper legal form, in which case it is called a *financial instrument*. The definition, by itself, is not very revealing. First, to describe financial assets more fully, the discussion compares the general characteristics of nonfinancial assets with those of financial assets. Then a classification of financial assets is presented. The remainder of the chapter defines and describes the most common form of financial assets listed in this classification.

Nonfinancial Wealth and Financial Assets

Wealth, assets, or capital can all be defined as part of the *stock* of economic goods at a point in time. An economic good is a good with a market price greater than zero.

Wealth can be divided into two parts: *financial* and *nonfinancial*. Nonfinancial wealth can be further divided into two parts: physical wealth and human capital.

Physical wealth consists of such things as factories, hotels, sidewalks, lampshades, and grocery carts. There are stocks of shoes, onions, potatoes, and rhubarb. All of these items have a value related to their physical form. In general, the more of them (or the larger they are) and the better condition they are in, the more valuable they are.

Human capital, on the other hand, is the present value of the future labor services embedded in the population. Three general characteristics of nonfinancial wealth will help to distinguish nonfinancial wealth from financial wealth.

1. The value of nonfinancial wealth is directly related to its physical form. This characteristic is least applicable to human capital, because it stretches the meaning of physical form to include intelligence, training, and, within wide latitudes, general health.
2. The transportation costs of moving physical wealth and the storage costs of holding physical wealth are substantial, relative to the value of the asset.
3. The income that flows from physical wealth is a direct addition to the national income of the society.

The first two characteristics are fairly straightforward. The third characteristic is based on the idea that goods and services add to individuals' welfare according to the value these individuals place on them. The total value of all the goods and services produced in a year in an economy is called the *value of the economy's national income*.

Consider the income from a truck that is rented out in a market where all costs and benefits are reflected in market prices. The rentals per year are a direct addition to national income. They are a measure of the value of the truck's services to individuals renting the truck.

The three general characteristics of financial assets that differentiate them from nonfinancial assets are:

Know this

1. The size and physical condition of a financial asset is not related to its value or to the services derived from it. For example, a $1 million debt instrument can be on a smaller, less attractive piece of paper than a $1000 debt instrument.
2. The cost of moving financial assets and the cost of storing them is negligible compared to the value of the financial asset.
3. The income from a financial asset is not a direct addition to national income.

These characteristics stand in sharp contrast to the three characteristics that describe nonfinancial assets. The third characteristic is illustrated with an example comparable to the truck rental example:

> Sorry Corporation, a manufacturer of weeping dolls, sends an interest payment on one unit of its debt to Happy Saver, a saver who forsakes the purchase of dolls and other things in order to buy a debt instrument.

No goods or services are associated with this payment. Therefore, it is not included in the accounting of national income. It is called a *transfer payment*.

Classification of Financial Assets

There are three types of financial assets.

1. *Money.* Money can be defined as those goods that are widely accepted in exchange for goods and services and for the payment of debt (they serve as a *medium of exchange*). (Some definitions also include other goods which can be inexpensively changed into the medium of exchange.)
2. *Debt instruments.* Debt instruments are sometimes broadly called *bonds* by economists. They are evidence of loans. Many debt instruments are issued formally by businesses and banking institutions and can be sold before maturity; that is, they are *marketable* or *negotiable*.
3. *Equities.* Equities are ownership rights in businesses. If the business is a corporation, they are called *stocks*.

The discussion turns next to money: its definition, functions, and some institutional details about money in the U.S. economy. Then debt instruments and equities are discussed, beginning with the legal basis and proceeding to institutional details.

Money: Definition and Functions

Money is usually thought of as something that is generally accepted as payment for goods and services and for the discharge of debt. This definition is at the core of most descriptions of money; it emphasizes the *medium of exchange* function of money. This description, however, does not nail down all the different things that may be considered money, so it is useful to look at the general set of functions or services that traditionally have been attributed to those goods considered money:

1. Medium of exchange.
2. Temporary abode of purchasing power.
3. Store of value.
4. Unit of account (sometimes called a *standard of value*).
5. Standard of deferred payment.

These five functions are discussed next in some detail.

1 ① A good used as a medium of exchange is widely accepted for the payment of debt and the purchase of goods and services. Examples are currency, coin, or checks drawn on deposits.

Some commonly used definitions of money, however, include items such as time deposits at commercial banks. These are not a medium of exchange. Consumer time deposits usually cannot be sold; they must be held to maturity (the termination date of the time deposit) to receive the full interest. The owner can then transfer time deposits into accounts on which a check may be written: a "checkable" deposit.

Some items that may generally be a medium of exchange, such as a $1000 bill or a personal check, may not always provide this service. Sellers may refuse to exchange goods and services for them. A $1 bill may not serve as a medium of exchange on a subway that requires a token.

Just as some items that usually serve as a medium of exchange do not always serve this function, other items that rarely serve as a medium of exchange sometimes do. Common stock is sometimes exchanged for the purchase of a corporation.

Obviously, there are exceptions to the definition. Nevertheless, the medium of exchange function forms the core of most definitions of money. In addition, other goods that can be inexpensively changed into the medium of exchange are sometimes treated as money. Savings deposits at a commercial bank can easily be transferred into demand deposits, which are a medium of exchange, since demand deposits can be transferred by check.

The value of the medium of exchange function can be viewed as depending both on a special kind of uncertainty—uncertainty about the size and timing of future receipts and expenditures—and on a reduction in the cost of making transactions.

The reduction in the cost of transactions afforded by the introduction of money occurs by the replacement of barter (trading without money) with a money system. Arranging barter trades can require large transactions costs.

A barter economy is one in which goods and services are exchanged without the use of money. Goods and services are traded for other goods and services. No good's value is determined primarily by its medium of exchange services (or the medium of exchange services of another good for which it can be inexpensively exchanged).

It is often held that in a barter economy buyers and sellers are not fortunate enough to enjoy a *double coincidence* in exchange and that this is the reason money was invented. The double coincidence occurs when both parties to a transaction wish to buy a good or service that the other party offers to sell, in exact exchange. Thus in a barter economy a double coincidence would occur if the customer for the bus desired to trade a pair of shoes for a bus ride, while the driver of the bus sought to trade a bus ride for the pair of shoes. The problem of the double coincidence could be lessened with a triangular trade: The customer goes off to find someone who will trade the pair of shoes for a belt, which the bus driver wants. This is messy. The customer misses the bus and the new driver wants a ticket to the hockey game. Because of the improbability of this double coincidence or various expeditious triangular trades, a good came into use as a medium of exchange. The costs of trading were thereby reduced.

The nature of the special kind of uncertainty can be understood by first imagining the opposite environment—complete certainty about all future receipts and expenditures. Imagine you knew for certain that you would buy a bunch of turnips for $3.26 twelve years from now on July 14, after receiving your $6379.56 paycheck on July 12. Your knowledge extends in this way through every last penny of receipts and expenditures to the moment of your death and even beyond—to the hidden ecstasy of your heirs, spending your estate with tears in their eyes. Your horizon of knowledge is far enough down the road to make even further knowledge of expenditures and receipts of negligible importance today.

Never mind the details. Ask yourself: "If everyone had this knowledge, would they need to carry checkbooks, currency, and coin?" All future transactions could be recorded in a giant computer bank, and changes in bank balances arising from here to the knowledge horizon could be cleared today. No checking accounts, currency, or coin would be needed.

The future is, however, unclear to us; but wondering about it does cause people to think in constructive ways. It pays to own a "temporary abode of purchasing power," that is, a precautionary amount of the medium of exchange to tide one over those rough spots where receipts are less than expenditures.

2 (2) The temporary abode of purchasing power function is thus related to the medium of exchange property and refers to the holding of money as a readily available means of negotiating future transactions. The uncertainty of receipts and payments of money requires that some money

be held as a precaution, even though it might not be needed immediately.

3 (3.) One way to *store wealth* is in the form of money. Nevertheless, it is not the only way to store wealth. Owning a house or a tract of land is also a way to store wealth. Therefore, the store of value function of money is not a unique function of money.

4 (4.) A unit of account is a basic number in a counting system. The generally accepted practice of translating the value of all transactions, wealth, and debts into a single monetary unit of account measurement, such as a dollar, is a great convenience. One can compare a car currently valued at $1000 with a house currently valued at $6000 and conclude that six of the cars could be traded for the house. However, the domestic monetary unit does not always serve as the unit of account. During the colonial period, Americans frequently kept their bookkeeping records in British pounds rather than domestic currency. Inhabitants of countries where foreign trade, including tourism, is a substantial part of their national income may keep their records and quote their prices in terms other than their domestic currency.

5 (5.) The standard of deferred payment function of money refers merely to the practice of calculating debts in terms of the unit of account used for money.

6 (6.) Uniformity in appearance is a characteristic of many forms of money. It can be added to the five functions of money to form a list of six commonly described money characteristics. Money of the same denomination (e.g., all $1 bills) is usually uniform in appearance. All U.S. paper dollars look alike; this is a convenience. The Susan B. Anthony $1 coin introduced in 1979 looked too much like a quarter, causing confusion.

A money system can work without being uniform in appearance. Until 1862, currency used in the United States was mostly a heterogeneous collection of notes of varying sizes and colors, issued by private banks. Since 1862, official U.S. currency has been printed by the government so that it is uniform in appearance.

Sometimes the characteristics of money are summarized with the word *moneyness*. Goods that have many of these characteristics and can be converted inexpensively to money are said to be near-monies. These goods include Treasury bills, insurance policies with immediate cash value, and term deposits (certificates of deposit) at depository intermediaries.

Institutional Characteristics of Money in the United States

Until 1973, virtually all checkable deposits in the United States were held at financial institutions called *commercial banks*. A depositor could write out a check ordering the bank to pay a designated party a given sum of money from the depositor's account. The basic medium of exchange concept of money used by the U.S. government consisted of those checkable deposits, called *demand deposits*, plus all the currency and coin held by the public outside the commercial banks. Government regulation prohibited the payment of interest on those demand deposits.

In 1973, other financial institutions that offer deposits (and, together with commercial banks, comprise what are called *depository institutions*) began to allow similar checkable accounts that paid interest to their depositors, just as did their traditional accounts, which could not be withdrawn by a depositor's check. These traditional accounts required the presentation of a passbook, either in person or by mail, to withdraw funds. These other depository institutions that we are referring to include savings and loan associations, mutual savings banks, and credit unions, also called *thrift institutions* or *thrifts*. One form of checkable account they offer is called a *NOW account* because depositors can withdraw their funds and order payment to a designated party with a negotiable order of withdrawal, which is similar to a check used at commercial banks. The difference is that NOW accounts pay interest. Commercial banks soon began to offer NOW accounts to compete with checkable accounts that pay interest.

A new, broader concept of money used as a medium of exchange, designed to reflect the growth in NOW accounts, was introduced by the government on February 7, 1980. The new concept was called *M1B* until January 1982, when it became *M1*. It includes the checkable deposits at all depository institutions, plus all the currency and coin held by the public outside banks, plus outstanding travelers checks of nonbank issuers (see Table 2-1).

A still broader concept of money, called *M2*, was officially redefined in February 1980 to include not only checkable deposits at all depository institutions but also all deposits that are accessible on demand plus consumer time deposits (see Table 2-1). An account is accessible on demand if the depositor can obtain his or her funds without prior notice, either by check or by presentation of a withdrawal notice (sometimes a passbook is used), either in person or by mail. This concept of money includes shares in investment organizations, called *money market funds*. It also includes accounts at depository institutions that are not checkable but that can be inexpensively transferred into checkable accounts and used as a medium of exchange. Time deposit accounts cannot be inexpensively transferred because they cannot be withdrawn until a particular date. Therefore, the large business time deposits are excluded from the concept of M2, although consumer time deposits (under $100,000) are included. (Since consumer time deposits cannot be sold—only returned to the bank at penalty rates before maturity—it can be argued that they should also be omitted from M2. The deciding factor is whether or not consumers treat them as assets that are as liquid as savings deposits and other accounts in M2.) Large business time deposits are included in *M3* and in an even larger aggregate which includes all liquid assets, as shown in Table 2-1.

TABLE 2-1

Concepts of U.S. Money, September 1981*
(Billions of Dollars)

Date	M1 Sum of Currency, Travelers Checks, Demand Deposits, and Other Checkable Deposits[†]	Addenda Overnight RPs at Commercial Banks plus Overnight Eurodollars[‡] NSA	Addenda Money Market Mutual Fund Balances (General Purpose and Broker/Dealer) NSA	M2 M1 Plus Overnight RPs and Eurodollars, MMMF Balances (General Purpose and Broker/Dealer), and Savings and Small Time Deposits[§]	M3 M2 plus Large Time Deposits, Term RPs and Institutions —Only MMMF Balances[¶]	L M3 plus Other Liquid Assets[‖]
September 1981	SA 431.2	39.6	130.4	SA 1778.1	SA 2138.0	SA 2577.3

*SA, seasonally adjusted; NSA, not seasonally adjusted.

[†]Averages of daily figures for (1) currency outside the Treasury, Federal Reserve banks, and the vaults of commercial banks; (2) traveler's checks of nonbank issuers; (3) demand deposits at all commercial banks other than those due to domestic banks, the U.S. government, and foreign banks and official institutions less cash items in the process of collection and Federal Reserve float; and (4) other checkable deposits (OCD) consisting of negotiable order of withdrawal (NOW) and automatic transfer service (ATS) accounts at banks and thrift institutions, credit union share draft accounts (CUSD), and demand deposits at thrift institutions. The currency and demand deposit components exclude the estimated amount of vault cash and demand deposits, respectively, held by thrift institutions to service their OCD liabilities.

[‡]Overnight (and continuing contract) RPs are those issued by commercial banks to other than depository institutions and money market mutual funds (general purpose and broker/dealer), and overnight Eurodollars are those issued by Caribbean branches of member banks to U.S. residents other than depository institutions and money market mutual funds (general purpose and broker/dealer).

[§]Includes savings and small-denomination time deposits (time deposits—including retail RPs—in amounts of less than $100,000) issued by commercial banks and thrift institutions. M2 will differ from the sum of components presented in subsequent tables by a consolidation adjustment that represents the estimated amount of demand deposits and vault cash held by thrift institutions to service time and savings deposits.

[¶]Includes large-denomination time deposits issued by commercial banks and thrift institutions in amounts of $100,000 or more, less holdings of domestic banks, thrift institutions, the U.S. government, money market mutual funds, and foreign banks and official institutions. M3 will differ from the sum of components presented in subsequent tables by a consolidation adjustment that represents the estimated amount of overnight RPs held by institutions-only money market mutual funds.

[‖]Other liquid assets include the nonbank public's holdings of U.S. Savings Bonds, short-term Treasury securities, commercial paper, bankers acceptances, and term Eurodollars net of money market mutual fund holdings of these assets.

A wide variety of other items could be included in the definition of money under the contention that they could be inexpensively converted into a medium of exchange. These include (1) government bonds; (2) available or unused consumer credit, such as that available with credit cards; (3) the cash value of life insurance policies; (4) bonds issued by private corporations; and (5) common stock.

As the list of items included in the definition of money becomes larger, money becomes an unwieldy concept for economic analysis. It is probably better to include in the definition of money only those goods that serve as a medium of exchange, as well as goods that can be changed very inexpensively into a medium of exchange.

Debt Instruments and Equities: Definitions

Debt instruments are claims against a money income fixed at a constant or variable rate of interest. In the case of a bond, this income usually consists of a stream of interest payments plus a final face-value payment at the time the debt instrument matures.

An equity, such as a stock, is a claim against a variable income. It is a claim against the residual between revenues and costs, the *profits*, plus the proceeds from the sale of any assets, after other, *more senior*, claims are paid. More senior claims include all liabilities, such as bonds that were issued; these claims must be paid before stock owners receive any income.

Securities is the general term for both debt instruments and equities.

Debt Instruments: Legal Basis

There are many types of *legal instruments* which are *evidence of debt*. Legally, debts that call for the payment of money and which can be transferred from one party to another before maturity are called *negotiable instruments*. The general characteristics of "negotiable instruments laws" grew out of centuries of practice in England comprising part of the common law and were first formally codified in the British Bills of Exchange Act of 1882. Uniformity in the treatment of negotiable instruments in the United States was furthered by the Uniform Negotiable Instruments law of 1897 and the Uniform Commercial Code of 1952. Both of these were submitted to individual states for adoption on these dates.

A *negotiable instrument* is a contract in writing, signed by the executing party, containing an unconditional promise or order to pay an exact amount of money on demand or at a specific time in the future, payable to the *bearer* or to the order of a *specified person* indicated in the contract with reasonable certainty.

There are two classes of negotiable instruments:

1. Promissory notes.
2. Drafts, or bills of exchange.

A *promissory note* is any written obligation which meets the proper legal conditions, whereby one person promises to pay another an exact sum of money. A generalized example is shown in Figure 2-1.

Date: January 2, 1982 Amount: $ 532.75

TERMS: Thirty days after date, I promise to pay to the order of: L. B. Nelson of St. Louis, Mo.
the amount of: Five Hundred thirty-two and 75/100 dollars.
Payable at: 5th National of St. Louis. Value received with interest at 12 %. No. 16 Date Due: Feb. 1, 1982

Signature: P. B. Pheebe

Figure 2-1

Example of a promissory note.

A *draft* or *bill of exchange* is a negotiable instrument with three parties to the agreement: the one who draws the order, the one who is to receive payment, and the one who is ordered to make payment. A commercial bank check is such an instrument. The depositor can order the commercial bank to make payment to someone else by means of a commercial bank check.

Drafts can be classified according to the time at which the payment must be made. Some drafts, such as commercial bank checks, are payable immediately at sight (or demand) during regular banking hours. Other drafts have a fixed date or are contingent on some action, such as the delivery of goods.

Bonds and Notes

A *bond* or *note* is part of a *group* of *formally* offered debt instruments. They are contracts that stipulate a series of fixed payments from the issuer to the holder of the bond or note. The payments are usually semiannual or annual but sometimes quarterly. The final payment also includes the face value of the bond or note. Bonds and notes may be offered by a private corporation, a state or local government unit, the federal government, or a foreign firm or government. Most bonds and notes are marketable: They may be sold. Some, such as U.S. Savings Bonds, cannot be sold. They can, however, be redeemed by the original owner. Notes have shorter maturities, generally a maximum original maturity of ten years or less, whereas bonds, normally classified as "long term," can have any maturity.

Most bonds or notes bear the following information:

1. The name of the maker (or issuer), such as the XYZ Corporation.
2. The *face value, par value,* or simply *par*, is the amount the maker is obligated to pay when the bond matures.
3. The maturity date, the date of the final payment. Some bonds have provisions allowing them to be redeemed by the issuer before maturity. They are called *call* provisions, and such a bond is *callable*.
4. The interest payments noted on the bond are often stated a percent of the face value to be paid each period. This is cal. the *coupon rate* because the fixed dollar interest payment ea payment period is often obtained by clipping the appropriat physical coupon and exchanging it for the payment.
5. The dates at which the interest payments are to be made.
6. In the cases of bonds or notes issued by corporations, the trustee, usually a trust company or large bank, is named. The trustee must see that the issuer complies with the terms of the bond or note. The trustee will send interest payments upon receipt of the coupons. If the bond or note is registered, interest payments will be sent automatically, without coupons.

The *original term to maturity* is the time between the date of issuance and the final payment (and return of the face value). The alternative meaning of *maturity* is the *time remaining from the present to the final payment*. A bond with a ten-year original term to maturity may have only a one-month maturity if the final payment is next month. Unless qualified with the term *original*, the term *maturity* is ordinarily used in the second sense.

Bonds need not have a maturity. They may pay a fixed dollar amount per year forever. Such bonds, called *consols* or *perpetuities*, have been sold by the British government. Preferred stock, discussed later, also has the characteristics of consols.

A consol may promise to pay $5 per year forever. If the consol is sold for $50, the yield is 10 percent. Because the arithmetic involved in computing the interest is much simpler for consols than for bonds with fixed maturities, consols are frequently used in economic analysis.

As a result of legislation in 1967, U.S. Treasury note maturities were extended to as much as seven years. Previously, Treasury notes were issued for maturities of one to a maximum of five years. Since 1976, notes have been issued with maturities up to ten years. The extension of the maturities on notes helped the Treasury's long-term financing operations because notes had no interest ceilings, whereas bonds had a $4\frac{1}{4}$ percent interest rate ceiling for a Treasury offering. Treasury bonds are currently issued with maturities of over ten years.

The term *principal* has several commonly used meanings, which may cause confusion. It is often used to refer to the *original market price* of a debt instrument. If a bond with a $100 face value is originally sold for $50, $50 is the principal or the original amount borrowed. *Deep discount bonds* are bonds that have sold at a price significantly below their face value. The repayment of the face value at maturity on these bonds therefore contains a capital gain, which is taxed at a lower rate than ordinary income. The current value of a debt instrument is usually simply referred to as its *current market price*, not its *principal*.

Sometimes the term *principal* is used to mean the par value or face value of a bond. This definition causes some confusion because the face value describes the final payment but not necessarily the amount paid for the bond. The amount paid for the bond is the market price at the time the bond was sold.

An example of a somewhat misleading use of the *face value* or *par value* of a bond is illustrated by a common method of estimating the current value of the debt of the United States. The current value of the U.S. national debt can be defined as the current value of federal government debt instruments outstanding (outside the holdings of the federal government). The current cost of reducing this debt is the current market price of the group of bonds that the government wishes to purchase. The cost is not the face value (or par value) of these debt instruments, unless they have matured and the par value is the only payment left.

The *par value* of a bond is printed on its face. It is the amount that the maker is obligated to pay when the bond matures, together with any coupon payments due at that time. Suppose, for example, that a one-year bond has a $100 par value plus a 5 percent (of par) coupon payment, both due in a single payment at the end of the year. The bond may sell for only $75. The bond owner will receive $75 principal plus a payment of $30 at the end of one year. Thirty dollars is 40 percent of $75, so the bond yields a 40 percent interest rate at a current price of $75.

Bonds can be classified by the type of security pledged as collateral. The following are examples:

1. *Mortgage bonds* are secured by fixed (immovable) property, such as buildings and permanent capital improvements on the land. Sometimes more than one mortgage is issued against the same fixed property. The "first mortgage" has first claim against the property in case of default, the "second mortgage" has second claim, and so on.
2. *Chattel mortgages* are secured by personal movable property such as a television set or an automobile.
3. *Equipment trust certificates* are secured by movable property of considerable value, such as airplanes or railroad rolling stock.
4. *Collateral trust bonds* are secured by bonds and stocks.
5. *Revenue or special tax bonds* are secured by general revenues or specific tax revenues, respectively, of a government.

Corporate bonds that are unsecured by specific properties, but rather by the firm's earning power, are sometimes called *debentures*.

TABLE 2-2

| | Bond Ratings* | |
	Moody's	Standard & Poor's
Highest quality	Aaa	AAA
High quality	Aa	AA
Upper medium quality	A	A
Medium to lower medium quality	Baa	BBB–BB
Speculative	Ba–B	B
In default or high probability of default	Caa and below	CCC and below

*The convention is that the Moody's rating comes first and Standard & Poor's rating uses only capital letters. *Example:* The top rating is Aaa/AAA.

Many economists have long advocated a bond in which the face value and/or the interest payments move up and down with the rate of change of the price level. Although this arrangement would protect bond holders from unexpected inflation, it would impose unexpected costs on borrowers, some of whom would have income that is not so protected. The arrangement is called *indexing* and the bond is called a *purchasing power bond* or a *bond with an escalator.*

Corporations that issue large numbers of bonds frequently pay one or both of the rating firms, Moody's or Standard & Poor's, to rate their bonds for *default risk.* Default risk is the risk of failing to make an interest payment and/or the final face value payment. The ratings are shown in Table 2-2.

Almost all newly issued bonds or bonds that are newly rated have ratings of Baa/BBB or above.

State and Municipal Bonds

Municipal bonds or *municipals* refer to bonds issued by governments of counties, cities, towns, villages, and other divisions within a state; *state bonds* are issued by state governments. Four general types of these bonds are:

1. *General obligation bonds,* secured by the general credit of the issuer.
2. The *revenue bond,* payable from revenues obtained from the operation of some facility, such as a tollway.
3. The *special tax bond,* secured by the payment of a particular tax such as a gasoline tax.
4. *Special assessment bonds,* which derive their income from special property which is financed by the bonds. State and munici-

pal bond income is generally exempt from federal income tax and from state and local taxes in the areas where the bonds are issued and in the District of Columbia. This income is not, however, exempt from federal inheritance taxes. The special tax treatment of these securities has induced buyers to bid up their prices relative to other bonds that are not tax exempt. Since higher bond prices mean lower interest rates, the result is that the yield on these "tax exempts" is close to the after-tax yield on other bonds of similar risk, for people in higher income tax brackets.

Bills

A *bill* usually refers to a marketable debt instrument, such as those issued by the U.S. Treasury, that matures in one year or less. They yield no interim coupon payments, only a final lump-sum payment.

Although the method for calculating the yield of bills is the same as that for all other bonds, the market convention for stating their yield is different. For example, assume that a $10,000 one-year Treasury bill is sold at a 5 percent discount, that is, for $9500.00. When the bill matures in one year, it can be redeemed for $10,000. The yield, 5.26 percent, is simply the discount ($500) divided by the purchase price ($9500). The market convention of describing this bill as being sold at a 5 percent discount can easily be confused as referring to yield when, in fact, the yield is different.

Stocks

Stocks are ownership rights (equities) in a corporation. The corporation's charter specifies the maximum authorized stock issue that can be outstanding. There are several important types of stock. *Common stock* is the basic form of ownership, usually allowing the holder to vote for the directors of the corporation. Usually, each share of common stock entitles the owner to one vote, but alternative systems are also used. Most votes are received by absentee ballots, each of which is called a *proxy*. Each share of common stock is a pro rata (in proportion to the total number of shares of common stock issued) claim against current and future earnings. Those earnings may be paid to the stockholders as dividends or retained in the corporation and invested to enhance future earnings. Because of the personal income tax on dividend income, stockholders may sometimes increase their after-tax income if the corporation reinvests the profits. As the corporate stock rises in value, stockholders may sell their stock. The increase in the value of their stock at the time of sale, if it has been held long enough, is taxed at a lower rate (the capital gains rate) than are the dividends. In 1982, 40 percent of the capital gain on a stock held at least one year was subject to income tax with a tax rate of 50 percent; the maximum effective tax on capital gains, therefore, is ordinarily 20 percent.

Preferred stock, the second type, has no voting rights unless dividends are not paid for a number of periods, often six quarters. Preferred stock pays a fixed dividend, stipulated in the corporation charter as a percentage of the par value of the stock. Each class of security has a different level of priority for claims against income and assets, with common stock generally given a lower priority than that of preferred stock or bonds. Preferred stock has the characteristic of a perpetual bond (a consol), a fixed money income stream.

The privilege of converting preferred stock (convertible preferred stock) and bonds (convertible bonds) into common stock, at specified prices, is sometimes stipulated. Preferred stock, convertible preferred stock, convertible bonds, and participating bonds (which in addition to interest income may share the income of the earnings) all share some characteristics of bonds and some characteristics of equities. The lines of demarcation among these financial assets are vague.

STUDY QUESTIONS

1. What is a financial asset, and how does it differ from a nonfinancial asset?

2. What is a purchasing power bond? Under what conditions would an issuer of these bonds be hurt by its indexing provision?

3. What is a third-party agreement for the payment of money? Give an example of a legal instrument that is a third-party agreement.

4. What is the difference between U.S. Treasury bills, bonds, and notes? Which are coupon issues, and which are sold at discount? Explain.

5. What concepts of money are currently used by the Federal Reserve, the U.S. central bank? Describe these concepts.

6. What reply can you make to those who argue that "debt is bad"? Comment on the relationship between this view and the view that credit is desirable. (You may wish to review your answer after reading about the functions of financial markets in Chapter 3.)

3

Financial Markets

Introduction

Although some securities, especially large blocks, are traded directly between buyers and sellers after private negotiation, the major places for trading securities in developed economies are financial markets. Those who view the price system as the most efficient allocator of funds see financial markets as remarkable institutions of a developed free society. Financial markets are generally very competitive. The bottom line—the rate of return—guides billions of dollars of funds that change hands in these markets each day. Financial markets perform a vital allocative function for the wealth of a complex economy.

The discussion of financial markets begins with a description of the types of financial markets. The less competitive *primary* financial markets for newly issued securities are discussed next. The discussion focuses on *underwriters*, who attempt to sell these new securities. Then the formal secondary markets are described. A classification of market participants is presented followed by three sections describing how markets operate. The important concept of an *efficient market* is introduced. The chapter ends with an assessment of the functions of financial markets.

Types of Financial Markets

A market is a formal or informal organization of buyers and sellers who conduct trades in particular commodities or services. The market may be located at a particular geographical meeting place, such as a shopping center (a retail market). A market may be organized over wide areas connected through phones or computer terminals. Although the trading room of the New York Stock Exchange is located in New York City, buyers and sellers who actively participate in this market may conduct their trades from distant locations. This is the *institutional* way of looking at a market.

The Baltic Exchange, one of the world's leading markets for the hire of maritime vessels, is an example of an informal market. It began in the middle of the 18th century at a coffee house, and its business is now carried on in the marble-columned hall of London's venerable St. Mary Axe building. Brokers, shipowners, and their agents gather from all over the world to gossip and negotiate business, and the deals that are agreed upon are communicated by telephone and telex so that maritime vessels, whether in port or under way, can be directed to pick up new cargoes.

Financial assets are traded in *financial markets*. These markets are also called money markets or capital markets. *Money markets* are for short-term financial assets (debt instruments under a year) and *capital markets* are for all longer-term financial assets. They may be *formal markets* organized with a set of rules for their operation, such as the New York Stock Exchange. Or they may be *informal markets*, where the existing laws of contract are observed but the market has no formal rules. The *third market* for stocks was such an informal organization for stocks that were not traded through an organized exchange. The New York money market, discussed in Chapter 20, is an informal market.

New financial assets are issued in *primary markets*. Financial assets that are resold are traded in *secondary markets*. Firms that specialize in trading either new or reissued financial assets are called *primary* and *secondary dealers*, respectively. Both new and reissued debt instruments are traded in the money market (discussed in Chapter 21). The New York Stock Exchange is a secondary market.

Financial assets that are claims for the future delivery of financial or nonfinancial assets are traded in the *futures markets*. *Spot markets* are for the exchange of assets in the present period.

Primary Financial Markets

New issues of marketable stocks and bonds are usually not sold to the public, but to underwriters. The underwriters may be brokerage firms (firms that primarily implement stock orders on the formal exchanges) or

investment banks (firms that primarily raise funds for corporations).[1]
Sometimes a group of investment banking houses and brokerage houses
join together to form an *underwriting syndicate* or *purchase group* to
sell a large new offering. A *purchase agreement* is a contract between
the purchase group and the issuer. The Securities Act of 1933 requires
registration of an offering with the Securities and Exchange Commission.
There is a waiting period of twenty days or more, which introduces
additional costs for the underwriters who must hold the offering. On
very large offerings the purchase group may tell its *syndicate* or *lead
manager*, as specified in the purchase group agreement, to offer the new
offering to a larger group of *investment banking* and *brokerage* firms,
called the *selling group*.

The largest underwriting firms as measured by estimates of the volume
of securities they handled during the first half of 1981 (in which
they acted as the sole underwriter or the lead manager) are shown in
Table 3-1.

Placing debt for large corporations is reported to be a lucrative activity.

ONE WAY TO BE A MILLIONAIRE IS TO BECOME A PARTNER; DON'T WEAR SHORT PANTS

Each summer, waves of anticipation roll through Salomon's headquarters at One New York Plaza as the executive committee mulls over a list of prospective new partners. The chosen ones are usually anointed in August or September. Of the current 62 partners, only three were named last year. Mr. Gutfreund stresses that in a firm of 2,500 employees, not everyone will be made a partner.

But although some nonpartners are paid in the vicinity of $200,000 a year, partnership remains the universal goal. "I wouldn't want to be them," says a young Salomon investment banker, referring to the nonpartners. He says he will seek a job elsewhere if he isn't named a partner by his 40th birthday.

TABLE 3-1

	Domestic Underwriting as Sole or Lead Manager (January 1, 1981–June 12, 1981)	
	Number of Issues	Dollar Volume* (billions)
Morgan Stanley & Co.	43	5.96
Salomon Brothers	41	5.32
Merrill Lynch	29	2.18
Goldman Sachs & Co.	23	2.50
First Boston Corp.	24	2.35

*Firms' estimates were used.
Source: The Wall Street Journal (June 17, 1981), p. 12.

The dream of partnership fuels a grueling work schedule for Salomon's young investment bankers, traders, and analysts. A recent initiate tells of arriving one chill morning at 7:15 "only to find 15 or 16 people already in line for coffee." That's how Salomon's executive partners want it. Henry Kaufman, the firm's famed chief economist and head of research, states: "We are looking for people who don't look at the endeavor as a 9-to-5 business. For some of us, it's a 24-hour business."

James Lowrey, a former Salomon partner who left recently to set up his own company, states it simply: "There are a lot of smart guys who came to Wall Street to be millionaires—that's why I came." Attaining partnership status at Salomon Brothers is widely believed to be a sure means of fulfilling that ambition. As a longtime institutional customer of Salomon puts it, "Being a partner in that firm is the closest thing to being a partner in the U.S. Treasury."[2]

The Banking Act of 1933 (also known as the Glass-Steagall Act after its Senate and House sponsors) restricted commercial banks to underwriting only U.S. government securities and general obligation state and municipal securities (as opposed to state and municipal revenue bonds, which may claim income only from a specified project). This part of the legislation was a reaction (perhaps a mistaken one) to the stock market crash and the depression of that period.

Underwriters mark up the securities from their buying price, the difference being called a *spread*. The securities are then sold to the public at this higher price. The purchase agreement may be organized, according to the liability of the underwriters, as one of the following:

1. *Straight agreement*, where the selling group is liable for the entire new issue they purchase.
2. *Standby agreement*, where only the original underwriters agree to take any unsold securities.
3. *Best effort agreement*, where unsold securities are returned to the issuer.

Sales of new securities through underwriting groups generally do not involve competitive auctions. The new issues may be rationed by non-price methods if the issuing price is perceived to be below the market value. A broker may call his or her best customers or best friends and let them in on the special buy of a specified number of securities.

The Public Utility Act of 1935 requires competitive bidding (instead of the system of private negotiation) for new public utility securities. A rule of the Interstate Commerce Commission also requires competitive bidding for railroad securities. Most new U.S. Treasury debt instruments are sold in competitive auctions, usually through the Federal Reserve. Some Treasury bonds have been sold at a fixed price without an auction.

New options and futures contracts are generally not sold through underwriters. Formal markets have been developed for trading many of these financial assets. Some are still sold through private negotiation with a dealer.

Formal Markets for Securities

Stocks and bonds that have already been sold to the public are often traded in the formal secondary markets listed in Table 3-2. Also, commodity future contracts and options are often traded in the formal markets listed in Table 3-2. The latter two types of financial assets are sold by the issuer directly in the markets, so these formal markets are really a combination of primary and secondary markets.

TABLE 3-2

Major Formal Markets for Securities in the United States and Canada (as of April 1982)

Commodities Futures Trading
  Chicago Board of Trade
    Wheat, corn, oats, soybeans, soybean oil, soybean meal, plywood, silver, Government National Mortgage Association securities, U.S. Treasury bonds and bills, ninety-day commercial paper, Eurodollars, and certificates of deposit
  MidAmerica Commodity Exchange
    Ninety-day Treasury bills
  Minneapolis Grain Exchange
    Wheat
  Kansas City Board of Trade
    Wheat, stock index (tied to the Value Line composite index)
  New York Cotton Exchange
    Cotton and orange juice
  New York Commodity Exchange
    Gold, silver, and copper
  New York Futures Exchange—a unit of the New York Stock Exchange
    Ninety-day Treasury bills
  New York Mercantile Exchange
    Maine potatoes, heating oil, platinum, palladium, silver coins, and foreign currency
  Coffee Sugar Cocoa Exchange
    Sugar, coffee, and cocoa
  Chicago Mercantile Exchange
    Cattle, hogs, pork bellies, fresh broilers, eggs, lumber, and Treasury bills
  American Commodities Exchange
    Government National Mortgage Association certificates
Options Trading
  Chicago Board Options Exchange
  American Stock Exchange
  Philadelphia Exchange
  Pacific Exchange
Bond Trading
  New York Exchange
  American Exchange
Stock Exchanges
  New York Stock Exchange
  National Association of Securities Dealers (NASDAQ) (over-the-counter trading)
  American Stock Exchange (AMEX)
  Boston, Midwest, Pacific, Philadelphia, Montreal, and Toronto stock exchanges

Market Participants

Participants in financial markets can be classified into four groups, according to their market behavior. They are *speculators, hedgers, arbitrageurs,* and *investors.* Although these market participants can be distinguished in a hypothetical model where they are limited to a particular activity, such a distinction is difficult, if not meaningless, in most financial markets. Most individuals who fit one classification also fit some or all of the other classifications. Nevertheless, it is useful to separate these activities conceptually so that the actions of market participants can be understood.

Many individuals and firms buy financial assets primarily for the income they receive from holding the assets. These individuals value stability of income more than the chance of making short-term profits. This income may be monetary, in the form of dividends and interest payments. These individuals and firms are *investors.* There is not always an operational way, short of psychoanalysis, to separate individual investors from other financial asset holders, called *speculators,* who would be willing to sell their holdings any time they could make a large enough profit. Also, hedgers who hold long-term assets in order to pay off long-term liabilities are difficult to separate from investors. A pension plan, for example, may hold long-term bonds that mature at the time lump-sum pension disbursements are anticipated.

Speculation occurs when an asset is held for resale at a higher price or is sold short for purchase at a lower price (short sales are explained later). A professional speculator trades frequently and in large amounts, making his or her income primarily from this activity. The frequency of trades and the primary income characteristics can be used to differentiate the specialist in speculation from other speculators, although the distinctions are not clear cut.

Some firms and individuals hold financial assets in order to *hedge.* Hedging occurs when two or more assets are held with the expectation that they will have offsetting price movements because of some nonrandom relationship between them. This differs from *diversification,* in which there is an expectation of offsetting price movements caused by random fluctuations. An individual diversifies because he or she expects that if the price of one asset falls from some expected level, another asset in the portfolio will have an offsetting price movement as a matter of random chance.

Many hedges have a simple *mechanical relationship,* such as the simultaneous purchase of both a stock and a *put option* on that stock. (A put option is a contract to sell a stock at a specified price on a future date. It is described more fully in Chapter 22.) Two or more assets are perfectly hedged if, regardless of price fluctuations, their aggregate value is expected to remain the same because of a mechanical relationship. If an asset is not hedged by another asset, the asset holder may be a speculator. He or she may not be a *voluntary* speculator, though; assets that would act as perfect hedges for his or her portfolio may not exist or may be too expensive to purchase. An individual's budget may not be large enough to obtain a hedge, or the individual may not consider the cost of the hedge to be worth the increase in protection.

Still another type of financial market participant is the *arbitrageur.* One form of arbitrage, *simple arbitrage,* takes place when an asset is bought and simultaneously sold at a higher price. For example, if a stock is bought for $5.00 on the Paris Bourse (stock exchange) and simultaneously sold for $5.25 on the New York Stock Exchange, the transaction is known as arbitrage. An arbitrageur must usually carry an inventory because all his or her sales cannot be made simultaneously with purchases. The arbitrageur, therefore, holds a speculative inventory ("takes a position") and cannot be easily distinguished from a speculator.

All three types of trading in financial assets (speculation, hedging, and arbitrage) perform useful functions. Hedging allows individuals who do not wish to take unnecessary gambles, or who are unfamiliar with market information they deem necessary for successful speculation, the opportunity to buy insurance. For example, farmers can ensure a price for their grains in advance. They can buy a futures contract that guarantees them a specific price in the future. The sellers may be buyers who also want to ensure against unfavorable price increases or speculators who risk their funds on the basis of their estimates of future prices. Farmers can then concentrate on farming rather than on speculation in grain prices.

Speculation, under normal conditions, reduces the amplitude of fluctuations in the prices of financial assets. Speculators try to buy when the asset is at a low price, thus bidding its price upward. They try to sell when the price of the asset is high, thus forcing the price downward. They reduce extreme price fluctuations in commodities such as food by inducing increased storage when food is abundant in summer and inventory reduction when it is scarce in winter.

Speculators can be destabilizing if they buy before the peak, causing prices to rise more than they would have, or if they sell before the trough, causing prices to fall more than they would have.

Arbitrageurs help to maintain a consistent set of prices for the same or "related" financial assets. This reduces the search costs of other traders who wish to buy or sell assets on the best possible terms.

Arbitrage cannot, even in principle, be separated from hedging or speculation if the following types of transactions are considered to be arbitrage: An asset with a lower rate of return is sold and an asset of equal value with a higher rate of return is purchased. Every trader may be thought of as attempting to arrange his or her trades so that he or she arbitrages the rates of return in this sense.

How Financial Markets Operate

Formal financial markets, such as the New York Stock Exchange, operate as competitive auctions. They differ in an essential respect from local auctions for nonfinancial assets such as jewelry, antiques, paintings, or cattle. The latter are organized around an auctioneer who continually repeats the highest price offered. If no higher price is offered, the item is sold to the highest bidder. There is only one seller, the auctioneer, and many potential buyers.

In competitive financial markets there are many sellers seeking to obtain the highest price possible and many buyers who wish the lowest price possible. Buyers and sellers from around the world may participate through third parties, such as brokers.

The buyers and sellers of financial assets could, if there were no formal market, negotiate their own trades with each other. These negotiations could lead to many different—sometimes widely different—prices for the same financial assets at the same time, if each pair of traders did not know instantly the prices of other trades.

In formal financial markets the equivalent of auctioneers exists to ensure that there is no more than one price for the same financial asset in the market at one time. Instant information is either relayed by modern communication systems or—as in the case of the New York Stock Exchange—by a *specialist* on the floor of the exchange (who specializes in trading the particular stock).

Instant information of *real-time* quotes assures buyers and sellers that they are trading at prices that reflect market conditions rather than a widely different price based on an incorrect estimate of the demand and supply for the financial asset.

The objective of one price that equates current demand and supply for an asset is as closely approximated in a competitive formal market for financial assets as it is in local nonfinancial markets with auctioneers. This objective is more closely met in financial markets than in worldwide transactions for nonfinancial assets such as jewelry or antiques. This is because financial markets cover a much broader area with many more participants and because it is less expensive for arbitrageurs to keep prices on different financial markets in line with each other.

As the auctioneer in Toledo, Ohio, points to a beautiful Persian rug and yells, "Who will give $1250?" a potential buyer in Sacramento, California, cannot reply. If it were 100 shares of General Motors stock, both the seller in Toledo and the buyer in Sacramento could place sell and buy orders, respectively, on the New York Stock Exchange within a matter of minutes. They need only visit a broker and make their wishes known. For a small fee (in proportion to the value of the asset) the order would be sent promptly to the New York Stock Exchange. General Motors stock is also sold on other exchanges, such as the Bourse in Paris, France. Arbitrageurs keep the price of GM on the Bourse and the New York Stock Exchange approximately the same. So there is worldwide participation in setting the price of GM stock.

In principle, arbitrageurs could keep the price of hand calculators nearly the same in Toledo, Sacramento, and Paris. For example, buying hand calculators in Sacramento, where such calculators are relatively cheap, and selling them in Paris, where they are relatively expensive, involves costly transportation charges. The price of hand calculators would rise in Sacramento as more are demanded and fall in Paris as more are supplied. The difference in prices between Sacramento and Paris would be reduced, but from arbitrage alone it would not fall below the transportation, transaction, import duty, and sales tax costs.

Why is it more difficult to completely arbitrage out price differences in nonfinancial markets than in financial markets? There are three reasons, which can be generalized from these examples:

1. Financial asset transactions require much smaller (as a proportion of the value of the asset) transaction costs. Transactions costs are the costs of making a transaction, including transportation costs.
2. Many financial assets can be easily standardized so that distant buyers and sellers will understand exactly the form of the asset. Bonds and stocks can easily be offered in standard form. The characteristics of the issuer may be widely different; these different characteristics are normally reflected in the price of the financial assets.
3. Modern communication systems rapidly broadcast prices of financial assets because their characteristics are easily summarized. Traders have equal and nearly costless information about market prices and the characteristics of the financial asset.

Transactions costs would be very high, approaching infinity, for land, such as the sale of Mount Everest to a Nebraska mountain climber eager to conquer it in his own home state. Land, machinery, and building prices may vary widely from place to place because the *location* of the asset is important to its value. Real estate sales people sometimes list the three most important attributes for the price of real estate as location, location, and location. Financial assets, because they have negligible transportation costs, may well sell at the same price downtown or uptown, in Paris, Sacramento, or Toledo. The form of financial assets can easily be standardized.

It is easy to change the form of a financial asset: They are *fungible*. For example, a bond with quarterly payments could easily be changed to a bond with annual or perpetual payments with the same yield and present value. Only the size of the individual payments need be altered. The cost of standardizing nonfinancial assets, such as used cars (ten years old, two doors) or hotels (six elevators, four entrances, red stone, fourteen stories, overlooking Lake Erie), is much higher.

Modern communication systems include worldwide computer and telephonic communications. Approximately 3100 stocks in the United States are sold entirely from computer listings by the National Association of Securities Dealers, Inc. (known as NASD). Although NASD is located at 1735 K Street Northwest in Washington, D.C., and its central computer is in New England, there is no trading room. Buy and sell orders are posted on computer screens. Orders are effected by phone or, in the case of some stocks, directly by computer signals. The major formal markets are linked together by an Intermarket Trading System (ITS), which provides buy and sell bids and offers from one exchange to another. These links are discussed in Chapter 21.

For these reasons, a nearly uniform single price for each traded asset is achieved simultaneously on all formal markets. The market price is valuable information not only to active market participants, but also to all those holding the financial asset who might want to sell, and to all those who do not hold the asset but might want to buy if the price is right.[3]

What Does the Market Price Mean in an Efficient Market?

Prices have an important meaning in an efficient market for financial assets. Ordinarily, in the context of *static* price theory, the equilibrium price on a free market equates the quantity supplied with the quantity demanded. The quantities demanded and supplied at each price depend on the present value of the future income the asset is expected to produce. Therefore, the market price of an asset provides valuable information about the value of an asset as it is currently being judged by market participants.

Although static price theory provides valuable tools of analysis, it must be critically amended to explain financial markets. First, there is the need to be sure that the asset has only one market price. Second, one must find out if that price is an equilibrium price. The more nonequilibrium the market prices of an asset, and the more widely dispersed they are, the less valuable market prices become as a guide to the value of the asset.[4]

To meet these objectives the market must have one price for each asset and achieve its equilibrium price instantly.[5] A perfectly competitive market can meet these criteria and therefore be *efficient* in providing information about an asset's value if the following conditions hold:

1. The transactions costs (such as brokerage fees, transportation taxes, transportation costs, and record keeping) must be negligible.
2. Assets must be standardized in form.
3. Equal and nearly costless information about the market price and the characteristics of the asset must be available to all market participants.

These conditions assure more than the existence of a unique price for an asset. They enable all available information about an asset to be utilized by market participants in determining the price. If, for example, good news, never before known, about General Motors profits is uncovered, the price of GM stock in such a market will be rapidly, almost instantly, bid up to take account of this information. This is not generally true in markets for nonfinancial assets because the transactions costs are not only substantially higher, but can be prohibitively high with rapid adjustment. Instant adjustment or even rapid adjustment is too costly.

Of course, a market cannot be efficient in the sense of incorporating all available information in the price of assets traded if it is not perfectly competitive. If, for example, large participants believe they can control, or at least affect, market prices by their transactions, considerations other than the present value of the future income from an asset will determine its market price. Therefore, a fourth condition for market efficiency is:

4. No market participant acts as though his or her transactions will affect the market price; instead, they take the market price as given.

This condition is not always met. However, the markets for most financial assets are very large and arbitrageurs and speculators are often ready to jump in and correct anomalies. It appears unlikely that the condition is seriously violated except in some futures markets where the value of substantially all of an underlying asset is small enough to be "cornered" by a monopolist.

Finally, an efficient market must be free of government restrictions on the price of assets sold:

5. No government restrictions that inhibit price movement are imposed.

Many of the futures markets have such inhibiting price regulations. Market prices may only move a designated amount in one trading day.

Market Efficiency and Economic Efficiency

The term *efficient markets* refers to markets in which all available information is rapidly—even immediately—incorporated (or discounted) into the price of the assets being sold on the markets. In this sense the word *efficiency* is used to indicate that markets rapidly and accurately reflect the value of the assets as evaluated by market participants (and by those who hold the asset or may purchase the asset at the right price).

If the market only slowly reached an equilibrium price that reflected this information, market prices would be more difficult to interpret as indicators of market participants' evaluations. This is because it would be very difficult to tell when the markets were in equilibrium and, therefore, when correct information about the market participants' assessment of value is reflected in the current market prices.

The meaning of *economic efficiency* is somewhat different. A production process is more efficient in the conventional economic sense as the ratio of usable output per unit of input increases. This concept can be applied to financial markets. The output of financial markets is the provision of services for allocating funds to where they can be used most profitably. The inputs in a financial market are the various costs of running the market. The costs are represented in brokerage fees. The benefits are tied to the profits that can be made by selling less profitable assets and buying more profitable assets in the market.

For example, prices of stocks are allowed to change on the New York Stock Exchange by $\frac{1}{8}$ of a dollar. Strictly from the standpoint of efficient markets—that is, showing precisely the present evaluation of an asset—it would be preferable to have smaller changes so that more exact prices could be ascertained. The changes might be to the nearest penny, $\frac{1}{100}$ of a dollar. However, from the standpoint of economic efficiency, the cost of the extra precision may be too high. Thus the market may be economically less efficient with this kind of a pricing system. The profits that can be gained from correcting, through trading, the value of a stock to its perceived underlying present value are evidently too small for changes under $\frac{1}{8}$ of a dollar.

This is not true on bond markets, where transactions often involve large sums. Gradations such as $\frac{1}{32}$ of a dollar are used.

Consideration of economic efficiency illuminates the fact that efficient markets, in the sense of markets with all available information incorporated into market prices, are not costless. As in other production processes, there is some optimum level of market efficiency where the rate of return based on the costs compared to the services of making a market efficient is at least as high as in other investments.

Stability and Instability

Stability in economics refers to the *probability* that an event will occur. If the probability remains constant (or nearly constant), the process is stable. For example, a fair coin has a .5 probability of heads. This does not mean that 50 percent of the tosses of the coin or every other toss will produce heads. It means that as the number of tosses increase, the average number of heads will approach 50 percent.

For financial markets, it is clear that an asset with a price soaring to infinity is unstable. What about something less dramatic. If all information is discounted into the price of stocks, only new information that cannot be predicted will affect stock prices. Because it cannot be predicted, the new information is random. *Random* means unpredictable. Stocks affected only by random events will change in a random manner. Is this unstable?

Extensive statistical tests of stock prices support the view that price changes do not react to information by shooting off to infinity or zero. Prices settle down to a new level which is different from the previous level by an amount that could not have been predicted prior to knowledge of the new information. In an efficient market almost all information should be discounted almost immediately into the price of the stock.

Therefore, it seems appropriate to use the following definition of *stability*: In the face of no additional information about the asset, its market price follows a predictable course relative to the average price of other assets and, after the dispersal of new information, the price of the asset adjusts to a new predictable course. Note carefully that this kind of stability does not require that changes in the price of the stock be known in advance, since this would be impossible without knowledge of information which has not yet unfolded.

Governments and some market participants like *orderly* financial markets. Orderly financial markets are markets in which the price of the financial assets does not change more than some acceptable difference from a notion of a normal price. There is usually no way to pin down the basis for these concepts of normal. However, traders can receive valuable information about market prices by being able to predict the levels that a government considers normal. In the foreign exchange market, governments often wish to prevent excessive swings in the international value of their currency. Traders can gain by buying when a currency is too low by government standards and selling after the government has intervened to increase the price.

The relation between orderly markets and stability is imprecise. Stability is determined by statistical tests on various parameters of the market prices. Orderliness often depends on a government official's conjectures. However, sometimes wild swings that appear disorderly are also clearly unstable. One does not always need a smoke alarm to tell that the barn is burning.

There are many tests for stability, some of which are formally carried out by government regulators and stock exchange officials. These individuals have the function of surveillance over the market. For example, trading in a stock may be halted for thirty minutes or more if an announcement is to be made that may affect the value of the stock. The officials watch the stock closely as trading is resumed to see if it settles down to a stable course.

There is a controversial question as to whether the stock price would fluctuate by a smaller amount if trading were not halted. Allowing trades that would eliminate excess demands or supplies might make the adjustment to equilibrium smoother than letting the pressures build for thirty minutes or more.

The Functions of Financial Markets

Adam Smith, in his famous book, *An Inquiry into the Nature and Causes of the Wealth of Nations,* first published in 1776, wrote the following title for Chapter III:

That the Division of Labor Is Limited by the Extent of the Market.

He went on to explain.

> When the market is very small, no person can have any encouragement to dedicate himself entirely to one employment, for want of the power to exchange all that surplus part of his labor, which is over and above his own consumption, for such parts of the produce of other men's labor as he has occasion for.[6]

These words from Smith's great classic have formed the primary rationale for explaining an important function of markets for nonfinancial wealth: *specialization in production.* Trading financial assets—claims to present and future income—adds an entirely new and fascinating dimension.

Nonfinancial markets allow specialization. Farmers, for example, can specialize in agricultural production and need not devote time to production of other goods that they produce less efficiently.

Financial markets, on the other hand, provide a means of allocating funds to where they can be used most profitably. Therefore, to Adam Smith's famous observation that markets allow specialization in production, a primary function of financial markets can be added: *the allocation of funds to the most profitable types of production.*

If financial markets work reasonably well, they play a major role in the allocation of wealth to its best possible uses. The transactions costs incurred to effect a better allocation of assets can be substantially reduced with the development of well-functioning financial markets.

Imagine that a firm in a country without well-developed financial markets needs funds to finance a very profitable new venture. The entrepreneur might call his or her friends and acquaintances, place ads in newspapers, or travel to distant lands to seek funds. Other people would be reluctant to buy the firm's equities or bonds since investors would probably be unfamiliar with the past history of the firm or the opinions of other investors about the present value of the firm.

Alternatively, suppose that this firm were in an advanced economy with developed financial markets. The firm might have its stock listed on a modern public stock exchange, such as the New York Stock Exchange. The price of the firm's stock conveys valuable information about the present value placed on the firm's future profits and cash flows. Buyers of the firm's stock would have a ready market for selling the stock. If the entrepreneur could convince people of the greater profitability of his or her new venture, compared to other available investment opportunities, the firm could rapidly acquire funds by selling stocks or bonds. The transactions costs, as well as the costs of substantial information about the firm to investors, are relatively small. A phone call to a stock broker can produce an offer to buy the stock, often a few minutes later, on the floor of a modern stock exchange or, in the case of NASD, on a computer network. Although new issues are not sold directly on the New York Stock Exchange, the price of a firm's stock on the exchange is related to the price of its stock in the market for new issues. Underwriters initially sell new stock, although it may be promptly listed on an exchange after it is introduced.

There is yet a third alternative to individual solicitation or listing on a financial market, which many would claim is a far more efficient and equitable form of allocating financial or nonfinancial wealth: the central government. This can be accomplished in many ways, ranging from elimination of financial markets and central government control of the factors of production to intervention in financial markets, for financial assets control may take many forms. The government may allocate credit. Government credit allocation in the United States has included a broad range of government policies. The federal government has guaranteed the debts of Chrysler Corporation and New York City. The federal government has also set up government or quasi-government agencies and corporations which borrow on a massive scale by selling debt instruments that benefit (through being considered more creditworthy) from their federal government sponsorship. These agencies and corporations then relend the funds to a particular industry. (An example of this is the U.S. single-family residential mortgage market discussed in Chapter 22.) There is a fine—perhaps invisible—line, from the standpoint of economic analysis, between this form of credit allocation and direct loans from the U.S. Treasury, which sells government debt to the public and then spends the proceeds on desired projects.

No matter how efficient a production process is, a decision as to how much of the economy's inputs should be devoted to it must still be made. It is a decision that involves other production processes that compete for the inputs. The effects on other production processes are difficult to estimate. The decision to help Chrysler (which produces automobiles) and New York City (which produces city services) with federal guarantees on their debt was a decision to transfer more to them and less to other productive processes. Central credit control is, therefore, based more on the benefits to the recipient productive processes than on the less discernible losses to the productive processes that receive less (or are denied) input. This does not mean that central control is always wrong; however, decision making can be biased by failing to analyze the costs of this type accurately.

Free financial markets, on the other hand, may not be biased toward the recipients of credit. The costs of credit compared to the expected returns are the focal points for decision making. Proponents of free financial markets believe that the most equitable arrangement is to bias production toward the most profitable production processes. Profits indicate the level of demand relative to costs under competitive conditions, where costs and benefits of a productive process are reflected in the prices. A mixture of free and regulated financial markets does not necessarily lead to the best allocation of funds. The distortions from regulations, interventions, and tax policies may negate much of the benefit of free markets.

Prices may fail to reflect all costs or benefits if substantial *externalities or neighborhood effects* exist. For example, if a firm does not include in its costs the pollution it produces, or fees for primary education do not include the full benefits to society from educating the citizens, negative or positive neighborhood effects arise, respectively. The way to correct misallocations of resources due to incorrect prices that, in turn, result from externalities, is not to intervene in financial markets. These markets may be functioning efficiently, and intervention by the government may well introduce new misallocations of resources that are unrelated to externalities. The misallocations resulting from externalities can be offset, to a large extent, with a system of appropriate taxes and subsidies for negative and positive externalities, respectively. Furthermore, a legal system should exist for suits and settlements arising from externalities, such as damages from pollution.

NOTES

1. The name *investment banking* was applied to many firms in the nineteenth and early twentieth centuries in the United States. Herman E. Kroos and Martin R. Blyn, in their *A History of Financial Intermediaries* (New York: Random House, Inc., 1971), p. 54, state: "If investment banking is defined to mean providing long-term capital, then all financial intermediaries, especially in early American history, were investment bankers. The stockholder lists of the early textile companies, for example, include the names of 35 commercial banks, 7 savings banks, 5 general insurance companies, 5 brokers, 2 private banks, and one life insurance company." The large *investment bankers* flourished from the latter half of the 1800s to World War I. They undertook a variety of activities, including the granting of large loans, the purchase and control of companies, and the formation of alliances with other financial intermediaries. Investment bankers borrowed large sums to finance their operations. Their controlling interest in other companies made them holding companies as well as financial intermediaries. J. P. Morgan and Company and Lehman Brothers are examples of large companies that bought and sold huge amounts of financial assets. In 1895, President Cleveland, on behalf of the U.S. Treasury, applied to J. P. Morgan and Company for a loan.
2. *The Wall Street Journal* (June 4, 1981), pp. 1, 12. Salomon Brothers was purchased by Philbro Corporation (for approximately $800 million) in 1981 and no longer has partners. Thomas W. Lippman reported in the *Washington Post* that Philbro (the world's largest publicly owned commodities trading company) is controlled by the diamond and minerals "empire" controlled by Harry F. Oppenheimer. Citing a report by Ruth Kaplan to be published by the Africa Fund, Lippman reported that Oppenheimer is chairman of two South African firms: the Anglo American Corporation ("the Western world's largest producer of gold, diamonds and platinum"—a quotation from Kaplan) and De Beer's ("marketing 80% of the world's diamonds including the Soviet Union's"—a quotation from Kaplan). These two firms control Minerals and Resources Corporation, based in Bermuda (called "Minorco"). "Oppenheimer is chairman of Minorco. . . . Also on the board of directors besides Wriston [Walter Wriston, Chairman of Citicorp] are Robert Chase, a partner in the New York law firm of Shearman and Sterling, which represents Citibank; Felix Rohatyn, head of the investment banking firm Lazard Frères; and Cedric Ritchie, Chairman of the Bank of Nova Scotia. . . . Minorco, according to SEC records, owns 18.5 million shares of Philbro, or 27.2 percent of all outstanding shares" [*Washington Post* (April 11, 1982), pp. G1–G2].
3. Trades of large quantities of stock, *block trades*, are often arranged through private negotiation. This saves brokerage fees, assures an agreed-upon price, and probably produces price outcomes fairly close to formal market outcomes.
4. The equilibrium price equates quantities supplied and demanded.
5. If everyone knew the equilibrium price, this information would make it unnecessary for the market continually to display equilibrium prices. The prob-

lem is that not everyone—perhaps no one—would know market clearing prices in a rapidly changing market.
6. Adam Smith, *An Inquiry into the Nature and Causes of the Wealth of Nations*, Edwin Cannan, ed. (New York: The Modern Library, 1937), p. 17.

STUDY QUESTIONS

1. Is the New York Stock Exchange a primary or a secondary market? Explain.

2. What is an underwriter, and what do underwriters do?

3. Describe four types of market participants.

4. What is an efficient market? Describe the conditions necessary to achieve an efficient market and the benefits derived for the economy.

5. What does the following statement mean? "The division of labor is limited by the extent of the market." Does this apply to financial markets? Explain.

6. What function does the financial market perform with respect to the allocation of funds?

7. What is meant by the economic efficiency of a financial market?

8. What are the meaning of stability, orderliness, and randomness with respect to financial markets?

9. Name some undesirable results that you might expect from unstable or disorderly markets.

4

Wealth, Income, Interest Rates, and the Flow-of-Funds

Introduction

Some basic concepts and modes of analysis used in understanding variables important in financial markets and the economy are discussed in this chapter. First, the concepts of *wealth* and *income* are described briefly. The discussion brings in the difference between nominal (or market values) and real values, which is a constant source of confusion to the untrained observer. Many readers will have previously studied this distinction and may proceed with only the summary description. Others may wish to read the elaboration in Appendix A at the end of this chapter, including the important component of this discussion, an explanation of price indexes.

Next, the concept of *income* studied in most introductory economic textbooks—one derived from national income concepts—is broadened to include *capital gains* and *losses*. Capital gains and losses are essential ingredients of the change in income as perceived by individuals who own assets, especially financial assets.

Next, the classic national income concepts of *savings* and *investment* are introduced. The relation between investment and the change in wealth is discussed. The important concept of *depreciation* and its relationship to the change in wealth is described. The concepts of *desired saving* and *investment* are discussed and the meaning of their relationship for the economy is shown. The difference between these definitions of saving and investment and those in common usage is discussed in Appendix B.

43

A discussion of the important concepts of the *rates of interest* that define the relation between wealth and income are introduced. This discussion ties together the basic triad of *assets, asset prices*, and *rates of interest*. The effects on interest rates of income tax rates and expected rates of inflation are described and depicted in simple algebraic relations.

One way to describe and analyze asset prices and interest rates for a large complex economy like the United States begins with a systematic summarizing accounting record called *flow-of-funds*. The concept of the flow-of-funds is perceived as "a system of social acconting in which (a) the economy is divided into a number of sectors and (b) a 'sources' and 'uses-of-funds statement' is constructed for each sector. When all these sector sources and uses-of-funds statements are placed side by side, we obtain (c) the flow-of-funds matrix for the economy as a whole."[1] This description is elaborated in the section, "What Is the Flow-of-Funds?" In the following section, some basic identities of flow-of-funds accounting are presented. Sector accounts are viewed in the next section. The use of the flow-of-funds in organizing hypotheses for forecasting interest rates is presented next. Finally, an application of flow-of-funds analysis to one participant, the federal government, is presented. Government borrowing is described and discussed. A word of caution in using flow-of-funds data and an important lesson illuminated by flow-of-funds analysis are presented in Appendix C.

Wealth and Income

Wealth is the *stock* of everything of value at an instant of time, as described in Chapter 2. Wealth, assets, or capital can be—and will be in this discussion—used to mean the same thing. Nominal wealth has the single dimension of dollars; that is, wealth may be measured in units of dollars. Income is the *flow* (stream) of services from wealth. Nominal income has the dimensions of dollars per unit of time. Thus a $10,000 rental house may yield an income (after all expenses) to the owner of $1500 per year.

Both income and wealth may also be expressed in real terms by dividing their nominal values by P, the price level of the goods and services used by the individuals whose behavior is being analyzed. (See Appendix A for an elaboration of the difference between nominal and real values and the development of price indexes.)

Capital Gains and Losses

Capital gains and *losses* are increases or decreases in the valuation of assets. The capital gains can be nominal or real capital gains, depending on whether or not they are divided by P, the price level.

Capital gains and losses are very important, even critical, in analyzing economic behavior in financial markets. Unfortunately, capital gains often have been either neglected in economic analysis or not explicitly noticed. The national income accounting concept of income defines income in terms of the proceeds earned by producing current output. Capital gains and losses are excluded from this narrow definition of income. The income (to labor and capital owners) from building a factory is part of national income. The rise or fall in the value of an existing factory is a capital gain that is not part of the national income accounting concept of income.

Yet the after-tax receipts of capital gains from selling an asset are for the recipient the same as the after-tax income from labor. Both enrich the individual. An individual may either sell the factory or retain ownership and receive its profits to obtain an income, *if income is defined broadly to include all payments to the individual.*

Because of a lower income tax rate on capital gains than on dividends, individuals in higher income tax brackets often prefer capital gains. They prefer the corporation to expand, reinvesting rather than distributing its earnings, and thus driving up the value of their stock. This is a capital gain they can earn by selling the stock. In effect, the corporation invests the individuals' earnings for them. (This is, incidentally, an important reason for mergers, the purchase of one corporation by another.)

Those analyzing the important variables related to financial markets normally must take into account capital gains and losses, for they are a substantial portion of the income (broadly defined) flows for those who trade financial assets. Capital gains and losses on nonfinancial wealth *do* enter national income accounting in the form of a variable called *depreciation*. This variable and its relation to the important concepts of saving, investment, and the change in the value of wealth are discussed in the next section.

Capital gains and losses of financial assets are brought into the analysis by changing interest rates. This procedure is described briefly in this chapter and discussed in more detail in Chapter 9 and Part IV.

Saving, Investment, Depreciation, and the Change in Nonfinancial Wealth

Let Y be the symbol for real income in a national income accounting definition of income. It can be broken into two parts: C/P, real consumption, and I/P, real net investment. (C is nominal consumption, I is nominal net investment, and P is the price level.) *Real consumption is that part of current output that is used up in the year. Real net investment is that part of current output that is not used up in the year.* Eating food, currently produced, is consumption. Building a factory for future use is investment.

The national income accounting definitions can be stated in symbols as follows:

$$Y = C/P + I/P \qquad \text{or} \qquad I/P = Y - C/P \tag{1}$$

The symbol I/P in Equation (1) is *net investment* (which is *gross investment* after *depreciation* is subtracted out). This is illustrated in Figure 4-1. That part of output that is not consumed is gross investment. It is shown as adding to the level (fluid in a vessel in Figure 4-1) of wealth. Part of the value of wealth declines (leaks out of the vessel) each period. This is called *depreciation* (or capital consumption).

Depreciation occurs because wealth:

1. Is used up,
2. Is worn out, and/or
3. Becomes obsolescent (a *capital loss*) or appreciates (a *capital gain*)—negative depreciation.

As inventories of goods manufactured in previous periods are consumed, (1) (using up wealth) occurs. As capital equipment wears out and becomes less productive (or requires maintenance expenditures to maintain its productivity), (2) occurs. Even if the physical wealth is maintained intact (say, an automobile on blocks that is never used), it may become less valuable (a better automobile—in the eyes of investors—may be built). This is called *obsolescence* and it shows up as a capital

Figure 4-1

Investment and nonfinancial wealth.

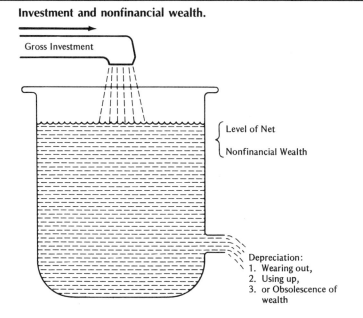

loss (3). The item of nonfinancial wealth may appreciate. A work of art from an old master, or an antique item, may gain in value through the years. This appreciation is *negative depreciation*—an awkward name for a simple capital gain.

National income equals national payments for the national product. *Gross national product* (GNP) is the market value of all final goods and services sold in a given year (no matter when they were produced). The primary deductions to obtain national income are depreciation and indirect taxes (such as sales taxes). The depreciation deduction subtracts out goods sold in the current year but produced in a previous year, that is, the using up of the capital stock. Some of the estimates used in national income accounting for recent years are shown in Table 4-1.

Net real investment is equal to the change in real nonfinancial wealth W/P, as depicted in Figure 4-1:

$$I/P = \Delta(W/P) \tag{2}$$

where Δ (the Greek capital letter delta) means "change in."

Real saving S/P is that part of real income that is not consumed:

$$S/P = Y - C/P \tag{3}$$

Comparing the equalities in Equations (1) and (3), the famous Keynesian equality is obtained for a closed economy:

$$S/P = I/P \tag{4}$$

Desired and Actual Saving and Investment

A central point of John Maynard Keynes's expenditure analysis—Keynesian analysis—can be made by defining actual and desired saving and investment. Individuals may desire to save and invest a different amount than they actually do save and invest. Therefore, desired real saving, $(S/P)^D$, and desired real investment, $(I/P)^D$, can be different from actual real saving, S/P, and actual real investment, I/P.

Desired levels of real saving and real investment are sometimes described as reflecting individuals' plans. They are formed before the event and are called *ex ante* variables. Actual levels of real saving and real investment are referred to as *ex post* variables, to indicate that they are realized "after the event." Their equality is given by Equation (4).

Suppose that from a position of equilibrium more real saving than investment is suddenly desired and that temporarily interest rate effects are ignored. Then

$$(S/P)^D > (I/P)^D \tag{5}$$

TABLE 4-1

National Income and Product Accounts: GNP Expenditures and Gross Saving, 1976–1981
(Billions of Dollars)

Account		Seasonally Adjusted Annual Rates					
		1976	1977	1978	1979	1980	1981*
Total GNP	1	1718.0	1918.0	2156.1	2413.9	2626.1	2881.6
Current outlays	2	1446.4	1600.0	1781.3	1984.7	2207.5	2408.1
Households	3	1084.3	1205.5	1348.7	1510.9	1672.8	1831.0
Of which consumer durables	4	156.8	178.8	199.3	212.3	211.9	227.0
State and local governments	5	232.9	250.6	279.2	305.9	335.8	357.7
U.S. government	6	129.2	143.9	153.4	167.9	198.9	219.4
Gross domestic investment	7	257.9	322.3	375.3	415.8	395.3	455.8
Private fixed investment	8	246.0	301.3	353.2	398.3	401.2	434.6
Residential construction	9	72.0	95.8	111.2	118.6	105.3	111.3
Mobile homes	10	3.0	3.9	4.5	5.0	4.4	5.2
1–4-family structures	11	59.2	78.7	89.8	91.4	77.1	80.8
Household purchases	12	55.0	73.0	86.8	90.7	77.2	84.0
Farm	13	1.1	1.5	1.8	1.8	2.0	2.2
Change in work in process on nonfarm	14	3.1	4.2	1.2	−1.2	−2.1	−5.4
Noncorporate	15	1.6	2.1	.6	−.6	−1.0	−2.7
Corporate	16	1.6	2.1	.6	−.6	−1.0	−2.7
Multifamily units	17	9.8	13.2	17.0	22.2	23.8	25.3
Households	18	2.6	3.8	5.8	10.9	12.3	13.6
Noncorporate business	19	5.7	7.7	9.3	10.1	10.4	10.6
Nonfinancial corp. business	20	.9	1.6	1.8	1.2	1.1	1.2
REITs	21	.5	.1	—	—	—	—
Nonresidential plant and equipment	22	174.1	205.5	242.0	279.7	296.0	323.3
Nonprofit institution (HH)	23	5.7	5.9	6.5	7.2	7.4	7.6
Farm	24	13.8	15.3	16.6	18.3	18.1	18.3
Nonfarm noncorporate business	25	18.3	26.1	33.0	38.9	42.5	45.5
Financial corporations	26	7.2	8.8	11.0	13.3	15.2	16.5
Nonfinancial corporate business	27	129.0	149.4	175.0	202.0	212.6	235.4
Inventories	28	11.8	21.0	22.1	17.5	−5.9	21.2
Farm	29	−2.0	.8	.4	4.1	−1.2	1.8
Nonfarm	30	13.9	20.2	21.8	13.4	−4.7	19.4
Noncorporate	31	1.0	1.7	1.9	−.2	−2.3	−.3
Corporate	32	12.8	18.5	19.9	13.5	−2.3	19.7
Net exports	33	13.8	−4.2	−.6	13.4	23.3	17.7
Exports	34	170.9	183.3	219.8	281.3	339.8	364.5
− Imports	35	157.1	187.5	220.4	267.9	316.5	346.8
Disposable personal income	36	1194.4	1311.5	1462.9	1641.7	1821.7	1986.1
Personal saving	37	82.5	74.1	76.3	86.2	101.3	105.1
Saving rate (percent)	38	6.9	5.6	5.2	5.2	5.6	5.3
Federal government surplus	39	−53.1	−46.4	−29.2	−14.8	−61.2	−49.8
State and local government surplus	40	16.6	28.1	29.0	26.7	29.1	35.9
Corporate profits, taxes, and dividends:							
Profits: total	41	166.3	192.6	223.3	255.4	245.5	224.9
Farms	42	.5	.4	.5	.6	.4	.9
Foreign	43	14.3	15.5	19.7	30.3	31.1	22.7
Financial corporations	44	17.1	23.5	29.3	31.6	30.6	24.0
Nonfinancial corporate business	45	134.5	153.1	173.8	192.8	183.3	177.3

TABLE 4-1 (*Continued*)

National Income and Product Accounts: GNP Expenditures and Gross Saving, 1976–1981
(Billions of Dollars)

Account		Seasonally Adjusted Annual Rates					
		1976	**1977**	**1978**	**1979**	**1980**	**1981***
Tax accruals: total	46	63.8	72.6	83.0	87.6	82.3	74.8
Farms	47	.2	.2	.3	.3	.3	.2
Financial corporations	48	11.2	13.1	15.6	17.9	19.2	18.6
Nonfinancial corporate business	49	52.4	59.2	67.1	69.5	62.9	56.0
Dividends: total	50	37.4	39.9	44.6	50.2	56.0	62.0
Farms	51	.1	.2	.2	.2	.2	.5
Financial corporations	52	−1.0	−1.8	−1.7	−2.4	−3.0	−3.3
Nonfinancial corporate business	53	38.2	41.6	46.2	52.3	58.8	64.8
Net dividends paid	54	29.9	31.7	35.9	37.1	40.2	48.7
⊣ Net foreign dividends received	55	8.2	9.8	10.3	15.2	18.6	16.1
Undistributed profits: total	56	65.1	80.1	95.7	117.6	107.2	88.1
Farms	57	.1	—	—	.1	—	.3
Financial corporations	58	6.8	12.2	15.4	16.1	14.4	8.6
Foreign	59	6.0	5.7	9.4	15.1	12.5	6.6
Nonfinancial corporate business	60	52.1	62.2	70.9	86.2	80.3	72.6
Domestic undistributed profits	61	43.9	52.3	60.6	71.0	61.7	56.5
+ Net foreign dividends received	62	8.2	9.8	10.3	15.2	18.6	16.1
Capital consumption adjustment:	63	−13.5	−12.0	−13.5	−15.9	−17.2	−14.7
Farms	64	−.2	−.2	−.3	−.4	−.5	−.6
Financial corporations	65	−.5	−.7	−1.1	−1.8	−2.7	−3.5
Nonfinancial corporate business	66	−12.9	−11.1	−12.1	−13.7	−14.0	−10.6
Total capital consumption	67	175.0	196.0	221.2	253.6	287.3	316.7
Owner-occupied homes (HH)	68	24.5	28.6	33.6	39.1	45.6	52.0
Nonprofit institutions (HH)	69	4.5	4.8	5.5	6.3	7.1	8.0
Farm noncorporate	70	9.9	11.2	12.6	14.3	16.4	18.0
Nonfarm noncorporate business	71	26.2	29.1	33.2	38.5	42.7	44.2
Total corporate	72	109.9	122.4	136.4	155.4	175.4	194.6
Financial business	73	5.1	5.7	6.7	7.9	9.6	10.9
Corporate farms	74	1.2	1.4	1.6	1.9	2.2	2.5
Nonfinancial corporate business	75	103.6	115.2	128.1	145.6	163.7	181.2
Memo: Capital consumption on consumer durables not included above	76	116.9	128.6	143.1	159.9	178.1	195.3
Total capital consumption including durables	77	291.9	324.6	364.2	413.6	465.4	512.0
Statistical discrepancy	78	5.1	4.4	6.4	2.2	−.7	−6.9
Profit tax rate (percent)	79	38.4	37.7	37.2	34.3	33.5	33.3
Personal tax rate (percent)	80	14.1	14.7	15.0	15.5	15.7	16.2

*2nd quarter estimates.
Source: Flow-of-Funds Accounts, 4th Quarter 1980 and 2nd Quarter 1981, Division of Research and Statistics, Board of Governors of the Federal Reserve System (February 1981), p. 1.

Individuals would increase their real saving at each level of real income by reducing their real consumption. Demand for goods and services, therefore, falls under the condition posed by Equation (5). Businesses cannot sell off their newly produced inventories and are thereby forced into *involuntary investment*. They must carry the inventory into the next year.

In these two ways—a decline in real income and a rise in involuntary investment—equilibrium as defined by the following equation is restored.

$$(S/P)^D = (I/P)^D \tag{6}$$

If from a position of equilibrium less real saving is suddenly desired than real investment, individuals would increase their real consumption spending, involuntary disinvestment would occur as inventories are run down, and income would rise to restore equilibrium.

Because this equilibrium statement is made in terms of the national income definition of income, receipts from capital gains are omitted. Yet, as stated previously, for the individual, the after-tax receipts from the sale of an asset that has risen in price (a capital gain) may be indistinguishable, as far as its effects on his or her spending are concerned, from after-tax labor income.

Since capital gains and losses are central to the study of financial markets, the national income Y should normally not be used as a complete measure of income. A broader measure of income that includes capital gains and losses should be used. For example, a rise in stock prices that is expected to be permanent increases individuals' current receipts and the value of their *financial wealth*. This increase in the value of their financial wealth can cause them to increase their spending even though both income, using a national income definition, and the value of their nonfinancial wealth are constant. Their *total wealth* does increase. One way to take account of capital gains and losses is a change in interest rates. Interest rates are described next.

Real, Nominal, and After-Tax Interest Rates

The *real rate of interest* can be viewed as simply the rate at which real wealth produces real income. A $10,000 house producing $1500 profits each year to the owner would have a real interest rate of 15 percent.

If the general price level steadily increased (i.e., inflation occurred), both the price of the house and the profits may go up with the inflation, preserving the real rate of interest. Thus a fall in this interest rate, at the same level of expected profits, also means a rise in the price of the house, a capital gain. A rise in this interest rate, at the same level of expected profits, also means a fall in the price of the house, a capital loss. Thus asset prices, the interest rate (or, as it is sometimes called, the rate of return) on an asset, and the expected (net) income from an asset are all related views of the asset. They are the triad of dimensions of an asset used throughout the study of financial assets and financial markets. (A convenient way to view them is presented in Chapter 9. In Part V, there is an elaboration of the meaning of the rate of return and a model of the relationship between the rate of return and asset prices. Here, the very important concept of the rate of interest and its relation to inflation and tax rates is described.)

Alternatively, consider a risk-free bond, which, for simplicity, is assumed to pay $1500 per year for every future year. (Such a bond is called a *perpetuity*.) The bond costs $10,000, so the yield is 15 percent, other things being the same. Other things rarely remain the same for the careful lender or borrower. For example, an inflation rate expected to be 25 percent per year would reduce the real value of the income stream by 25 percent a year. This effect can be stated generally in the following way. Unity plus the *nominal* rate of interest on bonds i_B is the compounding factor by which the investment in the bond increases each year. This is the compounding factor, which for readers who are not familiar with compound interest, is reviewed in Chapter 5. This compounding factor is simply $(1 + i_B)$. It equals the compounding factor for the real rate of interest (the interest rate with no inflationary expectations) multiplied by a compounding factor for inflation. If the inflation is expected to increase at a rate of λ (the Greek lowercase letter lambda) per year, the compounding factor for inflation is $1 + \lambda$. Thus

$$(1 + i_B) = (1 + r_B)(1 + \lambda) \tag{7}$$

Multiplying the right side out and subtracting unity from each side of Equation (7), the following expression for the nominal interest rate on bonds is obtained:

$$i_B = r_B + \lambda + r_B\lambda \tag{8}$$

The term $r_B\lambda$ is sometimes ignored on the grounds that it is small.[2] Then the nominal rate of interest on bonds is simply stated as the real rate on bonds plus the expected rate of inflation.

This is an equilibrium relationship to which market adjustments will lead if lenders and borrowers share these expectations of inflation, other things being the same. Lenders wish to cover themselves for the decline in the value of future interest payments and return of principal. Borrowers are willing to pay because the nominal return on the investments for which they wish to use the funds is also expected to rise by the rate of inflation.

Again, some important factors are not the same. This story is far from complete because the borrower (the bond seller) can deduct the interest payments from his or her income, reducing the borrower's taxes. Therefore, the government pays part of the interest. The borrower would be willing to pay a higher interest rate because of this subsidy. The lenders must pay tax on interest income (except for tax-exempt issues such as municipals), so that they need a higher rate of return to cover the real rate of interest plus the expected rate of inflation.

These tax considerations can be taken into account by looking at the effective real after-tax cost of funds, $r_{B,AT}$. If there were no expectation of inflation, it could be obtained by deducting the tax rate on income, K, from the nominal rate of interest, or simply

$$i_B(1 - K) = r_{B,AT} \qquad \text{(for } \lambda = 0) \tag{9}$$

with no expectation of inflation. Therefore, if inflation is expected at a rate of λ, Equation (7), using the tax rate adjustment in Equation (9), becomes

$$1 + i_B(1 - K) = (1 + r_{B,AT})(1 + \lambda) \tag{10}$$

Solving for the effective real after tax costs of funds, $r_{B,AT}$,

$$r_{B,AT} = \frac{1 + i_B(1 - K)}{1 + \lambda} - 1 \tag{11}$$

An example will illustrate the use of this formula. Suppose that the nominal market rate of interest is observed to be 17.5 percent per year; the inflation is expected to be 8 percent per year; and the effective tax rate is $33\frac{1}{3}$ percent. Then the effective real after-tax cost of funds is

$$\left\{ \frac{[1 + .175(1 - \frac{1}{3})]}{1.08} \right\} - 1 = .03395 \quad \text{or} \quad 3.4 \text{ percent}$$

It is easy to see from Equation (9) that a rise in tax rates will reduce the effective real after-tax cost of borrowing if all other conditions remain the same. However, a lower real return will cause suppliers of funds to provide less and demanders of funds to ask for more funds. To equilibriate demand and supply, the nominal interest rate must then rise. Thus a rise in tax rates on income leads to an increase in nominal or market rates of interest. This is the basis for a further analysis of the effect of tax rates on interest rates in Chapter 8.

What Is the Flow-of-Funds?

The flow-of-funds (FOF) definition given by Lawrence Ritter and presented in the introduction to this chapter grew out of research conducted in the 1950s and early 1960s, including the regular estimation and publication of flow-of-funds data by the Federal Reserve beginning in 1955.[3] William Freund and Edward Zinbarg drew attention to the importance of the Federal Reserve estimates.

The flow-of-funds statistics, now published regularly by the Federal Reserve System, have made an important, yet so far generally unexploited, contribution to financial market analysis. There are at least three advantages in utilizing the flow-of-funds accounts rather than traditional, privately compiled sources and uses of funds statements. (1) The flow-of-funds accounts are quarterly, whereas most sources and uses statements are annual or, at best, semiannual. (2) They possess a degree of internal consistency that a private agency would find difficult, if not impossible, to achieve. (3) They link financial with real transactions, thus facilitating the translation of business activity forecasts into financial forecasts.[4]

The flow-of-funds between participants in the economy is a flow of both money and securities. For example, if the government sells Treasury debt instruments to the public, the public pays money and the Treasury acquires debt. The size of the total debt in a period may become many times larger than the size of the money supply (defined, for example, as M1). This is because the money may change hands many times, while the recorded debt becomes larger and larger, as each transaction involving debt is cumulated into the total debt for the period. The total flow of debt and equities is given in the flow-of-funds accounts shown in Table 4-2.

Basic Identities of the Flow-of-Funds Analysis

The depiction of the flow-of-funds groups the transactors in the economy into sectors. Funds raised (financial assets sold) are estimated by sector and type of financial asset. The sources of funds (financial assets bought and new money issued) are estimated in Table 4-2B. A generalized balance sheet for each sector shows the sources and uses of funds in that sector. Increases in assets are treated as a use of funds, and increases in liabilities are treated as a source of funds. This is in keeping with the use of flow-of-funds analysis that undertakes "to spell out the types of financial flow that carry funds from where they are saved to where they are invested and to record the financial claims established by these flows."[5]

The sources and uses statement for a sector in a given time period takes the following general form.

Uses	Sources
Δ Real assets (investment or depreciation	Δ Liabilities (borrowing or repaying debt)
Δ Financial assets (lending or selling off part of the portfolio of financial assets)	Δ Net worth

As can be seen from the sources and uses statement that the change in net worth, Δ net worth, can arise from additions (or reductions) to the

TABLE 4-2

Flow-of-Funds in the United States, 1975–1981
A. Funds Raised in the U.S. Credit Markets
(Billions of Dollars; Half-Yearly Data Are at Seasonally Adjusted Annual Rates)*

Transaction Category, Sector	1975	1976	1977	1978	1979	1980	1981[†]
				Nonfinancial Sectors			
1 **Total funds raised**	**211.8**	**273.6**	**336.6**	**395.6**	**387.0**	**371.9**	**416.8**
2 Excluding equities	201.7	262.8	333.5	396.3	394.0	357.0	415.3
By sector and instrument							
3 U.S. government	85.4	69.0	56.8	53.7	37.4	79.2	89.0
4 Treasury securities	85.8	69.1	57.6	55.1	38.8	79.8	89.5
5 Agency issues and mortgages	−.4	−.1	−.9	−1.4	−1.4	−.6	−.5
6 All other nonfinancial sectors	126.4	204.6	279.9	342.0	349.6	292.7	327.9
7 Corporate equities	10.1	10.8	3.1	−.6	−7.1	15.0	1.6
8 Debt instruments	116.3	193.8	276.7	342.6	356.7	277.8	326.3
9 Private domestic nonfinancial sectors	114.9	185.0	266.0	308.7	328.6	263.4	292.6
10 Corporate equities	9.9	10.5	2.7	−.1	−7.8	12.9	.9
11 Debt instruments	105.0	174.5	263.2	308.8	336.4	250.6	291.7
12 Debt capital instruments	98.4	123.7	172.2	193.7	200.1	179.4	162.2
13 State and local obligations	16.1	15.7	21.9	26.1	21.8	26.9	27.8
14 Corporate bonds	27.2	22.8	21.0	20.1	21.2	30.4	20.5
Mortgages							
15 Home mortgages	39.5	64.0	96.3	108.5	113.7	81.7	76.1
16 Multifamily residential	**	3.9	7.4	9.4	7.8	8.5	5.4
17 Commercial	11.0	11.6	18.5	22.1	24.4	22.4	22.6
18 Farm	4.6	5.7	7.1	7.5	11.3	9.5	9.7
19 Other debt instruments	6.6	50.7	91.0	115.1	136.3	71.1	129.5
20 Consumer credit	9.6	25.4	40.2	47.6	46.3	2.3	29.2
21 Bank loans n.e.c.	−10.5	4.4	26.7	37.1	49.2	37.3	46.3
22 Open market paper	−2.6	4.0	2.9	5.2	11.1	6.6	16.9
23 Other	10.1	16.9	21.3	25.1	29.7	24.9	37.1
24 By borrowing sector	114.9	185.0	266.0	308.7	328.6	263.4	292.6
25 State and local governments	13.7	15.2	17.3	20.9	18.4	25.3	25.3
26 Households	49.6	89.6	139.1	164.3	170.6	101.7	126.8
27 Farm	8.5	10.2	12.3	15.0	20.8	14.5	23.0
28 Nonfarm noncorporate	1.4	5.7	12.7	15.3	14.0	15.8	16.8
29 Corporate	1.7	64.3	84.6	93.2	104.8	106.1	100.8
30 Foreign	11.5	19.6	13.9	33.2	21.0	29.3	35.2
31 Corporate equities	.2	.3	.4	−.5	.8	2.1	.6
32 Debt instruments	11.3	19.3	13.5	33.8	20.3	27.2	34.6
33 Bonds	6.2	8.6	5.1	4.2	3.9	.8	3.3
34 Bank loans n.e.c.	2.0	5.6	3.1	19.1	2.3	11.5	5.5
35 Open market paper	.3	1.9	2.4	6.6	11.2	10.1	20.6
36 U.S. government loans	2.8	3.3	3.0	3.9	3.0	4.7	5.2

TABLE 4-2 (*Continued*)

Flow-of-Funds in the United States, 1975–1981
A. Funds Raised in the U.S. Credit Markets
(Billions of Dollars; Half-Yearly Data Are at Seasonally Adjusted Annual Rates)

Transaction Category, Sector	1975	1976	1977	1978	1979	1980	1981[†]
	Financial Sectors						
37 **Total funds raised**	**9.7**	**23.4**	**51.4**	**76.8**	**84.3**	**66.7**	**90.9**
By instrument							
38 U.S. government related	10.3	15.1	21.9	36.7	48.2	43.0	38.7
39 Sponsored credit agency securities	2.3	3.3	7.0	23.1	24.3	24.4	24.0
40 Mortgage pool securities	7.1	12.2	16.1	13.6	24.0	18.6	14.7
41 Loans from U.S. government	.9	−.4	−1.2	0	0	0	0
42 Private financial sectors	−.6	8.2	29.5	40.1	36.0	23.7	52.2
43 Corporate equities	.5	−.2	2.6	1.8	2.5	6.2	10.4
44 Debt instruments	−1.1	8.4	26.9	38.3	33.6	17.5	41.9
45 Corporate bonds	3.2	9.8	10.1	7.5	7.8	7.1	−1.7
46 Mortgages	2.3	2.1	3.1	.9	−1.2	−.9	−2.9
47 Bank loans n.e.c.	−3.7	−3.7	−.3	2.8	−.4	−.5	4.6
48 Open market paper and RPs	1.1	2.2	9.6	14.6	18.2	4.6	23.8
49 Loans from Federal Home Loan Banks	−4.0	−2.0	4.3	12.5	9.2	7.1	18.0
By sector							
50 Sponsored credit agencies	3.2	2.9	5.8	23.1	24.3	24.4	24.0
51 Mortgage pools	7.1	12.2	16.1	13.6	24.0	18.6	14.7
52 Private financial sectors	−.6	8.2	29.5	40.1	36.0	23.7	52.2
53 Commercial banks	1.2	2.3	1.1	1.3	1.6	.5	.2
54 Bank affiliates	.6	5.4	2.0	7.2	6.5	6.9	6.9
55 Savings and loan associations	−2.3	.1	9.9	14.3	11.4	6.9	17.0
56 Other insurance companies	1.0	.9	1.4	.8	.9	.9	.9
57 Finance companies	.5	4.3	16.9	18.1	16.8	5.8	18.7
58 REITs	−1.3	−2.2	−2.3	−1.1	−.4	−1.7	−.8
59 Open-end investment companies	−.3	−2.4	.4	−.5	−.6	4.4	9.3
	All Sectors						
60 **Totals funds raised, by instrument**	**221.5**	**297.0**	**388.0**	**472.5**	**471.3**	**438.6**	**507.8**
61 Investment company shares	−.3	−2.4	.4	−.5	−.6	4.4	9.3
62 Other corporate equities	10.9	13.1	5.3	1.7	−4.0	16.8	2.6
63 Debt instruments	210.9	286.4	382.3	471.3	475.8	417.5	495.8
64 U.S. government securities	94.9	84.6	79.9	90.5	85.7	122.3	127.8
65 State and local obligations	16.1	15.7	21.9	26.1	21.8	26.9	27.8
66 Corporate and foreign bonds	36.7	41.2	36.1	31.8	32.8	38.4	22.1
67 Mortgages	57.2	87.2	132.3	148.3	155.9	121.1	110.9
68 Consumer credit	9.6	25.4	40.2	47.6	46.3	2.3	29.2
69 Bank loans n.e.c.	−12.2	6.2	29.5	59.0	51.0	48.4	56.4
70 Open market paper and RPs	−1.2	8.1	15.0	26.4	40.5	21.4	61.3
71 Other loans	9.8	17.8	27.4	41.5	41.9	36.7	60.3

TABLE 4-2 (*Continued*)

Flow-of-Funds in the United States, 1975–1981
B. Direct and Indirect Sources of Funds to Credit Markets*
(Billions of Dollars, Except as Noted; Half-Yearly Data Are at Seasonally Adjusted Annual Rates)

Transaction Category, Sector	1975	1976	1977	1978	1979	1980	1981[†]
1 **Total funds advanced in credit markets to nonfinancial sectors**	**201.7**	**262.8**	**333.5**	**396.3**	**394.0**	**357.0**	**415.3**
By public agencies and foreign							
2 Total net advances	39.6	49.8	79.2	101.9	74.0	92.1	103.0
3 U.S. government securities	18.0	23.1	34.9	36.1	−6.2	15.6	24.0
4 Residential mortgages	15.8	12.3	20.0	25.7	36.7	31.1	20.8
5 FHLB advances to savings and loans	−4.0	−2.0	4.3	12.5	9.2	7.1	18.0
6 Other loans and securities	9.8	16.4	20.1	27.6	34.3	38.2	40.3
Total advanced, by sector							
7 U.S. government	13.4	7.9	10.0	17.1	19.0	23.7	29.3
8 Sponsored credit agencies	11.6	16.8	22.4	39.9	53.4	43.8	40.4
9 Monetary authorities	8.5	9.8	7.1	7.0	7.7	4.5	−7.4
10 Foreign	6.1	15.2	39.6	38.0	−6.1	20.0	40.8
11 Agency borrowing not included in line 1	10.3	15.1	21.9	36.7	48.2	43.0	38.7
Private domestic funds advanced							
12 Total net advances	172.4	228.1	276.2	331.0	368.2	307.9	351.0
13 U.S. government securities	76.9	61.5	45.1	54.3	91.9	106.7	103.8
14 State and local obligations	16.1	15.7	21.9	26.1	21.8	26.9	27.8
15 Corporate and foreign bonds	32.8	30.5	22.2	22.4	24.0	26.2	17.3
16 Residential mortgages	23.6	55.5	83.7	92.1	84.6	59.1	60.7
17 Other mortgages and loans	18.9	62.9	107.7	148.6	155.1	96.2	159.4
18 LESS: Federal Home Loan Bank advances	−4.0	−2.0	4.3	12.5	9.2	7.1	18.0
Private financial intermediation							
19 Credit market funds advanced by private financial institutions	123.4	191.4	260.9	302.4	292.5	270.3	322.5
20 Commercial banking	29.4	59.6	87.6	128.7	121.1	99.7	101.4
21 Savings institutions	53.2	70.5	82.0	73.5	55.9	58.4	43.8
22 Insurance and pension funds	40.6	49.7	67.8	75.0	66.4	79.8	79.3
23 Other finance	.3	11.6	23.4	25.2	49.0	32.4	97.9
24 Sources of funds	123.4	191.4	260.9	302.4	292.5	270.3	322.5
25 Private domestic deposits	94.2	124.4	138.9	140.8	143.2	171.1	196.9
26 Credit market borrowing	−1.1	8.4	26.9	38.3	33.6	17.5	41.9
27 Other sources	30.3	58.5	95.1	123.2	115.7	81.6	83.7
28 Foreign funds	−8.7	−4.7	1.2	6.3	25.6	−22.3	−5.1
29 Treasury balances	−1.7	−.1	4.3	6.8	.4	−2.6	10.6
30 Insurance and pension reserves	29.7	34.3	50.1	62.2	47.8	64.1	61.6
31 Other, net	11.0	29.0	39.5	48.0	41.9	42.4	16.7
Private domestic nonfinancial investors							
32 Direct lending in credit markets	47.9	45.1	42.2	67.0	109.3	55.1	70.4
33 U.S. government securities	25.4	16.4	24.1	35.6	62.8	32.6	34.6
34 State and local obligations	8.4	3.3	−.8	1.4	1.4	3.1	19.7
35 Corporate and foreign bonds	8.9	11.8	−3.8	−2.9	10.3	3.6	−12.5
36 Commercial paper	−1.3	1.9	9.6	16.5	11.4	−3.8	7.2
37 Other	6.6	11.7	13.2	16.4	23.5	19.7	21.4

TABLE 4-2 (*Continued*)

Flow-of-Funds in the United States, 1975–1981
B. Direct and Indirect Sources of Funds to Credit Markets
(Billions of Dollars, Except as Noted; Half-Yearly Data Are at Seasonally Adjusted Annual Rates)

Transaction Category, Sector	1975	1976	1977	1978	1979	1980	1981[†]
38 Deposits and currency	101.2	133.4	148.5	152.1	152.6	182.3	202.6
39 Currency	6.2	7.3	8.3	9.3	7.9	10.3	4.7
40 Checkable deposits	9.4	10.4	17.2	16.3	19.2	4.2	29.9
41 Small time and savings accounts	97.3	123.7	93.5	63.5	61.7	80.9	11.3
42 Money market fund shares	1.3	**	.2	6.9	34.4	29.2	104.1
43 Large time deposits	−14.0	−12.0	25.8	46.6	21.2	50.3	43.9
44 Security RPs	.2	2.3	2.2	7.5	6.6	6.5	7.7
45 Foreign deposits	.8	1.7	1.3	2.0	1.5	.9	1.0
46 Total of credit market instruments, deposits and							
** currency**	**149.1**	**178.5**	**190.7**	**219.1**	**261.9**	**237.5**	**273.0**
47 Public support rate (in percent)	19.6	19.0	23.7	25.7	18.8	25.8	24.8
48 Private financial intermediation (in percent)	71.6	83.9	94.4	91.3	79.4	87.8	91.9
49 Total foreign funds	−2.6	10.5	40.8	44.3	19.5	−2.3	35.6
MEMO: Corporate equities not included above							
50 **Total net issues**	**10.6**	**10.6**	**5.7**	**1.2**	**−4.6**	**21.1**	**11.9**
51 Mutual fund shares	−.3	−2.4	.4	−.5	−.6	4.4	9.3
52 Other equiies	10.9	13.1	5.3	1.7	−4.0	16.8	2.6
53 Acquisitions by financial institutions	9.8	12.5	7.4	4.5	10.6	17.7	28.8
54 Other net purchases	.8	−1.9	−1.6	−3.4	−15.1	3.4	−16.9

*Full statements for sectors and transaction types quarterly, and annually for flows and for amounts outstanding, may be obtained from Flow of Funds Section, Division of Research and Statistics, Board of Governors of the Federal Reserve System, Washington, D.C. 20551.
[†]1981 figures are for January–June.
**Is smaller than 0.1.
Notes for part B by line number:
  1. Line 2 of table 1.58.
  2. Sum of lines 3–6 or 7–10.
  6. Includes farm and commercial mortgages.
 11. Credit market funds raised by federally sponsored credit agencies, and net issues of federally related mortgage pool securities.
 12. Line 1 less line 2 plus line 11. Also line 19 less line 26 plus line 32. Also sum of lines 27, 32, and 38 less lines 40 and 46.
 17. Includes farm and commercial mortgages.
 25. Line 38 less lines 40 and 46.
 26. Excludes equity issues and investment company shares. Includes line 18.
 28. Foreign deposits at commercial banks, bank borrowings from foreign branches, and liabilities of foreign banking agencies to foreign affiliates.
 29. Demand deposits at commercial banks.
 30. Excludes net investment of these reserves in corporate equities.
 31. Mainly retained earnings and net miscellaneous liabilities.
 32. Line 12 less line 19 plus line 26.
 33–37. Lines 13–17 less amounts acquired by private finance. Line 37 includes mortgages.
 39. Mainly an offset to line 9.
 46. Lines 32 plus 38, or line 12 less line 27 plus 39 and 45.
 47. Line 2/line 1.
 48. Line 19/line 12.
 49. Sum of lines 10 and 28.
 50, 52. Includes issues by financial institutions.
Source: Federal Reserve Bulletin (January 1982), p. A43.

assets through saving (not consuming up income) and reductions can occur through *dissaving* (consuming more than income). Also, capital gains (increases in the value of assets) can increase net worth. To eliminate capital gains and make flow-of-funds estimates conform to national income accounts, the Federal Reserve values securities at book value where possible.[6] (Roland Robinson's suggestion in 1963 that capital gains should be estimated separately would be a useful addition to this analysis. See Note 3.)

For each sector the sources and uses statement incorporates a basic accounting identity between changes in its assets and liabilities.

$$\Delta \text{ net worth} + \Delta \text{ liabilities} = \Delta \text{ real assets} + \Delta \text{ financial assets} \qquad (12)$$

This accounting identity reflects the familiar *T account*, where the value of assets equals the value of liabilities plus net worth. It reflects the convention that all assets are defined to be claimed by someone, either the individual or a firm in that sector statement (in which case it enters into net worth) or another firm or individual (in which case it is called a liability). The equation is in first-difference form; as before, Δ (delta) means "change in." This conforms with the *flow* variables in the flow-of-funds accounts.

If saving is defined to mean an increase in the value of one's wealth, saving equals Δ net worth. An individual or firms may save or increase its liabilities by borrowing. On the other side of the balance sheet, the value of its assets rise either in the form of real investment or lending (buying bonds). Thus Equation (12) may be rewritten as:

$$\text{saving} + \text{borrowing} = \text{investment} + \text{lending} \qquad (13)$$

For an economy (including the foreign sector) as a whole, borrowing equals lending because for every loan asset there is a financial liability somewhere.

Surplus and Deficit Units

Therefore, from Equation (13), saving equals investment. However, a sector or individual participant may invest more than it saves and therefore demand funds. That is, it may sell financial assets (bonds and stock). These units can be called *deficit units*. A *surplus unit* saves more than it invests. A surplus unit buys financial assets.[7]

A surplus unit can buy financial assets outright or go to a financial intermediary, such as a commercial bank, a savings and loan, or a mutual fund. They would buy the financial assets created by these financial intermediaries, such as bank deposits and shares. These become assets of the public and liabilities of the financial intermediaries.

Instead of buying financial assets from financial intermediaries, surplus units could go directly into the financial markets and buy financial assets. These surplus units include households, government entities, businesses—both financial and nonfinancial, and foreigners.

Government could be said to be saving when it takes in more income (from taxes) than it spends. It runs a surplus. The 1980 entry for the government in Table 4-1 is a negative number, indicating a $61.2 billion deficit.

Government and depository institutions also add a source of funds when they create additional money.

Meanwhile, investors need funds. They want to sell financial assets. Gross domestic investment in 1980 is shown in Table 4-1 to have been $395.3 billion, or 15 percent of GNP. Investors may borrow from financial intermediaries, go directly to the credit markets and sell financial assets, or use their savings.

The Sector Accounts

To organize these flow-of-funds accounts between different entities in the economy, the Federal Reserve divided the economy into twenty sectors and organized the flow-of-funds estimates around this classification. The twenty sectors are:

Households
Farm business
Nonfarm noncorporate business
Corporate nonfinancial business
State and local governments
Rest of the world
U.S. government
Monetary authorities
Commercial banks
Savings and loan associations
Mutual savings banks
Credit unions
Life insurance companies
Other insurance companies
Private pension funds
State and local government employee retirement funds
Finance companies
Real estate investment trusts
Open-end investment companies
Security brokers and dealers

All the sectors, beginning with "rest of the world," which include all the financial sectors, are specifically described in this book. The reader can find the timely data on these sectors by consulting the Federal Reserve's flow-of-funds accounts that appear in the monthly *Federal Reserve Bulletin* from the Board of Governors of the Federal Reserve System.

Table 4-3 is a hypothetical *flow-of-funds matrix* for an economy divided into four sectors: households, business, government, and financial intermediaries.

The table will serve to illustrate the way sectors are compiled and related in the flow-of-funds tables used by the Federal Reserve.

Households saved $100 billion, invested $40 billion, and put the remainder of their savings into financial assets. Savings exceeded investment by $60 billion, the size of the surplus for this sector.

Business saved $20 billion and invested $75 billion, causing a deficit for this sector of $55 billion. It was financed by a $55 billion increase in financial liabilities (borrowings).

Government ran a deficit of $5 billion (a form of dissaving) and borrowed $5 billion by selling bonds (increasing its financial liabilities). The government could also increase its financial liabilities by issuing money (the monetary base) to pay its bills. It is a $5 billion deficit sector.

The financial intermediary sector increased its financial liabilities by $60 billion (say, by increases in NOW accounts at banks) and bought $60 billion in financial assets. No saving or investment occurred, so this sector has neither a deficit nor surplus.

The sum of all sectors also shows no deficit or surplus.

This simplified example does not contain all the intersector flows-of-funds summarized in Table 4-2. It does bring out essential parts of the flow-of-funds analysis, the deficit and surplus of each sector and the nature of the intersector flows. Notice that total saving, $115 billion, equals total investment. The purchase of financial assets, or lending, $120 billion, equals borrowing. Households have purchased all their $60

TABLE 4-3

Hypothetical Flow-of-Funds Matrix for a Unit of Time*
(Billions of Dollars)

	Households		Business		Government		Financial Intermediaries		All Sectors	
	U	S	U	S	U	S	U	S	U	S
Saving (net worth)		100		20		−5				115
Investment	40		75						115	
Net change in financial assets	60							60	120	
Net change in financial liabilities				55		5		60		120
Totals	100	100	75	75	0	0	60	60	235	235
Sector surplus or deficit	60		(55)		(5)		0		0	

*U is uses of funds; S is sources of funds.

billion in financial assets from financial intermediaries. The economic health of sectors, the method of financing, the pressure on markets for investment funds and current interest rates, and the direction of international financial flows are some of the important information that comes from viewing the flow-of-funds matrix.

Interest Rate Forecasting

The demand and supply of loanable funds analysis for the determination of market interest rates presented in Chapter 8 generally uses as its source data flow-of-funds estimates from either the Federal Reserve or a private source. One method of organizing the data is to extrapolate from past history the flow-of-funds matrix for the next period. Expected interest rates, the level of economic activity, and any new flow-of-funds (such as might occur with a large federal goverment deficit) are all taken into account.

The preparation of an estimated flow-of-funds matrix is a large task because innumerable intersector flows must be estimated. If the estimates show that the equalities are not in balance, say, estimated borrowing exceeds estimated lending, interest rate forecasts must be adjusted (in this case, upward).

These kinds of forecasts are made regularly by many organizations that operate in the financial markets. They are important to both corporate officers who must plan financing and to participants in financial markets.

Much analysis is cast in terms of equilibrium rate of interest. This is true of the discussion in Part II of this book. If markets adjusted instantaneously to all new information, in the mode supposed by the efficient markets hypothesis, little would need saying about the yield or rate of return on each asset. The rate of return on all assets would be a given—it would simply be a piece of data—and would be equal, after corrections for risk, for all assets.

As useful as equilibrium analysis is in predicting the direction and probable final level of interest rates, equilibrium is not instantly achieved for all assets, not even financial assets. Knowledge of the sources and uses of the flow of funds of individual sectors is useful in predicting changes in the asset prices and the yield on assets. An increased demand for housing may, for example, nudge the yield on mortgage contracts or stocks of companies supplying the housing industry higher. The increased rate of return should promptly attract funds in the competitive capital markets, driving down the yield to equilibrium rates. The astute traders would see a chance to borrow at equilibrium rates and invest in these higher-yielding financial assets.

It is, in fact, the rise in yields above equilibrium rates that attracts more capital funds to the most profitable sectors, thus allowing financial markets to perform their allocative functions. Similarly, sectors with lower than expected earnings experience an excess supply of their securities, a sell-off that reduces the market value of their assets.

Government Borrowing: An Application of Flow-of-Funds Estimates

The percentage of new funds raised by the federal government in the economy from 1954 to 1980 is shown in Table 4-4 and Figure 4-2. It is evident that in years of big government deficits, such as 1975, the federal government (including government agencies) becomes a very large participant in the capital markets, an immense borrower of funds. Its share grew from an average of 2.7 percent from 1954 to 1960 to an average of 21

Figure 4-2

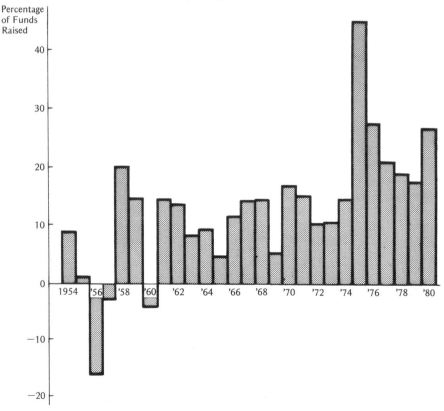

Percentage of total funds raised by federal government (including federal agencies) throught sales of securities, 1954–1980. *Source:* Flow-of-funds data from Federal Reserve, and unofficial U.S. Treasury computations.

TABLE 4-4

Funds Raised Through Various Categories of Obligations, as Percentages of Total Funds Raised for the Calender Years 1954–1980

	1954	1955	1956	1957	1958	1959	1960	1961	1962
Long-term funds									
Mortgages									
Home	31.7	28.5	34.9	26.2	22.9	21.9	26.9	24.0	23.7
Multifamily	1.8	1.9	1.9	1.7	4.4	3.5	5.1	5.3	5.1
Commercial	5.8	4.6	7.9	7.4	6.7	5.1	7.7	7.5	7.8
Farm	1.7	1.8	2.6	1.7	1.6	1.6	1.8	2.0	2.1
Total	40.9	36.8	47.3	37.0	35.6	32.2	41.4	38.8	38.6
Corporate securities									
Bonds	11.1	8.1	16.3	22.8	15.5	7.7	13.1	9.8	9.0
Stocks	7.2	4.4	8.7	8.6	5.7	4.2	4.0	5.4	1.0
Total	18.3	12.5	25.0	31.4	21.1	11.9	17.1	15.2	9.9
Total long-term	59.2	49.3	72.3	68.4	56.8	44.0	58.5	54.0	48.6
Government securities									
U.S. government	7.6	−.2	−18.1	−8.1	20.3	12.3	−5.3	12.5	10.1
Federal agencies	.2	.6	.7	5.3	.0	2.6	1.2	1.9	3.5
State and local governments	20.1	12.0	11.7	12.9	12.5	10.4	12.8	9.5	8.7
Total	28.0	12.4	−5.7	10.1	32.8	25.3	8.6	23.9	22.4
Short-term funds									
Business credit									
Open-market paper	.9	−.3	1.5	2.5	−.0	.5	5.3	1.6	2.1
Bank loans	−.7	16.6	16.7	5.1	−1.1	9.4	8.3	3.9	9.3
U.S. government loans	.4	.9	.7	.1	.3	.1	.2	.4	.7
Federal agency loans	−.1	1.3	−.2	.7	.7	2.0	−.0	1.6	1.7
Finance company loans	.0	1.1	.3	2.9	.1	2.4	4.6	.4	.3
Security RPs	−.2	−.4	−.0	−.3	.1	.4	−.6	.5	.1
Total	.3	19.2	19.0	11.0	.2	14.8	17.8	8.5	14.1
Consumer credit	4.8	16.2	12.7	8.9	1.2	13.4	10.6	4.7	10.2
Security credit	7.1	2.2	−2.1	−.8	3.9	.1	.9	4.2	1.1
Foreign loans									
Banks	1.6	.5	1.2	1.0	1.2	.4	.4	1.3	.7
U.S. government	−.7	−.1	.1	1.0	1.4	−.0	1.0	.9	1.2
Total	.9	.4	1.3	2.0	2.7	.4	1.4	2.2	1.8
Other loans									
U.S. government loans to sponsoring agencies	.0	.1	1.0	−.9	−0	.1	−.2	.1	−.0
U.S. government loans to S&L associations	−1.1	.0	.2	.5	.4	.3	.5	.4	.8
Loans to households	.9	.1	1.2	.8	2.0	1.6	2.0	1.9	1.1
Banks	.0	−.4	.3	−.6	1.0	.6	.1	.5	−.2
U.S. government	.1	.2	.2	.3	.3	.3	.5	.4	.4
Policy loans	.7	.4	.7	1.1	.7	.7	1.5	.9	.8
Total other loans	−.3	.3	2.4	.5	2.4	2.0	2.3	2.4	1.9
Total short-term funds	12.8	38.3	33.4	21.5	10.4	30.6	32.9	22.1	29.1
Total funds raised	100.0	100.0	100.0	100.0	100.0	100.0	100.0	100.0	100.0

TABLE 4-4 (*Continued*)

Funds Raised Through Various Categories of Obligations, as Percentages of Total Funds Raised for the Calender Years 1954–1980

	1963	1964	1965	1966	1967	1968	1969	1970	1971
Long-term funds									
Mortgages									
Home	24.5	22.7	20.6	15.5	15.9	14.9	15.1	13.7	17.2
Multifamily	4.7	6.1	4.4	3.9	3.9	2.9	4.1	6.2	5.7
Commercial	7.3	5.1	5.3	7.3	5.2	5.7	4.9	6.4	5.9
Farm	2.3	2.8	2.7	2.4	2.2	1.8	1.5	.7	1.4
Total	38.8	36.7	33.0	29.1	27.2	25.4	25.5	27.0	30.1
Corporate securities									
Bonds	8.9	9.0	9.7	14.3	18.3	12.3	11.5	20.9	13.5
Stocks	.2	2.0	.4	1.4	2.8	.5	4.3	6.9	7.8
Total	9.1	11.1	10.1	15.7	21.1	12.9	15.8	27.9	21.3
Total long-term	47.9	47.8	43.1	44.9	48.3	38.3	41.4	54.9	51.4
Government securities									
U.S. government	5.9	7.1	1.6	3.0	9.8	8.9	−1.1	11.6	14.9
Federal agencies	2.1	1.8	3.1	8.8	4.7	5.9	6.2	7.9	2.8
State and local governments	8.2	8.0	8.8	7.2	8.6	8.1	8.3	10.1	10.0
Total	16.2	17.0	13.5	19.0	23.2	23.0	13.4	29.6	27.6
Short-term funds									
Business credit									
Open-market paper	1.5	2.9	1.0	5.8	4.6	3.6	10.4	1.9	−.1
Bank loans	9.1	8.2	17.7	12.2	6.7	10.9	13.4	5.1	4.4
U.S. government loans	.6	.8	.7	.7	.8	.4	.4	.7	.4
Federal agency loans	2.4	1.1	1.2	2.0	−2.0	1.0	4.0	2.1	−1.1
Finance company loans	2.0	2.1	2.4	1.4	−.4	1.9	4.1	.3	.8
Security RPs	−.1	.7	1.5	−.1	−.0	.8	4.4	−3.7	2.1
Total	15.5	15.8	24.5	22.1	9.7	18.6	36.6	6.3	6.5
Consumer credit	12.7	13.1	12.8	8.4	6.3	9.8	9.0	4.8	8.4
Security credit	3.8	−.1	1.4	1.0	7.8	5.6	−5.5	−.7	2.2
Foreign loans									
Banks	.9	2.0	.7	−.1	−.4	−.3	−.2	−.2	1.1
U.S. government	1.7	2.2	1.8	1.6	2.8	1.9	1.7	1.2	1.0
Total	2.5	4.1	2.5	1.6	2.4	1.5	1.5	1.0	2.2
Other loans									
U.S. government loans to sponsoring agencies	−.1	.2	.2	−.3	−.1	.2	−.2	.0	.0
U.S. government loans to S&L associations	.3	.3	.4	.8	.2	.3	.6	.1	.2
Loans to households	1.1	1.8	1.6	2.6	2.3	2.7	3.3	4.0	1.5
Banks	.2	.8	.6	.0	.8	1.2	.8	1.7	.7
U.S. government	.3	.4	.3	.7	.4	.4	.4	.3	.2
Policy loans	.6	.6	.6	1.8	1.0	1.1	2.1	2.0	.6
Total other loans	1.3	2.3	2.2	3.1	2.4	3.2	3.7	4.1	1.7
Total short-term funds	35.9	35.2	43.4	36.1	28.5	38.7	45.3	15.6	21.0
Total funds raised	100.0	100.0	100.0	100.0	100.0	100.0	100.0	100.0	100.0

TABLE 4-4 (*Continued*)

Funds Raised Through Various Categories of Obligations, as Percentages of Total Funds Raised for the Calender Years 1954–1980

	1972	1973	1974	1975	1976	1977	1978	1979	1980
Long-term funds									
Mortgages									
Home	20.4	17.4	14.5	18.1	20.2	24.1	20.9	21.4	17.5
Multifamily	5.9	4.0	3.0	.0	.6	1.8	2.0	1.7	1.8
Commercial	7.8	7.4	6.6	4.9	4.2	4.5	4.6	5.1	4.8
Farm	1.7	2.1	2.2	2.0	1.9	2.1	2.0	3.2	3.0
Total	35.8	31.0	26.3	25.0	26.9	32.5	29.6	31.5	27.1
Corporate securities									
Bonds	8.5	5.3	10.4	15.9	11.5	8.8	6.3	6.5	7.7
Stocks	6.4	4.0	2.1	4.7	4.0	1.2	.9	1.5	2.9
Total	15.0	9.3	12.5	20.6	15.5	10.0	7.2	8.0	10.8
Total long-term	50.7	40.3	38.5	45.6	42.4	42.5	36.8	39.5	37.7
Government securities									
U.S. government	6.6	3.1	5.2	37.5	21.4	14.0	10.9	7.7	17.2
Federal agencies	4.3	7.9	9.7	5.4	5.9	6.5	8.0	10.1	10.1
State and local governments	6.8	5.7	7.2	7.1	4.8	5.7	5.6	3.8	5.4
Total	17.8	16.7	22.1	49.9	32.1	26.2	24.5	21.6	32.8
Short-term funds									
Business credit									
Open-market paper	.7	3.2	7.7	−.5	2.5	3.6	5.2	8.0	4.6
Bank loans	10.2	16.5	15.2	−6.5	−.2	5.8	7.3	9.3	6.8
U.S. government loans	.2	.5	1.0	1.3	.9	1.0	1.9	1.7	1.5
Federal agency loans	.4	3.3	4.0	−1.1	.1	1.6	2.9	2.9	2.3
Finance company loans	2.0	1.9	2.1	.9	1.7	2.5	1.6	1.4	.4
Security RPs	1.4	6.5	1.3	.7	4.3	3.0	4.1	3.7	4.5
Total	14.8	32.0	31.4	−5.2	9.3	17.5	23.1	27.0	20.1
Consumer credit	9.2	10.1	4.3	4.2	7.9	9.8	10.0	8.8	.5
Security credit	4.0	−3.1	−2.1	1.6	3.9	1.5	.1	.2	2.1
Foreign loans									
Banks	1.4	1.1	2.0	1.7	2.1	.7	3.6	.4	2.5
U.S. government	.7	.7	.7	1.2	1.0	.7	.8	.6	1.1
Total	2.1	1.7	2.7	2.9	3.1	1.5	4.4	1.0	3.6
Other loans									
U.S. government loans to sponsoring agencies	.0	.0	.3	.4	−.1	−.3	.0	.0	.0
U.S. government loans to S&L associations	.2	.1	.3	.1	.6	.0	−.3	.0	.2
Loans to households	1.1	2.3	2.1	.4	.8	1.2	1.4	1.9	3.1
Banks	.5	1.3	.7	−.5	.2	.7	.7	.7	1.2
U.S. government	.2	.1	.2	.2	.1	.1	.2	.3	.5
Policy loans	.4	.9	1.2	.7	.4	.4	.5	.9	1.4
Total other loans	1.3	2.4	2.7	.9	1.3	1.0	1.1	2.0	3.3
Total short-term funds	31.4	43.0	39.1	4.5	25.5	31.3	38.7	38.9	29.5
Total funds raised	100.0	100.0	100.0	100.0	100.0	100.0	100.0	100.0	100.0

percent in the 1970s. (Negative percentages reflect reductions in the federal debt.) The 1975 percentage of 42.9 stands out as a high point in the 26 years. Notice the precipitous rise in federal agencies' shares, to 10.1 percent in 1979 and 1980. Meanwhile, state and local governments' share dropped during the 1950s and 1960s, climbed in the early 1970s, and then fell again, as shown in Table 4-4.

The rise in federal debt was greater than the recorded deficits, due to the use of substantial off-budget items, not all of which are included in Table 4-4. Loan guarantees, direct loans (mostly made through the Federal Financing Bank, part of the Treasury), loans from government-sponsored enterprises (such as the Federal National Mortgage Association), and even federal tax exemptions for state and local government debt offerings raise credit.[8]

The analysis of the federal government deficit often employs estimates of the credit needs of the federal government. The deficit must be financed by borrowing (selling government securities) or printing money. The increasing proportion of credit raised by the government in the 1970s, as shown in Figure 4-2, has been a cause for concern. As the government enters the market, *it may crowd out* private investment.[9] Large new debt issues by the government temporarily reduce government security prices and raise the rate of interest the government pays. However, the funds flow back into the private sector because they are used to pay for the deficit. Other things being the same, the effect on interest rates should be only temporary. However, if the increased government supplies of securities are suddenly added to an increasing demand for private securities, the effect on interest rates could be longer lasting, pushing long-term private financing into future periods. Whether or not there is any permanent effect on interest rates from the change in government debt is discussed in Chapter 9.

Appendix A: Nominal and Real Values

The value of an asset can be described in either of two forms, *nominal* (or *money*) *values* or *real values*. Nominal values are uncorrected for inflation. In the case of *income*, nominal income is simply the money value of income. Since the *purchasing power* of *money* (the amount of goods and services that can be bought with a unit of money) changes, the measuring standard of nominal values changes.

To correct for changes in the monetary measuring standard, real values are used. Real values are the nominal values corrected for changes in the purchasing power of money using a *price index*.

A price index is the average price per dollar for the purchase of a given group of goods and services compared to their average price in a base period. If the average price is $1.00 in the first period and $1.15 in the second period, the price index in said to have increased 15 percent. The price index in period 2 is $1.15/$1.00 or, multiplying by 100 to make the first period equivalent to a base of 100, 115, a pure number with no units.

There is, in principle, an impossible problem in forming a price index. At any time, different market baskets of goods are consumed by different households; therefore, whenever there are changes in relative prices, a price index must fail to represent the change in the cost of buying a market basket for one or both of these households. The same problem applies over time to a given household, since the market basket of goods purchased in 1970 will not be the same as that purchased in 1982, as relative prices change.

In the United States, price indexes, which are estimated by departments in the federal government, are frequently used to describe price level changes. The *producers' price index* (of wholesale prices) and the *GNP deflator* (of all goods and services included in the gross national product) are estimated regularly. A number of price indexes result from extensive monthly surveys of the Bureau of Labor Statistics. Their *consumer price index* (CPI) is an index of prices based on a particular group of goods and services, called the *market basket*, which is supposed to include the types of things bought by most consumers. An index that is similar in its attempt to measure consumer prices is the *price of consumer expenditures* (PCE). The PCE index measures the average price on *all* consumer goods compared to a base period. (The different methods of calculating the CPI and the CPE are explained subsequently.)

These price indexes are all estimated from sample surveys using modern statistical procedures. The actual construction of a price index, together with some intuitive notion of what it means, can best be illustrated with a simple example. Suppose that two goods, A and B, are purchased in two periods, as shown in Table 4-5.

TABLE 4-5

	Period 1	**Period 2**
Price A	$10	$ 5
Price B	$ 6	$20
Quantity of A sold	10	11
Quantity of B sold	15	7

Forming a Price Index for Two Goods

Index Using Period 1 Weights: *

$$P_L = \frac{10(\$5) + 15(\$20)}{10(\$10) + 15(\$6)} = \frac{\$350}{\$190} = 1.84 \text{ (84 percent rise)}$$

Index Using Period 2 Weights: †

$$P_A = \frac{11(\$5) - 7(\$20)}{11(\$10) - 7(\$6)} = \frac{\$195}{\$152} = 1.28 \text{ (28 percent rise)}$$

*This is called a Laspeyres index, a method used for the CPI index.
†This is called a Paasche index, a method used for the PCE index. Both indexes are usually multiplied by 100 so that $P_L = 184$ and $P_A = 128$, which is equivalent to making the base year outlay equal 100.

The table shows first the money outlay for goods in the first period, $350, divided by the outlay for goods sold in the second period, $190, using in both cases the quantities sold in the first period (the use of base period quantities to weight the prices in both periods characterizes a *Laspeyres price index*). The calculation gives an index of 184 for the second period, or an 84 percent rise in the price level.

This method of calculating an index tends to overstate the rate of inflation. The calculation uses the same quantity in the second period of a good that has gone up in price, when relatively less is likely to be sold at the higher price. This weighting system gives too much weight to goods with rising prices and not enough weight to goods with falling prices.

If the quantities sold in the second period are used as weights, the inflation tends to be understated because the weights are biased in the other direction (this system of weighting, using current period quantities, characterizes a *Paasche price index*). The lower quantities sold in the second period for goods that have risen in price are also used for the first period. This method of forming an index gives too little weight to goods with rising prices. Thus the calculations in Table 4-5 indicate a smaller rate of inflation, 28 percent.

The price level P is estimated by the value of the price index. In Table 4-5, $P = 184$ or 128 in the second period according to the method selected for its calculation. The price level is a measure of the amount of goods and services that can be exchanged for a dollar, on the average, compared to a base year, or by calculating the percentage change, to any year after the base year. For example, if P doubles (P would equal 200 in the second period in Table 4-5), a $1 bill can, on the average, be exchanged for half as many units of goods and services. The *purchasing power* of a dollar declines by half. If the price index changes further, from 184 to 200, the price level rises by $\frac{16}{200}$, or 8 percent. The *exchange price* (or *real value*) of a dollar is given by $1/P$. The exchange price (or real value) of M units of money is M/P.

Appendix B: Saving and Investment Defined by Common Usage

This simplified Keynesian analysis presents definitions of saving and investment which do not conform to the popular usage of those terms. Most individuals consider the purchase of items such as stocks, bonds, or precious coins to be an act of investment. Investment, in this usage, is simply the acquisition of wealth. This concept of investment differs from the national income accounting definition, which defines the production of goods that are not used up in the current period as investment.

This definition of investment is broader than that used in the national income accounts. The acquisition of wealth by an individual may be divided into two parts. Some of the wealth is newly produced. This is investment in either the common usage or national income definition. Other wealth acquisition is merely a transfer of wealth with no new wealth being produced. Common usage includes this transaction in the concept of investment. Those who use national income accounting definitions consider this a *portfolio adjustment* that should not be part of national income.

Saving is in common usage defined to be the residual, after consumption, from all income. A broad definition of income includes capital gains, transfer payments, and income from the production of new goods and services. This is quite a useful concept as an important determinant in analysis of spending. All these parts of broadly defined income add to an individual's wealth; therefore, changes in this measure of income will probably be associated with changes in spending.

The use of capital gains to define income raises immense problems in defining the value of capital. Generally, income is defined at a given level of interest, which means that there are no capital gains or losses. Such a concept of income for the private sector has been used in a number of analyses.

Capital gains and losses are *balance sheet* changes. A balance sheet increase in the value of an asset such as a house is simply an increase in its market value. Balance sheet changes are vital for analyzing financial flows, as displayed subsequently in the flow-of-funds. Financial market observers generally cannot afford to wait for observable interest rate changes that reflect these balance sheet changes. They will want to keep a close watch on the flow-of-funds and on the values of portfolios.

Appendix C: Some Words of Caution

Finally, some words of caution about the meaning and accuracy of the flow-of-funds data and an important lesson illustrated by flow-of-funds analysis are presented. Suppose that the Katz Corporation borrows funds (by selling bonds) and invests the funds in bonds issued by the Quilt Corporation. Quilt then lends the excess cash it has to the Lilt Corporation by buying Lilt bonds. If each bond purchase was $100 million, $300 million in bonds were sold. However, there is no increase in funds available to the private sector. There may well be a better distribution of funds if Lilt can use the funds more profitably than Quilt or Katz.

The point of caution is that sources of funds in the flow-of-funds accounts is not a faultless indicator of the supply of new credit (loans) and new equity capital (funds available for stock purchases) because of a large and unknown amount of double counting the same funds.

The attempt to make the flow-of-funds estimates conform to national income concepts introduces some unsolved problems in the estimates by the Federal Reserve. In particular, the method for eliminating capital gains, discussed previously, is not satisfactory.

Another word of caution concerns the need to take account of both sides of a transaction, a lesson driven home by the flow-of-funds matrix. Failure to take account of both sides of a transaction can flaw an analysis. For example, a large purchase of gold, financed by U.S. dollar bank deposits, would not necessarily deplete the U.S. banking system's reserves if the sellers of gold redeposit the dollar deposits, which then flow back into U.S. banks.

NOTES

1. Lawrence S. Ritter, "The Flow-of-Funds Accounts: A New Approach to Financial Market Analysis," *Journal of Finance* (May 1963), p. 220.
2. The term $r_B\lambda$ is the premium over the real rate of interest for the decline in the purchasing power of a discrete interest payment during the year when that payment is made on the last day of the year. No such premium is paid on an account that pays continuous interest, as described in Chapter 5.
3. M. A. Copeland, *A Study of Moneyflows in the United States* (New York: National Bureau of Economic Research, 1952); *Flow of Funds in the United States*, Board of Governors of the Federal Reserve System (1955); Ritter, "The Flow-of-Funds Accounts," pp. 219–230; William C. Freund and Edward D. Zinbarg, "Application of Flow of Funds to Interest-Rate Forecasting," *Journal of Finance* (May 1963), pp. 231–248; and Stephen Taylor, "Uses of Flow-of-Funds Accounts in the Federal Reserve System," *Journal of Finance* (May 1963), pp. 249–258. Also read the interesting comment by Roland I. Robinson suggesting that capital gains and losses be estimated separately ["Comment," *Journal of Finance* (May 1963), pp. 262–263].
4. Freund and Zinbarg, "Application of Flow of Funds," p. 238.
5. Taylor, "Uses of Flow-of-Funds Accounts," p. 250.
6. The book value of a firm is its net worth, as recorded in its accounting records. It is sometimes expressed as dollars per share of stock. The book value of a bond is the value of it on the firm's books, an amount that may be changed to bring it into agreement with its amortized value.
7. A deficit unit invests more than it saves and therefore demands funds (sells financial assets). A surplus unit saves more than it invests (buys financial assets). Channeling funds from surplus units to deficit units is one of the primary functions of financial markets and financial intermediaries.

   One group of participants is composed of neither deficit nor surplus units when we employ the concept of income used in the national income accounts. As noted previously, this concept of income does not include capital gains or losses. Many individuals rearrange their portfolio of wealth to achieve capital gains or to limit capital losses. In the national income sense they are neither investors nor savers. Therefore, to the classification that begins with deficit and surplus units, a third category of participants, *portfolio traders*, can be added.

   One phenomenon that makes most citizens portfolio traders is inflation, the decline in the value of money and all assets denominated in money units, such as bonds, where their declining real value is not offset by increased interest payments. This causes individuals to economize on cash balances and bonds that do not pay a rate of interest to cover the expected rate of inflation, by rearranging their wealth. The costs of this *churning* (buying and selling financial assets) may be quite large since, although money balances must be reduced to avoid the tax of inflation, they must also be replenished to provide a medium of exchange. This churning is a wasteful use of resources and one of the most important costs of inflation.

8. See Herman B. Leonard and Elizabeth H. Rhyne, "Federal Credit and the 'Shadow Budget'," *The Public Interest* (Fall 1981) pp. 40–58.

9. See Roger W. Spencer and William P. Yohe, "The 'Crowding Out' of Private Expenditures by Fiscal Policy Actions," *Preview*, Federal Reserve Bank of St. Louis (October 1971), pp. 12–24; and V. Vance Roley, "The Financing of Federal Deficits: An Analysis of Crowding Out," *Economic Review*, Federal Reserve Bank of Kansas City (July–August 1981), pp. 16–29. The models used in these articles use national income concepts and therefore may not reflect balance sheet changes and certain nominal flows-of-funds that may be important parts of crowding out that are not easily picked up in market interest rates or current national income variables. Whether this is true or not is an important subject for further research. Spencer and Yohe touch on this issue, as does Robert Auerbach, who contends that the government budget constraint was not properly incorporated (Spencer and Yohe, p. 23). There have been a number of analyses that do take the government budget constraint into account, but this leads into an entire new line of analysis. For the interested reader, a sample is found in Robert Auerbach and Jack Rutner, "A Negative View of the Negative Money Multiplier: Comment," *Journal of Finance* (December 1977), pp. 1814–1817.

STUDY QUESTIONS

1. Define wealth, income (real and nominal), the flow-of-funds, and real and nominal interest rates.

2. What kind of income (in the eyes of the recipient) is not defined as income in a national income accounting sense? Do owners of stock generally make this distinction and prefer income in the national accounting sense?

3. What has happened over time to the role of the U.S. federal government as a participant in financial markets in financing the federal deficit? Explain.

4. Describe the Federal Reserve's flow-of-funds account estimates. What words of caution should be remembered in using these estimates?

5. Recalculate the numerical example used in this chapter for Equation (11) for the real cost of a one-year loan for a tax rate that is half as large as the one used. What effect would this tax reduction have on investments?

6. How do inflation and tax rates affect the computation of interest rates? Does it follow that deflation would be good for investment? Explain.

7. Depreciation is subtracted from GNP (together with other adjustments) to obtain an estimate of national income, the value of output in a year. What is depreciation? How does it occur? Is it always due to a physical change in a capital stock? Can it be viewed as an adjustment to avoid double counting wealth produced in a previous period? Explain.

8. Describe the concepts of saving, investment, and income.

9. Calculate both a Laspeyres and a Paasche price index based on the following information:

	Prices	
	Period 1	Period 2
Price of good A	$100	$200
Price of good B	$300	$200
Quantity of A	12	5
Quantity of B	8	18

10. What are some important problems in estimating a price index?

5

The Arithmetic of Interest Rates

Introduction

The price of an asset and its expected income are related by its interest rate (also called yield or rate of return). Whereas the price of an asset has the dimension of dollars, the expected *flow* of income has the dimension of dollars per unit of time. The interest rate is a pure number per unit of time, such as 5 percent a year. The interest rate shows the time dimension of an asset. To illuminate this view of the interest rate, consider its reciprocal. The reciprocal of the interest rate is called the *year's purchase*. The reciprocal of 5 percent a year is 1/.05/year, or 20 years. This means that a dollar invested at 5 percent interest will be repaid (at simple interest) in 20 years.

Interest rates thus measure the connecting link between the *stock* of assets and their expected *flow* of income (or payment stream). Learning the arithmetic of relationships between interest rates and these stocks and flows is a necessary first step for fruitful analysis.

There are a number of important statistics used to describe financial assets, including their price, the size of their payment stream, and their yield. These statistics can often be found in bond and annuity tables, provided that the characteristics of the financial asset conform to the assumptions in the table. Tables are certainly useful and should be used, just as a cashier making a retail sale uses a sales tax chart or a programmed calculation in the cash register. But understanding the nature of financial assets requires that the underlying computational procedures be known. These underlying computations reveal the relationship between the income, market value, and yield on a financial asset. The best way to become familiar with these relationships is to examine the underlying formulas and, most important of all, actually to calculate the statistics for different types of financial assets. It is possible to stare for a long time at a formula that gives the present value of a bond without understanding it. Substituting in actual values for a bond's income stream and yield and actually calculating the present value is, like a picture, worth a thousand words.

That learning experience can be more rewarding and enjoyable than many other trips to the land of mathematics. That is because the versatile hand computer takes almost all the drudgery out of the tedious arithmetic calculations. Multiplying (1.0675) by itself 25 times—as is required for a bond maturing in twenty-five years with a $6\frac{3}{4}$ percent yield—is a headache and a half with only pencil and paper. On many calculators, 1.0675 is punched in, the Y^x button is pushed, 25 is punched in, and then the = (equal) key is pushed. In a second, the answer, 5.119141, appears. The drudgery is gone. Only the satisfaction of learning the practical skills of computing statistics for financial assets on a modern calculator is involved.

It is necessary to have a calculator that contains at least the following features: (1) a Y^x key for raising a number to a higher power or for taking a root and (2) several memories, including a summation memory. If you wish to learn continuous compounding, your calculator should have natural logarithms. Business calculators programmed for the formulas in this chapter should not be used to learn these procedures.

The body of the chapter contains five basic sections: "Compounding Once a Year," "Discounting Once a Year," "Perpetuities," "Internal Rate of Return," and "Compounding More than Once a Year."

Appendix A introduces the annuity formula, a valuable tool for calculating the statistics not only of annuities, but also of bonds, sinking funds, mortgages, and general amortized loans. (The method of calculating the yield on a debt instrument such as a Treasury bill that has no coupon payments was shown in Chapter 2).

Appendix B presents continuous compounding and discounting and Appendix C contains two rule-of-thumb approximations for the time it takes asset values to double. Appendix D presents a frequently used procedure for calculating balance and interest payments on the periodic repayment of loans.

This chapter contains numerous examples, including twelve practice problems and detailed solutions. The first twelve study questions at the end of the chapter repeat the practice problems in the chapter, with different numbers, for further practice.

All payments on the financial assets in this chapter are treated as though there is no risk of default. The treatment of probability of default is discussed in Part IV.

Compounding Once a Year

Suppose that the interest payment on a savings account is to be calculated and added to the account once a year. This is called *compounding once a year*. If $100 were initially deposited and the interest rate were 5 percent per year, $5 interest would be paid at the end of the first year. This would increase the deposit balance to $105. During the entire second year, the deposit would have amounted to $105; the account would be paid 5 percent of that, or $5.25, on the last day of the second year. Interest would be earned on the interest earned in previous periods. At the end of the second year, the account would have a balance of $110.25 at the compound interest rate of 5 percent.

This example of compound interest can be put in more general form. If $100r$ is the (percentage) interest rate and R_1 is the value of the deposit at the end of the first year, then

$$\text{PV}(1 + r) = R_1 \tag{1}$$

where PV is called the present value of R_1. If R_1 is compounded for another year,

$$R_1(1 + r) = R_2 \tag{2}$$

where R_2 is the value of the deposit at the end of the second year. This process can be repeated for any number of years. Rather than write this long expression, the terms can be collected into a simpler general statement:

$$\text{PV}(1 + r)^Y = R_Y \qquad\qquad \textit{Compound Interest} \tag{3}$$

where Y is the number of years and R_Y is called the *return* at the end of the Yth year. This is the *compound interest* or *future value formula*. It is a basic formula of finance. Every formula in this chapter can be derived from Equation (3).

Returning to the mathematical example, suppose that $100 is left on deposit for three years at a 5 percent interest rate. The deposit grows to $105 at the end of the first year. Five percent of that plus the $105 equals $110.25, the value of the deposit at the end of the second year. Five percent of that is $5.5125, so that the deposit is $115.7625 at the end of the third year. If Equation (3) is used, the same result is obtained. First, multiply 1.05 by itself three times, which equals 1.157625. Multiply this product by the original principal, $100, and $115.7625 is obtained. This is the value of $100 compounded once a year, for three years, at 5 percent.

1 | PRACTICE PROBLEM

Compounding

Suppose that $752.39 is deposited in a savings account on January 1, 1928. How large would the balance be on March 4, 1988, if interest had been paid at a rate of $3\frac{1}{2}$ percent compounded and payable on December 31 of each year? Repeat for 10.5 percent interest.

Answer: The last compounding will have been December 31, 1987, which would have been the fifty-ninth yearly compounding. The compounding factor is unity plus the interest rate, 1.035. Taking the compounding factor up to the 59th power, it equals 7.611682. Multiply this amount by the original deposit, $752.39, to obtain the answer, $5726.95; at 10.5 percent the answer is $272,155.69.

Discounting Once a Year

The terms in Equation (3), the compound interest formula, can be rearranged so that they appear as

$$PV = \frac{R_Y}{(1 + r)^Y} \qquad \qquad \textit{Discounting or Present Value} \quad (4)$$

This is called the *discounting or present value formula.* The present value of future income discounted once a year, at the end of the year, at a rate of r is given by the discounting formula. In the previous example, the $110.25 expected at the end of the second year has a present value of $100 if it is discounted at 5 percent. If R_Y is expected in the Yth year, the present value can be obtained if the interest rate is known.

2 | PRACTICE PROBLEM

Discounting

If John's rich aunt leaves him $100,000 payable ten years after her death, what is its present value at the time of her death using a 7 percent interest rate (and assuming that the bequest is not taxed)? The answer is obtained by discounting $100,000 back ten years at 7 percent.

Answer:

$$\frac{\$100,000}{(1.07)^{10}} = \$50,834.93$$

PRACTICE PROBLEM | **3**

Discounting

Wilma suddenly remembers a savings account she opened seventy years earlier. She finds that it presently contains a balance of $146.06. How much did she originally deposit if the interest rate was 3 percent for the first forty years and 5 percent for the last thirty years?

The answer is found by first discounting $146.06 back thirty years at 5 percent:

$$\frac{\$146.06}{(1.05)^{30}} = \$33.795$$

Then that sum (saving the integers to the right of the decimal point for the accuracy needed for high powers—repeated compounding) is in turn discounted back forty years at 3 percent.

Answer:

$$\frac{\$33.795}{(1.03)^{40}} = \$10.36$$

The discounting formula can be put in general terms for a stream of income R_1, R_2, and so on, to R_N: a rate of discount r and an initial present value PV.

$$PV = \frac{R_1}{1 + r} + \frac{R_2}{(1 + r)^2} + \cdots + \frac{R_N}{(1 + r)^N} \quad \underline{\begin{array}{c}\textit{Present Value of an}\\ \textit{Income Stream}\end{array}} \quad (5)$$

This formula says that the present value is the discounted value of expected future returns. The time periods can begin in the present period 0 and continue to the termination of income in period N. The income stream in Equation (5) begins with an annual payment one year in the future.

PRACTICE PROBLEM | **4**

Discounting a Stream of Income

Suppose that a three-year bond has a coupon payment of $70.00 each year, a 7 percent coupon rate, and an annual (December 3) payment date. In the third year, the owner of the bond receives the $70.00 coupon payment plus the $1000 face value of the bond. The present value of $70.00 one year in the future is

$$\$65.42 = \frac{\$70}{1 + r}$$

Suppose that $r = .05$; then the present value of the bond is

$$\$1054.47 = \frac{\$70}{1.05} + \frac{\$70}{(1.05)^2} + \frac{\$1070}{(1.05)^3}$$

Now take out your calculator, clear it, and solve the equation. Here are some hints that are useful for most calculators. First, enter 1.05 on the calculator. If the calculator has a memory, store this in the memory; then divide by $70.00. Then take the reciprocal, 1/x. This should equal $66.6667. If the calculator has a summation memory, push the summation button. If it does not, record the number. Now recall 1.05 from the memory and square it. Divide it by $70.00 and take the reciprocal. Again, if the calculator has a summation button, sum this number into the summation memory; if it does not, record the number. Recall 1.05 from the memory and cube it; that is, take it up to the power of 3. This is 1.1576. Divide by $1070.00 and take the reciprocal. This is $924.30. Again, sum it into the memory or record it. Next, either recall the three amounts summed into the memory or add them up from the record you are keeping, to obtain the present value, $1054.47, rounding to the nearest penny.

Perpetuities

Equation (5) can be simplified if the income stream is the same for every future period. That is, $R_1 = R_2 = R_3 = \cdots = R_N$, where N is a very large number. This simplification is useful in analyses where the shape of the income stream is not important. It is used in Chapter 9 in the explanation of real interest rates.

A bond with such a perpetual income stream is called a *perpetuity*, or in the case of such bonds sold by the British government, a consol. Preferred stock that pays a perpetual income stream has these characteristics.

To simplify, let R be the yearly payment. Then Equation (5) can be rewritten as

$$PV = R\left[\frac{1}{1+r} + \frac{1}{(1+r)^2} + \cdots + \frac{1}{(1+r)^N}\right] \tag{6}$$

Simplifying, letting $L = 1/(1 + r)$ and calling the sum of the terms in the brackets S,

$$S = L + L^2 + \cdots + L^N \tag{7}$$

Multiply both sides of Equation (7) by L, subtract the resultant equation from Equation (7), and factor out S to obtain

$$S(1 - L) = L - L^{N+1} \tag{8}$$

L^{N+1} is a fraction multiplied by itself many times, so that its value approaches zero and may be discarded. Equation (8) then becomes, after dividing through by $(1 - L)$,

$$S = \frac{L}{1 - L} \tag{9}$$

or, substituting back in $1/(1 + r)$ for L,

$$S = \frac{\dfrac{1}{1 + r}}{1 - \dfrac{1}{1 + r}} = \frac{1}{1 + r - 1} = \frac{1}{r} \tag{10}$$

Then Equation (6) is dramatically simplified, since the sum of the terms in the brackets is simply $1/r$, to give the following formula for the value of a perpetuity:

$$PV = \frac{R}{r} \qquad\qquad Perpetuity \quad (11)$$

PRACTICE PROBLEM | **5**

Perpetuities

What is the present value of a perpetuity paying $10 a year if the interest rate is 4 percent?

Answer:

$$\frac{\$10}{.04} = \$250$$

Internal Rate of Return

In most cases, the buyer of a bond knows the present value, its present price on the market. The buyer also knows the payments stream. The unknown variable is the interest rate or yield or, as it is sometimes also called, the *internal rate of return*.

The value of the internal rate of return is found through a trial-and-error hunt called *iteration*. Iteration merely amounts to trying different interest rates in equations until one is obtained that is consistent with the present value, the price for which the bond is being sold in the market. Some business calculators find this internal rate of return merely by inserting the price and the dated payment pattern. Programmable calculators with enough memories and program steps can be programmed to look for the correct yield. If you have the time, you can insert different interest rates into the discount formula, solve for the present value for each interest rate, and correcting each time in the right direction, see if you can sail into port in this more tedious blindfolded navigational feat.

If other characteristics are the same, such as risk and call features, the buyer will want to choose the investment that gives the highest internal rate of return. An elaboration of the point is presented in Chapter 12. The possibility of obtaining more than one internal rate of return that satisfies Equation (5) (due to multiple roots) is shown to require an alternative to this investment rule.

Compounding More than Once a Year

Suppose that a depository intermediary compounds quarterly to calculate interest payments on deposits. Then, instead of paying r percent interest rate each quarter, it pays $r/4$, or $\frac{1}{4}$ of the yearly interest each quarter. Also, instead of compounding Y times in Y years, it compounds $4Y$ times.

More generally, suppose that the interest is compounded N times a year. Then r/N interest is paid each compounding time and compounding occurs NY times in Y years.

It is an easy matter to substitute these new values in Equation (3) for compounding N times a year.

$$\text{PV}\left(1 + \frac{r}{N}\right)^{NY} = R_Y \qquad \qquad \textit{Compounding More} \atop \textit{than Once a Year} \quad (12)$$

It turns out that Equation (12) is not only useful in calculating quarterly (four times), semiannual (two times), and other discrete values of N; it is also a step toward continuous compounding where N approaches infinity, as shown in Appendix B to this chapter. A higher interest payment is obtained for the same interest rate with more compoundings per year.

---

6 | PRACTICE PROBLEM

Compounding More than Once a Year

How large will a deposit of $400 become in ten years in a savings account paying 7 percent interest if compoundings are made: once at the end of the year, semiannually, quarterly, and daily?

Compounding once at the end of each year is given by Equation (3):

$$\$400(1.07)^{10} = \$786.86$$

Compounding semiannually (twice a year) is given by Equation (12):

$$\$400\left(1 + \frac{.07}{2}\right)^{(10)(2)} = \$400(1.035)^{20} = \$795.91$$

Compounding quarterly is also given by Equation (12):

$$\$400\left(1 + \frac{.07}{4}\right)^{(10)(4)} = \$400(1.0175)^{40} = \$800.64$$

Compounding daily, assuming a 365-day year is used, is also given by Equation (12):

$$\$400\left(1 + \frac{.07}{365}\right)^{(10)(365)} = \$400(1.0001918)^{3650} = \$805.45$$

The differences between the final deposit balances due to these different frequencies of compounding are not large. After a ten-year period, the difference in the final deposit balance between the daily compounding and the once-a-year compounding is $18.59, which has a present value (Equation 4), using 7 percent, of $9.45. Thus, if $409.45, instead of $400.00 had been compounded once a year, the same final balance as under daily compounding, $805.45, would have been obtained. Alternatively, an interest rate of 7.2501 percent, instead of 7 percent, could have been used for end-of-the year compounding, to achieve a final balance of $805.45. The difference in the final deposit balances with the different frequencies of compounding would be larger with either more years of growth or higher interest rates.

Appendix A: Annuity Formula: Applications for Financial Assets

1. Compound Value of an Annuity

Suppose that Walter Johnson began working at age 21 for the United Tool Company. Each month, $100 was invested for Walter by the United Tool Company at a 7 percent annual yield. How much would Mr. Johnson receive in addition to the customary gold watch at age 65 when he rose to speak at his retirement party? This method of saving is embodied in a contract called an *annuity*.

The solution begins by noticing that Mr. Johnson receives one month's interest rate on the last payment one month before he retires. That amount is $P(1 + r)$, from Equation (3), where P is the $100 monthly payment and r is the *monthly* interest rate (.07 per year/12). Two months interest is received on the payment made two months before retirement, giving a total of $P(1 + r)^2$ at retirement; and so on backward in time to his first payment, which occurred one month after he started. If N is the number of months Mr. Johnson worked at United Tool, that first month's payment would, at age 65, amount to $P(1 + r)^{N-1}$. Mr. Johnson will have worked 44 years, which (times 12 months) is 528 months, the value of N.

The sum S of the values of these monthly payments will be 100 times what will have accrued from monthly payments of $1; the latter sum can be painlessly computed from a formula derived as follows: For ease in notation, let $L^i = (1 + r)^i$, where i takes values from 1 (on the final payment) to $N - 1$ (on the first payment). Then

$$S = 1 + L + L^2 + \cdots + L^{N-1} \tag{13}$$

Multiply each side of Equation (13) by L, subtract the resultant equation from Equation (13), and factor out the S to obtain

$$S(1 - L) = 1 - L^N \tag{14}$$

Dividing through by $1 - L$ and substituting back $(1 + N)^i$ for L^i, Equation (14) becomes

$$S = \frac{1 - L^N}{1 - L} = \frac{1 - (1 + r)^N}{1 - (1 + r)} = \frac{1 - (1 + r)^N}{-r} \tag{15}$$

Multiplying the numerator and denominator of the fraction by -1 and allowing the payments to be a multiple of $1, or P dollars per month, the final value of the annuity after N periods is found:

$$P\left[\frac{(1 + r)^N - 1}{r}\right] = \text{FVA} \qquad \textit{Final Value of an Annuity} \tag{16}$$

where FVA is shorthand for *final value* of the *annuity*. From this equation, with $P = 100$, the value of Walter's annuity at age 65 can easily be calculated to be $352,535.39.

---

7 | PRACTICE PROBLEM

Compound Value of an Annuity

If $37 is put into an annuity each month for seven years and the interest rate is 8.5 percent per year, what is the final value of the annuity?

The answer is easily found from Equation (16):

$$\$37\left[\frac{\left(1 + \dfrac{.085}{12}\right)^{(7)(12)} - 1}{\dfrac{.085}{12}}\right] = \$37\left[\frac{(1.0070833)^{84} - 1}{.0070833}\right] = \$4227.05$$

Compound Value of an Annuity

How much should be deposited in a savings account each month if $10,000 is desired in four years and the account pays 6 percent interest, compounded monthly?

The problem is to find the size of the monthly payments. The number of months N is 48. Since the future value is known, Equation (16) may be used to find P.

$$P\left[\frac{\left(1 + \frac{.06}{12}\right)^{48} - 1}{\frac{.06}{12}}\right] = P\left[\frac{(1.005)^{48} - 1}{.005}\right] = \$10,000 \qquad P = \$184.85$$

2. Present Value of Annuities

The final value of an annuity is given by Equation (16). It is the sum of all future payments compounded to the date of final payout. The present value of that amount is found by discounting that sum back to the present period. The present value is found by dividing by $(1 + r)^N$, in the same manner as shown by Equation (4).[1]

$$P\left[\frac{\frac{(1 + r)^N - 1}{r}}{(1 + r)^N}\right] = \text{PVA} \tag{19A}$$

where PVA is shorthand for *present value* of the *annuity*. Equation (19A) can be simplified using the notation $(1 + r)^{-N}$ for $1/(1 + r)^N$.

$$\text{PVA} = P\left[\frac{1 - (1 + r)^{-N}}{r}\right] \qquad \textit{Present Value of an Annuity} \tag{19B}$$

For the example of the $100 straight annuity paid monthly for 528 months, using 7 percent per year interest, the present value is

$$\$100\left[\frac{1 - \left(1 + \frac{.07}{12}\right)^{-528}}{\frac{.07}{12}}\right] = \$100\left[\frac{1 - (1.005833)^{-528}}{.005833}\right] = \$16,347.90$$

There is a simple rule-of-thumb approximation for this computation shown in Note 1.

3. Present Value of Bonds

The PVA Equation (5) is useful in calculating the present value of bonds and other periodic incomes or payments. A bond has a series of equally spaced interest payments. In addition, if the bond is not a perpetuity, the return of the face value is due at maturity. Therefore, in Equation (5), insert the coupon payments each year. Then insert the final face value payment, which is usually the last payment, together with a coupon payment. Solve the formula by using a market rate of interest.

---

9 | PRACTICE PROBLEM

Present Value of a Bond

Suppose that a bond which yields 5 percent and matures in twenty years has semiannual interest payments of $70 and a final return of face value of $1000. What is its present value? Equation (5) requires a tedious series of computations. Instead, the present value of the interest payments PVA_I may first be calculated by using Equation (19B) for the present value of an annuity.

$$PVA_I = \$70 \left[\frac{1 - \left(1 + \frac{.05}{2}\right)^{(-20)(2)}}{\frac{.05}{2}} \right] = \$70 \left[\frac{1 - (1.025)^{-40}}{.025} \right] = \$1757.19$$

The present value of the return of the face value PVA_{FV} is obtained by using Equation (3).

$$PVA_{FV} = \frac{1000}{(1.025)^{40}} = \$372.43$$

Adding PVA_I to PVA_{FV}, the present value of the bond is obtained, $2129.62.[2]

4. Sinking Funds

Sinking funds are roughly the equivalent of the payment side of bonds. The debtor (the borrower) pays interest to the creditor (the lender) and deposits into his or her own account payments, which accumulate until the full principal borrowed is achieved. Then there is a lump-sum return of principal payment to the creditor at the termination date of the loan. The major difference between the computations for a sinking fund and a bond is that in a sinking fund the debtor may obtain interest on the account where the periodic payments are made. The interest from the account may be different from the interest on the loan.

Sinking Funds

Suppose that the Fence Company borrowed $125,000 for five years at 11 percent interest compounded quarterly. The principal is accumulated monthly in a savings account paying 6 percent interest. What is the interest cost of the loan and the size of the sinking fund payments?

The interest payment on $125,000 is simply 11 percent a year or $13,750 per year, since the balance is not reduced until the termination of the loan.

To find the offsetting interest payment and the size of the periodic payments into the deposit, use the annuity Equation (16). The final value of the annuity FVA is constrained by the need to return the principal, $125,000, and the interest rate in the savings account, which is 6 percent.

$$P\left[\frac{\left(1 + \frac{.06}{12}\right)^{60} - 1}{\frac{.06}{12}}\right] = P\left[\frac{(1.005)^{60} - 1}{.005}\right] = \$125,000$$

Solving for P gives $1791.60. Therefore, each three months these payments accumulate to three times $1791.60, which equals $5374.80. In addition, the interest payment to the creditor, the direct interest payment, is .11/4 times $125,000, which equals $3437.50. The total of these payments is $8812.30. This means that a loan of $125,000 will cost (as a close approximation) $8812.30 every quarter for five years. Equation (19B) may be used to find the interest rate that would equate this payment stream with a present value of $125,000.

$$\$8812.3\left[\frac{1 - (1 + r)^{-20}}{r}\right] = \$125,000$$

For ease in computation, divide through by $8812.30 to obtain

$$\frac{1 - (1 + r)^{-20}}{r} = \$14.1847$$

Either an annuity table may be consulted, or different values for r may be inserted until the correct value is obtained. (The Rule of 78 discussed in Appendix D provides a method for approximating the yield.) The value of r is 3.5216 percent or 14.848 percent, stated at a yearly rate; that is, if compounding quarterly, $(1.035216)^4 = 1.14848$. The high interest reflects the fact that in addition to the interest on the loan, funds must be tied up in the sinking fund at a lower return.[3] These funds lose the interest they could have earned if they had been used to reduce the principal. Mortgages or amortized loans allow the principal to be reduced with each payment. They are discussed next.

5. Mortgages and Amortization

Suppose that a homeowner wants to find out how much he or she owes on a thirty-year mortgage. If he or she borrowed $50,000.00 at 8.5 percent nine years (108 months) ago and has been making a payment of $384.46 each month (excluding other payments for taxes, insurance, etc.), the annuity formula, Equation (16), can be used in a new formulation to compute the balance. If no payments had been made on the mortgage, the balance would simply be found by inserting the original amount borrowed in the compound interest formula, Equation (3), with N now representing the number of months instead of Y. Since the homeowner has made monthly payments in the same form as an annuity, the annuity formulation in Equation (16) becomes an offsetting amount. The balance B_N after N months is

$$B_N = B_0 (1 + r)^N - P\left[\frac{(1 + r)^N - 1}{r}\right] \qquad \textit{Mortgage Balance} \quad (20)$$

where B_0 is the original amount borrowed and r is the monthly rate of interest (it is .085/12 or .0070833 in this example). The homeowner still owes $45,110.84, according to this formulation. On a more positive note, he or she has paid off $4889.16 of the loan, which, together with the down payment and capital gain, may make his or her net assets larger than nine years before.

An equivalent method of computation uses the present value of the payments that have not been made. Let j be the number of payments that have not been made. The present value of these payments is given by Equation (19B), where B_N is substituted for PVA to signify the balance after N payments:

$$B_N = P\left[\frac{1 - (1 + r)^{-j}}{r}\right] \qquad \textit{Mortgage Balance} \quad (21)$$

(Notice that $N + j$ is the total number of payments if the mortgage is not paid off before it matures.) This computation procedure, unlike Equation (20), does not require explicit introduction of the amount borrowed. Equation (20) has the advantage of being intuitively easy to understand, as in the example presented.

Either equation yields the same answer, except for small differences due to rounding errors. Rounding errors occur because the dollar amounts are rounded to the nearest penny. In the example presented, B_N obtained from Equation (21) is $45,111.75 after 108 payments, so that $j = 252$. There is a $0.91 difference between the answers given by the two computational procedures.

The mortgage formulations can also be used for any loan where the principal and interest are repaid in equal periodic payments. These loans are called *amortized loans*.

PRACTICE PROBLEM | **11**

Amortized Loan

Suppose that a ten-year loan of $50,000 from a bank is amortized. The interest rate is 7 percent compounded annually. How large are the periodic payments? How much is owed after the sixth payment?

The size of the periodic payments can be found by inserting these values in Equation (21) (using the fact that the balance left when $j = 10$—when no payments have been made—is $50,000):

$$\$50,000 = P\left[\frac{1 - (1.07)^{-10}}{.07}\right]$$

(handwritten: $266{,}000 = P\left[\dfrac{1 - (1.13)^{-30}}{.13}\right]$ 2220)

Solving for P yields $7118.88. The balance after the sixth payment is found by inserting the values in Equation (20):

$$B_6 = \$50,000(1.07)^6 - \$7118.88\left[\frac{(1.07)^6 - 1}{.07}\right]$$

Solving for B_N gives $24,113.10. This value may be checked by using the alternative computational procedure, Equation (21), with j equal to 4, the number of remaining payments.

$$B_6 = \$7118.88\left[\frac{1 - (1.07)^{-4}}{.07}\right] = \$24,113.15$$

with a $0.05 difference due to rounding.

Appendix B: Continuous Compounding and Discounting

Continuous or *instantaneous compounding* and *discounting* formulas are valuable tools for a number of reasons, including the following two. First, many growth processes are fairly continuous in nature. That is, compounding takes place at nearly every instant in time. It is the inability to gather data continuously that causes these processes to appear as discrete changes from the available estimates. Second, many depository institutions that have been subject to ceilings on the interest they pay their depositors have used continuous compounding. This allowed them to pay slightly higher interest amounts.

Suppose that a bank pays 5 percent interest on its accounts and pays that interest only once, on the last day of the year. A $1,000,000 deposit receives an interest payment of $50,000. If the bank compounded at every instant of time at the same 5 percent yearly interest rate, a

$1,000,000 deposit would receive $51,271 in interest payments over the year. At the end of the second year, the size of the deposits for annual and continuous compounding would be, respectively, $1,102,500 and $1,105,171 (which is .2 percent larger). At the end of fifty years, the size of the deposit would be $11,467,400 with annual compounding and $12,182,404 (or 6.2 percent larger) with continuous compounding.

The basis of continuous compounding and discounting is *Euler's e*. Leonard Euler (1707–1783) discovered that if M in the following equation is given larger and larger values, the right-hand value approaches a constant number, which has been named Euler's e. Suppose that M rises all the way up to infinity; then

$$\text{limit of } \left(1 + \frac{1}{M}\right)^M = 2.7182818284 \ldots = e \qquad \textit{Euler's e} \quad (22)$$

as M approaches infinity (where . . . means "and so on"). Euler's e can be approximated by 2.718 for most purposes. This degree of accuracy is attained if M is equal to 10,000. Take the reciprocal of 10,000 (= .0001), add 1, and raise this sum to a power of 10,000 to otain 2.718.

In order to show how Euler's e can be used, suppose that a bank compounds N times during the year. The appropriate compound interest formula is then Equation (12). As N becomes larger (i.e., the number of compoundings each year increases), the instantaneous rate of compounding is approached. Suppose that N approaches infinity. Euler's e enters the analysis. Let $1/M = r/N$, so that Equation (12) can be written as

$$\text{PV}\left[\left(1 + \frac{1}{M}\right)^M\right]^{r_Y} = R_Y \qquad (23)$$

As N approaches infinity, M approaches infinity and the expression in brackets in Equation (23) approaches Euler's e. Equation (23) then can be rewritten as

$$\text{PV}e^{r_Y} = R_Y \quad \text{ or } \quad \text{PV}(2.718\ldots)^{r_Y} = R_Y \qquad \begin{array}{c} \textit{Continuous} \\ \textit{Compounding} \end{array} \quad (24)$$

The interest rate, r in Equation (24), is referred to as the *instantaneous* or *continuous rate of interest*.

Stating interest in continuously compounded form yields a smaller number than stating interest in a discretely compounded form. If a $100 deposit grows to $105 in one year, the discrete rate of interest for compounding once a year on the last day of the year is 5 percent. Continuous compounding of $100 at 4.88 percent for one year also produces a deposit (at the end of the year) of $105.00. Generally, the continuous interest rate is not labeled differently from the corresponding interest rate under discrete compounding. These two types of interest rates can usually be differentiated by the way they are used.

PRACTICE PROBLEM | **12**

Continuous Interest

If a savings account is compounded continuously at 5 percent per year, how large will it be in fifteen years, starting from an initial balance of $1000? The answer is found by inserting these values in Equation (24).

$1000e^{(.05)(15)} = 2117

If compounding had taken place only once at the end of each year, the final balance would have been $38.07 smaller, as shown by inserting the values in Equation (3):

$1000(1.05)^{15} = 2078.93

Appendix C: The Rules of 70 and 72

Here is another very useful approximation for continuous compounding that requires no calculator. How long will it take $1 to double (to become $2) at a compound interest rate of r? Using Equation (13) (with units of dollars) yields

$$e^{rY} = 2 \qquad\qquad (25)$$

For those who know logarithms, transform Equation (15) into

$$r_Y = \ln 2 \quad\text{or}\quad Y = \frac{\ln 2}{r} = \frac{.70}{r} \qquad\qquad \textit{The Rule of 70} \quad (26)$$

Since $\ln 2 = .693$, which will be approximated as .70, divide .70 by the interest rate. The *Rule of 70* is divide 70 by the interest rate (in percentage form) to determine the number of years for doubling the value.

For example, if the interest rate is .05, one dollar would double in approximately 70/5, or 14 years. If the interest rate is 7 percent, one dollar will double in approximately 70/7, or 10 years. At a 10 percent inflation rate, college tuition should double every seven years.

For compounding once a year, instead of continuous compounding, the number 72 is divided by the percentage interest rate. In the example, using 5 percent, the approximate time period for doubling would be 72/5 = 14.4. This can be checked by inserting these values in Equation (3):

$1(1.05)^{14.4} = 2.02

Appendix D: The Rule of 78

Although Equations (15) and (19B) give precise values for future and present values of annuities for given uniform periodic payments and yield, an alternative approximation is sometimes used by creditors. It is also built into tables these creditors use when calculating the balance due if a loan is paid off before maturity. It is called the *Rule of 78*. The Federal Reserve notes:

> The Rule is recognized as a practical way to calculate rebates of interest. There are other methods, but this one is widely used, and it is reflected in a number of state lending laws.[4]

It also turns out that the Rule of 78 may be used in a very useful way to approximate the rate of interest on an annuity or a mortgage if the periodic payments and the amount borrowed are known.

The Rule of 78 is an algorithm (a procedure for solving a problem) based on the sum of the digits from 1 to the total number of payments. In a fifteen-payment loan that sum, S_{15}, is

$$S_{15} = 1 + 2 + 3 + 4 + 5 + 6 + 7 + 8 + 9 + 10 + 11$$
$$+ 12 + 13 + 14 + 15$$

There is a shortcut for the sum of the digits S_N, where N is the highest digit.

$$S_N = \frac{N}{2}(N + 1) \qquad \text{Sum of the Digits} \quad (27)$$

In the example, where $N = 15$, the sum of the digits is obtained from Equation (27):

$$S_{15} = \frac{15}{2}(15 + 1) = 120$$

In a twelve-period loan (a one-year loan payable monthly) the sum of the digits is 78, a result that explains the name of this rule.

The Rule of 78 specifies the amount of interest paid during each payment on a periodic equal-payment loan payback. Let T be the total interest paid throughout the loan. Then the amount of interest A_{V+1} paid on a given payment is

$$A_{V+1} = \left(\frac{N - V}{S_N}\right)T \qquad \begin{array}{l}\textit{Rule of 78}\\ \textit{for Interest} \quad (28)\\ \textit{Payments}\end{array}$$

where V is zero for the first payment, plus 1 for each succeeding payment, and $N - 1$ at the final paymnt.

For example, suppose that $3000 is borrowed for fifteen months. It is to be repaid in fifteen equal monthly payments of $215.00 (of interest plus principal). The total interest payment during all fifteen months is obtained by multiplying 15 by $215 to obtain $3225. This is $225 larger than the loan principal, so that $225 is the total interest T. The amount of interest paid in the first payment is obtained by substituting these values in Equation (28).

$$A_1 = \left(\frac{15 - 0}{120}\right)\$225 = \$28.125$$

This means that the remainder of the first $215 payment, or $186.875, is a reduction of the amount owed. Similarly, the interest on the fifth payment is

$$A_5 = \left(\frac{15 - 4}{120}\right)\$225 = \$20.63$$

leaving $194.37 for reduction of the debt.

The balance due after the fifth payment is the sum of the ten remaining payments (10 times $215 = $2150) minus the interest on those payments, which is excused. The interest on the remaining ten payments is calculated in the following way. Using Equation (28), summing over V going from 5 to 1, the desired total is $225/120 times the sum of the first ten digits. From Equation (27),

$$S_{10} = \frac{10}{2}(10 + 1) = 55$$

The interest left to be paid is, therefore, 55/120 of the total $225 = $103.12.[5] Subtracting that excused interest from the sum of the last ten payments, the balance is obtained.

$$\$2150 - \$103.13 = \$2046.87$$

Table 5-1 contains the data for all fifteen payments.

What is the interest on this loan? One easy way to approximate it roughly is to average the interest paid on the first and last payments. On the first payment the interest on the $3000 balance is seen from Table 5-1 to be

$$\frac{\$28.13}{\$3000} = .009367$$

The interest on the last payment when only $213.13 is owed is

$$\frac{\$1.87}{\$213.13} = .008774$$

TABLE 5-1

Payment Schedule for $3000 Fifteen-Payment Loan Using the Rule of 78

Monthly Payment Number	Interest	Reduction of Debt	Total Payment
1	$ 28.13	$ 186.87	$ 215.00
2	26.25	188.75	215.00
3	24.37	190.63	215.00
4	22.50	192.50	215.00
5	20.63	194.37	215.00
6	18.75	196.25	215.00
7	16.87	198.13	215.00
8	15.00	200.00	215.00
9	13.13	201.87	215.00
10	11.25	203.75	215.00
11	9.37	205.63	215.00
12	7.50	207.50	215.00
13	5.63	209.37	215.00
14	3.75	211.25	215.00
15	1.87	213.13	215.00
	$225.00	$3000.00	$3225.00

Adding these interest rates together and dividing by 2, the "average" interest rate is seen to be .00907: .907 percent per month, or on a yearly basis, 10.88 percent. The accuracy of the Rule of 78 in providing the correct interest rate for this loan can be checked by substituting this yield and the $215 payment amount into Equation (19), the present value of an annuity:

$$215\left[\frac{1 - (1.00907)^{-15}}{.00907}\right] = \$3002.55$$

Only a $2.55 error results.

This use of the Rule of 78 for finding the yield on an annuity where the original or final balance and the payment size are known is a useful approximation only when tables for these loans, or a business calculator, are not available.[6]

NOTES

1. The present value of an annuity can be derived from the formula for a perpetuity or consol. This alternative derivation also yields a useful approximation for long annuities. Think of an annuity with periodic payments of P as a consol with interest payments of P. The final payment after N periods on the annuity corresponds to the sale of the consol. To obtain the formula for the annuity, subtract the present value of the future sale of the consol,

$$\frac{P/r}{(1 + r)^N}$$

from the present value of a consol (Equation 11), P/r. The result is the present value of a periodic payment for N periods.

$$\frac{P}{r} - \frac{P/r}{(1+r)^N} = \frac{P}{r}\left[1 - \frac{1}{(1+r)^N}\right] = \frac{P}{r}\left[\frac{(1+r)^N - 1}{(1+r)^N}\right] \tag{17}$$

$$\frac{P}{r} - \frac{P/r}{(1+r)^N} = P\left[\frac{1 - (1+r)^{-N}}{r}\right] = \text{PVA} \tag{18}$$

For large values of N, PVA approaches P/r from the high side. In the example of the $100 per month annuity where $N = 528$, the approximation is

$$\frac{\$100}{.0058333} = \$17{,}142.86$$

which is $794.96 or 5 percent larger than the correct value. A more precise, but more cumbersome, approximation procedure is given in Appendix D.

2. As N becomes larger, the present value of the return of the face value approaches zero, so that the present value of the bond approaches the present value of the coupon payments, PVA in Equation (18) in Note 1. The value of PVA approaches the coupon payment divided by the interest rate. Except for very long bonds, this approximation is poor but is nevertheless used in bond listings in some newspapers.

3. To see this, assume that the creditor is a bank, which also maintains the sinking fund account. The bank obtains an account from which it can obtain funds at less than its lending rate. This spread between rates is gross income to the bank insofar as it can lend out the funds (after adjusting for the proportion held as reserves). Also, substituting the interest rate .11/4 and the loan amount $125,000 into Equation (19B), the solution for the periodic payment is $8208.97. This smaller payment could be used if the loan was amortized as explained in the next section.

4. *The Rule of 78's or What May Happen When You Pay Off a Loan Early,* Pamphlet, Department of Consumer Affairs, Federal Reserve Bank of Philadelphia (April 1979), p. 2.

5. The correct answer is $103.125. It is rounded down to $103.12 to conform to the payment schedule in Table 5-1, which preserves all payments at exactly $215.

6. For Practice Problem 10, where the yield on an annuity with a present value of $125,000 and a payment of $8812.30 is sought, the approximation is 3.4 percent. That is close enough to the correct yield of 3.5 percent to be useful in the iteration procedure.

STUDY QUESTIONS

1. Suppose that $10.67 is deposited in a savings account in August 3, 1979. How large would the balance be on March 5, 2016, if interest had been paid at a rate of $3\frac{1}{2}$ percent compounded and payable on December 31 of each year?

2. If Melvin Crost receives $75,000 payable when he is due to leave prison in fifteen years, what is its present value using a 25 percent interest rate, assuming no taxes?

3. If Melvin Crost puts all the funds from a robbery in a savings account paying 5 percent interest per year, when he enters prison to serve a

fifteen-year term, and the amount grows to $75,000, how much did he steal?

4. Suppose that a bond with a par value of $5000 and a 6 percent coupon payable once at the end of the year is eight years from maturity. What is its present value at an interest rate of 7.5 percent?

5. What is the present value of a perpetuity paying $176.48 forever if the bond yields a 12 percent return?

6. How large will a $3000 deposit become if it is compounded daily (using a 360-day year) from March 1 to July 1 of the following year?

7. If $1000 is paid into an annuity quarterly for seventeen years, what is the final value of the annuity?

8. How much should be deposited in a savings account each month if the account pays 4 percent interest compounded monthly and $1 million is desired in three years?

9. What is the present value of a bond with a par value of $7500, a coupon rate of 7.35 percent, semiannual payments, and twenty-nine-year maturity?

10. Suppose that the Sly Company borrowed $30 million for two years at 12 percent interest compounded quarterly from a bank where a sinking fund for the principal was accumulated in an account paying Sly Company 9 percent, compounded monthly. What is the interest cost of the loan and the size of the sinking fund payments?

11. Suppose that a thirty-year mortgage of $50,000 bears an 11 percent per year interest rate. How large are the periodic monthly payments? How much is owed after three years, ten years, and twenty-nine years?

12. If consumer prices increased at a 10 percent continuously compounded rate, how large would a $32,000-per-year pension be in ten years if it is indexed to this rate of inflation? How large would it be in twenty years?

Part II

Loanable Funds and the Rate of Interest

6

The Demand for Money

Introduction

The financial markets for securities and the demand and supply of money are closely related. The condition of equilibrium prices in the financial markets for securities, described in Chapter 3, means that at current prices and interest rates, there is not a move to shift out of securities into money or a move to reduce money balances and buy securities. (More precisely, there is not an excess supply of securities associated with an excess demand for money or an excess supply of money associated with an excess demand for securities.) An excess supply of money can be caused by rapid money growth that can occur by goverment action, as described in the next chapter and in greater detail in Chapter 23. The excess supply of money causes the prices of goods and services to rise (inflation), and it has effects on securities' prices. The effects on securities' prices are analyzed in Chapter 26, where it is also suggested that money supply changes sometimes follow changes in securities' prices because of government policies.

These effects of changes in the demand and supply of money are also associated with interest rate changes. The movement of funds back and forth between money and securities depends to a large extent on interest rates. Interest rates are affected significantly by changes in the demand and supply of money as well as the demand and supply of securities.

One way to view the determination of equilibrium interest rates is to look at the nominal rate of interest that would equate the quantities of real-money balances demanded and supplied. This popular approach simplifies the analysis of interest rates by concentrating on one asset, money—adjusted for the rate of inflation.

The cost of simplifying the analysis of equilibrium interest rates to a view of one asset, money, depends on the use made of the analysis. Markets for other assets may be moving toward different equilibrium interest rates. In a dynamic society constantly buffeted with new information that affects asset prices, a view of only one asset must be myopic. A view of only the demand and supply for money may not give correct information about the equilibrium yields on other assets. However, the demand for money *does* depend on the interest rates of other assets, as shown in this chapter. So the simplification is not a completely isolated view, especially when one considers that money is widely held and is important to the portfolio decisions of nearly all the participants in the society. In fact, a general description of the equilibrium interest rate for assets held in one's portfolio can be formulated around the correct proportions of the portfolio held in money form. So the popular demand and supply of money analysis can be a useful tool if the demand for money is properly formulated.

The study of the demand for money has a very long history, as briefly noted in the next section of this chapter. Then the determinants of the demand for money are discussed, including an interesting property alleged for consumer behavior, the absence of money illusion. The money-income relationship is commonly summarized by a variable called *velocity*, which is explained next. The demand for money by business firms is discussed in Appendix A of this chapter. Finally, in Appendix B the analysis in the chapter is used to explain equilibrium interest rates and the effect on these interest rates of the payment of interest on money. The supply of money is discussed in the following chapter.

Before proceeding, readers should review the official concepts of money used in the United States, as elaborated in Chapter 2.

A Perspective from the Past

The *demand for money* and the relation of money and the price level have been discussed by scholars for a number of centuries. The beginnings of this discussion can be traced back as far as Confucius. Skipping through the centuries, the subject is found in John Hale's "Discourse of the Common Weal of This Realm of England," written sometime before his death in 1571, and in John Locke's "Some Consideration of the Consequences of Lowering the Interest and Raising the Value of Money," written in 1692.[1]

It is probably difficult to find a well-known economist from Adam Smith (whose famous "An Inquiry into the Nature and Cause of the Wealth of Nations" was published in 1776) to the present time who has not devoted considerable space to the analysis of the demand for money and the relation of money and the price level. Many of these luminaries developed useful new analyses ("new" is a tenuous allegation in the presence of enterprising historians) or successfully reformulated hypotheses in a more useful way.

Throughout the history of this inquiry there is one frequently repeated assertion: The quantity of money is a primary determinant of the price level. Writing in his classic essay, "Of Money," David Hume (1711–1776) said: "Suppose four-fifths of all the money in Britain to be annihilated in one night. . . . Must not the price of all labour and commodities sink in proportion . . . ?"[2] The rigid version of this central theme in the history of monetary theory (as in Hume's isolated assertion) is that of strict proportionality between the quantity of nominal money and the price level.[3]

The apparent absurdity of this unqualified rigid version of strict proportionality between money and prices has been a focus of derision and confusion. As a statement about the change from one equilibrium position to another in a mathematical model, it can, of course, be made to be true. As a description of individual behavior- at the microeconomic level—it is inaccurate. Individuals may have offsetting behavior that allows the statement to be true for the economy as a whole under certain conditions. To go from the micro level to an explanation of how the economy as a whole—the macro level—can achieve strict proportionality between a nominal money supply increase and a price-level increase turns out to require some of the most brilliant academic acrobatics.[4] The conditions that are required for strict proportionality are unlikely to hold. Nevertheless, much insight can be gained about the demand for real-money balances from knowing something about one of the most important underlying principles involved in this age-old subject. This principle, the absence of money illusion, is discussed in a later section.

The Demand for Real-Money Balances

The demand for real-money balances, $(M/P)^D$, depends on:

1. Real income, Y/P (a national income aggregate).
2. Market interest rates on alternative assets, which are summarized by the rate of interest on bonds, i_B. These interest rates indicate the rate that could be earned if the money was not held. They are called the *opportunity costs* of holding money.
3. Other variables determining the public's tastes and preferences for real-money balances, Z.

In symbols, the equation is

$$\left(\frac{M}{P}\right)^D = F\left(\frac{Y}{P}, i_B, Z\right) \tag{1}$$

Each of the variables Y/P, i_B, and Z is reviewed in this chapter.

The Effect of Real Income

The influence of the real-income variable, Y/P, may be thought of in two ways. First, the greater real income, the more real purchases will be made, so that more real-money balances will be demanded. This motive for holding real balances was described by John Maynard Keynes as the *transactions demand* for money.

A second way to explain the effect of real income on the demand for real-money balances treats money as one asset in a portfolio of assets. At higher levels of real income, an individual's wealth is likely to be greater. The individual will have more assets, one of which will be real-money balances. Real wealth itself is a more desirable variable, but since estimates of wealth are very rough, real income is used. Real wealth and real income indicate the scale of an individual's portfolio and are called *scale variables*.

The Effect of Interest Rates

Why do individuals hold real-money balances?[5] They hold real-money balances because of the services and money income that money produces. A real-money balance is a given amount of purchasing power. It provides both medium of exchange services to make payments and store of value services.

At a given price level, individuals are viewed as increasing their money balances up to the point where additional services per dollar (the *marginal service yield*) equal the additional net costs per dollar. To illustrate this view, assume that:

1. The bond rate of interest i_B is 10 percent.
2. The interest rate (from a NOW deposit) on money R_M minus any storage costs per dollar C_M is 4 percent.
3. The marginal service yield i_M is unknown.

This statement says that an individual will increase his or her money balances until

$$i_M = i_B + C_M - R_M \tag{2}$$

Substituting in these values, $i_M = 6$ percent. Equation (2) is therefore a condition for equilibrium-desired real-money balances. If the individual values the services from real-money balances at more than 6 percent, he or she will sell off some other assets and add real-money balances. Simply stated, real-money balances would offer a higher net rate of return than other assets. This is a simplified version of the portfolio decision problem ignoring risk, which is discussed in detail in Part IV.

Traditionally, economists have stated the demand for money in terms of only one interest rate, i_B. The effect of changes in other interest rates on the demand for money, such as a change of NOW account interest, are handled separately. This type of analysis is demonstrated at the end of the chapter.

The Absence of Money Illusion

An important property often alleged for Equation (1), the demand for real-money balances, is worth learning if you do not want to be accused of having money illusion. Suppose that all money prices suddenly rise by 10 percent. This makes the real values of money and bonds fall; it also makes the value of money income fall. Suppose that each moneyholder simultaneously receives 10 percent more nominal money balances, 10 percent more money income, 10 percent more "money" assets (assets such as time deposits and bonds), and that there is no expectation of further price changes. This is a form of relabeling. It takes time to find out that all prices have risen by 10 percent and that, even though more units of dollars are needed to make the same real expenditures, there is just enough additional money and money income to buy as much as before and to save as much as before. In time, everyone will realize that his or her nominal income, his or her nominal money balance, and all nominal prices have risen in proportion to the price level.

A government decree that effectively changed the unit of account, including the units by which money income, nominal prices, and money balances are measured, could have achieved the same result, except that the government decree would provide more rapid announcement of the relabeling process.

To show what has happened in this example, let the Greek lowercase letter lambda, λ, be equal to 1.1, the compounding factor for a 10 percent increase in nominal money, nominal income, and the price level. Then Equation (1) becomes

$$\left(\frac{\lambda M}{\lambda P}\right)^{D} = f\left(\frac{\lambda Y}{\lambda P}, i_B, Z\right) = \left(\frac{M}{P}\right)^{D} \tag{3}$$

The property alleged for this equation is that, under these conditions, individuals do not change their behavior; they want the same real-money balances $(M/P)^{D}$.

If individuals do demand a different quantity of real-money balances at the higher price level, they are said to suffer from *money illusion*. They do not base their behavior on real variables, none of which has changed. They base their behavior on nominal variables. Many economic analyses, including some that define conditions of macroeconomic proportionality between nominal money balances and the price level, assume "no money illusion."

This property of Equation (1) is a powerful insight, but not a fully tested proposition. It requires that the services from real-money balances be independent of the nominal number of dollars in the real balances. The implicit income from 100 one-dollar bills is assumed to be the same as that from 200 one-dollar bills if the price level doubles (and there is no expectation of a further price change). This assumption may not hold for commodity money (money made out of a substance with a valuable alternative use, such as gold), but it seems plausible for fiat money balances (money that is not made out of or guaranteed to be convertible into a valuable substance, such as gold).

There are some costs and distribution effects arising from the adjustment process that could change income. It takes time to shop around and learn about prices. Some nominal prices are fixed by contracts that were made in the past, so the property will not hold until the contracts are revised or the assets involved are revalued.

In addition, every monetary variable must change in proportion, including exchange rates of the domestic currency with foreign currencies (adjusted for the change, if any, in the purchasing power of the foreign currencies).

Consider the following example, in which skid-row residents may incorrectly appear to have "liquor illusion." The consumption of alcohol by poor alcoholics might have been changed by the January 1, 1980, federally mandated switch to metric measurements of liquor bottles. The familiar 8-ounce (half-pint) bottle, which is so attractive to many skid-row residents, was changed to a 6.8-ounce bottle, the 200-milliliter bottle. There probably will not be liquor illusion, although there is a real change. Buyers on skid row must adjust the size of their inventories. At least temporarily, they must buy more or less than before. Given their inability to borrow, this may entail an adjustment in income-producing activities. Real consumption will change, but probably by a trivial amount.

The Income Velocity of Money

A common way to look at the relationship between money and income, with real or nominal variables, requires the introduction of a new concept, the *income velocity of money*, referred to in this chapter simply as *velocity*. National income data are used.

Income velocity is defined as the ratio of nominal income Y divided by the average stock of money M.

$$V = Y/M \tag{4}$$

The average stock of money M is measured in the same period as nominal income Y. Velocity is a number per unit of time. For example, using the third quarter of 1981, annualized estimates, M1 averaged

$430.3 billion and GNP was $2956.6 billion. Thus the M1 velocity, using a GNP estimate for income, was $2956.6/430.3, or 6.87 per year.

Equation (4) can be rearranged as

$$MV = Y \qquad (5)$$

The meaning of this equation can be illuminated with an example. Twenty students are in a classroom. Each student is given 10 one-dollar bills. The students are allowed to sell final goods and services to each other for one hour. Each student records the total money value of the final goods and services that he or she has sold. Assume that the total sales of all students amount to $600. Since there was a total of 200 one-dollar bills, each bill must have changed hands an average of three times (600/200). Nominal income is $600 and the income velocity is 3/u.t., where u.t. (unit of time) is one hour.

The concept of velocity can be stated in equivalent real terms as real income Y/P divided by real-money balances M/P, or simply Y/M.

$$V = \frac{Y/P}{M/P} = \frac{Y}{M} \qquad (6)$$

Equation (6) is identical to Equation (4), except that the income and money variables in Equation (4) have both been divided by P. The value of velocity has not changed. Rearranging Equation (6),

$$MV = PY \qquad (7)$$

This equation says that expenditures (money balances times their turnover) are equal to receipts (the "average" price times the quantity of goods and services in the national income accounts).

Dividing each side of Equation (7) by P yields

$$(M/P)\, V = Y \qquad (8)$$

At each level of real income, an increase in the demand for real balances is equivalent to a decline in velocity. One of these variables cannot go up without the other falling if real income is constant. *Therefore, the problem of finding the demand for money at each level of income can alternatively be defined as a problem of finding the value of velocity.*

If there is a *desired level of money balances* at some income, there is a *desired velocity*. Desired velocity, therefore, is also dependent on the interest rates discussed here. At higher bond interest rates, velocity rises, and with larger direct interest payments on money, velocity falls.

The concept of income velocity is a useful way to organize the relationship between money changes and changes in the price level and real income. It can be seen in Equation (7) that if velocity can be predicted, predictions of the relationships among the other variables, M, P, and Y, are simplified. Furthermore, this identity is a reminder that if a theory explains only the change in one of the variables, say, a rise in the price level, it is incomplete. There must be offsetting changes in M, V, or Y to preserve the equality of MV and PY.

Velocity and Expected Income

There have been a number of studies of the way income velocity changes over business cycles, *cyclical changes*, or over the long run, the *trend*. Velocity tends to rise during business expansions and fall during business contractions. This means that during business expansions, individuals hold less money per dollar of some measure of income—their demand for money per unit of real GNP declines. During business contractions, individuals hold more money per dollar of GNP.

Over a longer period of time, a different relationship has been observed. In tests of the long period from 1867 to the 1950s, real income and income velocity were found to move in opposite directions in the United States. That is, as income grew over this period, individuals tended to increase their demand for money per dollar of income. Therefore, an apparent contradiction arose. As income rose during business expansions, the demand for money declined, but as income rose over the long run, a least up to the 1950s, the demand for money increased.

One explanation for this contradiction is that money demand does not depend on current-period income, but instead depends "on the average yearly income individuals expect over a longer period of time."[6] Using this concept of *expected income*, a sudden rise in current income during a business cycle expansion will only slightly affect individuals' long-run expected income. Money demand that depends on expected income will not rise by as much as current income. Income velocity will rise. Similarly, during a business contraction, expected income will not fall by as much as current income. Money demand will not fall by as much as current income. Therefore, velocity calculated on the basis of current falling income will fall. This explanation is consistent with the long-run fall in velocity from 1867 until the 1950s, as the trend in income (both current and expected) was upward.

The Secular Decline to 1950 and the Subsequent Rise in Velocity

Figure 6-1 shows that the long-run decline in velocity appears to have ended in 1948 for the concept of money used before 1980. Old M1 was the demand deposits of commercial banks plus currency and coin held by the public. Old M2 was old M1 plus savings and time deposits, except

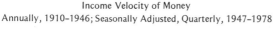

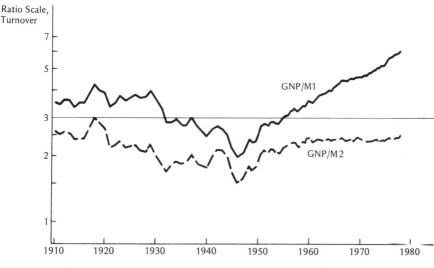

Figure 6-1

Income velocity of money defined as old M1 and old M2.* *Source: Historical Chart Book,* Board of Governors of the Federal Reserve System (1978), p. 5.

*Old M1 is the demand deposits of commercial banks plus currency and coin held by the public. Old M2 is old M1 plus savings and time deposits (except large CDs) at commercial banks.

for large certificates of deposit at commercial banks. What caused the long-run decline in velocity from at least the middle of the last century to the middle of this century? What caused the different behavior in velocity since approximately 1950?

The long-run decline in velocity from approximately 1850 to 1950 was probably caused in large part by growing confidence in the stability of the U.S. government, which issued the monetary base, and in the stability of the banking system, which created "bank money." This generated a willingness to hold an increasing proportion of income and wealth in the form of money. In addition, more of the transactions in the economy were conducted through the market, where money was used, and less output was manufactured in the home. Initially, the home was an important factor in the production of goods and services for the household. Many production processes, from making clothes to processing food for storage, were conducted in the home. Modern technology and specialization not only removed the necessity for most household production, but made home production a relatively inefficient use of labor. A huge increase of women in the work force accompanied this change. Increasing knowledge and sophistication about the use of banking facilities accompanied the change in velocity.

One variable that captures part of this trend is the degree of urbanization—the size of the population in metropolitan areas relative to rural areas. The degree of urbanization is a good candidate for the symbol Z in Equation (3), especially when trying to explain the demand for real-money balances in developing economies.

Beginning in the 1950s, interest rates in the United States began to rise. Most of the rise in interest rates can be attributed to rising rates of inflation, according to the explanation given in Chapter 4. The interest rate ceiling on time deposits at commercial banks, a large component of old M2, was raised to 5 percent in the 1950s. The interest rate ceiling for demand deposits at commercial banks, a major component of old M1 and the currently defined M1, was held constant at zero, except for gifts and free services that banks provided as a legal way to partially evade the prohibition on interest payments.

It therefore became more and more costly to hold demand deposits. As interest rates rose, depositors had increased incentives to economize on demand deposits. They switched more and more of their money to other assets. The quantity of M1 (as currently defined—for continuity) they demanded continued to fall relative to income; that is, the velocity of M1 rose. From the 1950s to 1982 the average yearly rate of rise of M1 has been 3.4 percent a year. Taking three-year averages—to smooth out business cycle variations—the deviations from this "trend" have generally not been large. Since competitive interest was paid on time deposits until the end of the 1970s, there was no such incentive to economize, and the demand for time deposits remained roughly constant relative to income, so that the velocity of old M2 was roughly constant in the 1960s and 1970s.

The payment of competitive interest rates on deposits, as authorized under the Depository Institutions Deregulation and Monetary Control Act of 1980, would again tend to lower the velocity of M1. There will be less incentive to economize on balances held in checkable accounts because of the lifting of ceiling rate limitations on interest payments.

The effect of the payment of interest on NOW accounts is discussed, using demand and supply analysis, in Appendix A.

Appendix A: The Demand for Money by Business Firms

Real-money balances can be thought of as a *factor of production* in a business firm, the same as other inputs, such as land, labor, and capital. It can be shown in price theory that each factor of production will be used up to the point where the additional output it produces per dollar of cost is equal to the additional output that could be produced by each of the other factors per dollar of their cost.

The *budget constraint* is the name given to the limitation placed on the amount of income available to a household in a given period. The budget constraint in a given period could be altered by a household if funds are borrowed against future income. The market for loans against future wage income is, however, imperfect. Households must borrow at a much higher rate than they can earn by lending. If one presumes that the budget constraint for a household cannot be significantly shifted in a given period because of the difficulties associated with borrowing, the idea of a fixed budget constraint for households may be a roughly correct approximation. Then income can be usefully employed to explain the real-money demand. This is not the case for business firms. The capital market will rapidly shift funds into firms that are expected to bring the greatest rate of return. Even if a firm has a small rate of profit in the current period, it may have a very large scale of operations because it is able to borrow in a capital market on the basis of expected increased profits in the future. The concept of a fixed budget constraint for a business firm operating in a fairly competitive capital market is untenable. In this respect, business firms differ from households and require a different development for the demand for real-money balances. Perhaps a more important determinant is whether or not the business is relatively money intensive, such as a financial intermediary might be.

Nevertheless, the *scale of operations* may have explanatory power on the strictly mechanical grounds that a larger business needs more real-money balances to operate. The real asset size and the total volume of transactions have been used as scale variables in tests of the demand for real-money balances by business firms.

The results of tests of business demand for real-money balances are not consistent.[7] Different results are obtained from *cross-section data* (estimates of different firms in the same time period) than from *time-series data* (data from successive time periods). Tests have shown that

> differences in manufacturing industries' demands for cash can be explained by differences in firm sizes. . . . What happens is that the velocity of cash (where velocity is sales divided by cash) at first declines and then rises, as firms increase in size. But the decline in velocity occurs only over a small fraction of the lower portion of the values the asset-size variable may take on.[8]

These results, which synthesize several investigators' findings, are interesting, but they tend to relate unsatisfactorily to theory and are therefore difficult to interpret. Test results in search of theoretical meaning may find many shoes that fit; unfortunately, they may walk off in several directions, tearing the theory apart.

One of the most difficult aspects of interpreting the business demand for real-money balances is the necessity of taking into account the output produced by real-money balances. Real-money balances are a factor of production that yields output for the business firm. The output produced by money in a business firm "is likely to be especially dependent on features of production and conditions affecting the smoothness and regularity of operations as well as those determining the size and scope of enterprises, the degree of vertical integration, and so forth."[9] A business firm that has many unexpected payments and/or receipts may find it more profitable to carry larger quantities of real-money balances than a firm of similar size (with the same amount of transactions and the same size assets) that has a smoother, more predictable flow of receipts and payments.

The analysis of the demand for real-money balances by business firms is further complicated by the necessity of distinguishing between manufacturing firms and financial intermediaries. The amount of reserves held by financial intermediaries depends to a large extent on the quantity of short-term liquid liabilities that they have issued to the public and on legal reserve requirements in the case of depository intermediaries. These financial intermediaries buy and sell assets in the money markets daily. The total volume of transactions is huge and is not related to their money balances in the same manner as is the volume of transactions of manufacturing firms.

Furthermore, new cash management techniques allow firms to economize on real-money balances. These techniques include lock-box systems under which bill payments are collected in post office boxes throughout the country and local banks immediately deposit the payments. This can be combined with zero-balance accounts: Bank accounts are reduced to zero each day and the funds are transferred to a central account for immediate investment. The implementation of cash management techniques is probably very uneven among firms, thus making an aggregate business demand for money schedule difficult to estimate.

A significant change in cash management practices that should affect the business demand for real-money balances will not originate with businesses. It involves a reduction in bank float. Bank float was as high as $7.7 billion in February 1980. The requirement of the Depository Institutions Deregulation and Monetary Control Act of 1980 that the Federal Reserve start charging banks for float by September 1981 should reduce float dramatically. Insofar as float is treated as a working balance by businesses using cash management techniques, they may be forced to carry more money or more very short-term loan instruments.

However, after lamenting the unsatisfactory state of estimates of the business demand for money, it can be said that the variables in the household demand for money (Equation 1) probably explain much of the relationship. This may be true because variables such as the relative number of business firms that are cash intensive, or the size distribution of business firms, do not change enough to offer much explanation over and above the commonly used variables, such as income and interest rates.

Appendix B: Interest Rate Equilibrium

It is customary to speak of the demand and supply of the *stock* of money at a given time. This is depicted in Figure 6-2. The supply of money S_M is assumed to be a vertical line; it is not discussed in this chapter. The demand for money at each nominal interest rate on bonds is shown along

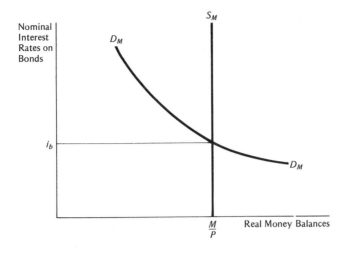

Nominal Interest Rates on Bonds

S_M

D_M

i_b

D_M

$\frac{M}{P}$ Real Money Balances

Figure 6-2

The demand and supply of the stock of money.

$D_M D_M$. The quantity of money demanded equals the quantity supplied at an interest rate of i_B. In equilibrium i_B is the same nominal interest rate that would be derived from the demand and supply of loanable funds analysis discussed in Chapter 8. If the interest rate were higher than i_B, the supply of money would exceed the demand; there would be excess supply. Normally, this would cause a switch into other assets, such as bonds. Bond prices would rise, reducing their interest yield toward i_B. Alternatively, an excess demand for money, at an interest rate below i_B, would normally reduce the demand for bonds and cause interest rates to move up toward i_B.

This analysis can be used to show the effect of paying interest on money. With the authorization on January 1, 1981, of nationwide interest-paying checking accounts at all depository institutions (commercial banks, savings and loans, mutual savings banks, and credit unions), it is also important to take into account direct interest payments on money. They are a deduction from the opportunity cost and the explicit cost that should be made in compounding the net cost of holding money.

Suppose that $100 is in such an account, paying 5 percent a year, and that this is an equilibrium level of money balances, which means that the level of real-money balances demanded has settled down to the position of equality between the quantities demanded and supplied at point A in Figure 6-3. Now, if bond interest rates rise from 8 percent to 10 percent, the equilibrium would change from A to B, and the quantity of real money balances demanded would fall, say, to $20 (given the same price level), as shown in Figure 6-3.

Suppose that direct interest payments on the checkable account are simultaneously raised from 5 to 7 percent. The same 3 percent difference between the bond yield and the direct interest paid on checking balances is maintained. Suppose that the demand for money shifts out to

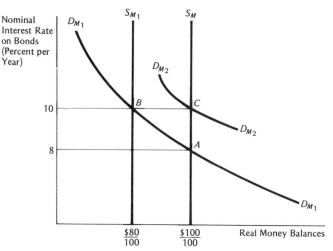

Figure 6-3

The demand and supply of real-money balances with an increase in demand.

$D_{M_2}D_{M_2}$. The original quantity of real-money balances, \$100/100, might still be held if real income is the same. The point is that tandem changes in interest payments on money tend to offset, to some extent, the effects on money demand of changes in the opportunity cost.

This outward shift in the demand for real-money balances is in the same direction as would occur with an increase in real income. In the case of the increase in the direct interest payments on money, it is more profitable to hold money at *every* interest rate on bonds. In the case of an increase in real income, the individual will desire to increase his or her wealth, including his or her real-money balance holdings, at every interest rate on bonds. These additional money balances will provide the additional services that the higher real income requires. The medium of exchange service is a fundamental determinant of the demand for more real-money balances.

There are three important reasons why one would not expect the effect of an increase in bond interest rates (on the demand for real-money balances) to be perfectly offset by a rise in the interest paid on money. First, part of the money supply (28 percent of M1B at the end of 1981) is currency on which no interest can be paid. Second, the *difference* between the bond interest rate and the interest rate paid on checking accounts is related to the cost and profits of depository institutions in providing services such as checking account services. These amounts explain the *difference* between the bond rate of interest and the interest rate paid on checking accounts. This difference is sometimes called the *cost of intermediation*, a name that will be more informative after financial intermediaries are discussed in Part V. If the cost of intermediation varies, interest payments on checking accounts will not be in lock step with bond interest rates. The third reason is that depository institutions may operate under ceiling rate limitations, which prevent them from raising the interest they can pay on checking accounts.

Although changes in the opportunity cost of holding money will not be completely offset, the advent of nationwide interest-paying checking accounts in 1981 and the subsequent planned removal of ceiling limitations on interest that can be paid to depositors should reduce the responsiveness of real-money balances demanded to changes in market interest rates.

NOTES

1. Edmund Whittaker, *Schools and Streams of Economic Thought* (Chicago: Rand McNally & Company, 1960), pp. 37, 66. Hugo Hegeland traces "the quantity theory of money" (a theory that emphasizes the demand for money) back to the writings of Confucius (551–479 B.C.) in his *The Quantity Theory of Money* (New York: Augustus M. Kelley, Publishers, 1969).
2. Whittaker, *Schools and Streams of Economic Thought*, p. 78.
3. This subject is discussed by Milton Friedman, "The Money-Quantity Theory," in *International Encyclopedia of the Social Sciences*, Vol. 10 (New York: Macmillan Publishing Co., Inc., 1968), pp. 432–447. For a description of what was called the "modern quantity theory" and famous studies, see Milton Friedman, ed., *Studies in the Quantity Theory of Money* (Chicago: University of Chicago Press, 1956), with contributions by Friedman, Phillip Cagan, John Klein, Eugene Lerner, and Richard Selden.
4. See Don Patinkin, *Money, Interest, and Prices* (New York: Harper & Row, Publishers, 1965). Conditions for strict proportionality on a macroeconomic level between nominal money balances and the price level at each level of real income have been elegantly developed. These conditions (roughly) include the requirements that the prices of all goods and services vary in the same proportion (as a composite good); that an excess demand for goods in one market can be reduced by a decrease in excess supply in other markets, so that equilibrium can be attained in all markets; that the distribution of wealth is unchanged; that the size and age profile of the population is constant with given tastes; that the money supply is fiat government issue; and that there is no expectation of changing prices. In general, the literature on this subject is too difficult for beginners. The curious reader may examine the nonmathematical parts of these few articles to obtain some flavor of the subject. The historical development of these conditions is reviewed by Kenneth Arrow and F. H. Hahn in *General Competitive Analysis* (San Francisco: Holden-Day, Inc., 1971), Chapter I. An excellent but advanced discussion of this subject may be found in Douglas Fisher, *Monetary Theory and the Demand for Money* (New York: Halsted Press, 1978), Chapter 3. On the same level of difficulty, an alternative to the Patinkin model that enlarges the model to provide a better description of real capital goods is given in Karl Brunner and Allan Meltzer, "Money, Debt, and Economic Activity," *Journal of Political Economy* (September–October 1972), pp. 951–977.
5. John Maynard Keynes brought in the effect of interest rates on the demand for money by describing two motives (in addition to the transaction demand, mentioned previously) for holding money. The *precautionary demand* for holding money is a demand for money as a contingency fund for emergencies. The fund would be reduced if interest rates on bonds rose, making the (opportunity) cost of fund higher. The *speculative demand* alleges that individuals buy more bonds and hold less money when bonds are less expensive; that is,

interest rates are higher. The description of both motives fails to fit modern cash management, which even consumers practice to keep their money balances (which pay less than market rates of interest) at a minimum. However, the inverse relationship between bond interest rates and money holdings that Keynes developed was the basis for much of the analysis that followed. For a review of the more recent analysis presented here, see Benjamin Klein, "Competitive Interest Payments on Bank Deposits and the Long Run Demand for Money," *American Economic Review* (December 1974), pp. 931–949; and David Laidler, *The Demand for Money, Theories and Evidence* (New York: Dun-Donnelly, 1977), especially "The Role of Interest Rates," pp. 122–130.

6. See Milton Friedman, *A Theory of the Consumption Function* (Princeton, N.J.: Princeton University Press, 1957), where *expected income* is called *permanent income*. See also Friedman, "The Demand for Money: Some Theoretical and Empirical Results," *Journal of Political Economy* (August 1959), reprinted in *The Optimum Quantity of Money and Other Essays* (Chicago: Aldine Publishing Company, 1969), pp. 111–139. Friedman could not explain all of the demand for money with permanent income.

Friedman has been criticized for not giving greater weight to the effect of interest rates on the demand for money, although some of the interest rate effect is captured by the single variable, permanent income. A classic and early study which shows that interest rates have a major effect on the demand for money is Henry A. Latane, "Cash Balances and the Interest Rate—A Pragmatic Approach," *Review of Economics and Statistics* (November 1954), pp. 456–460. Also see Stephen M. Goldfeld, "The Demand for Money Revisited," *Brookings Papers on Economic Activity*, No. 3 (Washington, D.C.: The Brookings Institution, 1973), pp. 577–638; Karl Brunner and Allan H. Meltzer, "Predicting Velocity: Implications for Theory and Policy," *Journal of Finance* (May 1963), pp. 319–354; Gregory Chow, "On the Short-Run and Long-Run Demand for Money," *Journal of Political Economy* (April 1966), pp. 111–131; and David Laidler, "The Rate of Interest and the Demand for Money—Some Empirical Evidence," *Journal of Political Economy* (December 1976), pp. 545–555.

7. An excellent summary of these studies up to the late 1960s is found in a book by William J. Frazier, Jr., *The Demand for Money* (New York: World Publishing Company, 1967). More recent work, which tends to be on a sophisticated theoretical level, includes Thomas Saving, "Transactions Costs and the Firm's Demand for Money," *American Economic Review* (June 1971), pp. 407–420; and Stanley Fisher, "Money and the Production Function," *Journal of Economic Inquiry* (December 1974), pp. 517–533.

8. Frazier, *The Demand for Money*, pp. 214–215.

9. Friedman, *Studies in the Quantity Theory*, p. 12.

STUDY QUESTIONS

1. What determines the household demand for money and the demand for money by business firms?

2. How would an increase in NOW account interest affect the demand for money? Carefully couch your answer in terms of other market interest rates.

3. What is money illusion?

4. What is expected income, and is it a good income variable for explaining the demand for money and velocity during business cycles?

5. How would an increase in service charges or a reduction in interest on NOW deposits affect income velocity?

6. How would a system of automatic transfer of money (with zero float) affect income velocity? Be careful. Income velocity is not a measure of the speed of payments; it is related to the proportion of income that individuals wish to hold as money. Would the loss of float cause households to hold more M1 as a proportion of income? Would it affect demand for real-money balances? Explain.

As $i \uparrow$ velocity rises. $m^0 \downarrow$

$\Delta B = DEF + \Delta BONDS + \Delta FLOA + \Delta US + \Delta DISC + \Delta G$

7

The Supply of Money

Introduction

The supply of money in the United States is the dollar amount of goods, defined as money in private circulation. The supply of money can be in nominal terms: simply the number of dollar units of money M. It can also be in real terms: the number of dollar units of money adjusted for changes in the purchasing power of money, M/P, where P is a price index.[1] The supply schedule of (real or nominal) money is the (real or nominal) quantity of money supplied at each interest rate, as shown in Figure 7-1.

The analysis of the quantity of money supplied can conveniently be divided into two parts. First, there is the part of the money supply created by the federal government. It is called the *monetary base*. In the United States the primary entity creating and contracting the monetary base is the Federal Reserve, the central bank of the United States. It is a large organization that performs many important functions, and it is described in more detail in Part V. Think of the Federal Reserve System as an arm of the federal government, not of the private sector. The Federal Reserve services and regulates much of the banking system and carries out monetary policy.

The monetary base, B, is composed of the currency and coin held by the public outside depository institutions, COB, plus the cash reserves

115

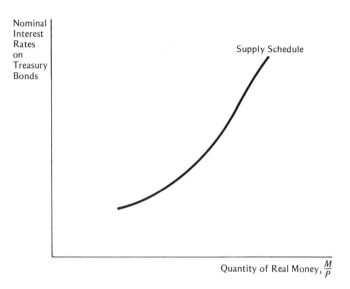

Figure 7-1

The supply schedule of real money.

(vault cash on their premises and deposits with the Federal Reserve) of the depository institutions, R.

$$B = COB + R \tag{1}$$

At the end of April 1982, the monetary base was $167.0 billion, of which $40.5 billion was cash reserves of depository institutions and $126.5 billion was currency and coins outside depository institutions. These aggregates and their relation to M1 can be seen in Table 7-1.

The methods by which the Federal Reserve manages the quantity of the monetary base in circulation are discussed briefly at the end of the chapter and are given more attention in Part V.

At this point it is important to note that this direct management of the monetary base is the primary tool of monetary policy.

Control of the monetary base is not the same as control of the entire money supply. M1, for example, was $440.4 billion at the end of December 1981. This amount was larger than the monetary base by $269.8 billion, so that the monetary base was 39 percent of M1. The $269.8 billion was created by the depository institutions through their practice of fractional reserve banking.

In this chapter a simplified view of fractional reserve banking and the relation between the monetary base and the part of the money supply created by private depository institutions is presented. The presentation is simplified, in part, by ignoring the currency and coin held by the public outside depository institutions. A more sophisticated relation between the monetary base and the entire money supply, which takes ac-

TABLE 7-1

The Components of M1 (January 1981)

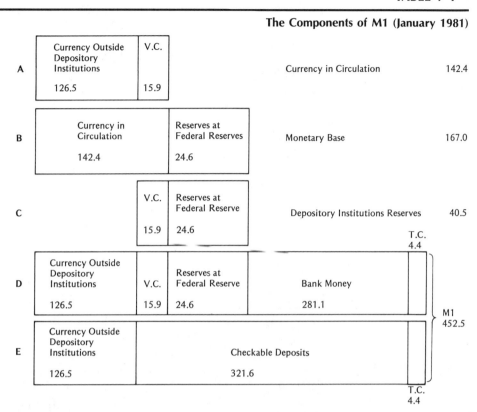

count of the currency and coin held outside depository institutions, is presented in the appendix to this chapter. A discussion of the depository institutions is presented in Part V.

Fractional Reserve Banking

Fractional reserve banking is the practice of keeping only a fraction of deposits in the form of reserves. Depository institutions (commercial banks, savings and loan associations, mutual savings banks, and credit unions) are able to do this because only a small fraction of their depositors is expected to turn up during any given day or week to withdraw their deposits. The bulk of deposits is invested in financial assets, from which the depository institutions earn most of their income.

Those income-earning financial assets range from bills, notes, and bonds issued by private corporations and by the federal, state, and municipal governments to mortgage loans for housing. Each type of financial institution has a different type of portfolio of assets, which reflects their area of special expertise in managing financial assets. This subject is discussed in Part II, where depository institutions are grouped with a larger class of financial institutions called financial intermediaries.

To demonstrate how depository institutions create money under the present system of fractional reserve banking, a hypothetical example of a commercial bank, Southwest National Bank, will be used. It is assumed that federal regulations require Southwest National Bank to hold a percentage of its deposits in the form of cash reserves. This is called the *reserve requirement*. The reserves may be held in the form of currency and coin on the premises, a form of reserves called *vault cash*. Or they may be held in a deposit at a regional Federal Reserve Bank.

Assume that the Southwest National Bank management, taking into account the reserve requirement and the projected amount of withdrawals and deposits, decides to keep 20 percent of its deposits in reserves.

The Southwest National Bank Creates Money

Under a fractional reserve banking system, banks create money. The money creation story can begin when John Jones deposits $1000 in currency in the Southwest National Bank.

The Southwest National is no charity. It is a profit-maximizing institution that can be expected to look eagerly for ways to earn income on the 80 percent of John Jones' deposit that it does not desire to hold. Alvin Bly comes to the bank with a loan application. Southwest National Bank makes an automobile loan for $800 to Mr. Bly. Mr. Bly gives the check drawn on the Southwest National Bank to an automobile retail dealer, Selma White. John Jones believes that his deposit of $1000 is in the bank, while Selma White, the automobile dealer, also believes she has a good check for $800. Fractional reserve banking has allowed the Southwest National Bank to create $800.

Money Creation in Accounting Form

It is customary to show how banks create money by using simple T accounts and double-entry bookkeeping. The presentation that follows is deceptively simple, but it helps to explain the principle of deposit expansion. Some important complications will be disregarded. The time it takes for bankers to adjust their portfolios so that they hold their desired reserves will be ignored. The value of the currency and coin held by the public outside depository institutions is assumed to be constant. At first, it will also be assumed that Southwest National Bank is the only available depository institution, so that all checks drawn on the bank are redeposited in the same bank.

TABLE 7-2

Assets	Liabilities
	Initial Deposit
(2) $1000 cash	(1) $1000 deposit by John Jones

Tables 7-2 through 7-6 display simple T accounts for the Southwest National Bank. Each T account displays an identity which states that:

1. The sum of the value of all *assets* (which are claims on future income and other commodities of value held by the bank) listed in the left-hand column of each T account is exactly equal to
2. The sum of the value of all *liabilities* (which are claims against the bank's assets by people or firms) listed in the right-hand column of each account.

The equality of assets and liabilities is equivalent to the statement that everything of value in the bank belongs to someone.

There are two types of liabilities:

1. *Equities*, claims of the owners of the banks.
2. *Other liabilities*, claims of persons or firms who are not owners of the bank: for example, deposits, which are claims of depositors on the bank.

The process of money creation is illustrated step by step in the T accounts for the bank in Tables 7-2 through 7-6. The time-honored rules of double-entry accounting are followed. They require that all entries be made at least twice.

In comes John Jones with a $1000 deposit, which is represented both as a $1000 liability (1) and a $1000 cash asset (2) in Table 7-2. The bank desires to maintain a 20 percent reserve ratio, so that $800 is available for the purchase of an income-earning asset. In comes Alvin Bly for an $800 automobile loan. The loan is made, causing a reduction in cash of $800 (3) and a new asset (4), the automobile loan shown in Table 7-3. In this step, $800 is created, since Alvin Bly has $800 that did not exist before.

TABLE 7-3

Assets	Liabilities
	$800 of Money Is Created
(2) $1000 cash	(1) $1000 deposit by John Jones
(3) −$800 cash	
(4) $800 auto loan to Alvin Bly	

TABLE 7-4

Redeposit of the New Money

Assets	Liabilities
(2) $1000 cash	(1) $1000 deposit by John Jones
(3) −$800 cash	(5) $800 deposit by auto dealer,
(4) $800 auto loan to Alvin Bly	Selma White
(6) $800 cash	

Selma White, the automobile dealer, deposits the $800 (5), adding $800 to the bank's cash assets (6), as shown in Table 7-4.

The bank now has $1800 in deposits and $1000 in reserves. The management desires to keep 20 percent of deposits, $360, as reserves and to use the remainder of its reserves, $640, for the purchase of income-earning assets. Therefore, the bank management decides to loan K Corporation $640. This loan reduces the bank's cash assets by $640 (7) to acquire the new business loan asset (8), as shown in Table 7-5. In this step, $640 is created, since K Corporation has $640 it did not have before.

K Corporation redeposits the $640, creating a new deposit (9) and adding $640 to the bank's cash assets (10), as shown in Table 7-6. Total

TABLE 7-5

Second Money Creation

Assets	Liabilities
(2) $1000 cash	(1) $1000 deposit by John Jones
(3) −$800 cash	(5) $800 deposit by auto dealer,
(4) $800 auto loan to Alvin Bly	Selma White
(6) $800 cash	
(7) −$640 cash	
(8) $640 business loan to K Corporation	

TABLE 7-6

Hypothetical Creation and Redeposit of $1440 by Southwest National Bank

Assets	Liabilities
(2) $1000 cash	(1) $1000 deposit by John Jones
(3) −$800 cash	(5) $800 deposit by auto dealer,
(4) $800 auto loan to Alvin Bly	Selma White
(6) $800 cash	(9) $640 deposit of the K Corporation
(7) −$640 cash	
(8) $640 business loan to K Corporation	
(10) $640 cash	

---

cash reserves of the Southwest National Bank are still $1000. The total deposits are now $2440. Since the desired reserve ratio is 20 percent, the desired reserve level is now $488 and the bank will desire to purchase $512 in additional income-earning assets. This process of money creation can continue if each income-earning asset purchased is redeposited at Southwest National Bank.

How Much Money Can the Entire Banking System Create?

In the example, the amount of desired reserves grows from $200 after the first deposit of $1000, to $360 after the second deposit of $800, and to $488 after the third deposit of $640. The desired reserves increase while the total reserves are constant at $1000. Eventually, the Southwest National Bank will have created so many deposits that all of the $1000 will be desired for reserves, and no additional earning assets will be purchased. The T-account example may be pursued to the limiting amount of deposits for the original deposit of $1000 in currency. A more convenient method that employs a few symbols may be used to find the answer. In order to generalize the result to the entire banking system (all depository institutions), the Southwest National Bank is replaced by the entire banking system. Instead of requiring redeposits in the Southwest National Bank, redeposits in similar accounts at any depository institutions will allow the money expansion process to proceed.

Let d be the average desired ratio of reserves to deposits, which in the previous example is .2. Then $1 - d$ (= .8) is the desired proportion of deposits an average bank management uses to buy income-earning assets. Let $L = 1 - d$.

If new deposits currently are $1, the bank purchases L times $1, or L of earning assets. The sum of L is redeposited in a bank, which loans out L times that amount, or L^2. This process is repeated a large number (N) of times, resulting in the following series:

$$S = \$1(1 + L + L^2 + \cdots + L^N) \tag{2}$$

The sum (S) of the numbers in the parentheses is the total dollar value of deposits that banks could create with an initial deposit of $1 in currency. Dropping the dollar sign for convenience, Equation (2) becomes

$$S = 1 + L + L^2 + L^3 + \cdots + L^N \tag{3}$$

Now a simple trick will be used to find the value of this series of L's. The equality in Equation (3) is unaltered by multiplying each side of the equation by L:

$$LS = L + L^2 + L^4 + \cdots + L^N + 1 \tag{4}$$

Subtract Equation (4) from Equation (3) to obtain

$$S(1 - L) = 1 - L^N + 1 \tag{5}$$

The fraction L approaches zero as it is multiplied by itself a great many times, so that $L^N + 1$ is approximately zero. This leaves (after substituting d for $1 - L$):

$$S = \frac{1}{1 - L} = \frac{1}{d} \tag{6}$$

This shows that the sum of the value of deposits (new money) of the entire banking system, D, created by an initial $1 deposit of currency is

$$D = \frac{\$1}{d} \tag{7}$$

If $d = .2$, D would be $5. If, as in the example, the initial deposit of currency were $1000, D would be $5000. In more general form, the preceding equation may be written as

$$D = \frac{R}{d} \quad \text{or} \quad d = \frac{R}{D} \tag{8}$$

where R represents the total cash reserves of the banking system.

The example and the derivation of Equation (7) are intended to give an intuitive feeling for money creation by the private banking system. The description will be modified in Chapter 18 to take account of varying amounts of cash held by the nonbank public. If, for example, Mr. Bly, in the example above, demanded his $800 loan in the form of currency that he put in a safety deposit box, no further expansion of money by the Southwest National Bank would have occurred. Most loans are made by increasing a depositor's account rather than in cash. Nevertheless, the analysis explains the fundamental principle of private bank expansion of the money supply.

The Control of the Money Supply

Recall in the example that the initial deposit was $1000 in currency. Currency is part of the monetary base. The monetary base, in turn, is controlled primarily by the Federal Reserve, the central bank of the United States. The Federal Reserve can directly affect the amount of the monetary base by two different methods: open-market operations and direct loans to depository institutions. The Federal Reserve is described in greater detail in Part V.

Open-market operations is the name applied to the Federal Reserve's special auctions at which securities, mostly U.S. Treasury securities, are bought from or sold to the private sector. When the Federal Reserve buys securities, it pays the private buyer new money—in the form of currency or bank reserves. This is an addition to the monetary base. If the Federal Reserve sells securities, it receives payment in the form of currency or bank reserves, which reduces the monetary base. Thus open-market operations can be used to change the size of the monetary base.

The Federal Reserve is also empowered to loan money directly to any depository institution with checkable accounts. The extension of those loans increases the monetary base, and their reduction reduces the monetary base. Those loans are said to be made through the Federal Reserve's *discount window* and are sometimes referred to as *discounts and advances* or simply *discounting*. (The use of the name "discount window" refers to the loan paper on which the Federal Reserve based its member bank loans in its early history. The loans were made at a discount from the value of the loan paper.)

The Federal Reserve can also influence the size of the money supply by changing the proportion of deposits that depository institutions must hold as reserves. This is called a *change in reserve requirements*.

These three Federal Reserve actions comprise its *monetary tools*. The monetary tools can be used to affect the size of the monetary aggregates, such as M1B and M2 and the level of interest rates.

Suppose that the monetary base is increased, causing the nominal money supply M to increase to M', as indicated in Figure 7-2. The supply of real-money balances may move from M/P to the lower level M'/P' if the price level rises (from P to P') by more than the increase in the nominal money supply.

Figure 7-2

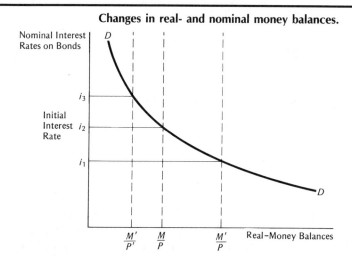

Changes in real- and nominal money balances.

The point to remember is that although the government has capabilities for directly controlling the monetary base and thereby influencing the size of the nominal money supply, it cannot directly control the real quantity of money, M/P. These relationships, which are examined in later chapters, make monetary policy a fascinating part of money and banking.

Appendix: The Money Expansion Multipliers

Important variables involved in the relationship between the monetary base and the money supply are illuminated by means of the *money expansion multipliers*. These multipliers are described first with special attention to two variables that determine the size of the multipliers: the public's desire for currency and coin relative to deposits and depository institutions' desire for reserves relative to deposits.

The *money expansion multiplier* (also called the *monetary base multiplier*) is derived from two other identities. The first states that the total money supply (M1) is equal to currency and coin outside depository institutions C plus checkable deposits at depository institutions D:

$$M1 = C + D \tag{9}$$

The second identity defines the monetary base B as equal to currency outside depository institutions C plus the reserves of depository institutions R:

$$B = C + R \tag{10}$$

If Equation (9) is divided by Equation (10) and the terms rearranged, Equation (11) is obtained:

$$M1 = B\left(\frac{C + D}{C + R}\right) \tag{11}$$

Dividing the numerator and the denominator of the fraction by D, the final identity is

$$M1 = B\left(\frac{C/D + 1}{C/D + R/D}\right) \tag{12}$$

The money supply is equal to the size of the monetary base multiplied by a ratio. The ratio in parentheses on the right side of Equation (12) is sometimes called the money expansion multiplier. If R/D declines in value, the denominator, $C/D + R/D$, becomes smaller and the money expansion multiplier becomes larger. If C/D declines in value, the numerator, $C/D + 1$, declines by a smaller proportion than the denominator, $C/D + R/D$. This is because the C/D ratio is added to 1 in the numerator and to a fraction R/D in the denominator. The same change added to both a larger number and a smaller number will increase the smaller number by a larger proportion.

Equation (11) classifies the determinants of the money supply into three groups. First, there are those government transactions that affect the size of the monetary base B. These transactions are open-market operations and discounting by the Federal Reserve. Second, there are those factors that affect the *currency ratio*, C/D. The size of the currency ratio is determined primarily by the public. The public decides what proportion of its money it wishes to keep in the form of currency and coin. The greater this proportion, the smaller is the currency and coin available to the banking system as a reserve for the expansion of the supply of bank money.

The third group of factors affecting the money supply is classified as the determinants of the *reserve ratio*, R/D. The managers of individual depository institutions determine the proportion of deposits they wish to keep in the form of reserves in order to meet reserve requirements and the liquidity needs of the bank. (For large city banks with quick access to the federal funds market and the Federal Reserve discount window and careful cash management, few if any excess reserves are carried. Liquidity needs that deplete reserves are offset with reserve injections that keep average excess reserves for the week near zero.) If the definition of money is M1, time deposits at commercial banks are not included in the money supply. Nevertheless, the managers of depository institutions will desire and are required to hold some reserves against their time deposits. The government deposits in commercial banks are also not included in the money supply. Depository institution managers may desire to hold reserves against government deposits. The proportion of checkable deposits maintained in the form of reserves by an individual depository institution will therefore depend on the distribution of deposits between checkable deposits, time deposits, and government deposits.

The manager of each depository institution must assess his or her expected average deposits and the expected variations about that average in the forthcoming period to ensure that there will be sufficient reserves to meet legal reserve requirements and the excess of withdrawals over deposits of funds by depositors.

The effect on the money supply of a change in either the currency ratio or the reserve ratio depends on whether the other changes as well. Suppose that the monetary base is constant at $100 billion. The currency ratio is assumed to be .2 and the reserve ratio is assumed to be .3. The total money supply is then determined from Equation (11):

$$\$240b = \$100b\left(\frac{.2 + 1}{.2 + .3}\right) = \$100b(2.4) \qquad (13)$$

(here "b" designates "billion"). The money expansion multiplier is 2.4. Therefore, the money supply is equal to $240 billion. Now, if the currency ratio is increased to .3, the expression becomes

$$\$216.67b = \$100b\left(\frac{.3 + 1}{.3 + 3}\right) = \$100b(2.1667) \tag{14}$$

The money expansion multiplier is equal to $2.1667, so the total money supply is $216.67 billion. The effect of increasing the currency ratio by .1 is a decrease in the money supply of $23.33 billion.

If, instead, the currency ratio remains at .2 and the reserve ratio increases to .4, the money expansion multiplier then equals 2 and the money supply equals $200 billion:

$$\$200b = \$100b\left(\frac{.2 + 1}{.2 + .4}\right) = \$100b(2) \tag{15}$$

which is a decline in the money supply of $40 billion compared to Equation (13).

Now suppose that both the currency and reserve ratios change together. Both increase by .1 from their values in Equation (13):

$$\$185.71b = \$100b\left(\frac{.3 + 1}{.3 + .4}\right) = \$100b(1.8571) \tag{16}$$

The money supply is reduced by $54.29 billion compared to Equation (12). The sum of the changes in the money supply caused by the changes in C/D and R/D, taken separately in Equations (13) and (14), is $63.33 billion. The $9 billion difference in Equation (15), where both C/D and R/D change, reflects the interaction between the ratios. The effect on the money supply of a change in one of these ratios is not independent; it depends on the size of the other.

NOTE

1. For those unfamiliar with price indexes, a description is provided in Appendix A of Chapter 4. Note that the description of the flow-of-funds in Chapter 4 is not wrong because it was stated in nominal terms. Rather, the demand and supply schedules for loanable funds must each be labeled for the price level for which they are applicable. As the price level changes, the demand and supply schedules for nominal loanable funds change.

STUDY QUESTIONS

1. Does the government create the basic media of exchange? Explain.

2. Can depository institutions create money? Explain.

3. What is fractional reserve banking?

4. Derive a formula that shows how much money can be created for a given increase in the monetary base. What simplifying assumptions are made in the derivation?

5. What part of the government controls the money supply, and how do they do it?

6. What source of financing deficits that is not available to state or local governments is available to the federal government?

7. What are the money expansion multipliers, and how are they derived? Discuss the determinants of B, C/D, and R/D.

7.

$$m1 = C + D$$

$$B = C + R$$

$C = $ Currency + Coin

$D = $ Deposits at Inst,

$R = $ Reserves

See to p. 124-5

$$m1 = B\left(\frac{C+D}{C+R}\right)$$

$$= B\left(\frac{C/D + 1}{C/D + R/D}\right)$$

8

The Demand and Supply of Loanable Funds

Introduction

The demand for loanable funds can be viewed as a desire to obtain funds by supplying financial assets. This can be accomplished by selling bonds and other securities.

The supply of loanable funds can be viewed as a desire to lend funds by demanding financial assets. This can be accomplished by buying bonds and other securities.

This chapter uses the demand and supply of loanable funds to explain nominal interest rates and the volume of loanable funds traded in a period. The nominal interest rate is the rate of interest observed on bonds. The term "bonds" is used as a general name for all debt instruments.

So far the demand and supply for loanable funds appears to be a simple run-of-the-mill demand and supply analysis, but appearances may be deceptive. As an abbreviated explanation the demand and supply of loanable funds are frequently called forth to show that market forces determine interest rates. However, the concept of loanable funds is not well understood.

Loanable funds is a concept that mixes financial assets such as bonds and stocks with the means of payment, money. The concept of loanable funds can be described by using the national income concepts of saving and investment, and changes in the demand and supply of money. Changes in the demand for money are shown to be equivalent to hoarding or dishoarding money.

The analysis begins with a discussion of hoarding and dishoarding. Saving and investment, explained in Chapter 4, are then brought into the picture. The discussion proceeds directly to a description of the demand and supply of loanable funds. In the last part of the chapter, the effects of inflationary expectations and income taxes on the equilibrium interest rate are analyzed from a loanable funds point of view.

The chapter uses a macroeconomic view insofar as it looks at a summary variable for the economy as a whole. Individual investor behavior is discussed in Part V. Also, the analysis in this chapter is simplified by holding the price level constant and by assuming that all securities are default-free perpetuities. This last simplification bypasses the problem of different interest rates on bonds with different maturities (discussed in Part III). It also ignores different interest rates due to different default risks (discussed in Part IV).

Finally, the inapplicability of loanable funds analysis to balance sheet changes (portfolio changes) is noted.

Changes in the Demand for Money

One view, called the "classical" analysis of the equilibrium rate of interest, is that the rate equates saving (and savers' expected rate of return) with investment (and investors' expected rate of return).[1] The work of John Maynard Keynes in 1936 asserted that the equilibrium rate of interest is affected significantly by the demand and supply of money.[2]

In the equilibrium described subsequently, the two views of the determination of the rate of interest are seen to be equivalent. However, saving and investment and the demand and supply of money play partially separate roles; and making the separation can be especially important in explaining changes in the interest rate that lead to new equilibrium positions.[3] These partially separate roles are important enough to warrant a separate look at the demand and supply of money as was done in Chapter 6.

In the analysis of loanable funds the *form* of the demand and supply of money must be changed. Saving and investment are *flow* concepts: a given number of dollars of saving or investment per period. These flow concepts measure the transfer of funds over a given time period. Money demand and supply are *stock* concepts: simply a given number of dollars with no time dimension. A stock concept is a photograph of inventories at one instant of time. *Changes* in the *stock* of money demanded is a flow concept: a stream of dollars added to or subtracted from an individual's stock of money per period.

Money demand is transformed into a flow variable: the increase or decrease in money demand. An increase in money demand is a desire to increase one's money balances. It has also been called a desire to increase one's hoard of money, or simply *hoarding money*. Its dimension is a flow: a given number of dollars per period. Money supply is transformed into the rate of change of the money supply, also a given number of dollars per period. Changes in both money demand and supply are plotted in Figure 8-1 for each nominal interest rate.

The equality between actual hoarding of money and the rate of change of the money supply is easy to show. Simply consider that no one can add a dollar to his or her hoard of money unless someone else reduces his or her hoard of money, if the total money supply is constant. *Net hoarding* (hoarding minus dishoarding) of money, therefore, is zero, by definition, when the money supply is constant. The only way that net hoarding can be positive is if the money supply is increased so that individuals can increase their holdings—their hoards—of money.[4] Therefore, net hoarding always equals the change in the money supply ΔM_S, where Δ is the Greek capital letter delta and is used to mean "change in."

In Figure 8-1, the change in the supply of money ΔM_S is upward sloping, indicating that the change in the money supply will be greater at a higher interest rate on bonds, i_2.[5]

Suppose that individuals try to increase their demand for money faster than money is supplied, as is shown at an interest rate of i_1 in Figure 8-1. The increase in the demand for money ΔM_D, or *desired net hoarding*, exceeds the change in the money supply by *ab*. Obviously, all individuals and other transactors together cannot accomplish this feat. Some transactors may attempt to sell bonds (borrow money) to increase their money balances. This action, viewed separately, will cause bond prices to fall or, equivalently, the interest rate on bonds to rise.[6] Equilibrium will be restored when the interest rate rises to a high enough level to discourage the increase in money demand at a rate that is more rapid than the change in the money supply. That interest rate is shown to be i_2

Figure 8-1

The relation between changes in the demand and supply of money.

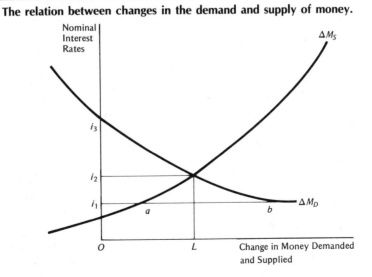

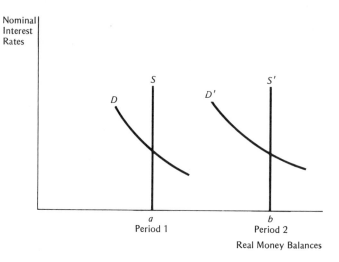

Figure 8-2

Changes in the stock demand for money between periods.

in Figure 8-1. The explanation of a falling interest rate above i_2 is left to Study Question 5 at the end of the chapter.

How does Figure 8-1 fit into the analysis of the demand and supply of money in Chapter 6? In Chapter 6 the stock demand and supply of money is described for one instant of time. If both the stock and flow demands for money are in *equilibrium* at a given price and a nominal rate of interest i_2, the correspondence can be shown in Figures 8-1 and 8-2. Equilibrium for a rate of growth of the money supply of OL in Figure 8-1 corresponds to a change in the money supply of ab in Figure 8-2. The stock demand and supply curves have shifted from D and S to D' and S'.[7]

The Demand and Supply

Suppose that the only supply of credit or loans to the economy was from those who saved and that they supplied exactly the amount they saved. Also, suppose that the only loan demand was from people (or corporations) who invested and that this demand exactly equaled desired investment. Then some interest rate could be found at which savers would obtain a high enough return so that they would desire to save exactly what investors would desire to invest. (This equilibrium interest rate was presented in Chapter 4.) Under the condition posed, this would explain the interest rate that cleared the market for the demand and supply of loans or credit.

However, the demand for loans in each period can be greater than desired investment by the amount by which individuals, corporations, and governments wish to increase their holdings of money. Also, the supply of loans can be greater in each period by the amount by which the money supply increases. Therefore, the demand and supply of loanable funds must include not only desired saving and desired investment but also desired changes in the demand for money (desired net hoarding) and changes in the money supply.

At some interest rate, lenders will be induced to offer the amount of loanable funds that borrowers will find profitable to demand. This interest rate is said to be determined by the demand and supply of loanable funds or, equivalently, the demand and supply of financial assets (or securities) in each period.

The supply of loanable funds or credit consists first of any funds that individuals or corporations desire to save. Second, the supply of loanable funds consists of the change in the money supply.

The demand for loanable funds consists, first, of desired investment, and second, of increases in the demand for money by individuals, corporations, or state and local government (desired net hoarding).

These components of the demand and supply of loanable funds are shown in Figure 8-3. The equilibrium nominal interest rate, OF, equates the change in the demand for money ΔM_D with the change in the money supply ΔM_S (equilibrium position A) and desired savings S^D with desired investment I^D (at equilibrium position B). The supply of loanable funds schedule is the (lateral) summation of two schedules: $S^D + \Delta M_S$. The demand for loanable funds schedule is the (lateral) summation of two other schedules: $I^D + \Delta M_D$. In equilibrium in Figure 8-3, these summations require that $FB + FA = FC$ or, equivalently, that $FA = BC$.

The demand and supply of loanable funds are depicted in Figure 8-4 without the underlying schedules. The supply schedule $S_L S_L$ slopes

Figure 8-3

Desired investment and saving, changes in the demand and supply of money, and the demand and supply of loanable funds.

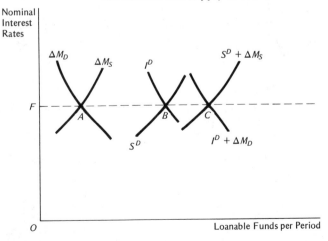

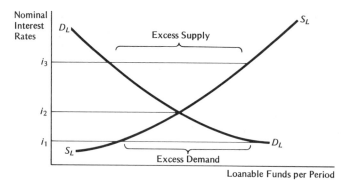

Figure 8-4

The demand and supply of loanable funds.

upward on the grounds that more will be saved (at a given level of income and prices) when the reward (the interest rate) is higher. The demand schedule $D_L D_L$ slopes downward on the assumptions that (1) (with a given stock of wealth and a given level of prices) more investment opportunities are profitable at lower interest rates and (2) there will be a greater demand to increase money holdings when interest rates on alternative assets such as bonds are lower.

The equilibrium interest rate i_2 in Figure 8-4 equates the amount of loanable funds supplied with those demanded. At a higher interest rate, such as i_1, there would be an excess demand and interest rates would rise.

Other things being the same, the following changes from a position of equilibrium will initially shift the demand for loanable funds $D_L D_L$ to the right and increase the nominal interest rate:

1. An increase in investment at each interest rate.
2. An increased demand for money at each interest rate.[8]

Other things being the same, the following changes from a position of equilibrium will initially increase nominal interest rates by shifting the supply of loanable funds to the left:

1. A decrease in saving at each interest rate.
2. A decrease in the money supply due to actions taken by the government or the private sector.

These relationships are readily apparent from examining the underlying curves in Figure 8-3. The analysis provides an interesting and easy way to see these partial relationships. They are partial because they do not simultaneously take into account changes in prices and real income.[9]

The Effect on Interest Rates of Income Tax Laws and Inflationary Expectations

The loanable funds analysis can be used to show the effects on observed market interest rates on bonds of income tax laws combined with inflationary expectations. Suppose that initially there is a given level of inflationary expectations and income tax rates. The demand and supply of loanable funds under these conditions are shown in Figure 8-5 as $D_L D_L$ and $S_L S_L$, respectively.

Then assume that suddenly there is an expectation of a more rapid inflation. The adjustment is shown in Figure 8-5. The initial equilibrium is at an interest rate of i_1. Savers will be unwilling to loan out the same amount of money at each interest rate as they were willing to loan before they revised their expectations about inflation. Another way of saying this is that bond buyers will demand higher interest on their bonds to cover the effect on their interest income and the return of principal of expected inflation. The supply of loanable funds $S_L S_L$ will therefore shift to the left to $S_L' S_L'$.

Borrowers will also recognize that the effects of inflation will increase their money income and the amount of funds they need to finance their investments. They will be willing to pay more interest on the bonds they sell. The demand for loanable funds $D_L D_L$ will shift to $D_L' D_L'$.

A full adjustment will cause the new equilibrium interest rate i_2 to exceed the prior equilibrium interest rate i_1 by approximately the increase in the expected rate of inflation. Neglecting the complications from tax laws, the Fisher relationship shown in Chapter 4 would provide an explanation of the difference between i_2 and i_1 in Figure 8-5. The difference between i_2 and i_1 is the increase in the expected rate of inflation.

Figure 8-5

The demand and supply of loanable funds adjusting to specified conditions.

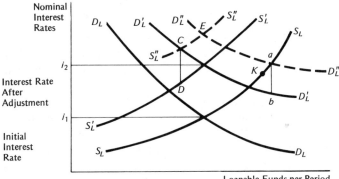

Now assume that tax laws allow interest payments to be deducted by borrowers and that lenders must pay tax on the increased interest income, as described in Chapter 4. The expectation of inflation has increased the rate of interest and also the size of the tax deduction for borrowers. Borrowers taking into account that larger tax deduction would further increase their demand for loanable funds. In effect, they are given a subsidy equal to ab in Figure 8-5. Meanwhile, lenders must pay a higher tax on their interest income, equal to CD. Both the demand and supply of loanable funds will shift to incorporate these tax and subsidy distortions. The demand increases to $D_L''D_L''$ and the supply decreases to $S_L''S_L''$, so that the new equilibrium is at E. The equilibrium interest rate is higher. Whether the same, greater, or smaller quantities of loanable funds are traded per period depends on the magnitude of these shifts.

If tax-exempt debt instruments such as state and municipal bonds (both referred to as municipals) are used, the aggregate demand for loanable funds will shift by a smaller amount than $D_L'D_L'$ to $D_L''D_L''$. This is because the borrowers, city and state governments, do not pay and are not directly affected by federal income tax laws. Their demand for loanable funds will not be affected by the tax laws. The final equilibrium would reflect the tax-exempt nature of interest received on municipals by lenders. If the expectation of inflation has put lenders in higher tax brackets, they will supply more loanable funds. Suppose (for simplicity in Figure 8-5, which will not gracefully take even one more line) that the supply of loanable funds moves down to S_LS_L as a result of lenders' increased exemption from taxes. The new equilibrium is at a position such as K, where more loanable funds are traded.[10] Since tax-exempt government bonds do not dominate the credit markets (they were 5.4 percent of funds raised in the flow-of-funds accounts for 1981 in Chapter 4), the supply of all loanable funds will not shift down by a great deal; in Figure 8-5, therefore, the equilibrium interest rate will not fall as far as i_2.

Balance Sheet Considerations

The criticism is sometimes correctly made that the foregoing analysis depends primarily on the flows of saving, investment, and money, whereas market interest rates depend to a large extent on portfolio changes.

For example, suppose that a family sells a car it owns and buys a bond. This is a portfolio change affecting the composition of their wealth, while leaving their saving, investment, and the change in their money demand unaffected. It is a change that could be observed only by looking at the composition of their balance sheet (or list) of wealth.

In this example, physical nonfinancial wealth producing nonpecuniary (nonmoney) services is traded for financial wealth, which yields pecuniary (money) returns. There are also continual shifts between different kinds of financial wealth. These portfolio changes may represent massive changes in the demands for particular types of assets, affecting their prices and yields.

Macroeconomics has little to say about these portfolio changes except some nearly platitudinous conjectures that there are some equilibrium proportions between the different kinds of assets that people hold. The field of finance has much more to say, as indicated in Part IV.

All this may mean that in the short run the equilibrium interest rate determination given by the loanable funds analysis may provide useful information about the effect of important macroeconomic variables on the rate of interest. The analysis in the next chapter applies to a longer period of time. The long-run fundamental determinants of the real rate of interest are discussed. This should be useful information even though it does not explain the short-run effects on real and nominal interest rates of important portfolio shifts such as a shift from bonds, stocks, and fiat money into gold during a world crisis.

NOTES

1. The word "classical" is a misnomer in the sense that most pre-Keynesian economists (before 1936) to which this term is applied were more interested in the rate of return from *capital* and saving rather than from *investment* and saving, a distinction that will be made meaningful in the next chapter. See Abba P. Lerner, "Alternative Formations of the Theory of Interest," in *The New Economics*, Seymour E. Harris, ed. (New York: Alfred A. Knopf, Inc., 1948), p. 634, footnote 1, for this point and pp. 634–654 for the rest of an eloquent presentation. The reader would also benefit from Lerner's "Interest Theory—Supply and Demand for Loans, or Supply and Demand for Cash?" also in *The New Economics*, pp. 655–661.
2. John Maynard Keynes (1887–1946) wrote innumerable articles and seventeen books. His second-to-last book became his most famous and spawned a whole new theory of macroeconomics. It is *The General Theory of Employment, Interest and Money* (New York: Harcourt Brace & World, Inc., 1964; first published in 1936), usually referred to as *The General Theory*.
3. *Partially separate* means that although all four functions are interrelated and are jointly affected by and affect changes in other variables, such as real income, each plays a distinct role in the analysis of loanable funds and the interest rate.
4. If the increase in the money supply is defined as dishoarding by the government or private institutions creating the money, net hoarding would always equal zero. Because the government is often assumed to run monetary policy with targets (such as price stability) that are different from other transactors, money supply changes are separated out and not considered part of hoarding or dishoarding.
5. The view that the level of the nominal money supply is larger at higher interest rates is controversial. It rests on the belief that at higher interest rates on bonds, depository institutions will borrow more from the Federal Reserve; depository institutions will reduce their excess reserves (reserves in excess of required reserves); and the monetary authorities will *accommodate* income changes with money supply changes. Depository institution borrowing does not depend on the level of the rate of interest on bonds; it depends on the difference between that rate and the borrowing rate (called

the *discount rate*). Excess reserves of depository institutions are usually so low—due to continual economizing—that there is little room for further economizing. For simplicity, accommodation is ruled out. Many economists believe it is a bad policy because it provides stimulus during inflation and restraint during contractions. Even if the *level* of the nominal money supply is invariant (does not vary) with interest rates, the *change* in the money supply may under special conditions.

From an initial equilibrium position income may rise to a higher (or lower) trend rate of growth. During the change, interest rates may also rise (or fall). Even if the monetary authorities are not accommodating income and interest rate changes over the business cycle, they may wish to increase (or decrease) the rate of growth of the money supply. In a sense, they are accommodating long-term, not short-term, trends in income. From the same initial quantity of money, the change in the money supply, equal to the change *ab* in Figure 8-2, would be larger with a higher interest rate under these conditions. Thus an upward-sloping change in the supply of money function could be consistent with the vertical level of the money supply function. This would be true if the former were considered only for adjustments to new equilibrium rates of income growth and the latter considered only for conditions of equilibrium growth in income.

If the ifs and buts are too numerous to tolerate, the vertical *M* supply curve may be assumed. The supply of loanable funds can still be considered upward sloping since, as is shown subsequently, the supply of loanable funds also contains a saving function, which is upward sloping.

6. Alternatively, transactors could individually attempt to hoard more money by reducing their consumption and *saving* more of their income, or by selling off their assets. Selling off their assets means that they run down their physical wealth (such as automobiles and houses) or exchange stocks, bonds, and other nonmonetary financial assets for money. Insofar as saving (the difference between an individual's income and consumption) is affected, the analysis requires a consideration of the saving function that is incorporated into the demand for loanable funds. Insofar as the individual is changing the proportion of his or her portfolio held as money (say, by trading bonds for money), equilibrium interest rates are affected if the schedule for desired net hoarding changes. A portfolio change from bonds to money temporarily increases desired net hoarding. Additional portfolio changes are discussed in the final section of this chapter.

7. In Chapter 6 it was shown that

$$MV = PY \tag{1}$$

where *M* is money, *V* is income velocity, *P* is the price level, and *Y* is real income. In rates of change, this equation becomes

$$\dot{M} + \dot{V} = \dot{P} + \dot{Y} \tag{2}$$

where dots above the letters mean rates of change.

If interest rates are constant at an equilibrium level, there is an equilibrium level of velocity, so that $\dot{V} = 0$. Then, if $\dot{M}$ is taken as the rate of change in money demand, it is, in equilibrium, equal to $\dot{P} + \dot{Y}$, or simply $\dot{Y}$ if the price level is constant. Therefore, *ab* in Figure 8-2 can, in equilibrium, equal the change in real income associated with the equilibrium rate of change of real income. Since real income is growing, *ab* will represent larger and larger changes over time.

8. The nominal values of investment and money demands here and the nominal values of the saving and money stock functions that follow all are based on a given rate of rise or level of prices. Therefore, the nominal and real values of these variables are the same.

9. The most popular elementary model for integrating prices and real income into this analysis is the Hicksian solution to macroeconomic equilibrium. It can be studied in compact form in Robert Auerbach's *Money, Banking, and Financial Markets* (New York: Macmillan Publishing Co., Inc., 1982), pp. 299–323.

10. The demand curve is unlikely to shift as far as the pretax position because only a small proportion of bonds are tax exempt. Also, the introduction of tax-exempt bonds to the analysis introduces a second interest rate at a lower level for these securities. The aggregate interest rate in this analysis would then become a weighted average of the two interest rates (where the weights are equal to the quantities of tax-exempt and nontax-exempt securities, in units paying $1 per year, sold in a base equilibrium period).

STUDY QUESTIONS

1. Using loanable funds analysis, analyze the effects on loanable funds traded and interest rates of:
   a. Credit allocation plans in which government authorization is required for loans and investments.
   b. Tax laws allowing saving to be deducted from income in computing income taxes.
   c. A portfolio shift in which some bonds are exchanged for stocks.
   d. A portfolio shift in which some bonds are exchanged for money.

2. What is the effect of a reduction in tax rates on equilibrium interest rates?

3. If there were a shortage of $5 bills (i.e., they are difficult to obtain without paying a premium for them), is it correct to say that net hoarding of $5 bills is positive? Is it correct to say that the velocity of $5 bills has declined?

4. If inflation is expected to slow down, what would happen to equilibrium interest rates given no change in tax laws? Use the loanable funds analysis to describe the results.

5. If the interest rate is above i_2 in Figure 8-1, explain the forces that cause the interest rate to fall to i_2.

6. Does the loanable funds analysis explain the effect of portfolio changes on the rate of interest? Explain.

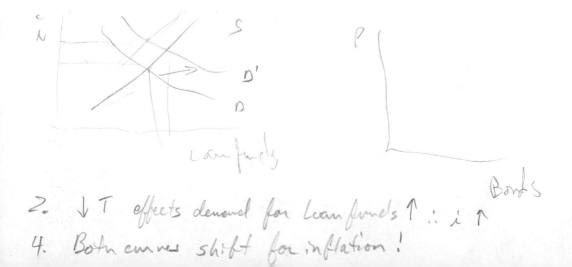

2. $\downarrow T$ effects demand for loan funds $\uparrow$ ∴ $i \uparrow$ Bonds

4. Both curves shift for inflation!

9

Determinants of the Real Rate of Interest

Introduction

The analysis of the market rate of interest in the preceding two chapters did not consider fundamental reasons why the society should settle down to or approach any long-run real rate of interest. Such a real rate of interest is an equilibrium rate of return on investment or, if the society has all the capital it wants, the equilibrium rate at which capital produces output. Recall from Chapter 4 that the real rate is less than the observable nominal rates of interest on default-free bonds by the premium for expected inflation and an adjustment for tax rates. The fundamental considerations that determine the equilibrium real rate of interest are discussed in this chapter.

The equilibrium real rate of interest depends on two different classes of determinants. On the productivity side, it depends on the rate at which factories and other production facilities can produce output. The other class of determinants is preferences—the amount of future consumption compared to present consumption which the society wants. In a free enterprise economy, the managers or owners of productive facilities, such as factories, are the demanders of capital. The ultimate wealth holders, the savers, supply the capital. Savers do not consume their entire income. They can use the income they save to buy securities from those who demand capital for productive processes. In this way, the savers acquire claims against future income.

The chapter begins with a discussion of two broad classes of bonds, inside and outside bonds. Outside bonds are thereafter deleted from the discussion until the final section of the chapter. The next section explains a commonly used simplifying device that transforms all securities into perpetuities paying $1 a year, called *consol equivalents*. This simplification allows securities to be added together and bypasses the problems of different interest rates on securities with different maturities (discussed in Part III).

The demand for capital by the managers or owners of productive processes, described subsequently, depends on the productivity of the productive processes and the cost of additions to the stock of capital of productive enterprises. These additions are called *net private investment*, a concept explained in Chapter 4.

The supply of capital at each interest rate by the ultimate wealth holders is shown to depend on their *time preference*. Time preference is the name applied to the preference for present relative to future consumption. It summarizes individuals' preferences for allocating consumption over time and is embodied in the rate at which an individual discounts future income to determine the present value to him or her of financial assets. This rate is called the *subjective rate of discount*. The concepts of time preference and the subjective rate of discount and their relation to equilibrium real rates of interest are discussed.

The underlying equilibrium real rate of interest equates the quantity of capital demanded by managers and owners of productive processes with the quantity supplied by ultimate wealth holders. Since the quantity of capital demanded by owners of productive processes depends, in the long run, on the productivity of the capital stock (output per unit of capital) and the supply of capital by savers depends on their time preferences, the following rough summary holds: In a market economy, the long-run real rate of interest emerges from equating, in the markets for capital, people's preference for future relative to present levels of consumption with their ability to produce the necessary output. This chapter elaborates this theoretical contention.

Inside and Outside Bonds

Since the real rate of interest will be shown to depend on the rate at which new output can be produced and the society's relative preference for that output now or later, transfers of funds that are not associated with the sale of new output can be ignored. These transfers of funds are called *transfer payments*. Transfer payments are payments between individuals in the society that are not associated with the production of new goods and services.

An example of transfer payments with respect to financial assets is the payment of interest between entities (individuals, corporations, and government units) in the domestic economy.

If, for example, the Calling Corporation makes an interest payment on its outstanding bonds owned by I. Save, there is no new output of goods and services produced. This is a transfer payment that is not part of and is not added into the estimate of national income, the value of output produced in a year.

Calling Corporation bonds are called *inside bonds* and are part of *inside wealth*. This is because the interest and return of principal payments on these bonds are transfer payments inside the economy. The fact that Calling Corporation owners feel poorer from the acquisition of this liability for these future payments, considered by itself, does reduce the value of their wealth. The bond owner, I. Save, feels wealthier because of the acquisition of this asset, considered in isolation.

For the society as a whole, a bond issued by the private sector is an asset to the owner and a liability to the issuer. Since net wealth equals assets minus liabilities, the bond is not an item of net wealth. Having been reduced to zero on the national accounting ledger, it produces no part of real output from an accounting viewpoint. Since no net wealth is created by more inside wealth and if saving and investment for the economy as a whole depend on the amount of net wealth, saving and investment are unaffected.[1] On these grounds, inside bonds and the remainder of inside wealth (which includes money created by the banking system) are deleted from the analysis in an attempt to lay bare the underlying determinants of the real rate of interest.

Outside bonds are part of *outside wealth*. Outside wealth includes federal government-issued bonds and money and net ownership of foreign securities. Outside bonds, such as U.S. Treasury bills, notes, and bonds, are sometimes included in the analysis. However, there is controversy, presented in the appendix to this chapter, over whether or not changes in the quantity of outside bonds affect the real rate of interest.

Federal government bonds are items of net wealth if the future taxes needed to pay the future income stream on these bonds are not considered by the public to be a fully offsetting liability. The public then finds itself richer because it owns this asset and no one feels poorer (by a fully offsetting amount) because of the interest and principal liability. The government's level of expenditures for investment is assumed to be unaffected by a change in its bond liability. If the public does not fully take into account the taxes it will have to pay in the future to make the interest payments, federal government bonds are part of net wealth. If the public does consider future taxes to pay the interest and principal on these bonds to be a fully offsetting liability, government bonds, owned by the taxpaying private sector, are not an item of net wealth.

Analysts are not in agreement as to whether future taxes for interest and principal on government bonds are fully taken into account by the public, although government bonds have been treated in most analyses as if they are part of outside wealth.

Even if they are part of outside wealth, changes in the quantity outstanding may not affect the real rate of interest, a point covered in the appendix.

Most analyses of real rates of interest subtract out one more component of wealth, broadly defined. They subtract human capital, which produces an expected stream of labor services. This subtraction is made on
the grounds that in a nonslave society the ownership and sale of human
beings is generally (professional sports arguably provides some exceptions) prohibited.

Now, what is left? The ultimate nonhuman real income-producing
wealth remains. The claims to this wealth are financial assets such as
stocks or direct ownership claims of unincorporated enterprises.

Consol Equivalents

The securities producing these income streams can be made more uniform, allowing simple demand and supply curves to be drawn, by transforming the securities into perpetuities or, as they will be called, *consol
equivalents*. Each such consol equivalent will be standardized so that it
pays an expected $1 a year.

This transformation can be easily understood through an example.
Suppose that a productive enterprise, a sandwich shop on a college cam-
pus with a three-year contract, has the following expected income (from
profits) stream (bypassing the procedures for calculation of expected income, which are covered in Part IV): $5000 in year 1, $7500 in year 2,
and $15,000 in year 3. Substituting these values into the present value
formula in Chapter 5, assuming for simplicity that these profits are paid
in a lump sum at the end of each year, and assuming that a 6 percent
market rate of interest is used, we have

$$\$23,986.24 = \frac{\$5000}{1.06} + \frac{\$7500}{(1.06)^2} + \frac{\$15,000}{(1.06)^3}$$

The formula for a perpetuity, given in Chapter 5, is

$$PV = R/r$$

where PV is present value, R is the constant income, and r is the interest
rate. To transform the foregoing income stream and present value into a
perpetuity with the *same yield and the same present value*, substitute
the values into the preceding equation:

$$\$23,986.24 = R/.06 \quad \text{or} \quad R = \$1439.17$$

This perpetuity is further transformed into 1439.17 consol equivalents
with the following values:

$$\$16.67 = \$1/.06$$

That is a perpetuity with a 6 percent per year yield and a perpetual income stream of $1 a year.

The Demand and Supply of Sources of Future Income

The demand and supply of sources of future income streams are shown in Figure 9-1.[2] The curves show the demand and supply of the quantity of consol equivalents, each producing expected perpetual income streams of a dollar a year. The vertical axis gives the price, or value, of these consol equivalents, which is simply $1/r$, where r is the interest rate. The horizontal axis is the quantity of consol equivalents. This description of Figure 9-1 refers to mechanics. What does it mean for the economy?

First, consider the supply of consol equivalents. The income streams from these assets are from the existing stock of productive capital: the factories and machines. Owners and managers who wish to expand the stock of capital would offer to supply a greater quantity of consol equivalents at each interest rate. The supply curve would move to the right at each interest rate. Such a desired increase in the capital stock from the sale of these consols is called *desired net investment*. Recall from Chapter 4 the equality between net investment and the change in the capital stock.

Savers who do not consume their income become the ultimate wealth owners when they buy the consol equivalents, the sources of these in-

Figure 9-1

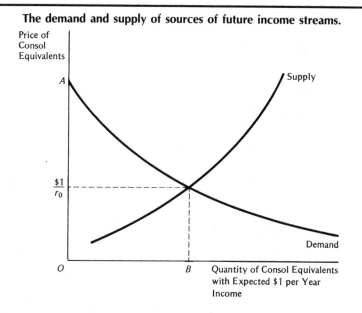

The demand and supply of sources of future income streams.

come streams. A desire to buy more of these sources of future income, instead of consuming their income, moves the demand curve in Figure 9-1 to the right at each interest rate. This is called *desired saving.*

The *shifts* in the demand and supply curves for the sources of income streams are, therefore, called *desired saving* and *desired investment*, respectively. The equilibrium price of the sources of income streams is a price of consol equivalents equal to $\$1/r_0$, where r_0 is the equilibrium real rate of interest.

This view of the determination of the long-run real rate of interest, using consol equivalents, illustrates a central point. *The real rate of interest used by individuals to translate income streams into present values determines how many consol equivalents they will demand at each market interest rate.* It determines the shape of the demand curve in Figure 9-1 and therefore plays a key role in the determination of the equilibrium real rate of interest.

Individuals in their role as consumers and savers must decide how much income to consume and how much to save. If they save, they can buy consol equivalents, provided that they value them at least as high as the market price. These choices affect the determination of the real rate of interest. They can bid up or down the prices of sources of future income streams—consol equivalents—and thereby play a major part in determining the equilibrium real rate of interest. The quantity that would be demanded at each market interest rate is depicted by the aggregate demand curve in Figure 9-1. Their preferences determine the rate of interest they will use to determine how valuable the consol equivalents are to them. A description of these preferences and how they affect asset prices is given in the next sections.

Before turning to that topic, Figure 9-1 can be further clarified. Suppose that the society settles down at an interest rate of r_0, so that the quantities of consol equivalents demanded and supplied are equal at OB in Figure 9-1. Since neither curve is shifting, there would be no desired net investment or desired saving. The society would merely consume its income, including in its consumption expenditures the maintenance of the constant stock of capital. This is called a *stationary state.*

The conditions necessary for society to settle down to a stationary state have been discussed through the centuries. With injustice to that literature, one type of stationary state is described. In the euphoric variety of stationary state, the economy is satiated with claims to future income. The return on net investment and saving (from current income) is zero and no one saves to increase his or her future income. Equilibrium in Figure 9-1 would be at the point where the demand curve, extended out to the right, eventually passes through the horizontal axis. This condition requires a zero real rate of interest, a requirement that is contradicted by the argument for positive time preference presented subsequently. An alternative explanation of Figure 9-1 is given.

The demand and supply schedules can alternatively be viewed as the *current* supply and demand curves for consol equivalents by owners and managers of productive enterprises and ultimate wealth holders, respectively. Many change their preferences, hopefully not so rapidly or in such an erratic manner as to make their demand or supply schedules of little value in analyzing the equilibrium real rate of interest. The schedules would then be predictable, but not stagnant as in a stationary state.

The Subjective Real Rate of Discount and Time Preference

The interest rate individuals use to discount future expected income streams to obtain present values is not observed in the market. It is the *subjective real interest rate* in each individual's mind that is fundamental to his or her valuation of securities. It is not a number that may be discovered and removed in a lobotomy. Rather, it is the summary statistic invented to describe individuals' evaluation of expected future income streams. *The same expected income stream can have many different present values depending on this subjective interest rate.*

Time preference plays a crucial role in determining the underlying real rate of interest in the following way. Individuals discount the future income stream of a security, say, a consol equivalent, using their subjective real rate of discount. If the present value they obtain is greater than the market price of the consol, they have an incentive to buy it. If it is lower, they would not want the consol. By bidding or not bidding for sources of future income or by trying to sell, they act to determine the underlying real rate of interest.

If an individual prefers present consumption over future consumption, a phenomenon called *positive time preference*, he or she must be discounting the future with a positive rate of discount to give consumption in the future a smaller value than the same amount of consumption in the current period. If individuals have a positive rate of discount, their subjective real rate of discount will be positive. Is this the norm? Analysts must do their most brilliant detective work in discovering whether positive time preference exists. The case is not closed.

First, in developing these ideas of time preference, a familiar example is used. Individuals must make decisions not only on how they will spend additional income in the present period, but also on how much they will consume now and how much they will consume in the future.[3] Suppose that an individual is indifferent between spending $100 today or loaning out his or her money (by buying a one-year government debt instrument) with the certain return of $110 one year in the future, given no expectation of inflation. The individual's subjective real rate of discount is then 10 percent per year. It is the rate by which he or she converts future income streams into present asset values. This subjective rate of discount is also the direct measure of the individual's time preference (defined more precisely in Note 4).

Unfortunately, these subjective rates of discount do not appear as summary statistics in the financial press because they are not directly observable. In the example above, the individual would more likely find that the market rate on loans is 10 percent. If he or she makes the loan, there is no direct report of the individual's underlying subjective real rate of discount. If it is less than 10 percent, he or she is being rewarded for postponing consumption by a greater amount than required. In other words, he or she would have paid a higher price for the consol equivalent. Given knowledge of this individual's loan rate, it is not clear what actions would be taken at a lower market interest rate. The objective of the analysis is to go in the other direction: that is, to see how an individual's preferences determine market interest rates. For this purpose, time preferences must be described.

A Geometric View of Time Preference

An individual is viewed as receiving satisfaction (or utility) from consumption, such as entertainment, food, shelter service, transportation services, and tourism. The individual rearranges his or her consumption stream over time so as to maximize his or her satisfaction (or utility).[4]

Figure 9-2

Time preference between two periods with three different types of indifference curves: Zero time preference, $U'U'$; Positive time preference, U_PU_P; and Negative time preference, U_NU_N.

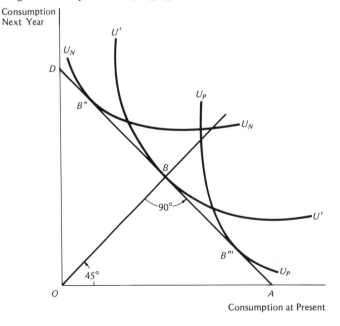

(The theoretical current/future trade-off is, for simplicity, framed under the implicit assumption of certainty about future endowments. In Part IV, considerations of risk in interest rate analysis are discussed.)

Assume for simplicity that there are only two periods, as shown in both Figures 9-2 and 9-3. One can consume at present or next year. The lines AD and $A'D'$, the *opportunity lines* in the two figures, show the possible allocations of consumption between the two periods at two different interest rates. To understand this, note that in Figure 9-2 when the real interest rate is zero, the minimum possible consumption in period 1 is OA. The maximum consumption in period 2 is OD. Even if no consumption is undertaken in period 1 and the funds are invested in bonds, no greater consumption could be attained in period 2, because the market interest rate is zero.

The interest rate shown along $A'D'$ in Figure 9-3 is positive. If OA' consumption in period 1 is forgone, the amount saved earns a positive interest, enabling the individual to consume OD' in period 2. Here $OD' > OA'$, because a positive interest payment in earned. OD' is equal to $(1 + r)OA'$, where r is the real rate of interest. So the slope (and tangent of angle $OA'D'$) of the opportunity line showing possible allocations of consumption is $-OD'/OA'$, or $-(1 + r)$, the negative sign indicating a negative slope. This is also the formula for the slope in Figure 9-2. In that case, $r = 0$ and the slope is simply -1.

Next, the curves showing the individual's preferences are described.

Figure 9-3

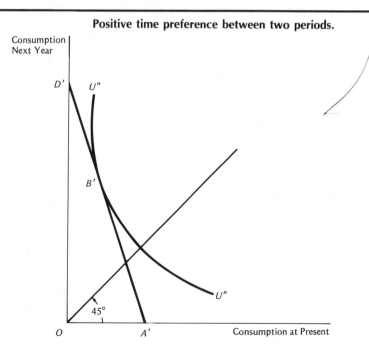

Positive time preference between two periods.

The curves $U'U'$ and $U''U'''$ are two possible indifference or utility curves for different individuals. They each show all the combinations of consumption this year and next between which an individual would be indifferent. The higher the utility curve, the greater the utility level.

Each utility curve is convex from the origin because as interest rates reach higher or lower extremes the individual has less and less incentive to push all consumption into either period. For example, if real interest rates continued to rise, there would be a shift of consumption from period 1 into period 2. But the amount of consumption that could be squeezed out of period 1 would be a smaller and smaller proportion of the change in interest rates. The loss in utility from additional subtractions from period 1 consumption would become larger and larger relative to the additional utility from increased consumption in period 2. The assumption is that more and more consumption in a period produces smaller and smaller increases in satisfaction relative to the decreased satisfaction from consuming less in the other period.

Given the initial allocations of consumption in period 1, OA in Figure 9-2 and OA' in Figure 9-3, how much consumption will be allocated to period 2 in each case? The market interest rate r determines the slope of the opportunity lines, $-(1 + r)$. In this way the maximum consumption in period 2 is determined to be OD and OD' in the two figures. The actual division of consumption between the two periods is determined by finding the point of highest utility along an opportunity line. This point is where the highest utility curve just touches—is tangent to—the opportunity line. It is B' in Figure 9-3, and either B, B'', or B''' in Figure 9-2, depending on the type of utility curve that is appropriate.

If with a real interest rate of zero, as in Figure 9-2 (i.e., there is no reward for saving), the individual divides consumption equally between the two periods, he or she is said to have *zero* or *neutral time preference*. That means that there is no preference for consuming more now or less later.[5] The tangency of the utility curve in Figure 9-2 at B (where the 45° line splits the quadrant) on utility curve $U'U'$ means that the highest degree of satisfaction (the highest utility that can be reached) can be achieved by splitting the consumption in this equal manner.

Alternatively, if the utility curve were $U_N U_N$, as in Figure 9-2, less would be consumed at present at a zero interest rate and there would be negative time preference. The utility curve $U_P U_P$ in Figure 9-2 shows positive time preference, more being consumed in the current period.[6]

Most periods have positive real interest rates, as depicted by the line $A'D'$ in Figure 9-3. With a reward for saving it is more difficult to determine time preference even though the intersection B can be ascertained from the individual's behavior. This is precisely because the individual is rewarded to postpone consumption and invest for future increased consumption. Of course, if it were possible to know that the shape of the utility curve is $U''U'''$, it would be clear that the individual had positive time preference. It is not known, so the important search for the value of time preference is more difficult.

Is There Positive Time Preference?

That there is positive time preference has been inferred from general observations. If there were zero or negative time preference plus a positive rate of interest, individuals, having no bias in favor of consumption at present, would reduce current consumption to starvation or subsistence levels to achieve future benefits. Because this behavior is not generally observed, some positive time preference is assumed.[7]

Weak as the evidence above is, it seems sensible to suspect that people have positive time preferences since they do not move most of their consumption into distant periods when interest rates are very low. The notion of a planning horizon beyond which individuals give no value to consumption is consistent with a weak form of positive time preference when the horizon is distant. As long as individuals allocate funds for future emergencies, for later years when their income will be lower, or for their heirs, there is reason to believe that their planning horizons are fairly far in the future.

Additional Determinants of Time Preference

Sometimes it is held that time preference is related to income. When people become poor, their time preference becomes higher. This is probably incorrect if it is assumed that they have a constant, low income stream. Some observers hold that poor people are as concerned about their future as individuals with higher income. In other words, the mere fact that people are poor does not necessarily mean that they have a different time preference then individuals with higher income.

What does seem important for time preference (summarized by the subjective real rate of discount)? First, there is the longevity of one's life and heirs. Strong positive time preference could be expected from an individual facing death, either by disease or war, with no family, friends, or charity to which to leave his or her estate. In the extreme—the imminent firing squad or during a nuclear attack—the utility curve in Figure 9-3 would become the horizontal axis. Time preference would be infinitely positive. An increase in positive time preference would result in a country that is about to collapse into anarchy or be subject to war. However, increased uncertainty about the time of one's death can either increase time preference, since an early death is possible, or decrease time preference, since a later death requires increased provision for the future. If, on the other hand, the average time of death is expected to be more distant because of medical advances, time preference may become less positive. Individuals may begin to save for the possibility of longer lives.

Second, increased pessimism (or reduced optimism) about the future economic condition of the economy, the threat of adverse economic events in the future, or a loss of faith in the stability of the society may cause individuals to increase their subjective rate of discount. They would place less present value on an investment even if its expected income stream is unaltered. The utility from present consumption is certain; that from future consumption may be less certain and/or expected to be severely reduced by the increased probability of a sick economy or an unstable society. The dollar a year from the consol equivalents may look better or worse depending on the latest news.

Changes in the subjective rate of discount may be the main source of variation in the prices of securities in many periods. These changes may often be relatively small and they may be frequent, since investors are continually confronted with news affecting general conditions in the economy and the society in the future.

The Demand and Supply of Capital

The demand and supply of sources of future income streams may be easily restated in an alternative formulation using more conventional demand and supply schedules, the demand and supply of capital in Figure 9-4. This alternative formulation in Figure 9-4 is merely an alternative way to look at the same analysis as in Figure 9-1. Instead of viewing

Figure 9-4

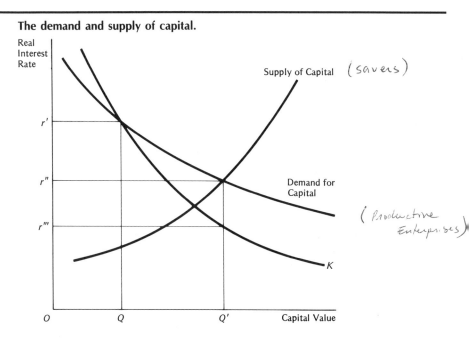

The demand and supply of capital.

savers as demanding sources of future income streams, this alternative formulation views them as supplying capital funds. Owners and managers of productive enterprises, who were viewed as the suppliers of future income streams to the society, are depicted here as the demanders of capital. The previous analysis emphasized the role of the interest rate in translating future expected income into present values. This way of depicting the determinants of the real rate of interest allows the demand for capital to be emphasized. The demand for capital is a downward-sloping curve in Figure 9-4 because it depends on cost and productivity considerations.

As more capital stock is produced, the rate of return from investing to produce still more capital stock declines if the following assumptions are correct:

1. The *cost* of producing more capital *rises* as more capital stock is produced; that is, there are *diminishing returns* to the production of capital.
2. The income stream from the capital stock requires an increasingly larger amount of capital per unit of output as the capital stock increases. That is, the productivity of capital declines as the capital stock increases. There are *diminishing returns* to the capital stock.

In other words, it gets more expensive to produce more capital and more is needed to produce the same number of additional $1 income streams.[8]

These assumptions may not hold if technological advances make either the production of capital cheaper or the productivity of the capital stock greater. Also, the assumptions may not hold if there is an increase in human capital which increases the productivity of nonhuman capital.[9]

The Mechanics of the Demand and Supply of Capital Schedules

The *K* curve has the property that the product of its distances to the horizontal and vertical axes is constant. This type of curve is known as a rectangular hyperbola. That is, the real interest rate, r, times the capital value is constant, since this product equals the constant number of units ($1 per year) expected from the constant capital stock.

If business owners and managers had no desire to change the capital stock, the *K* curve would be the demand for capital. However, at real rates of interest below r', the demand for capital is greater than the existing stock of capital. This difference between the desired and actual stock of capital is *desired net real investment* (defined in Chapter 4). If the real rate of interest were at r', savers (as shown along the supply curve of capital) would supply more funds and business managers would just maintain the existing stock of capital. The real rate of interest would fall because there would be an excess supply of capital funds.

If the real rate of interest fell below r''', investors would have an incentive to borrow but savers would have no incentive to lend at this low interest rate. So the real interest rate would rise because there would be an excess demand for capital funds.

Long-Run and Short-Run Interest Rates

What about the saving and investment curves shown in Chapter 8? The investment curve shows how fast the capital stock will be adjusted to the desired level at each rate of interest. The saving curve shows the amount of national income that will not be consumed at each rate of interest allowing investment goods to be produced.

The rate of return on investing depends on the same two considerations as the demand for capital stated previously: the cost of producing the capital stock and the productivity of the capital stock. The saving curve depends on time preference and the rate of return from saving.

In the short run, the real rate of interest depends on the savings and investment schedule and the demand and supply of money, as shown in Chapters 6 and 8. The real interest rate, which equates the demand and supply of capital, may be different from the short-run real interest rate, determined by the interaction of the demand and supply of money and real savings and investment. Without additional disturbances real interest rates will move toward the underlying real rate of interest determined by the productivity and the cost of producing the capital stock, and time preference. In Figure 9-4 this underlying real rate is r''.

Appendix: Outside Bonds and the Real Rate of Interest

If government bonds are considered outside wealth, what happens to the real rate of interest as a result of a purchase of these bonds from the public? This is part of a protracted, but stimulating, discussion in the academic literature.[10] If government bonds can affect the equilibrium real rate of interest, the analysis presented in this chapter would be false. That is because the underlying real rate of interest has been shown to depend on the productivity of the capital stock, the cost of its production, and time preference. This analysis is sometimes referred to as the *classical position*. It does not depend on government bond purchases.

The late Lloyd Metzler began the modern part of the debate with a brilliant analysis that showed that real rates of interest were affected by the quantity of government bonds held by the public. If the government bought some of these bonds, Metzler held that the public would try to save more at every interest rate, to restore its wealth. The increased saving would permanently lower real interest rates.

Many attacked this finding on a number of grounds, while others incorporated it into their analysis. One important reformulation of Metzler's analysis was as follows.[11] Since the government does not have to make payments on the bonds it has repurchased, the government's deficit will be less (it may even run a surplus). If this reduction in government expenditures is returned to the public as a tax reduction, private wealth may have a capital gain that exactly offsets the effects of less outside wealth. No real interest rate changes would occur.

In terms of Figure 9-4, the demand and supply of capital could be altered by changes in taxes. A permanent change in the tax on consumption or income would affect the supply of capital; a permanent change in the tax on capital (a corporate income tax change) would affect the demand for capital. Both would cause a change in underlying real interest rates.

Later analysts held that securities sold to the government at equilibrium prices are an exchange in which the private-sector market participants do not believe they have less wealth.[12] (If they did believe they were losing wealth, they would not agree to the trade.) If the tax rates are unaltered, there is no change in real private wealth and the underlying determinants of the real rate of interest described in this chapter are unaltered by the change in outside bonds.

NOTES

1. Changes in the distribution of wealth from transfer payments can affect saving and the real rate of interest if there are differences in the way people divide their additional income between saving and investment. This is apparent in transfers between different age groups, if older retired people have a higher marginal propensity to consume than do younger wage earners. Also, the conclusion that an increase in inside bonds does not change net wealth is directly opposite to the view expressed in Part I. There it was stated that financial assets and markets provide an efficient way to allocate wealth. That means that the existence of inside bonds produces real effects and therefore affects net wealth. No one has discovered a way to measure the net wealth created (or reduced) by a specific change in the amount of inside bonds. This should be an area of major concern since the real interest rate may be significantly affected.

2. For a further discussion, see Milton Friedman, "The Theory of Capital and the Rate of Interest," in *Price Theory* (Chicago: Aldine Publishing Company, first published in 1962), pp. 244–263.

3. See Mancur Olson and Martin J. Bailey, "Positive Time Preference," *Journal of Political Economy* (February 1981), pp. 1–25. An excellent bibliography on the rate of return from public investment is found in Raymond F. Mikesell, *The Rate of Discount for Evaluating Public Projects* (Washington, D.C.: American Enterprise Institute for Public Policy Research, 1977). Some of Olson and Bailey's conclusions are discussed in Note 7 below.

4. Let utility U be a function of the discounted value of consumption in different periods:

$$U = \sum_{t=0}^{N} \frac{f(C_t)}{(1 + r_D)^t}$$

where $f(C_t)$ is the function of real consumption in period t, r_D is the rate per period of positive time preference (the subjective real rate of discount), and N is the number of periods in the future that are taken into account by the individual, called his or her planning horizon. The level of r_D measures the concept of time preference used by Olson and Bailey, "Positive Time Preference."

5. One exception to this statement would be if there were severely declining marginal utility of consumption, so that the individual became satiated and postponed an equal amount to the next period. Another exception would be if the individual expected to have a lower income in the future. The analysis of time preference often bypasses this second complication by assuming that the individual's income stream is constant.

6. Given a zero rate of interest, a utility curve such as $U'U'$ with neutral or zero time preference intersects the 45° line at a 135° angle (measured from the x axis); a utility curve with negative time preference, such as $U_N U_N$, intersects the 45° line at a greater angle; and a utility curve with positive time preference, such as $U_P U_P$, intersects the 45° line at a smaller angle.

7. Olson and Bailey ("Positive Time Preference") cite this conventional conclusion and then they go further (pp. 12–14). Suppose that in a world with no capital stock, new techniques of production increase real interest rates because the demand for loanable funds increases while the supply is unchanged. In that situation, real interest rates, as registered in the market for loanable funds, would rise above the subjective real rate of discount which measures time preference. If the real interest rate exceeded the subjective real rate of discount by very much, what would be observed? Individuals would find that the value of a consol equivalent in the market was lower than their own evaluation of its present value. They would thereby be induced to buy consol equivalents and to reduce their consumption to "implausibly low levels of consumption" (p. 12). Since they do not do this, it is concluded that their time preference (their subjective rate of discount) is significantly positive and that "at least in those societies where real interest rates are very high and expected to remain so," the subjective real rate of discount (the time preference) "must exceed zero by more than a minuscule amount."

The argument for positive time preference then rests on two grounds. (1) The first argument is that people do not choose to move all but starvation levels of consumption to future periods when there is an interest reward for doing so. (2) The second argument is that a technological change raises the real rate of interest but not individuals' real rate of discount, so that with zero time preference consumption would be implausibly low.

These arguments for a significant positive rate of interest are cleverly conceived but still not strongly supported. The first argument is weak because it is difficult to define starvation levels. Although an individual could survive on leftovers (what others consider garbage), the minimum life-style in some advanced countries is considerably more. A middle-class family in the United States may be "struggling" along on meat twice a week, housing services from a $100,000 house, and only necessary trips in a $9000 automobile (using 1982 prices). Once this minimum level of living, below which it is psychologically very painful to go, is allowed, it is difficult to read positive time preference into their behavior. They may have zero or negative time preference for additional increments of consumption. That is, if interest rates were zero, they might move almost all additional consumption into future periods, because of a zero rate of time preference for additional current consumption.

The second argument for time preference may be true for short periods. A technological advance may temporarily increase the demand for loanable funds, but not the supply for loanable funds, at least initially. This would cause interest rates to rise. However, the supply of loanable funds depends on saving (and the rate of change of the money supply). As more income is expected, the saving curve would shift out to the right, as would the supply of loanable funds. Interest rates, which initially rose, would fall as the saving curve shifts out. As will be shown subsequently, the underlying real rate of interest might even fall below its initial position if the society approaches its desired stock of capital.

If more income is expected in the future, even individuals with negative time preference might straighten out their income stream by shifting consumption into the present period. Therefore, to observe positive time preference it is necessary to assume a constant income stream, an assumption that is violated by a technological change that requires a long time to implement.

8. If either of these two assumptions is invalid or works in the wrong direction, the effect of the remaining assumption can still be strong enough to cause a downward-sloping demand function for capital. If the economy was in a stationary state where desired investment is zero, only the second assumption would be applicable, since there would be no net investment.

9. More precisely, an increase in the stock of human capital increases the marginal productivity (referring to changes in total productivity as small additions of the stock are added) of the nonhuman capital stock. The stock of human capital can increase with population growth or with training and formal education.

10. The discussion began with a brilliant article by the late Lloyd Metzler, "Wealth, Saving, and the Rate of Interest," *Journal of Political Economy* (April 1951), pp. 93–116. Robert A. Mundell extended Metzler's work in "The Public Debt, Corporate Income Tax, and the Rate of Interest," *Journal of Political Economy* (December 1960), pp. 622–626. These two articles were followed by a number of articles, including John Wood, "Metzler on Classical Interest Theory," *Journal of Political Economy* (March 1980), pp. 135–148. Wood holds that Metzler's results improperly rely on bond trading at disequilibrium prices. Wood's bibliography (pp. 147–148) is a good reading list for this subject.

11. Mundell, "The Public Debt."

12. Wood in "Metzler on Classical Interest Theory" presents a provocative discussion of what he considers to be both Metzler's and Mundell's mistaken use of disequilibrium prices and their neglect of the fixed payment streams on government bonds. When payment streams are fixed on default-free debt instruments and the market is efficient (see Chapter 3), the price of the debt instrument may be assumed to approximate closely the equilibrium price.

STUDY QUESTIONS

1. What is time preference?

2. What causes the negative slope of the demand for capital by owners and managers of productive enterprises?

3. How is investment related to the demand for capital?

4. What is a consol equivalent? What is the consol equivalent for a three-year bond paying $100 the first year, $100 the second year, and $1100 the third year if the market interest rate is 10 percent?

5. Does the purchase of Treasury bills by the Federal Reserve change the equilibrium real rate of interest? In your answer, define outside bonds.

6. How would the discovery of a drug that could extend life by as much as ten years affect the subjective real rate of discount?

7. How do forecasts of high rates of inflation and the possibility of wage and price controls affect the real rate of interest?

8. If a stock has a fairly stable expected income flow (as a result of stable expected profits in the underlying company), why would the price of the stock vary with changes in uncertainty about other economic variables, such as the level of unemployment?

9. What evidence is there of positive time preference, and what difference does it make? In what sense, if any, does time preference set a limit to the real rate of growth in a society?

10. How would an earthquake that destroyed 20 percent of the housing in an economy affect house rentals and the real rate of interest?

↑ real rates

rental receipts p (little p) went up
more than P

Part III

The Term Structure of Interest Rates

10

The Pure Expectations
and Error-Learning Hypotheses

Introduction

In speaking about interest rates, it is common practice to speak of "the interest rate" as if there were only one. Usually, what is meant is the rate on a one-year government debt instrument (a U.S. Treasury bill) with no risk premium for default. (A *default risk premium* is an addition to the rate of return to cover the possibility that part of the payment stream will not be paid.) There is another dimension to returns on bonds besides default risk premiums. There are bonds of all different maturities. The relationship between yields on bonds of different maturities is called the *term structure of interest rates*. The use of bonds of similar default risk, such as all U.S. Treasury debt instruments or all top-rated corporate debt instruments, simplifies the analysis of the term structure of interest rates.

The term structure of interest rates can be pictured as in Figure 10-1. The bonds are arranged by maturity on the horizontal axis, and their respective yields are plotted against the vertical axis. A curve showing the term structure is called a *yield curve*. Three different hypothetical yield curves are depicted in Figure 10-1.

There are many theories of the term structure of interest rates.[1] Many are built on the basis of the pure expectations hypothesis, while others contradict it. The pure expectations hypothesis gives one explanation of the term structure of interest rates under specific conditions. It holds that the observable market interest rates on bonds of different maturities

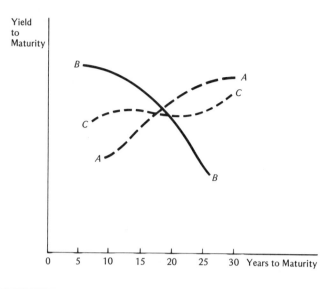

Figure 10-1

Three hypothetical yield curves.

imply future interest rates expected by the public to prevail in the future. These implied future rates are held to be unbiased estimates of the rates expected by the public in future years. This hypothesis is explained first.

The pure expectations hypothesis explains the *shape* of the term structure; it does not explain how the term structure *changes*. David Meiselman provided an explanation.[2] His theory, the error-learning hypothesis, is presented next with some suggestions for expanding it. The error-learning model is shown to present one very important determinant of changes in the term structure of interest rates.

In the discussion in Part III, the letters S and i are reserved for nominal rates and r for real rates of interest.

The Pure Expectations Hypothesis

Suppose that the rate of interest on a one-year default-free bond is 2 percent. The rate of interest that is expected to prevail on such one-year bonds in the following year is 7 percent. Then the rate of return on a two-year default-free bond sold at present might be expected to yield a return equivalent to the yield on a sequence of one-year bonds. Thus the one-year yields expected during the next two years would be related to the yield on two-year bonds presently observed in the market. The view that such a relationship exists is called the *pure expectations hypothesis.*[3]

Assume that a list of current yields on default-free bonds, bonds that differ only by their maturity (say, U.S. Treasury bills, notes, and bonds), is available. These current rates are sometimes called *spot rates*. The published rates of interest reflecting observable current market prices, the spot rates, are $S_1, S_2, S_3, \ldots, S_N$ for one year, two years, three years, and so forth, all the way out to a distant maturity of N years.

Now consider the one-year rates that are *expected* to prevail during the next N years on one-year bonds in each of these years. The yields expected on these one-year bonds are sometimes called *expected* or *implied forward rates*, sometimes simply *implied* or *forward rates*. Let i_1, $i_2, i_3, \ldots, i_N$ be the respective implied forward rates.

Refer to the compound interest formula (3) in Chapter 5. If \$1 is invested in a one-year bond, it will grow in value to $\$1(1 + S_1)$ in a year. This is the same amount as is obtained for the first year using the expected rate, $\$1(1 + i_1)$. The one-year interest that clears the market for one-year bonds is a reflection of what individuals expect that rate to be. So, for the first year,

$$1 + S_1 = 1 + i_1 \qquad \text{or} \qquad i_1 = S_1 \tag{1}$$

If funds are to be loaned out—that is, bonds are to be bought—there are two choices: (1) buy a two-year or (2) buy a series of two one-year bonds. If there are negligible transactions costs for buying and selling bonds and the same rate of return can be earned by either choice, then the return on the two-year bond $(1 + S_2)^2$ is equal to the combined return on the two one-year bonds $(1)(1 + i_1)(1 + i_2)$:

$$(1 + S_2)^2 = (1 + i_1)(1 + i_2) \tag{2}$$

or

$$1 + S_2 = \sqrt{(1 + i_1)(1 + i_2)} \tag{3}$$

The pure expectations hypothesis holds that this relationship between observable market rates of interest on bonds and the implied or expected forward rates is approximated in the bond markets.

The justification for this can be seen with an example. Suppose that the market rate on two-year bonds is 11 percent, and the market rate on one-year bonds is 10 percent. The values of the symbols are then $S_2 = .11$ and $S_1 = i_1 = .10$. From Equation (2) it is found that $i_2 = .12009$ is the consistent value for the expected one-year rate in year 2.

Suppose this were not true and that a rate of 15 percent were expected on one-year bonds during the second year. In that case, some individuals who held this expectation would sell two-year bonds, paying 11 percent on the loan. They would then buy a series of two one-year bonds earning 10 percent the first year and, if their expectations are correct, 15 percent the second year. The two-year return would be 12.472 percent, a 1.472-percentage-point profit. They could eliminate risk by simultaneously making contracts with borrowers (who also expect no less than 15 percent interest in the second year) to buy their bonds during the second year at 15 percent. This is called a *futures contract* and is discussed at the end of this chapter and in Chapter 22. This process is called *arbitrage*.

If no such futures contract exists, there would be uncertainty about the one-year rate in the second year. The transactions that would bring the rates in line would therefore involve speculation (taking a position that involves capital risk). For this reason, these transactions are not simple arbitrage. They can be called *speculative arbitrage*.

Suppose that markets are working perfectly in the sense that individuals can borrow funds at a rate at least as low as their lending rate. They could borrow at 11 percent and relend for a profit. They would merely be borrowing and relending for a profit. They would cease performing these transactions when there was no more expected profit in the transactions. This would occur when the equality, in Equation (3), between the observable market rate on two-year bonds is equal to the average (it is a geometric average) of the expected forward rates.[4]

Using the same type of reasoning, a formula for the implied forward rates for a bond of any maturity can be stated. Suppose that the observable market yield on an N-year bond is S_N. Then

$$1 + S_N = \sqrt[N]{(1 + i_1)(1 + i_2) \cdots (1 + i_N)} \tag{4}$$

This is the general relationship between expected forward rates and the corresponding observable market rate or spot rate if "any individual can buy and sell bonds of any maturity without affecting the rates."[5]

Finding a Single Implied Forward Rate

If the conditions for the equality in Equation (4) hold, the implied forward one-year interest rates can easily be calculated from a series of observable market interest rates for each period. The calculation can be illustrated by looking at relationships with observed two- and three-year rates. The two-year relationship is

$$(1 + S_2)^2 = (1 + i_1)(1 + i_2) \tag{5}$$

The three-year relationship is

$$(1 + S_3)^3 = (1 + i_1)(1 + i_2)(1 + i_3) \tag{6}$$

Now suppose that the rate observed on two-year bonds, S_2, is 4 percent, and the rate observed on three-year bonds, S_3, is 5 percent. What is the implied rate during the third year? To find the answer, divide Equation (6) by Equation (5):

$$\frac{(1 + S_3)^3}{(1 + S_2)^2} = 1 + i_3 \tag{7}$$

Substituting in the values for S_3 and S_2, the value of $1 + i_3$ can be found easily. It is 1.07. The forward rate implied by the current observable rates on two- and three-year bonds is 7 percent.

In more general form for any maturity, say, for bonds of N and N minus one year's maturity, Equation (7) becomes

$$i_N = \frac{(1 + S_N)^N}{(1 + S_{N-1})^{N-1}} - 1 \tag{8}$$

Here is an example of how Equation (8) can be used. The management of a firm decides to increase its inventory for one year, to take advantage of an expected increase in sales two years in the future. They need $1 million in funds at that time. How do they arrange to borrow the funds at today's interest rates if they do not need these funds for two years, and then only for a one-year loan? They would sell $1 million in three-year bonds; that is, they obtain a three-year loan from bond buyers. The management of the firm would also simultaneously buy $1 million in two-year bonds. For the first two years, they pay out the interest they receive on the two-year bond that they own to cover the interest on the three-year bond that they sold. At the end of the second year, the two-year bond matures and they have $1 million to spend on inventory for one year. At the end of the third year, they must pay back the holders of the three-year bonds.

What rate will they pay on this one-year loan? It is given by Equation (8). If three-year bonds currently have a 10 percent interest and two-year bonds have a 12 percent interest, i_N in Equation (8) is 6.1 percent.

The Error-Learning Hypothesis

David Meiselman produced one of the earliest statistically tested specifications of the way expectations of implied forward rates are formed in the pure expectations model.[6] In his *error-learning hypothesis*, participants in the bond market are held to adjust the yields on bonds by a fixed proportion of the difference between the actual spot one-year rate and the current one-year rate that had been expected in the previous period. The expression $(_tS_{1,t} - {_ti_{1,t-1}})$ is the forecasting error between the actual spot rate observed $_tS_{1,t}$ and the rate expected in the previous period to prevail in the current period $_ti_{1,t-1}$.

A key to the fancy notation is needed. The prescript (before i or S) gives the period when the rate takes effect. The first subscript (after each symbol) gives the duration of the loan (or maturity of the bond) for which the rate applies. The second subscript gives the period, for observed rates (S), that the rate was negotiated in the market, or for implied rates (i), the period that the expectation was formed. Thus $_{t+2}S_{30,t}$ is an observed rate on a thirty-year loan (a bond) that goes into effect two years from now (if t is defined as the current period). The loan was negotiated in the current period. The symbol $_ti_{1,t-1}$ is the rate expected one year ago to prevail in the current period (t) on one-year loans.

Let $E = (_tS_{1,t} - _ti_{1,t-1})$ be the forecasting error. The error-learning hypothesis holds that the change in expected rates for any period $t + N$ (where N is the number of periods forward) is determined as a proportion b of this forecasting error. The value of b is different for different expected rates. Its value was obtained by fitting the following relation to the data:

$$_{t+N}i_{1,t} - _{t+N}i_{1,t-1} = bE + C + u \tag{9}$$

The symbols C, a constant, and u, an error term, are explained subsequently.

For example, if last year this year's one-year rate ($_ti_{1,t-1}$) was expected to be 10 percent but the spot rate ($_tS_{1,t}$) turns out to be 12 percent, a 2 percent error is made. Meiselman estimated the proportion of the forecasting error (the value of the coefficient b) by which expected rates would change for different values of N in Equation (9). For $N = 1$, one year forward, the proportion was estimated to be .7. That proportion fell with more distant years down to .21 for $N = 8$. *Most of the change from a forecasting error was found to be in the shorter maturities.* The 2 percent forecasting error in the example would cause expectations of next year's one-year rate to be revised upward by 1.4 percentage points and the expected rate eight years out would be revised upward by .42 percentage point.

The entire yield curve is altered as rates are changed to take account of the forecasting error. Interest rates on bonds with more distant maturities, the *long rates*, adjust less rapidly because they are the average values of many implied one-year rates. Thus if the one-year rate expected for the current year turns out to be too high, the entire yield curve shifts downward. In Figure 10-2, such an adjustment is shown. Notice that the long rates are corrected least, since a change in the short rate is only a small part of the average on which long rates are held to depend.

The error-learning model describes how the yield curve changes as a result of differences in the observed spot interest rates from what was expected. It does not explain how changes in the observed spot rate come about. It does not explain the level of the term structure. The level of interest rates is the product of many forces, summarized earlier in Part II.

The error-learning model was held to be consistent with the efficient market hypothesis because the forecasting error was held to depend only on current information.[7] Actually, current expected rates depend on past spot rates, according to Equation (9), if the adjustment is not instantaneous.[8] Recall from Chapter 3 that in an efficient market all available information is immediately discounted into the prices of securities. The past history of a security contains no information about the future price of a security. Today's price (or yield) on a debt instrument, traded in an efficient market, is the price expected tomorrow, plus the

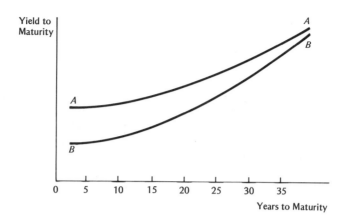

Yield to Maturity

Years to Maturity

Figure 10-2

A downward revision of a yield curve from *AA* to *BB* because the expected one year turned out to be too high under the pure expectations hypothesis.

cost of holding the debt instrument one day.[9] As new information is received, the spot rates at all maturities immediately adjust.

So what does the error-learning model show if debt instruments are traded in an efficient market? The test results can be interpreted to show that unexpected changes in observed short rates affect the near maturities more, and the distant maturities less. This is consistent with the pure expectations hypothesis, which holds that the long rates are averages of the expected short rates. That is an important, although not fully supported, finding.

The error term *u*, in Equation (9), has not been found to be random (unpredictable) from its own past history. This means that the error is partly predictable, and if it is predictable, it is part of the explanation of the change in expected rates.[10] Also, the constant term C has been found to be significant, so that even if there is no forecasting error the expected rates would change.

This leads to an expanded explanation of the term structure on the basis of the pure expectations model. Many kinds of information can affect the term structure in addition to the valuable information that the new one-year spot rate is different from what was expected. As will be shown in Chapter 12, a future inflation or recession could cause considerable movement in the term structure—a hump or a valley in rates for future years, respectively—without changing the current forecasting error. Long-term rates may move by more than short-term rates under such conditions. Many economic forces significantly affecting the rates expected to prevail in future years must be considered. These forces are in addition to the unexpected changes in the short-term rates on which the error-learning model focuses.[11] Nevertheless, the observable phenomenon of a new spot rate on one-year bonds that differs from what was expected can be expected to cause an important change in expectations. These changes may not be in large discrete jumps, but rather in small random changes, as new one-year bonds are issued each day.

The Rapid Increase in Financial Instruments of the Term Structure

There has been a rapid increase in the number of financial assets and a massive increase in the volume of financial assets that allow trading on future asset prices and rates of return beginning in the 1980s. This subject is discussed in Chapter 22. It is important to note these developments in connection with the expectations hypothesis of the term structure.

It is now possible, for example, to buy a contract (a *futures contract*) that allows the owner to purchase a ninety-day Treasury bill at a specified price and yield on a given date in the future. Thus the rate to be earned on a three-month Treasury bill next year can be nailed down in advance. When these instruments are available, the kind of *speculative* risk involved in buying a series of one-year loans as an alternative to buying a two-year bond is removed. The risk, and therefore the cost, of achieving equilibrium accurately reflecting future expectations are reduced.

NOTES

1. An excellent summary of the literature on the term structure of interest rates is given by Lester Telser in "A Critique of Some Recent Empirical Research on the Explanation of the Term Structure of Interest Rates," *The Journal of Political Economy* (August 1967), Supplement, *Issues in Monetary Research*, pp. 546–561. The classic statement of the expectations hypothesis is found in David Meiselman's *The Term Structure of Interest Rates* (Englewood Cliffs, N.J.: Prentice-Hall, Inc., 1962). Burton Malkiel presents an extensive development of alternative theories of the term structure of interest rates in his *The Term Structure of Interest Rates: Expectations and Behaviour Patterns* (Princeton, N.J.: Princeton University Press, 1966). An additional list of references on the term structure of interest rates is found in Note 1 of the next chapter.
2. Meiselman, *The Term Structure*.
3. The equation for this relationship was developed by John R. Hicks in *Value and Capital* (New York: Oxford University Press, 1946), Chapter XI, especially part 3, pp. 144–145.
4. To compute an arithmetic average, N numbers are added together and divided by N, whereas a geometric average is obtained by multiplying the numbers together and taking the Nth root. The arithmetic average of 7, 8, and 9 is 8, and the geometric average is 7.96, slightly lower.
5. Telser, "A Critique," p. 548. If this condition is true and Equation (4) holds, none of the implied forward rates should be negative. A negative rate would imply that lenders will pay borrowers to take their money. Yet Reuben Kessel, using Equation (9), found a period of nine days in September 1960 when a forward rate was negative. The conclusion is that Equation (4) is definitely not always true. It may, however, be a close approximation.
6. Meiselman, *The Term Structure*.
7. Ibid., p. 30.
8. If the adjustment is instantaneous, the error-learning model would take a different form from that shown in Equation (9). This is because the coeffi-

cient of adjustment b has the dimension of a number per unit time, such as $\frac{1}{4}$/year. The reciprocal of b is the time for a full adjustment, which, in this example, is four years. With instantaneous adjustment, the time period collapses toward zero, so that in this example b approaches infinity. To evaluate Equation (9), divide through by b and then let b go toward infinity to obtain

$$E = 0 \qquad \text{or} \qquad {}_tS_{1,t} = {}_ti_{1,t-1} \tag{10}$$

This equation simply says that the observed spot rate is the rate that was expected. From the standpoint of the way people set expectations, it is meaningful to say that individuals attach an error term (or a probability distribution for different outcomes) to their expectations of the one-year rate. Therefore, Equation (10) can be written as

$$_tS_{1,t} = {}_ti_{1,t-1} + u \tag{11}$$

If the market is efficient, the observed rates will instantaneously incorporate all information so that the last period's expected rate will also equal its observed spot rate. Equation (11) is then replaced by a series of observed spot rates that differ only by a random term. Such a series of random *first differences* (or *random walk*) is a form of a *Markov chain* that was originally held to describe stock prices in an efficient market. Paul Samuelson, using mathematical expectations, changed this description of efficient markets by showing the theory to be consistent with a *drift* up or down of prices that randomly changed around this trend. "Proof That Properly Anticipated Prices Fluctuate Randomly," *Industrial Management Review* (1965, No. 2), pp. 41–50.

A dependence of current expected rates on past spot rates can easily be shown if the adjustment is not instantaneous. Suppose that rates are constant, so that the same rate is expected next year. Now, if spot interest rates begin to rise unexpectedly, the change in expected rates will be a proportion, b, of the rise in interest rates. The new level of expected interest rates based on the forecasting error only is given by

$$_{t+1}i_{1,t} - {}_{t-1}S_{1,t-1} = b({}_tS_{1,t} - {}_{t-1}S_{1,t-1}) \tag{12}$$

[using $_{t+1}i_{1,t-1} = {}_ti_{1,t-1} = {}_{t-1}S_{1,t-1}$ under these conditions]

or

$$_{t+1}i_{1,t} = b_tS_{1,t} + (1 - b)_{t-1}S_{1,t-1} \tag{13}$$

since the spot rate observed in the last period was also the expected rate. The expected rate next period ($_{t+1}i_{1,t}$) is dependent on the previous spot rates. This process could be continued by substituting values of the relation in Equation (9) for future periods. This kind of adjustment model leads to distributed lags (a weighted average of past spot rates). In support of the existence of such lags, Benjamin Friedman asserts: "At least three conceptually distinct phenomena may account for investors' failure to adjust their portfolios fully and immediately to whatever equilibrium allocations are consistent with each period's new values of the relevant variables: transactions costs, expectation formation lags, and perception lags" ["Financial Flow Variables and the Short Run Determinations of Long-Term Interest Variables," *Journal of Political Economy* (August 1977), p. 665]. Michael Beenstock and J. Andrew Longbottom find a lag in the time it takes the domestic term structure to adjust to the international term structure for the United Kingdom ["The Term Structure of Interest Rates in a Small Open

Economy," *Journal of Money, Credit and Banking* (February 1981), pp. 44–59]. Thomas J. Sargent shows the correspondence of Meiselman's error-learning model with the theory of rational expectations [*Macroeconomic Theory* (New York: Academic Press, 1979), pp. 209–213].

9. The one-day holding cost is approximately the opportunity cost of alternative investments, which can be proxied by the market rate of interest for one day times the value of the security.

10. For a discussion of this point and a summary of early work supporting and criticizing the error-learning model, see Telser, "A Critique," with following comments by Burton Malkiel, pp. 561–564, and David I. Fand, pp. 565–568.

11. For some of the analysis and tests combining the postulates of efficient markets, see T. J. Sargent, "Rational Expectations and the Term Structure of Interest Rates," *Journal of Money, Credit and Banking* (February 1972), pp. 74–97; Thomas F. Cargill, "The Term Structure of Interest Rates—A Test of the Expectations Hypothesis," *Journal of Finance* (June 1975), pp. 761–777; Thomas F. Cargill and Robert A. Meyer, "The Term Structure of Inflationary Expectations and Market Efficiency," *Journal of Finance* (March 1980), pp. 57–70; and Robert A. Fildes and M. Desmond Fitzgerald, "Efficiency and Premiums in the Short-Term Money Market," *Journal of Money, Credit and Banking* (November 1980), pp. 615–629.

STUDY QUESTIONS

1. Plot the current term structure using yields on U.S. Treasury securities. Then make a new term structure curve using high-grade private securities.

2. Suppose that default-free ten-year bonds currently yield 10 percent and eleven-year bonds yield 10.2 percent. What is the implied forward rate during the eleventh year?

3. How could $1 million be borrowed ten years from now for a period of five years at rates given by current spot rates?

4. How could $1 million be loaned for four years beginning twelve years from the current date at rates given by current spot rates?

5. Under what conditions could future implied forward rates be negative using the pure expectations hypothesis?

6. What is the pure expectations hypothesis? Is the term structure it implies a product of its assumptions (true by definition), or does it require a particular type of market behavior? Explain.

7. What is Meiselman's error-learning model?

8. What important information for changes in the term structure of interest rates is suggested by Meiselman's error-learning model?

9. Under what conditions is the forecasting error in the error-learning model a random event? Consider the forecasting error in predicting tomorrow's one-day rate in an efficient market. What would be the size of the adjustment in expectations—the value of the adjustment coefficient in the error-learning hypothesis?

11

The Capital Risk and Market Segmentation Hypotheses

Introduction

After wading carefully through Chapter 10 on the pure expectation hypothesis, the reader will not welcome the following emphatic conclusion: "And maybe not." Nevertheless, two important alternative types of explanations of the term structure of interest rates are covered in this chapter.[1] They are the capital risk (or liquidity preference) and the market segmentation hypotheses.

Capital risk is the risk that the price of a bond will unexpectedly fall (interest rates will rise) if the bond is sold before it matures. Proponents of the capital risk, or liquidity preference, hypothesis believe that bond yields contain a premium for capital risk that is larger the longer the remaining term to maturity. Therefore, the claim of the pure expectations hypothesis—that the future expected rates implied by the observable market rates imply unbiased estimates of future expected rates—is held to be incorrect.

The pure expectations hypothesis assumes that the demand for long-term bonds is robust enough to bid away such a premium. Those who want long-term *income* (including those who wish to arrange financing for future periods, as shown in Chapter 10) may have a brisk demand for long-term bonds. According to the pure expectations theory, there is no chronic or congenital weakness in the market for long-term bonds because of insufficient demand by these participants to bid away liquidity premiums. The condition for the absence of such a congenital weakness can be stated in the following way. Those transactors desiring the safety of long-term *income* dominate those who seek to protect the *value of their capital.* These points are discussed together with the capital risk hypothesis.

This condition of robust demand for long-term bonds is shown to depend, in part, on *time preference,* explained in Chapter 9. The increased likelihood of more rapid inflation and a slower rate of output growth, for example, could make time preference more positive. This means that the rate at which individuals discount future income would increase. Future incomes would then become less important. In other words, the present value of securities would fall. Thus what looks like a congenital weakness may be a result of changes in time preference evidenced by higher real interest rates. The move by market participants into short-term financial assets, including money, may be produced by an increase in *positive time preference* due to the increased likelihood of certain future events.

The rapid rise in real interest rates and the accompanying plunge in bond prices that occurred in 1980 and 1981 may have been produced by a number of changes in the likelihood of particular future events which affected time preference. They are described in the next chapter.

A *fundamental condition for the validity of the pure expectations hypothesis collapses with a significant rise in positive time preference.* Real interest rates simply become too high for distant future income to remain important for many individuals. Individuals must be enticed to buy long-term bonds with a liquidity premium over and above what is predicted from the pure expectations hypothesis.[2] By the same reasoning, if time preference is not severely positive, the conditions of the pure expectations hypothesis may hold.

The second group of explanations of the term structure alleges that the yields on debt instruments of different maturities can vary, to a significant extent, independently of the implied forward rates. This can occur because arbitrage between different markets, where each type of security is sold, is imperfect and/or too costly. In addition to high transactions costs, there are a number of other conditions that could invalidate the pure expectations hypothesis. This group of hypotheses is called the *market segmentation hypothesis.* It is discussed after the capital risk hypothesis.

The market segmentation group of hypotheses of the term structure is not a unique classification, clearly separated from the preceeding groups of hypotheses. Even though the hypotheses in this group do not specifically *constrain* the yields of different maturities to some variant of the relationships shown either under the expectations hypothesis or the capital risk hypothesis, they are not necessarily inconsistent with either of the latter. Because a race horse is not constrained to a race track does not mean that a photograph of the horse running will be one in which the horse is not on the track.

There is controversy about whether or not unconstrained theories do give a true picture. Such a controversy surrounds an unconstrained hypothesis of the term structure of interest rates called the *preferred habitat hypothesis*. It is discussed last.

The Capital Risk Hypothesis

The *capital risk* or *liquidity preference hypothesis* of the term structure asserts that future rates implied from Equation (4) in Chapter 10 are a *combination* of expected rates and a liquidity premium. The liquidity premium pays for *capital risk*, the risk that the bond will unexpectedly fall in value and a loss will be incurred if it is sold prior to maturity. The fall in the price of the bond (a rise in interest rates) must be unexpected at the time of its purchase. If such a fall in price were expected, the price would have previously fallen. In other words, in a fairly efficient market this information would rapidly be discounted into the price of the bond.

The liquidity preference proponents claim that "risk aversion of lenders makes them value the stability of principal more than the stability of income."[3] That is, the desire to have ten years of money income from bonds is less important than the fear of a decline in the value of the bond during the ten-year period. The market is alleged to have a *congenital weakness* on one side, so that, for example, more risk is attached to ten-year bonds than to nine-year bonds. John Hicks, in his classic presentation, said: "Other things being equal, a person engaging in a long-term loan contract puts himself into a more risky position than he would be in if he refrained from making it, but there are some persons (and concerns) for whom this will not be true, because they are already committed to needing loan capital over extensive future periods." He goes on to say that "on the other side of the market" (the lenders) "there does not seem to be any similar propensity." He concludes that the market for long-term loans has "a constitutional weakness on one side," so that "if no extra return is offered for long lending, most people (and institutions) would prefer to lend short, at least in the sense that they would prefer to hold their money on deposit in some way or other." Hicks did not present evidence to support his view of "a constitutional weakness."[4] One conclusion drawn from this reasoning is that the risk premiums for capital risk will be larger the more distant the maturity.[5]

Suppose that L_j is the risk premium for the jth forward period. For example, the liquidity premium six years in the future is designated by L_6 or L_j, where $j = 6$. The liquidity premium five years in the future is L_5 or L_{j-1}. This notion of an increasing risk premium can be put in symbols.

$$L_{j-2} < L_{j-1} < L_j \tag{1}$$

This risk premium is combined with the implied future rates given by the pure expectations hypothesis. For every implied future one-year rate

i_j for the jth period forward in Equation (4) in Chapter 10, the associated risk premium must be added. An illustration of this is given in Figure 11-1. Curve AA is a yield curve that is consistent with expected future rates, according to the pure expectations hypothesis. Curve $A'A'$ includes liquidity premiums, in keeping with the liquidity preference hypothesis.

The term structure equation becomes a relation between an observed rate on a bond S_N for a term of N years to maturity, and an average of each year's sum of the implied rate and a liquidity premium.

$$1 + S_N = \sqrt[N]{(1 + i_1 + L_1)(1 + i_2 + L_2) \cdots (1 + i_N + L_N)} \tag{2}$$

where $\cdots$ means "and so on" and i_j is the nominal rate of interest.

Notice that in the error-learning model in Chapter 10 the forecasting error would be biased if there is a liquidity premium added to the expected rate. The biased forecasting error would be the difference between an observed one-year rate and the sum of the rate expected for that year plus a liquidity premium. Furthermore, if the liquidity premiums are not the same for different maturities, if instead they behave as in relation (1), then the constant term C in the estimating equation shown in Chapter 10 cannot represent the effect of the liquidity premiums. The liquidity premiums are embedded in the forecasting errors. The difference between the forward implied rate and the subsequently observed spot rate is not entirely a forecasting error. It is, at least in part, a liquidity premium.

In a famous presentation of the liquidity preference theory, the late Reuben Kessel estimated that the size of liquidity premiums changes at different maturities with changes in the business cycle, increasing during expansions and decreasing during contractions.[6] Since interest rates tended to rise during expansions, Kessel found that "it is the level of

Figure 11-1

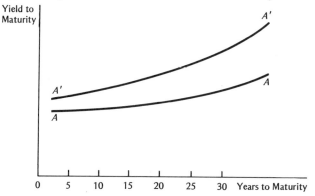

The liquidity preference hypothesis yield curve $A'A'$ compared to the expectations hypothesis yield curve AA for the same series of expected forward rates.

interest rates and not the stage of the cycle that determines the magnitude of liquidity premiums.[7] The implications of this analysis for interpreting yield curves are reviewed in the next chapter.

The Market Segmentation Hypothesis

Suppose that, from a position of equilibrium, the yields on twenty-year mortgages are constant as the yields on five-year U.S. Treasury notes double. One explanation is that each instrument is sold in somewhat unrelated markets. Market participants are not selling sufficient quantities of mortgages in one market and are not buying sufficient quantities of Treasury notes in another market to bring the rates in line with Equation (2), after allowance is made for differences in default risk. There are various hypotheses about this type of phenomenon, called *market segmentation* hypotheses.

Numerous frictions could produce market segmentation. These frictions include: legal restrictions; the lack of a homogeneous debt instrument that can be sold easily on a national market; crisis conditions that cause wild gyrations in yields; the absence of free markets with enough volume to provide continuous spot prices to prospective buyers and sellers; uncertainty about default risks; and lack of knowledge. A market is said to be *thin* if there are relatively few sales. In such a market, participants—bond brokers with inventories of a particular bond—may post prices that are not precisely consistent with market prices that would prevail if greater sales were being made.

Profits that can be earned by overcoming these frictions can be substantial. Modern technology for instantaneously communicating the prices and yields on financial assets to traders all over the world makes lack of knowledge a minor problem for many bonds. The ease of changing the form of financial assets to avoid some legal restrictions can make some of these frictions ineffective.

One of the most famous market segmentation theories was published by J. M. Culbertson in 1957. It is called the *hedging-pressure hypothesis*.[8] This hypothesis holds that market participants, such as large institutional investors, have preferences for particular maturities and will not change. Changes in expectations do not specifically enter into this theory of the term structure.

Depository institutions with short-term checkable deposits may hedge by holding short-term assets. Insurance companies with long-term pension funds may hedge their pension liabilities by investing primarily in long-term assets, such as long-term bonds. (Hedging pressure is widely referred to as *maturity matching* to minimize the exposure of a financial intermediary to fluctuations in net interest margin due to changes in the spread between assets and liabilities when one side of the balance sheet must be rolled over or readjusted more frequently than the other.)

This type of theory is likely to be very attractive to those who are close to the capital markets, such as brokers and bond dealers. The needs of the large participants they deal with daily are likely to influence their predictions. Practical men and women must react to the bullet in their knee rather than to the tide of battle. If the government unexpectedly announces that it will sell a large quantity of seven-year notes, the expectation may arise that spot prices on medium-term debt instruments will fall. The composition of the buy and sell orders is a good clue to short-run changes. The only trouble is that for many bond dealers the long run may well be tomorrow morning.

Once a longer period of six months or a year is taken into account, it seems likely that in modern markets in advanced economies with instant communication, some market participants will take advantage of arbitrage profits.

Meiselman points out that:

> One important implication of hedging pressure theory of the term structure is in direct conflict with a comparable implication of the expectations hypothesis. The expectations hypothesis implies that changes in the maturity composition of outstanding debt, when total debt is given, will have no long run effect on the term structure unless the changes in the supplies of or demands for securities of different maturities also affect either "the interest rate" or expectations of future rates.[9]

The *preferred habitat* is a variant of the hedging pressure theory.[10] Some prominent economists have subjected the theory to statistical tests, not all of which support the hypothesis. The test results that were viewed favorably have been questioned.[11]

The preferred habitat refers to definite holding periods for transactors who loan or borrow forward. The hedgers are held to dominate the market with their fixed preferences for particular periods for holding bonds or for borrowing. Risk premiums arise because of the composition of these preferred holding or borrowing periods. The risk premiums do not necessarily increase in size with more distant maturities, as in Equation (1).

Douglas Fisher questioned the kind of fixed habitat active speculators are alleged to have. He asserted that: "It is the essence of this (an active speculator or arbitrageur's) activity that he has no fixed 'habitat'."[12] Thus Fisher contended that active traders are likely to seek profits with little regard to the maturity of the debt instruments.

Conclusion

One conclusion can be drawn with respect to all these views of the term structure. The statistical tests of the term structure face such difficult data problems that a consensus has not yet been formed around one explanation. Analysts must match the conditions in the economy with the appropriate hypothesis. Some examples of applications are given in the next chapter.

NOTES

1. Some of the important books that include different explanations of the term structure of interest rates are J. R. Hicks, *Value and Capital, An Inquiry into Some Fundamental Principles of Economic Inquiry,* 2nd ed. (Oxford: Clarendon Press, 1946); Ruben A. Kessel, *The Cyclical Behavior of the Term Structure of Interest Rates,* National Bureau of Economic Research, Occasional Paper 91 (New York: Columbia University Press, 1965); John Maynard Keynes, *The General Theory of Employment, Interest and Money* (New York: Harcourt Brace & Company, 1936), pp. 202–204; David Meiselman, *The Term Structure of Interest Rates* (Englewood Cliffs, N.J.: Prentice-Hall, Inc., 1962); Burton Malkiel, *The Term Structure of Interest Rates: Expectations and Behavior Patterns* (Princeton, N.J.: Princeton University Press, 1966); and Friedrich A. Lutz, *The Theory of Interest Rates* (Chicago: Aldine Publishing Company, 1968). A bibliography of books and articles can be found in Terence C. Langetieg, "A Multivariate Model of the Term Structure," *Journal of Finance* (March 1980), p. 97, and in Robert J. Shiller, "The Volatility of Long-Term Interest Rates and Expectations Models of the Term Structure," *Journal of Political Economy* (December 1979), pp. 1217–1219.
2. A model explaining the term structure in terms of an individual maximizing utility over different periods was developed by Joseph E. Stiglitz, "A Consumption Oriented Theory of the Demand for Financial Assets and the Term Structure of Interest Rates," *Review of Economic Studies* (July 1970), pp. 321–352.
3. Lester Telser, "A Critique of Some Recent Empirical Research of the Term Structure of Interest Rates," *Journal of Political Economy* (August 1967), Supplement, *Issues in Monetary Research,* p. 546.
4. Hicks, *Value and Capital,* pp. 146–147.
5. The need for borrowers to pay risk premiums that increase in size the more distant the maturity was called "normal backwardation" by John Mayard Keynes in 1930 in his *A Treatise on Money,* Vol. II (London: Macmillan & Company/New York: Harcourt Brace & Company, 1930), pp. 142–144. It was also used by Hicks, *Value and Capital,* p. 147. One of the most famous theoretical statements supporting the opposite view—that long and short maturities, bills, and consols are close substitutes—is found in Lutz, *The Theory of Interest Rates.*
6. Kessel, *Cyclical Behavior.*
7. Ibid., p. 97.
8. J. M. Culbertson, "The Term Structure of Interest Rates," *Quarterly Journal of Economics* (November 1957), pp. 485–517.
9. Meiselman, *The Term Structure,* p. 49.
10. Franco Modigliani and R. Sutch, "Debt Management and the Term Structure of Interest Rates: An Empirical Analysis of Recent Experience," *Journal of Political Economy* (August 1967), pp. 569–589; and Franco Modigliani and R. Shiller, "Inflation, Rational Expectations and the Term Structure of Interest Rates," *Economica* (February 1973), pp. 12–43.
11. Douglas Fisher points out that the test equations have nonrandom errors, a problem discussed in Chapter 10 for the estimating equations in the error-learning model ["The Term Structure of Interest Rates," in *Monetary Theory and Policy,* Richard S. Thorn, ed. (New York: Praeger Publishers, 1976), p. 531]. Also, the method for estimating expected capital gains by fitting a

relation to past interest rates has a number of statistical and analytical problems, which leave the interpretation of the test results in doubt. For one thing, this requires that the financial markets not be efficient.

12. Fisher, "The Term Structure," p. 530. Parenthetically, Fisher also says: "It is probably better for empirical purposes to assume that he is hoping for transitory income rather than that he is organizing his future consumption" (ibid). Transitory income is, in consumption theory, unexpected income.

STUDY QUESTIONS

1. Describe the differences and similarities between the error-learning hypothesis, the capital risk hypothesis, and several market segmentation hypotheses of the term structure of interest rates.

2. Under what conditions is the pure expectations hypothesis valid? How do these conditions differ from the conditions necessary for market segmentation theories?

3. Under what time preference conditions would the error-learning model fail to explain changes in long-term expected rates?

4. Why is the hedging-pressure hypothesis inconsistent with the error-learning model? Explain why the effectiveness or ineffectiveness of arbitrage (or—more precisely—speculative arbitrage, as explained in Chapter 10) is crucial to differentiating between different theories of the term structure.

5. Suppose that there were only two assets, money and consols. Under what conditions would the yield on consols contain no liquidity premiums?

6. What determines the size of the liquidity premiums on long-term bonds in the capital risk and preferred habitat theories?

7. Does active heavy trading in markets reduce the likelihood of market segmentation compared to less active thin market trading? Explain.

12

Interpreting Yield Curves

Introduction

Yield curves are not merely an electrocardiogram showing the condition of an advanced market economy's bond market. They are more. Insofar as yield curves imply future expected interest rates and predictable risk premiums, they are a direct measure of individuals' views of the future. If this description of yield curves is accurate, they are better compared to notes from psychoanalysis than to an electrocardiogram. Door-to-door surveys seeking respondents' views of the future may well reveal what individuals think they ought to say, rather than the way they act on the basis of their beliefs. For example, an individual in the out (of the White House) party may loudly decry the forthcoming demise of the bond market and the economy, while an individual of the in party celebrates the soon-to-blossom era of good times for all. Meanwhile the public cynic buys twenty-year bonds and the public optimist shortens the maturity of his or her portfolio. The term structure, as depicted by the yield curve, adjusts to their transactions rather than to their rhetoric, although their public posturing can produce temporary disturbances.

This chapter uses the pure expectations and capital risk hypotheses to analyze yield curves. This is not an overly constrained analysis resting merely on a mechanical variant of the view that spot rates are averages of expected one-year rates. The determinants of interest rates and liquidity premiums are numerous and are the subject of study in both economics and finance. The assumption of effective arbitrage (or, more precisely, speculative arbitrage, as described in Chapter 10) is made. This assumption does eliminate market segmentation hypotheses from the discussion.

Many will view this omission as a serious flaw, and they are correct, especially for short-run analysis. The current demands and supplies of debt instruments may properly be viewed as having significant short-run effects. These effects are considered pervasive by many professional bond dealers. They are close to the market and must, for example, sell or buy inventories of debt instruments or obtain Treasury bills as collateral for repurchase agreements before they close down for a late lunch. The viewpoint in this chapter is longer run.

First the implications of the pure expectations hypothesis are discussed. The effects on the yield curve of expected future changes in income tax rates, inflation rates, and factors that affect the real rate of interest are considered. Then the liquidity premium implications are detailed. The analysis of yield curves in 1979 and 1980 by the Federal Reserve Bank of St. Louis is presented together with some problems that arise in their interpretation.

The Implications of the Capital Risk Hypothesis

In Chapter 4 the following relationship was described:

$$[1 + i_{B_j}(1 - K_j)] = (1 + r_{B,AT_j})(1 + \lambda_j) \tag{1}$$

where i_B is the nominal rate of interest on bonds, $r_{B,AT}$ is the real after-tax rate of interest, K is the rate of tax on income, and λ is the expected rate of inflation. The subscript j has been added to signify the period of time to which these variables apply. For example, if j is $T + Y$, the period may be four years in the future, where T is the present year.

Solving Equation (1) for the nominal rate of interest on bonds produces

$$i_{B_j} = \frac{(1 + r_{B,AT_j})(1 + \lambda_j) - 1}{1 - K_j} \tag{2}$$

This expression says that the nominal rate of interest is a real after-tax yield corrected for expected inflation and the tax rate on income. Notice that either an increase in the tax rate or the expectation of inflation is consistent with a higher nominal interest rate. This nominal rate of interest is inserted in the basic equation for the capital risk hypothesis described in Chapter 10, and it is repeated here:

$$1 + S_N = \sqrt[N]{(1 + i_1 + L_1)(1 + i_2 + L_2) \cdots (1 + i_N + L_N)} \tag{3}$$

Suppose that inflation is expected to rise to double its present rate during the next four years and that government countermeasures are then expected to cause a recession and bring inflation down. From Equation (2), the lambdas in each of the first four years will rise:

$$\lambda_4 > \lambda_3 > \lambda_2 > \lambda_1 \tag{4}$$

where the subcripts signify the years. Then inflation is expected to be held in check at a lower level. The yield curve, on the basis of these considerations only, will appear as curve *AA* in Figure 12-1. For the first four years the expected one-year nominal rates given in Equation (3) will be rising. The observable market yield on bonds with one, two, three, and four years' maturity should then be successively larger.

Now suppose that under the same conditions a significant tax cut is imposed. The expectations might produce a yield curve such as *AA'*, which is simply lower than *AA* because the *K* in Equation (2) for each period is smaller. If the tax cut is expected to produce huge deficits that will trigger temporarily higher real interest rates from an increased supply of government securities needed to finance them, *AA"A'* may be the yield curve.

Variables that are expected to affect the real rate of interest in future years also change the yield curve. For example, if the age profile, or age distribution, of the population is expected to change, so that there will be a smaller proportion of younger people in the future period, the real interest rate may change. The demand for loans may be greater for younger people than for older people because of the desire by younger people to borrow against future higher income during their lower-income periods. A changing age profile for the population can therefore change the term structure of interest rates.

Figure 12-1

Yield curves with four years of increasing inflation, AA, and large deficits AA"A'.

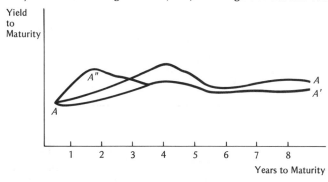

Business Cycles and the Yield Curve

Reuben Kessel combined the capital risk and pure expectation hypothesis in his elegant analysis of the term structure. Kessel observed:

> The joining of liquidity preference to expectations explains the lack of symmetry in the movement of short and long-term rates over the cycle. It explains why short rates do not exceed long-term rates at peaks by as much as they fall below long-term rates at troughs; why yield curves are positively sloped during most of the cycle; and why yield curves, when short-term rates are unusually high, never seem to be negatively sloped throughout their full length, but show humps near the short end.[1]

These observations can be understood by first assuming that interest rates are expected to remain constant. Given that expectation, the pure expectations hypothesis would indicate that long rates would equal short rates. Now add liquidity premiums that increase in size the more distant the maturity. The resultant yield curve, like A'A' in Figure 11-1, is upward sloping. That, according to Kessel, is a normal slope.

Now assume that a contraction occurs and interest rates fall. At the trough (the turning point before recovery) there are two forces pushing short-term rates below long-term rates: (1) Liquidity premiums are higher for long-term rates, and (2) interest rates are expected to rise or, more precisely, short-term rates are considered abnormally low.

Next assume a cyclical peak (the end of an expansion). The two forces

Figure 12-2

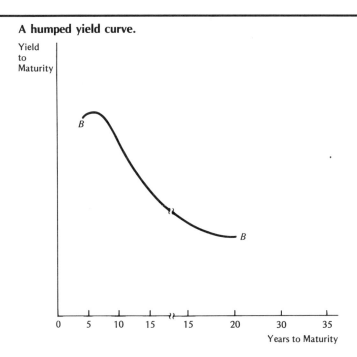

A humped yield curve.

now work in opposite directions: (1) Liquidity premiums are higher for long rates, and (2) expectations work in the opposite direction and, according to Kessel, this effect dominates. Short rates are considered abnormally high. Therefore, long rates rise above short rates by a larger absolute amount at a trough than the amount by which long rates exceed short rates at a peak. This liquidity preference-induced phenomenon exacerbates both the upslope and the downslope.

terrible!

What about the hump in the yield curve Kessel describes? If rates are expected to fall in the future, the yield curve may be humped as is curve *BB* in Figure 12-2. Forward implied rates rise and then fall, giving a hump to the yield curve for spot rates. Kessel holds that this yield curve is typical of a peak in a business cycle. The decline in interest rates is not immediately expected. Instead, the decline is expected to be gradual.

The 1979–1982 Yield Curves

The real rate of interest may vary widely. For example, suppose that there is an increase in uncertainty about the general economic outlook for the future. This is one plausible explanation for the leap upward of long-term rates in the United States in the fourth quarter of 1979, after they had fallen. Uncertainty caused a premium to be demanded by buyers on the yields of debt instruments. Security prices fell. There was increased uncertainty about future economic conditions in that period, following an announcement by the Federal Reserve that it would concentrate on slowing money growth. Uncertainty about the future further increased in November 1979 when the staff of the American Embassy in Iran was taken hostage and a major crisis ensued.

Commenting on this period, the Federal Reserve Bank of St. Louis presented the following hypothesis of how yield curves change with the business cycle.

> In general, the shape of the yield curve changes over a business cycle. At the beginning of an economic expansion, the yield curve is upward-sloping—short-term rates are lower than longer-term rates. As the expansion proceeds, short-term rates tend to rise faster than long-term rates, so the yield curve can become downward-sloping or inverted—short-term yields are higher than longer-term yields. Then, as economic activity declines, short-term interest rates decline faster relative to longer-term rates and the yield curve again flattens out, eventually becoming upward-sloping again before the next expansion begins.[2]

Then, in 1979 and 1980, the changes in the yield curve depicted in Figure 12-3 were described as follows:

> The shape of the yield curve for U.S. Treasury securities has changed dramatically between March 14, 1980, and May 5, 1980. Short-term yields are currently about the same as intermediate- and long-term yields, resulting in a flat yield curve. This contrasts with the downward-sloping yield

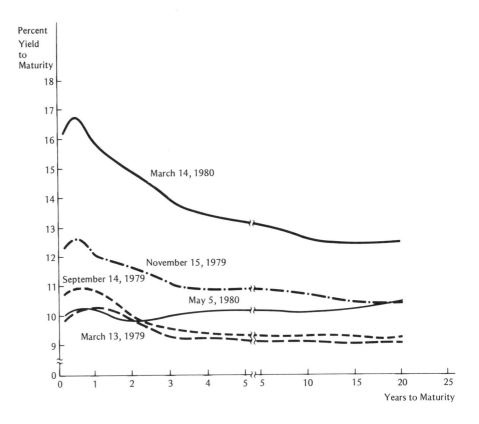

Figure 12-3

Yield curves in 1979 and 1980 on U.S. Government Securities. *Source:* **Federal Reserve Bank of St. Louis,** *U.S. Financial Data,* **May 7, 1980.**

curves that existed since late 1978. The last time such a change in the yield curve's shape occurred was during the 1974–75 recession. Current yields on short-term Treasury securities are at about the same levels as prevailed in March 1979. Current long-term yields, on the other hand, remain 100 to 150 basis points higher than they were a year ago.[3]

The evidence presented in Figure 12-3 is consistent with the view that yield curves change over the business cycle. However, if these changes over business cycles were predictable by market participants, the expected rates would already indicate cyclical movements, as in the yield curves in Figure 12-1. The current time period would be deleted and the y axis would move to the right as time elapsed. Long-term rates would change slightly, according to the expectations hypothesis, as each current year's rate dropped into history. The longer-term rates would then be averages of a slightly different set of forward rates. The phenomena described by the St. Louis Federal Reserve could occur under an expectations hypothesis only if the phases of the business cycle *changed* future expectations. Perhaps 1979 was a year of fundamental changes in long-term expectations, or perhaps there were changes in risk, as the preceding comments suggest. The interesting catch-22 of the expectations hypothesis is that the changes depicted in Figure 12-3 could not happen if the expectations embodied in previous yield curves were maintained, or at least not significantly changed. If the yield curves shift dramatically, it is an indication that the public is changing its views of the future, reducing the value of a single yield curve as an indicator of expectations.

Following Kessel's observations, the yield curves for March and November 1979 in Figure 12-3 indicate the expectation of a change to lower rates. By May 1980 the slightly upward-sloping curve indicates the expectations of higher rates. Rates fell to a low in the summer of 1980, then remained high until the third quarter of 1981. They then fell during the fourth quarter of 1981—short rates falling the farthest—and rose again in early 1982 until May, when short rates fell slightly. Amid these types of bobbing changes, the yield curve in May 1982 took the shape shown in Figure 12-4.

There was no longer any hump in yields at the short end of the term structure. There was a dip and then a rise, reflecting expectations of higher yields that tapered off slowly and slightly at more distant maturities. High projected federal government deficits, despite initial forecasts by the Reagan administration that the deficits would be small, and the threat of renewed fast money growth caused market participants to expect higher interest rates in the future. The changing patterns of the yield curve and the probable existence of substantial liquidity premiums both reflected a high level of uncertainty by those whose investments depend on future economic conditions.

The yield curve changed again dramatically in the summer of 1982, and short-term interest rates began to fall rapidly. The three-month Treasury bill rate fell below the discount rate (the rate that the Federal Reserve charges for loans, which was set at 12 percent) in the middle of July 1982. This decline appeared to be a response to slow money growth that had deepened the recession and reduced inflation. The Federal

Figure 12-4

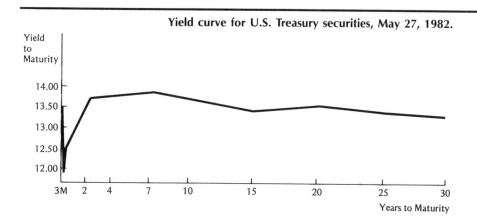

Yield curve for U.S. Treasury securities, May 27, 1982.

Reserve held the growth in the basic money supply (M1) for the six months ending in the week of August 10, 1982, to 1.8 percent and for the three months prior to August 10, 1982, to only .4 percent. This slow money growth made the recession worse and any recovery slower than would have occurred with more rapid money growth. It also helped to reduce expectations of inflation in the short run, probably down to the range of approximately 7 to 8 percent per year. By August 20, 1982, the three-month T-bill rate fell to 7 percent, having been at nearly 13 percent in June 1982 and 14 percent in February 1982. The yield curve took a positive slope.

The episode was associated with a rash of inaccurate analyses in the media. The dramatic fall in interest rates (dramatic since June 1982, less dramatic since the peak of February 1982) was held to be the result of a current rumor in financial markets that the Federal Reserve would ease money growth. The theories were buttressed with the observation that the Federal Reserve had lowered its discount rate in August and that this had been a fundamental factor causing interest rates to decline. They did not take into account that the Federal Reserve was catching up with the decline in rates, which had fallen below the discount rate a month before. The buyers of financial instruments—in a worldwide market—did not change the amount they were willing to pay for these securities because the Federal Reserve had decided to bring its lending rate in line with interest rates. That Federal Reserve action, the announcement by major banks of lower prime rates, and an announcement by Henry Kaufman of Salomon Brothers, did have powerful *announcement effects* on the stock markets. Henry Kaufman announced that he had been wrong in his predictions of higher interest rates. He abruptly changed his prediction to lower interest rates on the basis that the economy was weaker than he had anticipated. He criticized the slow-growth monetary policies. During the week of August 16–20, 1982, the stock market surged with record volume and rising prices. The announcement that even Henry Kaufman, who held a widely known prediction that interest rates would rise, was now convinced of lower interest rates helped trigger a reaction. To say that the decline in interest rates was a *result* of that announcement, the decline in the prime rate, the Federal Reserve's lower discount rate, and the rumor of faster money growth was myopic. It was harmful to the country because it led to government policies incorrectly believed to have immediate rather than long-run effects. It was harmful to individuals who based their investment decisions on these types of forecasts (see Chapters 25 and 26). The bouncing yield curves may well be reactions to that type of environment and to wide swings in the rate of growth of the money supply.

NOTES

1. Reuben A. Kessel, *The Cyclical Behavior of the Term Structure of Interest Rates*, National Bureau of Economic Research, Occasional Paper 91 (New York: Columbia University Press, 1965), p. 98.

2. *U.S. Financial Data*, Federal Reserve of St. Louis (May 7, 1980), p. 1.

3. Ibid.

STUDY QUESTIONS

1. Draw a yield curve for spot rates showing the effect of:
   a. An expected acceleration in inflation beginning in three months.
   b. A deceleration in inflation expected to begin in two years.
   c. Announcements of new policies by the government that create increased uncertainty about future economic events.
   d. An announcement of the implementation of price controls during an inflationary episode.

2. How does a liquidity premium change the term structure of interest rates?

3. What can be learned from the observation that yield curves frequently change during business cycles or when the Federal Reserve announces major policy shifts?

4. What would yield curves look like if people planned only eight years in advance? Is there evidence from yield curves of a planning horizon?

Part IV

Portfolio Selection

13

Criteria Under Certainty

Introduction

Decision rules for selecting a portfolio of assets are presented in this chapter. The discussion ignores the risks of default, capital loss due to unexpected increases in interest rates, or purchasing power risk due to unanticipated inflation. The decision rules are aimed at maximizing the investor's net worth.

The decision rules for selecting a portfolio of assets are presented under the additional assumption that investment opportunities are *mutually exclusive*. An investment option is mutually exclusive if the acceptance of the option excludes the acceptance of one or more other options. For examples, two alternative bond investments may be considered by an individual. If one is selected, the other will not be chosen. A firm may be investing in one of two furnaces for its plant. If one is chosen, the other will not be chosen.

If some investment options are not mutually exclusive, the decision rules would be reformulated in terms of mutually exclusive alternative *strategies,* where each strategy included a combination of contingent asset decisions. For example, if the selection of a new furnace for a plant is contingent on an investment in plant expansion, both investments together represent an investment strategy.

The chapter begins with a discussion of simplified equilibrium for an individual who holds four different types of assets. The discussion of equilibrium is simplified because considerations of risk that are important to the determination of portfolio equilibrium are not directly included. A number of important points are brought out by this simplified demonstration. The presence of substantial nonpecuniary (other than money) returns from holding some assets is one of these points.

The basic valuation formula for determining the present value of an asset is presented next. This equation ties future expected income payments, the *income stream*, to a present value, by discounting the income stream at a given rate of interest. For investment decisions the formula is reformulated in terms of future cash inflows and outflows and the name *net present value* is introduced. This second formula leads to two alternative investment decision rules: the *internal rate of return* and the *net present value* rules. The interest rate of return rule is based on the selection of investment options with the highest yield, and the net present value rule is based on selection of investment options that add most to an individual's or firm's net worth.

Although the net present value rule is preferred, for a number of reasons explained in the body of the chapter and in the two appendices, the internal rate of return rule is also important. It is important to know why an investment with a higher internal rate of return may, under certain conditions, be rejected in favor of an investment with a lower internal rate of return. Since the internal rate of return rule is commonly used—the primary calculation can often be made instantly on a business calculator—it is important to be able to tell an incredulous devotee of this rule why, in some cases, he or she should select the investment alternative with the lower internal rate of return.

Only under special conditions do these alternative investment rules produce contradictory results. If, for example, the investment options are stated in terms of their *terminal values*, as will be shown subsequently, they are both consistent rules.

Both the internal rate of return rule—when used with reinvestment considerations and/or a cutoff (or minimum) acceptance rate—and the net present value rule require that a subjective rate of discount or an "appropriate" market rate of interest be estimated. This estimation process can use knowledge of the term structure of interest rates, the availability and terms of futures contracts, and the determination of the current equilibrium rate of interest. Thus interest rate determination (discussed in Part II), the term structure of interest rates (discussed in Part III), and futures markets (discussed in Chapters 10 and 22) all enter into the investment decision process of selecting between alternative options. The specifications of those alternatives involves a much wider range of subjects throughout the field of finance.

A Portfolio of Assets

Suppose that an individual owns a Jones Corporation bond, some shares of common stock in the Smith Corporation, some money, and a group of personal assets, which will be treated as a simple commodity. These items are listed in Table 13-1

If the individual has no incentive to sell one of these assets and buy more of another, it could be assumed that each asset gives him or her the same total yield, provided that the different kinds of risks elaborated in the next chapter are ignored. This statement can be understood by breaking down the yield of each of the assets into two parts. First, there is the money yield. The bond has a rate of return of 10 percent a year. The 100 shares of common stock also yield 10 percent a year. The 100 U.S. dollars are in an interest-paying NOW account from which the individual receives a 5 percent rate of return. The group of private items (clothing, for example) has no money yield.

The second component of the total yield on each asset is the nonpecuniary yield. The nonpecuniary yield of money is the value of the (in-kind) services of money per dollar. Money yields many services, such as providing a temporary abode of purchasing power or being a medium of exchange, both of which were described in Chapter 2. If the individual is in the equilibrium position of having no incentive to reduce one asset and buy another in order to increase the total yield of his or her wealth, the total yield on each asset must be the same, as shown in Table 13-1. If it is assumed for simplicity that bonds and stocks yield no nonpecuniary return, it follows that the 100 dollars yield a 5 percent nonpecuniary rate of return and the group of personal items yields a 10 percent nonpecuniary rate of return.

What are the behavioral implications of this simple view of portfolio equilibrium? First, an individual can be expected to arrange the quantity of each asset held so that each yields the same rate of return, if considerations of risk are ignored. Second, if one asset has a greater yield, the individual will make some adjustments to increase this higher-yielding wealth and reduce the quantity of other assets.

As the quantity of an asset is reduced, its yield will normally rise. It will become more and more unprofitable to reduce drastically cash balances or personal possessions. Their nonpecuniary yield will normally

TABLE 13-1

Equilibrium Yields on Assets in an Individual's Portfolio* (percent)

	1 Jones Corporation Bond	100 Shares of Smith Corporation Common Stock	100 U.S. Dollars	Group of Personal Items
Money yield	10	10	5	0
Nonpecuniary yield	0	0	5	10
Total yield	10	10	10	10

*The different risks elaborated in the introduction to this chapter are all ignored.

rise rapidly as the individual stops maintaining his or her wardrobe and runs his or her money balances down.

If the dividends on the 100 shares of Smith Corporation common stock rise so that their yield is 11 percent, will the individual sell the Jones Corporation bond, which yields only 10 percent? The full answer must include the riskiness of the return on these assets. Given that the rate of return on each of these assets is uncertain, it is safer to hold a number of different bonds and stocks, so that if the rate of return falls on one asset, the entire portfolio of bonds and stocks may not suffer an equally unpleasant fate. This is the principle of *diversification*—do not put all your eggs in one basket.

It will be safer to hold bonds and stocks that are not in similar industries so that a problem in one industry will not depress the rate of return of the entire portfolio of bonds and stocks. Diversification can lead to investments in precious commodities such as gold and diamonds, real estate, and various forms of art, even if some of these investments have a lower expected yield.

The simple example of portfolio equilibrium depicted in Table 13-1 can be used to illustrate three important points in the analysis of portfolio selection. First, portfolio decisions include a wide range of assets, not just the traditional financial assets, stock and bonds, as well as decisions about changing the size of a portfolio.

The general alternatives shown in the example in Table 13-1 are incomplete. A decision to reduce one's holdings of stock in AT&T may not represent a *portfolio adjustment*. That is, the funds may not be reinvested in another asset. Instead, the funds may be spent on consumption. Broadly viewed, consumption expenditures can be thought of as an investment in human capital, but normally they are not thought of as a portfolio adjustment. Alternatively, income can be saved, rather than consumed, and an investor's portfolio can thereby be increased.

Second, the example is built on the hypothesis that, ignoring the risks discussed in the next chapter, individuals attempt to maximize the rate of return on the stock of wealth they hold. The investment rule they follow is to *shift into those assets with the highest yield*. This hypothesis is rather vacuous if it is merely taken to mean that in whatever proportions assets are held, that is the equilibrium where the portfolio reaches its highest yield position. The hypothesis must explain how changes in yields from a position of equilibrium affect the adjustment of assets in a portfolio. Suppose, for example, that the rate of return on real estate rises significantly. Other yields remain at a position that has been maintained for several periods. This analysis would predict that the demand for other assets would decline while the demand for real estate would rise. Although the rate of return rule works in this example, its use here is only a starting point. As will be shown subsequently, it is sometimes a faulty rule.

A third interesting point illuminated by this example is that nonpecuniary yields on many assets must be substantial. To see this, imagine an array of assets with no nonpecuniary yields. Again, ignoring risks, the individual would hold only the asset with the highest pecuniary rate of return. In the example in Table 13-1, the individual would place all of his or her wealth in stocks and bonds and hold no dollars or personal items such as clothing. The wide variety of assets held by individuals with a wide range of pecuniary rates of returns cannot be plausibly explained by considerations of risk alone. The wide range of assets held indicates that the nonpecuniary yields on many assets are significant.

Nonpecuniary yields can be affected by many different factors and these effects may produce predictable portfolio adjustments. For example, the implementation of effective price controls can reduce the nonpecuniary medium of exchange services from money. If the controls are expected to be permanent and effective, individuals will demand fewer real-money balances. The institution of higher levels of deposit insurance can increase the quality of deposit money and therefore its nonpecuniary yield. This will increase the demand for deposit money relative to currency.

The Basic Valuation Formula

The conventional basic view of the valuation of assets is that their price is the discounted value of their future income. The basic discount formula, derived in Chapter 5, for an asset is

$$\text{PV} = \frac{R_1}{1 + r} + \frac{R_2}{(1 + r)^2} + \cdots + \frac{R_N}{(1 + r)^N} \tag{1}$$

where PV is the present value, R_j is the return in the jth period, and N is the number of periods.

Equation (1) is the conventional present value formula for evaluating the present value, PV, from an asset, such as a bond. For example, consider a three-year bond with a face value of $1000 and a coupon rate of 7 percent. Its income stream, R_1, R_2, and R_3, consists of three yearly amounts, $70, $70, and $1070. Substituting these values into Equation (1) with an interest rate of 10 percent, the present value of $925.39 is obtained.

The income flow $70, $70, and $1070 in the three successive years may be returned to the investor. They are *cash inflows*. If the investor paid $925.39 for the bond, this is the *cash outflows*. Some of the income flow may be reinvested, so that the cash inflow eventually received by the investor is changed from its original form. For investment decisions, all cash outflows and inflows expected from an investment must be taken into account. An investment decision may be based on the *present value of cash inflows minus the present value of cash outflows*. The difference is called the *net present value*. The net present value calculation can be depicted from a transformation of Equation (1) that includes all cash inflows and outflows. If in any period j the cash inflow is R_j and the cash outflow I_j, Equation (1) can be rewritten as follows:

$$\text{NPV} = -I_0 + \frac{R_1 - I_1}{1 + r} + \frac{R_2 - I_2}{(1 + r)^2} + \cdots + \frac{R_N - I_N}{(1 + r)^N} \qquad (2)$$

where NPV is the net present value, I_0 is the initial cost of the investment, and j takes a value from 0 to N.

Internal Rate of Return and Net Present Value Investment Decision Rules

Two investment rules follow from Equation (2). The first depends on determining the value or r in Equation (2). Since the incomes and the costs, including the initial cost of an investment I_0, are usually known or estimated by the investor, the variable to be derived from Equation (2) is r. It is sometimes called the *internal rate of return*. This name reflects the fact that it is a derivation internal to the investment calculation, not a given datum. It is also the rate of return, yield, or rate of interest applicable to the investment.

The internal rate of return is derived from Equation (2) by setting the NPV equal to zero and finding an internal rate of return—a value for r—that is consistent with the cash inflow and outflow streams. There are a number of methods used to find a solution. Modern calculators and computers use *iteration*. Iteration consists of trying different numbers in the neighborhood of the answer and selecting the one that makes NPV closest to zero. Another graphical method is to insert a number of values of r and plot a net present value curve as shown in Figure 13-1. At r^*, where the curve crosses the horizontal axis, a solution for NPV = 0 is found.

The investment discussion rule that uses the internal rate of return as a criterion can be stated in several ways. In its general form, this decision rule is to select the investment option (or options) with the highest internal rate of return. In application, investors may have some minimum rate below which they would not accept any investment option.

The internal rate of return rule is generally easy to apply. Unfortunately, it can provide ambiguous or misleading information. As shown in Appendix A, there can be more than one positive solution for r in Equation (2). This is the problem of *multiple internal rates of return*. In addition, mutually exclusive investments sometimes produce conflicting criteria for investors between the internal rate of return rule and the rule described next, the *net present value rule*.

The net present value rule requires that the investor insert an appropriate interest rate into Equation (2) and calculate the NPV for each alternative investment option. The investor should choose the invest-

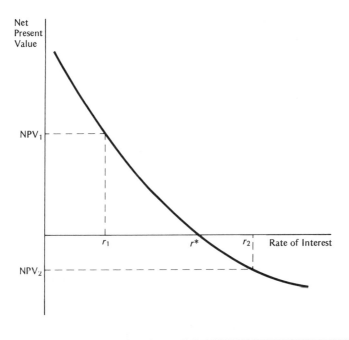

Figure 13-1

Net present values and interest rates.

ment option (or options) with the highest NPV. The appropriate rate of interest may be a market rate of interest; an arbitrary interest rate (used by a firm or government agency); or, for the individual, the subjective rate of discount (described in Chapter 9). A positive net present value is an increase in the investor's net worth. Therefore, the NPV rule conforms to the objective of investment, maximizing net worth.

The problem of conflicting investment decision criteria between the internal rate of return and net present value rules can often be remedied by considering reinvestment rates on expected cash inflows from the investment. These reinvestment rates are important, in any case, for determining the net present value or *additions to a firm or individual's net worth that can be expected from an investment*. That subject is discussed next.

Reinvestment and Terminal Values

The use of either investment decision rule often requires consideration of the shape of the income stream and the rate of return that can be earned on any income that is reinvested. An example illustrates this point. Suppose that an investor puts $100 in a savings and loan association passbook account paying 7 percent interest. What is the internal rate of return for this investment? The question appears simple at first glance. It is 7 percent. However, it is not clear.

To see this, suppose that the investor retains the deposit for three years. The yearly returns, including the initial $100 as a negative flow, would be $-$100, 0, 0, \$122.5043$. Using the valuation formula, Equation (2), yields

$$0 = -\$100 + \frac{0}{1.07} + \frac{0}{(1.07)^2} + \frac{\$122.5043}{(1.07)^3} \tag{3}$$

This equation is consistent with that payment stream, a payment stream that could alternatively be stated as

$$0 = -\$100 + \frac{\$122.5043}{(1.07)^3}$$

However, most investment streams do not take this form. Instead, income is returned each year, so that a payment stream with the same yield might be stated as

$$0 = -\$100 + \frac{\$7}{1.07} + \frac{\$7}{(1.07)^2} + \frac{\$107}{(1.07)^3} \tag{4}$$

What happens to the $7 returns in years 1 and 2?

The $7 cash inflows in years 1 and 2 can be reinvested. The expected return on these investments must be taken into account in judging the overall desirability of the investment. Thus the investor must (1) determine the expected profitability of future investments for reinvestment purposes and (2) take account of the riskiness of these future investments. Ignoring the problem of risk, Equation (4) could be rewritten as follows:

$$0 = -\$100 + \frac{\$7(1 + i_2)(1 + i_3) + \$7(1 + i_3) + \$107}{(1 + r)^3} \tag{5}$$

This equation takes into account that the $7 interest payment reinvested at the end of year 1 earns an i_2 rate of return during the second year and i_3 during the third year. The $7 interest payment reinvested at the end of year 2 earns i_3 interest during the third year. Suppose that $i_2 = i_3 = 7$ percent, the internal rate of return, r, of this investment, shown in Equation (4). Then Equation (5) becomes

$$0 = -\$100 + \frac{\$7(1.07)^2 + \$7(1.07) + \$107}{(1 + r)^3} \tag{6}$$

The *terminal value* is the value of the numeration of the fraction. It is \$122.5043. This value is exactly the same as Equation (3), where the internal rate of return is also shown to be 7 percent.

This example illustrates the important point that the *internal rate of return rule implicitly assumes that all payments will be reinvested at a rate of return equal to the internal rate of return on the investment.* This is not a surprising result with perfect certainty and an efficient capital market. If, for example, there was an opportunity to reinvest income from investment A at a higher rate of return in investment B, investment *B should be chosen in the first place. It has a higher rate of return. If there is no other investment that has a yield as high as the internal rate of return of investment* A, *the cash inflow should be reinvested in investment* A.

Unfortunately, life is not that simple. An individual faces an imperfect capital market where he or she may be able to borrow funds only at a higher rate than funds can be loaned. The individual's budget may, therefore, be constrained so that investment opportunities with high yields cannot be fully exploited. In this case, reinvestment in investment B could be at a higher rate if income from investment A increases the individual's available funds, say by increasing his or her credit rating. Investment A may be chosen by a firm that has not received funding for all its projects (because of an imperfection in the capital markets caused, for example, by insufficient knowledge of the firm's potential).

Suppose that the values of $i_2 = .09$/year and $i_3 = .11$/year. Suppose further, for simplicity, that there is no risk due to the availability of futures contracts, described in Chapter 22. Then, ignoring costs incurred in buying futures contracts, Equation (5) can be rewritten with these values:

$$0 = \$100 - \frac{\$7(1.09)\,(1.11) + \$7(1.11) + \$107}{(1 + r)^3} \tag{7}$$

Evaluating the numerator of this fraction, the *terminal value* of the investment is obtained. It is $123.299. The solution to Equation (7) is easily found by dividing by $100, rearranging terms, and multiplying by $(1 + r)^3$:

$$(1 + r)^3 = 1.23299 \tag{8}$$

Use a calculator to take the one-third power of the right-hand side of Equation (8), subtract 1, and the solution for r is found. The internal rate of return for this investment is 7.23 percent.

This indicates that a higher internal rate of return could be earned from an investment with an income stream of $7, $7, $107 in each of three years than from one with a final payment of $122.5043 (shown in Equation 3), even though both payment streams have the same internal rate of return. This is because reinvestment of the first investment's income stream produces a higher internal rate of return for the entire initial investment, including the return from the reinvestment of cash inflows.

The net present value rule is consistent with the internal rate of return rule when terminal values are used. A higher terminal value in Equation (3) or (5) produces a larger NPV as well as a larger internal rate of return.

Market Rates and Subjective Rates of Discount

The solution for r, the internal rate of return, is depicted in Figure 13-1 as r^*, where the net present value in Equation (2) is 0. Suppose that the interest rate used to discount the investment is less than r^*, say, r_1. Then the net present value is NPV_1. How could this happen? If the subjective rate of discount (discussed in Chapter 9) used by the individual or the market interest rate used by a firm is smaller than r^*, the net present value of the investment is considered to be greater than its present cost, giving rise to a positive net present value. Alternatively, suppose that the real subjective rate of discount is larger than r^*, say, r_2. The net present value, NPV_2, is a negative number. This means that the investment is not considered to be worth the cost to a given investor. In these cases, selection of the investment with the highest internal rate of return may lead to an incorrect investment decision. First, the investor's rate of discount or the market rate of interest appropriate to an investment of this type must be ascertained. Then the net present values of alternative investments are calculated. Among the acceptable investments the one (or more than one) with the highest net present value would be chosen. The investment decision requires that an interest rate be estimated first. Notice that the subjective rate of discount can be high enough so that no new investments are undertaken at their present costs.

The Net Present Value Criterion

The analysis has come full circle back to Part II, where the determination of the rate of interest was discussed.[1] It is sometimes necessary to determine equilibrium rates of interest implied by the market and use these rates to determine which investment opportunities have the highest present values. This is the net present value decision rule for investing. Portfolio selection would be much simpler if one could merely always select the investment with the higher internal rate of return. Selecting the investment with the higher internal rate of return may still be a very useful decision rule for many problems where the ambiguities presented in the preceding section and in the appendices do not arise.

Appendix A: Multiple Rates of Return

The number of rates of return (or roots) that will satisfy Equation (2) is, under normal conditions, equal to the highest power in the expression, that is, the number of possible roots equals N in Equation (2).[2] If the internal rate of return is being calculated on a twenty-year bond, there are usually twenty possible solutions for r. Some will be negative and

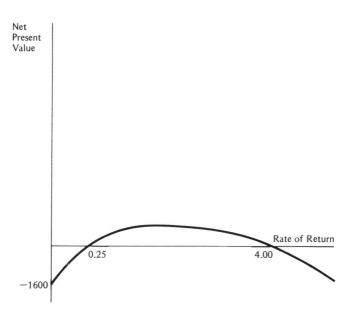

Figure 13-2

Net present values and rates of return for a machine with two internal rates of return solutions.

some will be imaginary numbers (numbers that contain the square root of minus one, $\sqrt{-1}$). The decision rule for picking the asset with the highest yield requires that only the positive roots be chosen. There may, however, be more than one positive root that solves Equation (2).

For example, suppose that a machine costing $1600 is expected to yield $10,000 during the first year and lose $10,000 during the second year.[3] Substituting these values in Equation (2) yields

$$-1600 + \frac{10,000}{1 + r} - \frac{10,000}{(1 + r)^2} = 0 \tag{9}$$

Two positive solutions for r are found: .25 (25%) and 4 (400%). These two positive solutions are shown in Figure 13-2. In cases such as this, an interest rate should be estimated and inserted in Equation (2). The decision rule for optimal investment, ignoring risks, then turns on the asset with the highest net present value.

Appendix B: Switching Between Investments

Another problem with the internal rate of return rule is given by example.[4] Suppose that there is an investment choice between two machines, *A* and *B*. Both machines cost $25. Their income streams are as

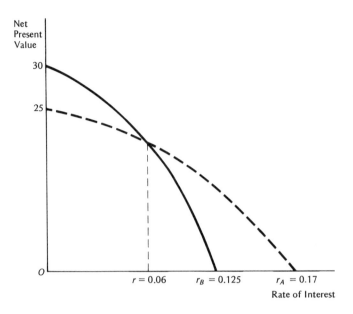

Figure 13-3

Net present values and interest rates for machines A and B.

follows. Machine A has a net income stream of $5 in each of the following ten years. Machine B has an increasing income stream of $1, $2, $3, $4, $5, $6, $7, $8, $9, $10 in each of the next ten years.

The net present values of each of these machines at different rates of discount are shown in Figure 13-3. The solution to Equation (2) for the present value of each of the machines is shown along the horizontal axis, where the net present value equals zero. For machines A and B the internal rates of return are $r_A = 0.17$ and $r_B = 0.125$.

On the basis of the internal rate of return criteria only, machine A should be selected. However, whenever the rate of interest is less than 6 percent, machine B has a higher net present value. At lower interest rates machine B, which has higher incomes further in the future, becomes more valuable. At interest rates higher than 6 percent, machine A, which has larger early incomes, becomes more valuable. The 6 percent interest rate is at a switching point. If there is another *switching point*— a lower rate where the original machine is selected—it would be called a *reswitching point.*[5] Since the objective is to maximize wealth, the machine with the higher present value should be selected. That calculation requires that an appropriate rate of interest be selected first.

NOTES

1. Real rates of interest are used to discount future income that is expected to be indexed for inflation. In the case of a fixed income stream for a bond, a premium for the decline in the real value of the income stream due to inflation must be added (as shown in Chapter 4) to compute the present value.

2. The number of positive roots of an equation $f(x) = 0$ does not exceed the number of variations of the sign of $f(x)$ (arranging the polynomial in descending powers of x), nor does the number of negative roots exceed the number of variations of $f(-x)$. This is called Descartes's rule of signs. Thus, for $x^3 + 5x - 7 = 0$, there is one variation in sign and therefore not more than one positive root. For $f(-x)$ the equation becomes $f(-x) = -x^3 - 5x - 7$ with no variation in signs and therefore no negative roots. Since there are three roots, two must be imaginary.

3. This example is taken from J. H. Lorie and L. J. Savage, "Three Problems in Rationing Capital," *Journal of Business* (1955), pp. 229–239, reprinted in Edwin H. Neave and John C. Wigintin, *Financial Management: Theory and Strategies* (Englewood Cliffs, N.J.: Prentice-Hall, Inc., 1981), p. 68. Other examples of this type are given in an excellent article by Jack Hirshleifer, "Risk, the Discount Rate, and Investment Decisions," *American Economic Review* (May 1961), pp. 112–120, reprinted in *The Theory of Business Finance: A Book of Readings*, Stephen H. Archer and Charles A. D'Ambrosio, eds. (New York: Macmillan Publishing Co., Inc., 1976), pp. 308–345. The investment option with an initial cost of −$1 and a two-year payment stream of $5 and −$6 is an example. It has both a 100 percent and a 200 percent internal rate of return.

4. The example is taken from A. Alchian, "The Rate of Interest, Fisher's Rate of Return over Cost, and Keynes' Internal Rate of Return," *American Economic Review* (December 1955), pp. 938–943, as reprinted in Eugene F. Fama and Merton H. Miller, *The Theory of Finance* (New York: Holt, Rinehart and Winston, 1972), p. 139.

5. Reswitching is an exception to some prior analysis that held a fall in interest rates would cause a change in methods of production. See G. C. Harcourt, *Some Cambridge Controversies in the Theory of Capital* (Cambridge, England: Cambridge University Press, 1972), especially Chapter 4, "A Child's Guide to the Double-Switching Debate," pp. 118–204. The child must be extremely sophisticated in economics to wade through this chapter.

STUDY QUESTIONS

1. Describe the net present value and internal rate of return rules for investment decisions. Explain what they are and the calculations needed in using them.

2. Are the internal rate of return and present value rules for investment decisions always consistent? Explain the conditions under which conflicts or ambiguities occur.

3. Are nonpecuniary returns important in portfolio selection? Explain.

4. Is it correct to hold that of two investment alternatives of equal present value, the one with the earlier payment stream is always preferable because the funds may be more rapidly reinvested to earn additional returns? Explain.

5. Does dissaving (consuming more than income) affect the value of an individual's wealth? Does portfolio adjustment, when income equals consumption, affect the value of an individual's wealth? Explain.

6. Construct income streams from hypothetical investments that have negative, positive, and imaginary solutions for the internal rate of

return. What investment selection rule should be used if there is more than one positive internal rate of return?

7. What part does reinvestment and the term structure of interest rates play in investment decisions?

8. Is the net present value rule inconsistent with the internal rate of return rule when terminal values are used? Explain.

9. Under what conditions with respect to the rate of discount should an investor not undertake any investments?

10. Explain the phenomenon of switching investments to the one with the lower internal rate of return.

14

Risk–Yield Trade-off Theories

Introduction

Portfolio selection under conditions of risk is discussed in this chapter.[1] The concept of risk can be defined as the chance of receiving a lower yield than expected with increased risk increasing the chance of lower yields. Decisions for the selection of a portfolio of assets are viewed as balancing the undesirability (to most people) of more risk against the desirability of higher yields. Like eating delicious fatty foods and risking the accompanying increased chance of arteriosclerosis, the investor is viewed as facing a set of opportunities where higher expected yields are available only at increased risk.

The development of a concise formulation for risk and expected income that uses conventional statistical measures has induced a growth industry in research, both analytical and empirical. This growth industry has also been stimulated by the use of time-series (data on the value of a variable through time) methods that are new to the fields of finance and economics. (Time-series methods are discussed in Chapters 25 and 26.) The new statistical methods are designed to take account of regularities in time series.[2] These statistical methods also led to the modern analysis of stock prices and to the debunking of simple decision rules for doing better than the stock market average.

The prevalent theory of portfolio selection under uncertainty is both succinct in the basic conditions that are assumed and often complex in its theoretical superstructure. The ability to deduce many useful conclusions on the basis of a few conditions can make the theory applicable to many environments, provided that the few conditions are applicable.

The development of these theories of portfolio selection under uncertainty has produced a number of testable hypotheses which are not the kind that could be conjured up from practical experience. Some of these, such as the capital market line, are presented in this chapter. The principle of diversification, which can be learned from practical experience alone, is given a concise basis in the theories of portfolio selection under uncertainty.

In addition, information on particular assets can be developed from these theories and is used by some brokerage and investment advisory firms to formulate investment advice. For example, the type of asset yields that have tended to fluctuate with the market in the past are said to have a high degree of *systematic* risk, as captured by a statistic called the *beta coefficient*. If markets are perfectly efficient, any such prior history that was believed to enhance or reduce the present value of the stock would already be discounted into the price of the asset.

The analysis in this chapter proceeds in the following sequence. First the concept of expected yield is developed. Then utility curves are used to depict preferences toward return and risk. Portfolio opportunities are presented next, as described by their expected risk and expected yield characteristics. The presentation of the concepts of efficient and inefficient portfolios enables the analysis to proceed to an analysis of the selection of an optimum portfolio. This optimum portfolio analysis combines the utility curve analysis of risk preferences with the analysis of portfolio opportunities.

The inclusion of one riskless asset in the portfolio allows the interesting *capital market line* to be presented. Three underlying assumptions are discussed. Given these assumptions, an amazing conclusion for the optimum portfolio is derived. It is that if there are any risky assets in the optimum portfolio, all risky assets will be held. Furthermore, these risky assets will be held in the same proportions (not necessarily the same quantities) by all investors holding risky assets in their optimum portfolio even though they have different preferences for risk. A portfolio composed of these proportions of all risky assets is called the *market portfolio*.

The final presentation is another schedule, which is a second cousin to the capital market line, showing how risk on each individual risky asset is related to the risk of the market portfolio. It is called the *security market line*. The security market line provides an explanation for equilibrium prices on individual assets. This development is called the *capital asset pricing model* (CAPM).

Most of the work done on the analysis presented in this chapter has used stocks as the primary examples of the assets in the portfolio. As the next chapter notes, the analysis should be thought of in a wider context. Thus the general word *asset* is used to describe the items in the portfolio and the individual, corporation, or government unit choosing the portfolio is called an *investor*.

Although formulas are presented for the capital market line and the security market line, they are not derived mathematically. Such a derivation requires taking the derivative of expected yields with respect to a measure of risk and evaluating the result at given values for the parameters. Instead, the formulas are obtained from the graphs of the functions. This allows the formulas to be compared and described without burdening the exposition with the rigorous proofs.

The Expected Yield

The *expected yield* $E(r)$, also called the *expected rate of return*, the *expected return*, and (somewhat ambiguously) the *return*, is a weighted average of different possible yields. The weights are probabilities P_i, which are constructed so that they add to 1 (unity).[3] The formula for the expected rate of return $E(r)$ is

$$E(r) = P_1 r_1 + P_2 r_2 + \cdots + P_N r_N \tag{1}$$

for N alternatives. The sum of all the P's is unity.

An example of the calculation of an expected yield according to Equation (1) is shown in Table 14-1. There are four possible alternative yields on the investment under consideration (column 1). The probabilities of these yields are given in column 2. The expected value of each alternative is found in column 3. It is the multiple of the other two columns. Adding column 3, it is seen that the total of the expected yields is 9.9 percent. Each possible outcome is weighted by its probability of occurring, to give the "weighted average" 9.9 percent. The weights, being probabilities, will always sum to unity. Thus 9.9 percent is the expected yield on the investment.

The *risk* of obtaining less than the expected yield is examined next. The statistical measure of risk is calculated from the variation around the

TABLE 14-1

		Expected Yield of an Asset
(1) **Possible** **Alternative** **Rates of Return (%)**	**(2)** **Probability** **of Each** **Alternative**	**(3)** **Expected Value** **of Each Alternative (%)** **(Column 1 × Column 2)**
8	.1	.8
9	.2	1.8
10	.4	4.0
11	.3	3.3
	(Unity) 1.0	Expected yield = 9.9

average of each alternative possibility. The total variation is measured by a statistic called a *variance* σ^2, the Greek lowercase letter sigma squared. The formula for the variance is simply the average squared difference from the expected yield, where again the average is weighted by the probabilities of each alternative.

$$\sigma^2 = P_1[r_1 - E(r)]^2 + P_2[r_2 - E(r)]^2 + \cdots + P_N[r_N - E(r)]^2 \qquad (2)$$

Using the example begun in Table 14-1, the calculation of this variance is shown in Table 14-2. Since the expected yield is 9.9 percent, the absolute deviation from this expectation is easy to obtain in column 3 of Table 14-2. These deviations are squared in column 4, eliminating negative signs. Multiplying again by the weights for each alternative (column 5), the weighted squared deviations are obtained in column 6. Adding this column up, the variance σ^2 is seen to be .89 percent. Since this number is a squared number, and the expected value is not used in squared form, the square root of the variance is taken to put it in the same units. The square root of the variance is called the *standard deviation* σ, simply sigma. The standard deviation σ is .94 percent. The expected yield on the asset is said to be 9.9 percent with a standard deviation of .94 percent.

The higher the standard deviation, the more risky the asset is held to be in this analysis. Standard deviation is therefore a direct measure of risk. Intuitively, this measure of risk is clear. If the rate of return on an asset has many wide swings (positive and negative) from its expected value, it is more likely to fall in price below its expected rate of return than an asset with less variation—a lower sigma.

Expected yields are more desirable the greater they are. Expected risk is more undesirable (for most people) the greater it is. The general approach in this analysis, to balance greater returns against greater risk according to the investor's taste for risk, is therefore a balance between expected yields and standard deviations of yields.

TABLE 14-2

The Variance of the Expected Yield on an Asset

(1) Possible Alternative Rates of Return (%)	(2) Expected Yield (%)	(3) Deviation (Column 1 − Column 2) (%)	(4) Squared Deviation (%)	(5) Probability of Each Alternative	(6) Weighted Squared Deviation (%)
8	9.9	−1.9	3.61	.1	.361
9	9.9	−0.9	.81	.2	.162
10	9.9	0.1	.01	.4	.004
11	9.9	1.1	1.21	.3	.363
					.89% = Variance, Σ^2

Standard deviation, Σ = .94%

Taste for Risk

The investor's taste for risk is depicted in terms of schedules of his or her preferences, called *utility curves* or *indifference curves*.[4]

Just as an intelligence test quotient (the "IQ") relates only to performance on a test, a utility or indifference curve shows the actions an individual, faced with a number of choices, would take. Neither measure is a penetrating or even casual peek into cerebral functions; they are both a summary statistic relating to performance. Although tests for fitting utility curves to individual behavior can be constructed, the usual approach is to make their construction broad enough to cover many types of behavior, yet specific enough to classify radically different preferences.

Utility schedules for three different types of investors are held to exist. They are shown in Figure 14-1 with only one of a similar family of utility curves for each type of investor.

Each curve has an expected return of *OA* at point *A* in Figure 14-1. At this point, there is no risk. Such a point would be applicable to a U.S. Treasury bill with a yield of *OA*, assuming that it has no risk of default. All three types of investors are assumed indifferent between this type of an investment—no risk and an expected yield of *OA*—and other investments with the risk-yield combinations shown along their respective utility schedules.

The *risk averter* would always select an investment with lower risk if asked to select between alternative investments with the same expected yields. The risk averter's utility curve slopes upward at a decreasing rate (concave from above), showing that he or she is indifferent between the

Figure 14-1

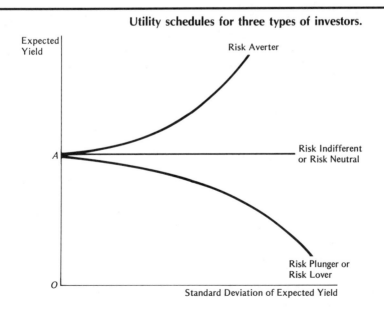

Utility schedules for three types of investors.

investment with no risk (at point A) and other investments with higher expected yields provided that the following is true: The expected yield must rise by a larger proportion than the increase in risk, the proportional increase in expected yield being larger for more risk aversion.

The *risk-indifferent* or *risk-neutral* individual is indifferent between other investments with the same expected yield as at point A regardless of their risk. The risk-indifferent individual has a horizontal yield curve. This case is a limiting position between the risk averter and the risk lover.

The *risk plunger* (or *risk lover*) obtains satisfaction from risk. Given the same expected yield, he or she prefers the investment that has the greater standard deviation of expected yield. The risk plunger's utility curve slopes down at an increasing rate (concave from below).

The risk averter's utility curve will be used in combination with portfolio opportunities to show how portfolio selection is made.

Portfolio Opportunities

The preceding section summarized individual preferences between risk and expected yields with utility curves. The other side of the portfolio decision problem is the presentation of the available opportunities. The problem is initially posed as one of dividing up a *fixed* amount of wealth, at a point in time, into proportions of different assets. The assumption that wealth is fixed can be subsequently dropped when allowance is made for borrowing against future income.

The decision problem is simplified, without changing the logic of this approach, by assuming that only two assets, 1 and 2, are available. The expected yields on these two assets are r_1 and r_2 and their associated variances are σ_1^1 and σ_2^2.

Next the expected yield, $E(r_P)$, of the portfolio composed of these two assets is derived. The respective proportions of assets 1 and 2 in the individual's portfolio of wealth are X_1 and X_2, where $X_1 + X_2 = 1$. Then the total expected yield $E(r_P)$ is simply

$$E(r_P) = X_1 E(r_1) + X_2 E(r_2) \tag{3}$$

The measurement of the risk of the portfolio of both assets together requires a new statistic, the covariance $\sigma_{1,2}$. The covariance is a measure of the association between the expected yields on each asset. If the yields on each asset were offsetting, the yield on the entire portfolio would be less than if the yields varied together.

For example, if the prices of two stocks in a portfolio with constant expected returns generally move in opposite directions, the rate of return on the portfolio will change by less than the yield on either asset. The principle of *diversification* holds that risk is reduced by holding some of each asset rather than by holding only one of them.

The prices of both stocks might always change together, say, because they are for corporations in the same industry. When the yield on one of the stocks went down, the other would follow in tandem.

To put this concept into more precise language, it is useful to follow the calculations of the covariance in Table 14-3. The yields presented for assets 1 and 2 in Table 14-3 are observations from five successive time periods. To calculate the mean (or average) yield, the five yields in the periods are added together and the total is divided by 5.

Notice an important difference between this computation of covariance and the previous computation of standard deviations. In Table 14-3 the computation of covariance uses data from past periods on the assumption the past history will apply to the future. The previous computations used probabilities of future events. Ideally, the investor should make projections about the future. Nevertheless, the calculation of covariances is usually done with prior information as in Table 14-3, a practice that contradicts the theory of perfectly efficient markets presented in Chapter 3.

The formula for the covariance of the yields on assets 1 and 2 is

$$\sigma_{1,2} = E\{[r_1 - E(r_1)][r_2 - E(r_2)]\} \tag{4}$$

This formula describes the covariance in terms of the deviations of each asset's yield from its mean. This is the formula behind the computation shown in Table 14-3. The sum of the multiples of each asset's deviation

TABLE 14-3

Computation of Covariance and Correlation for Yields on Two Assets

(1) Time Period	(2) Yield on Asset 1 (%)	(3) Yield on Asset 1 −6.8%* (%)	(4) Yield on Asset 2 (%)	(5) Yield on Asset 2 −11.2%† (%)	(6) Multiple of Percentage Point Deviations (Column 3 × Column 5)
1	5	−1.8	15	3.8	−6.84
2	2	−4.8	17	5.8	−27.84
3	7	0.2	9	−2.2	−.44
4	8	1.2	8	−3.2	−3.84
5	1.2	−5.2	7	−4.2	21.84
	Total 34		Total 56		Covariance = −60.8 /5 = −12.16
	Mean 34%/5 = 6.8%		Mean 56%/5 = 11.2%		

Variances $\Sigma_1 = 54.8/5 = 10.96$ $\Sigma_2 = 80.8/5 = 16.16$

Standard
deviations $\Sigma_1^2 = 3.31$ $\Sigma_2^2 = 4.02$

Correlation = $\rho_{1,2} = \dfrac{-12.16}{(3.31)(4.02)} = -0.91$

*Sum of the squared terms in column 3 is 54.8.
†Sum of the squared terms in column 5 is 80.8.

from its average (mean) yield is shown to be -60.18 in column 6. Dividing by 5 to obtain the average (mean), the covariance is found to be -12.16. This negative covariance indicates that as one of the asset's yield deviates positively from its mean, the other asset's yield deviates negatively.

The correlation statistic is a related measure of association that is frequently used. Unlike the covariance, which is in the units of the numbers being compared, the correlation statistic is standardized (or normalized) so that it can only vary from -1 to $+1$. This is done by dividing the covariance by the product of the standard deviation of the series of yields for each asset.

$$\rho_{1,2} = \frac{\sigma_{1,2}}{\sigma_1 \sigma_2} \tag{5}$$

This correlation statistic ρ (the Greek lowercase letter rho) is found to be $-.91$ in Table 14-3. Since -1 would be a perfectly offsetting correlation, $-.91$ can be seen to be a very high offsetting correlation between the two yields in the two assets. As one yield rises or falls relative to its mean, the yield on the other asset almost always changes in the opposite direction.

Armed with this measure of the manner in which the yields of the two assets are associated, the variance of the entire portfolio σ_P^2 can be computed from this formula:

$$\sigma_P^2 = X_1^2 \sigma_1^2 + 2X_1 X_2 \sigma_{1,2} + X_2^2 \sigma_2^2 \tag{6}$$

or, alternatively, using the correlation statistic and making the substitution from Equation (5),

$$\sigma_P^2 = X_1^2 \sigma_1^2 + 2X_1 X_2 \rho_{1,2} \sigma_1 \sigma_2 + X_2^2 \sigma_2^2 \tag{7}$$

If $\rho_{1,2} = 1$, perfect positive correlation, Equation (7) becomes

$$\sigma_P^2 = X_1^2 \sigma_1^2 + 2X_1 X_2 \sigma_1 \sigma_2 + X_2^2 \sigma_2^2 \tag{8}$$

which is the same as

$$\sigma_P^2 = (X_1 \sigma_1 + X_2 \sigma_2)^2 \tag{9}$$

The standard deviation of the portfolio, the measurement of its risk, is obtained by simply taking the square root of each side of Equation (9)

$$\sigma_P = X_1 \sigma_1 + X_2 \sigma_2 \tag{10}$$

The risk for the portfolio is in this case simply a weighted average of the risks of each asset. By varying the proportions held of each asset, it is easy to derive the linear (straight-line) relationship shown as AA' in Figure 14-2. At point A, only the asset with the lower risk (σ_1) is held

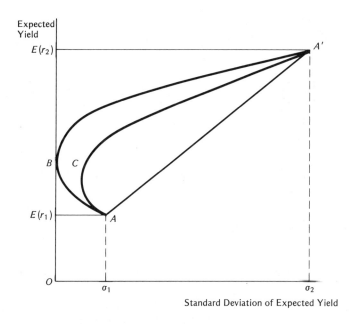

Figure 14-2

Loci of risk–yield combinations for investment opportunities.

($X_1 = 1$). At point A', only the asset with the higher risk is held ($X_1 = 0$). Along AA', different proportions of the two assets are held.

With perfect positive correlation, $\rho_{1,2} = 1$, diversification—holding more than one asset—must mean a lower expected yield than could be obtained by holding only asset 2. The expected yield–risk combinations would be at a point other than A' along AA'.

If the $\rho_{1,2}$ between the expected yield on the two assets is -1, perfect negative correlation, the variance of the yield on the portfolio is

$$\sigma_P^2 = X_1^2\sigma_1^2 - 2X_1X_2\sigma_1\sigma_2 + X_2^2\sigma_2^2 \tag{11}$$

and, following the same steps as shown for Equation (9), only this time with a minus sign, the standard deviation is

$$\sigma_P = X_1\sigma_1 - X_2\sigma_2 \tag{12}$$

Because the correlation is perfectly offsetting, it is now possible to derive a value for X_1 that makes σ_P in Equation (12) equal to zero. This is point B in Figure 14-2.[5] (Equations 13 and 14 are in footnote 5.) The portfolio of the two assets has no risk at this point, due to the expectation of perfectly offsetting variations in the yields of the two assets. With $\rho = -1$ the curve ABA' in Figure 14-2 traces out all the available expected yield–risk alternatives that can be achieved by changing the proportions of the two assets held.

The point B must be between the expected yields that can be earned by holding all of either asset. This is because some of each asset must be held to obtain the offsetting movements which reduce the portfolio risk σ_P to zero.

Limits have been set by showing portfolio opportunities when $\rho = -1$ and $\rho = +1$. Now the analysis of portfolio selection under uncertainty can proceed to a more general case.

The Efficient Frontier and Portfolio Selection

A portfolio is *efficient* rather than *inefficient* if no other available portfolio provides the same expected yield and lower risk, the same risk and higher expected yield, or both a higher expected yield and less risk.

Therefore, expected yield–risk combinations of assets 1 and 2 along AB in Figure 14-2 are inefficient. This is because there are alternative points along BA', directly above each point on AB, which give the investor a higher expected yield at the same risk.

The same logic can be applied to a curve showing the locus of available investments when the correlation is between -1 and $+1$. Such a curve is ACA' in Figure 14-2, where only CA' is efficient. The closer the correlation is to $+1$, the closer the curve ACA' is to the straight line AA'. The closer the correlation is to -1, the closer ACA' is to the curve (a parabola) ABA'. The *efficient frontier* CA' for investments is redrawn in Figure 14-3, again labeled CA'. Two utility curves from the family of

Figure 14-3

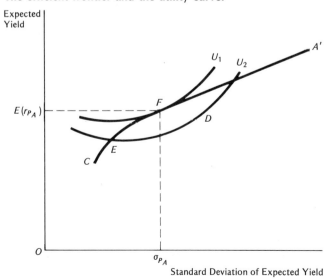

The efficient frontier and the utility curve.

Standard Deviation of Expected Yield

utility curves for a risk averter are drawn. Utility is greater along U_2 than along U_1. At E or D the available investment opportunities along the efficient frontier are on utility curve U_1. The highest level of utility can be reached at point F, where utility curve U_2 is just tangent to the efficient frontier of investment opportunities. The standard deviation of the portfolio at that point is σ_{P_A} and its expected yield is labeled $E(r_{P_A})$. This portfolio represents the optimum portfolio of assets 1 and 2 that can be selected by a risk averter with his or her tastes for risk.

If the individual was a risk lover (or plunger), the highest (downward-sloping) utility curve would pass through point A' in Figure 14-3. That would be the optimum portfolio: The risk plunger would hold only the more risky assets.

Such risk plunging is not merely a hypothetical construct. The chance of the largest profits arise by taking the most risky assets with the highest expected yield. Some individuals may naturally prefer such an alternative. Diversifiers reduce the risk of loss by holding assets which may, as a matter of chance, have offsetting movements in their yields. But diversification also reduces the chance for large gains. Anecdotal evidence from some successful stock traders reveals a taste for a portfolio of only one or two stocks which, although risky, have a chance of very big gains in price. Similarly, those after big gains may forgo costly hedges or limitations on losses. A short seller in the stock market, for example, may forgo a stop loss order in case the stock rises in price. Rather than take his or her insurance with a stop loss order, for what may be only a spike in the stock price series, all safeguards that may reduce the expected yield are bypassed.

The Capital Market Line

The analysis of portfolio selection under uncertainty may be extended to the entire portfolio, providing a range of interesting and useful implications. Three underlying assumptions are made. One asset that is devoid of risk will now be included in the portfolio. Such an asset might be a U.S. Treasury bill, if risk is understood to be default risk.[6]

The three underlying assumptions are: First, the market is efficient, so that prices and yields reflect all available information. This assumption allows continuous adjustment to equilibrium prices and yields on all assets. The analysis does not take into account time-consuming or costly adjustments to new information.

Second is the assumption that all investors have the same expectations about the probabilities of different alternatives, such as those displayed in Table 14-2. Thus they assign the same risk measure to each asset. This condition is called *homogeneous expectations of risk and rates of return*. The assumption of homogeneous expectations, defined in this way, does not require that all investors have the same tastes and preferences for risk, only that they assess each asset in the same way.[7]

Third, investors can *borrow* at the risk-free rate of interest. This simplification allows additions to the portfolio of assets of investors at a cost per dollar asset equal to the market rate of interest. Since the market rate of interest may be assumed to be earned from the riskless asset, a loan is shown as a negative amount of the riskless asset. The introduction of a riskless asset allows both simplification and development of testable assertions about portfolios.

Because it is riskless, the standard deviation of the expected yield from a riskless asset is zero, $\sigma_s = 0$. The riskless interest rate and the yield on the riskless asset is simply r_s.

Equations (3) and (7), for the expected yield and risk from the portfolio, take a simpler form with one risky asset. Suppose that an efficient frontier is derived, as previously shown, along CA' in Figure 14-4. Rather than just two risky assets, assume that the efficient frontier shows the risk–yield combinations for all risky assets. Now add in the possibility of holding the riskless asset. The new combined portfolio combination of the riskless asset and the risky assets has the following expected yield:

$$E(r_{cp}) = X_1 r_s + (1 - X_1)E(r_K) \tag{15}$$

where $E(r_{cp})$ is the expected yield on the combined portfolio and $E(r_K)$ is the expected yield on the risky assets. The standard deviation of the combined portfolio, σ_{cp}, and its measure of risk is

$$\sigma_{cp} = (1 - X_1)\sigma_{r_K} \tag{16}$$

Figure 14-4

The capital market line.

Note: X_1 is the proportion of the riskless asset in the combined portfolio. Borrowing at the risk-free rate of interest is denoted by a negative value for X_1. The market portfolio of risky assets has a yield–risk combination given at m. The capital market line is $r_s mD$.

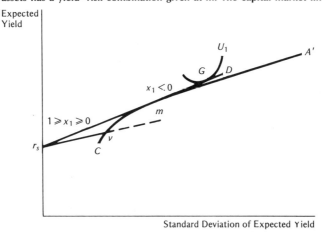

Standard Deviation of Expected Yield

where σ_{r_K} is the standard deviation of the risky assets. This formula is the same as Equation (6), with the covariance between the yield on the riskless and risky assets and the standard deviation of the yield on the riskless asset both equal to zero. This is because the yield on the riskless asset is treated as a constant. There is no correlation between a moving variable and a constant variable.

The next step in the analysis is to specify which combination of risky assets will be combined with the riskless asset. Suppose that the combination of risky assets associated with point v on the efficient frontier CA' in Figure 14-4 is selected. That combination of risky assets can be combined with various combinations of the riskless asset. These combinations produce a combined yield–risk locus of r_sv in Figure 14-4, a linear (straight-line) schedule. It begins with the point r_s, where only the riskless asset is held, and changes in proportion to the change in X_1, the proportion of the riskless asset in the portfolio. At point v only the combination of risky assets would be held; none of the riskless asset would be held.

Combined portfolios to the right of v along the dashed line may be held. This can be accomplished by borrowing at the risk-free rate of interest. Rather than receiving a yield at the risk-free rate of interest from the riskless asset, these portfolios require a payout at this rate of interest. The proportion of the portfolio invested at the risk-free rate of interest, X_1, becomes negative. The negative value of X_1 can be inserted in Equations (15) and (16) to obtain the expected yield and the standard deviation of the combined portfolio.

The portfolios with risk–yield combinations along the line running from r_s through v are inefficient relative to portfolios with higher efficient frontiers, such as similar linear combinations of the riskless asset with risky asset portfolios on CA' above v. This is true since a higher expected yield at the same risk can be obtained at these higher points.

This leads to the conclusion that the portfolio with the risk–yield combination at m is optimum. Rotating the straight line r_sv upward so that it is just tangent to CA' at m will produce an optimum portfolio. Along r_smD, combinations of the risky assets with positive or negative amounts of the riskless asset produce a yield–risk locus that is higher than any other that can be drawn. Maximum expected yield is afforded at the same risk as any corresponding point on a lower line such as r_sv.

At r_s only the riskless asset is held. Increased proportions of the risky asset are held along r_smD until at m only the risky assets are held. Beyond m, increasing amounts of the risky assets are held, financed by borrowing at the risk-free rate of interest. The line r_smD is called the *capital market line* (CML). The CML is the efficient frontier, given the three assumptions previously stated.

Notice that the optimum portfolio of the risky assets has the yield–risk combination given at point m, and other points along r_smD are attained by varying only the proportion of the riskless asset. Thus under the three assumptions, each investor will hold the same percentage of all risky assets. Jan Mossen described this very strong conclusion:

> What this means is that in equilibrium, prices must be such that *each individual will hold the same percentage of the total outstanding stock of all risky assets*. This percentage will of course be different for different individuals, but it means that if an individual holds, say 2 percent of all the units outstanding of one risky asset, he also holds 2 percent of the units outstanding of all the other risky assets. Note that we cannot conclude that he also holds the same percentage of the riskless asset; this proportion will depend upon his attitude toward risk, as expressed by his utility function.[8]

This combination of risky assets at point m in Figure 14-4 is called the *market portfolio of risky assets* or simply the *market portfolio*.

There is no incentive to hold a different combination of risky assets from those in the market portfolio. The only difference in the composition of efficient portfolios is the proportion of the riskless asset or borrowing at the risk-free rate of interest with which the market portfolio is combined.

The portfolio selected along the CML depends on the highest utility curve that can be reached. For example, for a risk averter with utility curve U_1 in Figure 14-4, the portfolio associated with the risk–yield combination at point G would be chosen.

The Capital Market Line Formula

The capital market line CML is redrawn in Figure 14-5 with the standard deviation of the yield on the market portfolio of risky assets and its expected yield $E(r_m)$ labeled on the axes. To find the equation of the CML, first find its slope. The slope of line $r_s m D$ in Figure 14-5 is

$$[E(r_m) - r_2]/\sigma_{r_m}$$

Next recall that a straight line on a graph can be represented as $y = a + bx$, where y and x are variables and a and b are constants. The intercept is a and the slope is b. Using the expression for the slope and r_s as the intercept for the CML, its formula is

$$E(r_{cp}) = r_s + \left[\frac{E(r_m) - r_s}{\sigma_{r_m}}\right]\sigma_{cp} \tag{17}$$

The y value is the expected yield of the combined portfolio $E(r_{cp})$ and the x value is the risk of the combined portfolio σ_{cp}.

This derivation of the CML will allow a simple transition to an expression for the yield–risk combinations obtained by holding different amounts of one risky security.

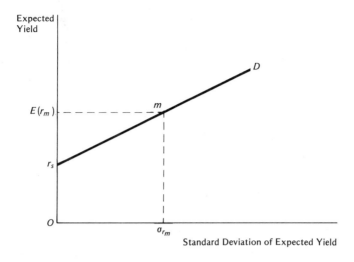

Figure 14-5

The capital market line.

The Security Market Line

The *security market line* (SML) is an extension of the analysis that shows the (equilibrium) relationship between each risky asset's yield and risk. The SML equilibrium yield can be transformed into an equivalent equilibrium price. The development of this price is called the *capital asset pricing model* (CAPM).

The risk for a single risky asset is divided in two parts in the analysis: the systematic and the unsystematic risk. The *systematic risk* is that part of the variation in the yield that is related to the entire market portfolio. The *unsystematic risk* is the independent variation in the yield of the asset.

A key point in the CAPM is that there is no way to diversify the systematic risk away. The efficient market portfolio exhibits this risk; it is the variation in the entire market from general economic activity. When the ship is bobbing, so are the passengers. If efficient portfolios diversify away unsystematic risk, their yields will move together with general economic activity. The rates of return of all efficient combinations of assets will, therefore, be perfectly correlated. These points were noted by William Sharpe, who developed the SML.[9] He summarized these points as follows:

> Although the theory itself implies only that rates of return from efficient combinations will be perfectly correlated, we might expect this would be due to their common dependence on the over-all level of economic activity. If so, diversification enables the investor to escape all but the risk resulting from swings in economic activity—this type of risk remains even

in efficient combination. And, since all other types can be avoided by diversification, only the responsiveness of an asset's rate of return to the level of economic activity is relevant in assessing its risk. Prices will adjust until there is a linear relationship between the magnitude of such responsiveness and expected return. Assets which are unaffected by changes in economic activity will return the pure interest rate; those which move with economic activity will promise appropriately higher expected rates of return.[10]

Sharpe suggested that the easiest way to understand the statistical measure of systematic risk, the beta coefficient, is to think of test-fitting a regression equation to data. Two variables would be fitted as shown in Figure 14-6. The yield from one asset (call it the jth asset) is plotted against the yield on the assets of the entire market—the yield on the market portfolio.[11] The regression line AB is the best linear fit to these data (it minimizes the run of the squared distances of each observation to the regression line). Some of the variation in the yield on asset j is due to the change in the yield in the market portfolio. That part of the variation is shown, an average, by the slope of the regression line AB. The slope is given by the coefficient of the regression, the beta coefficient.

The formula for the beta coefficient, β_j, is, by definition,

$$\beta_j = \frac{\sigma_{j,m}}{\sigma^2(r_m)} \tag{19}$$

the covariance of the yield of asset j with that of the market compared to the variance of the market portfolio. The larger the beta coefficient, the greater the return in a rising market and the greater the loss in a falling

Figure 14-6

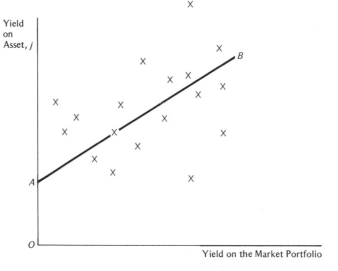

Yields on asset j and the market portfolio.

market, ignoring unsystematic risk (or assuming that its expected value is zero).

The SML is shown in Figure 14-7. The yield r_s on the vertical axis is the risk-free rate of return. In equilibrium it is the same for all assets, as shown in the simple portfolio demonstration in Chapter 13. The SML slopes upward, showing that as different assets (or portfolios of assets) have higher systematic risk, compared to the risk on the market portfolio, they require a higher expected yield $E(r_j)$ to be held in equilibrium. The SML is a general line for all equilibrium holdings of assets (or portfolios of assets). At point m on the SML the efficient portfolio of risky assets, the market portfolio, is held. This is the portfolio for which the CML is drawn.

The equation of the SML can be determined from the graph in the same way as was shown for the CML. The SML equation is

$$E(r_j) = r_s + \beta[E(r_m) - r_s] \qquad (20)$$

where β is the beta coefficient, $E(r_m)$ is the expected return on the market portfolio, and $E(r_j)$ is the expected return on asset j. Notice that at point m on the SML the covariance in Equation (19) that defines the beta coefficient becomes unity. Therefore, at point m the SML formula is the same as the CML formula. The expected return on the portfolio is $E(r_m)$ and the systematic risk is σ_{r_m}, again identical to the market portfolio.

Suppose that a beta coefficient for an asset is found by fitting Equation (18) to historical data series on its yield. Suppose further that a relatively high risk, such as OV in Figure 14-7 (high in terms of σ_{r_m}, the risk on the

Figure 14-7

The security market line.

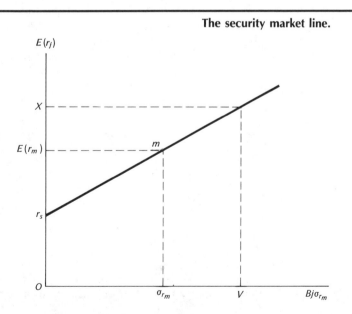

market portfolio) is found. This beta would require a high yield, OX, to be in equilibrium. The distance r_sX is the risk premium on this asset and Or_s is its risk-free rate of return. Thus if an asset's yield systematically varies by more than that of the market, it requires a greater risk premium to obtain equilibrium in the market. If it varies by less than the market portfolio, it requires a lower risk premium than the market portfolio.

The SML is, therefore, a general linear schedule, for efficient or inefficient portfolios, measuring how large a risk premium each asset must have to reach its equilibrium yield.

If the asset's expected yield is plotted on Figure 14-7 and found to be far above the SML, it is undervalued; if it is far below the SML, it is overvalued, provided that the following condition is true: The beta coefficient must be a good forecasting tool. The conditions described for the CML, especially the requirement of efficient markets, contradict that condition. This does not mean that the concept of the SML is invalid. Problems with the beta coefficient forecasting properties are discussed in the following chapter. Regardless of the forecasting problems, the security market line is a rigorously developed concept for explaining equilibrium prices.

To translate a yield into a price, the following formula can be used:

$$P_1 = \frac{E(V_2) - \beta[E(r_m) - r_s]}{1 + r_s} \tag{21}$$

where P_1 is the price in the current period and $E(V_2)$ is the expected value of a firm's net income plus liquidation value in the market in period 2. Notice from the SML formula that $\beta[E(r_m) - r_s]$ is the risk premium. It is subtracted from the expected value in period 2 in Equation (21) and then discounted back to period 1, at the risk-free rate of interest. The larger the risk premium on the yield, the smaller the price. Thus the SML can be used, together with an estimate of the value of future earnings and the value of the firm, to obtain the equilibrium price. This explanation of price is called the *capital asset pricing model.*[12]

NOTES

1. Pioneering work on the analysis in this chapter was developed by Harry Markowitz, *Portfolio Selection: Efficient Diversification of Investments* (New York: John Wiley & Sons, Inc., 1959); James Tobin, "Liquidity Preference as Behavior Towards Risk," *Review of Economic Studies* (February 1958), pp. 65–86; and William F. Sharpe, "A Simplified Model for Portfolio Analysis," *Management Science* (January 1963), pp. 277–293. For an up-to-date bibliography on this subject, see the latest articles in such journals as the *Journal of Finance* or the *Journal of Financial and Quantitative Analysis.*

   No bibliography on this subject is complete without Franco Modigliani and Merton Miller, "The Cost of Capital, Corporation Finance and the Theory of Investment," *American Economic Review* (June 1958), pp. 261–297. That article presented a hypothesis on risk and corporate finance. The riskiness of a firm can increase if the firm borrows funds, raising its ratio of debt to equity. This ratio is called the *leverage factor*. Offsetting the effect of increased leverage on firms' stock prices are the assets obtained with borrowed funds that will produce a yield that benefits equity holders. Suppose that debt is borrowed at the risk-free rate of return. In addition, assume that all investors have homogeneous expectations of yields and the riskiness of yields on earnings of firms. Also assume that there are no taxes on individuals' income from corporations. Now add in an efficient market where investors can combine the stock of different firms to produce any aggregate level of leverage factor they desire for their entire portfolio and where market prices of stock exactly incorporate the effect of the riskiness of increased leverage and the offsetting effect of increased income from assets obtained with borrowed funds. Miller and Modigliani are able to show that under these conditions the present value of each firm's equity and its cost of new capital are unaffected by the degree of leverage. The Miller-Modigliani hypothesis also holds that the cost of equity is equal to the average cost of capital plus a risk premium that depends on the leverage factor. Essentially, the M-M hypothesis holds that investors are able to diversify their portfolios to obtain any desired level of corporate debt while the corporations take actions that maximize the present value of their firms.

2. Regularities in time series are also called *periodicities*; *seasonals*—when they occur yearly; *cycles*—when they occur in intervals greater than a year; and *trends*—for the largest regularities. They are measured by *autocorrelations*—the correlation of movements in a series with its own prior movements (see Chapters 25 and 26).

3. A probability is the weight placed on the chance of an event occurring. The weights on all possible alternatives are calibrated (or normalized) so they add to unity. If they are stated in percentage form, they add to 100 percent. A familiar example is the fair coin, which, at each toss, has a 50 percent probability of landing heads up and a 50 percent probability of landing tails up.

4. A utility curve measures the magnitude of the preferences, with higher utility curves indicating a greater utility or welfare level than lower ones. The individual is assumed to be able to decide that a given utility curve of expected yields and standard deviations is, say, four times better than a given lower utility curve. An alternative to these *cardinal* methods of counting is *ordinal* methods of counting preferences. These involve interpreting the curves as merely ranked relative to one another, with the individual assumed to be able to say only that one level is better than another, and not necessarily by how much. The analysis here can use either interpretation of indifference or utility curves.

5. Since $X_2 = 1 - X_1$, Equation (12) becomes

$$\sigma_p = X_1\sigma_1 - (1 - X_1)\sigma_2 \tag{13}$$

Setting σ_p equal to zero and solving for X_1,

$$X_1 = \frac{\sigma_2}{\sigma_1 + \sigma_2} \tag{14}$$

This corresponds to point B in Figure 14-4.

6. The riskless asset might also be money, as in Tobin's article "Liquidity Preference."

7. This implies that changes in the level of wealth do not change an investor's assessment of risk and rates of return and that changes in the distribution of income and wealth have no such effect.

8. Jan Mossen, "Equilibrium in a Capital Asset Market," *The Theory of Business Finance, A Book of Readings*, Stephen H. Archer and Charles A. D'Ambrosio, eds. (New York: Macmillan Publishing Co., Inc., 1976), p. 283,

reprinted from *Econometrica* (October 1966), pp. 768–783. The statement also holds that if an individual holds any risky assets, he or she holds some of every risky asset.

9. William F. Sharpe, "Capital Asset Prices: A Theory of Market Equilibrium Under Risk," *Journal of Finance* (September 1964), pp. 425–442, reprinted in Archer and D'Ambrosio, *Readings*, pp. 215–232.

10. Sharpe, "Capital Asset Prices," in Archer and D'Ambrosio, *Readings*, p. 232.

11. The equation of the regression line is

$$E(r_j) = A_j + \beta_j[E(r_m)] + e \tag{18}$$

where $E(r_j)$ is the yield on asset j, A_j and B_j are constants that are derived from the estimation procedure, and e is the error.

12. The capital asset pricing model was developed by Sharpe, "Capital Asset Prices"; John Lintner, "The Valuation of Risky Assets and the Selection of Risky Investments in Stock Portfolios and Capital Budgets," *Review of Economics and Statistics* (February 1965), pp. 13–37, in Archer and D'Ambrosio, *Readings*, pp. 233–275; and Fisher Black, "Capital Market Equilibrium with Restricted Borrowing," *Journal of Business* (July 1972), pp. 444–454.

STUDY QUESTIONS

1. What is the expected yield?

2. Use utility curves to explain risk aversion.

3. How are portfolio opportunities pictured in the capital asset pricing model?

4. Explain the meaning of the capital market line and the market portfolio.

5. What is the security market line?

6. How can beta coefficients for individual assets be estimated, and how can they be used in determining if an asset should be bought or sold?

15

Some Perspectives for Further Research

Introduction

The decision theories for portfolio selection presented in Chapters 13 and 14 are part of a sophisticated, rational, useful methodology. Faced with managing portfolios or giving advice to investors, the theories provide concrete and practical strategies capable of quantification and calculation in computer programs. They are also rich in findings that contradict some of the long-held folklore ideas described in Chapter 1. Useful rules for selection of assets, such as the net present value rule or the selection of the most efficient portfolio, are difficult to beat.

There were some problems in explaining stock prices in recent periods. During the 1970s and early 1980s, stock prices were considered to be undervalued in the market by many of those who used these analyses. That is, stock prices were lower than the theories predicted. Undervaluation can be explained away as an aberration if it is short-lived; but when it is observed for twelve years (1970–1982), the explanation rather than the event begins to look aberrant. That such problems existed is not surprising. Economic conditions changed rapidly in the early 1970s from moderate to more rapid inflation and from low to rapidly rising interest rates. Such erratic changes in conditions offer a chance to test theories under the most trying conditions. Problems that appear in the theories can be analyzed with a view to improving the theories. There are intriguing avenues for further research.

The discussion of these problems that surfaced in the 1970–1982 period can take two avenues of inquiry. One is to suggest changes in the parameters of the analysis. For example, perhaps investors are using a higher rate of return than has been estimated. Perhaps they are using a consistently wrong rate of return even though this implies inefficient market information. Perhaps they are consistently making errors in evaluating assets because of inflation. These subjects are discussed in the next two sections. In the following section the size of the market portfolio is discussed. Limiting it to equities may cause problems in evaluating and identifying systematic risk.

Second, there may be fundamental problems with the concepts and analysis presented. Perhaps the market is not as efficient as many believe it to be. If it is not, then equity prices may not be at their equilibrium values, as is required by the capital asset pricing model. Perhaps variances of prices or yields are not complete or conceptually correct measures of risk. Perhaps nonpecuniary returns, which are not directly observable and therefore difficult to quantify, should be incorporated in the analysis. Perhaps under certain conditions, the formation of expected returns cannot be rationalized by using concepts of probabilities. The combination of prior judgments and actual events, both denoted in probability terms, can be combined in simple Bayesian analysis. That analysis is described under these conditions and shown to produce a *probability collapse*. An important implication of such a result is that the assumption of homogeneous expectations, used in the capital asset pricing model, does not apply. These fundamental questions of the analysis of portfolio selection are discussed in the last four sections of the chapter. Then a short conclusion follows.

Rates of Return on Nonfinancial Capital

The paradox we explore in this paper is the fall of the market valuation of our sample of 187 firms despite the relative constancy of the calculated productivity of their capital stock.[1]

So wrote William Brainard, John Shoven, and Laurence Weiss at a 1980 seminar at the Brookings Institution. Robert Hall, one of the discussants, said:

The verdict is a strong confirmation of the hypothesis of gross undervaluation of corporate earnings. All respectable economic explanations of the weak stock market are found wanting.[2]

Phillip Cagan commented:

The stock market has lately become a subject of intensified research to discover why real stock prices are so low in an inflationary environment. In the traditional view, stocks protect against inflation and should be bid up relative to earnings when inflation escalates. As Brainard, Shoven, and Weiss show, the market value of companies relative to replacement cost of capital (the q ratio) fell by more than half from 1968 to 1977. . . . The authors derive internal rates of return which generally show a doubling over the 1968–77 period. This implies that average returns to capital explain none of the decline in q.[3]

Cagan's insightful reference to the q ratio has far-reaching implications.[4] The q ratio is the market value of a company (as measured by its equity prices) compared to the replacement cost of its capital. When the q ratio is low enough, it is less expensive to buy capital from another firm by buying its equities than to build the capital stock. The q ratio, therefore, affects real investment.

Brainard, Shoven, and Weiss allege that even with pessimistic projections of future earnings, "the real discount rate required to equate market and present values has shown a dramatic increase from an average of less than 5 percent in the last half of the 1960s to an average of more than 10 percent in 1974–79."[5]

On the basis of these findings, the solution of the undervalued market prices, relative to estimates from theories of portfolio selection, may appear to be clear. There was a sharply increased risk premium in the 1970s compared to earlier periods. Time preference became much more positive. With a high enough estimated rate of discount the puzzle disappears.

But is this justified? It is important to remember that if a parameter in a theory cannot be predicted without very wide tolerances, the explanatory power of the theory suffers. It is one thing to say that a real rate of return can be found which is consistent with stock prices; it is quite another to say that a consistent rate of return can be predicted on the basis of analysis. The first solution fits the events to an arbitrary number and may provide little or no information about the past or the future. The second solution looks for determinants of behavior.

Brainard, Shoven, and Weiss suggest that the variables they use to estimate risk "are important in explaining market value, but changes in their value do not explain much of the puzzle."[6] Thus they call attention to the problems of identifying determinants of risk.

Factors such as the rapid inflation of the 1970s and early 1980s may contribute to interest rate increases by more than in the past because economic instability increases risk. The incorporation into the interest rate of inflationary expectations, described in Chapter 4, may understate the relationship. That explanation sought to explain the increase in the nominal rate over the real rate by an inflation premium, adjusted for tax rates. An additional adjustment, a risk premium for rapidly changing rates of inflation, should perhaps be added.

Modigliani–Cohn Hypothesis

Franco Modigliani and Richard Cohn believe inflation causes errors in evaluating corporate assets.[7] The first error results from the failure of investors to take into account the reduction in the real value of the firms' nominal liabilities during periods of inflation. The second error is the use of the nominal rather than the real interest rate as the subjective rate of discount.

The first error should lead to a relatively higher undervaluation of firms with high debt-to-equity ratios compared to firms with lower debt-to-equity ratios and similar earnings characteristics. Such a relationship has not been generally observed.[8]

Findings of a relationship between inflation and undervaluation of stocks by the market, plus estimates of risk-free rates of discounts that behave like government bond yields, give circumstantial support to the second error. Theoretically, the confusion of the nominal with the real rate of interest violates important assumptions usually made about economic behavior. It is not necessary that investors know the meaning of these terms, only that they do not suffer from *intertemporal* (over time) *money illusion*. That is, they do not regard a 10 percent increase in expected nominal profits in the following year as enhancing their real wealth if they also expect 10 percent inflation.

Such an intertemporal money illusion would cause a number of peculiar forms of investor behavior. An example pertaining to the reverse of inflation—deflation—illuminates this point. During a deep depression when deflation is expected—pulling the nominal rate below the real rate—stock prices would be bid up. Rising demand for stock during a depression that is deep enough to cause the price level to fall is not likely to be observed before the recovery is generally expected.

An alternative explanation to the negative impact of inflation on equity prices is that rising rates of inflation reduce the real returns being discounted. That is, the problem could be in the economy and the tax system rather than in the equity markets.[9] The phenomenon of rapid inflation and high rates of unemployment has been named *stagflation*. This phenomenon has been observed repeatedly in many countries since 1970.[10] Stagflation may be reflected in business firms by increased costs of planning in an unsteady state of inflation and increased risk premiums on the rate at which future earnings are discounted. These changes are likely to cause output and employment to be reduced to lower levels.

Also, the tax system taxes capital gains that result from inflation. This lowers the real after-tax return from holding assets. Tax effects from inflation may be more severe for equities, since other parts of the tax laws also affect firms' after-tax profits.[11]

However, explanations of the underdevaluation of stock prices by the market relative to estimates from a version of the capital asset pricing model generally take these effects into account. Future earnings are forecast on the pessimistic end of the spectrum of plausible expected earnings. Pointing to these inflation-induced problems without further elaboration does not solve the problem of identifying whether the expected earnings variables or the subjective rates of discount or both have been incorrectly estimated. Therefore, it does appear that the Modigliani–Cohn hypothesis is controversial and tentative, yet a very important area for further analysis.

Widening the Market Portfolio

The market portfolio of assets, as conventionally viewed, may be too small.[12] The analysis has focused primarily on stock prices. Systematic risk is usually taken to mean the variance in the entire stock market. That is the basis for estimating the beta coefficient. It is, of course, an incomplete view, since individuals can and do move into other assets. Real estate; commodities such as gold, silver, diamonds, works of art, stamps, precious coins, and oil; and other financial assets are part of a complete portfolio. Diversification against systematic risk, narrowly defined for the stock market only, is possible by moving into these other assets.

In an even broader context, diversification can be achieved by investing in human capital: that is, investing in education and training. Even consumption enhances future earnings. Without the consumption of food and the provision of housing services, future productive services (and those of unborn heirs) would be eliminated.

The idea of diversifying through the enhancement of human capital may at first glance seem farfetched, and in addition, a fatal harpoon in conventional ideas about diversification. Pity the reader who foresakes other activities to read this book but who does not understand the need to enhance human capital. When nonhuman capital falls in value relative to human capital, those diversified into human capital will have higher expected income.

Having said all that, it may still be true that there is no way to diversify against general business fluctuations. Human and nonhuman capital both fall in value during a deep depression. The beta coefficient, estimated from equity prices alone, may pick up the systematic risk for many other assets. Still, as noted in the previous section, inflation appears to have a negative impact on equity prices. Diversification to reduce the risk of inflation may, therefore, include the purchase of real estate, commodities such as gold and silver, and investments in certain types of training and education. The nominal returns on these alternatives may rise with inflation and the real returns may do better than investments in stocks.

The alleged undervaluation of equity prices in the market might not be inconsistent with the conclusions of the analysis in Chapters 13 and 14 if a larger group of assets is considered. The problems with enlarging the group of assets are numerous. There are insufficient estimates for the additional assets. There are conceptual problems in measuring expected returns in owner-occupied houses or from investments in human capital. Therefore, as operational decision tools and data sources, the analysis in Chapters 13 and 14 would have to be developed further to solve these problems.

Questioning Market Efficiency

The efficient markets hypothesis describes markets such as the New York Stock Exchange well enough to justify the general conclusion that it plausibly explains most price movements. However, it is not precisely correct, even though it is approximately true. The six doubts that are raised here put that approximation in perspective and offer a fundamental reason for questioning the results of portfolio decision theory, which assumes perfectly efficient markets.

All available information is not instantly discounted into housing prices, for example. It takes time and expense to change the stock of houses. This causes long cycles over many years in housing prices during the adjustment process. The past history of housing prices does contain information about future prices. This process cannot be described as a random walk of prices or a fair games model (where no information outside the current price improves a forecast of future prices).

What are the consequences of inefficient markets? Once market prices can be assumed to be out of equilibrium for significant intervals, the information content of the current price of an asset is reduced. Past information on the asset's prices, other characteristics of the asset and the firm that issued it, and expected conditions in the industry and the economy help to identify the adjustment process. Traders can buy at a trough and sell at a peak by correctly anticipating these turning points. Modern statistical techniques used to find cycles and seasonals in data are discussed in Chapters 25 and 26.

The reader should be warned that extremely sensitive statistical procedures have been use to test stock prices and that very little in the way of refutation of the efficient markets hypothesis has been found. Nevertheless, at least six doubts remain.[13]

First, there is the existence of a huge volume of assets created by financial intermediaries. If the efficient markets hypothesis were true, individual investors should be equally able to select their own portfolios. Many investors buy assets from financial intermediaries, undoubtedly because they value the decision-making services that these intermediaries provide. If efficient markets require rational, informed behavior, it is somewhat inconsistent and fatuous to classify all investors who value financial intermediaries' services highly as either irrational or uninformed. Their actions could be justified under an efficient market explanation only as a payment for diversification. For a small investment, the financial intermediary gives these investors a wide portfolio of assets. It seems likely, however, that many individuals buy assets created by financial intermediaries in order to employ experts to manage their funds. In addition to the possibility that some individuals specializing in equity trading have superior knowledge or skill in trading, there is a second possibility that explains the purchase of these services. There may be economies of scale in the production of information and transactions services (such as brokerage fees). This second possibility means that available information would be more valuable to some people than to others, a violation of the fair game model that characterizes perfectly efficient markets.

Second, there are many traders on the floors of the stock exchanges who make a living by trading stock for themselves. They even pay large sums for a seat on a stock exchange. In addition, there are many individuals throughout the society who have for many years earned their living buying and selling securities. Their success cannot be dismissed as a random run or a lucky exception if it is sustained over a number of years.

Third, decision making is expensive. Events, especially significant events such as the beginning of a war, the imposition of price controls, or an oil boycott, may impose especially large decision costs that require a long period of portfolio adjustments. Those who have some insight into this adjustment process may reap better-than-average profits. For example, the downward fall of stock prices after the October 1979 announcement by the Federal Reserve, interpreted at the time to mean a monetary contraction, did not have the characteristics of instantaneous adjustment to new information.

Fourth, if all economic data were reported on a day-to-day basis, most of them would look random. The reasons are that it takes time for people to adjust to new conditions and that there are innumerable disturbances that affect to some extent their day-to-day behavior. In addition, it is impossible to distinguish a random from a nearly random series. Special care should be taken in calling a process efficient because it cannot be explained statistically on the basis of prior changes. As more observations become available—say, in fifty years—it may become crystal clear that there were trends and cycles that could not easily be picked up with the data available. (The problem of testing in the face of trends and cycles in data collected over time is reviewed in Part VIII.)

Fifth, when new information about a stock does become known, random though it may be, a number of individuals must attempt to buy or sell the stock to take advantage of the new information so that it does get discounted into the price of the stock. For these people, the price changes are not random. The adjustment process may not be smooth. There may be undershooting and overshooting from which the smart trader can profit. "Selling into good news" about a corporation can be profitable if overshooting is expected.

Sixth, some analysts, using sophisticated statistical methodologies, believe their results show that the variances in stock prices are too large to be justified in terms of new information.[14] One suggestion made by Robert Shiller is that markets are subject to fads.[15]

A Correct Measure of Risk

Is the variance of prices or yields a correct measure of risk? To approach this question, which is fundamental to the analysis of portfolio selection under uncertainty, an example is posed. Suppose that a stock, say, the Pens Railroad, settles down to a price of $4 per share. The railroad is perceived by many to have a finite chance of bankruptcy. Is lack of variance in its almost constant price a measure of its riskless nature? It may be a sign of agreement about the stock's expected earnings by traders. It is more likely that such an agreement could occur when there is an overriding factor, such as the significant chance of bankruptcy, rather than a host of interrelated factors, affecting its price. This statement is not applicable to a perfectly efficient market. Such a market would reach equilibrium almost instantaneously with all relevant information discounted into the assets' prices.

However, if the market is not perfectly efficient with homogeneous expectations, the stock prices of large, relatively sound, firms with many product lines could fluctuate precisely because the cost of instant decision making on multiple events that continually affect their earnings stream is high. Yet the diversified nature of these firms and/or the soundness of their financial condition make them appear more attractive, relative to other firms with the same expected yield, to risk averters.

Thus a higher variance in the price of the stock of this large company than that of Pens Railroad may not be a sign that it is relatively more risky, where risk is the probability of receiving less than the expected earnings stream.

Many would agree with this conclusion, even those fully supporting variance as a measure of risk. The finite probability of bankruptcy skews the probability distribution of Pens Railroad to the right (see Figure 15-1). That is, there is some slight probability of higher earnings, but the bulk of the weight on future alternative (consol-equivalent) income streams is near zero and the probability distribution is chopped off at zero. To take account of this, a relative of the variance statistic, the *third moment*, is sometimes suggested.[16] In addition, the expected value of the bankruptcy costs—the cost of liquidating the company to obtain its asset values—may simply be discounted into the stock price.

Still, the variance (and the third moment) may not give a good measure of risk. Consider an alternative example to show that a risky stock need not have a skewed distribution. Suppose that the C.C.I. Communications System relies for its profits primarily on a future court decision which will allow it to use the facilities of other firms at a low price. If the court decision is negative, the firm's profits are expected to drop by 90 percent of their present level. If it is positive, the profits are expected to rise by an equal percentage. Again, the profit impact of an overriding factor may be easier to assess than multiple other factors. The price of the stock may settle down at a particular price as investors find themselves in general agreement about the probable outcome of this single, easily quantifiable major factor. There is no skewed distribution.

Again, the lack of variance may reflect investor agreement rather than lack of risk. The large company previously mentioned might be less risky than C.C.I. Communications System. It is less risky because the probability of a large percentage decline in earnings is less.

Again, the caveat must be added that these conclusions do not apply in a perfectly efficient market where there are homogeneous expecta-

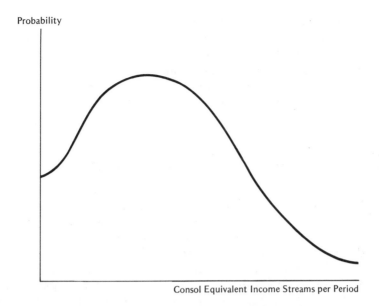

Probability

Consol Equivalent Income Streams per Period

Figure 15-1

Hypothetical skewed probability distribution around Pens Railroad consol equivalent income stream with a finite chance of bankruptcy.*

*This probability distribution with very small probability for larger values is described as skewed to the right.

tions or even large classes of individuals with homogeneous expectations, but such may not be the state of the world.

Nonpecuniary Returns

The simple portfolio equilibrium demonstration presented in Chapter 13 illuminated the presence of significant nonpecuniary returns on many assets. The use by investors of financial intermediaries, discussed in Part V, is based on the nonpecuniary returns that are provided by the financial assets these firms create. Holding these assets has been largely overlooked. These nonpecuniary returns include the reduction in capital risk, purchasing power risk, and default risk. These assets should be included in the market portfolio.

The rise in money market funds, an investment intermediary discussed in Chapter 19, occurred in the late 1970s, part of the period when the undervaluation of stocks by the capital asset pricing model occurred. Among other services, the money market funds provided diversification and liquidity services. The most important nonpecuniary service of money market funds was the small size of minimum investments compared to the lowest denomination of the assets bought by the money market funds. This service allowed money market funds to compete with depository institutions that provided a similar but lower-yield service. The value of these nonpecuniary services should be added to the pecuniary return obtained. Money market funds afforded a way to obtain a pecuniary yield that was less than the market yield by an amount equal to the percentage cost of their managerial fees.

Probability Collapse and Bayesian Analysis

Probabilities are used as weights for alternative possible incomes in each period in calculating expected value. This calculation is described in Chapter 14. The derivation of probabilities may take the general form developed in Bayesian statistics.[17] In that form an investor begins by formulating his or her probabilities for different alternatives. In Table 15-1 probabilities for three alternatives are assumed to have been selected by the investor to represent his or her judgments. Column 2 presents these probabilities. They are called, in Bayesian terminology, either *prior probabilities* or simply *priors*.

The third column of Table 15-1 gives the results of actual events, or in statistics language, trials. This is the frequency with which each alternative actually occurred. Sometimes this number is called a *conditional probability* because the priors are combined with this number to obtain the joint probabilities in column 4. The priors are conditional on the outcome of actual events.

Assume that the number of trials is significantly large, large enough to warrant revising the investor's priors. The mathematics of probability theory requires that the priors and the frequencies of actual events be multiplied to obtain the joint probabilities. The first alternative, for example, was expected to occur 1 percent of the time. It actually occurred .495 percent of the time. The sum of the joint probabilities is .0197.

To obtain a set of final or revised probabilities—the *posterior probabilities* or *posteriors* in column 5—the joint probabilities must be refor-

TABLE 15-1

Bayesian Probability Analysis*

(1) Alternative	(2) Prior Probability	(3) Frequency of Events	(4) Joint Probability	(5) Posterior Probability
1	.01	.495	.00495	.25
2	.01	.495	.00495	.25
3	.98	.01	.0098	.50
			.0197	

*Columns 2, 3, and 5 are normalized to sum to unity.

mulated so they add to unity. This is done by finding the fraction of the sum of the joint probabilities represented by each. For alternative 1, the calculation is .00495/.0197 = .25. This reformulation is called *normalizing to sum to unity.*

The resulting posterior probabilities are 25 percent, 25 percent, and 50 percent. The posteriors can then be used as priors for combination with additional events.

The priors and the frequency of events are set up in Table 15-1 to show an episode in which events turned out almost exactly opposite to what was expected. The priors and the frequency of events are almost perfectly negatively related.[18] The individual thought one alternative would happen, but events turned out much differently. He or she was virtually positive alternative 3 would occur, as shown by the 98 percent probability attached to it. It turned out that it virtually never occurred. Combining such strongly held convictions with just enough trials to warrant reevaluation, the individual is shown now to believe that alternative 3 has a 50 percent chance of occurring. If reevaluation were attempted before any trial produced alternative 3, the results would have been quite different. The joint probability for alternative 3 would have been zero, and the posteriors would have been 50 percent, 50 percent, and zero for alternatives 1, 2, and 3, respectively. That would have been even a more dramatic shift in strongly held convictions. Only 1 out of 100 trials that results in alternative 3 can change that zero percent probability to 50 percent. One event out of 100 changes the posterior from 0 to 50 percent, from a final strong belief in the event never happening to the belief it will happen 50 percent of the time. Little confidence can be put in the likelihood of such an immense change from both prior strongly held beliefs and from the occurrence of 1 out of 100 trials.

The posterior probabilities are blown up to deceptively different size in the process of normalizing joint probabilities that sum to approximately zero. The situation in which prior judgments (or prior trials) are almost exactly opposite to additional trials is reflected by the approximately zero sum for the joint probabilities. It is a signal of what might be called a *probability collapse.*

In the example presented in Table 15-1 a probability collapse has occurred. This means that differences in the posteriors are insignificant. This concept of insignificance is not used here as a statistical measure; it relates to what is called *economic insignificance.*

An additional example further illustrates this point. A tiny amount of new construction starts in the northern United States in one December period may look like an investment boom when it is seasonally adjusted. The seasonal adjustment procedure puts great weight on previous December estimates when there were virtually no construction starts. A tiny increase is a very large percentage increase of a number close to zero. Little economic significance can be found in the statistical result that shows an investment boom.

The effect of a probability collapse on computing expected values is shown in Table 15-2, using the same probabilities as Table 15-1 and

TABLE 15-2

Expected Values for Income in Period 2 Using Probabilities from Table 15-1

Alternative	Alternative Income in Period 2	Prior Probability	Value 1	Frequency of Events	Value 2	Posterior Probability	Value 3
1	$ 100	.01	$ 1	.495	$ 49.50	.25	$ 25
2	1,000	.01	10	.495	495.00	.25	250
3	10,000	.98	9,800	.01	100.00	.50	5,000
			Expected value 1 $9,811		Expected value 2 $644.50		Expected value 3 $5,275

these arbitrary alternative income levels. The priors would have given an expected income of $9811. The frequency of actual events, used as weights, gives an expected value of $644.50. The posteriors give the expected value that is obtained in this simplified Bayesian analysis, $5275.

A truer picture of the positions would reflect the approximately zero joint probabilities. The investor would be unable to decide and would call it a toss-up. That is, he or she would in effect assign equal probabilities to each plausible alternative, one-third to each.[19] The expected value of the income shown in Table 15-2 would then be $3700, nearly 30 percent smaller than is obtained by combining prior expectations with actual events in the Bayesian analysis. The uncertainty in selecting these present values would be reflected in higher subjective rates of discount.

The examples in Tables 15-1 and 15-2 are a caricature of the 1970–1982 period. In that period, events frequently turned out to be different than the consensus forecast of many professional forecasters. Although priors and conditional probabilities were not perfectly negatively correlated, there is reason to suspect that the sum of the joint probabilities approached a probability collapse in many periods.

Under these conditions, the expected income from assets may approach some mean of equally weighted alternatives. The subjective rate of discount will rise dramatically given the risk of making a decision in this environment. The value of the probability and the span of plausible alternatives for the expected income of an asset cannot be given a measure of central tendency, such as a variance, under these conditions (see Note 19). Therefore, the assumption of homogeneous valuations of risk and expected value that is made in the capital asset pricing model may be unrealistic under these conditions. If this were the case, wide swings in market prices of the type previously described (by Schiller) may occur. The higgling and haggling over erratic and unexpectedly low market prices under these conditions is consistent with a breakdown in deriving expected incomes under conditions approaching a probability collapse.

Conclusion

Much of the analysis developed for portfolio selection theory is based on logical extensions of conventional price theory. It offers the best foundation for understanding financial markets and for developing principles of portfolio selection. The nagging doubts raised in this chapter are part of the constant barrage of doubt that must be aimed at any analysis in the hope of finding a better way.

These portfolio selection theories have many useful applications and they form the basis for a continuing massive research effort. Eugene F. Fama and Merton H. Miller, in their classic 1972 textbook on this subject, gave a general assessment of the state of the portfolio selection theories when they explained that they omitted specific examples of investment decisions throughout their book,

> purporting to show how to apply the theory, in precise, quantitative terms, to real world decision problems. This omission is less a move to save space than a reflection of our belief that the potential contribution of the theory of finance to the decision making process, although substantial, is still essentially indirect. The theory can often help expose the inconsistencies in existing procedures; it can help keep the really critical questions from getting lost in the inevitable maze of technical detail; and it can help prevent the too easy, unthinking acceptance of either the old cliches or new fads. But the theory of finance has not yet been brought, and perhaps never will be, to the cookbook stage.[20]

The stock price explanations and predictions that were cooked up for the 1970–1982 period were a bit sour. They were probably no worse and probably much better than most other predictions. The economic variables in this period generally changed more rapidly than in the prior twenty-four years. Few, if any, precise and detailed forecasts turned out to be correct, although a number of plausible backcasts can now be made to approximately fit these prior events.

NOTES

1. William C. Brainard, John B. Shoven, and Laurence Weiss, "The Financial Valuation of the Return to Capital," *Brookings Papers on Economic Activity*, No. 2 (Washington, D.C.: The Brookings Institution, 1981), pp. 453–511.
2. Robert E. Hall, discussion of Brainard, Shoven, and Weiss, "Financial Valuation," pp. 506–507.
3. Phillip Cagan, discussion of Brainard, Shoven, and Weiss, "Financial Valuation," pp. 503–504.
4. The *q* statistic was developed by James Tobin and William C. Brainard, "Asset Markets and the Cost of Capital," in *Economic Progress, Present Values and Public Policy: Essays in Honor of William Fellner*, Bela Balasso and Richard R. Nelson, eds. (Amsterdam: North-Holland Publishing Company, 1977), pp. 235–262f. The idea was discussed by John Maynard Keynes in his classic book. "But the daily revaluations of the Stock Exchange, though they are primarily made to facilitate transfers of old investments between one individual and another, inevitably exert a decisive influence on the rate of

current investment. For there is no sense in building a new enterprise at a cost greater than that at which a similar existing enterprise can be purchased; whilst there is an inducement to spend on a new project what may seem an extravagant sum, if it can be floated on the Stock Exchange at an immediate profit" [*The General Theory of Employment, Interest and Money* (New York: Harcourt Brace & World, Inc., 1964 printing of original 1936 edition), p. 151].

5. Brainard, Shoven, and Weiss, "Financial Valuation," p. 501.

6. Ibid.

7. Franco Modigliani and Richard A. Cohn, "Inflation, Rational Valuation, and the Market," *Financial Analysts Journal* (March–April 1979), pp. 24–44.

8. Brainard, Shoven, and Weiss, "Financial Valuation," p. 497. They do not find evidence of this error in evaluation. They do find support for the second error on the grounds that their estimate of risk-free internal rates of return closely resemble bond rates (p. 498). Richard A. Cohn and Donald R. Lessard find negative correlations between stock prices and inflation or nominal interest rates among most industrialized countries and therefore conclude: "While inflation may be proxying for some set of real variables which is producing the effects we observe, it is tempting to conclude that systematic errors in valuation are made when there is significant inflation" ["Are the Markets Efficient? Tests of Alternative Hypotheses, the Effect of Inflation on Stock Prices: International Evidence," *Journal of Finance* (May 1981), p. 288]. A bibliography of work on inflation and stock prices is presented.

9. John Lintner suggests this alternative for "at least part" of the observed relationship between equity prices and inflation ["Discussion," *Journal of Finance* (May 1981), pp. 310–311].

10. This point is made by Milton Friedman, "Nobel Lecture: Inflation and Unemployment," *Journal of Political Economy* (June 1977), pp. 451–472.

11. Marcelle Arak examines the effect of taxes during inflationary periods on inventory profits, understated depreciation allowances, nominal debt and debt servicing, and the personal capital gains tax ["Inflation and Stock Values," *Quarterly Review*, Federal Reserve Bank of New York (Winter 1980–1981), pp. 3–13].

12. This is a frequent suggestion. See, for example, the discussion of the Brainard, Shovin, and Weiss, "Financial Valuation," where Robert E. Hall makes this point and then says: "Certainly, real returns to bonds have not risen, and this is a serious obstacle to this line of argument" (p. 508).

13. A number of tests that contradict the existence of a perfectly efficient market hypothesis have been made. Only the following report and those in Note 14 are presented here. A recent working paper published by the National Bureau of Economic Research analyzes the buy and sell recommendations of a brokerage firm from 1964 to 1970. The study concluded that investors following these recommendations earned a rate of return that averaged approximately two percentage points above broad stock market averages. A follow-up study made from a random sample of 2500 accounts of the firm found that investors following the recommendations tended to do better than the market average, especially if they acted several days in advance of the formal recommendations on the basis of "information leakage" [Kenneth L. Stanley, Wilbur G. Lewellen, and Gary G. Schlarbaum, "Further Evidence on the Value of Professional Investment Research," *National Bureau of Economic Research, Reprint 217* (Spring 1981), reprinted from *The Journal of Financial Research* (Spring 1981), pp. 1–9]. This study must be regarded as very tentative until it has met the test of criticism by the economics and finance profession.

14. Robert J. Schiller, "The Use of Volatility Measures in Assessing Market Efficiency," *Journal of Finance* (May 1981), pp. 291–304; and Stephen Lekoy

and Richard Porter, "The Present Value Relation: Test Based on Implied Variance Bounds," *Econometrica* (March 1981), pp. 555–574.

15. Schiller, "The Use of Volatility Measures," p. 304.

16. The mean is sometimes called the *first moment* of a distribution. The variance is the *second moment* because it contains squared terms. The *third moment* contains cubed terms. The kth moment about the expected value of v is $E[v_i - E(v)]^k$. If $k = 2$, it is the second moment, the variance. If $k = 3$, it is the third moment.

17. Bayesian statistical methods were introduced to many students studying decision theory in the post-World War II era by Robert Schlaifer in *Probability and Statistics for Business Decisions: An Introduction to Managerial Economomics Under Uncertainty* (New York: McGraw-Hill Book Company, 1959).

18. The correlation coefficient is -1.

19. This is reflected in a diagram of probabilities, such as is shown in Figure 15-1, as a horizontal probability distribution. The value of a probability for a single option is always $1/N$, where N is the arbitrary number of options.

20. Eugene F. Fama and Merton H. Miller, *The Theory of Finance* (New York: Holt, Rinehart and Winston, 1972), p. VIII.

STUDY QUESTIONS

1. What is meant by the undervaluation of assets in the period 1970–1982?

2. Discuss the Modigliani–Cohn hypothesis about errors that cause incorrect valuation of stocks during inflation.

3. What effect does widening the market portfolio have on the definition of systematic risk? Explain.

4. Discuss six doubts about stock market efficiency.

5. Is the standard deviation a complete and accurate measure of risk? Explain.

6. How do nonpecuniary returns affect yields? What class of financial assets have relatively high nonpecuniary returns? Should they be included in the market portfolio? Explain.

7. What is Bayesian analysis?

8. What is a probability collapse, when does it occur, and what are its implications for stock prices?

Part V

Financial Intermediaries

16

Functions

Introduction

Attention was directed in Chapters 13 and 15 to the importance of non-pecuniary returns from assets created by financial intermediaries. These assets are purchased by the public. The financial intermediaries then channel these funds into financial markets. In 1980, for example, $357 billion was advanced in credit markets to nonfinancial sectors, and private financial intermediaries advanced 76 percent of that amount to credit markets. Thus financial intermediaries are massive participants in the financial markets.

In addition to the need to discuss financial intermediaries for an understanding of financial markets, the financial intermediaries are deserving of attention for another very important reason. The assets they create (assets of the public, liabilities of the financial intermediaries) are often closely related to and sometimes part of the money supply. Financial intermediaries, therefore, are part of the money creation process.

The reasons for studying financial intermediaries do not stop with these two. The nature of the services they offer, the competition for these services, the characteristics and the relationships to other economic variables of all the assets they create, and their role in the Euro-dollar market (discussed in Chapter 24) are all important areas of study in domestic and international economies and finance. In this chapter the discussion centers around the importance, the functions, and the types of financial intermediaries, and the movement toward deregulation and homogenization of financial intermediaries in the late 1970s and early 1980s.

The Vital Connection

There is some evidence that the proportion of income saved by rich countries or rich people is not very different from that saved by poor countries or poor people. Since income saved is available for investment (equal to investment in an economy without foreign trade by the method of defining investment in Chapter 4), why do poor countries and poor people invest so little of their income? The answer may well be that they do save and do invest, but in a form that does not produce factories, machines, tractors, automatic home television recording sets, or more efficient methods of farming.

In some countries in current times, individuals may invest in gold jewelry to hang around their necks. In the Middle Ages, individuals invested in beautiful, costly religious edifices such as Notre Dame Cathedral. All of these things produce great psychic income, but they are not the *reproducible capital*—the factories and machines or more efficient techniques of production—that breed material wealth.

What if a poor peasant girl in a developing country who saved part of her meager income to buy a gold necklace had instead taken her funds and placed them on deposit in a business called a savings and loan association? In short order, the savings and loan would invest most of the money in residential housing. But this is not to be. The peasant girl in many countries would certainly not trust her money to a business over which she has no control. Why not enjoy the beauty of her jewelry rather than some future interest payment that is uncertain? So no such business exists. The handicraft industry that makes gold necklaces, as well as gold necklace importers, may prosper. However, these recipients of funds may also fail to invest in reproducible capital.

The savings and loan association in the United States may have the nearly complete trust of its customers. The savings and loan association is one type of financial institution called *financial intermediaries*. Indeed, the very existence of numerous financial intermediaries may be the vital connection for much of the population between saving and the "form" of investment needed for a modern affluent society.

A Definition

Financial intermediaries can be private firms or governmental units. They obtain funds by selling financial assets (claims against themselves) with relatively low pecuniary (money) yields which they create and for which they are liable. Financial intermediaries use these funds to buy financial assets issued by others, yielding higher pecuniary returns. The financial intermediaries receive most of their income from these assets with a higher pecuniary yield. The income covers both the cost of their operations and the payments they make on the financial assets they create. These assets are assets to the public, which holds them, and liabilities to the financial intermediaries that issue them.

A requirement that the financial intermediary not be in the business of managing or seeking controlling interest in other firms could be added to exclude firms called *holding companies*, which are not generally viewed as financial intermediaries. A holding company, unlike a financial intermediary, owns stock in other firms for the purpose of ownership and/or control.

Financial intermediaries should be distinguished from firms that create financial assets with special characteristics and then charge an explicit fee for those instruments.[1] Those firms earn most or all of their income from this fee rather than from financial assets issued by others, which they buy. They are providing and selling a service for which they are directly paid.

Financial intermediaries can also be thought of as taking funds from lenders (savers) and giving these funds to borrowers (investors). The financial intermediary facilitates the exchange of funds between borrowers and lenders by helping to bring borrowers and lenders together. The word "intermediary" and the general name of the services supplied by financial intermediaries, *financial intermediation*, imply this position of middleman or, more accurately, *middle participants* (to include women and corporations) in the exchange of financial assets.

The criterion of middleman sometimes turns out to be a difficult way to isolate financial intermediaries. Just about everyone is a middle participant in the flow-of-funds created by buying and selling financial assets.[2] From the viewpoint of the flow-of-funds between transactors in an economy, the middleman definition can be a circular way to designate some transactors as middlemen and others as the economic units at the beginning and end of the transfer of funds.[3] As an example, assume that a firm borrows from a bank and redeposits the money in the bank. Which is more in the middle, the firm or the bank?

Intermediation Services

Why do buyers of financial assets created by financial intermediaries accept a lower yield than they would obtain by directly buying the financial assets in the financial intermediary's portfolio? The answer is that financial intermediaries provide the following *intermediation services*:

1. *Changing denominations.* Want to buy a $1000 piece of a portfolio of $10,000 Treasury bills? Contact a money market fund.

Here the denomination is reduced; it can also be increased, allowing a large investment to be used to purchase assets of lower denomination.

2. *Changing the timing of income.* Want to invest a small sum every month and receive no return until age 65? Contact a financial intermediary offering pension plans.

3. *Providing liquidity.* Want to put your funds where they can be retrieved on demand or transferred by check? Contact a depository intermediary or money market fund.

4. *Reducing risks.* Pooling of assets in a large portfolio can reduce the risk of default, compared to putting all your eggs in one company's basket. If the financial intermediary gives its customers a percentage of the income of its portfolio, capital and purchasing power risks may also be reduced. If the funds are available on demand at a fixed nominal amount, as in a demand deposit at a bank, capital and purchasing power risks can be avoided.

Thus, when the financial intermediary sells the financial assets it creates, it includes in the sale a group of services that make the asset more valuable than is indicated from the money income of the asset alone.

When funds are deposited with financial intermediaries, it is called *intermediation*, whereas *disintermediation* refers to withdrawal of funds from intermediaries. Disintermediation occurs, for example, when market interest rates rise sufficiently above the interest paid on deposits at savings and loan associations.

Types of Financial Intermediaries

Financial intermediaries can be divided into three groups (Table 16-1):

1. Depository intermediaries.
2. Contractual intermediaries.
3. Investment intermediaries.

The *depository intermediaries* consist of commercial banks and the thrifts, mutual savings banks, savings and loan associations, and credit unions. The depository intermediaries have common characteristics.

1. They all issue deposits (credit unions call them *share accounts*) that, except for time deposits that carry specific maturity dates, are normally *payable on demand*. That means that the deposits are accessible by presentation of a withdrawal form (and sometimes a passbook) in person, by mail, or by check.

2. All are authorized to offer checkable deposits.

TABLE 16-1

The Size of Financial Intermediaries in the U.S. Economy, September 1981* (Billions of Dollars)

	Assets
Depository intermediaries	
1. Commercial banks	1617.1
2. Savings and loan associations	654.6
3. Mutual savings banks	175.2
4. Credit unions	73.7
Contractual intermediaries	
1. Life insurance companies[†]	521.4
2. Other insurance companies[‡]	214.2
3. Private noninsured pension plans[§]	295.32
4. State and local government pension plans[¶]	222.1
Investment intermediaries	
1. Open-end investment companies (mutuals)	208.7
2. Closed-end investment companies	26.4
3. Domestic finance companies	168.1

*The estimates do not include brokerage firms' checkable asset accounts discussed in Chapter 20. Merrill Lynch had $13 billion in these accounts in 1981.
[†]Estimate from surveys for year-end 1981 provided by the American Council of Life Insurance.
[‡]Preliminary estimate.
[§]This estimate was found by extrapolating from the 1980 estimate the growth rate between 1979 and 1980.
[¶]End of 1981.
Source: American Council of Life Insurance; Insurance Information Institute; *Federal Reserve Bulletin; Securities and Exchange Commission, Annual Report 1981.*

3. All can obtain federal deposit insurance for $100,000 of deposits for each depositor if they meet federal regulations and the premia. Some have chosen insurance funds run by their state government. Thus deposits are relatively default-free.
4. The deposits of depository intermediaries have many of the properties of money. Some of these deposits are included in basic concepts of money, such as all checkable deposits in depository intermediaries, which are included in M1.
5. All are subject to federal reserve requirements to be phased in by 1988.
6. All can purchase services from the Federal Reserve after September 1981.

The *investment intermediaries* consist of investment companies and finance companies. The investment companies issue shares of ownership in their portfolios of assets. The investment companies specialize in the purchase of different types of financial assets, such as gold or oil stocks. The *money market funds* are investment companies that specialize in buying short-term, relatively default-free debt instruments, such as U.S. Treasury bills and commercial bank certificates of deposit. The shares in the money market funds have many of the characteristics of deposits in depository intermediaries. However, unlike deposits created by the depository intermediaries, the shares issued by investment intermediaries are not claims to a fixed nominal (money) value. Rather, they are a share in the variable value and income of the portfolio minus management fees of the money market funds.

Finance companies are investment intermediaries that hold a portfolio of loans to consumers and businesses on which they earn their income. They sell debt instruments and stock to raise funds.

Contractual intermediaries consist of insurance companies and pension funds. These intermediaries create credit instruments that form a contractual relationship with the buyer, such as an insurance plan that includes savings and loan privileges, an annuity, or a pension. They hold diverse portfolios that include bonds, common stocks, real estate, and other permissible alternatives.

Homogenization of Financial Intermediaries

At least two factors have tended to create differences between financial intermediaries. First, specialization in the management of particular types of assets and liabilities caused differences. Second, government regulations enforced the areas of specialization and created some noncompetitive barriers. Examples of the first factor are the specialization of savings and loan associations in mortgages and insurance companies in life insurance. An example of the second factor is the partially effective government limitation of checking account privileges to the depository intermediaries.

A number of forces have tended to erode these differences. One such force was the rapid rise in interest rates during the 1970s. This caused depositors in depository institutions to look for alternatives to the depositories' accounts that were subject to relatively low ceiling rate regulations on the payment of interest. Money market funds and stock brokerage firms began offering check-writing accounts that paid market rates of interest.

Another force tending toward a reduction in differences between financial intermediaries was the vertical expansion of financial intermediaries into related fields under hands off or look the other way policies of the government. The alternative characterizations of government actions depend on whether it was part of formal or informal policy.

The U.S. federal government acknowledged and tremendously accelerated the trend toward homogenization of the financial intermediaries during the Carter and Reagan presidencies. The Depository Institutions Deregulation and Monetary Control Act of 1980 was pushed through Congress primarily by Henry Reuss, former chairman of the Committee on Banking, Finance, and Urban Affairs. The administration under

Carter did little to help during the $2\frac{1}{2}$-year fight for this legislation, although they did set the tone for deregulation by deregulating the airline industry. The Monetary Control Act of 1980 (a short title for the legislation; technically, it applies only to the first part) went far toward reducing the regulatory constraints that restrained the homogenization of the depository intermediaries.

A huge push toward homogenization occurred during the beginning of the Reagan administration in its drive for general deregulation. The government constraints that caused barriers against homogenization were to be removed; the government regulators were told to pursue a deregulation policy; and the general tone for deregulation and homogenization spread through the financial intermediaries.

Deregulation and homogenization are not synonyms. There may be valid reasons, of the type Adam Smith described (see Chapter 3), for specialization. A vague policy of deregulation may, through subsidies, taxes, and remaining regulations, erode desirable types of specialization.

Government control is, as described in the next chapter, extremely complex and often misunderstood in its effects on the economy. It carries complex benefits and costs that sometimes can cause the controlled to dance to a tune that no one thought the government was playing. For example, through the discount window, the Federal Reserve gives enormous subsidies to depository institutions when its lending rate (the discount rate) is less than the market rate. These subsidies flow not only into depository institutions' banking activities, but into many other activities through holding companies that own most of the commercial banks. (These holding companies are described in Chapter 18.) Activities of these holding companies include insurance underwriting, mortgage banking, and consumer finance. Unfortunately, a vague policy of deregulation without substantial reform may be sauce to the goose but not to the gander. It may even lead to areas of monopoly power for a favored few. It may not produce a *level playing field* where all competitors face the same regulations. (See Chapter 20 for a discussion of the competition between commercial banks and thrifts over IRAs.)

On the other side of the argument is the risk of monopoly power by the industries that are formally sheltered from competitors by government regulations. The one (or two)-bank town, where a commercial bank had monopoly power on trust activities, business loans, and checking accounts, was not uncommon in the United States from the 1930s, when one-third of the banks in the country closed, until the Monetary Control Act of 1980 gave other depository intermediaries similar powers.

The consensus of many observers seems to be that the homogenization process, like a rolling stone, is gaining momentum and will not be stopped. It is very probable, however, that like other massive changes in business, the changes are better characterized by a pendulum. Deregulation and homogenization will proceed until problems arise that reverse or arrest the process. These problems may take the form of unwanted monopoly power through the vertical integration of giant firms into many industries; the development of diseconomies of scale in some firms beyond some point of expansion; and the public's sudden awareness that it desires some of the personalized and seemingly inefficient personal services it formerly received—leading to a revival of specialized firms.

One of the most important innovations affecting these changes is the widespread installation of home computers and word processors. The technology exists for receiving and ordering nearly all financial intermediary services from consumers' homes in a more precise and rapid manner than at present. Telephone, computer, and data processing companies may then be able to offer many financial services through direct linkage with financial intermediaries. At some point in this development, especially in view of the traumatic effects of immense and rapid change, the public may use the government to swing the pendulum forcibly back the other way.

Importance of Financial Intermediaries

The introduction to this chapter illuminated the vital link between savings and investment that financial intermediaries can provide. The data for the U.S. economy presented in Table 16-2 underline this presentation in an emphatic way. From 1975 to the first half of 1980, the average credit provided by financial intermediaries was 73 percent of the funds advanced in credit markets to nonfinancial sectors. This comparison is not meant to imply that funds raised by financial intermediaries are earmarked for nonfinancial corporations. A true picture of the flow-of-funds is much more complex. The comparison does indicate that financial intermediaries are a major part of the credit markets and that intermediation is a major activity in the U.S. economy. Financial intermediaries are not just the vital link; they are a major part of the chain connecting saving with productive investments.

TABLE 16-2

**Direct and Indirect Sources of Funds to the Credit Markets:
A Comparison of Total Funds Advanced to Nonfinancial Sectors and
Funds Advanced by Financial Intermediaries, 1975–1980***

	1975	1976	1977	1978	1979	1980
1. Total funds advanced in credit to nonfinancial sectors	201.7	262.8	333.5	396.3	394.0	357.0
2. Credit market funds advanced by private financial intermediaries	123.4	191.4	260.9	302.4	292.5	270.3
3. Row 2 ÷ row 1 × 100	61	73	78	76	74	76

*Rows 1 and 2 are billions of dollars. The data in row 3 are percentages.
Source: Federal Reserve Bulletin (December 1981), p. A45.

NOTES

1. There have been proposals to require banks to carry 100 percent of their deposits in reserves. If these reserves were held sterile—earning no interest—the banks would not be financial intermediaries earning their income primarily from the spread between the interest received on the financial assets they bought and the interest paid to their depositors. Instead, they would charge explicit fees to cover their costs, fees that would be paid by their depositors.
2. Donald Hester has noted that the "extent of middlemanness (as a measure of financial intermediation) in the economy is unknown" ["Financial Disintermediation and Policy," *Journal of Money, Credit and Banking* (August 1969), p. 602].
3. John Gurley and Edward Shaw, in *Money in a Theory of Finance* (Washington, D.C.: The Brookings Institution, 1960), posited a middleman type of classification system in which financial intermediaries create "indirect securities" while "spending units" (which include corporations producing goods and services) produce "primary securities." Intermediaries buy primary securities and sell indirect securities. This classification is useful in a formal model where the world can be simplified to illuminate certain relationships.

STUDY QUESTIONS

1. What are financial intermediaries?

2. What do financial intermediaries do?

3. What would be the effect on investment if financial intermediaries did not develop in an economy?

4. What forces have accelerated the homogenization of the financial intermediaries? Will this process continue? Explain.

17

Regulators and Changing Regulations for Depository Intermediaries

Introduction

The activities of financial intermediaries are closely tied to government regulators and regulations. The depository intermediaries not only have extensive government regulation, they also have experienced sweeping changes in these regulations since 1980. These sweeping regulatory changes have been induced by distortions resulting from rising market interest rates in the presence of government-imposed ceiling regulations on the payment of interest on deposits at depository intermediaries.

In this chapter the major regulators are discussed. The Federal Reserve is given the most attention because of its importance in a number of areas. The Federal Home Loan Bank is noted briefly. An additional description of its structure is found in the description of savings and loan associations in the following chapter. The Federal Deposit Insurance Corporation, which has broad regulatory powers, is also discussed in this chapter.

A description is presented of the changing regulations affecting depository intermediaries, the relationship of these changes with rising market interest rates, and ceiling rate limitations on interest paid to depositors. The final section discusses the implications of usury laws on loans and changes in usury laws authorized in 1980 legislation.

253

The Federal Reserve

The Federal Reserve is the central bank of the United States. It has primary responsibility for controlling the nation's money supply.

The money creation process was described in Chapter 7. In this chapter the Federal Reserve discount window is further described. A further description of reserve requirements is given in a special chapter on liabilities of depository institutions (Chapter 19). A further description of open-market activities is presented in Chapter 23, which focuses on Federal Reserve participation in financial markets. The Federal Reserve regulates part of the banking system and has a number of other functions described subsequently. Some commercial banks are private members of the Federal Reserve System. The relationship between these commercial banks and the Federal Reserve system of banks is described in Chapter 18. The governmental and semigovernmental part of the Federal Reserve structure is discussed in this chapter.

The Board of Governors

The headquarters of the Federal Reserve, where the Board of Governors (sometimes called "the Board") is located, is in Washington, D.C. The Board of Governors is composed of seven members (see Figure 17-1). The Washington headquarters contains many more individuals, who work in support of the Board of Governors or the central committee for controlling the nation's money supply, the Federal Open-Market Committee (FOMC). The FOMC is discussed subsequently. Several hundred economists and statisticians, a cadre of lawyers, and numerous supporting personnel work in these buildings.

The United States is divided into twelve Federal Reserve districts, each with a regional Federal Reserve bank. These districts, the twelve regional banks, and their twenty-five branches—in an additional twenty-five cities—are shown on the map in Figure 17-2. (Twelve Federal facilities that are not classified as branches are also listed in Figure 17-2.) The Federal Reserve has over 22,000 employees, including approximately 500 economists in research departments at the Board and the twelve regional Reserve banks.

The Board of Governors is composed of seven members, each of whom is appointed by the president of the United States, subject to Senate confirmation. The term of office is fourteen years. Appointment dates are staggered, so that only one appointment is made every two years unless a member leaves the Board before the end of his or her term. Thus a president can appoint two members during a four-year term of office if no member leaves before the end of his or her term.

The chairman and vice-chairman of the Board of Governors of the Federal Reserve System are appointed by the president, subject to con-

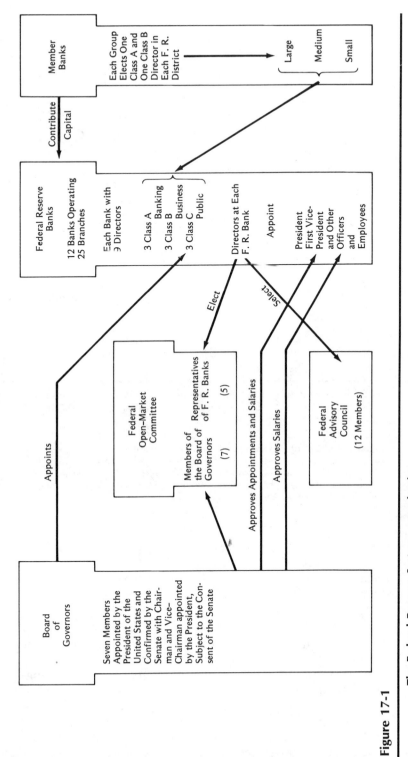

Figure 17-1

The Federal Reserve System: organization.

Additional facilities are listed in Figure 17-2.

Reserve Bank Cities ○
Branch Bank Cities ●
District Boundaries ——
Branch Territory Boundaries ———
Board of Governors of the Federal Reserve System ★

Note: Alaska is in the Seattle Branch Territory and
Hawaii in that served by the head office of the
Federal Reserve Bank of San Francisco. Both
are in the Twelfth District.

District numbers and corresponding letter symbols:

1 Boston A	4 Cleveland D	7 Chicago G	10 Kansas City J
2 New York B	5 Richmond E	8 St. Louis H	11 Dallas K
3 Philadelphia C	6 Atlanta F	9 Minneapolis I	12 San Francisco L

Figure 17-2

Federal Reserve map of the United States.* *Source: Fundamental Facts About United States Money,* **Federal Reserve Bank of Atlanta (July 1979), inside cover and p. 3.**

*Additional offices of these Banks are located at Lewiston, Maine; Windsor Locks, Connecticut; Cranford, New Jersey; Jericho, New York; Utica at Oriskany, New York; Columbus, Ohio; Columbia, South Carolina; Charleston, West Virginia; Des Moines, Iowa; Indianapolis, Indiana; and Milwaukee, Wisconsin. There is a communications and record center in Culpepper, Virginia.

sent by the Senate, to serve a term of four years (see Table 17-1). They are part of the seven-member Board of Governors and may finish the remainder of their fourteen-year terms as ordinary Board members when their four-year term ends or be reappointed as chairman or vice chairman.

The Board has the final word on all major decisions inside the Federal Reserve except those pertaining to control of the money supply through open-market operations, which are handled by the FOMC. The Board sets reserve requirements within the legal range and may implement the supplemental reserve requirements described in Chapter 19. The Board must approve changes in the rate of interest charged on loans to depository institutions, called the *discount rate.* Technically, the Board does not have authority to change the discount rate; the regional Federal Reserve must approve it. In practice, the Board sets the discount rate, the New York bank adopts it, and the Boards of Directors of the other re-

TABLE 17-1

Federal Reserve Board Chairmen	

Following are the twelve chairmen who have served the Board (designated "governor" before August 23, 1933) since its inception:

1. Charles S. Hamlin	Aug. 10, 1914–Aug. 9, 1916
2. W. P. G. Harding	Aug. 10, 1916–Aug. 9, 1922
3. Daniel R. Crissinger	May 1, 1923–Sept. 15, 1927
4. Roy A. Young	Oct. 4, 1927–Aug. 31, 1930
5. Eugene Meyer	Sept. 16, 1930–May 10, 1933
6. Eugene R. Black	May 19, 1933–Aug. 15, 1934
7. Marriner S. Eccles	Nov. 15, 1934–Jan. 31, 1948
8. Thomas B. McCabe	Apr. 15, 1948–Mar. 31, 1951
9. William McChesney Martin, Jr.	Apr. 2, 1951–Jan. 31, 1970
10. Arthur F. Burns	Feb. 1, 1970–Jan. 31, 1978
11. G. William Miller	Mar. 8, 1978–Aug. 6, 1979
12. Paul Volcker	Aug. 6, 1979–

gional banks rubber-stamp their agreement, with an occasional recalcitrant regional Reserve bank delaying for several weeks (for which they have authority).

The Federal Open-Market Committee

The Federal Open-Market Committee (FOMC) is one of the most powerful economic policy groups in the government. It formulates Federal Reserve open-market policy, and by doing so, affects the supply of money, interest rates, inflation, the level of economic activity, and the international exchange value of the U.S. dollar.

The FOMC is comprised of the seven members of the Board of Governors plus five representatives of the reserve banks, who may be either Federal Reserve bank presidents or vice-presidents. The president or vice-president of the New York Federal Reserve Bank is always on the FOMC. Each of the other four Reserve bank members is from one of the following four groups, which send a member to the FOMC on a rotating basis for one-year terms beginning March 1: (1) Boston, Philadelphia, and Richmond; (2) Cleveland and Chicago; (3) Atlanta, Dallas, and St. Louis; (4) Minneapolis, Kansas City, and San Francisco.

The FOMC meets formally nine or ten times a year. It determines the policy for the purchase and sale of securities by the Federal Reserve. These transactions, which create or contract the monetary base, are called *open-market operations*. (The monetary base consists of that part of the money supply that is a liability of the federal government: cash balances of the nonbank public and the depository intermediaries that may be held in Federal Reserve accounts.) The New York Federal Reserve Bank executes all open-market operations for the system.

The manager of the System Open-Market Account carries out the open-market activities in the New York bank. The manager may at times ask for a special conference telephone meeting of the FOMC, even though it is not in session. The mechanics of open-market operations are discussed in Chapter 23.

The Regional Banks of the Federal Reserve

Each of the twelve regional Federal Reserve banks was organized as a separate corporation. These regional Federal Reserve banks should be distinguished from private commercial banks, which may or may not be members of the Federal Reserve System. Every national bank must join the Federal Reserve System. State banks may elect to join.

Each member bank must subscribe to stock in the Reserve bank corporation. It must buy an amount of stock equal in value to 3 percent of the value of its capital, plus any surplus (from profits) in the bank, with another 3 percent subject to call by the Reserve bank. The stocks held by the member banks are different from stocks issued by private banks. The stocks receive a fixed return, currently 6 percent, and do not give their owners proprietary rights (i.e., the legal rights of ownership and control that normally belong to stockholders).

The member banks in each district elect six of the nine members of the board of directors of the Reserve bank in their district. The directors of each of the reserve banks are classified into three groups, consisting of three members each. (The following detail is presented to delineate clearly the composition of the group that has local authority in the Federal Reserve System.)

1. *Class A directors* must be members of the stockholding banks.
2. *Class B directors* must consist of members "with due but not exclusive consideration to the interests of agriculture, commerce, industry, services, labor and consumers," provided that they are not officers, directors, employees, or stockholders of any bank. The Federal Reserve Reform Act of 1977, quoted here, broadened representation of Class B directors from a prior limitation to "commerce, agriculture or some other industrial pursuit."
3. The three *Class C directors* are chosen by the Board of Governors and cannot be officers, directors, employees, or stockholders of any bank. The same language for Class B directors applies to those eligible to be Class C directors.

Directors of Reserve banks and branches are limited to one or two full three-year terms. The chairman and deputy chairman of each Reserve bank's board of directors are appointed by the Board of Governors from the three Class C directors. Class A and B directors are elected by the member banks; one director in each class is chosen by the small member banks, one by the member banks of medium size, and one by the larger member banks. The chairman, by statute, is made the Federal Reserve Agent. As Federal Reserve Agent, he or she acts as a representative of the Board of Governors and has responsibility for obtaining new currency (Federal Reserve notes) and maintaining custody of unissued notes in the Federal Reserve vaults.

Although the nine members of the Board of Directors manage their Federal Reserve bank mostly subject to the approval of the Board of Governors, they do have considerable authority, since bank regulatory actions are administered and initiated in the regional banks. The president and vice-president, who serve five-year terms, are elected by the Board of Directors, subject to approval by the Board of Governors. Prior to 1935, the boards of directors' authority, both in the supervision of their Federal Reserve banks and in the policy decisions of the entire Federal Reserve System, was much broader.

The Federal Reserve banks are empowered to make loans to depository institutions, to provide check-clearing services, to act as a depository for reserves of all depository institutions, and to transfer these funds between Federal Reserve banks. The Federal Reserve banks also act as fiscal agents for the U.S. Treasury by conducting the Treasury's sales of U.S. Treasury obligations. Federal Reserve banks supply research facilities for the member banks and publish a large number of reports and periodicals (over 3 million copies in 1979) for the public for little or no charge.

The Federal Advisory Council (FAC) is composed of twelve members, each one of whom represents one of the twelve Reserve banks. Prior to the 1930s, the FAC had considerable power, but it is now empowered with only advisory functions. It confers directly with the Board of Governors and makes recommendations on the operations of the system. The FAC frequently assists in developing answers to many of the general problems of banking and finance with which the Board must deal.

Discounts and Advances

The Federal Reserve Act of 1913 gave to each of the Federal Reserve banks the authority to make loans to private commercial banks that were members of the Federal Reserve system. The Depository Institutions Deregulation and Monetary Control Act of 1980 gave all depository institutions (credit unions, savings and loan associations, mutual savings banks, and all commercial banks) that have checkable accounts access to these loans on an equal basis. With the authorization in the same law for nationwide checkable accounts for all depository institutions, the number of potential consumer borrowers increased from slightly over 5600 member banks in 1980 to over 40,000 depository institutions.

These loans are of two forms, *discounts* (sometimes called *rediscounts*) and *advances*, although they are both usually referred to as *dis-*

counting. Certain types of commercial, agricultural, and industrial paper may be given to the Reserve banks by member banks in return for a loan equal to the value of the collateral minus a discount, that is, a discounted loan. A member bank may also obtain a direct advance on which interest must be paid and against which eligible paper must be deposited with the reserve bank. Virtually all borrowing is at present in the form of advances against which government securities are used as collateral.

The interest rate charged by the reserve bank to the depository institution is called the *discount rate.* Each Reserve bank's board of directors sets each Federal Reserve bank's discount rates at least once each month, subject to the approval of the Board of Governors. In the post-World War II period, this has usually meant that the Board initiates a discount rate and the twelve regional Federal Reserve banks adopt it within a two-week period. The discount rates from 1930 to 1980 are shown in Figures 17-3 and 17-4.

The officials at the Federal Reserve banks may deny a depository institution permission for a loan. The exact effect of nonprice rationing (including the threat of denial) on the volume of member-bank borrowing is difficult to determine. No precise policy of influencing depository institutions is discernible, although the objectives of member-bank borrowing privileges have been studied frequently, and the original Federal Reserve Act has been amended to redefine the objectives a number of times.[1]

In the post-World War II period, there has been extensive use of the discount facilities. In 1945, the daily average December borrowing amounted to $334 million. Borrowing rose to nearly $3.5 billion in 1974, partly because of a loan of $1.75 billion to the troubled Franklin National Bank in New York, which failed. In June 1981, total borrowings by member banks was $2.0 billion.

Although most borrowing is for short periods—no more than a few days—under Regulation A, as amended in August 1976, a seasonal borrowing privilege for longer-term borrowing was liberalized. Banks suffering seasonal deposit drains borrow for as long as four weeks. Also, following the Depository Institutions Deregulation and Monetary Control Act of 1980, which opened the discount window to thrifts, there is an extended credit facility for SLs.

The level of the federal discount rate, taken by itself, is a misleading determinant of the quantity of loans demanded from the Federal Reserve by banks. It is the "difference" between money market rates on other relatively risk-free, short-term debt instruments, primarily the federal funds rate, and the discount rate that should be used in predicting bank borrowing. If the discount rate is less than other short-term money market rates, banks have an incentive to increase their profits by obtaining loans from the reserve banks rather than from these more expensive sources. When the discount rate is below other short-term market rates of interest, banks receive a subsidy from the Federal Reserve in the form of a discount from market rates of interest on money they desire to borrow. Examine Figure 17-4: When the federal funds rate rose far above the

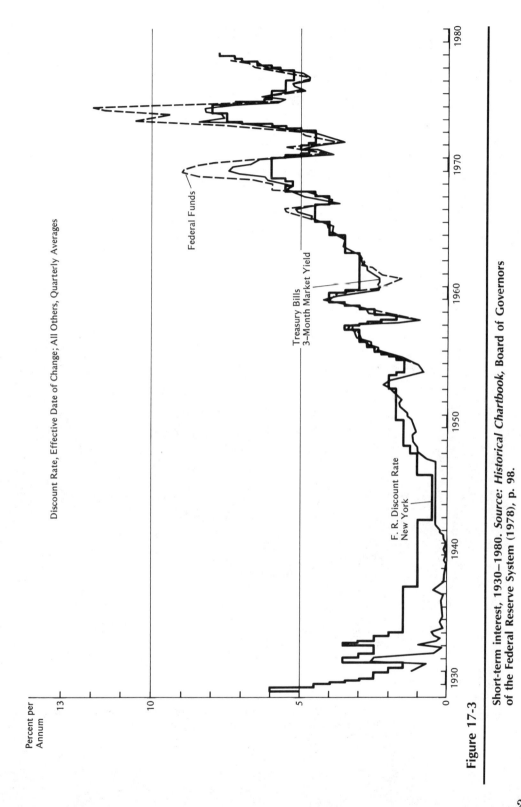

Percent per
Annum

Discount Rate, Effective Date of Change; All Others, Quarterly Averages

Federal Funds

Treasury Bills
3–Month Market Yield

F. R. Discount Rate
New York

Figure 17-3

Short-term interest, 1930–1980. *Source: Historical Chartbook*, **Board of Governors of the Federal Reserve System (1978), p. 98.**

261

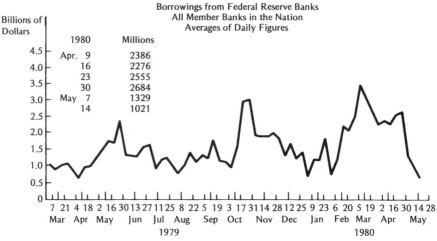

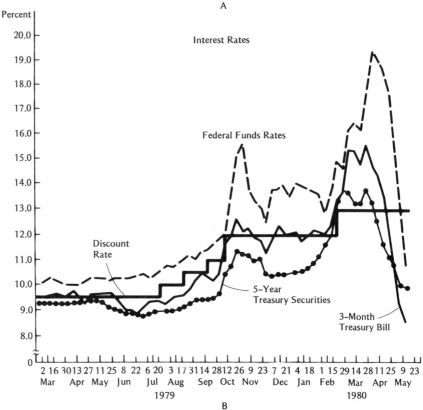

Figure 17-4

Borrowings from the Federal Reserve and the federal funds rates, discount rates, and selected market rates, from March 1979 to May 1980. *Source: U.S. Financial Data,* Federal Reserve Bank of St. Louis (release of May 16, 1980).

discount rate (October and November 1979 and March and April 1980), borrowings were substantial. In May 1980, as the federal funds rate fell, finally becoming lower than the discount rate, borrowing was sharply reduced.

The difference between the Federal Reserve discount rate and other short-term rates of interest is not the only important variable for predicting the quantity of loans demanded by member banks. Some consideration must be given to changes in the Federal Reserve's attitude or policy of discouraging "excessive borrowing" by member banks.

Changes in the discount rate usually receive wide attention. The announcement may temporarily cause changes in economic variables, such as increased fluctuations in stock market prices. These *announcement effects* are sometimes interpreted as the major effect of discount rate changes. It is sometimes said, for example, that an increase in the Federal Reserve discount rate is a signal that the Federal Reserve is raising market interest rates, or that the Federal Reserve thinks rates will rise and is leading the way. Neither conclusion may be true; both are usually wrong. The Federal Reserve discount rate is only one interest rate among many other interest rates on other assets throughout the domestic economy and worldwide financial markets. The Federal Reserve cannot raise interest rates directly. It can change the monetary base and thereby influence interest rates. A change in the Federal Reserve discount rate does not mean that all these other interest rates are thereby also changed. Very often, market interest rates may have risen previously. The rise in the discount rate may merely reflect an effort by the Federal Reserve to bring the discount rate more in line with other market rates of interest.

Member-bank borrowing can significantly affect bank reserves and therefore the potential quantity of money. The change in bank reserves from this source is often very erratic, difficult to predict, and a major source or error, or *leakage*, in the relationship between open-market policy and some desired level of bank reserves. Because of these problems, many economists have made suggestions for changing the Federal Reserve policy on bank borrowing. Many economists think that bank borrowing should be at penalty rates and never subsidized at less than market rates so that it must be allocated on a nonprice basis. The penalty rate could be some permanent high rate, such as a level equal to short-term market rates of interest plus a fixed amount.

Bank Supervision and Regulation by the Federal Reserve

Each of the twelve Federal Reserve banks supervises and examines the state member banks in its districts. Branch and merger applications are processed, applications for membership or termination of membership of banks in the Federal Reserve system are reviewed, and reports on the condition of member banks are examined. Bank examiners are sent out by the reserve banks, but an examination usually "amounts to little more than making routine examinations and requiring the submission of condition and earning reports." All bank holding companies are regulated by the Federal Reserve, which must pass on all mergers and acquisitions.

Specific Credit Regulations by the Federal Reserve

The Federal Reserve has, at times, been given power to regulate the terms of consumer installment credit. From 1941 to 1947, in 1948, during the Korean War until 1952, and again beginning on March 14, 1980, the Board of Governors exercised control over the terms of consumer installment credit. The Credit Control Act of December 23, 1969 (Section 205), provided that "whenever the President determines that such action is necessary or appropriate for the general purpose of preventing or controlling inflation generated by the extension of credit in an excessive volume, the President may authorize the Board to regulate and control any or all extensions of credit."

On March 14, 1980, President Carter authorized the Federal Reserve to implement a number of actions under the 1969 Credit Control Act. The actions were terminated four months later. These actions were summarized in the policy directive of the April 25, 1980, FOMC meeting:

> On March 14 the President announced a broad program of fiscal, energy, credit, and other measures designed to moderate and reduce inflationary forces in a manner that can also lay the groundwork for a return to stable economic growth. Consistent with that objective and with the continuing intent of the Federal Reserve System to restrain growth in money and credit during 1980, the Board of Governors took the following actions to reinforce the effectiveness of the measures announced in October 1979: (1) A specific credit restraint program; (2) A special deposit requirement for all lenders on increases in certain types of consumer credit; (3) An increase in the marginal reserve requirement on managed liabilities of large member banks; (4) A special deposit requirement on increases in managed liabilities of large non-member banks; (5) A special deposit requirement on increases in total assets of money market mutual funds; (6) A surcharge of 3 percentage points on frequent borrowing of large member banks from Federal Reserve Banks.

The imposition of these credit controls caused a sharp contraction in consumer credit and a decline in the ratio of currency to deposits (over what it would have been on the basis of past relationships) as individuals pulled money out of their bank accounts to substitute for credit card purchases. This latter effect caused the money supply to contract. Both effects, together with the surge in interest rates to 20 percent, caused a sharp business decline in 1980 and a jump in the unemployment rate to 7.5 percent by May 1980. The Credit Control Act of 1969 was subsequently legislated to expire in June 1982.

The Federal Reserve Board also regulates the payment of interest on bank deposits. Since the Banking Acts of 1933 and 1935, explicit money interest payments have been prohibited on demand deposits of Federal Reserve member banks and nonmember banks, respectively. Legislation passed in 1980 set up a committee (the Depository Institutions Deregulation Committee) of government regulators to remove interest rate ceilings on accounts by March 31, 1986 (see Exhibit 17-1).

Exhibit 17-1

```
            DEPOSITORY INSTITUTIONS DEREGULATION COMMITTEE
                           PRESS RELEASE

COMPTROLLER OF THE CURRENCY
FEDERAL DEPOSIT INSURANCE CORPORATION
FEDERAL HOME LOAN BANK BOARD
FEDERAL RESERVE BOARD
NATIONAL CREDIT UNION ADMINISTRATION
TREASURY DEPARTMENT

For immediate release                        May 7, 1980

The Depository Institutions Deregulation Committee today
announced that at its first meeting it elected Paul A.
Volcker, Chairman of the Federal Reserve Board, as Its
Chairman.  Irvine H. Sprague, Chairman of the Federal
Deposit Insurance Corporation, was named Vice Chairman.

The Committee was created by the Depository Institutions
Deregulation and Monetary Control Act of 1980, signed on
March 31.  Title II of that Act transferred to the newly
formed Committee the authority to set interest rate
ceilings on deposits of commercial banks, mutual savings
banks and savings and loan associations.  The
Committee's assignment under the Act is to provide for
the orderly phase-out of interest rate ceilings over a
six-year period and eventually to provide depositors
with a market rate of return on their savings.

Members of the Committee are the Secretary of the
Treasury and the chairmen of the Federal Reserve Board,
Federal Deposit Insurance Corporation, Federal Home Loan
Bank Board and the National Credit Union Administration
Board.  The Comptroller of the Currency serves as a
nonvoting member.

In its first substantive action, the Committee requested
comment by June 9 on a proposal to prohibit any premium
or gifts given by an institution upon the opening of a
new account or an addition to an existing account.
Premiums are now limited to $5 (at wholesale, exclusive
of packaging and shipping costs) for deposits of less
than $5,000 and to $10 for deposits of $5,000 or more.

In addition, the Committee proposed to limit any
finder's fees to third parties to cash payments and to
regard any finder's fees as interest to the depositor.

Comment was requested on this proposal, also by June 9.
```

The Securities Exchange Act of 1934 gave the Federal Reserve Board control over margin requirements on loans for the purchase of stocks. The Reserve Board controls margin requirements for stocks on domestic stock exchanges and, as of February 26, 1982, 1509 over-the-counter stocks. The Act was a consequence of the stock market declines in and after 1929. The purpose of the Act was to restrict the use of loans for speculative purposes. Milton Friedman argued against this particular type of credit control and against its supervision by the Board of Governors:

> Because of their dramatic quality, movements in stock prices command more attention from the system and others than their role as a source rather than as a reflection of economic changes justifies. . . . I see no justification for singling out credit extended to purchase or hold securities for special attention. But if this is to be done it should be as part of a policy directed at regulation of security markets and by an agency charged with special responsibilities for such markets, not by the Federal Reserve System.[2]

The eligibility requirements that the Federal Reserve has imposed on collateral for loans it extends to depository institutions are another tool of specific credit policy. Although this policy tool has not been used in recent years, it is well illustrated in a letter sent by the Federal Reserve Board to the Federal Reserve banks on February 2, 1929, the year of the great stock market crash.

> The Federal Reserve Act does not, in the opinion of the Federal Reserve Board, contemplate the use of resources of the Federal Reserve Banks in the creation or extension of speculative credit. A member bank is not within its reasonable claims for rediscount facilities at its Federal Reserve bank when it borrows either for the purpose of making speculative loans or for the purpose of maintaining speculative loans.[3]

Payments Mechanism Functions of the Federal Reserve

The provision of currency and coin, check-clearing services, wire transfer of money, and automated clearing houses for checks are some of the services the Federal Reserve renders to help maintain an efficient payments system in the United States.

Check clearing and the provision of currency and coin cost the Federal Reserve $460 million in 1979 when these services were provided at zero cost to member banks. Legislation passed in 1980 required the Federal Reserve to begin charging for these services by September 1981 and to offer them to all depository institutions on an equal basis, whether or not they were members. The Federal Reserve generally complied except for the charge required on float.

Most of the paper currency in the United States consists of Federal Reserve notes issued in denominations of $1, $2, $5, $10, $20, $50, and $100. The greenbacks, or U.S. notes that the Treasury began printing after the Legal Tender Acts of 1862, are no longer issued by the Treasury, except for the $100 denomination notes.

The Federal Reserve has primary responsibility for supervising and maintaining the quantity of currency and coin in circulation in the United States. When a purchase is made in a retail store, for example, the currency and coins are usually deposited in a depository institution. The depository institution, through its correspondent or directly, deposits most of the currency and coin at the regional Federal Reserve bank or its branch. Expert handlers at the Federal Reserve check the currency for counterfeits. Mutilated coins and worn-out currency are replaced.

The life of a dollar bill was, on average, approximately three years in 1941 and five years in 1976. The actual printing of new paper money and the minting of coins at the Bureau of Engraving and Printing and the Bureau of the Mint are under the jurisdiction of the U.S. Treasury.

The Federal Reserve also provides a Federal Reserve Communications System, or *Fedwire*, through which member banks can transfer their funds and securities. The regional Federal Reserve banks and their branches operate Automated Clearinghouses (ACHs). These computerized systems substitute electronic transfers for actually transporting paper checks. They have been used mostly for recurring transactions, such as direct deposit of payrolls or mortgage payments.

Other Federal Regulatory Agencies for Depository Institutions

The Federal Home Loan Bank Board (FHLBB) supervises savings and loan associations and mutual savings banks, which are its members. Mutual savings banks can also become members of the Federal Reserve System.

The National Credit Union Administration supervises member credit unions. The Central Liquidity Facility for credit unions, which is under the aegis of the National Credit Union Administration, borrows funds from the private sector, which it in turn can lend to credit unions.

Regulation is also administered by federal agencies that provide deposit insurance. The Federal Deposit Insurance Corporation (FDIC) sells insurance for deposits in commercial banks and mutual savings banks. The Federal Savings and Loan Insurance Corporation (FSLIC) sells insurance for deposits in savings and loan associations and mutual savings banks. The National Credit Union Administration sells insurance for credit union deposits: Federal Share Insurance. The deposit insurance from these three federal agencies was raised from $40,000 to $100,000 for each depositor in 1980.

Finally, the Federal Financial Institutions Examination Council (FFIEC), set up in 1978, coordinates information found by examiners of the various federal bank regulatory agencies. This in important, since many of the commercial banks and thrift institutions are examined by examiners from more than one federal regulatory agency. As a result of a desire to guard and preserve exclusive jurisdiction to an agency's area of control, sometimes referred to in Washington as "turf," agency personnel may be tempted to hold information for their own action, when in fact it could be combined with information found by other regulatory agencies into something more useful. In addition, of course, the FFIEC can save other agencies and the taxpayers the cost of obtaining the same information. The coordinating council should dent this problem for bank examination.

Federal Deposit Insurance

The FDIC, an independent federal agency (not under the aegis of another agency or department), was established by the Banking Act of 1933. The FDIC insurance on bank deposits, originally limited to a maximum of $2400, was first issued on January 1, 1934. The maximum insurance was increased a number of times, reaching $100,000 per depositor at each insured bank in 1980. All commercial and mutual savings banks that are members of the Federal Reserve system are required to carry FDIC insurance. Nonmember commercial banks and mutual savings banks may obtain FDIC insurance, but they must first satisfy the general requirements of the FDIC.

The premiums that banks must pay for FDIC insurance were set by statute at $\frac{1}{12}$ of 1 percent of total "assessible deposits." The banks pay half of this premium twice a year on their average assessible deposits in the preceding half-year. The assessible deposits are approximately equal to a bank's total deposits, plus uninvested trust funds, minus some deductions. These deductions include $16\frac{2}{3}$ percent of demand deposits and 1 percent of time and savings deposits.

The FDIC was formed as a corporation, with its entire income consisting of assessments on insured banks. The corporation is authorized to use, but never has used, borrowing privileges of up to $3 billion from the U.S. Treasury.

The FDIC has powers to examine insured banks; to prescribe various rules and regulations; and in some cases, to pass on mergers or consolidations. It has the power to subpoena any officer or employee or any books or records of insured banks that are relevant to its investigations. In addition, the Financial Institutions Regulatory Act of 1978 provides financial institution supervisory agencies, such as the FDIC, with other powers, such as civil money penalties, cease and desist orders, the power of removal and suspension of insiders (those who own a significant portion of the stock in the bank), and the power to approve or disapprove of foreign branches of state nonmember banks.

It is interesting that the Banking Act of 1933 also provided that interest on demand deposits be prohibited and that the FDIC police this regulation for nonmember insured banks and enforce ceiling rates of interest on time and savings deposits. The legislation passed in 1980 to remove ceiling rates over a six-year period included the chairman of the FDIC on the five-member deregulation committee.

The most important and overwhelmingly successful results of the creation of the FDIC has been the virtual elimination of bank runs and the substantial reduction in the number of bank failures. Between 1934 and 1980, there has been an average of only 12.3 insured bank failures per year. This statistic gives a somewhat misleading picture, since bank failures tapered off from a high level in the 1930s. In the post-World War II period, from 1947 to 1980, there was an average of only 6.4 failures per year. Of the 568 banks that failed from 1934 to 1980, most (551) were small, with total assets under $100 million, except for ten banks. The two largest banks that failed in the post-World War II period, with total assets over $1 billion, were United States National Bank of San Diego, California (failed October 18, 1973, with total assets of $1.3 billion), and the Franklin National Bank of New York City (failed October 8, 1974, with total assets of $3.7 billion).

Table 17-2 displays the large and growing number of bank failures up to the advent of the FDIC deposit insurance in 1934. It is evident that the establishment of the Federal Reserve at the end of 1913 did not stop bank suspensions; they kept growing until 1934. Indeed, the presumed function of the Federal Reserve as the lender of last resort may have caused some banks to reduce their reserves and other liquid assets below the level that ordinarily would have been considered prudent. The bankers thought the Federal Reserve stood ready to help them in time of bank runs, but in the period of the greatest number of banks runs, 1930–1933, the Federal Reserve failed to lend the banks much money. One-third of the banks closed permanently during this period.

In 1975, the FDIC had 200 people dealing with bank failures and 1600 field examiners were employed in their Division of Bank Supervisors, examining the 8800 nonmember banks. At that time, the Comptroller of the Currency had 2200 examiners for the 4700 national banks. The Federal Reserve employed another 699 examiners for the 1070 state member banks. The individual 550 states had 1800 examiners in their banking departments, who also examined and supervised state-chartered banks. (The numbers here for examiners and banks are approximate.)

The FDIC developed a list of problem banks which they thought might require insurance funds if corrective actions were not taken. Those banks included national banks and state member and nonmember banks. In 1974, there were about 175 banks on this list, with slightly over 50 of these categorized as having "serious problems." The lists were kept secret, since news of serious illness in a bank can mean immediate death as depositors run for their money.

TABLE 17-2

Total Number of Bank Suspensions in Selected Years, 1865–1969*

Year	Total Number of Suspensions	Total Number of Insured Bank Suspensions	Total Number of Noninsured Bank Suspensions
1865	6	.	6
1875	28	.	28
1885	46	.	46
1895	124	.	124
1905	80	.	80
1915	152	.	152
1925	618	Before	618
1926	976	FDIC	976
1927	669	insurance	669
1928	499	.	499
1929	659	.	659
1930	1352	.	1252
1931	2294	.	2294
1932	1456	.	1456
1933	4004	.	4004
1934	61	9	52
1935	32	26	6
1936	72	69	3
1937	83	76	7
1938	80	73	7
1939	72	60	12
1940	48	43	5
1950	5	4	1
1960	2	1	1
1969	9	9	0
1975	14	13	1
1976	17	16	1
1977	6	6	0
1978	7	7	0
1979	10	10	0
1980	10	10	0

*These figures include mutual savings banks and commercial banks, both of which were insured by the FDIC. There were 1807 noninsured and 14,150 insured banks in 1934.
Source: Historical Statistics of the U.S.: Colonial to 1957 (Washington, D.C.: U.S. Government Printing Office, 1960), pp. 633–637; *1980 Annual Report,* FDIC, p. 290.

Market Rates and Ceiling Rates

The Banking Acts of 1933 and 1935 prohibited the payment of *explicit pecuniary* (money) *interest* on demand deposits by Federal Reserve member banks and nonmember commercial banks, respectively. The words "explicit pecuniary" should be stressed, because "free" services, including convenient branch banks and "gifts" for demand depositors, have partially substituted for money interest payments. Regulation Q of the Federal Reserve Act allows the Board of Governors, the governing body of the Federal Reserve System, to set maximum rates that may be paid on all time deposits of both member (effective 1933) and insured nonmember (effective 1936) banks, and for the savings depositories owned and operated by the federal government in the Postal Savings System, which were run by neighborhood post offices from 1911 until they were closed in 1966.

The setting of maximum interest rates on deposits by the Federal Reserve has had a number of predictable effects. Assume that the federal government were to set a maximum price of ten cents a pound on flour for sale to millers. When the market price is nine cents, no one would be concerned. If the demand for bread were to increase, so that millers would be willing to pay fifteen cents per pound, the millers would rejoice. No miller would have to pay more than ten cents, and they would gain profit, at least in the short run, until farmers shifted into other grains. What if other firms that were not covered by the price control started buying the flour at eleven cents a pound and the millers ran short of flour? Now the millers would complain and ask that the price controls either be made to cover everyone or be abandoned.

When interest rates were low in the depression of the 1930s, Regulation Q was not an effective constraint. In the post-World War II period, when market rates were sufficiently above ceiling rates, there was massive disintermediation from savings and time deposits in commercial banks and thrifts.

The reader may ask why the regulations prohibiting the payment of interest on demand deposits were enacted. One reason given is that if banks were allowed to pay any interest, they would attract more funds than they could "safely" handle. This argument might also be restated as an argument against price competition that could be applied to any industry.

In the 1950s and 1960s, market interest rates frequently went above ceiling rates payable on time deposits at commercial banks. This is shown in Figure 17-5 for commercial banks. Interest payments on demand deposits at commercial banks were prohibited.

In 1966, interest rate limitations were extended to savings and loan associations and mutual savings banks, although at a higher level than those that applied to commercial banks. From 1973 to 1980, the difference was one-fourth of a percentage point on most savings and time deposits. Legislation enacted in 1980 (the Depository Institutions Deregulation and Monetary Control Act of 1980) directed that the ceiling rate limitations, including the differential, be phased out by March 31, 1986.

In 1973, 1974, and again after 1977, market rates soared above ceiling rates, as shown in Figure 17-5. In the first episode, 1973–1974, there was a massive drain of funds out of depository intermediaries. This is called disintermediation, as noted in the preceding chapter.

In the 1978–1980 period, the depository intermediaries were allowed to offer consumer time deposits with yields that were tied to market rates

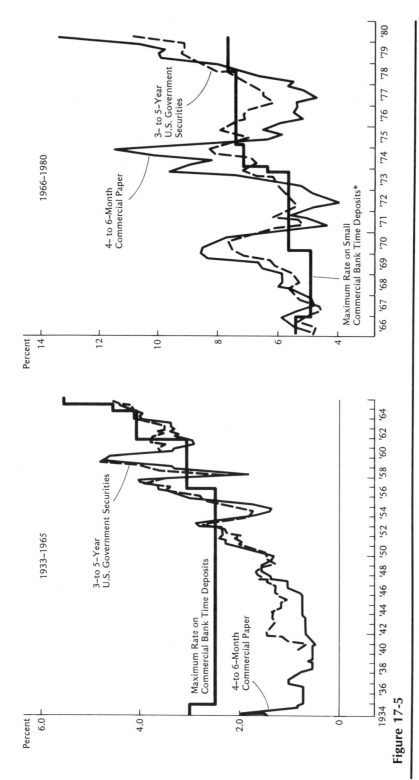

Figure 17-5

Selected market interest rates and ceiling rates on commercial bank time deposits, 1934–1980. *Source:* Scott Winningham and Donald Hagan, "Regulation Q: An Historical Perspective," *Economic Review,* Federal Reserve Bank of Kansas City (April 1980), pp. 4, 7.

*Except for "wild card" certificates in 1973 and three floating-rate certificates since June 1978. "Wild card" certificates was the name applied to CDs with denominations of $1000 or more and maturities of four years or more.

(called *money market certificates*), and disintermediation was not as serious for the depository intermediaries, except for the shift to money market funds discussed subsequently. (Since 1970, short term—less than ninety days' maturity—and since 1973, all business time deposits, called *certificates of deposit*, in denominations of $100,000 or more have had no ceiling limitations.)

The legislation in 1980 and much of the story of depository intermediaries in the 1970s, including the huge growth of money market funds, were a result of market interest rates rising through the ceiling, the ceiling rate on money interest payments that could be paid to depositors at the depository intermediaries.

NOWs, ATSs, Share Drafts, and Remotes

Prior to 1972, only commercial banks and a few savings banks (with state deposit insurance) offered third-party payment services—checking accounts. A thrift institution (savings and loan associations, mutual savings banks, and credit unions) would, upon presentation of a passbook—in person or by mail—issue a check drawn on its account at a commercial bank. The thrift did not offer the depositor the opportunity to withdraw and transfer his or her funds by check. The thrifts paid interest on their deposits, and it was presumed to be illegal to offer checking services for these deposits.

Or was it? In July 1970, a mutual savings bank in Massachusetts proposed a plan to the state banking commissioner to allow checking-type accounts by means of third-party "negotiable orders of withdrawal," or NOW accounts. Those accounts would pay interest just as other savings accounts but would be accessible by check. Savings and loan associations have been permitted by the Housing Act of 1970 to make preauthorized transfers from savings accounts for household-related bills since September 1970, but NOW accounts were a clearly broadened power, and the Massachusetts state banking commissioner said no to the proposal. However, in May 1972, the Massachusetts Supreme Judicial Court unanimously allowed MSBs in Massachusetts to offer NOW accounts. In September 1972, a savings bank in New Hampshire began offering NOWs. The NOW account cat was out of the bag and the U.S. Congress gave chase when in August 1973 all depository institutions in Massachusetts and New Hampshire except credit unions were authorized by federal law to offer NOWs. In 1976, federal legislation authorized NOW accounts in the states of Connecticut, Maine, Rhode Island, and Vermont; and the Financial Institutions Regulatory Act allowed them in New York in 1979.

Legislation submitted by the Carter administration for the Federal Reserve in the 95th Congress (1977 and 1978) would have extended NOW accounts nationwide. Unfortunately for the success of this provision, the proposal also contained authority for the Federal Reserve to pay interest on the reserves it required of its 5628 member banks. This additional ornament—intended to help the Federal Reserve hold on to its member banks—did not win the necessary support from a budget-minded Congress. It died in the Senate, and hearings were never held in the House of Representatives.

Despite federal legislation confining NOWs to New England and New York, checking deposits and remote cash-dispensing machines began to spread. In January 1974, First Federal Savings and Loan of Lincoln, Nebraska, installed automatic terminal facilities (ATFs) or remotes in two supermarkets, allowing remote cash withdrawals from savings accounts. Other savings and loan associations adopted such systems.

Also in 1974, money market mutual funds began offering their shareholders withdrawals by check. In 1974, some federal credit unions began offering checking accounts, called share drafts.

Why had all this happened? Higher market interest rates combined with a prohibition against the payment of interest on demand deposits at commercial banks made it profitable to sell substitutes for commercial bank deposits. That is, alternative types of third-party payment systems developed.

The Federal Reserve, under pressure from those compelling forces in the economy and still without a successful bill in Congress that would authorize nationwide NOW accounts, authorized a new type of account. On November 1, 1978, commercial banks were authorized to offer savings accounts that could be automatically transferred to checking accounts (automatic transfer services or ATS accounts) whenever funds were needed to cover a check. Although large minimum balances were imposed by the private banks on these ATS accounts, they were a means of paying interest on checking accounts.

On April 20, 1979, the U.S. Court of Appeals in Washington ruled that all interest-paying checking accounts, except those specifically authorized by Congress to operate in the six New England states and New York, were illegal. All ATS accounts, share draft accounts at credit unions, and the remote cash-disbursing units of savings and loan associations (ATFs) would be illegal. The court delayed the effective date of its ruling until January 1980 to give Congress a chance to act.

An excerpt from the now defunct *Washington Star* of April 21, 1979, reports on this decision. It also captures part of the scramble in the thrifts and commercial banking industries to obtain favorable government regulations while at the same time dodging the regulations that did exist, such as the prohibition against interest payments on demand deposits (page A6, a jump from a page 1 story):

> The decision covers three different suits. In each one, a section of the industry is trying to take away the interest-bearing checking account from another while at the same time trying to keep its own account.
>
> The American Bankers Association, which represents commercial banks and benefits from the automatic transfer account, sued the National Credit Union Administration in an effort to take away the share draft account.

The United States League of Savings Associations, which represents the savings and loan industry and has the remote service unit, sued the Fed and the FDIC to take away the automatic transfer.

And the Independent Bankers Association of America, which could benefit from the new accounts, sued the Federal Home Loan Bank Board, which regulates the savings and loan industry, to take away the remote service unit.

In its decision, the court recognized the narrowing of differences among financial institutions and said it was a change that should be addressed by Congress.

. . . Three separate and distinct types of financial institutions created . . . to serve different public needs have now become . . . three separate but homogeneous types of financial institutions offering virtually identical services to the public, all without the benefit of congressional consideration. . . .

Congress reacted with a three-month extension—until April 1980—that also contained a provision that gave NOW accounts to New Jersey.

Then at the last moment, March 31, 1980, after two and a half years of hearings in both the House of Representatives and the Senate and a prolonged battle between interest groups, a major bill was passed and signed into law. The Depository Institutions Deregulation and Monetary Control Act of 1980 (or simply Monetary Control Act of 1980) authorized nationwide NOW accounts and provided that the ceilings on interest on accounts be phased out over a six-year period. The law also extended the types of assets the thrifts were authorized to buy, moved toward eliminating state usury ceilings, and imposed federal reserve requirements on all depository institutions that offered checkable deposits or business certificates of deposits with maturities of less than four years. It increased federal deposit insurance from $40,000 per depositor at a financial depository to $100,000.

Usury Laws

Laws prohibiting the payment of interest above a ceiling rate grew out of centuries of belief that the payment of interest is a form of extortion since it is a transfer of funds to an individual who performs no labor in return. The major religions have, in their history, teachings against the sins of interest payment. Some communist countries, following Marxist ideology that defines value in units of labor, attempt to prohibit all interest payments.

Viewed in economic terms as the opportunity cost of forgone consumption; the rate of productivity (both described in Chapter 9); or, simply, the rate of change of price of a stored commodity per unit time (elaborated subsequently), it can be seen that no law can prevent the presence of the rate of interest. Usury laws change the allocation of credit, often in favor of those who find ways to legally and illegally evade them. A usury law also can impose a loss in welfare to the economy with no fully offsetting benefit to anyone. Such welfare losses arise from depriving credit to those who would have borrowed at a lower rate before evasion costs and monopolistic criminal (juice) loans above the usury interest rate ceilings, raise the rates, and reduce the quantity supplied. This is called a *dead weight loss*, that is, a welfare loss to the society that is not offset by benefits to someone else. Usury laws are an inducement, as strong as prohibition, for criminals to make loans above ceiling rates. Usury laws severely hurt lenders and borrowers in the 1970s when market rates rose above the ceiling rates of the individual states. Consumer loans, such as on credit cards, incurred a loss at state usury ceilings. Efforts were made to curtail credit card credit. Mortgage lending in many states came to a halt, or where it was legal, lenders raised the price of the house to compensate. These increases in the price of the house are called *points*. Each point is 1 percent of the cost of the house and is paid to the lender.

The system of points on mortgages illuminates the principle that usury ceilings can be made ineffective without price controls. To see this, consider that a rate of interest can be viewed as the rate of change of the price of a stored commodity minus storage costs per dollar, both per unit time. Thus a quantity of wheat that is stored may be expected to rise in price from $3.50 a bushel to $3.885 a bushel in one year. This is an 11 percent real rate of interest minus storage costs per dollar to the holder. The cost of storage per dollar of wheat will not exceed the expected rate of price rise per period or the rate of return from storing wheat will be zero. Effective price controls could lower the rate of return or interest from holding the commodity. These price controls could make the rate of return from storing wheat lower than alternative investments. None would be stored in the summer when the price is low to be sold in the winter when the price is high. The population would starve to death unless home storage and other legal and illegal ways were found to evade the price control distortion.

The necessity of either price controls or the prevention of part of the sales price being paid to the lender, to make usury laws effective, is readily apparent for nominal interest rates, the observable rate on a loan. Consider two financing arrangements for the purchase of a used automobile. Both require no money down and a $1250 payment in one year. The first arrangement is usurious (violates the assumed 18 percent state usury law). It is listed as a $1000 automobile financed by a loan requiring 25 percent interest. The second financing arrangement involves an 18 percent loan, with the automobile priced at $1059.32. Since the payments are identical, the borrowers should be indifferent. If he or she objects to 18 percent, because of interest rate illusion, a 1 percent loan arrangement with the same $1250 final payment can be arranged. In that case, the automobile will be priced at $1237.62. A zero interest rate can also be arranged for those who decline to pay any interest.

The Depository Institutions and Monetary Control Act of 1980 (Public Law 96-221) had provisions for, at least temporarily, eliminating some usury ceiling distortions. State usury laws limiting the amount of interest that could be charged on various kinds of loans by all federally insured lenders (primarily the depository intermediaries) were provisionally overridden. The term "provisionally" is used because the states were given the right to individually override this part of the federal law. Business and agriculture loan usury laws of the states were overridden for three years unless the states revoked that provision sooner.

Federal usury limits in terms of percentage points above the Federal Reserve discount rate were mandated for various kinds of loans. The usury ceiling for credit unions was raised from 12 to 15 percent and the National Credit Union Administration was authorized to raise the ceiling further.

NOTES

1. This is part of the preamble to the Federal Reserve Act of 1913.
2. Milton Friedman, *A Program for Monetary Stability* (New York: Fordham University Press, 1960), p. 27.
3. *Fifth Annual Report of the Federal Reserve Board*, 1928, p. 8.

STUDY QUESTIONS

1. What is the Federal Reserve, and what nonmonetary regulatory functions does it perform? Explain.

2. Describe the functions of the Board of Governors and the FOMC of the Federal Reserve.

3. What functions are performed by the regional banks of the Federal Reserve?

4. How do market interest rates affect advances from the Federal Reserve?

5. What regulatory powers does the FDIC have?

6. What changes affecting depository institutions were related to usury market interest rates and ceiling rates?

7. Explain the rise of NOWs, AFTs, share drafts, and remotes.

8. What is the purpose of the Federal Financial Examination Council?

9. No usury laws prevent the interest rates from ever rising above the legal ceiling. Why? Explain.

18

Depository Intermediaries

Introduction

The depository intermediaries all have an important common characteristic. They create liabilities that are either included in common concepts of money or are only one step away and have many of the properties of money. The number of total assets of the depository intermediaries are shown by type in Table 18-1. Commercial banks dominate this group, although the relatively small credit unions are most numerous. The average size of the 14,720 commercial banks in September 1981 had $109.8 million in total assets and the average size of the 21,306 credit unions had $0.1 million. The average size of the 4439 saving and loan associations (SLs) was $147.5 million in assets, and the 456 mutual savings banks (MSBs) had an average of $384.2 million in assets.

On January 1, 1981, all depository intermediaries were authorized to issue checkable consumer accounts on which interest could be paid, with ceiling limitations that were scheduled to be completely removed by 1986.

TABLE 18-1

The Assets and Number of Depository Intermediaries, September 1981

	Number	Total Assets (Billions of Dollars)	Percentage of Total Assets
All commercial banks	14,720	1,617.1	64.2
Savings and loan associations	4,439	654.6	26.0
Mutual savings banks	456	175.2	7.0
Credit unions	21,360*	73.7	2.9
Total	40,921	2,520.6	

*End of 1981.
Source: *Federal Reserve Bulletin* (December 1981), pp. A17 and A29; Federal Home Loan Bank Board and Savings and Loan League; National Association of Mutual Savings Banks; National Credit Union Administration.

Commercial Banks

Commercial banks had 61 percent of the deposits of depository intermediaries in June 1981. The commercial banks had a near monopoly in the provision of checking services until 1973, when NOW accounts were introduced in New England. Then in 1981, interest-paying checking accounts were authorized for all depository institutions. Will the different depository institutions retain their specialized characteristics and their market share, or will there be a general homogenization—so that they become more and more alike—with the thrifts gaining ground on the commercial banks? To answer those questions with some perspective, the reader must first gain some understanding of the nature of the commercial banking industry.

Banking institutions associated with commercial banks that are operated by the government should be distinguished from the private part of the banking system. This is a little confusion because of the Federal Reserve System. The Board of Governors of the Federal Reserve in Washington, D.C., and the twelve regional Federal Reserve banks and their branches, are essentially run by the government. The purist must note that the twelve regional Federal Reserve banks are nominally organized as private corporations. They are, however, supposed to operate with national goals rather than for profit maximization.

Private commercial banks and mutual savings banks can join the Federal Reserve System. As Table 18-2 indicates, 5492 private banks (37.3 percent of all commercial banks) were Federal Reserve member banks (or simply member banks) in December 1981. These member banks had 74.1 percent of checkable deposits and 66.0 percent of noncheckable savings deposits plus time deposits, or 68.8 percent of the total deposits.

In addition to the option of membership in the Federal Reserve System, private commercial banks may purchase federal insurance for their

TABLE 18-2

Classification of the Number and Amount of Domestic Deposits of U.S. Commercial Banks by Insurance Status, Federal Reserve Membership, and Type of Charter,* December 1981[†,‡]
(Deposits in Billions of Dollars)

	(1)	(2)	(3)	(4)	(5)	(6)	(7)	(8)
	All Commercial Banks	Insured Commercial Banks					Uninsured Commercial Banks	Insured and Uninsured
			Members of the Federal Reserve			Nonmember State Banks (Col. 2 − Col. 3)	Uninsured State Banks (Col. 1 − Col. 2)	State Banks (Cols. 5 + 6 + 7)
	Total	Total	Total	National Banks	State Banks			
Number	14,738	14,426	5,492	4,471	1,021	8,934	312	10,267
Percentage	100	97.9	37.3	30.3	6.9	60.6	2.1	69.6
Checkable deposits, demand ATS,[§] NOW								
Amount	452.949	449.118	335.438	254.126	81.312	113.680	3.831	198.823
Percentage	100	99.2	74.1	56.1	18.0	25.1	0.8	43.9
Other deposits[¶]								
Amount	862.383	821.939	568.914	456.412	112.502	253.025	40.446	405.973
Percentage	100	95.3	66.0	52.9	13.0	29.3	4.7	47.1
Total net								
Amount	1,315.335	1,271.058	904.352	710.539	193.813	366.706	44.277	604.796
Percentage	100	96.6	68.8	54.0	14.7	27.9	3.4	46.0

*State or national charter.
[†]Call data estimates.
[‡]Totals may reflect small rounding errors and deposits are unadjusted so that they include government deposits, domestic interbank deposits, and bank float.
[§]Automatic transfer service deposits.
[¶]Includes noncheckable savings and time deposits.
Source: Board of Governors of the Federal Reserve Board, unpublished.

depositors from the Federal Deposit Insurance Corporation (FDIC). The FDIC is a federal agency that provides insurance and regulation for insured banks. Most commercial banks (97.9 percent, with 96.6 percent of deposits) have this insurance.

Individuals who wish to open a bank must receive a charter from either a state government or the federal government. Prior to the Civil War, the federal government granted only a few charters to private commercial banks. The First Bank of the United States (1791–1811) and the Second Bank of the United States (1816–1836) operated under federal charters and served as the primary banker for the federal government. Other commercial banks operated under state charters until the passage of the National Banking Act of 1863, which allowed private commercial banks to operate under federal charters. The federal charters are issued by the Office of the Comptroller of the Currency, whose office supervises the national banks. The Comptroller of the Currency is part of the Treasury Department. Federally chartered private banks are referred to as *national banks*, while private banks operating under state charters are referred to as *state banks*. National banks can be identified by the word "national" in their name; or instead of the word "national," the letters NA are added to indicate "national association."

All national banks must be Federal Reserve members, and all Federal Reserve member banks must carry FDIC insurance. Most state banks, 60.6 percent, with 27.9 percent of total deposits, are not Federal Reserve members, as shown in Table 18-2. There were 4471 national banks (30.3 percent) and 10,267 state banks (69.6 percent) in December 1981.

Correspondent Banks

Commercial banks that supply services to other commercial banks are called *correspondent banks*. The correspondent bank is paid indirectly, in the form of income from deposit balances maintained by its bank customers, as well as by direct money payments. Small banks may have five or six correspondent banks, which provide many services: bookkeeping services (especially those that require large computers); assistance in the sale or purchase of assets (including consolidation of purchases with other buyers); and the provision of information about capital markets (including the sale of equity shares in their banks). Large banks may have as many as thirty correspondent banks that provide services and representation in other localities [including banks that provide services and representation in other localities (including foreign countries)] and specialized services that the correspondents can offer at a smaller cost.

The Federal Reserve has until 1981 provided free check-clearing facilities to its members, but nonmember banks relied entirely on correspondent banks to clear their checks. The correspondent banks often clear nonmember banks' checks through the Federal Reserve. In 1979, the Federal Reserve cleared 32 billion checks, totaling $35 trillion. Before September 1981, the Federal Reserve was required by law to charge a fee for its check-clearing services and to make these services available to all depository intermediaries.

Branch Banking

All states have some form of *branch banking*: that is, banking locations other than their main facilities. There were 41,902 deposit branches operating on December 31, 1980. The location of those branches is often limited by state law, and banks are forbidden from operating in more than one of the fifty states.[1] In some states, commercial banks have been allowed to open branch offices within a given distance from their main office or within the county where their main office is located. In some states, bank offices (not branches) are limited to particular functions, such as business other than the reception or withdrawal of deposits.

Laws governing the number and type of branches a bank may have affect the amount of deposits it can obtain, as well as the type of local competition it faces from other banks and financial intermediaries. Where branch banking is limited, substitutes for branch banks develop. The currency exchange found, for example, throughout the Chicago area is one such substitute that provides services for transferring funds. Currency exchanges cash checks, sell money orders and travelers checks, and provide other associated services.

Bank of America, the country's largest bank, located in California where branching is allowed, had 1092 branches at the end of 1977. The Continental Illinois Bank and Trust Co. and the First National Bank, the two largest banks in Illinois, had no branches outside the downtown Chicago area, since Illinois has tight restrictions on branches.

The use of automatic terminal facilities (ATFs), or remotes, for depositing and withdrawing money opened a new method for banks to obtain branches. Regulations for those remote terminals were more favorable for thrift institutions than for commercial banks, however. The Federal Home Loan Board authorized off-premises bank terminals. The First Federal Savings and Loan Association of Lincoln, Nebraska, opened branch terminals in the Hinky Dinky Food Stores.

Commercial banks faced a tougher obstacle. An important banking act, the McFadden Act of 1927, carefully defined branches in a manner that the U.S. Circuit Court of Appeals in Illinois interpreted as a prohibition against these remote terminals. Therefore, Illinois banks were not able to open the remote terminals. National banks are only allowed to open branches if it is permitted by the individual state laws.

The concept of what a branch is has been completely muddied by the invention of remote terminals. It is possible, for example, for an individual to use his or her telephone as a remote bank terminal for many kinds of bank business. The telephone could be plugged into a computer at the bank by dialing a particular number (the personal identification number or PIN), and the individual could punch a code into the telephone with appropriate instructions. A telephone call could, for example, be used to transfer money to a food market's account. Separate calls need not be placed if the food store rented lines and the customer merely placed an identification card (and punched a secret number) in a terminal permanently in service. In this way, the food market could instantly be paid for its sale of food to the customer without waiting for a check to clear. Bank One, an Ohio bank holding company, demonstrated a home banking computer that utilized a telephone and the homeowner's television set in 1980. This is a remote phone terminal for private homes. If developments such as these are implemented, the gray area of what is and is not a branch will need to be clarified.

Up to this point, the discussion has dealt only with branches authorized to receive deposits. Banks, through their holding company organizations, can open branches throughout the country that offer all services except the reception or withdrawal of funds from deposits. These may take the form of loan offices; consumer credit card facilities; or, in Washington, D.C., an office for lobbying and gathering information on laws and regulations relevant to the bank. In addition, holding companies may control a number of banks in a single state. Although these subsidiary banks have different names, many in the field would view them as similar to branches, especially in analyses of competition between depository institutions.

Bank Holding Companies

A bank holding company is a company that holds controlling stock in one or more commercial banks. By 1978, bank holding companies had become the predominant organizational form of commercial banking in the United States, with 71 percent of all domestic bank deposits in holding company banks. As of December 31, 1980, 3057 registered bank holding companies were in existence. A sample of 409 bank holding companies that each had more than $100 million in assets at year-end 1980 owned banks with deposits of $985.6 billion, or approximately 66.5 percent of deposits in U.S. banks.[2]

The Banking Act of 1933, which also established deposit insurance, provided mild regulation for bank holding companies. A bank holding company was defined in that law as "any corporation, business trust association or similar organization which owns or controls directly or indirectly either a majority of the shares of the capital stock of a member bank or more than 50 percent of the number of shares voted for the election of directors of any one bank at the preceding election or controls in any manner the election of the majority of directors of any one bank." This Act covered only those holding companies that own Federal Reserve member banks.

The Banking Act of 1935 provided an exemption for most one-bank holding companies, that is, holding companies that own only one bank.

Pressure mounted for some legislation, including a plea by President Franklin Roosevelt in a special message to Congress in 1938. This pressure did not produce federal legislation until the Bank Holding Company Act of 1956 was passed. This Act set a new standard for a bank holding company as an organization owning 25 percent or more of the stock of two or more banks. It gave the Federal Reserve the power to supervise bank holding companies and to approve or disapprove of their acquisition of additional banks, whether or not the banks were members. Existing interstate holding companies were allowed to retain their subsidiary banks. This practice is known as *grandfathering in existing structures* and explains why some holding companies own banks in more than one state. The Act required that future interstate acquisitions be subject to specific authorization by individual state law. Such authorization did not exist in any state, so that the formation of nationwide bank holding companies was halted.

One of the primary reasons for forming holding companies, other than the obvious reason of acquiring chains of additional banks, is to engage in certain activities that are not allowed to banks. These activities include mortgage banking and the development of out-of-state consumer finance companies. A 1956 law allowed multibank holding companies to operate safe depository companies, to liquidate property acquired by subsidiary banks, to own and manage holding company property, and to provide services to subsidiary banks. The Federal Reserve Board was permitted to allow or deny other nonbank activities, such as the operation of an insurance company, if these activities were closely related to the business of banking. During the 1970s, bank holding companies purchased a number of existing firms in related fields, as shown in Table 18-3.

This expansion of commercial banks into other fields can be viewed as part of a process of making banks more like other financial intermediaries, a process induced by the desire to compete more effectively. The process is not one-directional. Other financial intermediaries, such as brokerage houses, which originally made their income on commissions from buying and selling securities, are becoming more like banks, as some of them offer services that closely resemble bank deposit services.

In 1966, amendments to the 1956 Act were passed that expanded the number of organizations that were covered to registered investment companies and their affiliates; religious, charitable, and educational institutions; and nonbusiness long-term trusts. The Alfred I. du Pont es-

TABLE 18-3

Number of Approved Acquisitions of Nonbank Firms by Bank Holding Companies, by Activity, 1971–1977

Activity	1971	1972	1973	1974	1975	1976	1977	Total
Mortgage banking	2	11	34	33	13	3	12	108
Consumer finance*	2	26	231	160	8	58	14	499
Factoring	0	4	3	2	0	2	2	13
Insurance agencies	0	13	25	34	33	26	10	141
Insurance underwriting	0	0	13	13	13	17	8	64
Trust activities	1	1	4	1	3	3	1	14
Leasing	1	1	8	4	3	14	5	36
Community development	0	0	0	0	0	0	2	2
Financial advice	0	0	5	11	1	1	9	27
Data processing	0	1	6	6	4	4	16	37
Others	0	2	3	0	4	10	16	35
Total	6	59	332	264	82	136	95	976

*Includes commercial finance.
Source: *Federal Reserve Bulletin* (January 1980), p. 4.

tate, which controlled 31 banks, and Financial General Corporation, which through subsidiaries owned 21 banks in five states and the District of Columbia, are two examples of organizations that were brought under the Bank Holding Company Act of 1956.

As multibank holding companies grew rapidly, new amendments were passed in 1970 which allowed the Board of Governors to determine that a corporation is a bank holding company if it controls a bank, even without owning 25 percent of the stock.

Meanwhile, one-bank holding companies were also growing very rapidly, from 550 in 1965 to 1440 at the end of 1970. Favorable tax treatment and ease in raising funds were important reasons for this growth. Bank investors found that by forming a one-bank holding company to own their bank, the bank could circumvent the ceiling interest rates that could be paid on deposits and raise money directly by having the bank holding company sell debt instruments, which had the advantage of no ceiling rate and the disadvantage of no FDIC insurance. In addition, nonbank activities of one-bank holding companies, such as loan agencies, could cross state lines and expand throughout the country. Representative Wright Patman, former chairman of the House Banking Committee, introduced a bill that was enacted into law at the end of 1970, which finally brought one-bank holding companies under the regulatory apparatus of the Federal Reserve.

From 1971 to 1976, bank holding companies continued to grow rapidly. The Board of Governors received 745 applications to form new bank holding companies, and only 37 were denied. The board approved acquisitions of 1377 subsidiary banks by existing holding companies, including 288 newly organized subsidiary banks (called *de novo banks*). Holding companies were operating in all fifty states and the District of Columbia.

There was concern as to whether or not multibank holding companies were a vehicle whereby one or a few banks in a state could buy out most of the banks within a state and exert monopolistic control over the banking industry in that state. At the end of 1976, bank holding companies held 10 percent or less of the deposits in one state; 10 to 30 percent in six states; 30 to 50 percent in nine states and the District of Columbia; 50 to 75 percent in twenty-six states; and 75 percent in nine states.[3]

The effect on competition of having a significant number of banks in one state, but no more than one in each locale, owned by one holding company is difficult to ascertain. Nevertheless, because a line cannot be drawn around capital markets, the market for loans and deposits must be affected. It is improbable that a borrower could go down the road to the next town and receive a truly independent, competitive bid on a checking account service or a loan if both banks had the same owner and the same loan policies. In addition, ownership of a substantial segment of an entire state's banking industry can provide political power, power that could be used against competitors. On the other side of this argument is the contention that the small, independent, hometown bank can be a very powerful monopoly unless bank branches, subsidiary holding company banks, and other depository intermediaries come to town. The small, independent, hometown banker may take his monopoly power in terms of favors to the "good old boy network" rather than allocating services to the highest bidder. Competition can be effective medicine for eliminating this form of rationing.

Income and Portfolio of Commercial Banks

A summary of the assets and liabilities of commercial banks in 1980 is shown in Table 18-4, and the income and operating expenses of commercial banks are shown in Table 18-5. What are the central points of these tables?

First, excluding interbank loans, commercial banks made almost one-third of their loans to businesses: $256.2 billion, or 32.1 percent. Commercial banks are the primary depository intermediary lending to businesses.

Second, 75 percent of their loans and investments was loans, and 25 percent was securities. The securities part of the portfolio of commercial banks has been growing at a much slower rate than the loan part. This division in income-earning assets is reflected in the income record in

TABLE 18-4

Assets and Liabilities of U.S. Commercial Banks, February 1980 (Billions of Dollars)

Assets	
Loans and investments	1143.7
Loans, gross	857.1
Interbank	58.0
Commercial and industrial	542.9
U.S. Treasury securities	93.6
Other securities	192.9
Cash assets, total	149.9
Currency and coin	17.1
Reserves with Federal Reserve banks	30.7
Balances with depository institutions	43.4
Cash items in process of collection	58.7
Other assets	65.1
Total assets/total liabilities and capital	1358.7
Liabilities	
Deposits	1029.1
Demand	358.7
Savings	200.0
Time	470.4
Borrowings	145.1
Other liabilities	81.6
Residual (assets less liabilities)	102.9

Source: Federal Reserve Bulletin (March 1980), Table A.16.

TABLE 18-5

Income and Expenses of 14,395 Insured Commercial Banks for Six Months Ending June 30, 1978

Sources and Disposition of Income	Amount (Thousands of Dollars)	Percent of Income and Operating Expense
Operating income—total	52,634,160	6.4 Income from loans
Interest and fees on loans	34,957,228	
Interest on balances with banks	3,006,829	5.7
income on federal funds sold and securities purchased under agreements to resell in domestic offices	1,658,569 ⎫	
Interest on U.S. Treasury securities	3,243,482 ⎪	
Interest on obligations of other U.S. government agencies and corporations	1,369,954 ⎬	18.3 Interest and dividend income
Income on obligations of states and political subdivisions of the U.S.	2,849,804 ⎪	
Interest on other bonds, notes, and debentures	465,589 ⎪	
Dividends on stock	60,737 ⎭	
Income from direct lease financing	401,965	0.8
Income from fiduciary activities	1,046,029	2.0
Service charges on deposit accounts in domestic offices	979,120 ⎫	4.5
Other service charges, commissions, and fees	1,381,071 ⎭	
Other income	1,213,783	2.3
		100
Operating expenses—total	45,425,905	
Salaries and employee benefits	8,964,643	19.7 Salaries
Interest on time certificates of deposit of $100,000 or more issued by domestic offices	4,946,134 ⎫	
Interest on deposits in foreign offices	6,343,941 ⎬	50.5 Interest and deposits
Interest on other deposits	11,641,049 ⎭	
Expense of federal funds purchased and securities sold under agreements to repurchase in domestic offices	3,143,451 ⎫	8.7 Interest on
Interest on other borrowed money	571,774 ⎬	loans to
Interest on subordinated notes and debentures	217,095 ⎭	banks
Occupancy expense of bank premises, gross	1,918,261	
Less: Rental income	293,105 ⎫	
Occupancy expense of bank premises, net	1,625,156 ⎪	
Furniture and equipment expense	1,069,006 ⎬	21.1 Other
Provision for possible loan losses	1,563,753 ⎪	
Other expenses	5,339,903 ⎭	
		100
Income before income taxes and securities gains or losses	7,208,225	
Applicable income taxes	1,952,230	
Income before securities gains or losses	5,256,025	
Securities gains (losses), gross	81,180-	
Applicable income taxes	47,334-	
Securities gains (losses), net	33,846-	
Income before extraordinary items	5,222,179	
Extraordinary items, gross	13,336	
Applicable income taxes	4,722-	
Extraordinary items, net	18,058	
Net income	5,240,237	

Source: Assets and Liabilities: Commercial and Mutual Savings Banks, June 30, 1978, Board of Governors of the Federal Reserve System, Federal Deposit Insurance Corporation, Office of the Comptroller of the Currency, p. 126.

Table 18-5, where 66.4 percent of the income comes from interest on loans and 18.3 percent from securities.

Third, 50.5 percent of the operating expenses was interest on deposits.

A less important, but interesting, point is that commercial banks earned significant income from their interbank deposits in other banks, 5.7 percent of their income.

The Prime Rate

Commercial banks have an entire range of rates for loans to borrowers, ostensibly hinged to their *prime rate*. Sometimes, short-term business loan rates are made to float up and down with the prime rate. The prime rate can be defined as the advertised rate presumably available to the most creditworthy business borrowers for ninety-day loans, although there is no consensus on which short maturity is meant. Other commercial bank loan rates are supposed to be higher, according to different levels of default risk, administrative costs, and different maturities.

The Federal Reserve conducts quarterly surveys of bank lending practices. The survey includes 20,000 loans at 340 commercial banks (see Table 18-6).

TABLE 18-6

Short-Term Business Lending Below the Prime Rate by Selected Classes of Banks, 1979–1981*

	Percent of Gross Loan Extensions Made at Rates Below Prime							Spread Between Prime Rate and Weighted Average Rate on Loans Made Below Prime (Basis Points)[†]						
	1979		1980				1981	1979		1980				1981
Class of Bank	Aug. 7–12	Nov. 6–11	Feb. 4–9	May 5–10	Aug. 4–8	Nov. 3–8	Feb. 2–7	Aug. 7–12	Nov. 6–11	Feb. 4–9	May 5–10	Aug. 4–8	Nov. 3–8	Feb. 2–7
48 large	37.2	19.8	50.0	53.0	57.9	20.3	71.5	58	118	123	413	108	65	181
13 money center	44.7	25.0	55.2	61.1	59.4	22.5	60.6	56	114	116	433	107	45	179
Large nonmoney center	21.9	9.9	38.7	32.9	54.1	15.1	53.0	64	138	138	310	110	130	189
Large New York City	46.9	28.9	67.0	60.7	61.7	21.3	78.9	60	118	118	426	99	32	177
Large non-New York City	24.3	12.1	29.8	45.1	52.3	19.0	60.6	51	120	130	392	123	113	187
Medium and smaller	21.2	26.6	15.2	26.8	16.3	16.0	23.2	107	174	211	247	120	177	309

*Calculations are made on prime rates reported by respondent banks. There are approximately 340 banks in the survey, which report on approximately 20,000 loans.

[†]A basis point is $\frac{1}{100}$ of a percentage point. Thus 426 basis points is 4.26 percentage points.

Source: "Surveys of Terms of Bank Lending," Board of Governors of the Federal Reserve System, reprinted in the Staff Report for the Committee on Banking, Finance and Urban Affairs, U.S. House of Representatives, *An Analysis of Prime Rate Lending Practices at the Ten Largest United States Banks,* conducted under the direction of Robert Auerbach, economist for the Committee (Washington, D.C.: U.S. Government Printing Office, April 1981).

These surveys indicate a sharp increase in below-prime-rate lending beginning in 1980. The large New York banks made more than 60 percent of their business loans below their publicly announced prime rate in four of the five quarters from the first quarter of 1980 through the first quarter of 1981.

Although this period in 1980 stands out with its significantly higher percentage of below-prime-rate short-term loans by large banks, the practice of making below-prime-rate loans appears to be have been quite pervasive and on the increase throughout the period from 1977 to February 1981, the years for which estimates were available. Bank loans at below prime rates rose from 8.8 percent in 1977, to 16.1 percent in 1978, to 32.6 percent in 1979, and to 58.8 percent of all new loans in May 1980 at 48 large banks surveyed by the Federal Reserve. Many of these below-prime-rate loans may be explained on the grounds that they had a higher "effective" rate because of special provisions. One such provision is the requirement of the borrower in some loans to hold some average-sized deposit balance at the lending bank, a "compensating balance." Incomplete information from other sources indicates that some large corporate borrowers received large discounts off the prime rate.[4]

Why do the banks follow this practice rather than simply lowering the prime? One possible answer from price theory is that the banks are practicing price discrimination. This is a practice of charging different prices for the same commodity because of the ability to separate classes of customers, according to their demand curves (more precisely, according to their different elasticities of demand). Price discrimination is a form of monopolistic pricing that injures certain groups (those with less elastic demands).

In the 1970s, Citibank, the second largest bank in the country, often played the role of the bellwether bank for prime rate changes. The change would then spread to many other commercial banks. Before 1979, Citibank's prime was generally set equal to the average rate on prime commercial paper of the previous four weeks, plus an additional amount, which ranged from $\frac{3}{4}$ to $1\frac{1}{4}$ percentage points. In 1979, Citibank substituted the four-week average rate on three-month business certificates of deposit and made the "spread" between that average and their prime rate equal to $1\frac{1}{2}$ percentage points. This spread was not always adhered to because of other considerations. In 1980 (when prime rates peaked at 20 percent in April), the formula for setting the prime was, at least temporarily, dropped.

Mutual Savings Banks

Mutual savings banks (MSBs) (sometimes called "savings banks") are chartered in 17 states and Puerto Rico but are found primarily in the New England and Middle Atlantic states.[5] New York State, Massachusetts, Pennsylvania, and Connecticut held approximately 85 percent of the MSB deposits in the United States, with 63 percent of these deposits in New York, in 1978. The 473 MSBs in existence in 1978 all received charters from the individual states (no federal charters) and were jointly owned by the depositors. In 1980, some MSBs applied for federal charters at the Federal Home Loan Bank Board, and the first one was granted in September 1980. In September 1981 there were 456 MSBs with assets of $175.2 billion.

The original purpose for MSBs was to provide a safe depository for small savers. (A brief description of the history of MSBs is presented in the next section.) MSBs create short-term financial assets that take the form of very liquid savings deposits. Some of these accounts are checkable. These accounts, as well as regular passbook savings accounts at all MSBs, earn interest. Profits earned by the MSBs are divided between the depositors on the basis of the size of their deposits, but not exceeding any ceiling regulations on interest payments. The Federal Deposit Insurance Corporation insures eligible deposits of MSBs and commercial banks up to $100,000 for each depositor at a bank.

MSBs' experience with substantial declines in the value of their investments in mortgages during the deep depressions of the 1930s caused them to reduce their holdings of higher-interest mortgage loans and to increase their holdings of government securities. Since the late 1940s, they have again increased their holdings of mortgages, until in September 1981, mortgage loans constituted 57 percent of their financial assets, as indicated in Table 18-7. Mortgage holdings were nearly the same in

TABLE 18-7

Assets and Liabilities of Mutual Savings Banks, August 1981 (Billions of Dollars)

Assets	175.072
Loans	
Mortgages	100.2
Other	14.6
Securities	
U.S. government	9.4
State and local government	2.3
Corporate and other	38.3
Cash	4.8
Other assets	5.5
Liabilities	175.072
Deposits	153.4
Regular*	153.1
Ordinary savings	49.1
Time and other	101.9
Other	2.4
Other liabilities	11.1
General reserve accounts	10.5

*Excludes checking, club, and school accounts.
Source: Federal Reserve Bulletin (December 1981), p. A2.

1980, on average, as in September 1981, reflecting the effect of high interest rates, a housing industry slump, and general recession in this recent period.

Today, with interest-paying checking accounts, large MSBs such as the Bowery Savings Bank of New York City (which began in 1834), with $4.7 billion in deposits, look more and more like commercial banks that have a large proportion of their deposits in consumer savings accounts.

In 1980, MSBs were authorized to accept deposits from corporate customers (business accounts) and invest up to 5 percent of their assets in commercial loans. They were allowed to issue credit cards and to offer trust services (management of estates). Those broader powers, which allowed MSBs to become more like commercial banks, were extended, in large part, to reduce the burden imposed by lifting by 1986 the one-fourth percentage point higher interest (compared to commercial banks) they and savings and loan associations were allowed to pay on regular savings accounts.

The difficulties experienced by savings and loan associations, described in the next section, also befell MSBs. There was similar merger activity. On March 27, 1982, The New York Bank for Savings, which had already acquired Union Dime Savings, became a division of Buffalo Savings Bank. It advertised that it has thus become the largest savings bank in the United States, with more than $9 billion in total assets.

Savings and Loan Associations

Savings and loan associations (SLs) are found in every state, in the District of Columbia, and in Puerto Rico and Guam. There were 4709 SLs in September 1979, mostly small. Only 84 had assets of $1 billion or more and these SLs had 30.1 percent of the total assets of all SLs. SLs are the third largest private financial intermediaries (after commercial banks and insurance companies), with $654.6 billion in assets as of September 1981. The original purpose for their development was mortgage finance rather than as a safe depository for savings as was true of MSBs. They are the principal source of first-mortgage residential loans for residences in the United States, with 79 percent of their assets invested in mortgages, as indicated in Table 18-8. Many SLs are cooperative associations, in which each depositor owns a "pro rata" share, based on his or her account size, as in the mutual savings banks. Other SLs issue common stock. Some holding companies may control five or six SLs, and one may control fifteen.[6] SLs can obtain state or federal charters. In 1979, 1989 had federal charters and 2720 had state charters. Nearly all federal SLs are mutuals, while state SLs can, depending on the state's laws, be owned by stockholders. There were 805 stock-owned SLs in 1979.

At the end of 1981 there were 93 SL holding companies. Sears, Roebuck and Co.[7] (with assets of $34.5 billion) was the largest SL holding company. Its SL, the Allstate Savings and Loan Association, Los Ange-

TABLE 18-8

Assets and Liabilities of All Savings and Loan Associations, September 1981
(Billions of Dollars)

Assets		Liabilities	
Total assets	654.6	a. Savings capital	514.9
a. Mortgages*	518.4	b. Borrowed money	87.3
b. Cash and		FHLB[†] 40.3	
investment		Other 15.0	
securities	59.2	c. Loans in process	7.1
c. Other	77.1	d. Other	15.1
		e. Net worth[‡]	30.2

*Mortgages are 79 percent of assets.
[†] These are advances from the Federal Home Loan Bank.
[‡] New worth included undistributed income to depositors of mutual savings and loans.
Source: Federal Reserve Bulletin (December 1981), p. A29.

les, was the twentieth largest SL, with $2.27 billion in deposits. The second largest SL holding company was H. F. Ahmonson and Company, Los Angeles, a nondiversified holding company. It controls the largest SL, Home Savings of America, Los Angeles, with assets of $15 billion. If it were a commercial bank holding company, it would have been the twentieth largest.

SLs offer savings and checking accounts that can be insured by the Federal Savings and Loan Insurance Corporation, up to $100,000 for each depositor. Certificates of deposits with specified maturities are now important liabilities, as are regular savings accounts which are payable on demand.

Home financing organizations have been reported as existing in ancient Egypt, China, and the South Sea Islands. The Birmingham Building Society, established in 1781, was the first recorded firm that rose in response to the need for small-home financing in Great Britain. The English building societies were a product of the rapidly growing mine and factory towns in Great Britain's period of early industrialism.

The Birmingham Building Society was organized in a pub, where its founders and owners were also its sole participants. Members were fined if they did not show up at the "Fountain" in Cheapside on the first Monday of every month with half a guinea for each share they owned. When the fund became large enough, a lottery was held to determine who would obtain the first home loan. The recipient would repay the loan plus interest. Then another member would be granted a loan. When all the members had repaid their loans, the funds were divided among the shareholders, and the Birmingham Building Society was terminated.

The Oxford Provident, organized in 1831 in the small factory town of Frankfort, Pennsylvania, was the first such building and loan society in the United States. Its operation was similar in many ways to the Birmingham Building Society. It was operated with the sole purpose of providing loans to its members. No depositor could withdraw funds unless he or she terminated membership in the association, gave one month's notice, and paid a penalty fee. The loans were allocated in a different manner from those given by the Birmingham Building Society. When the fund reached $500, a loan was made to the member who agreed to pay the highest interest rate.

During the early history of banking in the United States there were several important differences between the MSBs and the SLs that influenced their growth. Initially, the MSBs offered small-deposit accounts, which could not be readily obtained from other financial intermediaries. Early commercial banks did not encourage small accounts. (Some commercial banks still discourage small accounts.) The practice precipitated a rapid growth of MSBs from ten banks and $1 million in deposits in 1820 to 620 banks and $819 million in deposits by 1880. Then came the banking panic of 1873, which was followed by 123 suspensions of savings banks from 1875 to 1879. This setback ended the period of greatest growth for MSBs.

MSBs operated under *permanent charters*, which allowed depositors to enter or leave the association at any time. SLs first used *terminating charters*, which made membership open only to original members. After 1854, *serial charters* allowed new groups of members to enter the associations under separate loan plans. Slowly, the SLs adopted permanent charters. They continued to emphasize regular savings, with fines and withdrawal fees for the delinquent.

The more liquid deposits of MSBs were a major factor in the more rapid growth of MSBs to the 1920s. In 1910, MSBs and commercial banks had approximately equal amounts of either of these competitors. By 1920, commercial bank savings deposits had grown much more rapidly than either MSB deposits or those of the smaller SL industry.

The post-World War I building boom caused a rapid expansion of SLs, which the MSBs did not experience. In 1929, there were 3709 more SLs than in 1930, with more than three times the amount of assets. Then came the depression of the 1930s. In 1929, the 12,342 SLs had $8.7 billion in assets, which included 24 percent of all nonfarm residential mortgages outstanding in the United States.

In 1935 and 1936, real estate owned outright by SLs from mortgage foreclosures amounted to 20 percent of their assets, compared to 2 or 3 percent in the 1920s. Most of this was sold at a profit during the 1940s. Mortgage loans could not rapidly be converted into cash when SLs were hit by large withdrawals. In addition, most cash reserves of SLs were held as deposits at commercial banks, many of which failed. By 1940, there were 4821 fewer SLs than in 1929, a decline of 39 percent. The SLs held $5.7 billion in assets in 1940, which was a decline in money terms of nearly $3 billion, or 34 percent. The decline in real terms, adjusted for a decline in prices, was much less: roughly 7 percent.

Was this a bad record? Kroos and Blyn claim that "No other financial intermediary, not even the commercial banking system, was more hard hit by the depression than the savings and loan industry."[8] Another analyst says: "Depressions in the 1890s and especially in the 1930s caused lapses in its overall growth and a fair number of failures, but, on the whole, SLs survived the depressions very well. In fact, they survived better than banks. . . ."[9]

The extremely rapid growth of SLs in the 1920s and in the post-World War II decades was a result in large part of the residential housing booms of the post-World War I and II periods. The loss of 4821 SLs during the 1930s and the default of many SL accounts made the 1930s, viewed separately, a catastrophic period for the owners and depositors of many SLs.

The SLs emerged from the 1930s with unprecedented federal supervision and assistance. The Reconstruction Finance Corporation had given $18 million to failing SLs. The Home Owners Loan Corporation gave $3 billion in mortgage credit between mid-1933 and mid-1936, with SLs directly receiving $800 million. The Federal Home Loan Bank (FHLB) was established in 1932 to supervise and provide credit to SLs for mortgages. The Federal Savings and Loan Insurance Corporation (FSLIC) was created in 1934 to issue deposit insurance to SLs. Federal chartering of SLs began with the federal government authorized to invest $1 million in each new SL so chartered. All federally chartered SLs have federal insurance. Three-fourth of the state-chartered SLs are members of the FHLB and have federal insurance.

The Federal Home Loan Bank (FHLB) has its headquarters, which is called the Federal Home Loan Bank Board (FHLBB), in Washington, D.C. It is controlled by a three-person board, employing approximately 1200 people throughout the country. It controls twelve district Federal Home Loan Banks, which supervise the SL industry. Each of the twelve district banks is a separate corporation nominally owned by stockholders, which are mostly SLs. The approval of the FHLBB in Washington is required before any major action is taken.

In 1980, SLs were authorized to issue credit cards and to offer trust services (management of estates). They were also allowed to invest up to 20 percent of their assets in consumer and commercial loans.

During 1981 and 1982 there was increasing concern that many SLs would be mortally wounded by the interest rate squeeze that had gripped the industry since 1979. SLs had made long-term mortgage commitments at rates considerably lower than market rates of interest in that period. Their income from mortgages did not cover their expense for new money that was bought at market rates.[10]

The *Washington Post* reported a run on an SL in New England in February 1982, allegedly started by a newspaper story about trouble in the SLs.[11] On the problems of SLs, the *Washington Post* continued:

> Based on an analysis of mid-1981 data, *The Wall Street Journal* has projected that 200 are in danger of failing. It quoted an unnamed official this week as saying that 40 troubled S&Ls are expected to be merged into healthier ones this month. Thus far in 1982 there has been an average of one supervisory merger a week, some of them involving several ailing S&Ls.

Last week the savings industry testified before a Senate subcommittee in favor of a bill to facilitate the sale of low interest rate mortgages to investors who would have the right to claim tax losses. In this way S&Ls and mutual savings banks hope to get rid of their old mortgages and use the funds for making new mortgages at higher rates or for other types of investments.

The U.S. League of Savings Associations claims its members have some $300 billion in low yield loans on their books. The Joint Tax Committee has estimated allowing investors to buy them for tax losses would mean a drain of $30 billion on the Treasury. The Treasury, which last week opposed the bill as bad tax policy, put the revenue loss at $50 billion.

Emergency legislation to aid mutual savings banks and savings and loans passed the House last fall, but it is stalled in the Senate, where the banking committee chairman wishes to make it part of a comprehensive reform of the financial services industry.[12]

The Wall Street Journal reported in February 1982 that Richard Pratt, chairman of the FHLBB, said that approximately 3800 SLs and 400 MSBs were experiencing a "quiet run."

Serious Trouble

There's no question the industry is in serious trouble. Three weeks ago, Richard Pratt, chairman of the Federal Home Loan Bank Board, told a builders' convention that the nation's 3,800 S&Ls are experiencing a "quiet run." In 1981, withdrawals at the S&Ls and about 400 mutual savings banks exceeded deposits by $39 billion, and their losses exceeded $6 billion. Mr. Pratt told the builders that about 400 S&Ls have an average net worth of 1.5% of assets and a loss rate that would exhaust their reserves within 12 months.

The S&L industry would like the administration and Congress to adopt a bailout plan that would involve a "warehousing" of the low-yielding mortgage loans that are hurting the thrifts. Under such a plan, the federal government would acquire the mortgages temporarily, paying the S&Ls market or near-market rates on them.[13]

Also, it was reported that Andrew S. Carron of the Brookings Institution (a research institute in Washington, D.C.), after a one-year study, predicted in February 1982 that more than 1000 SLs, or 609 with a so-called optimistic forecast, would fail by the end of 1983.[14] The optimistic forecast was based on a scenario where the new thirteen-week U.S. Treasury bills, auctioned February 23, 1982, with a 12.43 percent yield, would have an average yield in 1982 of 10.5 percent and continue to decline in 1983.

No aid (or as it was called, bail-out bill) for SLs and MSBs had passed the U.S. Congress by February 1982. Early in the Reagan administration, House Banking Committee chairman Fernand St Germain met with Paul Volcker, chairman of the Federal Reserve, and Richard T. Pratt, chairman of the FHLB. There was support among these individuals for a bill to assist troubled thrifts, but President Reagan announced his opposition to a bail-out, and action in the House of Representatives ceased at that time. In February 1982, Chairman St Germain, a Democrat, proposed a $7.5 billion emergency fund, the *Home Mortgage Capital Stability Fund*, for the FDIC, the FHLBB, and the National Credit Union Administration, NCUA, "to administer a program of direct capital assistance for home mortgage lending institutions whose net worth slips below two percent of assets." Although that proposal did not proceed, a different one initially passed the House Banking Committee. On May 11, 1982, the House Banking Committee passed a St Germain bill (by a 25-to-15 vote) that would give federal guarantees of net worth to thrifts that had net worth valuation of less than 2 percent of assets. The thrift industry supported the legislation because they thought it would do away with forced mergers. A bill with this provision was passed by Congress in September 1982. It was called the Garns-St Germain Depository Institute Act of 1982.

In 1981, Congress authorized savings certificates—the *All Savers Certificate*—for depository intermediaries that could pay up to $1000 ($2000 on a joint tax return) tax-free interest. These tax-free certificates had one-year maturities and could not be issued after January 1, 1983. The rate of interest was fixed at 70 percent of the one-year Treasury bill rate. The Reagan administration accepted the provision for the All Savers Certificates with reluctance because it was tied to their main tax bill in 1981. Whether the All Savers Certificate was of any help to thrifts in trouble is a matter for further testing. It did provide a substantial inflow of funds to commercial banks, which were not the target for assistance. It also reduced the demand for tax exempts, driving up their yield, at a time that federal aid to states and cities was being reduced.

SLs that were in trouble were allowed to merge with other SLs, even across state lines. The Federal Savings and Loan Insurance Corporation gave financial assistance as an inducement for these mergers. The FHLBB reportedly arranged eleven mergers in 1980 and 23 in 1981.[15] The large SLs merged with a number of troubled SLs in this period (see Table 18-9). An example of the mergers arranged by the Federal Home Loan Bank Board with financial assistance from the Federal Savings and Loan Insurance Corporation (FSLIC) was reported by the Associated Press wire service in February 1982.

4-Way SL Merger Arranged in Chicago

AP—Three Chicago-area savings institutions have been merged into a fourth to form the nation's seventh-largest savings and loan association, federal regulators said.

It was the sixth time this year that the government has provided financial help to bring off a merger in the financially troubled thrift industry.

In the latest case, the Federal Home Loan Bank Board approved the merger of North West Federal Savings and Loan Association of Chicago, Alliance Savings and Loan Association of Chicago, and Unity Savings Association of suburban Norridge, Ill., into Talman Home Federal Savings and Loan Association of Chicago.

The merger of the four institutions gives Talman, up to now the nation's 12th largest SL, more than $6.3 billion in assets, according to the board.

According to the board's announcement, the Federal Savings and Loan Insurance Corp. "will purchase for cash $10 million of income capital certificates from Talman to facilitate the transaction"—in other words, FSLIC will lend Talman $10 million.

TABLE 18-9

The Biggest SLs and Their Recent Acquisitions Reported as of February 1982

	Assets (Billions)
Home Savings of America, Los Angeles	$14.5
Nine SLs in Illinois, Texas, Missouri, and Florida	1.9
Great Western Savings, Beverly Hills	10.6
None	
American Savings, Los Angeles	9.7
None	
California Federal, Los Angeles	8.4
Four SLs in Georgia and Florida	0.9
Glendale Federal, Glendale	7.8
First Federal Savings and Loan Association, Broward County, Florida	2.6
First Nationwide Savings, San Francisco	7.0
West Side Federal, New York, and Washington Savings, Miami Beach, Florida	3.9
Home Federal Savings, San Diego	5.2
None	

Source: Federal Home Loan Bank of San Francisco estimates as reported in the *Wall Street Journal* (February 17, 1982), p. 27.

Other terms were not disclosed, except that Talman will repay FSLIC out of profits. The $7 billion corporations insures depositors' accounts in SLs.

Alliance account holders must approve the transaction, which requires Alliance to switch from a state to a federal charter.[16] ·

The Federal Savings and Loan Insurance Corporation allowed some creative accounting to help SLs.

Accounting Tactic Allowed

The FSLIC is also continuing to allow—and extending the scope of—an accounting tactic that inflates the earnings of the combined entity in voluntary mergers. The device, called the *purchase method of accounting,* allows an SL to treat the loss represented by a merger as *"good will"* amortized over as much as 40 years. But income and payoffs from the discounted mortgages can be taken into income over 10 to 12 years, resulting in substantially improved earnings for the first few years.

In 1981, the purchase method was used to increase the earnings of healthy SLs acquiring sick ones.[17]

Also, Chairman Pratt of the Federal Home Loan Bank Board fought to keep passbook savings accounts' ceiling rates from rising even to 6 percent in 1981, when short-term market rates were near 15 percent. He did this by either gaining or joining a majority of the six members of the Depository Institutions Deregulation Committee. This committee was set up by Congress in 1980 to remove gradually all ceiling rate restrictions on depository accounts by 1986. As can be seen from Table 18-10, little was done to raise the basic deposit rates during 1980 and 1981.

TABLE 18-10

Depository Institutions Deregulation Committee Changes in Interest Rate Ceilings on Deposits in 1980 and 1981

Date of Meeting	Effective Date of Change	Type of Deposit	Nature of Change
May 29, 1980	June 2, 1980	Small savers certificates (time deposits with maturities of 30 months or more, no minimum denomination)	*Prior ceilings:* Commercial banks were permitted to pay the yield on 2½-year Treasury securities less 75 basis points, and thrift institutions were permitted to pay 25 basis points more than commercial banks. The maximum interest rates permissible, however, were 11.75 percent at commercial banks and 12 percent at thrift institutions. *Changes:* Ceiling rates relative to yield on 2½-year Treasury securities raised 50 basis points. Ceiling rates will not fall below 9.25 percent at commercial banks or 9.50 percent at thrift institutions. The maximum ceiling rates of 11.75 and 12 percent were retained.
May 29, 1980	June 5, 1980	Money market certificates (time deposits in denominations of $10,000 or more with maturities of six months)	Raised the ceiling rate from the discount yield on six-month Treasury bills established at the most recent auction to that rate plus 25 basis points at both commercial banks and thrift institutions.*
October 9, 1980	December 31,1980	NOW accounts	Set the ceiling rate on NOW accounts at 5.25 percent for commercial banks, mutual savings banks, and savings and loan associations. The ceiling rate on interest-bearing checkable deposits was 5 percent until December 31, 1980.
June 25, 1981	August 1, 1981	Small savers certificates	Eliminated caps on these ceiling rates of 11.75 percent at commercial banks and 12 percent at thrift institutions. With the caps lifted, thrift institutions may pay the yield on 2½-year Treasury securities, and commercial banks may pay 25 basis points less.
September 3, 1981	October 1, 1981	All Savers Certificates	Adopted rules for All Savers Certificates specified in the Economic Recovery Act of 1981.
September 22, 1981	November 1, 1981	Money market certificates	Depository institutions are now permitted to pay the higher of the discount rate on six-month Treasury bills at the most recent auction, plus 25 basis points, or the average auction rate in the past four weeks, plus 25 basis points.
September 22, 1981	November 1, 1981	IRA/Keogh accounts	Created a new category of IRA/Keogh account with minimum maturity of 1½ years, no regulated interest rate ceiling, and no minimum denomination.

*Other changes in the ceiling rate on money market certificates are relevant when the yield on six-month Treasury bills falls below 8.75 percent.

Source: R. Alton Gilbert, "Will the Removal of Regulation Q Raise Mortgage Interest Rates?" *Review,* Federal Reserve Bank of St. Louis (December 1981), p. 7.

Credit Unions

Credit unions are consumer cooperatives with the objectives of providing loans and a means of regular savings to their members. The officers of a credit union are members who serve without compensation, except for the treasurer in some instances.[18] Business managers are often hired to run the credit union. Savings are deposited as shares, and interest is returned to the members as dividends. Credit unions operate under state and federal charters. At the end of 1981, there were 21,306 state and federal credit unions (12,440 federal and 8866 state).[19]

All federally chartered credit unions and approximately 54.4 percent of credit unions with state charters had federal deposit insurance. The National Credit Union Administration provides federal insurance up to $100,000 per depositor to all federal credit unions and to approximately 45 percent of the state-chartered credit unions.

Credit unions' members must have a common bond, such as a common place of employment. However, the restriction of a common bond can be mitigated. The Cincinnati-based Everybody's Credit Union was organized to serve the poor in nineteen counties. There are credit unions for hairdressers in Connnecticut; for inmates of Oregon State Penitentiary; for individuals with the last name of Lee in San Francisco; for the owners of Arabian horses in Burbank, California; and a credit union called "Alaska USA" with branches throughout Alaska and a service center in Denver, Colorado.

Credit union deposits are usually called *shares*, and their checkable deposits are called *share drafts*. Eighty-nine percent of the credit unions' liabilities were member shares or deposits (see Table 18-11). Where were the member shares invested? Seventy-six percent of the assets were loans back to the credit union members. These loans were for durable goods such as automobiles, furniture, home furnishings, and household appliances. Loans were also made to consolidate debts; to finance vacations; and to pay medical, dental, and funeral expenses. Table 18-11 lists the assets and liabilities of credit unions in 1981.

Credit unions originated in the nineteenth century in Germany. They were closely connected with moral and humanitarian goals and were

TABLE 18-11

Assets and Liabilities of Credit Unions, September 1981* (millions of dollars)					
Total assets	73.7		Savings	65.7	
Federal	40.5		Federal		
State	33.2		(shares)	36.6	(90.4%)
Loans outstanding	50.2	(76.4%	State (shares		
State	27.1	(66.9%	and deposits)	29.1	(87.7%)
Federal	23.0	(69.3%)			

*The ratios of savings (shares and deposits) to assets and for state and federally chartered credit unions, taken separately, loans to assets are shown in parentheses.

frequently organized in and supported by churches. They emphasized self-help for the impoverished. Credit unions first started in the United States in 1909, but they did not develop rapidly until after 1930. Edward Filene, part-owner of a department store in Boston, was one of the most important of a group of credit union promoters until his death in 1937. It is estimated that he spent $1 million supporting the work of the Credit Union National Extension Bureau, which promoted credit union formation. Credit unions paid as high as 8 percent return to their members to attract funds in the 1920s. They did well during the depression of the 1930s, increasing in number and in total assets. In 1934, federal charters were granted. By 1940, there were 3756 federally chartered credit unions and 5176 operating under state charters. The total number of credit unions declined during World War II to 8615 in 1945; however, they grew rapidly in the postwar period. In 1965, there were 16.8 million members of credit unions. Credit unions were the third largest source of consumer credit in the United States, with 15.7 percent of the market, compared to 4 percent in 1950.

The enormous expansion of credit unions has been due in large part to favorable government actions such as the tax-exempt status; the higher interest payments that credit unions are allowed to pay on their deposits; their new power to make mortgage loans up to thirty years for one- to four-unit residential property; the extension to twelve years on the maximum time allowed on unsecured loans; the allowance to participate in loans with other credit unions; and finally, the ability to offer checkable accounts. Credit union checks, called share drafts, were begun by the National Credit Union Administration in October of 1974.

Liquidity has been an ever-increasing problem for credit unions. Many credit unions receive deposits from their customers throughout the fall, winter, and spring and then suffer massive withdrawals in the summer as the members of the credit union go on vacation. Federal credit union liquidations (closings) rose to 326 in 1980. Government regulators forced 258 of these into involuntary liquidations, mostly because of insolvency (21 percent of the 258 were due to plant closings).

To provide for more efficient interlending among credit unions, every state has at least one credit union league. They are nonprofit cooperatives of individual credit unions fully financed by member dues. Fifty-seven of these in thirty-five states are called *centrals*. They lend funds to individual credit unions and provide a clearinghouse for interlending between credit unions. In addition, the Credit Union National Association (CUNA) opened the U.S. Central Credit Union in 1974 to provide for interstate lending and to allow U.S. centrals to borrow more easily from outside the credit union industry.

An important legislative victory for the credit union industry, which will enable credit unions to obtain more funds, occurred with the passage of the Financial Institutions Regulatory Act in the dying hours of the 95th Congress in 1978. The bill, which began as the Safe Banking Act, originally was aimed primarily at remedying practices in the commercial banking industry that came to light following a report from the Comptroller of the Currency on banking practices of Bert Lance, director of the Office of Management and Budget during the early part of the Carter administration. The hearings in the House were chaired by Representative Fernand J. St Germain, chairman of the House Banking Subcommittee on Financial Institutions, Supervision, Regulation and Insurance. St Germain and the chairman of the full banking committee, Henry Reuss, helped to promote Title 18, which created a Central Liquidity Facility for the credit unions. It is interesting that this bill, which covered so many reforms and provisions affecting depository intermediaries, was given little chance of passing the 95th Congress, but nevertheless passed the House and then after an all-night session was passed through the Senate on a voice vote of the few members present at 7:00 A.M. It was signed into law and the credit unions received a Central Liquidity Facility (CLF).

The CLF was authorized to provide more funds for credit unions. The CLF can borrow from the public and loan the funds to the credit union industry. It is administered by the Administrator of the National Credit Union Administration, the federal regulatory agency.

The supervision of credit unions has an interesting history. The Federal Credit Union Act was passed in 1934 "to establish a Federal credit union system, to establish a further market for securities of the United States and to make more available to people of small means credit for provident purposes through a national system of cooperative credit, thereby helping to stabilize the credit structure of the United States." The Act was first administered by the Farm Credit Administration. In 1942, the administration was transferred to the Federal Deposit Insurance Corporation. In 1948, Congress transferred the administration to a Bureau of Federal Credit Unions, which become one of the program bureaus of the Social Security Administration subject to the direction of the Commissioner of Social Security. The National Credit Union Administration Act of 1970 established an independent agency, the National Credit Union Administration, directed by an Administrator appointed by the president with the advice and consent of the Senate. An advisory board was set up with six members, one from each of the six regions with the indicated headquarters city: (1) Boston, (2) Harrisburg, (3) Atlanta, (4) Toledo, (5) Austin, and (6) San Francisco. Finally, the Financial Institutions Regulatory Act of 1978 established a three-member board to supervise insured credit unions to be appointed by the president and approved by the Senate, replacing the single administrator, and called the National Credit Union Board.

On May 1, 1982, interest rate ceilings on payments to accounts at federally chartered credit unions were removed. Immediately, some credit unions raised their interest payments from about 7 percent to 11 percent.

The Mutual Form of Ownership

Daniel Defoe in his "Essay on Projects" in 1698 and Jeremy Bentham in his plan for a "frugality bank" both proposed the establishment of early forms of mutual savings banks in Great Britain. Workers would pay a portion of their wages into a central fund and earn a return from investing the consolidated funds. The establishment of many of these types of savings plans among the labor force can be attributed in large part to the emergence of a new *value attitude system,* which no longer condemned the hoarding of worldly goods in excess of subsistence needs.[20]

At the same time, MSBs developed with early cooperative, communal ideas, which, since the 1920s, may have impeded their growth relative to other intermediaries, such as commercial banks and savings and loan associations. One of these impediments is emphasized by Teck:

> First, there is no personal profit incentive to form a mutual savings bank. Founders and trustees receive no salaries, and traditionally, prohibitions against special privileges and self dealing have been broadly interpreted and enforced.[21]

Thus in this mutual or cooperative form of ownership by the depositors, the "original" capital investment is paid back to the founders. Does this mean that depositors in a MSB receive a higher yield on their deposits because they also share in the profits? Because there are no stockholders, it is sometimes argued, the depositors' share must be greater. This is an irrelevant argument if ceiling interest rates prevent the depositors from being paid the "profits" made on loans and investments of the MSBs. Suppose that this is not the case; there are no effective ceiling rates.

The mutual form of organization poses a handicap in obtaining funds. It prevents the management from raising funds in the equity markets (i.e., selling stocks) when they can be obtained more inexpensively. There has been substantial pressure from the industry, from the Federal Home Loan Bank Board, and from some private studies to allow more thrifts to become stock-issuing corporations.[22] Consumer groups and some members of Congress have opposed it, sometimes on the grounds that the mutual distribution of profits is more equitable.

The type of financial asset created by thrifts organized as mutuals may be desirable for the less sophisticated, less affluent depositors. The deposit claim is money or a good that can easily be converted into money. It may be viewed as partly a bond with its principle guaranteed by trusted insurance; partly an equity with a claim to expected profits; and in some thrifts, partly a loan commitment for consumer loans. The cost to a small depositor of putting together a portfolio of assets with these attributes may exceed the intermediation fees and the cost of eliminating equity financing, reflected in his or her mutual deposit yield. This may be a rather vacuous line of argument. Suppose that a deposit at another depository intermediary down the street, organized as a stock corporation, pays a sufficiently higher yield to compensate for the MSBs' extra services and that the small depositor is indifferent between receiving income that is labeled interest rather than profits. He or she may move the deposit to the depository down the street.

NOTES

1. The Pepper-McFadden Act, usually known as the "McFadden Act," liberalized the branching rules for national banks in an effort to make them more competitive with state banks, but did not allow national banks to branch across state lines. Edge Act corporations are allowed to join banks together across state lines to conduct foreign business. These corporations can be owned by many banks. One has seventeen U.S. banks.

2. See *The Bank Holding Company Movement of 1978: A Compendium*, a study by the staff of the Board of Governors of the Federal Reserve System (September 1978), p. 63. These particular data come from the *Annual Statistical Digest 1972–76*, pp. 311–314.

3. Ibid.

4. See, for example, *The American Banker*, a daily trade publication of the commercial banking industry, for May 9, 1980. A page 1 headline story reports that 6 to 7 percentage points discount off the prime rate were being given to some large borrowers at large banks. Also, see the staff report for the Committee on Banking, Finance and Urban Affairs, U.S. House of Representatives, *An Analysis of Prime Rate Lending Practices at the Ten Largest United States Banks*, conducted under the direction of Robert Auerbach, economist for the Committee (Washington, D.C.: U.S. Government Printing Office, April 1981). Compensating balance requirements are discussed in Chapter 19.

5. Information on mutual savings banks can be found in George J. Benston, "Savings Banking and the Public Interest," *Journal of Money, Credit and Banking* (February 1972), pp. 133–266; Alan Teck, *Mutual Savings Banks and Loan Associations: Aspects of Growth* (New York: Columbia University Press, 1968); Benton E. Gup, *Financial Intermediaries, An Introduction* (Boston: Houghton Mifflin Company, 1886); and Herman E. Kroos and Martin R. Blyn, *A History of Financial Intermediaries* (New York: Random House, Inc., 1971).

6. Some holding companies have even gained control of mutual SLs by purchasing from the depositors proxies to vote.

7. L. Michael Cacaci, "Quarter of S&L Holding Firms Primarily in Other Business," *American Banker* (May 12, 1982), pp. 1, 26.

8. Kroos and Blyn, *A History*, p. 191.

9. Thomas Marvell, *The Federal Home Loan Bank Board* (New York: Praeger Publishers, 1969), pp. 7–8. This provocative history of the regulation of SLs contains a number of case studies. See also Gup, *Financial Intermediaries*, and Kroos and Blyn, *A History*.

10. The savings capital (which includes deposits and borrowed funds) generally rose from $430.9 billion in 1978 to $510.9 billion in 1980 and then to $$514.9 in September 1981, as shown in Table 18-8. Borrowed funds (from the Federal Home Loan Bank Board and other sources) for those periods (levels and percentages of above amounts) were 42.9 billion (10 percent), $64.5 billion (12.6 percent), and $87.8 billion (17.1 percent), respectively. These increasingly large amounts of borrowings as a percentage of savings capital reflected the plight of problem SLs.

11. Nancy L. Ross, "SL's Depositors Panic After Report of Big Loss," *Washington Post* (February 11, 1982), pp. C9, C13.

12. Ibid., p. C13. The U.S. League of Savings Associations is an industry association, and the chairman of the Senate banking committee is Jake Garn.

13. G. Christian Hill and John Andrew, "U.S. Expected to Cut Costly Efforts to Force Mergers of Troubled SLs," *The Wall Street Journal* (February 17, 1982), p. 27.

14. Reported in the *Washington Post* (February 22, 1982), p. 1; and Timothy D. Schellhardt, "Bailout of Troubled Thrifts Would Meet Strong Reagan Opposition, Aide Asserts," *The Wall Street Journal* (February 23, 1982), p. 56.

15. Associated Press wire service, "4-Way SL Merger Arranged in Chicago," *Washington Post* (February 22, 1982), p. 9.

16. Ibid.

17. Hill and Andrew, "U.S. Expected to Cut," p. 27.

18. See Olin P. Pugh's "Credit Unions: From Consumer Movement to National Market Force," *Bankers Magazine* (January–February 1980), pp. 19–27. See also Gup, *Financial Intermediaries*, and Kroos and Blyn, *A History.*

19. These estimates are from sample surveys taken by the National Credit Union Administration. The percentage of state-chartered credit unions is from their estimates for December 1980.

20. For an excellent description of the conflicting value attitude systems between the emerging capitalistic ethic and Judeo-Christian beliefs, see Walter Weisskopf, *The Psychology of Economics* (Chicago: University of Chicago Press, 1955).

21. Teck, *Mutual Savings Banks*, p. 148.

22. A study published by the Federal Reserve Bank of New York and the New York State Banking Department in 1974 recommended that MSBs be permitted to convert to stock form and operate as savings banks or commercial banks. This recommendation has continued to be voiced by many others since that time [Leonard Lapidus, Suzanne Cutler, Patrick Page Kildoyle, and Arthur L. Castro, *Public Policy Toward Mutual Savings Banks in New York State*, Federal Reserve Bank of New York and New York State Banking Department (June 1974)].

STUDY QUESTIONS

1. What are the major similarities and differences between commercial banks, savings and loan associations, and credit unions?

2. What are the differences and similarities between a branch bank, a correspondent bank, and a subsidiary bank in a holding company?

3. What is the prime rate?

4. How do commercial banks earn most of their income? Review the details of their portfolio of assets.

19

Liabilities of Depository Intermediaries

Deposits

Deposits are *claims* against depository institutions by depositors. Estimates of these deposits must be adjusted to fit into the common concepts of money. These concepts attempt to restrict the concept of money to the holdings of the *nonbank* public. Therefore, it is necessary to adjust gross deposits to the deposits recorded on the books of the nonbank public. Three aggregates must be deducted to obtain the deposits on the books of the nonbank public:

1. Federal government deposits.
2. Interbank deposits.
3. Bank float.

Federal government deposits in private commercial banks are substantial. They are mostly deposits of income tax withheld by employers, in special accounts of the U.S. Treasury called *tax and loan accounts*. Tax and loan deposits amounted to $12.8 billion in October 1981.

Interbank deposits are deposits of one depository intermediary in another. They amounted to $58 billion for commercial banks alone in February 1980. The adoption of the new money concept M1 in 1980 required more attention to interbank deposits of the thrifts, mostly with commercial banks, which also must be deducted.

The third deduction from gross demand deposits is bank float. The estimate of bank float is made by the Federal Reserve and is called *Federal Reserve float*.

Commercial bank deposits, including demand deposits, are subject to immediate withdrawal during regular banking hours at the request of the depositor, with the exception of certain time deposits, discussed in this section. Demand deposits may be withdrawn in the form of currency or coin, or they may be transferred to another account at any commercial bank. "Demand deposits at commercial banks can be transferred by bank check" and are sometimes called *checking accounts*. No money interest is paid on demand deposits. Checkable NOW accounts, which are available to consumers but not business depositors, pay interest. Technically, they are savings accounts that are accessible by a negotiable order of withdrawal.

Savings deposits at commercial banks and thrifts can usually be withdrawn as currency or coin, or as a cashier's check of the bank (a check drawn against the issuing bank); they may be transferred into the depositor's demand deposit account at the same bank, although technically the bank may refuse to withdraw or transfer a savings account for thirty days.

Time deposit accounts with specified maturities are exceptions to the convention that commercial bank deposits should be convertible to cash on demand. Prior to the date of maturity, the bank may refuse to exchange such a time deposit claim or may impose a penalty fee. The time deposit pays interest, giving it one of the characteristics of other private bonds.

Prior to 1976, a savings deposit at a commercial bank could be held only by a private individual or certain nonprofit organizations. Since 1976, corporations may have savings accounts of $150,000 or less. Ownership of savings account claims is sometimes evidenced by passbooks, which may be presented during regular banking hours for immediate withdrawal of the depositor's funds, although the bank may legally delay payment for thirty days. A bank would never, unless absolutely necessary, invoke such a waiting period, since it would seriously harm its deposit business.

Corporations and private firms, as well as some wealthy individuals, have, in an increasing volume since 1961, deposited their money in special time deposits for which large-denomination marketable *certificates of deposit* (CDs) (over $100,000) with specified maturities are given as evidence of their claims. CDs are negotiable, which means that they can be sold to others prior to their maturity date, and they pay market-determined rates of interest. The popularity of CDs was a result in part of the prohibition until 1976, and then the limitation, of savings accounts held by businesses.

Consumer or *personal time deposits* include CDs in denominations of less than $100,000. They are nonnegotiable; that is, they cannot be sold and must be returned to the issuing bank by the original purchaser. Until 1976, there were effective ceilings on interest payments. In 1978, consumer CDs were first authorized with ceiling interest yields closer to market interest rates. They were called *money market certificates.* Consumer CDs' interest payments will be allowed to vary without any restrictions if ceiling rate limitations are removed by 1986, as was directed by federal legislation passed in 1980.

Also, in 1982, banks started making arrangements with money market funds to offer depositors the following service, called a money fund *sweep* service. Money is transferred automatically back and forth into a money market fund so as to maintain a given minimum balance in a NOW account. See Chapter 20 for a description of money market funds and an additional discussion of sweep services.

Reserves

In the broadest sense, reserves of depository intermediaries are the assets a bank holds that may be exchanged for depositors' withdrawal claims. It is conceivable that a depositor who had originally deposited money would take an asset other than money. A bank could return a bond or any goods not included in the concept of money in exchange for a depositor's claim.

The depositor expects currency or coins, or a check that can be deposited to another bank account in return for his or her claim. These expectations are reinforced by government regulations for domestic bank deposits. The depositor may appear at the teller's window and request currency and coins, or he or she may sign an instrument such as a check or a negotiable order of withdrawal (NOW), which orders the bank to transfer funds to another bank. The bank must be ready with cash assets to meet demands for withdrawals that exceed deposits. Therefore, bankers store money on their premises (vault cash), and they hold "clearing balances," either as part of their reserves at the Federal Reserve or as correspondent balances at other banks.

Depository intermediaries store funds in other depository intermediaries. Those interbank deposits disappear from the total reserves of the entire banking system when the reserves of all banks are aggregated according to conventional accounting practices. The depository to which an interbank deposit is due has an asset exactly equal to the deposit liability of the depository from which the deposit is due. The interbank deposit liabilities exactly cancel the interbank assets for the banking system as a whole.

There are close substitutes for reserves in a bank's portfolio. Other nonmoney assets that may be converted into reserves at little cost are excluded from the definition of reserves used here. An overnight loan to another financial depository is an asset considered to be a very close substitute for money reserves.

TABLE 19-1

Federal Reserve Member Bank Reserve Requirements Prior to March 31, 1980*
(To Be Phased Out by September 1, 1983)

Type of Deposit, and Deposit Interval (Millions of Dollars)	Requirements in Effect February 29, 1980		Previous Requirements	
	Percent of Deposits	Effective Date	Percent of Deposits	Effective Date
Net demand[†]				
0–2	7	12/30/76	$7\frac{1}{2}$	2/13/75
2–10	$9\frac{1}{2}$	12/30/76	10	2/13/75
10–100	$11\frac{3}{4}$	12/30/76	12	2/13/75
100–400	$12\frac{3}{4}$	12/30/76	13	2/13/75
Over 400	$16\frac{1}{4}$	12/30/76	$16\frac{1}{2}$	2/13/75
Time and savings[†,‡,§]				
Savings	3	3/16/67	$3\frac{1}{2}$	3/2/67
Time[¶]				
0–5, by maturity				
30–179 days	3	3/16/67	$3\frac{1}{2}$	3/2/67
180 days to 4 years	$2\frac{1}{2}$	1/8/76	3	3/16/67
4 years or more	1	10/30/75	3	3/16/67
Over 5, by maturity				
30–179 days	6	12/12/74	5	10/1/70
180 days to 4 years	$2\frac{1}{2}$	1/8/76	3	12/12/74
4 years or more	1	10/30/75	3	12/12/74

	Legal Limits	
	Minimum	Maximum
Net demand		
Reserve city banks	10	22 -
Other banks	7	14
Time	3	10
Borrowings from foreign banks	0	22

* For changes in reserve requirements beginning 1963, see Board's *Annual Statistical Digest, 1971–1975,* and for prior changes, see Board's *Annual Report* for 1976, table 13. *Note:* Required reserves must be held in the form of deposits with Federal Reserve banks or vault cash.

[†] (a) Requirement schedules are graduated, and each deposit interval applies to that part of the deposits of each bank. Demand deposits subject to reserve requirements are gross demand deposits minus cash items in process of collection and demand balances due from domestic banks.

(b) The Federal Reserve Act specifies different ranges of requirements for reserve city banks and for other banks. Reserve cities are designated under a criterion adopted effective Nov. 9, 1972, by which a bank having net demand deposits of more than $400 million is considered to have the character of business of a reserve city bank. The presence of the head office of such a bank constitutes designation of that place as a reserve city. Cities in which there are Federal Reserve banks or branches are also reserve cities. Any banks having net demand deposits of $400 million or less are considered to have the character of business of banks outside of reserve cities and are permitted to maintain reserves at ratios set for banks not in reserve cities. For details, see the Board's Regulation D.

(c) Effective Aug. 24, 1978, the Regulation M reserve requirements on net balances due from domestic banks to their foreign branches and on deposits that foreign branches lend to U.S. residents were reduced to zero from 4 percent and 1 percent, respectively. The Regulation D reserve requirement on borrowings from unrelated banks abroad was also reduced to zero from 4 percent.

(d) Effective with the reserve computation period beginning Nov. 16, 1978, domestic deposits of Edge corporations are subject to the same reserve requirements as deposits of member banks.

[‡] Negotiable order of withdrawal (NOW) accounts and time deposits such as Christmas and vacation club accounts are subject to the same requirements as savings deposits.

Required Reserves

Reserve requirements specify the type and amount of reserves that banks must hold to fulfill government regulations. The type of reserves that may be used to fulfill federal reserve requirements are called *legal reserves*. Legal reserves are equal to reserves on deposit at the Federal Reserve banks and all vault cash. (Correspondent balances of banks that are passed through, dollar for dollar, to the Federal Reserve also qualify as legal reserves under the Monetary Control Act of 1980.) The required reserve ratio is a fraction, with required reserves in the numerator and deposits in the denominator, RR/D. Multiplying this ratio by 100, one obtains the percentage of required reserves.

The Federal Reserve has in the past imposed a complex set of reserve requirements on all its member banks, as indicated in Table 19-1. Notice especially footnote ¶ to this table, which details supplementary and marginal reserve requirements imposed during 1978 and 1979, when President Carter switched from an anti-recession to an anti-inflation program, which included higher reserve requirements.

As of March 31, 1980, the reserve requirements of all of the more than 42,000 depository institutions in the United States were a wild and woolly mess. The nonmember state commercial banks were subject to different reserve requirements in every state. Unlike the Federal Reserve, which required that reserves be held as vault cash or deposits at the Federal Reserve, state regulations allowed reserve requirements to be satisfied by the holding of vault cash; by interbank deposits; and by the holding of securities of the U.S. government, as well as those of the states and local governments. In Alaska and California, gold served as a reserve. Louisiana specified that in addition to cash reserves of a least 20 percent, banks are required to hold up to 80 percent of demand deposits in bills of exchange or discounted paper maturing within one year, or U.S., state, and local securities. New York had one reserve requirement for New York City, Albany, and Buffalo and another reserve requirement for the rest of the state. Some states based reserve requirements on populations. Some states allowed cash items collected in ten days to be counted to meet reserve requirements. The examples of state reserve requirements can be extended on and on until the reader receives the

---

§ The average reserve requirement on savings and other time deposits must be at least 3 percent, the minimum specified by law.

¶ Effective Nov. 2, 1978, a supplementary reserve requirement of 2 percent was imposed on large time deposits of $100,000 or more, obligations of affiliates, and ineligible acceptances.

Effective with the reserve maintenance period beginning Oct. 25, 1979, a marginal reserve requirement of 8 percent was added to managed liabilities in excess of a base amount. Managed liabilities are defined as large time deposits. Eurodollar borrowings, repurchase agreements against U.S. government and federal agency securities, federal funds borrowings from nonmember institutions, and certain other obligations. In general, the base for the marginal reserve requirement is $100 million or the average amount of the managed liabilities held by a member bank, Edge corporation, or family of U.S. branches and agencies of a foreign bank for the two statement weeks ending Sept. 26, 1979.

full view of the collage. The reader may name the composite either a "hodgepodge" or a "tribute to the dual banking system."

The *dual banking system* is the name applied to the concept of regulation that allows some of the banking system to be regulated by the states and some to be regulated by the federal government. Proponents of the dual banking system saw the composite as a striking example of the kind of innovation and regulation needed in a free society. Those in favor of more uniform regulations might note that even Adam Smith, the author of the classic and now ancient treatise on capitalism and free enterprise in 1776, thought the government should have control of the supply of money. Reserve requirement levels affect the quality of money that banks can create.

Reserve Requirements After 1980

To rationalize and simplify the reserve requirement structure and to make the required reserve ratios more uniform for all depository institutions, a new system of reserve requirements was signed into law on March 31, 1980. It was to be phased in over a four-year period for member banks and an eight-year period (ending September 3, 1987) for other depository institutions (except for nonmember commercial banks in Hawaii, which will not be completely phased in until January 7, 1993).

The new reserve requirements, shown in Table 19-2, apply only to checkable accounts and business certificates of deposits. All other deposits will have no reserve requirements. The initial "regular" reserve requirements on checkable accounts are 3 percent on the first $25 million and 12 percent above that amount. The Federal Reserve is given authority to vary the reserve requirement on checkable deposits over $25 million from 8 to 14 percent. The $25 million breakpoint will be adjusted every year-end by 80 percent of the percentage change in total checkable deposits in all depository institutions during the year ending the previous June 30. Thus the percentage of depository institutions with less than the breakpoint amount of checkable accounts will only slowly diminish as these deposits grow larger through the years. In 1982 the breakpoint was increased to $26 million.

The initial regular reserve requirement on business CDs with maturities of less than $3\frac{1}{2}$ years is 3 percent, with authority given to the Federal Reserve to vary this requirement between 0 and 9 percent.

In addition, the Federal Reserve may impose supplementary reserve requirements on all checkable accounts, provided that at least the amount of reserves that could be raised at the previously mentioned initial reserve requirement levels are being held.[1] Unlike the regular reserve requirements, which can be satisfied by holdings of vault cash or deposits at a Federal Reserve bank, the supplemental reserve requirements must be held at a Federal Reserve Bank. The supplemental reserve requirement may be varied by the Federal Reserve from 0 to 4

TABLE 19-2

**Reserve Requirements on Domestic Deposits Authorized by the
Depository Institutions Deregulation and Monetary Control Act of 1980 for
All Depository Institutions in the United States
(To Be Totally Phased In by 1993)**

	Initial Level	Legal Limits
1. Regular reserve requirement percentages with no interest payments satisfied by vault cash or deposits at a Federal Reserve bank*		
a. Checkable accounts[†]		
First $26 million	3	No variation
Over $26 million	12	8 to 14
b. NOW personal time accounts of less than $3\frac{1}{2}$ years maturity[‡]	3	0 to 9
2. Supplemental reserve requirements with interest paid on reserves satisfied by deposits at Federal Reserve banks only*,[§]		
a. Checkable accounts	0	0 to 4

* "Federal Reserve bank" means a regional or branch Federal Reserve bank, not a private member bank. However, a nonmember bank may meet reserve requirements by an interbank deposit at a member bank if the member bank passes these deposits on, dollar for dollar, to a Federal Reserve bank. These pass-through accounts can also be maintained at a Federal Home Loan Bank or the National Credit Union Administration Central Liquidity Facility.

[†] Checkable accounts are called *transactions accounts* in the legislation. The Board of Governors of the Federal Reserve was given discretion in determining which accounts are accessible by a check-type instrument. In 1981, these transactions accounts included demand deposit accounts, share-draft accounts, NOW accounts, ATS accounts, and telephone transfer accounts that are accessed more than three times a month. The $26 million cutoff (effective in 1982) will be changed each year by 80 percent of the change in checkable deposits of all depository institutions.

[‡] These are business certificates of deposit. Individual accounts of less than $3\frac{1}{2}$ years maturity that are transferable to checking accounts would also bear 3 percent reserves, if such accounts arise. The $3\frac{1}{2}$-year criterion became effective 4/29/82. In addition there was a 3 percent reserve requirement on all Eurocurrency liabilities, effective 11/13/80.

[§] The interest rate will be no higher than the average interest rate on the Federal Reserve's own portfolio of financial assets.

percent. Unlike the regular reserve requirements, the Federal Reserve is authorized to pay interest to the depository intermediaries for reserves held under the supplementary reserve requirements.

The Board of Governors of the Federal Reserve may impose any reserve requirements in a national emergency situation, under the authorization of the Monetary Control Act of 1980. It must consult with the "appropriate committees of the House and the Senate" and promptly issue an explanatory report to the Congress. This emergency reserve requirement action may not be extended for more than 180 days without the vote of a least five of the seven members of the Board of Governors.

Reserve requirements were first introduced by the state of Virginia in 1837. However, until March 31, 1980, there had never been mandatory federal reserve requirements on depository institutions located in the states. Bank managers could decide whether or not they wanted to belong to the Federal Reserve System, where federal reserve requirements were imposed. Even the management of a national bank, which must be a Federal Reserve member bank, could opt to change to a state charter and drop Federal Reserve membership, and with it federal reserve requirements. Only national banks in Washington, D.C., or in the U.S. possessions had no such option, since state charters were not available to them. Those banks were required to belong to the Federal Reserve and thus had mandatory federal reserve requirements.

High interest rates made Federal Reserve requirements especially burdensome in the late 1970s. That is, the higher the market interest rate, the higher was the opportunity cost of interest forgone on sterile reserves. Member banks began jumping from the Federal Reserve ship, and a large exodus was predicted. Thus the historic legislation that was pushed to remedy this problem by imposing mandatory reserve requirements was frequently called the Membership Bill. It made the membership problem largely irrelevant by keeping membership voluntary, while imposing the same reserve requirement schedule on all nonmember depository institutions.

Float

Float occurs because the records of the money balances of the parties to a transaction are not simultaneously adjusted to show the transfer of money. There is a delay between the time the recorded money balances of the person or firm receiving the money are increased and the time the recorded money balances of the person or firm paying the money are reduced.

Total float is composed of two parts: mail float and bank float. *Mail float* occurs when an individual or firm mails or delivers a check to another individual or firm before the check is deposited in a bank. Mail float increases the recorded money supply because the individual's deposit at the bank is not reduced, even though the individual has used part of the deposit to make a payment. The bank cannot brings its books up to date until the check is received. When the check is received by the bank, there is still a problem of float until the check finds its way to the checkwriter's bank. That second part of float is discussed next.

Bank float arises when one bank is credited with a deposit, but the deposits of the bank on which the check was drawn have not yet been reduced. The funds that must be collected through the check-clearing system are called *uncollected cash items* or *items in the process of collection*. A rise in bank float increases bank reserves and deposits.

The Federal Reserve defines float as the difference between *uncollected cash items* and *deferred availability cash items*. Deferred availability cash items are deposits that have not yet been credited to the bank that received the deposit. The reduction of this item from bank reserves is proper, but it is probably incorrect to compute the float on the money supply.[2]

The Managed Liabilities

Of special importance both to the process by which depository institutions adjust their reserve position and to monetary policy are the *managed liabilities*. These are

1. Negotiable certificates of deposit over $100,000.
2. Eurodollar borrowings (including overnight deposits at Caribbean branches of U.S. banks, included in M2. (This subject is discussed in Part VII.)
3. Federal funds borrowings.
4. Short-term repurchase agreements.

These managed liabilities allow banks to obtain funds in the same manner as regular deposits, except that:

1. They pay market rates of interest.
2. They have different reserve requirements than checkable accounts (unless they are defined by the Board of Governors as checkable deposits subject to the same requirements).
3. They can, rapidly and at small expense, change the amount of their managed liabilities.

If demand deposits decline, drawing down reserves, for example, an individual commercial bank can attract funds by immediately increasing its managed liabilities. Even if managed liabilities are not included in the concept of money, such changes can cause erratic movements in the money supply. This is because of the different reserve requirements behind managed liabilities and regular deposits and the substitution of managed liabilities for bank deposits.

This problem is vividly illustrated by the advent of the equivalent of overnight borrowings from nonbank depositors to banks in the 1970s. Some large nonbank depositors made the following arrangements. Their deposits were regularly drawn out of their account shortly before the bank closed each day. The bank then sold a Treasury bill to the depositor and agreed to buy it back at the same price in the morning, when the funds were replaced in the depositor's account. This repurchase agreement arrangement allowed the depositor to receive market interest on his or her bank account. Because reserve requirements were calculated on closing balances, the bank needed to carry no required reserves against these deposits. The depositor's funds were safe overnight, since ownership of a Treasury bill was passed to the depositor.

Although the amount of these automatic arrangements was believed to be relatively small, large corporate and local government customers who made specific arrangements early in the day had much larger amounts of overnight repurchase agreements. Overnight domestic repurchase agreements plus overnight agreements to nonbank customers from Caribbean branches of member banks amounted to $33.6 billion in Novem-

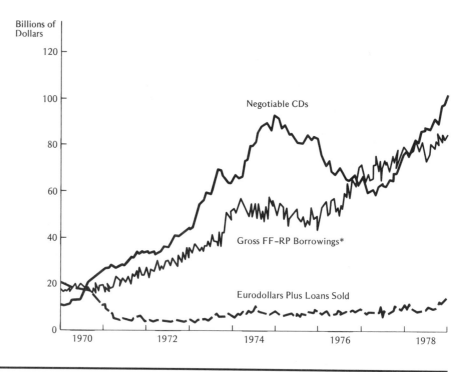

Figure 19-1

Principal managed liabilities of large U.S. commercial banks. *Source:* Thomas Simpson, *The Market for Federal Funds and Repurchase Agreements,* Staff Studies, Board of Governors of the Federal Reserve System (July 1979), p. 9.

*FF-PP borrowings are federal funds and repurchase agreement transactions.

ber 1981. This amount was 7.7 percent of the size of M1. It is not included in the estimates of M1; it is added into M2. Those bank customers treated overnight repurchase agreements as investments similar to other short-term, relatively default-free securities.[3] The rapid growth to huge levels of the major managed liabilities in large U.S. banks is shown in Figure 19-1.

The Federal Funds Market

The Fedwire is an important part of the payments mechanism for transactions between banks involving federal funds. Federal funds are immediately available funds that can be transferred through the Fedwire. The federal funds market is a short-term loan market with the important function of allocating reserves to banks that need reserves.

Some federal funds loans are made directly between commercial banks; other federal funds loans are arranged with money market dealers who also maintain a position in the market. Private corporations, mutual savings banks, and foreign banks may also enter the market, although tl market has been primarily made up of domestic commercial banks ar New York money market dealers.

There are a number of important aspects of the federal funds mark that explain its widespread use by commercial banks for short-term a justments in their reserve position. Federal funds loans are a way for banks to obtain funds and to legally pay market rates of interest. Since 1964, member banks could borrow not only from other members, but also from savings and loan associations, agencies of the U.S. government, and nonbank securities dealers.

Federal funds are payable "immediately"; that is, there is same-day clearing. Ordinary checks drawn on individuals, banks, or other business firms take at least one day to clear and to be made available to member banks for meeting their legal reserve requirements. Banks in the federal funds market can use federal funds and obtain same-day clearing for immediate additions to their reserve position.

A frequent type of federal funds transaction is a one-day overnight loan between member banks, in which the Federal Reserve debits the lender's account and credits the borrower's account on the same day. No collateral is exchanged. The loan is considered an unsecured loan and is limited by bank regulations to a percentage of the lending bank's capital plus surplus. Some federal funds are secured with government securi- ties. The large size of this market in unsecured, uninsured loans raises the possibility of injury to the banking industry if a large bank were to have financial problems and be unable to honor its federal funds borrow- ings. Presumably, the Federal Reserve would come to the rescue.

Banks also use *repurchase agreements* (RPs) to obtain short-term funds. In an overnight repurchase agreement, a security, such as a U.S. Treasury bill, might be sold to another bank, with the agreement to re- purchase it at the same price the following day. It is generally believed that the lending bank has a high degree of protection from default, since that bank owns the Treasury bill until the repurchase agreement is ter- minated the following day. Thus repurchase agreements are "secured" borrowings, whereas federal funds borrowings are generally unsecured. These transactions are therefore slightly different from federal funds loans.

The market for federal funds and repurchase agreements grew rapidly during the 1970s, as Figure 19-2 illustrates. Total nondeposit funds at commercial banks (mostly federal funds, RPs, and other borrowings from nonbanks) were estimated to be $119.8 billion in October 1981.

The rate of interest on federal funds—the *funds rate*—is closely watched at the trading desk of the Federal Reserve Bank of New York as a signal of the reserve position of the banking system. Market dealers and banks that participate in the federal funds market may post slightly different and varying rates during the day. All depository institutions with federal reserve requirements end their reporting week and must come up with their required reserves (an average for the week) by the close of business on Wednesday. A perceived surplus in the system

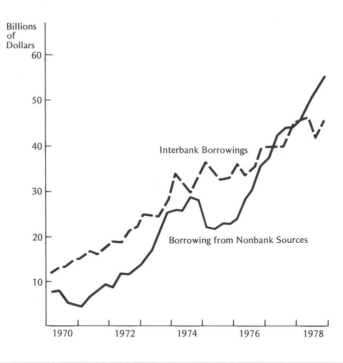

Figure 19-2

Federal funds and repurchase agreement loans to commercial banks. *Source:* **Thomas D. Simpson, *The Market for Federal Funds and Repurchase Agreements,* Staff Studies, Board of Governors of the Federal Reserve System (July 1979), p. 7.**

sends the federal funds rate plummeting downward, and an expected shortage sends the rate shooting upward, with perceptions sometimes shifting rapidly on Wednesday afternoon. The federal funds rate is, therefore, very erratic and unstable on Wednesdays because of the *Wednesday scramble* in and out of reserves.

Compensating Balance Requirements for Borrowers

Borrowers from commercial banks are frequently asked to maintain an *average* bank deposit balance *exceeding some minimum* amount *over the period of their loan*. This requirement is called a *compensating balance requirement*. The average compensating balance requirement is typically 10 percent of the line of credit available to the borrower and an additional 10 percent of the loan outstanding. Compensating balance requirements are most frequently applied by large banks to finance companies and industrial firms that maintain large lines of credit. A large firm may maintain one of its demand deposit accounts with the bank from which it also borrows funds.

Numerous explanations of reasons for the existence of compensating balance requirements have been given. Nevins Baxter and Harold Shapiro report the reasons given by banks in a survey they conducted almost twenty years ago,[4] shown in Table 19-3, from a questionnaire with limited selections, but still useful in analyzing the reasons for compensating balances.

Reliable evidence on the relationship between compensating balances and other variables is difficult to obtain because of the lack of data on informal compensating balance requirements. These occur when a banker suggests that a borrower open an account at the bank and maintain an average balance greater than some minimum amount. Compensating balance arrangements may be made even when the borrower normally maintains more than the minimum required average balance. Therefore, the analyses of the reasons for these compensating balances must be based on hypotheses that have not been rigorously tested.

First, some alternative explanations of compensating requirements will be examined. Does the compensating balance requirement make a bank loan less risky? If so, is this a major reason for the compensating balance requirements [reason (f) in Table 19-3]? If a borrower is required to maintain a minimum average deposit, will not the bank be assured of the existence of some liquid assets in case of a default on the loan? The bank cannot be so assured unless it has knowledge of the claims of other creditors against the borrower and is sure that it will legally be able to stop withdrawals by the depositor. A bank may not confiscate a private deposit without proper legal procedures which are also available to other creditors, who may take precedence. The borrower could furnish a financial statement to the bank, and the bank could take action to claim the cash assets of a borrower in default, even if the borrower had no money in an account at the bank. It is true that the bank may have superior knowledge of at least part of the day-to-day fluctua-

TABLE 19-3

Bankers' Reasons for Employing Compensating Balance Requirements	Percentage of Affirmative Replies in the Baxter–Shapiro Survey
(a) To increase deposits	83.2
(b) To increase net earnings	69.5
(c) To increase lending capacity	53.7
(d) To change the effective rate of interest	49.3
(e) To compensate the bank in lieu of service charges	40.3
(f) To increase the quality of loan asset	40.3
(g) To lend to a large number of consumers at the prime rate	17.4

Source: Nevins Baxter and Harold Shapiro, "Compensating Balance Requirements: The Results of a Survey," *Journal of Finance* (September 1964), p. 490.

tions in the borrower's cash assets if the borrower has an account at the bank. This advantage would appear to be of minor importance with the large firms, which are the largest owners of compensating balances.

Even if compensating balances afford the lending bank superior knowledge, compared to other lenders, of part of the borrower's cash position, this knowledge does not, by itself, explain the existence of compensating balance requirements. Rather than impose such requirements, the bank may charge slightly more interest on the loan, to pay for the increased risk. No compensating balance requirements would then be applied. The bank would lose whatever extra knowledge it obtained from watching the borrower's compensating balances, but it would be exactly repaid by higher interest rates on the loan. For some small loans the information provided by a compensating balance may be less expensive per dollar borrowed than prolonged credit investigations. In this case, it is cheaper for the borrower to maintain a compensating balance than to pay for such an investigation in the form of higher interest rates.

Usury laws have prohibited sufficiently high interest rates to cover default risk on loans to some borrowers. In this case, compensating balance requirements may be the only way to lower the recorded interest rates. Usury laws are probably a minor factor in explaining compensating balances since they are held primarily by large borrowers. Many of these large borrowers would maintain large deposit balances without the compensating balance requirements.

Assume that the maximum legal interest rates are too high to be relevant and that no interest is paid on bank deposits either in the form of money payments or services in kind. A simple example will illuminate some of the misconceptions about the reasons for compensating balances under these conditions. Suppose that a borrower desires a bank loan of $80. With a compensating balance of 20 percent, $100 must be borrowed to obtain $80 principal. If the borrower intends to keep an absolute minimum balance of $20 which will not be withdrawn, he or she would be indifferent between an $80 loan at 10 percent interest or a $100 loan at 8 percent with a $20 compensating balance requirement. However, if he or she views the compensating balance requirement as an *average* balance requirement (as it is usually stated by lending banks), he or she will not be indifferent between the two loan agreements. The $100 loan at 8 percent with a $20 loan compensating balance is superior because he or she not only receives an $80 loan, but also $20 which may be used as long as an *average* balance of $20 is maintained. Should he or she suddenly need $5, the balance can be reduced to $15 and replenished in a later period so that the $20 average balance is maintained. If $20 is usually in the bank, as may be true of larger borrowers, the distinction between these two loans—with and without compensating balance requirements—disappears.

Should the bank be indifferent between the two loan options? First, suppose that a bank has $80 in excess reserves over and above its desired reserves. The $80 may be called *surplus reserves*. If the bank makes an $80 loan at 10 percent interest, it earns $8. If, however, the bank requires compensating balances, it would make a $100 loan at 8 percent interest with a $20 compensating balance. The bank would again make $8 interest. In addition, the bank would need to keep additional reserves for the $20 compensating balance. The additional reserves needed for the compensating balance would draw the bank's reserves below its desired level. The bank would be forced to sell an interest-earning asset to restore reserves to their desired level. The compensating loan option pays the bank $8 interest minus the income lost on the income-earning asset that must be sold.

If the bank had more than $80 in surplus reserves, it would still be more profitable to loan $80 at 10 percent interest with no compensating balance. A $100 loan at 8 percent interest with a $20 compensating balance still requires additional reserves for the compensating balance that could have been used to buy other income-earning assets. The income on the $100 loan is then $8 minus the income forgone on income-earning assets that could have been purchased with the additional reserves for the $20 compensating balance.

In the examples above it is clear that the bank would earn less using loans with compensating balances rather than loans of equivalent interest to the borrower with no compensating balances. Compensating balances are an unprofitable way to increase deposits, net earnings, or lending capacity in this example [reason (a), (b), or (c) in Table 19-3]. The fact that these reasons appear in the survey of bankers may be an indication of the difficulties of perceiving generalizations, when one's vantage point is too proximate to the event. Nevertheless, the forgoing logical argument must be supported by more evidence before it can be confidently accepted. Yet no answers appear as consistent with the information that exists on compensating balances by many large borrowers as the following. Compensating balance requirements are primarily a way of paying interest on demand deposits. This answer is similar to replies (e) and (g) in Table 19-3. Large depositors receive interest payments in the form of a discount on their loans.

The payment of interest on bank deposits to those who hold compensating balances is not only a method to circumvent the prohibition of direct money payments of interest on demand deposits. It is also a way to discriminate on interest payments between depositors. Large depositors may cost the bank less per dollar of deposits (economies of scale). The bank may wish to pay a higher interest rate on their deposits. It can do this through a system of discounts on their loans without advertising different interest payments to different depositors. This is one explanation that is consistent with the existence of compensating balances before the prohibition of interest payments on demand deposits in the 1930s. It may also apply to consumer loans after 1986, when the ceiling rate limitations on the payment of interest on consumer checking accounts is scheduled to be removed.

NOTES

1. The reason for this provision is that both chairmen of the banking committees, Henry Reuss in the U.S. House of Representatives and William Proxmire in the Senate, did not want the Federal Reserve to pay interest on reserves to the commercial banks, as is allowed under the supplemental reserves requirements. They did not want the Federal Reserve to lower the reserve ratios to the bottom of the allowable range and substitute a supplemental requirement that allowed those interest payments. The Monetary Control Act of 1980 further requires the affirmative vote of at least five of the seven members of the Board of Governors and consultation with other regulators before the supplemental reserve requirements can be imposed. They can only be imposed to enhance monetary policy and not as a means of reducing the cost burden of the basic reserve requirements.

2. The subtraction of deferred availability cash items on the Federal Reserve records to obtain a concept of Federal Reserve float is important for bank reserves but may be incorrect for demand deposits. Suppose that money is defined as the "nonbank" public's holdings of commercial bank demand deposits and currency and coin. An "increase" in "uncollected cash items" means that there is an increase in the value of checks that have been deposited in one bank and not yet deducted from the account on which they are drawn at another bank. Nancy West in the example may well know that she has, say, four days before she must cover her check in California—illegal though that practice may be. The existence of "deferred availability cash items" is a deduction she does not make.

3. Thomas D. Simpson, *The Market for Federal Funds and Repurchase Agreements*, Staff Studies, Board of Governors of the Federal Reserve System (July 1979), p. 97, footnote 79.

4. Nevins Baxter and Harold Shapiro, "Compensating Balance Requirements: The Results of a Survey," *Journal of Business* (September 1964), pp. 483–496.

STUDY QUESTIONS

1. Why and how are depository intermediaries checkable deposits adjusted to obtain an estimate of the nonbank public's deposits?

2. What happened to federal reserve requirements in 1980? Describe federal reserve requirements before and after 1980.

3. What is float? Why is it important?

4. What are the managed liabilities of banks? How do banks use these managed liabilities? What part do interest rates play in selecting a portfolio of managed liabilities? What part is played in the selection of managed liabilities by reserve requirements? Are managed liabilities money?

5. What is the federal funds market?

6. How does a federal funds loan differ from an overnight repurchase agreement between banks?

7. Explain why compensating balances may be thought of as a means to pay interest on deposits and to pay different interest rates to different customers.

20

Investment and Contractual Intermediaries

Introduction

Investment and contractual intermediaries are discussed in this chapter. The immense changes in these intermediaries during the 1970s and early 1980s cannot easily be comprehended. Imagine the birth and growth to giant size of the money market funds, which grew to $180 billion in assets by 1982 starting from zero in 1972. Also, keep in mind that attention is often turned, by media coverage, to the depository intermediaries because they have massive federal regulation and sponsorship. The national news coverage is centered in Washington, D.C. The huge insurance industry is largely under state control and receives relatively little national news coverage. It is primarily a contractual intermediary that must be carefully considered in plans for deregulation and a level playing field, noted in Chapter 16. Pension funds, trust funds, finance companies, investment companies, stock brokerage houses, and other insurance companies are all fascinating industries that everyone interested in financial markets should carefully study.

Why should they be studied? These financial intermediaries are massive participants in the financial markets. They are also entering more and more of the same areas as the depository institutions, and a full understanding of the services and portfolios of either type of intermediary requires an understanding of the other. A rereading of the section "Homogenization of Financial Intermediaries" in Chapter 16 will aid in gaining perspective for this chapter. The final section of the chapter describes the present and proposed financial intermediary services to be offered by the largest retailer of dry goods and household equipment, such as hardware, in the United States, Sears, Roebuck and Company. To the trend toward the homogenization of financial intermediaries, the possibilities for financial intermediation services from other firms must be added, as is illustrated with this example.

Investment Intermediaries

The major financial intermediaries classified as *investment intermediaries* are *investment companies* and *finance companies*. Brokerage firms that offer money market funds and checkable accounts are also discussed. The major financial assets created by investment companies are pro rata (in proportion to) shares in their portfolio of financial assets. The major financial assets created by finance companies are debt instruments, often short-term commercial paper. These financial assets created by investment intermediaries are very liquid; some (money market shares) are even included in the definition of money (M2).

Investment Companies

Investment companies sell shares to their customers and purchase income-earning financial assets issued by others. Each shareowner has a pro rata share in the investment company's assets. The investment company's income-earning portfolio of financial assets may either be limited to particular assets in which they specialize, or it may be diversified with many types of financial assets. Unlike holding companies, investment companies do not acquire equities with the primary objective of ownership or control. They may purchase financial assets in only one industry, such as gold mining or oil. They may purchase more conservative securities, such as government bonds. Some specialize in municipal bonds in order to receive preferential tax treatment. Others may invest in equities with reliable dividends to assure continuous income, or they may invest in equities with little or no dividends in order to obtain income only from the lower-taxed capital gains.

Investment companies may be classified as follows:

1. The *fixed or fixed trust* investment company offers certificates for a proportional part of the portfolio (a *unit* of the portfolio). The portfolio is selected by the promoters and remains virtually intact, with little discretionary management.

2. The *open-end* or *mutual funds* investment companies constantly offer to sell new shares. The shares are sold directly by the company (or by a broker-dealer or underwriter). The mutuals continually adjust their portfolio of assets.
3. *Closed-end* investment companies issue a "limited" number of shares of common stock. These stocks are traded in regular financial markets. They may also issue marketable bonds or borrow from other firms in limited amounts.

The history of investment intermediaries is entwined with the history of other financial intermediaries in the United States. Before the Civil War, many financial intermediaries held a wide range of assets in their portfolios. The name "investment bankers" has been applied to many financial intermediaries that held large amounts of common stock and long-term bonds, but despite their similar name and their holdings of securities, they were not the specific forerunners of investment companies.[1] The term *investment banker* is now sometimes applied to firms specialized in underwriting new issues of securities. The underwriting function, viewed separately, does not include the creation of a different financial asset from those that are sold, as is specified in the definition of financial intermediaries in Chapter 16. Underwriters can probably better be classified for most analyses as firms that earn their income from specific fees, rather than the kind of spread in interest rates described in the definition of financial intermediaries in Chapter 16. These fees depend on the markup on the securities they underwrite.

In a broad way, investment banking in its earlier form and investment companies are related by their purchase of securities. However, investment companies, such as mutual funds, did not flourish in the United States until the 1920s, when there was widespread interest in participating in the stock market. Small investors could buy claims against a diversified portfolio of equities. Their appeal to small investors also distinguishes them from large investment bankers.

The demand for securities diminished with the dramatic fall in the prices of stocks in the 1930s. The value of investment companies' portfolios fell rapidly. There was an adverse reaction to the "management" of funds by the investment company management. Some of this criticism was undoubtedly unwarranted. After all, the public invested in investment companies in order to benefit from a diversified portfolio of stocks. They would not invest in an investment company that held only cash in anticipation of a general stock price decline. Why pay a management fee for holding cash?

This adverse reaction led to the formation of fixed (trust) investment companies in which the management was obligated to purchase a particular group of assets. *Certificates of participation* in these companies could be exchanged for either a proportion of the specified assets in the investment company's portfolio, or for the proceeds of the sales of this "unit" of the portfolio. The fixed trust rapidly diminished in importance due to the public's distaste for its rigid portfolio.

There were less than 20 mutuals by 1929. The value of their assets fell less than the stock market average. They grew from $75 million in assets in 1932 to $506 million in 1936 as they again attracted widespread investor interest.

The post-World War II period of growth in investment companies was influenced by a continuing rise in stock prices and by government regulation. The Investment Company Act of 1940 prohibited investment companies from buying on margin. They could not invest in companies where their management owned more than a prescribed amount of equity. Sales charges on contractual plans of payment (*front-end loads*) were limited to 9 percent of the total amount invested during the plan. Registered investment companies were required to have a net worth of $100,000 before they launched a new fund with a public offering of funds.

Perhaps the most severe limitations of the 1940 Investment Company Act pertained to borrowing. Borrowing was limited to 33 percent of the net assets of the investment funds, and mutuals were prohibited from issuing bonds or preferred stock. These prohibitions prevented investment companies from holding a large proportion of bonds relative to equities. New financial assets, such as dual-funds shares, partially abrogated the regulations by inventing equities that had the fixed-income characteristics of bonds.

The Investment Company Act of 1940 was probably a minor factor in the restoration of public confidence in investment companies. A major factor in restoring public confidence was the rising value of the stock in their portfolios. There was greater public demand for the new mutual funds than the older closed-end companies. The closed-end companies were probably more adversely affected by restrictions on borrowing since their stock issue was limited. "By 1968 there were only 14 diversified closed-end companies, compared with 240 mutual funds."[2] Some mutual funds were aggressively sold with commissions of 8 percent to 9 percent on sales up to $10,000. Funds that charge separately for these costs are called *load funds*. Other mutual funds take their management fees solely from the income on their portfolio. The financial assets of open-end funds, excluding money market funds, rose in value from $15.8 billion in 1959 to $47.6 billion in 1970, up to $56 billion at the end of 1973 and then down to $51.7 billion in September 1981.

In 1962, the Self-Employed Individuals Tax Retirement Act (Keogh Act) permitted self-employed individuals to set up retirement programs that allowed contributions that were deductible from taxable income. Taxes are payable on the later payouts from the pension plan. The Keogh Act programs are allowed to invest in a special series of government bonds, certain life insurance contracts, special trust accounts at banks, and mutual funds. Many mutual funds began offering Keogh plans, which puts them partially in the pension business along with contractual intermediaries.

The 1981 tax act (the Economic Recovery Act of 1981) allowed larger contributions by self-employed individuals to their Keogh plan, contributions that could be deducted from their current income. They were allowed to deduct the lesser of $15,000 or 15 percent of net self-employment earnings.

The 1981 tax act also allowed deductible contributions for employed individuals already in qualified pension plans, up to $2000 for an individual ($2250 if a nonworking spouse is included). The *individual retirement accounts*, IRAs, had not previously been allowed for individuals in pension plans. The Employee Retirement Security Act of 1974 authorized IRAs for employees who worked for employers with no pension plans. Not only are the contributions deductible from taxable income, the earnings on the invested funds are also tax free if they are not withdrawn. The earliest funds can be withdrawn without a special tax penalty is at age $59\frac{1}{2}$. At that time payouts are treated as regular taxable income.

The mutual funds, together with many other types of financial intermediaries, offered these types of pensions. The pension part of their operations makes them partially contractual intermediaries.

Money Market Funds

A giant investment company suddenly appeared on the scene in 1978, the money market mutual funds, or as they are more commonly called, the money market funds (MMFs). The MMFs are mutual funds that specialize in a portfolio of very liquid short-term debt instruments, such as U.S. Treasury bills and certificates of deposits from large domestic and foreign banks. A customer may have purchased a share in these funds for minimum investments, such as $500, $1000, or $5000, in 1982. Funds may be withdrawn from the MMFs by mail, by telephone, or in many cases, by a check for $500 or more.

The giant group of MMFs grew to over $197.1 billion in aggregate shares by May 1982. The first MMF had begun to offer shares only a few years earlier, in 1972, and by the end of 1977, the total value of MMF assets was a comparatively small $3 to $4 billion. Growth began to accelerate in 1978 and then to boom in 1979. In 1982 there were approximately 150 MMFs, each with $100 million or more in assets.[3]

The explanation of the explosion in MMFs is not hard to find. Market interest rates shot up in 1978 and 1979, and the interest rates on checking accounts and passbook savings accounts at the depository intermediaries were held down by government regulation. The spread between the yields at the five largest MMFs and the passbook savings account ceiling at thrift intermediaries is shown in Figure 20-1. Superimposed on this figure is the value of the *monthly change in MMF*. The spread rose from the middle of 1977 until the end of 1978, with the most rapid increase at the end of 1978. Investment in MMFs also rose after a slight lag and then, in the beginning of 1979, with a huge jump. In March 1980, MMFs were temporarily required to hold a 15 percent reserve at the

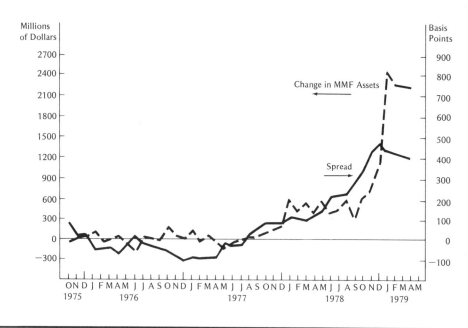

Figure 20-1

Change in the size of money market funds and the spread between their yield and the ceiling rate on passbook savings accounts at thrifts. *Source:* Timothy Q. Cook and Jeremy G. Duffield, "Money Market Mutual Funds: A Reaction to Government Regulation or a Lasting Financial Innovation?" *Economic Review*, Federal Reserve Bank of Richmond (July–August 1979), p. 27.

Federal Reserve on any new deposits as part of President Carter's program to restrain credit.

There were a number of similar investment intermediaries that grew during the 1970s.[4] They all invested primarily in short-term money market securities. Along with money market funds they are called *short-term investment pools* (STIPs). They include short-term tax-exempt funds (which invest in short-term tax-exempt securities), a Treasury bill pool, short-term investment trusts (which invest primarily in Eurodollar CDs), and short-term investment funds (which are pooled accounts of bank trust departments which invest mostly in commercial paper). All these STIPs resemble MMFs and grew for the same reasons.

MMFs can be divided into three groups: (1) *Institutional funds* are available only through institutional investors. Noninstitutional MMFs, available to all investors, are divided into two groups. Some are available through (2) *stockbrokers* and *dealers*. Others are available to all investors. These are (3) *general-purpose MMFs*. The assets of these three groups are shown in Table 20-1.

Are MMFs a temporary phenomenon?[5] No, they are probably not temporary unless they are ended by government regulation. They would be injured slightly if they were prohibited from offering withdrawals by check and they would suffer to a larger extent if reserve requirements were permanently imposed. Many individuals, induced by the large

TABLE 20-1

Assets of Money Market Funds, 1978–1981 (Assets in Billions of Dollars and Percentage of Total; Average Account Size in Thousands of Dollars)

End of Month	Total Assets ($)	Broker/Dealer			General Purpose			Institutional		
		Assets ($)	Assets (%)	Average Account Size ($)	Assets ($)	Assets (%)	Average Account Size ($)	Assets ($)	Assets (%)	Average Account Size ($)
December 1976	3.4	.4	12	16.7	2.4	70	16.6	.6	18	78.5
December 1977	3.9	.8	20	17.0	2.1	53	17.3	1.0	27	84.8
December 1978	10.9	3.7	34	16.9	3.9	36	19.5	3.3	31	63.9
December 1979	45.2	22.9	51	16.6	12.7	28	15.8	9.7	21	73.6
December 1980	74.4	38.9	52	14.3	21.6	29	11.8	14.0	19	65.0
November 1981	181.6	93.7	52	17.3	54.2	30	12.5	33.7	18	140.1

Source: Quarterly Review, Federal Reserve Bank of New York (Winter 1981–1982), p. 11.

spread in 1978 and 1979, learned how to hold a portfolio of high-grade debt instruments, including negotiable certificates of deposit with minimum denominations of $100,000, by buying shares in MMFs. Brokers and their customers have learned to transfer money to brokerage house MMFs when cash accumulates in the customer's accounts. The services provided by MMFs were evidently so attractive that during 1976, when the spread shown in Figure 20-1 was negative, there was still growth in MMFs during some months. Since the ceilings on intermediaries are to be removed by 1986, the MMFs will then be facing much more intense competition, and their relative size should diminish substantially.

Some insight into the future of MMFs when banks pay market rates of interest can be found by studying Canadian MMFs. Depository institutions in Canada may pay market rates on savings.[6] In 1982, Canadian banks paid 12 percent on day-to-day savings accounts and $17\frac{3}{4}$ percent on one-year maturity accounts, available at $1000 minimum. In March 1982, the third Canadian MMF went into operation and a fourth MMF was being formed. One inducement to invest in these funds was suggested to be their more rapid adjustment to market rates. Still the total amount in funds was small. The oldest fund, AGF-MMF, had approximately $30 million and the other fund in existence in March 1982 had $6 million. The new MMF being formed in Canada was advertised to be investing in Canadian Treasury bills, bank term deposits, and A-rated corporate short-term notes.

The depository intermediaries guarantee the depositor a fixed nominal sum, whereas the MMFs promise only a pro rata share of the value of their total portfolio, which can vary. Precisely because MMFs offer a different type of asset, one that can vary in nominal value and therefore can pay a slightly greater rate of return on average, some should be demanded.

Are accounts at MMFs money? They are included in M2 in the United States. They are limited as a medium of exchange (because of the $500 minimum check size) with a capital risk of getting back a smaller nominal amount than invested. Tests may determine if some measure of the value of shares at MMFs or shares in any of the STIPs allow better predictions of the price level and other variables to justify including them in the concept of money.

In 1982, some U.S. banks began offering a service called a money fund *sweep* service. Banks made arrangements with money market funds to transfer funds in and out of depositor's accounts so as to maintain a constant minimum balance. All kinds of minimum balance requirements, including IRA or money market fund certificates, were suggested. Some banks reportedly favored for their sweep accounts institutional MMFs that did not offer similar services to the public.

The reaction of the federal and state bank regulators, the Reagan administration, and the Congress was not clear in early 1982. In effect, the sweep service made negotiable certificates of deposits (in denominations of $100,000 or more) easily available to the depositors, insofar as the MMFs in the sweep service bought them. However, since FDIC insurance was $100,000 per depositor, these CDs would not be fully insured if a MMF exceeded that amount of CDs purchased at a single bank. In addition, the MMFs are not insured against shortages due to fraud, embezzlement, and mistakes in record keeping. If the sweep service caught on, the medium of exchange in the United States, if it is defined to include sweep service accounts, would lose some of its insured coverage. That may be viewed by many as a nonproblem, especially if the ceiling rates on interest payments on NOW accounts are removed by 1986, as scheduled. Most banks would then lose the incentive to offer sweep services.

Stockbrokers

There are many firms that buy and sell securities for customers on a commission basis. Some medium-sized regional firms often follow the equities of the firms in their region closely.[7] Some firms specialize in a single market such as tax-exempt bonds. Some firms are called *discounters* since they offer minimal service and research, but their fees are usually less than half those charged by the full-service firms.[8] Some firms are geared to dealing only with institutions and individuals of wealth: six- and seven-figure portfolios.[9] These firms include large firms, often with offices in major cities. Many of the firms limited to large investors offer a broad range of services, such as underwriting or, as it is also called, investment banking.

The very large brokerage houses offering a wide range of services to the public include Shearson; Bache; Dean Witter Reynolds; E. F. Hutton; Paine Webber; Smith Barney Harris Upham; Drexel Burnham Lambert; Kidder Peabody; and the largest, Merrill Lynch, Pierce, Fenner and Smith, Inc. (often called simply Merrill Lynch).

Merrill Lynch, Pierce, Fenner and Smith, Inc., the largest stockbroker in the United States, had five MMFs with assets of $38.5 billion on February 11, 1982.[10] These MMFs run by stockbrokerage firms make these brokers part investment intermediaries.

Stockbrokers also offer pension plans: Keogh and IRA plans and *Simplified Employee Pension Plans* (SEPs)—IRA plans established by an employer for employees. These investments make stockbrokers part contractual intermediaries.

Merrill Lynch also offers a special type of account accessible by check which they call a *cash management account.* (Dean Witter Reynolds' similar plan is called *active assets account.* In 1981 and 1982, other large brokerage businesses, including Shearson/American Express, Bache Halsey Stuart Fields, and E. F. Hutton, unvailed similar plans.) Thirteen billion dollars was held in its cash management accounts in 1981. The investor selects his or her portfolio of financial assets, including Merrill Lynch MMFs. A check may be written on Bank One of Ohio. The check is drawn against the value of the cash assets (such as MMF shares) plus the unused margin on securities in the Merrill Lynch cash management account. The portfolio must be valued at $20,000 or more. (One regional brokerage planned a minimum of only $1000.) The device allows market rates of interest to be earned on deposited funds and it reduces the transactions costs of shifting from securities into a medium of exchange and back again. In addition, interest payments on margin credit is generally deductible from taxable income. The cash management account makes Merrill Lynch partly a depository intermediary.

The cash management account is in large part a device to circumvent ceiling rate legal limitations for interest payments on depository intermediaries' accounts. If those ceilings are allowed to rise closer to market rates (since they are scheduled for complete removal by 1986), the cash management account will meet stiffer competition. There have been suggestions to bring these activities under the same regulations that apply to other depositories. These suggestions, as well as their alleged futility, were reported in a 1982 article in *The New York Times* entitled the "National Bank of Merrill Lynch."[11] The article, "Quartering the Bull," began by showing the sources of Merrill Lynch's 1981 revenues, using the bull in Merrill Lynch's advertising to identify the company).[12] They were reported to have earned 45.4 percent of their revenue from interest on margin accounts, 22.8 percent from commissions on securities trading, 10.9 percent on their own portfolio, 8.6 percent on underwriting and acquisition advice, 5.2 percent on real estate, 4.2 percent on insurance, and 2.9 percent on other activities, such as management and service fees.

The article also noted:

> Bountiful, Utah, is a tranquil farm community of barely 40,000 people. It is also the home of the Utah Bank and Trust Company. Utah Bank's deposits, now some $41 million, have slid about $1 million in the last two years.

Morris H. Atwood, the president, says he isn't sure who has been rustling his long-loyal checking account customers but high on the list of suspects he puts Merrill Lynch & Company, the financial services firm that offers customers high-yielding money-market funds with check-writing privileges.

So Mr. Atwood and Utah's other small-town bankers set out to do what thousands of their big-city brethren have pondered doing for a couple of years. They set out to stop Merrill Lynch. The bankers went to their friends in the Legislature and got an amendment to a pending bill to put Merrill and firms like it under the wing of the state banking department. That in turn would have just about put Merrill out of the checking account business in Utah. However, Merrill and its allies in the securities industry lobbied fiercely against the amendment, and succeeded in killing it.

It was the most serious assault yet against Merrill Lynch's exceptional new service and it could well be the last. Wall Street's biggest stock broker has progressed so far into the business of commercial banking and other financial services that nothing seems likely to stop it. Today, with some $23 billion in its Ready Assets money fund, the nation's biggest, and $13 billion in its more flexible Cash Management Account, Merrill's holdings of deposit-like client funds exceed the domestic deposits of Citibank by $16 billion. And unlike most bank checking accounts, both of Merrill's pay substantial interest.

In what seemed like grudging recognition of this fact, Walter B. Wriston, chairman of the board of Citicorp, remarked before a Senate banking committee last fall, at a time of higher interest rates, "The genie will never go back into the bottle. People know the difference between 17 percent and 5 percent, and so the whole system has to adjust to it."[13]

One place the bull was certainly not quartered was in one of the three classes of financial intermediaries; it ran through all three classifications.

Finance Companies

Finance companies held $168.1 billion in financial assets in the third quarter of 1981 (see Table 20-2). In general, there are three types of finance companies: *sales finance companies* and *consumer finance companies*, both for consumers, and *business* or *commercial finance companies* for businesses.

Finance companies borrow funds from other financial intermediaries and they sell their own credit instruments in the financial markets. They are licensed and supervised by diverse state laws. Domestic finance companies had $84.5 billion in consumer loans and $76.9 billion in business loans in the third quarter of 1981. The finance companies had borrowed $14.7 billion from the commercial banks and raised $51.2 billion through the sale of commercial paper.

Consumer finance companies specialize in small loans directly to consumers. Many of the consumer finance companies also purchase some consumer loans made by other companies. For example, an automobile dealer may sell an automobile for $12,000 financed by a $8000 loan and $4000 down payment. The dealer may be able to obtain a greater return

TABLE 20-2

Domestic Finance Companies, Third Quarter 1981 (Billions of Dollars)

Assets	168.1	Liabilities	168.1
Accounts receivable, gross		Bank loans	14.7
Consumer	84.5	Commercial paper	51.2
Business	76.9	Debt	
Total	161.3	Short-term	11.9
Less reserve for unearned		Long-term	50.7
income and loans	27.7	Other	17.1
Accounts receivable, net	133.6	Equity	22.4
Other	34.5		

Source: Federal Reserve Bulletin (December 1981), p. A39.

on his or her capital by investing in additional cars rather than additional loan paper. He or she sells the loan to a finance company and the purchaser usually is asked to make direct payments to the finance company. Consumer loan companies have supplied approximately 20 percent of all consumer credit.

Most of the loans for automobiles and other installment credit owned by finance companies are held by *sales finance companies*. They are free from many of the regulations applicable to direct small loan *consumer finance companies*. The sales finance companies make a number of different types of loans. They may buy installment loans from retailers, especially automobile dealers. They may lend money to retailers. Many have extensive insurance operations.

A few sales finance companies supply factoring services, but these are mostly offered by *factoring companies*. A factor loans money to a business firm, but requires that all the firm's customers (the accounts receivable) pay the factor instead of the firm. The factor takes a percentage of the accounts receivable and sends the remainder to the firm.

There is not a clear distinction between a sales finance company and a consumer finance company where state regulations allow both types of finance companies to make similar loans.

Finance companies finance much of their operations through very short-term *commercial paper*. Commercial paper is discussed in the next chapter. Finance companies such as General Motors Acceptance Corporation, Commercial Credit Corporation, CIT Financial Corporation, and Sears, Roebuck Acceptance Corporation directly buy and sell short-term commercial paper on the prime commercial paper market. In the third quarter of 1981, commercial paper liabilities of finance companies was 3.5 times larger than bank loans (see Table 20-2).

There are commercial finance companies that specialize in many types of business loans. Some firms specialize in housing credit (mortgage companies). Other firms (building trusts) make short-term loans for the construction of buildings. The federal government makes business loans and loan guarantees that are described in Part VII.

Finance companies have been affected by the general movement toward deregulation and the expansion into new financial services beginning in the late 1970s. Some finance companies have established nationwide computer facilities for transferring funds. Beneficial Corporation developed a revolving loan system in about half the states, where the law permits. It operates through regular checkable accounts at a commercial bank, which Beneficial acquired for that purpose. Household Finance purchased a savings and loan in California, and Gulf and Western's Associates purchased a consumer credit card operation in California.

Contractual Intermediaries

The major contractual intermediaries, with the value of their financial assets (in billions of dollars) at the end of 1980 are[14]

1. Life insurance companies $479.2
2. Other insurance companies   197.7
3. Private pension funds   256.9
4. State and local government pension funds   185.2

Contractual intermediaries create credit instruments that form a contractual relationship with the buyer, such as an annuity or pension. The terms of payments by the buyers and the obligations of the issuer vary according to the contract. Under stipulated conditions at specified times they can be converted into an exact amount of money and/or a specified share of earnings, or a loan at a specified interest rate. The claims against contractual intermediaries provide the holder with an asset that can be very liquid, often at a distant date.

Contractual intermediaries directly sell services such as life and property insurance. The administrative costs or operating expenses added to a premium are called the "load factor." Insofar as the premiums just cover these costs plus the actuarial cost of the insurance, no financial intermediation takes place. Services are sold for a fee. However, the premiums are invested and earn income. This allows a portion of the insurance companies income to come from the spread between the return on their portfolio and the return they pay on the financial assets—insurance policies they create. Insurance policies may be viewed from an economic viewpoint as a debt instrument with the interest contingent on specific events, such as a fire (casualty insurance), a death (life insurance), or the attainment of a particular age (savings plan, or in the 1800s—tontine). These types of insurance policies are discussed in the next two sections.

Insurance companies create other types of financial assets than insurance policies. They create pension and annuity plans. They also have money market funds, making them partly investment intermediaries.

Life Insurance Companies

Life insurance companies had financial assets of $509.5 billion in September 1981. Their assets are listed in Table 20-3.

Despite stringent regulations affecting life insurance companies' portfolios in each of the fifty states, their aggregate portfolios contain a slightly wider range of assets than commercial banks, MSBs, and SLs. They own a substantial amount of common and preferred stock for pension funds as well as corporate bonds. They invest in both residential and commercial mortgages, and own substantial real estate. They hold securities from federal and local government units and from foreign governments.

Life insurers are the major source among institutional investors (followed by pension funds and other insurance companies) that supply long-term funds. The need of these financial intermediaries for long-term financial assets as a hedge against their long-term liabilities was one reason advanced by David Meiselman for the strength in the long-term bond market and the absence of either a liquidity premium on long-term bonds or congenital weakness in that market. This assertion about the term structure of interest rates and opposing views was presented in Part III.

A key distinction in comparing life insurance companies with other financial intermediaries is that they grew under the individual state laws. The decision of the U.S. Supreme Court in *Paul v. Virginia* in 1869 held that "issuing a policy of insurance is not a transaction of commerce" and "such contracts are not inter-state transactions, though the parties may be domiciled in different states." This decision blocked federal regulation for a long time. Federal regulation imposes costs and benefits (such as the discount window and free services—before 1981—from the

TABLE 20-3

Assets of Life Insurance Companies, September 1981 (Billions of Dollars)

Securities	
Government	24.3
U.S.	7.7
State and local	7.0
Foreign	9.6
Business	250.3
Bonds	205.9
Stocks	44.4
Mortgages	137.0
Real estate	17.8
Policy loans	47.0
Other assets	33.0
Total assets	509.5

Source: Federal Reserve Bulletin (January 1982), p. A29.

Federal Reserve). Thus a vague call for deregulation leaving some financial intermediaries under federal supervision and some under state supervision may not produce the level playing field discussed in Chapter 17.

Life insurance companies' incomes are subject to lower tax rates than incomes received by nonfinancial corporations. Therefore, tax-free, lower-yield municipal obligations have had less appeal to these insurance companies.[15]

Life insurance companies began to grow rapidly in the 1840s in the United States. The appeal of the mutual form of organization and aggressive selling stimulated their growth. There was only one life insurance company in the United States until 1769, but by 1840 there were five, and forty-eight in 1850.[16] The most rapid period of growth for life insurance companies was the late nineteenth century. Among the developments that made life insurance companies the fastest-growing financial intermediary in this period were the reintroduction of the *tontine* and the sale of industrial life insurance.

The tontine insurance plan originated in seventeenth-century France and had been introduced in the United States in the early 1800s, but fell out of favor. In the form of the tontine introduced by Equitable, the full face value plus accumulated dividends were paid only to the members of a group of policyholders who survived a given period, such as ten or fifteen years; estates of members who died during this period received only the face value; and those who let their policies lapse received nothing. Policyholders bet on their superior longevity. Life expectancy at birth, even as late as 1882, for males and females in Massachusetts, was only 41.7 and 43.5 years, respectively. In the late 1800s, many thought they might live much longer and did not want their premiums raised because they had to pay for those who died at a younger age. On December 31, 1868, Equitable announced to its agents the new "Tontine Dividend Life Assurance Policies" in a pamphlet dated December 22.

> There are many persons who from vigorous health, comfortable position in life, great family vitality, or from a hopefulness of disposition, which often secures the end it anticipates, are very confident of living long, and yet feel the duty of making some provision against the great calamity of early death, which *may* come by accident or sudden disease, even to the most robust. . . . Again, this class of persons are apt to think that they are better risks than the average of individuals assured by Life Companies, and that if all assurants are placed in the same class, their own superior vitality will not receive its due reward, but that much of the profit derived from them, will be used to pay the losses occurring among weaker and shorter lived risks.[17]

Was this form of the tontine a good buy, or was it as Herman Kroos and Martin R. Blyn describe?

> The tontine feature, coupled with aggressive salesmanship, enabled a few companies to take over the business. . . . Tontines benefited the capital markets and, at least in the short run, the companies that wrote them, but these benefits came at the expense of policyholders, who voluntarily par-

ticipated in what was essentially a swindle. The word "swindle" may seem excessively harsh, but it was a swindle because most of those who participated really did not understand what they were participating in.[18]

Whether or not these criticisms are justified, it is probably fortuitous that the extreme form of the tontine, where all funds go to the sole survivor of a group, was never popular in the United States because it was thought to encourage homicide.

Industrial life insurance originated in 1854 in England and was introduced in the United States in the 1870s. It is distinguished from other life insurance by its small face value and small payments. Metropolitan Life sold industrial life insurance policies worth $25 million.

In 1890 the assets of life insurance companies were thirty-two times as large as they were in 1860. The struggle of the life insurance companies to increase their size so they controlled vast assets drew public indignation and further government control. Even so, the life insurance companies continued to grow with only a moderate decline in the early part of the 1930s depression.

The difficulty incurred by the policyholders in maintaining premium payments during the depression of the 1930s and the reduction in the real value of these hard-won savings due to inflated post-World War II prices caused many investors to shift to other assets. The relative size of life insurance companies compared to other financial intermediaries declined, although life insurance companies continued a rapid growth.

The composition of assets they issued changed. Life insurance with combined savings plans, such as endowment or retirement income, became a smaller share of total life insurance sales. Term insurance, which provides little or no savings, grew from about 10 percent of ordinary life insurance in 1950 to 54 percent in 1981. This has had an important effect on the maturity of investments that life insurance companies must buy to match their insurance liabilities. Life insurance liabilities can be matched with long-term bonds. Term insurance liabilities require shorter-maturity debt instruments.

Much of the relative decline in the 1970s in pension funds held by life insurance companies as a proportion of total pension funds was due to increased competition from other sources. These sources were given advantages by government regulations. From 1959 to 1961, life insurance pension funds were taxed at a higher rate. In 1961, life insurance pension funds' income was exempted from taxation. In 1962, the state of New York amended its law permitting life insurance companies to keep "separate accounts" for pension reserves and to invest in the wider range of assets permitted trust companies, including limited amounts of common stock. This was undertaken to maintain the competitive position of the state's private insurance firms. New York has occupied the position of leadership in setting regulations for life insurance companies. Between 1959 and 1970 the pension fund reserves of life insurance companies grew by over 40 percent to $41 billion, while the assets of other private noninsured pension funds grew less rapidly, by approximately 32 percent to $106 billion.

And then came the 1970s. "Change has been whirling through the life insurance business, converting it to something far different from what it was five years ago," wrote Carol Loomis in 1980.[19] Rising rates of inflation and interest rates, as well as the rapid increase in employer insurance plans as a fringe benefit, brought many changes. The rate of return on policyholders' savings was estimated to average under 5 percent in the policies of 100 companies examined.[20] In this respect, policyholders paid a high opportunity cost by not having their savings invested in assets that were more in line with the rising market interest rates. However, policyholders benefited from policy loan rates that were also low. The policy loans stood at $47 billion in September 1981 (see Table 20-3). This was $5.6 billion more than the 1980 average. These interest rate squeezes are examples of the effects of rapid inflation and the accompanying high interest rates of the 1970s and early 1980s on long-term contracts made on the basis of the lower levels of inflation and interest rates that existed in all earlier peacetime periods in the United States. One result has been that beginning in 1973, when inflation rapidly accelerated, the growth in ordinary life insurance (which accumulates cash value) declined while term insurance (which contains no cash value) accelerated.

Nevertheless, the industry kept growing rapidly due to the increase in insurance plans sold to businesses (group insurance policies) and the increase in pension plans. Life insurance companies premiums from group health ($22.3 billion) and group life ($8.5 billion) exceeded the premiums they received from ordinary life insurance ($29.5 billion) in 1980.

Other Insurance Companies

Other insurance companies offer insurance against many different types of risk. The *fire and casualty* insurance companies cover risks of fire, automobile accident and theft, workmen's compensation, and so on. *Multiple-line* insurance companies offer property and casualty insurance, and a miscellaneous group of other firms provide protection against different specific risks. They held 73.7 percent of their investments in bonds in 1980, mostly state, municipal, and federal bonds. Common stock represented 20.1 percent, preferred stock 5 percent, and other investments 1.2 percent.[21]

Some of these types of general insurance companies existed in the colonial period in the United States. They grew rapidly in the nineteenth century, with some major setbacks due to disasters. The Chicago Fire of 1871, for example, caused the bankruptcy of sixty-eight fire insurance companies. The introduction of the automobile caused a large growth of casualty insurance companies in the 1920s. Many general insurance companies adopted *multiple-line* insurance instead of specializing in one type of insurance. There was competition from *specialty firms* which sold insurance on a few types of risks (such as automobile insurance) at a low price (sometimes 20 percent lower). Specialty firms developed continuous membership policies and other cost-saving techniques. Specialty companies such as State Farm and Allstate used their own sales force rather than the alternative system of selling insurance through independent agencies.

The post-World War II period had been marked by innovation in the sale of all kinds of insurance, tailored to the changing needs of consumers and firms. The specialty firms, such as State Farm, branched into other types of insurance, such as home insurance. The transfer to the government of health insurance for the elderly covered by Social Security has been a major post-World War II development.

The rapid inflation in the 1970s and early 1980s has played an important role in casualty life insurance. The December 1979 to December 1980 rise in the U.S. consumer price index was 12.4 percent. Premiums for insurance rose in response as underwriting losses rose, in part, from inflation.

Inflation was not the sole culprit. There were fifty-one catastrophies, such as major windstorms, in 1980 causing insurers to pay out $1.2 billion. There were also other large insured losses. The property and casualty insurance business was hit by a *net loss* of $3.33 billion on underwriting operations in 1980. This was the second highest loss in the industry's history; a net loss of $4.2 billion was incurred in 1975. The other major gross underwriting payouts were as follows: Although the number of traffic accidents dropped, economic loss rose 2 percent, to $57.5 billion. Property losses from fire rose 15.6 percent, to $5.6 billion. Losses from robbery, burglary, larceny, and vehicle theft were up 28 percent, to $9 billion. The $100 million Las Vegas MGM Grand Hotel fire in November 1980 was the largest single insured loss.

Private, State, and Local Government Pension Plans

Pension plans can be classified as insured or noninsured. Insured pension plans are administered by insurance companies. Noninsured plans are usually separate entities managed by a committee appointed by a sponsoring organization, which in turn uses the services of a financial intermediary, such as a bank, for safeguarding the assets and investing the premiums. The private noninsured plans have been introduced by corporations, unions, and nonprofit organizations. Some pension plans are operated by the federal government (railroad retirement and Social Security plans) and by state and local governments.

Noninsured pension plans had assets of $256.9 billion at the end of 1980, while insured plans amounted to $165.8 billion. As shown in Table 20-4, they held substantial amounts of stocks, amounting to $110.94 billion, or approximately 50 percent of their assets at the end of 1979.

TABLE 20-4

Distribution of Assets of Noninsured Pension Plans (Book Value at End of 1979; Billions of Dollars)

U.S. government securities	22.96
Corporate and other bonds	59.54
Stocks	
Preferred	1.35
Common	110.94
Mortgages	3.09
Cash	8.61
Other	17.48
Total	223.47

Source: 1980 Pension Facts (Washington, D.C.: American Council of Life Insurance, n.d.), p. 20.

Pension plans began in the United States in the 1870s as *industrial* plans. American Express Company was first in 1879, followed by only approximately twelve similar plans by 1900. Private pension funds for employees grew more rapidly until 1929, when there were 397 plans covering 3.7 million employees, or one-eighth of the labor force. Unions, beginning in 1900 with the Pattern Makers' League of North America, also offered pension plans. Most early industrial plans were entirely paid by the employer. During the 1930s, private pension plan growth was moderate, with only 15 percent of the labor force covered in 1937.

After 1940, however, there was a huge expansion. A Supreme Court decision in 1949 contributed to this rapid growth. Employers generally had given pension plans on a selective basis. The Supreme Court, by declining to review a National Labor Relations Board rule, let stand the decision that required Inland Steel Company to bargain with its employees over wages and other conditions of employment, including pension benefits. Pension plans became part of the fringe benefits for which labor unions bargained together with higher wage rates. In the twenty years following World War II, more than half the workers in private employment were covered by private pension plans. There were 26 million persons covered in 1963 compared to 6.4 million in 1945. Private pension funds grew from $1 billion in 1940 to over $70 billion in 1967 and $256.9 billion at the end of 1980. There were 24.9 million people in private pension plans not yet receiving pension and 5.4 million people receiving pensions in 1975.

The Internal Revenue Service grants noninsured pension plans tax-exempt status if they meet certain requirements. Since 1958, when the Welfare and Pension Plan Disclosure Act was passed, they must provide financial information to the Department of Labor.

Extensive pension reform legislation to take effect between 1975 and 1981 was contained in the Employee Retirement Income Security Act of 1974 (ERISA). The act covered regulations regarding vesting time (the time one must work before being entitled to receive retirement benefits). Employers were required to choose one of three plans for vesting. (1) An individual could be vested with full entitlement to benefits after ten years of service. (2) An individual could be vested after five years of service starting with entitlement to 25 percent of the pension plan and working up to 100 percent of the pension plan by fifteen years of service. (3) The third plan is known as the "Rule of 45." An employee is entitled to 50 percent vesting when his or her age plus number of years of service (employment) add to 45. Thus, if an individual is 45 years old, he or she would immediately receive 50 percent vesting. The Rule of 45 allows for 10 percent vesting for each succeeding year until full vesting is achieved.

ERISA also required that indicia (evidence) of ownership of foreign assets by employee benefit plans be maintained in locations under the jurisdiction of U.S. district courts, or as specified by regulations of the Secretary of Labor. Regulations were eased in 1981 to allow banks to keep indicia in a foreign bank or other specified place under regulation by the foreign government. For example, Chase Manhattan Bank and Mitsubishi Bank of California (through the worldwide facilities of Mitsubishi Bank of Japan) have provided *global master custodianship* for foreign investments of pension plans.

ERISA specified that those who manage a pension plan's assets must do so for the sole benefit of the participants. There are prohibitions against engaging in specified transactions between the plan and the sponsoring company. The Pension Benefit Guaranty Corporation (PBGC) was established by ERISA to guarantee certain pension benefits if an employer terminates a plan that has insufficient funds to pay benefits to the participants. PBGC was given the right to claim 30 percent of the equity of a bankrupt firm with pension liabilities.

In 1979, the number of persons insured for retirement benefits was 135.8 million. President Carter's Commission on Pension Policy found in 1979 that 45 percent of all private industry employees at least 18 years of age were covered by pensions in their current jobs.

Self-employed individuals, such as doctors and lawyers, increasingly have formed corporations because of the generous allowances for income that can be sheltered from income tax provided it is set aside for pensions. Congressman Charles B. Rangel attempted to lower the amount of income eligible for shelter each year; it was lowered to $30,000 after 1982.

Private pension plans compete with *state, local,* and *federal government pension plans.* State laws authorizing pensions for the handicapped were adopted in a number of states after 1900. In 1920, the retirement system for federal civil service employees was established. These plans were small compared to the old age "insurance" program of the federal government enacted into law in 1935 in the Social Security Act. By 1939 there were 22.9 million employed persons covered (and 17.8 million employed persons uncovered) for old age, survivors, and disability insurance under Social Security.

The Advisory Council on Social Security appointed by Caspar W. Weinberger, secretary of HEW, in April 1977 and chaired by W. Allen Wallis, then chancellor of the University of Rochester, reported back with dismal projections.[22] In 1976, there were 31 beneficiaries receiving social security payments for every 100 workers. In the year 2035, as a greater proportion of the population will be over 65 years of age, there will be 51 beneficiaries for every 100 workers, more than one beneficiary for every two workers.[23] Since the Social Security System has little funding, almost all payments will come from current receipts. Will such a transfer of income and associated high labor tax be politically feasible? The question may be drawn toward a resolution earlier than anticipated. Although the report recommended a proposed tax rate as a percent of covered wages of 10.9 percent for 1986 and then increasing to 16.1 percent in 2025, it is scheduled to be close to that in 1990. Amendments to the Social Security Act in 1977 increased the Social Security wage tax of 5.85 percent on employer and employee (a combined rate of 11.7 percent) in 1977, by a series of increases to 7.65 percent in 1990 (a combined rate of 15.3 percent of wages). The taxable portion of wages (the earnings base) was raised in a series of steps from $16,500 in 1977 to $29,700 in 1981, with provisions for automatic adjustments to $42,600 in 1987. On a labor income of $42,600, the combined payment at 15.3 percent would be $6517.80.

The question of the political feasibility of such a transfer is broader than questioning the specification of the correct rate of the Social Security employment tax or the form of government-owned pension plans. As the country becomes wealthier and as a greater proportion of the population exceeds 65 years of age, two conditions will exist regardless of the form of Social Security. One condition is that a smaller proportion of the population will be working. Second, an increasing amount of the income produced by workers will go to nonworkers. That increasing amount may or may not be an increasing proportion of the worker's income, depending on the rate of increase of productivity.

The important consideration for political acceptance is the form of the transfer. One suggestion is that the government insure minimum income only to poor people, regardless of age. The major part of the transfer to older people, that to more affluent individuals, could be made more palatable if it was made through private financial intermediaries. The cost of such pension plans would be borne by those purchasing the plans on the basis of expected cost.

There will be fewer arbitrary changes in tax rates, as there are with the present government plans, to fit financing needs that everyone knows are incorrectly specified. The government is in the position of pleasing a political constituency with large pension benefits and suffering politically from adequately raising the costs. Therefore, adequate financing is achieved only for short periods and when crisis demands. Under these conditions, payments and benefits for individuals have little or no meaningful relationship. The concept of an annuity or an insurance policy loses its meaning and with it much of the rationality and justification for payments by younger workers. Of course, changes in the basic public pension plans cannot be so rapid that they pull the rug out from those who have counted on them. Such changes must be slowly phased in over many years.

The Social Security Administration, operating under these considerations, does not have the characteristics of a financial intermediary, in general, or a pension and insurance fund, in particular. Within the Social Security Administration and to some extent in Congress, the label of insurance is cherished and tightly held.[24] It provides a rationale for raising employment taxes. The workers' reactions would be less adverse if individuals thought that their contributions were an actuarially correct payment for the insurance and annuity benefits; that a sound trust fund was being built up so that future generations of workers would not need to face unexpectedly higher tax rates. But that is not the case, as Edwin L. Dale, Jr., assistant director of the Office of Management and Budget for public affairs during the Reagan administration so vividly described:

> As everyone knows and acknowledges, the main Social Security trust fund, the one that pays old age and survivors' benefits, is technically bankrupt. The solution to the problem, for the short run at least, is to have this fund borrow from the disabililty and Medicare trust funds so that the checks can go out on time and in the full amount due.
> The administration and Congress agreed on that solution last year. But the legislation permitting the interfund borrowing expires at the end of 1982. There is no doubt that it, or an alternative means of keeping the checks flowing, will be passed this year, but it still has to be identified in the budget as proposed legislation.[25]

The projections of a deficit in Social Security's main trust fund, the Old Age and Survivors Trust Fund, shown in Table 20-5, take into account the affects of indexing the payments on the U.S. consumer price index. That is an improper way to tie these payments to the standard of living in the United States for two reasons. First, the index is currently seriously flawed. Second, the standard of living should be measured by real income (say, national income) or real consumption per capita. If prices rise but real national income and real consumption do not, more

TABLE 20-5

Outlays, Income, and Balances for the Old Age and Survivors Insurance Trust Fund (Billions of Dollars)

	Actual*			Projections†					
	1970	1975	1980	1981	1982	1983	1984	1985	1986
Outlays	$27.3	$56.7	$103.2	$122.6	$141.4	$158.7	$178.0	$199.3	$222.6
Income	31.7	58.8	100.1	117.8	129.0	143.0	159.1	181.9	203.7
Year-end balance (fiscal year)	32.6	39.9	24.6	19.7	7.4	−8.2	−27.1	−44.5	−63.5

* *Social Security Bulletin* (April 1981), p. 43.
† *Paying for Social Security: Funding Options for the Near Term* (Congressional Budget Office of the Congress of the United States, February 1981).
Source: Reprinted in Neil A. Stevens, "Indexation of Social Security Benefits—A Reform in Need of Reform," *Review*, Federal Reserve Bank of St. Louis (June–July 1981), p. 4.

will go to Social Security recipients. There will be a redistribution of real income toward Social Security recipients. This could occur, for example, with an imported-oil price rise. Internal prices would rise, while the oil price rise would act as an external tax, tending to reduce real income. Social Security payments should be indexed on an aggregate such as nominal national income or nominal consumption, in order to maintain the share of output going to recipients.[26]

State and local government pension plans covering state and local government employees grew from $2.5 billion in total assets in 1940 to $185.2 billion at the end of 1980. There are over 2000 of these funds. They have many of the characteristics of financial intermediaries, except that state and local governments can raise income through their powers to tax. They hold corporate securities, which is an interesting form of government ownership.

Despite the competition from government pension plans, private plans grew rapidly in the same periods. In fact, they grew much more rapidly than nominal national income. They were also combined with profit sharing and tailored to a wide variety of needs.

Why do people prefer this method of holding corporate credit instruments? Why not invest in one of the large mutual funds that has a similar, widely diversified portfolio? Employees could purchase a portfolio of similar assets without the mandatory pension contributions and the bias in most pension plans against employees who leave or retire before they are vested. In some company plans, high employee turnover means an increase in forfeited benefits which accrue disproportionately to the higher-paid, longer-tenured employees. Why should employees bargain for fringe benefits that increase the costs of changing jobs? Why not bargain for higher wages rather than equivalent employer outlays for pension funds?

The primary reason for the post-World War II surge in private pension fund growth appears to be the increase in personal and corporate taxes and the preferential tax treatment given pension funds. Employees have an incentive to take their pay in forms other than highly taxed money wage income. Favorable tax treatment is given to both contributions and income earned from assets invested by pension funds.

Personal Trust Funds

Personal trust funds (including managed estates) are assets placed in the care of administrators (formerly called "fiduciaries") who are often employed by financial intermediaries in their trust departments. The administrators of trust funds are very close in concept to investment companies and therefore are sometimes treated as financial intermediaries. Commercial banks provide trust services. In 1980, the value of assets in personal trust funds and estates managed by banks was $229 billion, as shown in Table 20-6. For comparison, consider that the income of the Old Age and Survivors Insurance Trust Fund for 1980 (shown in Table

TABLE 20-6

Personal Trusts and Estates Administered by Banks* (Asset Holdings at Year-Ends; Billions of Dollars)

		1969	1970	1971	1972	1973	1974	1975	1976	1977	1978	1979	1980
1	Total assets	132.761	135.411	159.678	183.104	170.640	142.615	164.862	192.750	189.575	179.325	200.564	228.992
2	Deposits + credit market instruments	34.145	36.926	42.000	45.532	49.632	51.916	57.124	66.168	71.381	69.016	76.926	79.948
3	Total deposits	3.478	3.808	4.858	5.710	5.917	6.235	5.938	7.022	7.665	6.936	7.123	7.217
4	Demand deposits	1.748	1.681	1.694	1.843	1.898	1.795	1.594	1.614	1.563	1.849	1.880	1.881
5	Time + savings accounts	1.730	2.127	3.164	3.867	4.019	4.440	4.344	5.408	6.102	5.087	5.243	5.336
6	Credit market instruments	30.667	33.118	37.142	39.822	43.715	45.681	51.186	59.146	63.716	62.080	69.803	72.731
7	U.S. government securities	8.860	9.566	8.803	8.628	10.012	11.623	14.094	15.753	17.021	15.713	19.154	21.287
8	State and local government securities	10.953	11.879	14.033	15.208	16.184	15.046	16.494	19.986	22.108	21.278	22.750	20.994
9	Other S-T obligations†	.0	.0	.0	.0	.0	.0	.0	.0	.0	9.071	12.294	14.446
10	Other securities	8.662	9.354	11.884	13.527	14.938	16.069	17.752	20.443	21.618	13.149	12.399	12.070
11	Mortgages	2.192	2.319	2.422	2.459	2.581	2.943	2.846	2.964	2.969	2.869	3.206	3.934
12	Corporate equities—common	88.438	87.199	104.899	123.835	107.200	76.120	91.350	109.611	100.284	92.700	104.244	124.765
13	—preferred	2.900	3.018	3.543	3.748	2.727	2.012	2.923	2.656	2.234	2.449	1.859	1.967
14	Real estate	5.473	6.210	6.814	7.450	8.151	9.158	10.141	10.820	11.883	12.183	13.830	18.347
15	All other assets	1.805	2.058	2.422	2.539	2.930	3.409	3.324	3.495	3.793	2.977	3.705	3.965

*Coverage:
1968–1977   All insured commercial banks; total trust assets.
1978   Insured commercial banks and 8 Federal Reserve member noninsured trust companies; trust assets over which bank has investment discretion. Omission of nondiscretionary trusts beginning 1978 makes the totals not comparable with earlier years.
1979–1980   Insured commercial and mutual savings banks, F.R. member trust companies, nonmember nondeposit trust companies owned by bank holding companies. Discretionary assets only. Mutual savings banks and trust companies introduced in 1979 held about 2 percent of total 1979 assets.
† Included in line 10 before 1978.
Source: Flow of Funds Accounts, Assets and Liabilities Outstanding 1975–80, Board of Governors of the Federal Reserve System (September 1981), p. 58.

20-5) was only 44 percent of that amount; the assets of all noninsured pension funds in 1979 (shown in Table 20-4) amounted to $223 billion, also less than that amount; and the total assets of life insurance companies (shown in Table 20-3) was 2.2 times larger.

The amount of common stock managed in these trust funds, $125 billion, makes banks major institutional participants in the stock markets. Banks manage investment funds in their trust departments.[27]

Funds are frequently placed in trust under agreements that have the characteristics of pensions or life insurance claims. The agreements often stipulate payments to the individual after his or her retirement or to his or her heirs. Income from these trusts is frequently taxed at a lower rate. In addition to this stimulant to the formation of trust agreements, trusts provide continuous "responsible" management of an estate according to the directions of the agreement. It allows the management of an estate to be under the direction of its founder even after his or her death. His or her beneficiaries may be inexperienced in handling the estate and may benefit from the managerial services of the trust officer.

Private trust funds may take a variety of forms. They may be held by a fiduciary who is not connected with a financial intermediary, such as a lawyer or a friend. Some of the common forms of trust agreements are sometimes differentiated by special characteristics that relate to tax treatment, portfolio management, privacy with respect to ownership and value of assets, and the transfer of assets to one's heirs.

A *living trust* is made during an individual's lifetime, with stipulations about the chain of succession to the income in the trust. It provides some privacy and reductions in costs during the legal proceedings (in probate court) when the income from the assets is transferred to another individual. It may be *revocable* or *irrevocable*, depending on the desire to retain the right to alter its provisions. An *irrevocable living trust* may have some tax advantages if the assets are not transferred to an heir but only the income from these assets is paid. A *land trust* is formed for real estate assets; a *testamentary trust* is established in a will to be effectuated at the time of death. It can provide for a smoother, less costly transfer of wealth. A *short-term trust* may shift income to a person in a lower tax bracket for a given period and then provide for the return of the principal. A *blind trust* provides the owner with no specific information on the composition of its portfolio. It is used by some government officials to avoid conflicts of interest between their activities and the chance of profit on their private assets.

Administrators of trust funds, such as commercial banks, manage vast amounts of securities, often with considerable latitude. There is the potential conflict of interest problem that commercial banks can loan money at favorable terms to firms in which they hold substantial equities in their trust department.

Sears, Roebuck and Company

Sears, Roebuck and Company, the largest retail sales firm in the United States, owns Dean Witter Reynolds, one of the largest stockbrokers. Sears also owns one of the largest private insurance companies, Allstate; the Allstate Savings and Loan with more than 100 branches in California; and one of the large private mortgage insurance companies, PMI. In February 1982, Sears' chairman, Edward R. Telling, predicted that Sears will become "an important a factor in financial services as we are in consumer sales."[28] He said that Sears planned to have borrowing facilities for home mortgages; electronic funds transfer systems throughout the United States; two-way communications with homes through computers and telephones; and a credit card that allows customers to deposit or withdraw funds from every outlet.

These plans were generally consistent with the policy of deregulation of the banking system of the Reagan administration. Whether or not regulators and existing laws (such as the prohibition against deposit banking across state lines), as well as diseconomies, if any, to managing such diverse operations, impair these plans was not clear in 1982.

The homogenization of financial intermediaries plus the possibility of integrating them into other firms is illustrated by Sears' present and planned financial intermediation services. As is evident, their present and planned operations put them in all three categories of financial intermediaries.

NOTES

1. See Chapter 3 and Herman E. Kroos and Martin R. Blyn, *A History of Financial Intermediaries* (New York: Random House, Inc., 1971), p. 54.
2. Ibid., p. 244.
3. The estimate of aggregate shares is published by the Federal Reserve Board each week. This estimate is from *Federal Reserve Statistical Release*, Board of Governors of the Federal Reserve System (June 25, 1982), p. 1, Table 1. The number of MMFs with at least $100 million in assets is from *Donoghue's Money Fund Report* (Holliston, Mass.), as reported by *The New York Times* (February 14, 1982), p. F-11.
4. Timothy Q. Cook and Jeremy G. Duffield, "Short-Term Investment Pools," *Economic Review*, Federal Reserve Bank of Richmond (Sepember–October 1980), pp. 3–24.
5. Timothy Q. Cook and Jeremy G. Duffield, "Money Market Mutual Funds: A Reaction to Government Regulation or a Lasting Financial Innovation?" *Economic Review*, Federal Reserve Bank of Richmond (July–August 1979), pp. 15–31.
6. The 1967 Bank Act eliminated ceiling rate restrictions and allowed the banks in Canada to offer more competitive rates. See Laurie Landy, "Financial Innovation in Canada," *Quarterly Review*, Federal Reserve Bank of New York (Autumn 1980), pp. 1–8. The estimates of Canadian MMFs presented here are from "Canada's 3rd Money Fund Launched," *The American Banker* (March 5, 1982), p. 3. The new MMF in Canada was Bolton Tremblay Funds, Inc., and the proposed composition of its portfolio as announced by its president is noted in the article above (p. 70).
7. The classification and name of brokerage articles is taken from Laurence J. De Maria, "How to Pick a Stockbroker," *The New York Times* (February 21, 1982), p. 14. His names for the classifications are the *survivors* (the medium-sized regional firms); the *discounters*; the *Guccis* (firms specializing in large investors); the *specialty houses* (firms specializing in specific markets); and the *outsiders* (firms that are not members of the New York Stock Exchange or other exchanges).
8. Ibid.
9. Ibid.
10. *Donoghue's Money Fund Report.*
11. Robert J. Cole, "The National Bank of Merrill Lynch," *The New York Times* (February 7, 1982), p. F1.
12. Ibid.
13. Ibid.
14. The total value of life insurance company assets is found in *1981 Life Insurance Fact Book* (Washington, D.C.: American Council of Life Insurance, 1981), p. 69. Information on other insurance companies can be found in *Insurance Facts* (New York: Insurance Information Institute, 1981–82 ed.). The estimates of 1980 assets is found on p. 4. The assets of private pension plans and state and local pension plans are found on p. 51 of the same book.
15. Herbert E. Dougall, *Capital Markets and Institutions* (Englewood Cliffs, N.J.: Prentice-Hall, Inc., 1965), p. 5.
16. *Historical Statistics of the United States, Colonial Times to 1957*, Bureau of the Census and Social Science Research Council, U.S. Department of Commerce (Washington, D.C.: U.S. Government Printing Office, 1960), p. 672.
17. R. Carlyle Buley, *The Equitable Life Assurance Society of the United States 1859–1964*, Vol. 1 (New York: Appelton-Century Crofts, 1967), p. 93.
18. Kroos and Blyn, *A History*, p. 110. The last sentence of the quotation is from p. 110, footnote 19. They point out: "When the plan was at its height, Equitable was writing $300 million a year. In the ten years from 1885 to 1894, the company wrote a total of $1.4 billion. Of this amount, $463 million lapsed, two-thirds in tontines" (p. 110).

19. Carol J. Loomis, "Life Isn't What It Used to Be, and Neither Are the Inflation-Buffeted Insurance Companies That Sell the Product," *Fortune* (July 14, 1980), p. 86.
20. The study conducted by Consumers Union is reported by Loomis, "Life," p. 88.
21. *Insurance Facts*, p. 19.
22. "Report of the Advisory Council on Social Security" (Washington, D.C.: U.S. Department of Health, Education and Welfare, 1975).
23. Similar estimates are found in "Report of the Advisory Council on Social Security," and Frank M. Kleiler's interesting *Can We Afford Early Retirement?* (Baltimore: The Johns Hopkins University Press, 1978), p. 7.
24. This is in keeping with the original principles of Social Security legislation accepted by President Franklin Roosevelt and by the Congress. James H. Schultz summarizes the six principles involved, including this one: "Social security benefits were to be a matter of right; there was to be no *means test*. Workers were to earn their benefits through participation and contribution to the program. The system was to be self-supporting through these worker contributions, together with so-called employee contributions" [*The Economics of Aging* (Belmont, Calif.: Wadsworth Publishing Company, Inc., 1980), p. 95]. The employer contributions are partly and perhaps substantially borne by the worker, given that the demand for labor is downward sloping.
25. Edwin L. Dale, Jr., "Stockman Didn't Slash That Much," *The Washington Post* (February 16, 1982), p. A19.
26. I am thankful to Jack Reitner for discussions on this point.
27. The size of these fixed-income funds for 1981 is reported in the daily banking newspaper, *The American Banker* (February 25, 1982), pp. 10, 12, 13. The classification of all trust department business as contractual or investment intermediaries is not meaningful.
28. Jerry Knight, "Sears Is Planning Super Credit Card for Transactions," *Washington Post*, p. C11.

STUDY QUESTIONS

1. Describe the difference between contractual and investment intermediaries.

2. Explain the rapid rise in money market funds in the late 1970s.

3. How do finance companies raise funds?

4. What financial intermediation services are performed by stockbrokers? Use the definition of financial intermediaries given in Chapter 16.

5. What problems were faced by life insurance companies in the 1970s and early 1980s as a result of rising interest rates?

6. Describe the financial intermediation services of private pension funds.

7. In what sense are administrators of personal trust funds financial intermediaries?

8. Is the Social Security system in the United States a financial intermediary? Explain.

Part VI

Financial Markets

21

The Money Market

Introduction

The name *money market*, as in "New York money market," is frequently used to designate a group of markets where low-default-risk, very liquid, large-denomination, short-term debt instruments are traded. Sometimes reference is made to the money market in an entire country, such as the U.S. money market. New York and London have been leading money market centers for the past century.

The U.S. money market may be divided into markets for particular debt instruments, such as prime commercial paper, Eurodollars, bankers' acceptances, Treasury bills, negotiable certificates of deposit, loans to government securities dealers, repurchase agreements, and federal funds. The money market institutions have been described as follows:

> At the center of the money market are numerous "money market banks," including the large banks in New York and other important financial centers; about 34 government securities dealers, some of which are large banks; a dozen odd commercial paper dealers; a few bankers' acceptance dealers; and a number of money brokers who specialize in finding short-term funds for money market borrowers and placing such funds for money market lenders. The most important money market brokers are the major Federal Funds brokers in New York.[1]

The most important single participant in the money market is the Federal Reserve. Their participation is discussed separately in Chapter 23.

Eurodollars are also discussed separately in Chapter 29, as were federal funds in Chapter 19. In this chapter, attention is given to other major financial assets traded in U.S. money markets. The discussion of the Federal Financing Bank includes longer-term loans and loan guarantees that are not part of the money market.

Functions

The money markets provide an efficient way for large firms, including large financial intermediaries, to:

1. Economize on their cash balances by loaning money for short periods at prevailing yields when they have short periods of excess cash.
2. Economize on their cash balances by having a ready market for short-term borrowing, which enables them to hold less money for temporary unexpected cash drains.
3. Reduce brokerage fees, search costs, and other transactions costs incurred in buying and selling short-term debt instruments.
4. Through *rollovers*, continuous renewal of loans, long-term needs can also be financed.

Short-Term Interest Rates

The volumes outstanding and daily average volume of selected money market instruments in December 1980 are shown in Table 21-1. The huge average daily volume of federal funds and repurchase agreements, $82.8 billion, is due to Federal Reserve operations and the popularity of those types of financial assets. Treasury bills, with their default-free reputation, their short maturities, and their relatively small minimum denomination, are the single most important financial asset in the U.S. money markets. They are used for collateral on repurchase agreements and they are widely traded and held by institutions and households. The Treasury bill, or T-bill, rate is the basic default-risk-free financial asset used in the construction of the capital market line and the security market line in Chapter 14. The T-bill yield is thus a basic rate in theory and in practice. It can vary widely in its relationship from the repurchase agreement rate as the Federal Reserve moves into the market with its huge sales and purchases of repurchase agreements. Since repurchase agreements require collateral, such as T-bills or CDs, the entrance of the Federal Reserve into the market to buy huge quantities of repurchase agreements sets off a search for the collateral. Yields bounce around. The T-bill yield can also vary widely with the federal funds rate during the *Wednesday scramble*, the settlement day for federal reserve requirements at all covered depository institutions (potentially over 40,000).

TABLE 21-1

Selected Money Market Instruments: Volume Outstanding and Volume of Trading, December 1980 (Millions of Dollars)

	Volume Outstanding	Volume of Transactions (Daily Average)
U.S. government securities		
Treasury bills	216,104	13,751*
Other 1 year or less	81,281	466*
Federal agencies, within 1 year	31,637[+]	1,285*
Negotiable certificates of deposit	116,374	2,472*
Bankers' acceptances	54,744	
Commercial paper placed through dealers	56,985	
Directly placed commercial paper		
of financial companies	68,083	
Federal funds and repurchase agreements		82,753[‡]

*Figures include only transactions of U.S. government security dealers reporting to the Federal Reserve Bank of New York (average of five weeks ending in December).
[+]Federally sponsored agency debt with an original maturity of one year or less as of December 1979.
[‡]Gross funds purchased in federal funds and repurchase agreements (one day and continuing contract) by banks with assets of $1 billion or more on December 31, 1977 (average of five weeks ending in December).
Sources: "Dealer Transactions in U.S. Government and Agency Securities and Negotiable Certificates of Deposit," *Federal Reserve Bulletin;* Federal Reserve Bank of New York; various federally sponsored credit agencies, as compiled and published in James Parthemos, "The Money Market," in *Instruments of the Money Market,* Federal Reserve Bank of Richmond (1981), p. 4.

Many of these depository institutions use the federal funds market to reduce surplus reserves or acquire reserves in meeting their Federal Reserve requirements.

The yields on five short-term financial assets are shown in Figure 21-1: three-month and one-year T-bills, four- to six-month prime commercial paper, federal funds, and three-month certificates of deposits sold in the secondary market. The prime rate and the Federal Reserve discount rate are also shown. The yields on the five assets are shown separately because superimposing all on the same graph makes them appear roughly to correspond. However, spreads between yields on different assets exist and change over time. Each of these assets has special characteristics. Federal funds have the shortest maturity, often one day. Different maturities explain one reason for a spread between yields on federal funds and that of other assets. Also, differences in default risk cause spreads in yields.

The Federal Reserve does not consummate its auctions at a single uniform price or yield (a Dutch auction) but instead accepts all prices above or below a cutoff price. This means that many different yields on repurchase agreements clear the market at one time. (The conditions for an efficient market, discussed in Chapter 3, are, therefore, violated. The allocative functions performed by a single market-clearing price are im-

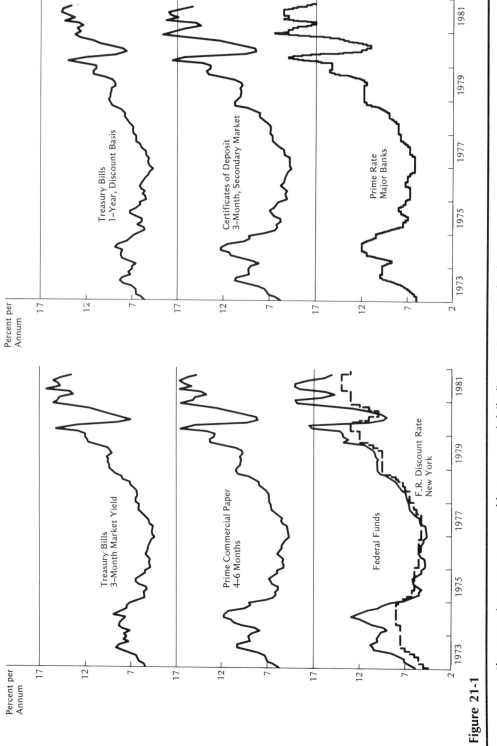

Figure 21-1

Short-term interest rates, monthly averages of daily figures. *Source: Federal Reserve Chart Book,* Board of Governors of the Federal Reserve System (November 1981), p. 72.

354

paired. Although attention in the media is sometimes directed at the prime rate or the T-bill rate, the huge volume of repurchase agreements used by the Federal Reserve and others makes these repurchase agreement yields as important, if not more important, than the prime in understanding the yields on the short-term money markets. As noted in Chapter 18, the prime is not a market rate; it is instead an advertised rate with ambiguous meaning.

Business Certificates of Deposit

The market for large *business certificates of deposit* or *negotiable certificates of deposit* (CDs) in denominations of $100,000 or more has been active since 1961.[2] It is a money market specializing in the sale of marketable, interest-yielding deposit certificates with specified maturity dates, issued by four types of financial intermediaries. Domestic CDs are issued by U.S. banks. Dollar-denominated CDs issued by banks outside the United States are called Euro CDs. The CDs issued by U.S. branches of foreign banks are called Yankee CDs. Thrift CDs is the name used to designate CDs issued by domestic thrifts.

The holder of a CD who wishes to exchange it for money before its maturity date may ask a money market participant (often a commercial bank) to arrange a sale through a specialized dealer. In 1977, Morgan Guaranty Trust Company introduced rollover CDs, or rolypoly CDs, in minimum denominations of $5 million. There is an active secondary market in CDs centered in New York. There are approximately twenty-five dealers in CDs.

The CD is an instrument that allows the depository intermediaries to raise funds at competitive market rates. It is called one of their *managed liabilities*. Since they loan out funds at their lending rates, they would normally keep their advertised prime above the CD rate. As noted previously, the prime rate formula that had been used by Citibank set the prime $1\frac{1}{2}$ percentage points above the previous three-week average of ninety-day (three-month) CDs sold in the secondary market.

The yield on three-month CDs is usually higher than three-month T-bills. T-bills have a lower default risk and are exempt from state and local tax. This may explain the existence of the spread, but not its variation. The value of reducing default risk during a recession may increase, causing the CD–T-bill spread to widen, as it did in 1974.

Bankers' Acceptances

Bankers' acceptances often arise in foreign trade.[3] A business buying goods from abroad where it is not well known and does not have other credit arrangements will first obtain a letter of credit from its own bank.

The letter will authorize the foreign seller to draw a draft on the company's bank. A *draft*, or *bill of exchange*, as it is sometimes called, is a debt instrument. It can be made payable on sight, that is, upon presentation (a *sight draft*), payable upon arrival of merchandise (an *arrival draft*), or payable in a fixed number of days (a *time draft*). A sight draft can be made payable in, say, thirty days after it is presented to the bank against which it is drawn. This draft can be discounted at the seller's bank so that the seller receives immediate payment. If this is done, the draft can be sent via correspondent banks back to the domestic bank against which it is drawn. The domestic bank can buy the draft, a short-term loan agreement to be paid by the company buying the goods abroad. This action would tie up bank funds. Alternatively, the bank can stamp the draft "accepted," with the appropriate signature, thereby indicating that the bank guarantees the draft, and then sell it in the secondary market. There are approximately fifteen dealers.

Dollar volume of U.S. bankers' acceptances reached $66.3 billion in October 1981. They were heavily used in international trade by Japanese, Korean, and other Asian traders. Money market funds became important investors in bankers' acceptances. They owned 12 percent of outstanding bankers' acceptances in December 1980.

Commercial Paper

The *commercial paper* market is a market for short-term, low-risk debt instruments issued by many different types of borrowers.[4] There was $164 billion in commercial paper outstanding in October 1981. Large finance companies, bank holding companies, utilities, trust funds, college endowment funds, and other large commercial institutional investors are participants in this market. Savings and loan associations and mutual savings banks were given permission to invest in commercial paper in 1980 (see Table 21-2). Some firms sell directly in the market. Other participants sell first to dealers, who then sell the commercial paper. There are six major commercial paper dealers. There are no secondary markets. Commercial paper may sometimes be redeemed early if there is an urgent need for funds, but this practice is discouraged.

Commercial paper is rated by Moody's, Standard and Poor's, and Fitch. From highest to lowest, the ratings are P-1, P-2, and P-3 for Moody's; A-1, A-2, and A-3 for Standard and Poor's; and F-1, F-2, and F-3 for Fitch. In the middle of 1980 approximately 75 percent of the commercial paper had the highest rating and could be called *prime commercial paper*. Firms issuing commercial paper often have backup lines of credit from commercial banks. The cost of these backup lines is often paid with compensating balances at the bank.

This specialized part of the money market offers a rapid way to meet short-term needs for money or to economize on money balances with

TABLE 21-2

Industry Grouping of Commercial Paper Issuers Rated by Moody's, November 3, 1980

Industry Grouping	Number of Firms Rated	Percentage of Total Firms Rated
Industrial	370	42.0
Public utilities	193	21.9
Finance	155	17.6
Bank holding	119	13.6
Mortgage finance	9	1.0
Insurance	25	2.8
Transportation	10	1.1
Total	881	100.0

Source: Peter A Abken, "Commercial Paper," *Instruments of the Money Market,* Federal Reserve Bank of Richmond (1981), p. 96, from Information supplied by Moody's.

short-term loans, frequently of less than thirty days' duration, which are called *weekend paper.* Many firms have different demands for cash during different seasons of the year. They can make loans and borrow in this market according to their seasonal demands.

Notes (short-term bonds) are in multiples of $100,000, with denominations sometimes exceeding $5 million. The average size is $2 million. Maturities usually range from twenty to forty-five days.

Loan paper with more than 270 days to maturity must be registered with the Securities and Exchange Commission, and its volume is insignificant.

The commercial paper market is not new. In the first decade of the 1900s, dealers began to sell commercial paper in the open market. The market grew rapidly, and by 1920 there were between 4000 and 5000 corporations issuing commercial paper on a regular basis. The volume of paper fell during the Great Depression and then increased after World War II, accelerating sharply in the late 1960s.

Dramatic events in the 1970s drew attention to risks of defaults. The Penn Central Railroad failed in 1970, with $82 million outstanding in commercial paper. The oil embargo of the United States in 1973 hurt utility company profits and made it more difficult for utility companies to sell their commercial paper in 1974. In addition, real estate investment trusts (REITs), which raised money for financing construction, began to have a credit problem and their paper became more difficult to sell. All this made buyers of commercial paper very conscious of the quality of the paper.

In early 1975, as a result of these problems, the spread in interest rates between the highest-quality paper and medium-quality paper was a full percentage point. Eventually, the extreme selectivity of investors, triggered by the experiences of the early 1970s, began to recede, so that by the end of 1976, the spread had narrowed to three-eighths of a percentage point. However, yields on paper are strongly affected by ratings issued by such bond-rating companies as Moody's.

One recent innovation is the issuance of tax-exempt commercial paper by state and municipal governments and qualified nonprofit organizations.

Repurchase Agreements

Repurchase agreements or *repos* are a type of financial assets developed for a period of high interest rates when it is profitable to keep funds earning market interest rates every possible day. Repurchase agreements can be tailored to any short-term time period and they provide a vehicle for relatively default-free loans.

A repurchase agreement is an agreement to buy back an asset, typically a U.S. Treasury or federal agency debt instrument, at a given price. It forms the basis for a loan. For example, the lender buys a Treasury bill from the borrower for five days, after which the lender sells it back at the original price plus interest on the loan plus an amount to cover the risk of less worthy collateral when applicable. The interest is not determined by the interest on the collateral used, but rather by the interest in the market for repos. This interest is associated with the interest on federal funds, the federal funds rate, another short-term debt instrument. The T-bill is usually called collateral, although since ownership is passed to the lender, it presumably involves legal ownership, but this has not been precisely clarified. Sometimes these agreements are called *reverse repurchase agreements* or *matched sales agreements* when viewed from the lender's side of the transaction, since the lender sells the security back to the borrower. A reverse repo can be arranged to obtain government securities on which a new repo is sold. The lender buys the security and then sells it on a shorter-term repurchase agreement. Large banks and government security dealers often combine transactions in this manner.

The market for repurchase agreements was deeply affected by the failure in 1982 of two relatively small dealers in the so-called United Government securities market. Drysdale Government Securities closed in May and Lombard-Wall in August 1982. Since they failed to pay borrowed money against which repos were pledged, lenders in this market became much more cautious.

Presumably, the lenders would learn from this episode of failing dealers to conduct credit analyses on borrowers and to avoid concentrating business with one firm. Bigger discounts on loan collateral, and agreements that permit a call for additional collateral when interest rates rise, would also be required. There also might be a demand by lenders that pledged securities must actually be delivered so that they cannot be

TABLE 21-3

Outstanding Repurchase Agreements of Commerical Banks with the Nonbank Public, 1969–1979 (Billions of Dollars)

Year-End	Amount
1969	4.9
1970	2.8
1972	6.1
1973	13.3
1976	26.8
1979	42.8

Source: Norman N. Bowsher, "Repurchase Agreements," *Instruments of the Money Market,* Federal Reserve Bank of Richmond (1981), p. 56.

pledged for other loans and to ensure that borrowers have the securities they are pledging.

Repos are usually in amounts of $1 million or more. The government security dealers are important participants in the repurchase market since they trade with the Federal Reserve almost exclusively in repos and reverse repos. This activity and the dealers are described in Chapter 23. Many large entities trade repurchase agreements: large nonfinancial corporations, state and local governments, depository institutions, and foreign banks and foreign official institutions. Large banks are usually borrowers of repurchase agreements. The huge amounts borrowed by banks in recent years, shown in Table 21-3, give an indication of the rapid growth in repurchase agreement trading. Large banks, those that had at least $1 billion in assets in 1977, had $53.2 billion in repos on November 25, 1981. Of that amount, 93 percent were one-day and continuing (receivable) contracts and only 7 percent were for other maturities.

Commercial banks make extensive use of federal funds and repurchase agreements to manage their cash position. Transactions are settled with funds that are made immediately available to the borrowing bank. Since repos have collateral and federal funds do not, the repo rate is generally less than the federal funds rate.

Treasury Securities

The U.S. Treasury sells large quantities of government securities to finance government operations and to refinance maturing debt (see Chapter 2 for a description of bills, notes, and bonds and the method of calculating the yield on a bill). Treasury open-market activities are sometimes labeled *debt management*. The Treasury can issue new government debt instruments and sell them to the public. The Federal Reserve cannot issue new debt instruments; the Federal Reserve can buy and sell only existing government securities. Since 1951, Treasury sales and retirement of debt instruments have been conducted in in cooperation with the Federal Reserve. The Federal Reserve may choose to offset, with its own open-market operations, any effects of Treasury operations that are not desired.

The Federal Reserve acts as the agent for the Treasury in the sale of Treasury securities: bills, notes, and bonds. Auctions are conducted through each of the Federal Reserve banks and the main Treasury building in Washington, D.C., for the sale of Treasury bills, often every week. Predominantly financial institutions, but also anyone else who has the minimum amount of funds, usually $10,000, necessary to buy the smallest denomination issued may place a *tender* offer.

Figure 21-2 is a sample tender for Treasury bills. The buyer may enter a "noncompetitive tender offer," in which he or she agrees to buy the bills at the average price of accepted competitive bids. The signed and filled-out tender offer, plus a cashier's check or a certified check, must be received by a Federal Reserve bank or by the Treasury in Washington, D.C., by a specific time. When the auction ends, the tender offer with the highest competitive bids, plus the noncompetitive tender offers, are accepted.

In recent years, longer-term maturities—notes and bonds—have been offered mostly through auctions to the highest bidder, although some fixed-price sales have been held. In the past, these securities were sold on a subscription basis, with a preannounced price and coupon rate. Auctions have been held on the basis of price or the equivalent yield (*price auction* or *yield auction*). In these auctions, all accepted bids pay the price that was submitted on each bid. Only four times (as of 1977) was a single price equal to the lowest accepted offer uniformly applied to all accepted bids. This uniform price auction is called a *Dutch auction*.

An interest rate ceiling on Treasury bonds of $4\frac{1}{4}$ percent was imposed from 1917 to 1971. As market interest rates rose, Congress began granting the Treasury limited authority to issue bonds at interest rates above $4\frac{1}{4}$ percent.

An *advanced refunding technique* was introduced in 1960. It consists of exchanging new bonds for old bonds far in advance of the maturity date on the older bonds. The reason given for advanced refunding is that some investors prefer long-term bonds. When bonds that these investors own approach their maturity dates, they are in effect short-term bonds. Their owners may then desire to sell them and acquire new long-term bonds. Individuals who have a preference for short-term bonds then buy these bonds in the secondary market. The advanced refunding technique allows the long-term investor to exchange his or her bond before it becomes a short-term bond. A more direct, more efficient, less expensive technique for achieving this result would be the sale of consols. Consols have no maturity; they are a debt instrument with a constant perpetual income stream.

FORM PG 4432–2
Dept. of the Treasury
Bur. of the Public Dept.

**TENDER FOR TREASURY BILLS
IN BOOK-ENTRY FORM AT THE
DEPARTMENT OF THE TREASURY
26-WEEK BILLS ONLY**

FOR OFFICIAL USE ONLY

FRB Request No. _____

Issue Date _____

Due Date _____

Cusip No. 912793 _____

MAIL TO:

☐ Bureau of the Public Dept. Securities Transactions Branch
Room 2134, Main Treasury, Washington, D. C. 20226
☐ Federal Reserve Bank or Branch
of your District at: _____

**BEFORE COMPLETING THIS FORM READ THE
ACCOMPANYING INSTRUCTIONS CAREFULLY**

ACCOUNT NO.

Pursuant to the provisions of Department of the Treasury Circular, Public Dept Series No. 27–78, the public announcement issued by the Department of the Treasury, and the regulations set forth in Department Circular, Public Dept Series No. 26–76. I hereby submit this tender, in accordance with the terms as marked, for currently offered U.S. Treasury bills for my account. (Competitive tenders must be expressed on the basis of 100, with three decimals. Fractions may not be used.) I understand that noncompetitive tenders will be accepted in full at the average price of accepted competitive bids and that a noncompetitive tender by any one bidder may not exceed $500,000.

TYPE OF BID
NONCOMPETITIVE ☐   or   COMPETITIVE ☐   at: Price _____

AMOUNT OF TENDER $ _____ .
(Minimum of $10,000. Over $10,000 must be in multiples of $5,000.)

ACCOUNT IDENTIFICATION: (Please type or print clearly using a ball–point pen because this information will be used as a mailing label.)

Depositor(s) _____

_____

_____

Address _____

_____

_____

PRIVACY ACT NOTICE

The individually identifiable information required on this form is necessary to permit the tender to be processed and the bills to be issued, in accordance with the general regulations governing United States book–entry Treasury bills (Department Circular PD Series No. 26–76). The transaction will not be completed unless all required data is furnished.

ALPHA-CROSS REF.

DEPOSITOR(S) IDENTIFICATION NUMBER

SOCIAL SECURITY NUMBER
FIRST NAMED ☐☐☐ – ☐☐ – ☐☐☐☐   OR   EMPLOYER IDENTIFICATION NO. ☐☐ – ☐☐☐☐☐☐☐

SOCIAL SECURITY NUMBER
SECOND NAMED ☐☐☐ – ☐☐ – ☐☐☐☐

DISPOSITION OF PROCEEDS

The per amount of the account will be paid at maturity unless you elect to have Treasury reinvest (roll-over) the proceeds of the maturing bills. (See below)
☐ I hereby request noncompetitive reinvestment of the proceeds in book–entry Treasury bills.

METHOD OF PAYMENT
TOTAL
SUBMITTED $ _____ Cash $ _____ Check $ _____   Maturing Treasury Securities $ _____

DEPOSITOR'S AUTHORIZATION

Signature _____ Date _____   Telephone Number During Business hours (_____) _____

Area Code

FOR OFFICIAL USE ONLY

Received by _____ Date _____

STATEMENT OF ACCOUNT		Issue Discount Price $		Amount of Discount $		
Date	Transaction	Per Amount Transacted		Account Balance	Authority Reference	Validation
		Decrease	Increase			
		$	$	$		

A   DEPARTMENT OF THE TREASURY COPY

Figure 21-2

Sample tender for Treasury bills.

TABLE 21-4

Holdings of Short-Term Marketable U.S. Securities (End-of-Year Flow-of-Funds Estimates in Billions)

Year	Foreigners $	Foreigners %	Federal Reserve $	Federal Reserve %	Households $	Households %	Commercial Banks $	Commercial Banks %	State and Local Governments $	State and Local Governments %	Private Nonbank Financial Institutions $	Private Nonbank Financial Institutions %	Nonfinancial Corporate Business $	Nonfinancial Corporate Business %
1960	7.7	8.8	19.2	22.1	10.6	12.1	22.9	26.3	7.6	8.8	5.8	6.6	13.3	15.2
1961	7.1	7.2	18.3	18.7	10.8	11.0	33.5	34.3	8.0	8.2	7.6	7.8	12.5	12.8
1962	9.2	9.4	20.7	21.1	12.6	12.8	27.8	28.3	9.0	9.1	8.4	8.5	10.7	10.8
1963	8.7	8.7	25.6	25.7	16.3	16.4	24.2	24.3	9.2	9.2	7.2	7.2	8.5	8.5
1964	8.5	8.1	28.2	27.0	15.8	15.1	28.3	27.1	8.4	8.0	7.7	7.4	7.5	7.2
1965	7.6	7.1	31.9	29.6	18.0	16.8	26.2	24.4	10.5	9.7	7.3	6.8	6.0	5.6
1966	6.7	6.2	36.5	33.5	19.3	17.7	21.5	20.0	11.5	10.6	8.5	7.8	4.7	4.3
1967	7.6	6.5	39.2	33.6	18.9	16.2	27.0	23.2	12.2	10.5	8.6	7.4	3.1	2.6
1968	5.9	5.0	32.6	27.8	25.7	21.9	28.6	24.4	11.5	9.8	10.0	8.5	3.0	2.5
1969	3.7	2.9	37.6	29.6	34.7	27.3	24.3	19.1	14.1	11.1	9.0	7.1	3.8	3.0
1970	11.5	8.8	38.5	29.3	21.0	16.0	30.1	22.9	14.8	11.3	10.8	8.2	4.7	3.6
1971	25.4	19.8	39.5	30.8	8.5	6.6	25.2	19.6	13.5	10.5	7.8	6.1	8.4	6.6
1972	27.7	18.7	41.2	28.8	9.7	6.8	30.8	21.6	18.1	12.7	10.4	7.3	5.8	4.0
1973	21.0	13.8	50.6	33.3	25.7	16.9	28.3	18.6	16.2	10.6	9.7	6.3	.9	.6
1974	28.6	17.7	50.5	31.2	36.2	22.3	26.9	16.6	9.0	5.5	10.1	6.2	.6	.4
1975	35.3	16.3	52.4	24.3	41.0	19.0	48.8	22.6	12.7	5.9	15.9	7.3	10.0	4.6
1976	38.6	16.2	58.6	24.6	31.6	13.3	56.5	23.8	16.7	7.0	23.4	9.9	12.4	5.2
1977	46.7	18.0	61.7	23.8	48.4	18.7	52.0	20.0	19.6	7.6	24.3	9.4	6.7	2.6
1978	60.6	22.3	62.1	22.8	59.1	21.7	41.7	15.3	24.4	9.0	23.7	8.7	.5	.2
1979	42.1	14.5	68.9	23.7	86.5	29.8	40.8	14.0	24.9	8.6	27.1	9.3	.1	.0

Source: Timothy Q. Cook and Jimmie R. Monhollen, "Treasury Bills," *Instruments of the Money Market,* Federal Reserve Bank of Richmond (1981), p. 7.

Treasury bills are the main debt instruments in the money market.[5] From 1929 until 1934 maturities of thirty, sixty, and ninety days were offered. Then 182- and 273-day maturities were offered to reduce the number of refundings. Ninety-one-day bills were used after 1937 and were supplemented in 1958 with six-month bills and in 1959 with one-year bills. A nine-month maturity was tried and discontinued in 1972. From 1972 to 1982 the maturities were ninety-one days, six months, and a year. A thirteen-week maturity was issued in 1982.

As Table 21-4 indicates, Treasury bills are widely held. This results in large part from their relatively low minimum denomination ($10,000 since 1970) compared to other money market instruments. Notice that in 1974 and 1979, as inflation accelerated, households dramatically increased their holdings of T-bills. This is probably evidence of increased uncertainty and positive time preference. Households switched into shorter-term default-free assets. If interest rates rose unexpectedly, they would be protected against capital loss by the short maturities.

Federal Agency Securities

The volume of federally sponsored agencies securities is a large and rapidly growing part of the debt of the federal government, as indicated

TABLE 21-5

Federal Credit Agencies

I. Mortgage-related federal credit agencies
   1. Federal National Mortgage Association
   2. Federal Home Loan Bank System
   3. Federal Home Loan Mortgage Corporation
   4. Federal Housing Administration
   5. Veterans Administration
   6. Government National Mortgage Association
II. The farm credit system
   1. Federal Land Banks
   2. Federal Intermediate Credit Banks
   3. Bank for Cooperatives
III. Miscellaneous credit agencies
   1. Export-Import Bank of the United States
   2. Rural Electrification Administration
   3. Student Loan Marketing Association
   4. Federal Financing Bank

in the flow-of-funds tables in Chapter 4.[6] A list of these agencies is presented in Table 21-5. Short-term debt, sold either at a discount or with a coupon, comprised 23.5 percent of the volume issued in 1979 and is an important part of the money markets. *Consolidated systemwide bonds*, sold by the Farm Credit Banks with maturities of six and nine months, are issued in *book-entry form* (see Table 21-6). Book-entry form means that no physical debt instrument is sent, only a record is kept. There is an active secondary market in the short-term debt instruments of the Farm Credit Banks, the Federal Home Loan Banks, and the Federal National Mortgage Association.

TABLE 21-6

Characteristics of Short-Term Agency Securities

Issuer	Type	Maturities	Form	Offering Schedule	Minimum Denomination	Tax Exemption
Farm Credit Banks	Consolidated systemwide bonds	6- and 9-month	Book entry	Monthly	$ 5,000	State and local
	Consolidated systemwide discount notes	5 to 270 days	Certificate	Daily	$ 50,000	State and local
Federal Home Loan Banks	Consolidated discount notes	30 to 270 days	Certificate	Daily	$100,000	State and local
Federal National Mortgage Association	Discount notes	30 to 270 days	Certificate	Daily	$ 5,000*	None

*Minimum purchase of $50,000.
Source: Donna Howell, "Federally Sponsored Credit Agency Securities," *Instruments of the Money Market,* Federal Reserve Bank of Richmond (1981), p. 25.

TABLE 21-7

Federal Financing Bank Holdings, December 31, 1981* (Millions of Dollars)

On-budget agency debt	
Tennessee Valley Authority	$ 11,390.0
Export-Import Bank	12,741.3
NCUA—Central Liquidity Facility	90.2
Total	24,221.5
Off-budget agency debt	
U.S. Postal Service	1,288.0
U.S. Railway Association	202.4
Total	1,490.4
Agency assets	
Farmers Home Administration	48,821.0
DHHS—Health Maintenance Organization	119.0
DHHS—Medical Facilities	150.5
Overseas Private Investment Corporation	24.3
Rural Electrification Administration—CBO	2,595.3
Small Business Administration	64.9
Total	51,775.0
Government guaranteed loans	
DOD—Foreign Military Sales	9,702.8
DED—Student Loan Marketing Assn.	4,600.0
DOE—Geothermal Loans	22.4
DOE—Hybrid Vehicles	2.2
DOE—Synthetic Fuels	39.9
DHUD—Community Development Block Grant	76.6
DHUD—New Communities	33.5
DHUD—Public Housing Notes	1,195.9
General Services Administration	412.0
DOI—Guam Power Authority	36.0
DOI—Virgin Islands	29.9
NASA—Space Communications Company	683.1
Rural Electrification Administration	13,516.3
SBA—Small Business Investment Companies	624.3
TVA—Seven States Energy Corporation	1,014.7
DOT—Amtrak	844.2
DOT—Emergency Rail Services Act	70.2
DOT—Title V, RRRR Act	118.8
DOT—WMATA	177.0
Total	33,211.2
Grand total[†]	$110,697.9

*NCUA, National Credit Union Administration; DHHS, Department of Health and Human Services; DOD, Department of Defense; DED, Department of Education; DOE, Department of Energy; DHUD or HUD, Department of Housing and Human Development; DOI, Department of the Interior; NASA, National Aeronautics and Space Administration; SBA, Small Business Administration; TVA, Tennessee Valley Authority; DOT, Department of Transportation.
[†]Figures may not total due to rounding.
Source: Federal Financing Bank News, Department of the Treasury (January 29, 1982), p. 7.

TABLE 21-8

Federal Financing Bank: Three December 1981 Commitments

Borrower	Amount	Guarantor	Commitment Expires	Maturity
El Salvador	$16,500,000	DOD	12/5/83	12/5/93
Kenosha, Wisconsin	1,100,000	HUD	6/1/82	6/1/02
Philadelphia Authority for Industrial Development	10,000,000	HUD	10/1/82	10/1/02

Source: Federal Financing Bank News, Department of the Treasury (January 29, 1982), p. 6.

The major housing agencies are discussed in the next chapter in connection with the mortgage market.

The Farm Credit Agencies are organized like the Federal Reserve and the Federal Home Loan Bank system into twelve districts with twelve regional banks for each of these credit agencies. Twelve appears to be a favorite number for subdividing federally sponsored agencies and monthly subperiods of a year.

The Federal Financing Bank was established in 1974 inside the Treasury to consolidate the borrowing activity of government agencies. Except for one issue of $1.5 billion of eight-month notes issued in July 1974, the Federal Financing Bank has obtained all its funds from the Treasury. It also consolidates loan guarantees to government agencies and departments.

As shown in Table 21-7, the Federal Financing Bank financed $24.2 billion in on-budget agency debt (including $90 million for the National Credit Union Administration), $1.5 billion off its agency debt, and they held $51.8 in agency assets. They also guaranteed $110.6 in government loans.

Examples of the Federal Financing Banks guaranteed loan activities are given by three guaranteed loans in December 1981, shown in Table 21-8. Notice that each of these loan guarantees has a government department guarantor.

NOTES

1. James Parthemos, "The Money Market," in *Instruments of the Money Market*, Timothy Q. Cook and Bruce J. Summers, eds., Federal Reserve Bank of Richmond (1981), pp. 1–6.
2. Bruce J. Summers, "Negotiable Certificates of Deposit," in *Instruments of the Money Market*, pp. 73–93.
3. Jeremy G. Duffield and Bruce J. Summers, "Bankers' Acceptances," in *Instruments of the Money Market*, pp. 114–122; "Bankers' Acceptances," *Economic Review*, Federal Reserve Bank of Cleveland (July 1970), p. 8; and Joy

S. Joines, "Bankers' Acceptances," in *Instruments of the Money Market*, pp. 77–84.

4. Peter A. Abken, "Commercial Paper," in *Instruments of the Money Market*, pp. 94–113; and Evelyn M. Hurley, "The Commercial Paper Market," *Federal Reserve Bulletin* (June 1977), pp. 525–536.

5. Timothy Q. Cook and Jimmie R. Monhollen, "Treasury Bills," in *Instruments of the Money Market*, pp. 7–19; James F. Tucker, "Buying Treasury Securities at Federal Reserve Banks," *Economic Review*, Federal Reserve Bank of Richmond (1980); and Timothy Q. Cook, "Determinants of the Spread Between Treasury Bill and Private Sector Money Market Rates," *Journal of Economics and Business* (Spring 1981), pp. 177–187.

6. Donna Howell, "Federally Sponsored Credit Agency Securities," in *Instruments of the Money Market*, pp. 20–29; and Benton F. Gup, *Financial Intermediaries, An Introduction* (Boston: Houghton Mifflin Company, 1980), pp. 414–435.

STUDY QUESTIONS

1. What is the money market?

2. What functions does the money market serve?

3. Describe the characteristics of negotiable CDs, bankers' accceptances, commercial paper, repos, T-bills, and federal agency securities.

4. What functions are performed by the Federal Financing Bank?

5. Describe the relationship of the yields on the assets listed in Study Question 3.

22

The Stock, Bond, Options, Futures, and Mortgage Markets

Introduction

The markets for financial assets have experienced immense institutional changes in recent years due to unstable economic conditions, especially rapidly rising interest rates and inflation. Not only managers of financial intermediaries, but also managers of nonfinancial firms are learning such formerly esoteric financial practices as hedging a comitment for future loans. They may execute a hedge in the futures market or a straddle in the stock market. Although covered arbitrage (discussed in Chapter 28) has been commonplace in international finance, these new domestic financial practices have not.

In this chapter these developments are summarized, and stock, corporate bond, options, futures, and mortgage markets are discussed.

It is interesting to note that the term *capital markets* has been used to designate markets for longer-maturity financial assets such as corporate bonds and stocks, and mortgages. The *money markets* is a term used to designate markets for shorter-maturity assets. Some of the hedging practices described subsequently, which tie together long and short securities, blur this distinction.

These are not undesirable developments, however painful the imprecision in classification may be. They provide a very important beneficial function. New financial practices, such as a CD–Treasury bond straddle, reduce market segmentation and increase efficiency (incorporating all available information into market prices) across different maturities and different financial assets. In the same manner as described for efficient markets in Chapter 3, these new practices improve the functioning of financial markets so that funds can be more efficiently allocated to their most profitable uses.

Of course, these rapid changes are traumatic for many regulators and lawmakers. There is a justified concern to protect the public interest. Their reaction is discussed in Chapter 24.

The Stock Markets

After a stock is sold to the first group of purchasers in the primary market, it is traded on one of the many *secondary stock markets*. The best known secondary stock market is the New York Stock Exchange, located on Wall Street in New York City. There are many other secondary markets throughout the world. In 1979, there were ten exchanges that were registered with the Securities and Exchange Commission operating in the United States. Those exchanges in the United States outside New York City are sometimes called *regional exchanges*. They provide *continuous auction markets* and are organized under formal rules for trading. Trading on the New York Stock Exchange accounts for 78.4 percent of the total dollar volume on all exchanges. Approximately 2200 stocks are traded on the New York Stock Exchange. These securities markets operate at one location. They receive orders from around the world through a network of brokers and dealers who are members of the exchange. Private stockbrokerage businesses, in turn, act as agents for the public in buying and selling stocks and bonds. The stockbrokerage firms hold stock on account for customers and loan customers money to purchase stocks "on margin."

In addition, there are active secondary stock markets that are not centered in one geographical location. The over-the-counter market in the United States includes 30,000 to 40,000 different common stocks, most of which are not actively traded. On February 8, 1971, part of the over-the-counter market was tied into a computer system called NASDAQ, an acronym for the National Association of Securities Dealers Automated Quotations. In 1981 approximately 3100 stocks were listed by NASDAQ. Dealers and brokers all over the United States were able to receive instant information from their computer terminals. Approximately thirty stocks could be traded through these computer facilities without even a phone order in 1981. The beginning of a system to tie New York Stock Exchange stocks into a computer listing was operating in 1981. (See Chapter 24 for a discussion of several experiments with consolidated, continuous price quotations and interconnections between exchanges.)

There are many indexes of the prices of financial assets. The most famous stock price index is the Dow Jones and Company, Inc., index of thirty industrial stocks. DJ also has indexes of transportation and utilities stocks that are published daily in the largest circulation newspaper in the United States, Dow Jones' *Wall Street Journal.* Standard and Poor's index of 350 stocks is used for tests in Chapter 26. The New York Stock Exchange Index of stocks on that exchange is a broader index.

These indexes are formed by somewhat the same procedures as shown for price indexes in Appendix A of Chapter 4, except that they must also take account of changes in the definitions of a unit of a stock. Units are changed by actions, such as a *stock split,* increasing the number of present shares by some multiple or dividing existing shares into a number of new shares. (Reverse splits reduce the shares outstanding.) A change in an index shows the percentage changes in average prices from an arbitrarily based period usually assigned a value of 100. The absolute change in an index is not a measure of a specific dollars and cents change, as it is often mistakenly called.

The number of U.S. shareholders in mid-1975 was estimated to be 26.27 million.[1] More than 100 million people held shares indirectly through financial intermediaries. The New York Stock Exchange reported:

> Despite increasing activity by institutions, the Exchange expects that individuals will continue to hold the majority of the shares listed on the Exchange in the foreseeable future. Ten of the most widely owned companies are American Telephone & Telegraph, 3,000,000 shareholders, General Motors, 11,300,000; Exxon, 725,000; International Business Machines, 575,000; General Electric, 525,000; General Telephone & Electronics, 475,000; Ford Motor Co. 325,000; U.S. Steel, 300,000; Texaco, 300,000.[2]

There were 115 institutions that had discretionary authority over their stock holdings with over $1 billion in stock holdings as of September 1981. The sixty largest are listed in Table 22-1. These large institutional investors account for the rising amount of *block transactions.* In 1965, the New York Stock Exchange reported 2171 block transactions amounting to $1.8 billion; in 1977 there were 54,275, amounting to $33.99 billion. The New York Stock Exchange Public Transaction Study for the fourth quarter of 1980 reported that the proportion of trading by NYSE members on their own account exceeded the proportion done by public individuals for the first time in their surveys (26.9 percent to 25.7 percent in number of shares and 30.2 percent to 19.8 percent in the value of shares traded, respectively). This was interpreted as reflecting increased block trading and arbitrage activities in the fourth quarter of 1980. The Federal Reserve flow-of-funds accounts shows pension funds as the biggest buyers of stocks and households (a residual that includes individuals, personal trusts, and nonprofit institutions) as the biggest seller. Commercial banks remained the biggest institutional participants, with trading for their pension accounts being the largest part of their stock trading by dollar volume (21 percent) and personal trusts by number of transactions (38 percent).[3]

Many block trades are negotiated. They sometimes trade in the *third market.* The third market is a market for stocks listed on the New York

TABLE 22-1

Sixty Largest Stockholdings of Institutions with Discretionary Authority over Stock Holdings in the United States on September 30, 1981 (Millions of Dollars)

1. J. P. Morgan & Co., Inc., New York	$12,494.5
2. College Retirement Equities Fund, New York	8,264.7
3. Bankers Trust New York Corp.	7,109.7
4. Prudential Insurance Co., Newark, N.J.	6,669.7
5. Fayez Sarofim & Co., Houston	6,251.9
6. Citicorp, New York	6,160.9
7. T. Rowe Price Associates, Baltimore	6,017.7
8. Batterymarch Financial Management, Boston	5,348.3
9. Putnam Management Co., Boston	5,245.0
10. State Street Research & Management, Boston	5,210.6
11. Wells Fargo Bank NA, San Francisco	5,205.1
12. Harris Trust & Savings Bank, Chicago	5,156.9
13. Mellon National Corp., Pittsburgh	4,977.5
14. Donaldson, Lufkin & Jenrette Securities Corp., New York	4,745.3
15. Bank of California NA, San Francisco	4,578.1
16. Wellington/Thorndike, Boston	4,545.0
17. U.S. Steel & Carnegie Pension Fund, Pittsburgh	4,374.0
18. Equitable Life Assurance Society, New York	4,328.0
19. Chemical New York Corp.	4,273.1
20. Chase Manhattan Corp., New York	4,192.9
21. First Interstate Bancorp., Los Angeles	4,053.7
22. Crocker National Corp., San Francisco	3,995.8
23. California Public Employees Ret. System, Sacramento	3,941.6
24. Capital Guardian Trust Co., Los Angeles	3,917.2
25. Northern Trust Corp., Chicago	3,771.6
26. Manufacturers Hanover Corp., New York	3,644.4
27. AmeriTrust, Cleveland	3,590.0
28. General Electric Pension Trust, Stamford, Conn.	3,526.4
29. Scudder Stevens & Clark, New York	3,318.5
30. National City Bank, Cleveland	3,300.6
31. First National Boston Corp.	3,206.0
32. Lord, Abbett & Co., New York	3,191.7
33. American National Bank & Trust Co., Chicago	3,075.9
34. Stein Roe & Farnham, Chicago	2,995.0
35. NBD Bancorp., Inc., Detroit	2,908.5
36. New York State Teachers Retirement, Albany	2,907.1
37. Teledyne, Inc., Los Angeles	2,902.7
38. Bank of New York	2,893.0
39. United States Trust Co., New York	2,883.7
40. Centerre Bancorp., St. Louis	2,867.4
41. Delaware Management Co. Inc., Philadelphia	2,847.7
42. Capital Research & Management Co., Los Angeles	2,832.1
43. Continental Illinois National Bank & Trust Co., Chicago	2,780.1
44. E. I. du Pont de Nemours, Wilmington, Del.	2,652.0
45. State Farm Mutual Automobile Ins. Co., Bloomington, Ill.	2,625.7
46. Loomis, Sayles & Co., Inc., Boston	2,587.4
47. Jennison Associates Capital Corp., New York	2,578.6
48. Kemper Financial Services Inc., Chicago	2,545.0
49. Eberstadt Asset Management, New York	2,475.6
50. FMR Corp., Boston	2,437.2
51. Oppenheimer & Co., New York	2,308.4
52. Aetna Life & Casualty Co., Hartford	2,304.3

TABLE 22-1 *(Continued)*

Sixty Largest Stockholdings of Institutions with Discretionary Authority over Stock Holdings in the United States on September 30, 1981 (Millions of Dollars)

53. University of California, Berkeley	2,286.5
54. Fiduciary Trust Co., New York	2,284.8
55. Gulf Oil Corp., Pittsburgh	2,265.5
56. Pioneering Management Corp., Boston	2,247.3
57. Wilmington Trust Co., Del.	2,243.4
58. Provident National Corp., Philadelphia	2,211.0
59. First Chicago Corp.	2,195.4
60. First City Bancorp., Dallas	2,183.3

Source: The rankings are compiled from 13-F reports filed with the Securities and Exchange Commission. Computer Directions Advisors Inc., a Silver Springs, Md., firm, collates the reports under a contract with SEC. Investors with discretionary authority over stock holdings valued at more than $100 million are required to report their holdings each quarter to the SEC. Reprinted in *The American Banker* (March 4, 1982), p. 10.

Stock Exchange that is not conducted through the New York Stock Exchange. Stocks sold in the third market are said to be sold *"off the Board."* Before 1975, when fixed commissions on the New York stock exchange were ended, the high commission fees caused increased trading volume off the Board.

In addition to the third market, the large institutional block traders often bypass both stockbrokers and stock exchanges and negotiate between themselves. This is called the *fourth market*. There are apparently no data on the size of the fourth market. Desk-top computer terminals link approximately 150 institutional traders in the fourth market by a system called *Instinet*.

Still, many block trades are conducted on the formal stock exchanges, especially in view of the negotiated commission schedule available on the New York exchange since 1975. Discounts and reciprocal agreements (where, for example, a stockbroker agrees to give return business to a financial intermediary) are made. Some consulting firms have been reported to accept their fees in "soft money." This requires the customer, say a bank, to give a specified amount of its brokerage business to a particular stockbroker, which then pays the consulting firm its fee.

Why is the bank, in the soft money payment arrangement noted above, prevented from obtaining its own discount at the brokerage? It may be that such a price is not available to other customers making trades of comparable size. Where the seller of a service can isolate groups of customers according to their elasticities of demand for a product, and charge each group a different price for the same quantity of service, there is *price discrimination*. This practice injures those with more inelastic demands. It would appear that demands are inelastic in the example above for customers who have no knowledge of alternative brokerage fees for the same service. Free access to commission charges and terms may, to a large extent, remedy this problem.

The New York Stock Exchange

A group of New York City brokers who had been trading securities under a buttonwood tree on Wall Street in 1792 authored the first agreement in the history of the New York Stock Exchange.[4] The Buttonwood Agreement increased the importance of brokers relative to auctioneers. At first, government stocks were traded at the Tontine Coffee House. In 1817, a more formal organization, the New York Stock and Exchange Board, was organized under a constitution. Its name was changed to the New York Exchange in 1863. It is sometimes called the *Big Board*. Regular trading sessions were scheduled, officers were elected, and the rules for the induction and regulation of members were formalized. As late as 1835, no industrial stock was traded. The New York Stock and Exchange Board handled government, utility, and transportation bonds. By 1856, fewer than twenty different industrial stocks were traded.

Up until 1840, markets for financial assets in other parts of the country were as important as those in New York City. State Street in Boston and Chestnut Street in Philadelphia were as influential as Wall Street. Nevertheless, the seeds of New York's prominence and the dominance of the New York Stock Exchange were planted early. With the opening of the Erie Canal (1823), New York enjoyed increased trade. Commercial paper to finance trade was handled in increasing amounts by New York banks. The New York banks also received more deposits, which allowed them to increase their *call loan* business to finance the sale of securities. These loans were considered to be desirable by the banks since they were very liquid short-term loans.

A second factor, which eventually gave New York City dominance in both the money market and the stock markets, was the demise of the Second Bank of the United States, which had been chartered to handle the banking business of the federal government. With its collapse in Philadelphia in 1842, more country bank reserves were sent to New York City.

The volume of business on the New York Stock Exchange reached 700,000 shares on a record day in 1879, and 1 million shares per day were traded in 1886. A new high of over 3 million shares traded in one day was reached in 1901, but this record was not surpassed until 1916. In the following decades the exchange suffered from the publication of reports of fraudulent practices such as the sale of phony stock issues. Annual reports were not always informative or available. When the exchange asked a railroad for its report shortly after the Civil War, the company replied that it makes "no reports and publishes no statements—and has done nothing of the sort for the last five years."[5] The exchange began to regulate itself with stock registration and, eventually, required public financial reports of listed stocks.

With public confidence restored and a "new era" of great expectations, trading volume rose from 173 million shares in 1921 to more than a billion in 1929. Stock prices reached their peak of 254 on September 7,

1929 (on the Standard and Poor's Index of ninety common stocks). At first there was an orderly decline in stock prices, then a short rally, and finally a plunge, beginning October 23. The day of greatest panic, "Black Tuesday," was October 29, on which the Dow Jones Industrial Average of stocks fell 12 percent (60 percent below its September 29 peak) and 16.4 million shares were traded (compared to the daily September average of slightly more than 4 million shares). The Dow Jones Industrial Average fell from 381 on September 3, 1929, to its low of 36 in 1932 and did not regain its 1929 peak for twenty-five years. During 1929, the American Telephone and Telegraph Company stock dropped from a high of $310\frac{1}{4}$ to $199\frac{1}{2}$; General Electric dropped from $396\frac{1}{4}$ to $168\frac{1}{8}$; and White Sewing Machine, which had been selling at $48, closed at $11 on Black Tuesday, with a block of stock reportedly being bought at $1 by an employee on the stock exchange floor.

The belief that the October crash produced many suicides has been challenged on the grounds that the suicide rate was relatively low in the United States in October and November of 1929, but for many the results were painful.

> One of the worst victims was Clarence Birdseye, who started Birdseye Foods on a pittance, sold it to General Foods for $30 million, and put the entire sum into the market not long before the crash. His fortune was obliterated. Another big victim was William C. Durant, the founder of General Motors. After his fortune was wiped out, Mr. Durant ended up running a bowling alley in Flint, Michigan.[6]

The 1929 stock market crash had momentous effects throughout the country and much of the world. It has been the subject of many books, which characterize the entire period of the 1930s as the aftermath of the stock market crash of 1929. This type of analysis is mostly wrong. The country was already in an economic decline, although the decline was certainly accelerated by the stock market's negative impact on investment and on the value of the public's stock of wealth. However, the stock market is but one market among many. The economy did not fall into two depressions in the 1930s solely or even primarily because of the October 1929 stock market crash. The severe business contraction, which had begun before October, would have ended in late 1930 or 1931 if additional events had not occurred. The most important of these were the collapse of a large number of commercial banks and the accompanying huge decline in the quantity of money in circulation—it decreased by fully one-third.

Beginning at the end of World War II, volume again grew in the securities markets. In 1967, all U.S. stock exchanges had a volume (in stocks and bonds) of approximately $768 billion, of which $131 billion was traded on the New York Stock Exchange. By 1981, trading volume often exceeded $50 million shares of stock. After the Federal Reserve made an announcement on October 6, 1979, which was interpreted as a signal that money supply growth would be dramatically lowered, stock market activity was stimulated to a new record day; 81 million shares traded on

October 10, 1979. Then on November 6, 1980, one day after Ronald Reagan was elected president (defeating the incumbent, Jimmy Carter), the New York Stock Exchange hit a new one-day trading record, 84.3 million shares.

The New York Stock Exchange went through a number of crises in the late 1960s and early 1970s. There was record volume that was difficult to handle and a record number of failures to complete transactions by delivery of the stock that had been offered (called "fails"). "Third" and "fourth" markets (informal arrangements for sales outside the formal exchanges), which were not subject to the New York Stock Exchange's arbitrary commission schedule, developed, and the number of organizations that were members of the New York Stock Exchange declined.

The New York Stock Exchange began to reorganize in August 1971 on the basis of the Martin Report. In January 1971 the New York Stock Exchange asked William McChesney Martin, formerly chairman of the Federal Reserve Board and the first paid president of the New York Stock Exchange when it had previously reorganized in 1938, to submit recommendations for reform. The New York Stock Exchange also decided to incorporate (February 18, 1971) and so did some regional exchanges. The Martin Report urged greater use of modern communications systems. In 1971 the boards of the New York Stock Exchange and the American Exchange authorized these exchanges to move toward establishing a new Securities Industries Automation Corporation (SIAC) as recommended in the Martin Report. This was intended to provide a single consolidated record of the price of stock on all exchanges, a move that would integrate the New York Stock Exchange, the American Stock Exchange, and the regional exchanges. In 1975, Congress ordered the Securities and Exchange Commission and the securities industry to develop a National Market System (NMS) for consolidated reporting of the price of a stock, even though it is sold on more than one exchange. This Composite Quotations System would supply quoted offers to buy and sell from all market participants that were quoting prices near current trading prices. (See Chapter 24 for a discussion of consolidated price quotations and suspension of the New York Stock Exchange restrictions on off-board trading on selected stocks.)

Beginning May 1, 1975, the fixed commission rate schedule of the New York Exchange was completely abandoned in favor of competitive rates set by the stockbrokers.

Due to the failure of a number of brokerage houses hit by rising volume and increased costs, the Congress passed the Securities Investor Protection Act of 1970, which created the Securities Investor Protection Corporation (SIPC). The SIPC insures customers of member brokers against the losses that are incurred if a broker goes bankrupt. The SIPC has no direct funding from the government but can borrow up to $1 billion from the U.S. Treasury.

The New York Stock Exchange is an organization of *member* firms and individuals. The available *seats* for members on the Exchange have numbered 1366 since 1953. In addition, there can be *allied members* (such as a general partner in a member firm who is not a member) and *approved persons* (such as a director of a member corporation). Seats on the New York Stock Exchange sold for prices that varied from $515,000 to $200,000 in 1969, then fell in the 1970s; a seat sold for $45,000 in October 1977 and $90,000 in October 1978. In 1929, the "bad old days," seats varied from $550,000 to $625,000.

The exchange is run by twenty directors: ten public representatives and ten brokers. In addition, there is a full-time paid chairman of the board.

Members trade on the floor of the New York Stock Exchange in one or more of the following capacities:

1. *Commission brokers* act on orders from the public relayed through brokers.
2. *Specialists* buy and sell particular stocks which are assigned to them. They keep a list of *limit* and *stop orders* and take a position by buying, selling, and holding the stocks they are assigned. They attempt to provide more continuous trading in a stock at prices that are closer to their concept of normal. Thus a stock that has been selling for $10 might be bought by a specialist for $9.75 rather than letting it fall to $9.00 if the specialist believes that most trades will take place around $10. An attempt is made to prevent prices in successive transactions from being conducted at more than one-eighth of a dollar per share difference. The specialist must make "effective execution of commission orders" and provide "maintenance, insofar as reasonably practicable, of a fair and orderly market on the Exchange" in the assigned stocks (Rule 108). The specialist can act as agent for other brokers or as a dealer for his own account, carrying out his or her functions. The approximately 400 specialists are evaluated quarterly by the floor brokers they serve.
3. *Odd-lot dealers* buy and sell stocks for which orders have been received for less than the standard 100-share multiples.
4. *Floor brokers* trade for other members on a commission basis. These floor brokers are popularly known as $2 brokers, the standard commission formerly paid for executing a 100-share order.
5. *Registered traders* trade primarily for themselves. (There are approximately 100 registered traders.)
6. *Bond brokers* trade bonds in the exchange's Bond Room.

The huge volume of stocks actively traded on the Big Board make it a fairly competitive market, which precludes any substantial collusive action or sustained domination by a small group of traders.

Some practices probably reduce the degree of competition. The limitation on membership can be reflected in monopolistic prices for seats on the exchange. It might be advantageous to allow more specialists in each stock. The single specialist in a stock has special information. He or she has schedules for a particular stock for all limit and stop orders. These orders are entrusted to the specialist by other exchange members. The orders specify a *floor* or *ceiling* price (*limit orders* to sell or buy, respectively) and/or directions to buy or sell if a given price is reached (*stop loss* orders). For example, a limit order might instruct the specialist to sell XYZ for $50 or better, whereas a stop loss order would instruct the specialist to sell XYZ if the price falls below $50. The specialist therefore has important information for predicting the future price of stocks that is not available to other market participants.

There are similar participants in the over-the-counter markets. Many firms or individuals can act as specialists in a security by actively buying, selling, carrying an inventory of the stock, and accepting some type of limit orders. Limited numbers of specialists on the Big Board (no more than one in each stock) may reduce the competition in the provision of these services. The specialist, however, is probably prevented from making substantial monopoly profits on the Big Board by other traders. If other traders suspected that a market was being made around prices that differed from their concept of normal, they would rapidly adjust their bids and offers to the new information.

The Stock Market and the Economy

Stock prices are sometimes said to be a symptom or a reaction, either to past conditions or expected future conditions in the economy. This may be true in large part, but the size of the stock market reaction may well change these future conditions. For example, if it is thought that the economy is going into a recession, so that the profits of companies with stocks sold on the New York Stock Exchange will take an unexpected dive the following year, stock prices may immediately fall. If the stock prices fall by a huge amount, this reaction of stock prices could make the recession bigger than expected. This is because people who own stocks will suffer a significant decline in their wealth. If this decline is thought to be long term, these individuals may dramatically reduce their spending.

For example, the stock market fell in the third quarter of 1978, measured by the Dow Jones Index of twenty-nine leading industrial stocks. The market fell 15.2 percent (108.8 percent at an annual rate) in the ten weeks following September 8, 1978. Since the total value of stocks outstanding listed on the New York Stock Exchange in September was $883.9 billion, this decline amounted to $134.5 billion reduction in the value of wealth held primarily by U.S. residents. Such a decline in wealth could easily lead many individuals to cut back on spending if they thought the decline was not a temporary dip and could throw the country into a recession.

Unfortunately, as Paul Samuelson, the Nobel laureate, reminds us: "The market has forecast nine of the last five recessions."[7] If individuals regard the decline in stock prices as temporary, some may start spending their money furiously to buy up companies at a low price, creating chains of new spending, which would to some extent offset the stock market decline. Investment in new plants and equipment may be curtailed by low stock prices. It can become less expensive to buy this capital in another company by buying up their stock at the low prices.

It may well be that one of the reasons for a stock market decline is the attempt to sell off stocks in order to invest funds in other parts of the economy, such as the home building industry, in which case the stock market's decline may to some extent be the result of another sector's expansion. Economists blandly call this a *portfolio adjustment*; those with long positions in the stock market call it murder.[8]

The New York Stock Exchange's biggest volume day was, up to that time, Wednesday, August 18, 1982, when 132.7 million shares were traded. On Tuesday, August 17, 1982, the Dow Jones Industrial Average rose a record 38.81 points. Some details of this episode are presented at the end of Chapter 12. On October 7, 1982, a record 147 million shares were sold.

The Corporate Bond Market

New corporate bonds are sold to the public in two ways. In *private placements*, bonds are placed directly with particular lenders. Life insurance companies often acquire bonds by this method. The decline in private placements from about one-half in the 1953–1964 period to one-third in 1977 reflects the reduced share of life insurance companies in bond acquisitions.[9]

The other and more common method of selling corporate bonds is by public offering handled by underwriters (investment banking firms), described in Chapter 2. During the 1920s, most public offerings were handled by commercial banks. The Glass-Steagall Act (the Banking Act of 1933) terminated bank underwriting of corporate bonds. Investment banking firms have been the major underwriters since that time.

The secondary market for corporate bonds is sometimes considered rather thin because most corporate bonds are purchased by large institutional buyers. However, secondary bond markets such as those found in the New York Stock Exchange bond room appear to be competitive and to be an efficient market. The special government bond market is discussed in Chapter 23 and the Eurobond market is discussed in Chapter 29.

An important new innovation in corporate bond issuance went into effect in 1982. A new rule by the Securities and Exchange Commission (S-3 registration form for publicly issued debt under SEC Rule 462A), commonly known as "shelf registration," will permit an issuer to register by issue of bonds with the SEC. The issuer will not have to sell them all at once. They can be sold in parts whenever there is a need for funds or a more favorable market. Finance companies and banks have previously been able to use that method of issuing bonds. This may mean that investment bankers can be bypassed in some cases and corporations can enter the market without the prior announcement that registration of new issues has formerly provided.

The most important developments in the corporate bond markets in the early 1980s, with wide swings up and down in interest rates at levels in the double digits, is the shortening of maturities. It was predicted that more than half of the corporate bonds sold in 1982 would be for maturities of ten years or less.[10] The most interesting and far-reaching response to high interest rates has come in the options and futures markets, discussed next.

The Stock Options Market

A *stock option* is a financial asset that gives the owner the right to buy or sell a stock at a particular price before a specified date. The terms used in the options market are listed below, with definitions 4 through 14 taken from the prospectus of the Options Clearing Corporation, a private corporation that clears option contracts.

1. An option to sell a *put*.
2. An option to buy a *call*.
3. The price at which the option owner can buy or sell the stock is the *exercise price*, the *striking price*, or the *strike price*.
4. *Underlying security*: the Security subject to being purchased or sold upon the exercise of an option. In the case of stock options, this is sometimes referred to as the underlying stock.
5. *Class of options*: options of the same type (i.e., put or call) covering the same underlying security.
6. *Series of options*: options of the same class having the same exercise price and expiration time and the same unit of trading.
7. *Expiration time*: the latest time in the expiration month when an option may be exercised by a clearing member at the Clearing Corporation. Holders of options should determine from their brokers the earlier exercise cutoff time, which is the latest time a customer may instruct his or her broker to exercise an option so that the exercise notice may be received "at the Clearing Corporation" prior to the expiration time.
8. *Premium*: the aggregate price of an option agreed upon between the buyer and writer or their agents in a transaction on the floor of an exchange.
9. *Opening purchase transaction*: a transaction in which an investor intends to become the holder of an option.
10. *Opening sale transaction*: a transaction in which an investor intends to become the writer of an option.

11. *Closing purchase transaction*: a transaction in which an investor who is obligated as a writer of an option intends to terminate his or her obligation as a writer. This is accomplished by "purchasing" in a closing purchase transaction an option of the same series as the option previously written. Such a transaction has the effect, upon acceptance by the Clearing Corporation, of canceling the investor's preexisting position as a writer, instead of resulting in the issuance of an option to the investor.

12. *Closing sale transaction*: a transaction in which an investor who is the holder of an outstanding option intends to liquidate his or her position as holder. This is accomplished by "selling" in a closing sale transaction an option of the same series as the option previously purchased. Such a transaction has the effect, upon acceptance by the Clearing Corporation, of liquidating the investor's preexisting position as a holder of the option, instead of resulting in the investor assuming the obligations of a writer.

13. *Covered call writer*: a writer of a call who, as long as he or she remains obligated as a writer, owns the shares or other units of underlying security covered by the call, or holds on a share-for-share basis a call of the same class as the call written where the exercise price of the call held is equal to or less than the exercise price of the call written.

14. *Uncovered call writer*: a writer of a call who is not a covered call writer.[11]

Before 1973, stock options were offered by private dealers. The options dealer charged a premium for these financial instruments. Options for many stocks are now heavily traded on formal exchanges. The formal trading of options began with options on sixteen stocks on the Chicago Board Options Exchange (CBOE) on April 23, 1973. There are now hundreds of different stock options traded on a number of formal exchanges, including the Chicago CBOE, the American Exchange in New York, the Philadelphia Exchange, and the Pacific Exchange.

The standards of the options exchanges for selection and maintenance of underlying stocks for options trading on the exchanges serviced by the Options Clearing Corporation include:

(A) A minimum of 8,000,000 shares owned by persons other than directors, officers, principal stockholders, and others required to report their stock holdings under Section 16(a) of the Exchange Act.

(B) A minimum of 10,000 shareholders.

(C) Trading volume on all markets on which the underlying stock is traded off at least 2,000,000 shares per year in each of the two previous calender years.

(D) The market price of the underlying stock shall have been at least $10.00 per share each business day of the six calender months preceding the date of selection as measured by the lowest closing price recorded in any market on which the underlying stock traded on each of the subject days.

(E) The issuer and its significant subsidiaries have not during the past three years defaulted in the payment of any dividend or sinking fund installment on any preferred stock or in the payment of any principal, interest, or sinking fund installment on any indebtedness for borrowed money, or in the payment of rentals under long-term leases.

(F) The issuer and its consolidated subsidiaries had an aggregate net income, after taxes, but before extraordinary items net of tax effect, of a least $1,000,000 in each of three of the last four fiscal years, including the most recent fiscal year.[12]

Options or rights to buy stock issued by the corporation that issues the underlying stock are called *warrants*. They are traded on stock exchanges. Warrants may have more distant original maturities than puts and calls currently have, extending out to more than a year.

If one has not traded options, the entire subject sounds complicated and even boring. A small position in options will clarify these problems rapidly. In place of that some oversimplified examples may do.

Bill Frank owns 100 shares of common stock in General Wheel, which he believes will not rise significantly in price in the next six months. If a call option for General Wheel is traded on an exchange, Bill Frank might try to make some extra money without selling his stock. Bill Frank would take his 100 shares of General Wheel to a broker and write a call option on them for sale on an exchange. (In this example, Bill Frank has a covered call since he owns the underlying stock.) The price of a share of General Wheel is $60 on the day in January that the call is written. An April call on 100 shares of General Wheel has a striking price of $65. It is called an *April 65 call*. The call option on 100 shares is currently selling on an exchange for $3.25 a share, or $325 for 100 shares. Bill Frank receives $325 (minus brokerage fees) on a call option that expires at the end of the second week in April.

Tom Pass believes differently. He buys the call for $325 because he expects the price of General Wheel to rise significantly. If the price of General Wheel does rise above $65, the call option would be said to be *in the money*.

Suppose that the price of General Wheel rises to $75. Then the April 65 call would rise to at least to $10 a share (or higher if a further rise is expected and the expiration date is not at hand). Why has the call risen in price to $10 or higher? Because the owner of such a call could exercise it and buy a share of General Wheel for $65 and then turn around and sell the same share at its current market price of $75, making a $10 profit minus brokerage fees. Tom Pass, like most stock options market participants, would not exercise his call; he would instead sell it in the market.

If the price of General Wheel does not rise to $65 before the end of the second week in April, Bill Frank makes his profit on selling the call, and he is not forced to sell his 100 shares at $65 each. Instead, he retains ownership of the 100 shares.

A put may be bought in place of a riskier short sale. A common stock may be *sold short* in anticipation of a price decline. An individual may sell a stock short that he or she does not currently own. Think of this transaction as involving a loan of stock from a stockbroker that the short seller must return within a stated time period. The short sale is riskier than a put in terms of the limits on the loss that could occur. The possible loss on a short sale theoretically has no limit if the stock keeps rising, but the put owner can only lose the cost of the put plus brokerage fees.

Assume, for example, that an individual, Mr. Williams, expects XYZ stocks to fall in price from $15 to $5 per share. Williams does not own this stock. He sells the stock short at $15 per share for ninety days by borrowing the stock from the broker. If he sells 100 shares, he receives $1500.00. If the stock falls to $5.00 per share before ninety days have passed, Williams repays the dealer by buying the stock for $5.00 and returning it to the broker. He then makes $1000.00 minus brokerage fees. If the stock were to rise to $20 a share, Williams would lose $500 plus brokerage fees.

Rather than sell short, Mr. Williams may simply buy a put for the stock. Assume that a put with a $10 striking price is available. The put costs $1.75 a share, or $175 for 100 shares. Then if the price of the stock falls to $5, Williams can exercise his put and make at least $500, minus the $175 cost of the put and brokerage fees. If the stock price rises, Williams can only lose $175 plus brokerage fees.

Stock options are financial assets that allow individuals to take a position on stocks at a small fraction of the cost of the stock. They also offer a way to hedge against unfavorable price changes on stocks.

Puts and calls may be used to *straddle the market*. A straddle can be executed by buying a put and call on the same stock. If the market falls, the put goes up in price and the call falls in price (to at most zero). If the market rises, the call goes up in price and the put falls in price (to at most zero). Straddling the market can be profitable if there are wide swings—either up or down—in the price of the underlying stock.

On September 8, 1981, Commodity Futures Trading Commission (CFTC), one of the federal government regulators that regulates financial markets (see Chapter 24), approved a three-year pilot program for trading commodity options on futures contracts. An option on a futures contract gives the right to buy or sell futures at a specified price. A plan by the Chicago Options Exchange would provide options holders the right to buy or sell an 8 percent Government National Mortgage Association (GNMA) security (described subsequently) at a fixed percentage of their $100,000 face value. In line with CFTC's pilot program, options holders would have the right to buy or sell GNMA contracts at a stipulated price, not the GNMA security itself. The congressional oversight committees in the Senate and House of Representatives have thirty business days to review CFTS's program.

The Futures Market

A *futures contract* is a legal instrument by which an individual agrees to buy or sell a commodity or financial asset at a fixed price in the future. Depository institutions use financial asset futures contracts to hedge against unfavorable changes in interest rates that would reduce the value of their loan portfolio. The futures contract may call for delivery as long as eighteen months in the future. Few of these purchase orders result in deliveries. Roughly 98 percent of all commodity futures contracts are settled by offset rather than delivery, as explained in the example. *Buy* contracts are purchased if prices are expected to rise, and *sell* contracts are purchased if prices are expected to fall. There are eleven federally licensed commodity futures exchanges in the United States:

American Commodities Exchange.
New York Mercantile Exchange.
Chicago Board of Trade.
Kansas City Board of Trade.
Chicago Mercantile Exchange.
Commodity Exchange, Inc., New York.
MidAmerica Commodity Exchange, Chicago.
Minneapolis Grain Exchange.
New York Cotton Exchange.
Coffee, Sugar & Cocoa Exchange, Inc.
New York Futures Exchange.

Commodity futures trading began with the establishment of the Chicago Board of Trade on April 3, 1848. It grew rapidly in the 1970s. Approximately fifty different commodity futures contracts are currently traded. The total number of commodity futures contracts traded increased from 15.6 million in 1970 to 76.0 million in 1978.[13]

Unstable economic conditions, especially rising rates of interest, gave an impetus to trading financial asset futures contracts in formal futures markets in the 1970s. Currency futures—called *selling currency forward*—have long been an important ingredient of international finance. They are discussed in Chapter 28. Forward contracts have been written for other financial assets in the past. Forward contracts are agreements between two partners. In a futures market a clearing corporation takes the risk that the other party is creditworthy and reliable.[14]

A number of types of futures contracts for financial assets began being traded in the formal futures market in the 1970s. Exchanges where futures contracts for financial assets were traded in 1982 were

Chicago Board of Trade.
Chicago Mercantile Exchange.
International Monetary Market, a division of the Chicago Mercantile Exchange, and the Kansas City Board of Trade.
MidAmerica Commodity Exchange.
New York Futures Exchange, a unit of the New York Stock Exchange.

A gold futures market opened in London. (The reader may decide whether this is a commodity futures market or a financial asset futures market depending on his or her preference.)

LONDON—The London Gold Futures Market is slated to open on April 19, [1982].

The 100-ounce contracts will be priced in sterling.

Keith Smith, chairman of the new exchange, said he was confident about the new market's future even though gold's price has fallen steadily since January 1980.

"In spite of the decline, the gold market has been very active in the past few months so we believe that the exchange will be successful," Mr. Smith said.

There will be 38 floor members. Apart from London Metal Exchange traders and the five London bullion houses, the following U.S. companies are members: J. Aaron & Co. (UK) Ltd.; Bache Halsey Stuart Shields Inc.; Merrill Lynch, Pierce, Fenner & Smith Ltd.; New York London Futures Ltd. and Shearson/American Express Ltd. The seats cost $101,000 each.[15]

"The world's first offshore—and completely automated financial futures exchange" was scheduled to open in Bermuda in June 1982.[16]

In 1981, financial asset futures reached new records in growth. The number of financial futures contracts traded increased from approximately 1.6 million in January to 2.6 million in November, approximately 42 percent of the number of commodity future contracts traded in November.[17] In November 1981, the record number of futures contracts traded on one day in one market, held by soybean futures contracts, was broken by Treasury bond futures contracts on the Chicago Board of Trade.

On February 24, 1982, the Kansas City Board of Trade began selling future contracts on an index of stocks. More than 2000 were traded the first day. First-day volume in these stock index futures was double the normal volume in futures for hard, red winter wheat, for which it is the biggest market.

Futures contracts based on stock indexes were also approved for trading on the Chicago Board of Trade and the Commodity Exchange Inc. in New York City in 1982. (They were approved by the Commodity Futures Trading Commission, a federal government agency described in Chapter 22.) The Chicago Board of Trade planned to trade contracts based on the Dow Jones Index of thirty industrial stock prices and the Commodity Exchange Inc. planned to trade indexes based on Standard and Poor's 500-stock index. Dow Jones and Company refused to permit its name and index to be used; Standard and Poor's also refused to allow its name to be used by the Commodity Exchange Inc. Standard and Poor's had given exclusive license to the Chicago Mercantile Exchange to trade futures contracts based on the S&P index. The Commodity Exchange Inc. and the Chicago Board of Trade tried to circumvent the refusals by inventing clone indexes identical to DJ and S&P indexes. Lawsuits over copyright and trademark infringements followed and by May 1982, restraining court injunctions were in place.

In March 1982, the Commodity Futures Trading Commission (discussed in Chapter 24) approved a ninety-day T-bill contract for the MidAmerica Commodity Exchange in Chicago. The contract's $500,000 face value was one-half that of similar contracts traded on the Chicago Mercantile Exchange. Settlement of the contract is by cash rather than

TABLE 22-2

Unofficial Summary of Contract Specifications for U.S. Treasury Bond Futures Traded at the Chicago Board of Trade (Subject to Change) and Price Quotations for July 29, 1981

Basic trading unit	U.S. Treasury bonds with $100,000 face value
Deliverable grade	U.S. Treasury bonds. Maturing at least 15 years from delivery day if not callable; and if callable are not so for at least 15 years from delivery day
Delivery method	Federal Reserve book entry wire transfer system. Invoice is adjusted for coupon rates and maturity or call dates
Price quotation	Percentage of par, e.g., 94-01 or $94\frac{1}{32}$
Minimum fluctuation	$\frac{1}{32}$ of a point or $31.25 per contract
Daily price limit	$\frac{64}{32}$ ($2,000 per contract) above and below the previous day's settlement price
Initial margin	$2,000 per contract
Maintenance margin	$1,500 per contract
Hedging margin	$1,500 per contract
Hours of trading	8:00 A.M. to 2:00 P.M. (Chicago time)
Ticker symbol	US

Note: Above is as of July 1981. Margins are subject to change. Margins required by member firms may exceed CBT contract margins. For full details on all specifications, see Chicago Board of Trade Rules and Regulations.

Prices for Treasury bonds at the Chicago Board of Trade as quoted in *The Wall Street Journal* on Wednesday, July 29, 1981:

The price for Sept. 1981 opened at 62-03 (62 and $\frac{3}{32}$nds) and settled at 61-29 (61 and $\frac{29}{32}$nds)

This settlement price translates into a yield of 13.574. (Futures market yields are based on a hypothetical 8% 20-year bond and are provided as interest rate reference points only.)

Treasury Bonds (CBT)—$100,000; pts. 32nds of 100%

	Open	High	Low	Settle	Chg.	Yield Settle	Yield Chg.	Open Interest
Sept.	62-03	62-03	61-17	61-29	−3	13.574	+.020	51,342
Dec.	63-00	63-00	62-16	62-26	−3	13.379	+.020	34,458
Mar. 82	63-22	63-22	63-08	63-17	−4	13.227	+.026	27,733
June	64-07	64-07	63-27	64-03	−4	13.111	+.026	27,010
Sept.	64-23	64-23	64-10	64-19	−4	13.009	+.026	27,243
Dec.	65-07	65-07	64-24	65-01	−4	12.920	+.025	28,079
Mar. 83	65-16	65-16	65-05	65-13	−4	12.845	+.024	22,758
June	65-19	65-24	65-17	65-24	−4	12.778	+.025	17,445
Sept.	66-06	66-06	65-27	66-02	−4	12.716	+.024	23,463
Dec.	66-14	66-14	66-09	66-11	−4	12.661	+.024	21,852
Mar. 84	66-22	66-22	66-13	66-19	−4	12.613	+.024	20,842
June	66-29	66-29	66-24	66-26	−4	12.571	+.024	9,960
Sept.	66-31	67-01	66-31	67-01	−4	12.529	+.023	2,645
Dec.	67-06	67-08	67-06	67-08	−4	12.488	+.024	562

Est. vol. 40,000; vol. Mon. 49,719; open int. 315,392, +1,761.

Volume for Tuesday, July 28, was estimated at 40,000

Actual volume for Monday, July 27, was 49,719

Open interest—contracts not yet offset by opposite transactions or delivery—reached 315,392 on Monday, July 27

(Treasury bond contracts are traded in $100,000 units. Minimum price fluctuations are $\frac{1}{32}$nd of a point. One point is $1,000, so $\frac{1}{32}$nd of a point is $1,000 ÷ 32, or $31.25.)

Source: U.S. Treasury Bond Futures, Chicago Board of Trade, Marketing Department (distributed 1982), p. 5.

delivery of the actual T-bills. Also in 1982, specialists firms on the New York Stock Exchange planned to trade on the New York Futures Exchange (then only eighteen months old). Stock index trading was also planned for the Mercantile and the Chicago Board of Trade.

The following hypothetical example illustrates the mechanics of futures contracts in a generalized form. Assume that Jones has entered a futures contract to buy a given quantity of commodity X at $1000 six months hence. This is called a *long position*. Jones expects the price to rise above $1000. The other party to the futures contract, Smith, agrees to sell a given quantity of commodity X at $1000 six months hence. Smith expects the price to fall. This is called a *short position*. Smith does not own commodity X but must deliver cash equal to the value of the commodity if he wishes to terminate his contract. (Parties to a contract need not actually trade with each other in the future; long and short positions are matched through clearinghouses such as the Chicago Board of Trade Clearing Corporation.) Now assume that the price of a contract on commodity X, scheduled for the same delivery date, rises in price to $1200. Jones may decide to take his profit; he sells his contract for $1200. Smith, fearing a higher price and a bigger loss, wishes to terminate his short position. In effect, Smith pays off the owner of a buy contract, Jones, by delivery of $1200 rather than actually delivering commodity X. The original contract is canceled with a loss of $200 to Smith and a gain of $200 to Jones, neglecting brokerage fees.

In this manner, most futures contracts do not result in the delivery of the commodity. Many more people than those actually interested in taking future delivery on a commodity are thus able to act on the market in an attempt to predict future prices.

Partial unofficial summaries of futures contract specifications (subject to change) for future contracts on U.S. Treasury bonds, certificates of deposit, Government National Mortgage Association contracts, and collateralized depository receipts are shown in Tables 22-2, 22-3, and 22-4. These contract specifications describe the underlying financial instrument. They also describe the daily limit allowed for price movements and the margin requirement (a discussion of the relationship of limits and margin requirements is presented in Chapter 24). The margin requirements, the percentage of cash required, are very small compared to the current 50 percent margin on stock. Two thousand dollars are required for a $100,000-face-value U.S. Treasury bond futures contract. Prices fluctuate on these contracts by at least $\frac{1}{32}$ of a point, defined as $1000. Thus minimum fluctuations are $31.25.

The example at the bottom of Table 22-2 shows that a gain on July 29, 1981, for those holding September 1981 contracts amounts to a .02 percentage-point increase in the yield. This is calculated on a hypothetical 8 percent twenty-year coupon bond, the artificial bond used to report price movements. A .02 percentage-point increase in the yield is equivalent to a fall in the hypothetical bond price of $93.75.[18] A full percentage-point change would, using this basis, therefore amount to a $4812.50 change in price.

TABLE 22-3

Unofficial Summary of Contract Specifications for Certificate of Deposit Futures Contract Traded at the Chicago Board of Trade (Subject to Change)

Basic trading unit	Domestic Certificate of Deposit $1,000,000 face value
Deliverable grade	Domestic Certificate of Deposit approved as deliverable by the CBT. The Certificate must have an original issuance date which is not earlier than the first business day of the calendar month three months prior to the delivery month . . . and which matures on a business day early in the third month following delivery month
Delivery instrument	Domestic Certificate of Deposit
Delivery method	Domestic Certificate of Deposit versus funds deposited in New York
Minimum fluctuation	$\frac{1}{100}$th of 1% of $1,000,000 on a 90-day basis ($25 contract)
Price quotation	Index: 100 minus yield, e.g., $100 - 10.27 = 89.73$
Daily price limit	$\frac{80}{100}$ ($2000 per contract) above or below the previous day's settlement price
Trading months	March, June, September and December plus other contract months as approved by the CBT and CFTC
Ticker symbol	BC
Trading hours	7:30 A.M. to 2 P.M., Chicago time

Source: Domestic Certificate of Deposit Futures, Chicago Board of Trade, Marketing Department (distributed 1982), p. 2.

TABLE 22-4

Unofficial Summary of Contract Specifications for Government National Mortgage Association (GNMA) Collateralized Depository Receipt Futures Contract Traded at the Chicago Board of Trade (Subject to Change)

Basic trading unit	$100,000 principal balance of GNMA 8% coupon or equivalent
Deliverable grade	Modified pass-through mortgage-backed certificates guaranteed by GNMA, with coupons of an equivalent principal balance based on an 8% coupon yielding 7.96% at par. Based on the assumption of a 30-year certificate prepaid in the 12th year
Delivery method	GNMA Collateralized Depositary Receipt (CDR)
Price quotation	Percentage of par, e.g., 64-01 or $64\frac{1}{32}$
Minimum fluctuation	$\frac{1}{32}$ of a point ($31.25 per contract)
Daily price limit	$\frac{64}{32}$ ($2,000 per contract) above and below the previous day's settlement price
Initial margin	$2,000 per contract
Maintenance margin	$1,500 per contract
Hedging margin	$1,500 per contract
Trading hours	8:00 A.M. to 2:00 P.M. (Chicago time)
Ticker symbol	M

Note: As of October 1981. For full details on all specifications, see *Chicago Board of Trade Rules and Regulations.*

Source: GNMA CDR Futures, Chicago Board of Trade, Marketing Division (distributed 1982), p. 2.

The yields on T-bond futures that cleared the market on July 29, 1981, were very close to the mark for Treasury bonds eight months later, as of March 1982. (The future yield in Table 22-2 for March 1982 is 13.2 and the actual March 26, 1982, Treasury bond yield turned out to be 13.69.) How do they look from the reader's vantage point in time?

The financial market provides a vehicle for hedging against unfavorable interest rate changes. For example, suppose that the treasurer of a company expects to receive $1 million in three months which will be invested in bonds. He or she wishes to protect against unfavorable and unexpected increases in the price of bonds. The treasurer goes long by buying futures contracts on Treasury bonds. If bond prices rise, the futures contracts will rise in value. If bond prices do not rise, the $1 million can be invested at a lower price and the futures contract can be sold. In this way, current expectations for interest rates and bond prices can be nailed down for future purchases. In Exhibit 22-1, the Chicago Board of Trade gives an example of a hedge for a savings and loan association that wishes to issue certificates of deposit.

A common trading technique in futures markets called *spreading* involves the simultaneous purchase and sale of different but related futures contracts. (A straddle usually refers to straddling the price on an

Exhibit 22-1

Hedging to "unlock" a fixed CD rate. *Source: Domestic Certificate of Deposit Futures,* **Chicago Board of Trade, Marketing Department (distributed 1982), p. 11.**

Background: On February 1, an S&L issues 90-day CDS at the current rate of 14.25%. Although interest rates appear to be declining steadily, the liability manager is unable to wait for a more favorable market environment because he needs funds immediately. To increase the marketability of his CD issuance, he chooses a 90-day CD rather than a shorter maturity.

Objective: To minimize the effects of being locked into a fixed rate in a declining rate environment, the manager buys 10 June CD futures contracts at 86.15.

Cash Market	Futures Market
February 1	February 1
Issues $10 million in 90-day CDs at a rate of 14.25% Interest expense: $356,250	Buys 10 June CD futures contracts at 86.15 (13.85%)
	Basis: −40
May 1	May 1
Rolls over $10 million in maturing CDs for another 90 days at 12.50%	Sells 10 June CD futures contracts at 87.90 (12.10%)
	Basis: −40
Opportunity Loss: 175 basis points (14.25% − 12.50%) or $43,750	**Gain:** 175 basis points (87.90 − 86.15) or $43,750

Results: Even though the S&L was locked into a 14.25% CD rate for 90 days, hedging allowed the manager to benefit as CD rates declined to 12.50%. The gain on his futures position offset the foregone interest savings exactly, making his effective borrowing cost from **February to May 12.50%**.

asset, such as buying a put and call on the same stock. Spread and straddle are sometimes used as synonyms.) They may differ by delivery
months; they may be related commodities or financial assets on the same
exchange; or related commodities or financial assets on different exchanges. (An intracommodity spread uses commodity futures contracts
for the same commodity in different months.) The futures contracts for
delivery during closest months are called *nearbys* and ones for more
distant months are called *deferreds*.

Here is an example of how a spread can be used.[19] A trader could
execute a spread transaction to reflect his or her expectations about the
interest rate yield curve. For example, when the yield curve is positive,
the nearbys will trade at a premium (positive spread) to deferreds. If
short-term interest rates rise and the yield curve flattens, the spread between the nearbys and the deferreds will tend to weaken. In this situation, a trader could profit from "selling the spread"—selling (shorting)
the nearby month and buying (going long) the deferred month. This is
known as a *bear spread*.

The bear spread is based on the expectation that during a period of
rising short-term interest rates the nearby month's price movement will
tend to outpace the deferreds month's price. (Recall from Chapter 10 that
longer rates are geometric averages of shorter rates and, under the error-
learning model, tend to change less rapidly.) Thus the nearby month will
fall in price faster than the deferred month, causing the spread to weaken
in favor of the trader.

When the yield curve is negative, the nearbys will trade at a discount
(negative spread) to the deferreds. If the yield curve becomes more positive (prices rise), the spread will tend to strengthen. In this situation, a
trader could profit from "buying the spread"—buying (going long) the
nearby month and selling (shorting) the deferred month. This is known
as a *bull spread*.

In this case, the nearby month is likely to outpace the deferred month
in terms of its price change. In an upward-trending, or bull, market, the
nearby month is likely to rise in price faster than the deferred month.
Thus the spread strengthens in favor of the trader.

Futures markets perform valuable functions. One function is to improve the allocation of the commodity over time. For example, without
future contracts, individuals might store an insufficient amount of food
in the summer for use the following winter. Extreme scarcity can occur
in the winter if there is no way for the price system adequately to reflect
next winter's expected food prices during the summer, when food is
abundant. Speculators would not be induced to buy food in the summer
and store it for winter. It is this kind of speculation that brings down
winter prices and raises summer prices of food, provides a better allocation of food over the seasons, and induces some individuals to specialize
in the storage of food in a manner that is more efficient than if each
household provided separate storage.

Futures traders also perform the important function of bearing the
risks of unfavorable future price movements. Some producers and buy-

ers of commodities or financial assets (such as loan commitments by banks) may be reluctant to gamble on future prices and may lack knowledge or funds to speculate on market conditions six months in the future. Futures trading allows the risk to be borne by those in the futures market who agree to buy or sell at a particular price, months before the commodity or financial asset is delivered.

An example of this second function can be found in the futures markets for currency. Suppose that American Wheel, Inc., wants to buy some merchandise in Germany for delivery sixty days later. The merchandise may already be on order, so that the necessity of a payment in German marks is definite. Rather than speculate on the price of German marks sixty days later, American Wheel may acquire a contract for the delivery of German marks in sixty days at a stipulated price. This is called *buying German marks forward*. The seller of the contract, perhaps a professional speculator, bears the risk of unfavorable increases in the price of German marks.

The Secondary Mortgage Market

The *secondary mortgage market* is a market in which mortgages that have already been negotiated are traded. The secondary mortgage market is sometimes included in the markets referred to as the money market. However, mortgages are long-term debts and might be more appropriately classified with long-term bonds in the conventional bond markets, or classified separately because of their distinctive features.

The private participants in the secondary mortgage market include private investors and mortgage brokers who buy and sell mortgages. The federal or quasi-federal participants are huge and operate nationally. The story of the secondary mortgage market is the story of its giant participants.

The Federal National Mortgage Association (FNMA), also known as "Fannie Mae," is the largest single supplier of funds for residential housing. Fannie Mae is a government-sponsored mortgage investment corporation nominally owned by its stockholders with a portfolio of residential mortgage loans outstanding in the third quarter of 1981 amounting to $54.2 billion (see Table 22-5). Its stock is sold on the New York Stock Exchange at a price that ranged between $6¾ and $12 in 1981.

Fannie Mae is not a primary lender. It lends money to institutions such as savings and loan associations, which themselves negotiate mortgage loans directly with the homeowners. Homeowners continue to send their monthly payments to the original lenders and are not aware that Fannie Mae owns the mortgage. In 1979, approximately 3500 organizations that make or purchase mortgages were eligible to sell their mortgages to Fannie Mae. Fannie Mae buys their mortgages at a special auction. In 1981, Fannie Mae acquired approximately 90,000 mortgages, roughly one in every twenty written in the United States.[20] It borrowed

TABLE 22-5

Mortgage Debt Outstanding, Third Quarter 1981* (Millions of Dollars)

Type of Holder and Type of Property		Type of Holder and Type of Property	
1 All holders	1,525,101	35 Federal Housing and Veterans	6,014
2 1- to 4-family	1,010,241	Administration	
3 Multifamily	140,253	36 1- to 4-family	2,224
4 Commercial	272,884	37 Multifamily	3,790
5 Farm	101,723	38 Federal National Mortgage Association	59,682
6 Major financial institutions	1,037,853	39 1- to 4-family	54,227
7 Commercial banks†	282,404	40 Multifamily	5,455
8 1- to 4-family	171,560	41 Federal Land Banks	44,708
9 Multifamily	13,132	42 1- to 4-family	2,605
10 Commercial	88,251	43 Farm	42,103
11 Farm	9,461	44 Federal Home Loan Mortgage	
12 Mutual savings banks	100,200	Corporation	5,432
13 1- to 4-family	65,551	45 1- to 4-family	4,166
14 Multifamily	17,405	46 Multifamily	1,266
15 Commercial	17,184	47 Mortgage pools or trusts‡	155,487
16 Farm	60	48 Government National Mortgage	
17 Savings and loan associations	518,132	Association	103,750
18 1- to 4-family	433,107	49 1- to 4-family	101,068
19 Multifamily	38,290	50 Multifamily	2,682
20 Commercial	46,735	51 Federal Home Loan Mortgage	
21 Life insurance companies	131,117	Corporation	17,936
22 1- to 4-family	17,889	52 1- to 4-family	14,401
23 Multifamily	19,872	53 Multifamily	3,535
24 Commercial	86,207	54 Farmers Home Administration	33,801
25 Farm	13,149	55 1- to 4-family	16,900
26 Federal and related agencies	124,511	56 Multifamily	3,172
27 Government National Mortgage		57 Commercial	5,631
Association	4,380	58 Farm	8,098
28 1- to 4-family	690	59 Individual and others§	207,250
29 Multifamily	3,690	60 1- to 4-family	124,088
30 Farmers Home Administration	4,295	61 Multifamily	27,400
31 1- to 4-family	1,765	62 Commercial	28,225
32 Multifamily	564	63 Farm	27,537
33 Commercial	651		
34 Farm	1,315		

*Based on data from various institutional and governmental sources, with some quarters estimated in part by the Federal Reserve in conjunction with the Federal Home Loan Bank Board and the Department of Commerce. Separation of nonfarm mortgage debt by type of property, if not reported directly, and interpolations and extrapolations when required, are estimated mainly by the Federal Reserve. Multifamily debt refers to loans on structures of five or more units.
†Includes loans held by nondeposit trust companies but not bank trust departments.
‡Outstanding principal balances of mortgages backing securities insured or guaranteed by the agency indicated.
§Other holders include mortgage companies, real estate investment trusts, state and local credit agencies, state and local retirement funds, noninsured pension funds, credit unions, and U.S. agencies for which amounts are small or separate data are not readily available.
Source: Federal Reserve Bulletin (December 1981), p. A41.

$40.4 billion in the financial markets, of which all but $3.6 billion was used to refinance maturing bonds and notes. For the first time, it lost money ($190.4 million), reflecting the general interest rate squeeze the thrift industry faced. Fannie Mae announced plans to buy *adjustable rate mortgages*, ARMs (mortgages that tie their interest return to a market rate between specified limits) and bought some *second mortgages* (mortgage loans that are subordinate to first mortgages in case of default). Fannie Mae was tracking seventy-five different types of ARMs in 1982. One problem in buying different types of mortgages is that the uniformity needed for competitive auctions with many participants could be impaired.

Fannie Mae has nearly 1100 employees, with headquarters in Washington, D.C. The chairman and chief operating officer in 1982 was David O. Maxwell, who was paid $225,000 a year, reflecting the designation of Fannie Mae as a private corporation that can offer salaries that are not under the lid imposed on federal government employees.

Fannie Mae is run by a board of fifteen directors, five of whom are appointed by the President of the United States. There is federal supervision in addition to the requirement that five appointments be made by the President. The secretary of Housing and Urban Development (HUD) can at times fix the aggregate amount of dividends that are paid by Fannie Mae in a year. The secretary of HUD can also require that a reasonable proportion of the corporation's mortgage purchases be "related to the national goal of providing adequate housing for low- and moderate-income families, but with reasonable economic return to the corporation." Offerings of stock and debt obligations must be approved by the secretary of HUD. The secretary of the Treasury must approve the issuance of various forms of debt securities.

With all this government supervision, it is quite evident that Fannie Mae is unlike the normal private corporation. It is, in large part, a government-created and government-organized corporation that has moved substantial amounts of capital funds out of other sectors into the housing market.

Fannie Mae has relatives. Freddie Mac, the Federal Home Loan Mortgage Corporation (FHLMC), was established July 24, 1970, by the Emergency Home Finance Act. It also purchases residential mortgages. The board of directors is comprised of the three members of the Federal Home Loan Bank Board, whose chairman is also the chairman of the FHLMC. The corporation is technically privately owned through the sale of nonvoting common stock issuable only to the twelve Federal Home Loan Banks.

Fannie Mae was originally chartered under the National Housing Act of February 1938 as the National Mortgage Association of Washington. In 1968, it was partitioned into two corporations, Ginnie Mae and the new Fannie Mae, described above. Ginnie Mae is the corporation entirely within the government; it is in HUD, under the direct supervision of the secretary of HUD.

All of these agencies either raise money by selling debt instruments in the private financial markets or they guarantee the debt raised by private lenders. Ginnie fully guarantees borrowings by private mortgage lenders. These debt instruments can often be especially attractive for investors who want investments with little default risk. Since the government either directly owns, or in large part supervises, these corporations, it is expected that the federal government will keep them from suffering a default. Ginnie Mae guaranteed "loan certificates" are advertised as follows:

> The certificates are sold by GNMA dealers or by mortgage originators in face values as low as $25,000. The purchaser of a GNMA certificate receives a standardized, highly marketable instrument with interest payments comparable to, or higher than, those for other debt instruments. The purchaser is guaranteed timely payments of principal and interest by the Government National Mortgage Association even if the individual homeowner or GNMA issuer defaults. GNMA certificates are backed by the full faith and credit of the U.S. government.[21]

The question arises as to whether a dollar spent from funds borrowed by the Mae sisters and cousin Freddie is a government or private expenditure. Is there a difference between an expenditure in the housing industry financed by the U.S. Treasury or Fannie Mae (or any of her relatives) selling a bond to the public? In both cases the allocation of funds to the housing industry is largely determined by the federal government.

Appendix: Tax-Exempt Securities Markets

Countries, cities, towns, villages, tax districts, or simply a civil division of a state may issue *municipal bonds* and states may issue *state bonds*. Both are *tax exempt* and are loosely referred to as *municipals*. Most municipals are *bearer bonds* (they are the property of whoever holds them) and are usually issued in $5000 units. Although the Sixteenth (income tax) Amendment allowed the federal government to tax income "from whatever source derived," federal legislation exempted the coupon income from these securities from federal taxation. Their capital gains are not exempted from income tax and these securities are not exempt from federal inheritance tax. State income tax exemptions are also generally provided for coupon income on state securities for the residents of the issuing state.

Both municipal bonds and state bonds may be *general obligation bonds* secured by the full faith and credit of the issuing political entity. They may also be based on particular expected general tax revenues or tax revenues from a particular source. These are special tax bonds (see Table 22-6). Tax-exempts secured by revenue from the specific property that it finances are called *revenue bonds*. They are sometimes called nonguaranteed bonds since they are not secured by the full faith and credit of the issuer.

One distinguising difference between the liabilities of municipal bonds and state bonds is that a state cannot be sued without its consent, whereas municipalities may be sued in the event of default. States have defaulted during major depressions, such as in 1837–1839 and the 1930s. (For example, Arkansas defaulted in 1932, after which payments were

TABLE 22-6

New Security Issues of State and Local Governments, 1978–1980
(Millions of Dollars)

Type of Issue or Issuer, or Use	1978	1979	1980
1 All issues, new and refunding*	48,607	43,490	48,462
Type of issue			
2 General obligation	17,854	12,109	14,100
3 Revenue	30,658	31,256	34,267
4 Housing Assistance Administration†	....	....	....
5 U.S. government loans	95	125	95
Type of issuer			
6 State	6,632	4,314	5,304
7 Special district and statutory authority	24,156	23,434	26,972
8 Municipalities, counties, townships, school districts	17,718	15,617	16,090
9 Issues for new capital, total	37,629	41,505	46,736
Use of proceeds			
10 Education	5,003	5,130	4,572
11 Transportation	3,460	2,441	2,621
12 Utilities and conservation	9,026	8,594	8,149
13 Social welfare	10,494	15,968	19,958
14 Industrial aid	3,526	3,836	3,974
15 Other purposes	6,120	5,536	7,462

*Par amounts of long-term issues based on date of sale.
†Only bonds sold pursuant to the 1949 Housing Act, which are secured by contract requiring the Housing Assistance Administration to make annual contributions to the local authority.
Source: Public Securities Association, *Federal Reserve Bulletin,* Board of Governors (December 1981), p. A36.

extended and resumed in later years.) To enhance their credit rating, some states include a provision in their bond obligations that provides the consent to sue in the event of default. Municipal bonds are generally not secured by specific assets. The liabilities are generally revenues from these specific assets.

Although tax-exempts have traditionally been used to finance assets for public use (such as roads, schools, and public buildings), since the early 1960s tax-exempt bonds have been increasingly issued to raise funds for private businesses and residential home buyers. These tax-exempt bonds used to raise money for the private sector are called *industrial development bonds* (IDBs). The state of Mississippi in 1936 allowed counties and cities to issue tax-exempts to construct buildings for lease to private firms.[22] In the 1960s IDBs were secured by property or receipts of specific projects and by 1968, 10 percent of all long-term tax-exempts were IDB revenue bonds. In 1967 the U.S. Treasury ruled that IDB interest income was subject to federal taxation. The following year the U.S. Congress passed the Expenditure Control Act of 1968, which overruled the Treasury and limited tax exemption on IDBs to small issuers (under $10 million) and to funding certain types of investment projects. These projects included the following: privately owned facilities, sewage facilities, electric energy and gas facilities, airports, docks, pollution control facilities, water facilities (which are subject to government regulation), and industrial parks (administered by a tax-exempt entity). IDBs have also been used to finance residential morgages. This practice increased rapidly when Chicago issued $100 million IDBs for this use in July 1978. The threat to Treasury revenues caused a law to be passed in 1980 prohibiting residential mortgages from being funded from IDBs after December 31, 1983 (the Mortgage Subsidy Bond Act of 1980). The Reagan administration announced in 1982 that in an effort to increase revenues, it would impose more limitations on IDBs.[23]

The default risk of tax-exempts is related to the general condition of the economy and the level of unemployment in the specific locale. Another important factor is the condition of the finances of the individual political entity, a consideration that has remained in center stage since the New York City crisis in the 1970s.

In 1976, after decades in which no large state or city was perceived to be in serious financial trouble, the municipal market was sharply affected by the threat that New York City would go bankrupt.[24] (New York City did not go bankrupt; it received federal assistance.) Not only the municipals from New York City but also the municipals from other northern cities with shaky finances (in addition to the severe financial strain from the 1973–1975 recession) drew attention as investments with dramatically increased default risk. (For example, Cleveland's financial situation was especially grim in 1978.) The spread between New York City municipals and those rated Aaa (the top rating by Moody's) approached 200 basis points during the crisis.[25] From 1960 to 1976 the spread between tax-exempts rated Baa and Aaa by Moody had been approximately 60 basis points. The spread in the tax-exempt market became larger than the spread between corporate bonds with the same ratings. There was, as a result of the New York crisis, a "flight to quality" in the market for municipals. That is, there was a greater emphasis on quality in the tax-exempt market as a result of the New York crisis.

The secondary markets are over-the-counter, with primary activity by large institutional investors. The primary market has a number of unique characteristics. Competitive bidding is required by municipalities in issuing new tax-exempts. Announcements of new issues, containing specifications and asking for bids, are placed in local papers and national media such as the *Daily Bond Buyer*. Municipals are not subject to registration with the Securities and Exchange Commission (described in Chapter 24), so that a standard *prospectus*, distributed with a new corporate bond, that contains a financial statement may not be circulated. An *offering circular* that gives the details of the new issue may be circulated. (The issues are subject to the antifraud provisions of the Securities Act of 1933.) A number of papers are required from the issuer, such as a copy of the minutes giving details and authorization for the issue by the appropriate government entity.

The marketing of new issues is awarded to underwriters, often commercial banks, that submit bids with the lowest interest rate cost. Although commercial banks are prohibited from underwriting most non-guaranteed bonds (revenue bonds), they are very active in underwriting general obligation bonds. The customers that buy from the underwriters are often commerical banks and other institutional buyers. The Tax Reform Act of 1976 allowed mutual funds to specialize in tax-exempts. These so-called *short-term investment pools* began with short-term tax-exempts in 1977. (They are described in Chapter 20.) The rapid growth of these funds came in part because of the financial intermediary service they provided: accessibility to a diversified portfolio of high-grade tax-exempts that are often available with check-writing privileges.

Beginning in the 1974–1975 recession, a new controversial technique for reducing tax obligations on returns from taxable bonds was invented. Buyers interested in current income were sold a strip of coupons from the bond and buyers interested in lump-sum income at a reduced (capital gains) rate were sold the return of face value of the bonds. These bonds were called *strip bonds*.

The procedure was controversial because zero-coupon bonds (bonds that only have a return of face-value payment) are subject to regular income tax rates instead of the lower capital gains rate. The discount on these zero-coupon bonds is treated for tax purposes as if it were earned over the life of the bond. (It is amortized for tax purposes.) In May 1982 the Treasury proposed legislation to require companies that issue zero-coupon bonds to deduct interest payments from taxes on a different schedule that applied a higher tax rate.

Finding the strip bonds for nonrecorded Treasury bearer bonds may be elusive. The Treasury was reported in 1982 to fear that as much as $20 billion worth of Treasury bonds and notes could be stripped without clear records of the purchase price.[26] If the bonds were, in effect, sold at a discount at the time of issue to those purchasing the return of face value, it was held that these should be treated as zero-coupon discount bonds for tax purposes.

In addition, brokerage firms began offering zero-coupon bonds collateralized by U.S. government bonds. Merrill Lynch was first in August 1982 with *Treasury Investment Growth Receipts*, called *Tigers*.

The controversy over strip bonds and zero-coupon bonds is an interesting example of the blurred difference between income defined in a national income accounting sense and capital gains, discussed in Chapter 4. For the ultimate wealth holder, a series of lump-sum return of face-value payments (originally purchased at a discount) are equivalent to an identical series of interest payments with the same yield, except for their different rate of taxation. For example (using simple numbers for clarity), compare two alternatives with a 7 percent interest rate. In the first alternative, a two-year bond is purchased for $12.65. It has two yearly payments of $7 each (and no other payments). Alternatively, two future lump-sum payments could be purchased. The first pays $7 in one year and costs $6.54. The second pays $7 in two years and costs $6.11. The cost of the two lump-sum payments and their income stream is identical to those of the two-year bond.

Treating the capital gain income on the lump-sum payments differently than the interest payments produces misallocations of resources. One of these misallocations is the time and resources spent in transforming financial assets into a form that yields income at the lower tax rate.

NOTES

1. *Understanding the New York Stock Exchange* (New York: New York Stock Exchange, Inc., 1976), p. 44.
2. *Understanding the New York Stock Exchange*, p. 45.
3. See the *1978 Fact Book*, New York Stock Exchange (1978), p. 70, and the *American Banker* (May 13, 1982), pp. 12 and 14, for a summary of the NYSE's Public Transaction Study (the first in five years) and the part of that study called the Bank Equity Transaction Study (that had not been done for seventeen years). Banks, the biggest institutional trader, lost ground in the 1970s according to these survey results (36.5 percent of share volume in 1979, 32.6 percent in 1980).
4. For a broad historical view, see Lance Davis, Jonathan Hughes, and Duncan McDougall, *American Economic History* (Homewood, Ill.: Richard D. Irwin, Inc., 1965), Chapter 13. For data on the New York Stock Exchange, see the annual *New York Stock Exchange Fact Book* and the monthly *Federal Reserve Bulletins*.
5. *Understanding Financial Statements*, New York Stock Exchange, Inc. (March 1981), p. 1.
6. The suicide rate is discussed by John Galbraith, *The Great Crash, 1929* (New York: Time, Inc., 1961), pp. 131–132. The quotation is from William G. Shepherd, Jr., "Recollections of Some Who Were There," *The New York Times* (September 23, 1979), p. F9.
7. *Newsweek* (November 11, 1978), p. 90. It turned out that real gross national product growth was negative for the second quarter of 1979. However, using the criterion that a recession is a period in which at least two consecutive quarters display negative growth, the first half of 1979 did not qualify because the first quarter had a positive growth rate.
8. A *long position* involves the ownership of stock, the value of which is reduced by a fall in stock prices. A *short position* ("selling short") involves the sale of stock that in effect is loaned to the seller for a given period (on which interest must be paid). The short seller can replace the stock at a profit if the price of the stock *falls* by enough to offset his or her transactions costs. An example of a short sale is given subsequently.
9. Burton Zwick, "The Market for Corporate Bonds," *Quarterly Review*, Federal Reserve Bank of New York (Autumn 1977), p. 29.
10. "Bonds and Beyond: Long Term Get Tougher," *Business Week* (March 1, 1982), p. 47. Some experts hold that changes in *bond duration* and yield volatility is the best measure of the price volatility of a bond. Bond duration is the length of time before a stream of payments from a bond generates one-half its present value [Jess B. Yarvitz, "The Relative Importance of Duration and Yield Volatility on Bond Price Volatility," *Journal of Money, Credit and Banking* (February 1977), pt. I, pp. 97–102].
11. *Prospectus*, The Options Clearing Corporation (October 30, 1981), pp. 3–4. The four exchanges are

Chicago Board Options Exchange, Inc.
American Stock Exchange, Inc.
Philadephia Stock Exchange, Inc.
Pacific Stock Exchange, Inc.

12. Ibid., p. 14.
13. *The ABC's of Commodities*, New York Mercantile Exchange (1980), p. 8.
14. There are other important differences between a forward and a futures contract. In a forward contract no money changes hands until the termination date. The equilibrium forward price must continually change over time in a way such that the newly created forward contracts will always have a zero value when they are made. See John Cox, Jonathan Ingersoll, Jr., and Stephen Ross, "The Relation Between Forward Price and Futures Prices," *Journal of Financial Economics* (Amsterdam: North-Holland Publishing Company/Rochester, N.Y.: Graduate School of Management, University of Rochester, December 1981), pp. 321–346.
15. "Gold Futures Market Opens April 19 in London," *The Wall Street Journal* (February 19, 1982), p. 33.
16. John Morris, "Bermuda Future Exchange Keeps Plans Close to Vest," *American Banker* (March 9, 1982), p. 2.
17. Anne Mackay Smith, "Financial Futures Blossomed in 1981, Most Others Slid," *The Wall Street Journal* (January 4, 1982), p. 21.
18. For Treasury bond and Treasury note futures, the 8 percent coupon is the standard against which other coupons are measured. If a coupon other that 8 percent is delivered, substitute instruments are priced, by means of a *conversion factor*, at an effective 8 percent yield.
19. The example is taken from *An Introduction to Financial Futures*, Chicago Board of Trade (distributed 1982), pp. 54–56.
20. Some of the information in this and the following paragraph are from Clyde H. Farnsworth, "Trying to Stem Fannie Mae's Losses," *The New York Times* (May 16, 1982), p. 6. Farnsworth describes the Fannie Mae headquarters as a building that "looks like an English manor—an elegantly proportional, Williamsburg-styled, red brick mansion" that is not in the downtown Washington, D.C., area. Despite these cosmetic differences as well as its sale of stock and different salary schedule, it is a government-created and government-sponsored corporation.
21. *There's More to Ginnie Mae Than Meets the Eye*, Chicago Board of Trade (January 25, 1980), p. 1.
22. Daniel E. Laufenberg, "Industrial Development Bonds: Some Aspects of the Current Controversy," *Federal Reserve Bulletin* (March 1982), pp. 135–141.
23. Howard Glickman, "Curbs May Cut Private Issues," *American Banker* (March 2, 1982), p. 11.
24. Lynn E. Broune and Richard F. Syran, "The Municipal Market Since the New York City Crisis," *New England Economic Review*, Federal Reserve Bank of Boston (July–August 1979), pp. 11–26.
25. The ratings by Moody's and Standard & Poor's are Moody's—Aaa, Aa, A1, A; Baa1, Baa, Ba, B; Caa, Ca, C; Standard & Poor's—AAA, AA(+/−), A(+/−), BBB(+/−); BB(+/−), B; D. Municipal bonds investors generally desire municipals rated at least Baa or BBB.
26. "Strips Tempt the Bond Trade," *Business Week* (May 3, 1982), p. 111.

STUDY QUESTIONS

1. What functions does a specialist on the floor of the New York Stock Exchange perform? How does this differ (if it does) from a specialist in the over-the-counter market? Are there any differences in the organization of specialists in these two markets?

2. What is the difference between a futures and a forward contract?

3. Do the Mae sisters or cousin Freddie Mac change the allocation of resources? Can a case be made that the bedroom suburbs of the middle class were heavily subsidized, whereas the inner city was further deprived, by the allocation of huge amounts of funds to thrifts by these sisters and their cousins?

4. Does a significant decline in stock prices affect economic activity? Note that it is helpful here to differentiate declines that are expected to persist from those that are expected to be temporary. With respect to the cycles of expansion and contraction in the economy, is the stock market a reflection of them, a cause of them, or both?

5. Describe each of the markets discussed in this chapter.

6. Describe a hedge, a spread, and a straddle.

7. Look up the prices and striking prices of a put and call option (where both are traded) and then look up the price of the corresponding stock. Do the option prices reveal any information about market participants' expectations?

8. Find the futures price for U.S. Treasury bills (reported daily in *The Wall Street Journal*). What information does this market convey about future short-term interest rates?

9. In 1976, savings and loan associations held only 44 percent of the mortages they originated. The home buyers continued to send the SLs their monthly payments. How do you explain this?

Part VII

Government and Financial Markets

23

Federal Reserve Participation and the Relation to Other Government Transactions

Introduction

The volume of the Federal Reserve's sales and purchases of repurchase agreements was in the trillions of dollars in the 1980s. Their participation in the money markets is, in a word, immense. They operate in a special government securities market with private dealers, whose participation must be approved by the Federal Reserve. A brief description of the general purposes—the *ultimate targets*—of Federal Reserve monetary policy is presented first. Then the specific targets of Federal Reserve monetary policy, formally given as twelve-month targets for monetary growth, are discussed. Next the operating instruments used by the personnel of the *open-market desk*, or *desk* as it is called, that carry out open-market operations are presented. This is followed by a description of a hypothetical open-market purchase. A discussion of alleged churning at the open-market desk (unnecessary buying and selling) and the reasons for it follow.

The remainder of the chapter details some very useful accounting identities and their components. These relationships can be used to analyze open-market operations and the associated financing of government operation. The diligent reader who conquers these relationships will benefit from understanding the government budget constraint or monetary base identity. It allows the Federal Reserve open-market operation to be combined with the transactions of the rest of the U.S. government in determining the total effect of government transactions on the money supply.

The Ultimate Targets

Official *ultimate targets for economic policy* were stated in the Employment Act of 1946 (Public Law 79-304). The legislation of 1946 set forth the following declaration of policy:

> The Congress declares that it is the continuing policy and responsibility of the Federal Government to use all practicable means consistent with its needs and obligations and other essential considerations of national policy, with the assistance and cooperation of industry, agriculture, labor, and State and local governments, to coordinate and utilize all its plans, functions, and resources for the purpose of creating and maintaining, in a manner calculated to foster and promote free competitive enterprise and the general welfare, conditions under which there will be afforded useful employment opportunities, including self-employment, for those able, willing, and seeking to work, and to promote *maximum employment, production,* and *purchasing power.*

Presumably, the Federal Reserve is guided, to some extent, by those ultimate targets. In its statement of purposes to the public, the Federal Reserve asserted:

> From the outset (of the establishment of the Federal Reserve), it was recognized that the original purposes of the System were in fact aspects of broader U.S. economic and financial objectives. Over the years, economic stability and growth, a high level of employment, stability in the purchasing power of the dollar, and reasonable balance in transactions with foreign countries have come to be recognized as primary objectives of governmental economic policy.
>
>   Such objectives have been articulated in many acts of Congress, including particularly the Employment Act of 1946.[1]

It is interesting that the Federal Reserve statement added balance of payments considerations to the triumvirate of objectives actually "articulated" in the 1946 Act (employment, purchasing power, and production).

The international objective can be inconsistent with the objectives of the Employment Act of 1946.[2] If the Federal Reserve does follow those "four" objectives, then both higher real interest rates to improve the international balance of payments and lower real rates to promote investment can be consistent with its ultimate targets.

It is difficult to determine what a poorly specified ultimate target means. The ultimate target "reasonable balance with foreign countries" has much less precision than the three objectives of the Employment Act. Even these three objectives are not too clear because there is no specification of whether they are long-run or short-run objectives.

To fathom what "reasonable balance with foreign countries" might mean to the Federal Reserve, it is sometimes necessary to see what it has done to implement this balance.[3] Presumably, when the Federal Reserve intervenes by buying U.S. dollars and selling foreign currencies, it is implementing this foreign objective. At a July 29, 1977, oversight hearing on monetary policy, Chairman Henry Reuss of the U.S. House of

Representatives Banking Committee said the following to Chairman Arthur Burns of the Federal Reserve:

> If the dollar depreciates, we have to pay more for essential imports, and that is going to add to our price levels. Furthermore, although our soybeans become cheaper to foreigners, we may need them at home, but some foreigner can grab them because of the lower international price, and that may hurt. . . .
>
> On the other side of the coin . . . the prevention of overvalued competitive currencies, like the mark and the yen, hurts the other two goals of national policy, namely maximum production and maximum employment, because if the dollar is overvalued vis-à-vis other currencies, then we export less and people lose jobs at home in the export industries. We import more and people lose jobs at home in import-competitive industries.
>
> So, my way out of that dilemma has always been to go with Adam Smith and say, "Let the market—supply and demand—determine the price of the dollar, and keep our hands off of it, absent disorderly markets."[4]

Chairman Reuss then asked Chairman Burns when the Federal Reserve actually does intervene. Chairman Burns replied:

> The Federal Reserve has a certain responsibility for the position of the dollar in the exchange markets. Our broad policy is, as you know, to intervene only in the event of disorderly markets. But I must say to you in all honesty that no two of us may agree as to the precise definition of a disorderly market or the precise way to recognize one when it exists. And I must say that when I see the dollar, which is intrinsically strong, depreciating against currencies of countries whose economy is demonstrably weak, I sometimes ask myself the question whether the market is an orderly market.[5]

Thus it appears that the fourth ultimate target of the Federal Reserve is the preservation of the international value of the U.S. dollar at a level that is judged to be "correct." "Incorrect" levels are most likely to arise when the international value of the U.S. dollar falls rapidly. This definition is similar to the analogy drawn by Chairman William Proxmire of the Senate Banking Committee in response to Federal Reserve replies. He said it was like nailing a custard pie to the wall.

Twelve-Month Monetary Target Ranges

Beginning in 1975, the Federal Reserve began to present twelve-month target ranges for monetary growth in the banking committees of the House and Senate of the U.S. Congress, under House Concurrent Resolution 133. At first this was done quarterly. Then, under the Humphrey-Hawkins bill, the Federal Reserve reported twice a year (in February and July).

In the period from March 1975 to the third quarter of 1979, the old medium of exchange concept, M1, missed the fifteen target ranges 47 percent of the time. For the period March 1975 to the fourth quarter of

1979, the old M2 and M3 missed their separate sixteen target ranges 31 percent and 44 percent of the time, respectively. Consider this record in the light of the ability of the Federal Reserve to move the target ranges each quarter from 1975 to 1980. The yearly target ranges for 1980 through 1982 are shown in Figure 23-1. Notice that the 1981 target range (the dashed lines above 1981) begins above the target range for 1980. The Federal Reserve does not plan its successive target ranges from where it planned to be. It builds in the errors by setting the new target range from where average yearly growth actually is. This changing of target ranges to build in errors is called *drift* in the target range. The Federal Reserve explained the 1981 drift by the introduction of nationwide NOW accounts, which were claimed to have artificially pushed up actual growth. A new monetary aggregate was invented for 1981 that subtracted out all NOW accounts that were transferred in from savings accounts. The claim that these funds were not the same as other M1 money and therefore could be disregarded was not borne out by velocity numbers for 1981.

Figure 23-1

Federal Reserve twelve-month targets 1980–1982 (dashed lines) and actual monthly growth 1980–March 1982 (solid line).*

*Target ranges are from fourth quarter of the previous year to the fourth quarter of the following year.

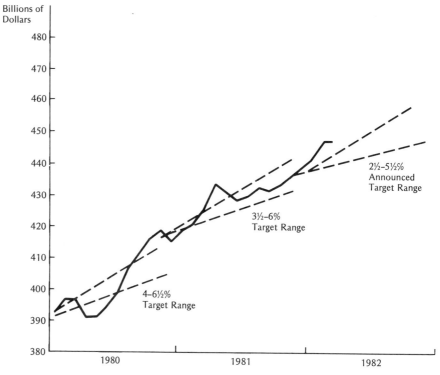

The rate of rise of velocity, 4.08 percent, in 1981 was not far from the average 3.4 percent rate of increase that it has generally followed since the Korean War in the 1950s. By dropping this adjustment at the end of 1981, the Federal Reserve was, in effect, saying that these NOW accounts transferred in from savings accounts had suddenly become M1.

As Figure 23-1 shows, actual monthly growth during 1980, 1981, and the beginning of 1982 was very erratic. No one could expect the Federal Reserve to come in close to the mark in a single month, but as Figure 23-1 indicates, some of the swings in money growth persisted over a number of months. There was controversy as to why the Federal Reserve could not and/or would not produce smoother monetary growth. One of the suggestions advanced, in part, to facilitate monetary control, would have a profound effect on the financial markets for repurchase agreements and bonds. That suggestion is discussed subsequently in the section entitled "Churning."

Whatever one's view on the desirability of better monetary control, the Federal Reserve's record since the inception of public announcements of its yearly targets (March 1975)—for both yearly growth and shorter-run monetary stability—has not been good. Announcing that it would do one thing and then failing to do it nearly 50 percent of the time severely injured the credibility of the Federal Reserve. The consequences are substantial. When the central bank of the Federal Republic of Germany announces from Bonn that the rate of growth of its money supply will be reduced, the adjustment process is rapid. Inflation soon slows. But when the U.S. Federal Reserve makes an announcement, after this record, confusion abounds.

Financial experts who specialize in reading between the lines of Federal Reserve announcements and who keep close track of monetary policies often opt for some variety of the "unintended reversal." An announcement by the Federal Reserve of slow money growth is interpreted as indicating a short period of very slow growth that will be followed by very rapid growth, which will raise money growth far above its previous level. The interpretations are not always that simple. Many experts believe that the poor record was caused by a preoccupation with the federal funds rate target and a neglect of the money supply targets. Therefore, interpretations of Federal Reserve monetary policy have been dependent on expected interest rate changes and expected Federal Reserve responses.

Operating Instruments

The Federal Reserve sets two-month targets to achieve the longer-run targets. Then the Federal Reserve must go one more step backward and determine the best *operating instrument* to change those intermediate targets. Open-market operations directly affect the monetary base. All or part of the monetary base may be viewed as the operating instrument. The desired level of those variables is the *immediate target* of the Federal Reserve open-market desk.

The operating instrument may be thought of as the entire monetary base. However, the open-market trading desk does not control borrowing at the discount windows of the twelve regional Reserve banks. Therefore, the desk could be said to have the *nonborrowed base, NB,* as its operating instrument, that is, the monetary base, *B,* minus borrowings, *BOR:*

$$NB = B - BOR \tag{1}$$

Subtracting currency outside depository institutions from the monetary base gives reserves of depository institutions *R.* The open-market trading desk uses the value of *nonborrowed reserves, NR,* as an immediate target.

$$NR = R - BOR \tag{2}$$

where *R* is total reserves. Nonborrowed reserves are only one step away from *free reserves, FR,* which also have served as an immediate target. Subtracting required reserves from total reserves gives *excess reserves, ER.* Free reserves are excess reserves minus borrowings:

$$FR = EX - BOR \tag{3}$$

For each individual bank, a higher level of free reserves is sometimes viewed as indicating a greater potential for expansion of loans and investments. For the economy as a whole, it can be a misleading variable as an indicator of a "tight" or "loose" money supply policy. This can be seen from the following example. Suppose there is heavy borrowing, so that *BOR* in Equation (3) rises. According to the monetary base identity developed in this chapter, the money supply would expand. In recent decades, with efficient cash management, the depository institutions normally carry small excess reserves. The free reserve variable *FR* in Equation (3) will fall, even turning negative. Negative free reserves are then sometimes incorrectly alleged to signify "tight money" when, in fact, the monetary aggregates are growing rapidly.

In practice, the Federal Reserve has targeted on a *total reserve path* covering the four weeks after the short-run targets are set at its FOMC meetings. This is converted into a *nonborrowed reserve path* by subtracting out an assumption about borrowing from the discount window. Each week's nonborrowed reserve target is updated on Friday on the basis of the most recent data. The immediate target in this procedure is nonborrowed reserves. The objective is to hit the short-run intermediate targets.

The Desk in Action

The system's open-market manager, who manages open-market operations at the New York Federal Reserve trading desk, often begins the day with early morning conferences with dealers in the New York money market. It is said that this is done to "get a feel for the market." Information about the prices, yields, quantities, and qualities of debt instruments traded the day before, as well as the opinions of money market dealers, are given.

The open-market manager consults the FOMC instructions and may participate in a number of telephone conferences with the Board of Governors (members or staff) and occasionally with all the members of the FOMC in Washington, D.C., and the regional banks. The chairman of the Board of Governors and the FOMC may, in our hypothetical example, say, "O.K., Peter, that action seems proper this morning." Peter Sternlight, the extremely able systems open-market manager in 1982, may then consult with the Treasury by phone to check on any transactions it may be making that would affect the monetary base. The decision is made by Sternlight. "We'll go into the market at 10:30 (A.M.) and buy $3.5 billion."

Sternlight walks into the room on the eighth floor of the New York Federal Reserve Bank, where the trading desk is located. Approximately ten security traders are seated at several rows of desks against a backdrop of an array of yields and prices of debt instruments that covers two walls. Each trader has a telephone console on his or her desk that is connected with three or four of the thirty-four approved private dealers in the U.S. government security market (see Table 23-1). They must be approved by the Federal Reserve. The private dealers are, in turn, brokers for large private customers, such as commercial banks, insurance companies, and large finance companies.

Sternlight's assistant tells the traders to notify the market. The traders push the buttons on their consoles and, via private lines, buzzers sound in the trading rooms of the dealers in the special government securities markets. The Federal Reserve trader announces, "We will be in the market shortly," and then hangs up. Sirens have sounded in the government securities markets; billions of dollars of securities will be bought or sold in the next half hour.

Then the second round commences ten minutes later, shortly after 10:40 A.M. The Federal Reserve traders tell the private dealers which securities the Federal Reserve will purchase. The phone calls are then terminated and the private dealers may reconnoiter, perhaps by phone, with some of their customers. These customers may be domestic commercial banks and domestic insurance and finance companies.

Suppose, for example, that the buy list includes a particular maturity of U.S. Treasury notes and that a bank, First Bank of Kansas City, Missouri, wishes to sell $10 million of these notes. The dealer informs a

TABLE 23-1

Government Securities Dealers Reporting to the Federal Reserve Bank of New York, May 20, 1981

Dealer	Address
ACLI Government Securities Inc.	140 South Dearborn St. Chicago, IL 60603
Bache Halsey Stuart Shields, Inc.	Bache Plaza 100 Gold Street New York, NY 10039
Bank of America NT & SA	555 California Street P.O. Box 37003 San Francisco, CA 94137
Bankers Trust Company	16 Wall Street New York, NY 10015
A. G. Becker Incorporated	55 Water Street New York, NY 10041
Briggs, Schaedle & Co., Inc.	67 Wall Street New York, NY 10005
Carroll McEntee & McGinley	40 Wall Street New York, NY 10005
The Chase Manhattan Bank, N.A.	1 Chase Manhattan Plaza New York, NY 10081
Chemical Bank	20 Pine Street New York, NY 10005
Citibank, N.A.	399 Park Avenue New York, NY 10043
Continental Illinois National Bank and Trust Company of Chicago	231 South LaSalle Street Chicago, IL 60693
Crocker National Bank	P. O. Box 38006 San Francisco, CA 94138
Dean Witter Reynolds Incorporated	130 Liberty Street New York, NY 10006
Discount Corporation of New York	58 Pine Street New York, NY 10005
Donaldson, Lufkin & Jenrette Securities Corporation	140 Broadway New York, NY 10005
The First Boston Corporation	20 Exchange Place New York, NY 10005
The First National Bank of Chicago	1 First National Plaza Chicago, IL 60670
Goldman, Sachs & Co.	55 Broad Street New York, NY 10004
Harris Trust and Savings Bank	1 Chase Manhattan Plaza New York, NY 10005
E. F. Hutton & Co., Inc.	One Battery Park Plaza New York, NY 10004
Kidder, Peabody & Co., Inc.	10 Hanover Square New York, NY 10005

TABLE 23-1 (*Continued*)

Government Securities Dealers Reporting to the Federal Reserve Bank of New York, May 20, 1981

Dealer	Address
Aubrey G. Lanston & Co., Inc.	20 Broad Street New York, NY 10003
Lehman Government Securities Incorporated	55 Water Street New York, NY 10041
Merrill Lynch Government Securities, Inc.	One Liberty Plaza New York, NY 10080
Morgan Guaranty Trust Company of New York	23 Wall Street New York, NY 10015
Morgan Stanley & Co., Inc.	1251 Avenue of the Americas New York, NY 10020
The Northern Trust Company	50 South LaSalle Street Chicago, IL 60675
Paine, Webber, Jackson & Curtin Incorporated	1221 Avenue of the Americas New York, NY 10020
Wm. E. Pollock Government Securities Inc.	160 Water Street New York, NY 10038
Chas. E. Quincey & Co.	60 Broad Street New York, NY 10004
Salomon Brothers	One New York Plaza New York, NY 10004
The Securities Groups New York Hanseatic Division	500 Park Avenue New York, NY 10022
Smith Barney, Harris Upham & Co., Incorporated	1345 Avenue of the Americas New York, NY 10019
United California Bank	707 Wilshire Boulevard Los Angeles, LA 90017

Federal Reserve trader of the First Bank offer (the price and quantity) in one of the several rounds of calls to the private dealers. Within thirty minutes from the time the initial calls were made, the open-market manager calls for a last round and the auction ends. The quantities and asking prices given by the dealers are recorded on separate pieces of paper. The open-market manager and his assistants place the pieces of paper on a large board at the end of the room in order of the asking price (lowest first). He or she then selects for purchase $3.5 billion of the offers with the lowest asking prices to sell. The traders call the private dealers and notify them which offers to sell have been accepted. Three and one-half billion dollars in U.S. Treasury notes have been purchased by the open-market desk, with delivery and payment on the same day. The monetary base is increased by $3.5 billion.

First Bank of Kansas City, Missouri, which offered, through their private dealer in the government securities market, to sell $10 million in

U.S. Treasury notes, has an acceptable offer. The Kansas City Federal Reserve Bank wire room receives the acceptance through the Federal Reserve's special wire service, with central facilities in a huge underground cave in Culpeper, Virginia, near Washington, D.C. First Bank can take delivery of cash in an armored truck or, more likely, deposit the funds in its account at the Federal Reserve for reinvestment in the money markets later the same day. The securities sold by First Bank are already at the Federal Reserve of Kansas City, Missouri. The Federal Reserve provides vault and inventory services for securities of banks.

The records of open-market operations of the Federal Reserve through Wednesday, together with estimates of changes in the U.S. money supply, are accumulated and usually released to the press at a weekly press conference in New York City.

The Federal Reserve conducts most of its open-market operations (over 95 percent) in repurchase agreements. The desk purchases securities from a dealer under a contract, which obligates the dealer to repurchase the securities at the same price on or before a particular date. The interest dealers pay on the money they receive is determined by the same open-market auction. These contracts are called *repurchase agreements*, or simply *repos*. They have the same effect on the monetary base as an outright purchase of securities. They expand the monetary base. Repurchase agreements are not made by the Federal Reserve for more than fifteen days.

The open-market desk can reduce the monetary base by a technique known as *matched sale-purchase transactions*, or *reverse repos*. The open-market desk sells Treasury bills and simultaneously buys the same Treasury bills for delivery one or more days later.

The open-market operations of the Federal Reserve can be said to be either *dynamic* or *defensive*. Dynamic open-market operations are performed to affect bank reserves and thereby to affect the money supply and interest rates. Defensive operations are designed to offset disturbances to the level of bank reserves. These disturbances can arise from operations of the Treasury and government agencies, which affect bank reserves, as shown by the monetary base identity (4) in this chapter. They also arise from changes in the distribution of deposits in the banking system (which affects the amount of required reserves that are held by depository institutions) and from numerous other sources, discussed in the next chapter. The application of this classification to short-run Federal Reserve operations is somewhat blurred for individuals outside the Federal Reserve. This is because it is very difficult, if not frequently impossible, to tell if the Federal Reserve is purposely moving to a new target or is offsetting a disturbance.

Churning

Total sales and purchases at the New York trading desk were approximately $800 billion in 1980, whereas the net change in the Federal Reserve's portfolio was $4.5 billion. Thus there was an incredible amount of transactions for a relatively small net change in the Federal Reserve's portfolio, indicating that the Federal Reserve had objectives other than gradually and smoothly changing the monetary base and that it was reacting to many disturbances. Are all these transactions necessary to achieve its objectives, or is this an example of *churning*: unnecessary buying and selling that runs up transactions costs? This is an interesting question that attracted the attention of a few—not many—people. Fernand J. St Germain, Chairman of the Committee on Banking, Finance and Urban Affairs of the U.S. House of Representatives, inquired about this subject in June 1981 (see Exhibit 23-1; the $1.634-trillion figure from the *Federal Reserve Bulletin* includes transactions for foreign central banks). Milton Friedman, in an article published in 1982 said:

> In the year 1980, the Federal Reserve made gross open market purchases of securities of something over $800 billion, and gross transactions, including sales of maturities being rolled over, of more than double that amount. The net change in the portfolio was $4.5 billion. The open market desk therefore made $184 worth of purchases gross and roughly twice that amount of transactions (purchases plus sales) in order to add one dollar to its portfolio. Why all this churning? *It accounts for something like one-quarter to one-half of all the transactions of U.S. government securities dealers other than the Fed itself.* It generates millions of dollars of fees for the dealers involved.[6]

Is this immense amount of buying and selling short-term repurchase agreements necessary to achieve the objectives the Federal Reserve has announced: namely, monetary objectives of targeted money growth and targeted interest rate changes? Both targets are stated as ranges between which no action is taken.[7] Obviously, the Federal Reserve has thought that their activities in the financial markets was necessary. Here are some reasons the Federal Reserve gives for their immense number of purchases and sales. They frequently desire to offset changes in the federal funds rate. They intervene when the federal funds rate is near the end of the target range. (After October 1976, they said that intervention would be undertaken only if the federal funds rate appeared to remain persistently outside the target range.) Also, insofar as the federal funds rate is thought to be an indicator of depository institution reserve changes, the Federal Reserve may go into the market in response to federal funds rate changes even when the federal funds rate is not outside its target range. This was especially true before 1979, but to the same extent, may still be true. In 1977, the Federal Reserve reported:

> One objective of current operating procedure is to insulate the monetary aggregates to the extent feasible from the effects of supply-related disturbances by limiting associated movements in the funds rate. These supply shocks include movements in noncontrolled factors affecting nonborrowed reserved—such as float or Treasury deposits at the Reserve Banks—and changes in the amount of excess reserves that banks wish to hold. If open market operations have the effect of stabilizing the Federal funds rate, they will at the same time substantially moderate—although not necessarily eliminate—the effects of supply-related disturbances "on the monetary aggregates."[8]

FERNAND J. ST GERMAIN, R.I., CHAIRMAN
HENRY S. REUSS, WIS.
HENRY S. GONZALEZ, TEX.
JOSEPH G. MINISH, N.J.
FRANK ANNUNZIO, ILL.
PARREN J. MITCHELL, MD.
WALTER E. FAUNTROY, D.C.
STEPHEN L. NEAL, N.C.
JERRY M. PATTERSON, CALIF.
JAMES J. BLANCHARD, MICH.
CARROLL HUBBARD, JR., KY.
JOHN J. LAFALCE, N.Y.
DAVID W. EVANS, IND.
NORMAN E. D'AMOURS, N.H.
STANLEY N. LUNDINE, N.Y.
MARY ROSE OAKAR, OHIO
JIM MATTOX, TEX.
BRUCE F. VENTO, MINN.
DOUG BARNARD, JR., GA.
ROBERT GARCIA, N.Y.
MIKE LOWRY, WASH.
CHARLES E. SCHUMER, N.Y.
BARNEY FRANK, MASS.
BILL PATMAN, TEX.
WILLIAM J. COYNE, PA.

J. WILLIAM STANTON, OHIO
CHALMERS P. WYLIE, OHIO
STEWART B. McKINNEY, CONN.
GEORGE HANSEN, IDAHO
HENRY J. HYDE, ILL.
JIM LEACH, IOWA
THOMAS B. EVANS, JR., DEL.
RON PAUL, TEX.
ED BETHUNE, ARK.
NORMAN D. SHUMWAY, CALIF.
STAN PARRIS, VA.
ED WEBER, OHIO
BILL McCOLLUM, FLA.
GREGORY W. CARMAN, N.Y.
GEORGE C. WORTLEY, N.Y.
MARGE ROUKEMA, N.Y.
BILL LOWERY, CALIF.
JAMES K. COYNE, PA.

U.S. HOUSE OF REPRESENTATIVES

COMMITTEE ON BANKING, FINANCE AND URBAN AFFAIRS

NINETY-SEVENTH CONGRESS
2129 RAYBURN HOUSE OFFICE BUILDING
WASHINGTON, D.C. 20515

225-4247

June.12, 1981

Mr. Anthony M. Solomon, President
The Federal Reserve Bank of New York
33 Liberty Street
New York, New York 10045

Dear Mr. Solomon:

Federal open market transactions records (Federal Reserve Bulletin, April 1981, page A10) indicate that the Federal Reserve conducted $1.634 trillion in sales and purchases of repurchase agreements (including matched securities) in 1980 through its New York open market desk with governmental securities dealers. (The 34 dealers operating on this market on April 2, 1981 are attached.) These transactions constituted 99 percent of total purchases and sales at the open market desk. In a year in which the Federal Reserve was ostensibly on an aggregates target and when M1-B changed by $25 billion (December to December), the huge amount of repurchase agreement transactions poses some questions.

First, to help answer these questions would you provide me a summary for May and November, 1980, of:

a. Interest rates, amounts and maturities on repurchase agreements and matched sales submitted during the auctions at the desk, indicating which were accepted and which were not;

b. The Federal funds rate in effect at the time; and

c. The average repurchase agreement rates in effect during that time.

Second, would you describe the rationale for the Federal Reserve's 1980 open market desk policy and any changes that are being carried out in 1981?

Third, I assume that you closely monitor the transactions costs to the Federal Reserve and the gross profits to the government securities dealers which result directly from these operations. Would you give me your estimate of the gross profits made by the government dealers from these repurchase agreement transactions during 1980?

I would appreciate your answer as soon as possible so that my staff can study the material prior to receiving the Federal Reserve's July 20 report.

Sincerely,

Fernand J. St Germain
Chairman

Exhibit 23-1

Insofar as the federal funds rate maintains some sort of relationship with other rates, as would be expected in competitive markets, and insofar as the markets are efficient, this operating procedure is a prescription for nearly unlimited intervention with little success in causing interest rate changes to be far from a random walk. (See Chapter 3 on efficient markets.) Insofar as the funds rate is temporarily controlled, there are very large profits to be made by those who understand the temporary effects of the Fed's intervention.

The fine tuning of the federal funds rate before 1979 is emphasized in the description of open-market operations written by Paul Meek and published by the New York Federal Reserve Bank in June 1978:

Getting the "Feel" of the Market

Well before 10:00 A.M. the Government securities market has usually become active. By then several traders around the Fed's desk are trying to learn from dealers whether any trend is developing. Other traders are getting a rundown from the Bank's foreign department about orders to be executed for foreign accounts. Reports have arrived on dealer positions, and on reserve positions and Federal funds transactions the day before at major banks in New York and other cities. On hand is a report giving the distribution of reserves among money market banks, other reserve city banks, and country banks. Shortly after 10 o'clock, two clerks update the quotation board with the latest "runs" of prices and yields obtained by telephone by dealers. The Fed's traders already know from their conversations with dealers what the board shows: prices are steady. They also know that there has been little trading except among dealers who are testing each other's markets by "hitting a bid"—that is, selling securities at the price bid by another dealer. Fed funds are quoted $5\frac{7}{8}$ percent bid, 6 percent offered, which is a shade higher than yesterday's average rate of $5\frac{1}{4}$ percent and well above the Fed's $5\frac{1}{2}$ percent discount rate.

One staff member calls the nonbank dealers to find out how much new money will be needed to replace loans maturing today or to finance securities being delivered today. A few minutes before 11 A.M., his tabulation shows that the dealers need loans of about $4.5 billion to finance their present securities holdings. Money was available at the close yesterday at $5\frac{3}{4}$ percent, but several dealers think money may be more expensive and harder to get today.

The desk officer, who has just been joined by the Deputy Account Manager and another officer, summarizes developments for them. Together, they review the newest projection of factors affecting bank reserves over the next six weeks, a research report received only moments before. The projection indicates that float on Monday was $500 million less than expected. Revised projections suggest the Fed must inject more reserves in the current week to hold the Fed funds rate around $5\frac{3}{4}$ percent. The officers begin to formulate the day's plan of action; the Deputy Manager checks with the Manager by phone and writes out the day's program. A last-minute contact with the traders indicates that banks and others are beginning to sell Treasury bills to dealers in greater volume than buyers are taking from them. Dealers are raising the rates they are bidding for Treasury bills, that is, prices are beginning to decline.

Meanwhile, a staff call is made to the Board of Governors in Washington and to the office of one of the Reserve Bank presidents currently on the FOMC. The New York staff provides information on the full range of data available on bank reserves and the money and Government securities markets. Thus, the Reserve Bank President will have before him the data on which the desk's plan of action is based. The officers hurry to an adjoining office to participate in the key telephone conversation that formalizes the day's strategy—the 11:15 conference call.

The Conference Call

"Washington and San Francisco are standing by," announces the telephone operator, completing the three-way telephone hookup that enables the Account Manager to review developments with the staff of the Board and the Reserve Bank president on the call. Sitting in on the conversation at the New York end today are the President of the Bank, the Manager and Deputy Manger of the System Acount, and the officers of the securities department. Seated directly behind a telephone microphone, one of the officers speaks:

"Conditions have changed somewhat since we spoke yesterday. The Government securities market opened this morning with very few changes in prices and rates, and with little activity. But Treasury bill rates now seem to be rising. There are some indications that long-term investors are holding off to see how the market will take the $200 million bond issue of the XYZ Corporation tomorrow. Fed funds opened at $5\frac{7}{8}$ percent bid, $\frac{1}{8}$ rate percentage point above yesterday's closing rate, and funds are well bid at that rate. Dealer financing needs this morning opened at about $4.5 billion. The banks have raised their call loan rates on dealer loans from 6 to $6\frac{1}{4}$ percent.

"Yesterday, we had a shortfall in reserves that more tha offset what we put in. We look for a sharp decline in reserves today and tomorrow as currency in circulation increases and float drops. Banks here and in Chicago seem under special pressure and have been very heavy buyers of Federal funds on each of the last three business days. Banks in several other major cities show reserve deficiencies. Today's $550 million call on the "C" banks will add to pressure on the money market banks."

The officer then reads the Manager's proposed plan for the day.

"In view of the expected stringency in reserves, the Account plans to purchase securities for cash. If the market continues to tighten, we may buy as much as $500 million of Treasury bills. We can use repurchase agreements to supply additional reserves if needed."

The conversation is, of course, more detailed and laced with the verbal shortcuts familiar to people operating in the money market. Prospective developments in the next couple of weeks are discussed. The Board participants may report about possible M1 and M2 revisions. The San Francisco Reserve Bank president will express his view on the proposed action.

The call is usually completed by 11:30. A staff member at the Board promptly summarizes the call in a memorandum sent to each Board member and a telegram is sent to each Reserve Bank president.

The Decision

Shortly before noon, conditions begin to jell rapidly and indicate a sharp increase in reserve pressures. Fed funds are heavily bid for at $5\frac{13}{16}$ percent. New York City banks and other participants in the funds market report that funds are hard to find. Dealers report little progress in meeting their financing needs by borrowing on a secured basis from their out-of-town sources, even at $5\frac{7}{8}$ percent.

The Manager reviews the evidence and gives the final go ahead: "The market has really started tightening up. We'd better move in right away in size to prevent this from getting out of hand. Let's go in and buy about $500 million in Treasury bills for cash today." As we have seen, within thirty minutes the Fed's traders purchase $523 million in Treasury bills for cash in a market "go-around."

Fed officers continue to watch the situation after the "go-around" is completed at around 12:30 P.M. The Fed funds rate eases back to $5\frac{7}{8}$ bid for a time, but then the brokers report that bids appear to be building while the supply available remains limited. Given the persistent tightness, the Manager approves the desk officer's recommendation that the System purchase about $1 billion of Treasury and federal agency securities under overnight repurchase agreements. Perhaps $100 million of bankers' acceptances will be bought under similar contracts.

By 1:00, the additional injection of reserves has been made, bringing the day's total to over $1.5 billion. Better balance returns to the Federal funds market, but the officers will not know until the next day whether the shortage of reserves reflected a sharper-than-expected drop in float or something else. A daily telegram to the Board and Reserve Banks will summarize the day's developments.

Private market traders will debate whether the Fed's action that day sought simply to head off the developing strain in the market or whether it had broad policy significance. Analysts may conclude that the Federal Reserve's double-barreled entry suggests that $5\frac{3}{4}$ percent is still the desk's objective. On another occasion, if analysts were worried at the strength in the M1 and M2 data published in recent weeks, they might quickly conclude that the Federal funds rate objective was being raised—were the desk to appear slow in supplying reserves. But today the reserve strains that threatened to become acute have disappeared.

Tomorrow is another day. . . .[9]

Although the federal funds target bands were broadened in October 1979, the federal funds rate might still serve as a signal for controlling reserves. The emphasis since 1979 has, however, been stated by Federal Reserve officials to be one of controlling nonborrowed reserves, while using the discount window as a "cushion" for offsetting unexpected changes in reserves.

The cushion is especially necessary because of the method of computing legal reserve requirements, in effect since 1968. Required reserves for the current week are calculated on the basis of deposits two weeks earlier. This system is called *lagged reserve requirements*. If reserves are pulled out during the current week and deposits begin to fall, depository institutions are forced to the discount window. No amount of borrowing from each other through the federal funds market can restore total reserves.

But as borrowing at the discount window increases, the total monetary base that supports deposits tends to rise. This tends to offset the effect of the open-market operations taken to reduce the money supply. Most experts inside and outside the Federal Reserve believe that lagged reserve requirements cause large variance in the federal funds rate and in the money supply.

The Federal Reserve said that lagged reserve requirements

heightened unexpected movements in excess reserves, requiring additional bank adjustments in the form of Federal funds transactions or member bank borrowing.[10]

Chairman Volcker of the Federal Reserve wrote on August 11, 1980, that the Board of Governors "was disposed toward" the system of concurrent or *synchronous reserve requirements* (where required reserves depend on the current week's deposits) in effect until 1968 (see Exhibits 23-2 and 23-3). There was concern that synchronous reserve requirements would impose undue costs on banks because they would have to keep close track of their current week's deposit in order to come up with the proper average reserves for the week by Wednesday, the settlement date. Finally, in September of 1982 the Federal Reserve announced that

BOARD OF GOVERNORS
OF THE
FEDERAL RESERVE SYSTEM
WASHINGTON, D.C. 20551

PAUL A. VOLCKER
CHAIRMAN

October 18, 1979

The Honorable Henry S. Reuss
Chairman
Committee on Banking, Finance
    and Urban Affairs
House of Representatives
Washington, D.C.   20515

Dear Chairman Reuss:

        I am not only sympathetic with the views you expressed in your
letter of October 12 on the subject of lagged reserve accounting, but
have asked that planning go forward on the matter. Concurrent reserve
requirements would be more consistent with the System's new approach to
monetary policy operations that places more weight on reserves. At the
same time, I am not convinced that the existing two week lag between
deposits and required reserves is an important complication in achieving
reserve and monetary targets over a period of three to six months or so.

        In all the circumstances, the Board has preferred to maintain
lagged reserve accounting at least for the immediate future in the hope
the membership problem can soon be resolved. There is little doubt that
such a change will be resisted by many small- and medium-sized banks for,
from their standpoint, legitimate reasons.

        In any event, we will complete our planning and studies so that
we will be prepared to act promptly should the Board feel that present
operating procedures reveal a more compelling and urgent need than we
now assume.

                            Sincerely,

                            Paul

Exhibit 23-2

---

synchronous reserve requirements would be reinstituted on February 2, 1984.

In 1982, Milton Friedman, then an adviser to President Reagan, advocated a return to synchronous reserve requirements and an end to churning.[11] He suggested that the Federal Reserve set targets for the monetary base over the next three or six months. Assume, for example, that a $10 billion increase is targeted for the monetary base over the next

BOARD OF GOVERNORS
OF THE
FEDERAL RESERVE SYSTEM
WASHINGTON, D. C. 20551

PAUL A. VOLCKER
CHAIRMAN

RECEIVED

August 11, 1980

AUG 15 1980

Banking, Finance & Urban Affairs Committee

The Honorable Henry S. Reuss
Chairman
Committee on Banking, Finance
  and Urban Affairs
House of Representatives
Washington, D.C.   20515

Dear Henry:

Thank you for your letter of July 31 concerning contemporaneous reserve accounting. Last Tuesday, the Board took up the issue of returning to contemporaneous reserve accounting in connection with its final action on Regulation D. After reviewing the comments received from the public on this issue, and after weighing the benefits against the burdens imposed on depository institutions, the Board concluded that it was disposed toward adopting contemporaneous reserve accounting in 1981. The Board plans to discuss the operational aspects with depository institutions to insure that the implementation of contemporaneous reserve accounting can proceed smoothly.

Sincerely,

Paul

P.S. As you will recognize, this is still short of a final decision. In any event, it simply didn't appear practical now.   Pav

Exhibit 23-3

six months. The Federal Reserve would go into the market only once a week, say, each Monday morning. It would buy $\frac{1}{26}$ of $10 billion, or $384.62 million in securities, plus the amount needed to replace maturing securities. If the single monetary aggregate designated for targeting got off course, the base target could be adjusted at the end of the three- or six-month period. A penalty rate would be put in place at the discount window to reduce substantially the amount of borrowing. Changes in borrowing at the discount window can alter the monetary base, moving it off the targeted rate of growth.

Such a plan would end fine tuning of the money supply. Short-run variance in the money supply may increase, but this conclusion is controversial since fine tuning at the open-market desk may introduce disturbances. Long-run money growth, it is argued, would be perceived as being more reliably within the projected target ranges.

> It would leave to the market the day-to-day and seasonal adjustments that the market is well qualified to handle—and could do more effectively if it knew precisely what the Federal Reserve intended to do, then in the present state of uncertainty with the weekly guessing game about the Fed intentions that follows each Friday's release of the figures on the money supply.[12]

Such a mode of operation would dramatically change the money markets. If the Federal Reserve operated with longer-term Treasury securities as would be appropriate under such a policy, there would be a reduction in repurchase agreement volume. Short-term Treasury bills, used as collateral in repurchase agreements, would be traded in a smaller volume market unless the Federal Reserve directly concentrated on them in open-market operations, as it did before it settled on repurchase agreements as the main instrument.

The Federal Reserve's Assets and Liabilities

Table 23-2 presents a generalized T-account classification of the Federal Reserve's assets and liabilities, consolidated to include all twelve regional Federal Reserve banks. Table 23-3 presents a specific itemized T account of these assets and liabilities for December 1981. This record is a starting point for gaining insight into the Federal Reserve's transactions that change the monetary base. A brief description of each of the classes of assets and liabilities follows.

TABLE 23-2

Generalized Accounting Record of the Federal Reserve's Assets and Liabilities*	
Assets	**Liabilities and Capital Accounts**

1. Cash assets
    a. Coin and currency
    b. Gold certificates
    c. Special drawing rights certificates
2. Loans to depository institutions
3. Uncollected cash items
4. Securities held
5. Miscellaneous assets
	6. Federal Reserve notes outstanding
	7. Deposits from depository institutions, international organizations, foreign central banks, and from the U.S. Treasury
	8. Deferred-availability cash items
	9. Other liabilities and capital accounts

*The basic accounting identity holds: Assets = liabilities + equity (or capital accounts).

TABLE 23-3

The Federal Reserve's Assets and Liabilities, December 1981* (Billions of Dollars)

Assets		Liabilities and Capital Accounts	
Gold certificates (and special drawing rights	14.5	Federal Reserve notes	129.1
Coin	.4	Deposits from banks	24.3
Loans to depository institutions	.2	U.S. Treasury account	3.5
U.S. and agency securities held†	136.7	Foreign and other accounts	1.3
Cash items in process of collections	7.5	Deferred-availability cash items	5.3
Other assets	10.1	Other liabilities and capital accounts	5.9
Total	169.4	Total	169.4

*Consolidated for all twelve regional Federal Reserve Banks. End-of-month estimates: slight inaccuracy because of rounding.
†Bankers acceptances, in relatively small amounts, are frequently held.
Source: *Federal Reserve Bulletin* (December 1981), p. A11.

First the assets, as numbered in Table 23-2, are identified (the estimates are from December 1981):

1a. The metal *coin and currency* are held by the Federal Reserve banks in their vaults in order to supply depository institutions, as part of the Federal Reserve's central bank function of maintaining the payments system described in Chapter 22. They held $400 million in coins.

1b. and c. *Gold certificates* and *special drawing rights certificates (SDR certificates)* arise in transactions with the U.S. Treasury. They amounted to $14.5 billion. The gold certificates are claims against the Treasury's gold. The SDR certificates are claims against the Treasury's SDRs, an international money issued by the International Monetary Fund.

2. *Loans to depository institutions* are also called *discounting* and are said to be made through the discount window at each regional Federal Reserve bank. Legislation passed in March 1980 gave authorization for all depository institutions with checkable accounts to borrow from the Federal Reserve. Since nationwide NOW accounts (a form of checkable account) were also authorized by this legislation, beginning in 1981, the serv-

3. and 8. *Uncollected cash items*, an asset, minus the liability, *deferred-availability cash items*, equals Federal Reserve float. Bank float results from the failure to record simultaneously the balances in the account where a check is deposited and in the account from which it is drawn. Float amounted to $2.2 billion.

4. The *securities held* by the Federal Reserve amounted to $136.7 billion. They comprise its portfolio of U.S. government and federal agency obligations, from which it earned $10.1 billion in 1979, or 98 percent of its current "earnings." The word *earnings* has quotation marks since these interest payments are from the U.S. Treasury and government agencies to the Federal Reserve. A consolidated balance sheet of the government, where the Federal Reserve is defined as part of the government, would net them out at zero. The transfers would be internal ones. Most of these funds that are not used for expenses are returned to the U.S. Treasury as "interest on Federal Reserve notes." This rebate amounted to $9.3 billion in 1979.

5. The *miscellaneous assets* ($10.2 billion) include the real estate, buildings, and equipment of the Federal Reserve.

The liabilities, as numbered in Table 23-3, are described next.

6. The *Federal Reserve notes*, amounting to $129.1 billion, are the bulk (90 percent) of the currency and coin in circulation. Examine a U.S. dollar bill, which is a Federal Reserve note. The name, number of the Federal Reserve district, and the letter of the alphabet corresponding to that number identify the regional Federal Reserve Bank that originally issued it. Technically, it is a liability of that Federal Reserve bank, although an attempt to return it would produce only a blank stare.

7. *Deposits* from depository institutions amounted to $24.3 billion. International organizations, foreign central banks, the U.S. Treasury, and government-sponsored agencies accounts also hold deposits at the Federal Reserve.

8. See 3.

9. *Other liabilities and capital accounts* ($5.9 billion) include the accumulated funds paid in to the regional Federal Reserve bank by member banks in the district for their stock. (The total paid in amounted to $1.3 billion.) Capital accounts also include the "profits" of the Federal Reserve, which are to be paid (back) to the U.S. Treasury, and accrued dividends for the 6 percent return on member bank stock.

Notice that Table 23-3 embodies the accounting identity that equates the total value of assets, something of value, to the total value of liabilities plus capital (or equity), the claims against the assets. It is a statement reflecting double-entry bookkeeping, the rule requiring everything to be entered at least twice.

Sources and Uses of Reserves

By rearranging the assets and liabilities in Table 23-2 and adding a few items from the Treasury, the accounting balance sheet for sources and

TABLE 23-4

Factors Affecting Reserve Accounts, November 1981*† (Billions of Dollars)

Supplying Reserve Funds	
1. Federal Reserve credit	
(4) Securities held	136.7
(2) Loans to depository institutions	.2
(3–8) Federal Reserve float	2.2
(5) Miscellaneous assets	10.1
2. (1a, 1b) gold and SDR accounts	14.5
3. Treasury currency outstanding	13.7
Total	177.4
Absorbing Reserve Funds	
1. Currency in circulation	141.9
2. Treasury cash holdings	.5
3. (7) Deposits with Federal Reserve except member banks‡	4.7
4. (9) Other Federal Reserve liabilities and capital	6.0
Total	153.1
5. (7) Reserve accounts	24.2

*Note: Number in parentheses refer to items in Table 23–2.
†Consolidated for all twelve regional Federal Reserve banks; end-of-month estimates: slight inaccuracy because of rounding.
‡Also excluded Edge Act corporations, U.S. agencies, and branches of foreign banks.
Source: Federal Reserve Bulletin (December 1981), p. A4.

uses of reserves shown in Table 23-4 is obtained. It is very similar to the T account in Table 23-3 except for these three changes:

1. Federal Reserve float has been consolidated into one item.
2. The currency created by the Treasury, "Treasury currency outstanding," is added as a source of funds. There was $13.7 billion of this currency.
3. The use of funds includes all the currency in circulation ($141.9 billion) and cash held by the Treasury ($0.5 billion).

The changes bring into the picture all the currency and coin that is created by the U.S. Treasury and the Federal Reserve. The accounting record is arranged in Table 23-3 so that all the factors that supply funds that could be used for reserves are separated from all the factors that use these funds. The residual is the reserves of member banks.

Because of the reserve requirements in the Depository Institutions Deregulation and Monetary Control Act of 1980, which will be phased in over eight years in all depository institutions instead of just member banks, it is appropriate to change slightly the accounting statement so that the reserves of all depository institutions are separated out as a residual. This is done in Table 23-4. Following convention, the assets of the Federal Reserve, except gold and the SDR certificate accounts, are brought under a variable called "Federal Reserve credit."

The sources and uses statement of private depository reserves (Table 23-5) is a useful classification for determining the effect of government

TABLE 23-5

Sources and Uses of Private Depository Institutions' Reserves

$$
\begin{bmatrix}
\text{1. Federal Reserve credit} \\
+ \\
\text{2. Gold and SDR certificate accounts} \\
+ \\
\text{3. Treasury currency outstanding}
\end{bmatrix}
=
\begin{bmatrix}
\text{4. Currency in circulation} \\
+ \\
\text{5. Treasury cash holdings} \\
+ \\
\text{6. Deposits with the Federal Reserve except private depository institution reserves} \\
+ \\
\text{7. Other Federal Reserve liabilities and capital} \\
+ \\
\text{8. Private depository institutions' reserves}
\end{bmatrix}
$$

$$
\text{where Federal Reserve credit} =
\begin{bmatrix}
\text{Securities held} \\
+ \\
\text{Loans to depository institutions} \\
+ \\
\text{Float} \\
+ \\
\text{Other Federal Reserve assets}
\end{bmatrix}
$$

transactions on reserves. For example, an open-market operation in which the trading desk at the New York Federal Reserve bought U.S. securities would increase "Federal Reserve credit," item 1 in Table 23-5. One of the other items must change to preserve the identity that defines a use for every source of reserve. This identity is in the spirit of the saying, "Everyone (a source) must be somewhere (a use)." Other things in the identity being the same, reserves of private institutions would increase.

The other figures that are not likely to be changed by the open-market purchase alone and therefore can be assumed to be constant are item 2, "Gold and SDR certificate accounts"; item 3, "Treasury currency outstanding"; item 5, "Treasury cash holding"; and item 7, "Other Federal Reserve liabilities and capital."

The other things that might change are as follows. The bond seller (to the Federal Reserve) may wish some cash. In that case, the Federal Reserve will increase its note issue and item 4, "Currency in circulation," will increase. If the bond seller is a foreign central bank, the proceeds may be deposited at the Federal Reserve, which will increase item 6.

The Government Budget Constraint or Monetary Base Identity

A final useful identity is called the *government budget constraint* or *monetary base identity.*[13] This relationship will tie together the transactions of the government that affect not only the reserves of depository institutions but also the rest of the monetary base: currency and coin outside depository institutions.

A fuller but simple view of the transactions of the U.S. Treasury is needed to obtain the monetary base identity. An easy way to understand the Treasury's transactions is to ask how it finances the government deficit. The deficit is the difference between expenditures for goods and services the federal government buys, plus transfer payments, and the taxes it collects. Notice that the question does not ask how deficits are *financed* by the federal government as a whole. That second question can be answered after the Federal Reserve is brought into the picture and the monetary base identity, in all its glory, shines forth.

Table 23-6 shows the different ways the Treasury and U.S. federal government agencies finance their deficits. They can sell bonds, item 2. The Treasury can use the funds it has on deposit at the Federal Reserve, item 3; it can use its own cash holdings, item 4; or it can use its deposits at commercial banks, item 5. Finally, the Treasury can sometimes obtain funds by creating more of its own currency, item 6, although this alternative is no longer an important source of funds.

The monetary base identity shown in Table 23-7 is then obtained by (1) putting the items in Table 23-5 in the form of changes, (2) substituting into Table 23-5 the Treasury identity in Table 23-6, and (3) consolidating transactions of the Federal Reserve and the U.S. Treasury.[14] The government budget constraint or monetary base identity can also be viewed as the equality between the change in the monetary base and the different ways it can be changed.

This second view is evident if the symbols shown in Table 23-7 are written in equation form:

$$\Delta B = DEF + \Delta BOND + \Delta DIS + \Delta FLOA + \Delta G + \Delta US \qquad (4)$$

The use of this identity in understanding the relationship between government transactions and the monetary base is illuminated by a closer examination of the individual variables.

TABLE 23-6

U.S. Treasury Financing of Its Deficit

1. [The deficit, DEF]	=	⌈ 2. Bonds sold by Treasury (Treasury borrowing)*
		−
		3. Change in Treasury deposits at the Federal Reserve
		−
		4. Change in Treasury cash holdings
		−
		5. Change in Treasury deposits at private banks, ΔU.S.
		+
		⌊ 6. Change in Treasury cash outstanding

*Sales of U.S. agency securities are included.

TABLE 23-7

The Monetary Base or Government Budget Constraint Identity*

| 1. Change in the monetary base, ΔB
  a. Change in reserves on deposit
    at the Federal Reserve
    +
  b. Change in currency
    (1) Held as reserves at depository
      institutions (vault cash)

    (2) Held by the nonbank public | = | 2. The deficit (*DEF*)
   +
3. Change in securities held by the
   federal Reserve minus bonds
   sold by the Treasury, $\Delta Bond$
   +
4. Change in loans through the dis-
   count window, $\Delta DISC$

5. Change in Federal Reserve float,
   $\Delta FLOA$
   +
6. Change in gold stock, ΔG
   +
7. Change in Treasury accounts in
   private banks, ΔUS |

*All changes refer to dollar values of the changes.

The Federal Deficit

The *federal deficit (DEF)* is the cash value of expenditures minus income of the government, involving goods, services, and transfer payments (mostly taxes), but excluding transactions in gold. It is item 2 in Table 23-7. This is a cash deficit as opposed to an accrual deficit. (An *accrual deficit* records taxes and expenditures at the time they become due rather than at the time the actual exchange of cash is made.)

If the other components of the change in the monetary base on the right side of Equation (4) are all equal to zero, a deficit increases the monetary base and a surplus (a negative deficit) decreases the monetary base. If, however, the deficit equals the value of government bond *sales* (the negative of bond purchases) to the public ($DEF = -\Delta BOND$), and the other components of the change in the monetary base equal zero, the change in the monetary base is zero.

A deficit of this type, where it is accompanied by an equal amount of bond sales, was used as a policy variable by John Maynard Keynes in *The General Theory of Employment, Interest and Money.*[15] In Keynes's analysis, which became the foundation of much of macroeconomics, a *borrowed budgetary deficit* or *loan expenditure*, as he called it, was a major policy tool with which the government affected total real income. One of the most prominent controversies in the postwar period has been about the relative effects on nominal and real income of a borrowed budgetary deficit versus a change in the money supply. Equation (4) included important government variables in this controversy. The identity ties together the fiscal and monetary policy actions of the government. *Pure fiscal policy actions* can be identified with the level of a borrowed federal deficit. This is a deficit that is "financed" by the equivalent of borrowing from the public, leaving the monetary base unchanged.[16] *Pure monetary policy* actions can be identified with a change in the monetary base (or a more broadly defined concept of money) when the deficit is zero.

   In statistical tests of the effects of monetary and fiscal policy, neither the deficit nor the change in the monetary base is usually found to be equal to zero. An attempt is made to isolate the separate effects of monetary and fiscal variables on the variable to be explained (such as real or nominal income).

Bond Transactions

The variable $\Delta BOND$ is the consolidated value of the purchases minus the sales of bonds by the Federal Reserve and the rest of the government to the public. This is item 3 in Table 23-7. If all the other variables on the right side of Equation (4) are equal to zero, a purchase of bonds increases the monetary base and a sale of bonds decreases the monetary base.

Federal Reserve Loans to Depository Institutions

Federal Reserve loans to depository institutions, or *discounting*, ΔDIS in Equation (4), is the net increase in these loans. When the Federal Reserve increases the volume of loans to depository institutions, and other components of the change in the monetary base are equal to zero, the monetary base increases.

Float

An increase in item 5 in Table 23-7, "Federal Reserve float," $\Delta FLOA$, increases the monetary base. It creates double counting of reserves credited to the depository institution where the check is deposited but not yet deducted from the depository institution from which the check is drawn.

Government Deposits at Private Depositories

The change in government deposits at commercial banks, ΔUS, is part of the monetary base identity. This is because a change in these deposits, when the other components of the right-hand side of Equation (4) equal zero, changes the monetary base. The Treasury may withdraw funds from its deposits at commercial banks and deposit them at its account at the Federal Reserve, thereby reducing the size of the monetary base.

The Treasury uses its accounts at the Federal Reserve banks for making payments. The money stored in deposits at commercial banks can be shifted to the Federal Reserve accounts. Commercial banks are usually given an advance warning if the Treasury expects to make a withdrawal. The Federal Reserve System, acting as the agent for the Treasury, announces a *call date* and the percentage of funds that the Treasury expects to withdraw.

Until 1978, substantial amounts of federal government funds were placed on deposit in commercial banks at a zero rate of interest return. Most of these funds were in *tax and loan accounts.* Tax and loan accounts are Treasury accounts authorized to receive corporate income taxes, excise taxes, unemployment insurance taxes, and payroll withholding taxes.[17] The commercial bank receiving these funds gives the depositor a depository receipt, which is used when his or her next tax form is sent to the Internal Revenue Service, as evidence that the tax was paid. Because the commercial bank could buy income-earning assets with these funds, they were especially profitable before 1978.

The profitability of tax and loan accounts to private banks was reduced by a 1977 law, which took effect in November 1978. It required each tax and loan private bank depository to select one of two options. It could either pay interest to the Treasury on its tax and loan balance (the *note option*), or it could immediately—by the next day—remit to the Treasury any such funds received (the *remittance option*). Under the note option, the bank pays an interest equal to 25 basis points less than the average federal funds rate for the week. Thus if the federal funds rate is 12 percent, the bank pays the Treasury $11\frac{3}{4}$ percent. Funds held under the remittance option are subject to regular reserve requirements, but funds credited to the note option are free from reserve requirements.

During October 1981, the Treasury had $16.3 billion in tax and loan accounts and $3.5 billion in its accounts at the Federal Reserve banks.

It is frequently argued that government deposits of tax proceeds in private bank accounts (tax and loan accounts) promote increased monetary stability because they do not change the monetary base. In Equation (4) the tax payment by the taxpayer is a *negative deficit* (a surplus), which is equal to an offsetting change in government deposits at commercial banks.

$$DEF + \Delta US = 0 \tag{5}$$

The monetary base is constant.

The deposit of tax proceeds into tax and loan accounts, however, does change the money supply, although by less than if the taxes were deposited in the Treasury's account at the Federal Reserve. Government deposits at private banks are not part of the private money supply, defined as M1, so that the money supply declines with the transfer of funds from private to government accounts, although not by as much as if the monetary base changed. Of course, the Federal Reserve could rapidly offset changes in the monetary base through open-market operations.

Gold

Item 6 in Table 23-7 is the change in the stock of gold, ΔG, held by the federal government, measured by the cash value of transactions in gold. When the Treasury buys $100 in gold, the monetary base rises by $100 if all the other components of ΔB in Equation (4) equal zero.

Only the value of dollars actually exchanged for gold are used to compute ΔG. A change in the value of the Treasury's gold stock, arising from the way it is valued (capital gains and losses), has no effect on the monetary base. For example, in 1934, the official U.S. price of gold was raised from the price of a year earlier, which was $20.67 an ounce, to $35.00 an ounce. This action by itself had no effect on the monetary base. In August 1971, the U.S. Treasury ceased an unlimited commitment to buy and sell gold from foreigners; the "gold window" was closed. Since 1971, the Treasury has occasionally sold some of its gold at market prices.

The bookkeeping entries of a Treasury gold transaction with the private sector have been found to be as fascinating as any other story about those shiny ingots of precious metal, which are buried in vaults and believed to mysteriously "back the money supply in circulation." Suppose that Reginald Marsh sold $100 in gold to the Treasury; Marsh received a $100 deposit, which was placed in his account at Southwest National Bank, which also thereby gained $100 in reserves, items 1 and 2 in the T accounts in Table 23-8. The Treasury paid Marsh by a check against its account at the Federal Reserve (items 3, 4, and 5) and the Treasury increased its gold stock, item 6. Next, Southwestern National Bank cleared Marsh's check at the FRB (items 7 and 8).

TABLE 23-8

T Accounts Reflecting Balance Sheet Entries from $100 Purchase of Gold by the U.S. Treasury

U.S. Treasury		Federal Reserve		Southwest National Bank	
Period 1	$100 gold (6); −$100 deposit at FRB (5)		−$100 reserves (3); $100 reserves (8)	−$100 Treasury deposit (4); $100 deposit from Southwest National Bank (7)	$100 reserves (2)	$100 deposit to Marsh (1)
Period 2	$100 deposit at F.R. (9)	$100 gold certificate outstanding (10)	$100 gold certificate (11)	$100 Treasury deposit (12)		

But this was not the end of the story. The Treasury replenished its account at the Federal Reserve by giving the Federal Reserve a gold certificate, for which the Treasury received $100 (items 9, 10, 11, and 12).

When the Treasury sold gold, the gold was frequently moved by armored car from the U.S. Assay Office in New York on the East River five blocks to the Federal Reserve Bank of New York on Liberty Street. The Federal Reserve vault is 50 feet below sea level and 76 feet below street level. Many foreign countries store some of their gold in this vault at the New York Federal Reserve Bank. Each working day, gold bars are wheeled between the various countries' storage compartments, on instructions for international payments, rather than the countries' incurring expensive shipping and insurance charges from transporting the gold between countries.

It is a weird and fascinating sight if one understands the implications. Men far underground, with steel covers over their shoes (to prevent injury if one of the bars drops), tote bars between compartments in the basement of the New York Federal Reserve Bank to settle a debt between Norway and Germany that arose from sardine imports into Germany. Many of the gold bars weigh 400 troy ounces (12 troy ounces to a pound), or $33\frac{1}{3}$ pounds. Many of these bars are stamped with the insignia of the Soviet Union, which, along with South Africa, mines much of the world's gold.

Expanding and Contracting the Monetary Base

Any combination of changes in the variables on the right side of Equation (4) that add to a positive number will increase the monetary base. The government can then be said to be expanding the monetary base, or *running the printing press* and putting money in circulation. The name often given to these relationships is *financing*. If, for example, a deficit of $10 billion occurs in the same period in which $10 billion in bonds are sold to the public, the deficit is said to be *financed by borrowing*. However, if a number of variables change in the period of the deficit, there is no mileage to be gained in economic analysis by pretending that particular sources of funds are earmarked for the deficit and other sources are not.

Mechanical Relationships Between the Components of the Change in the Monetary Base

The accounting relationships between the components of the change in the monetary base are illustrated with five examples, based on the monetary base identity:

1. The government incurs a deficit of $100 (*DEF* = $100) in the same period in which $100 in bonds are sold (Δ*BOND* = −$100); the sum of the other components of the change in the monetary base is zero. The aggregate change in the monetary base is then zero. The deficit is a borrowed deficit, financed by bond sales.
2. The government incurs a deficit of $100 (*DEF* = $100). All other components of the change in the monetary base sum to zero. The deficit is financed by "printing" money (Δ*B* = $100).
3. The government incurs a deficit of $200 (*DEF* = $200) in the same period in which all tax receipts of $100 are deposited in tax and loan accounts (Δ*US* = $100) and all other components of the change in the monetary base sum to zero. The monetary base must increase by $300 (Δ*B* = $300).
4. The government purchases $10 in gold (Δ*C* = $10) in the same period in which Federal Reserve bank float increases by $20 (Δ*FLOA* = $20) and the government incurs a $30 surplus (*DEF* = −$30). The monetary base is constant.
5. The Federal Reserve buys $100 in bonds (Δ*BOND* = $100) and the Treasury makes a call on tax and loan accounts of $50 (Δ*US* = −$50). The Treasury sells $50 in bonds to the public (Δ*BOND* = −$50) and the government runs a $70 deficit (*DEF* = $70). The first three Treasury and the Federal Reserve transactions have offsetting effects on the monetary base. The monetary base increases by $70.

These seemingly complex sets of government transactions can easily be analyzed for their direct effect on the monetary base by simply substituting the values into the variables of the *monetary base identity*. Much of the confusion and many of the mistakes that have arisen in discussions of the direct relationships of fiscal policy and other types of government transactions with the monetary base and the money supply are eliminated by this procedure.

NOTES

1. *The Federal Reserve System, Purposes and Functions*, Board of Governors of the Federal Reserve System (September 1974), p. 1.
2. The emergence of balance-of-payment problems did not appear in the President's *Council of Economic Advisers' Report* until 1960. Both the annual reports and the CEA were authorized by the Employment Act of 1946. See Reuben E. Slesinger, *National Economic Policy: The Presidential Papers* (New York: D. Van Nostrand Company, 1968) for a review of the Act and all the CEA reports to 1967.
3. One can study actions of interventions or read the following elaboration in *The Federal Reserve System: Purposes and Functions* without gaining a very precise idea of what the Board of Governors and the FOMC have in mind. Are they turning to foreign exchange intervention and a policy of high interest rates and away from emphasis on the monetary targets and domestic con-

siderations? Such a question often arises in monetary policy oversight hearings. Here is some custard pie ready for nailing to the wall (pp. 91–92):

"The Board of Governors and the FOMC take account of the U.S. balance of payments, movements in exchange rates, and other international economic and financial developments in making U.S. monetary policy.

"The Board of Governors takes various actions of a regulatory or supervisory nature that affects the international transactions and foreign operations of U.S. banks and the U.S. activities of foreign banks.

"In forming the judgments about prospective economic developments that underlie monetary policy decisions, Federal Reserve policy-makers regularly take into account the relationships that link the domestic economy to the rest of the world—for example, the forces that affect foreign demand for U.S. goods and services, the determinants of supply and demand in this country for U.S. products that compete with imports, the factors influencing international flows of funds, and the effects of international flows of funds on domestic financial markets. These relationships are viewed from two related perspectives. First, developments in the rest of the world may have significant implications for the domestic economic objectives of the United States and for the use of monetary policy in attaining these objectives. Second, economic developments in this country have important influences on the net balance of goods and services transactions and the net flow of long-term and liquid capital between the United States and foreign countries, which in turn affect the international value of the dollar and the international reserve position of the United States."

There is nothing inherently wrong with imprecise targets from the standpoint of a governmental unit that desires to ensure a broad scope for future actions. For the analyst, however, it is useful to know what, if any, limits are put on future actions. How precise are the targets for future actions?

4. *Hearings Before the Committee on Banking, Finance and Urban Affairs, House of Representatives, on the Conduct of Monetary Policy*, p. 97.
5. Ibid., p. 98.
6. Milton Friedman, "Monetary Policy," *Journal of Money, Credit and Banking* (January 1982), p. 113, emphasis added. Friedman later revised his estimates of gross transactions to $800 billion. "A Reply by Milton Friedman," *Journal of Money, Credit and Banking* (August 1982), pp. 404–406.
7. In October 1979 the Federal Reserve announced that it would change its operating procedures so as to emphasize control of the money supply. It then widened the permissible band—before intervention—on the federal funds rate.
8. "Analysis of the Impact of Lagged Reserve Accounting," a report prepared by the Staff of the Board of Governors of the Federal Reserve System (October 6, 1977), p. 15.
9. Paul Meek, *Open Market Operations*, Federal Reserve Bank of New York (June 1978), pp. 19–20.
10. Staff of the Board of Governors, "Analysis." p. 7. Also see the statements of Peter D. Sternlight and Stephen H. Axilrod, who spoke for the negative in "Is the Federal Reserve's Monetary Control Policy Misdirected? Resolved 'That the Federal Reserve's Current Operating Procedure for Controlling Money Should Be Replaced'," *Journal of Money, Credit and Banking* (February 1982), pp. 119–147. Also read Allan H. Meltzer and Robert H. Rasche's affirmative views in that debate.
11. Friedman, "Monetary Policy," p. 117.
12. Ibid.
13. The concept of the government budget constraint has been developed by Carl Christ in "A Model of Monetary and Fiscal Policy Effects on the Money Stocks, Price Level and Real Output," *Journal of Money, Credit and Banking* (November 1969), pp. 683–705; and by Robert Auerbach in "An Estima-

tion Procedure for the Federal Cash Deficit Applied to the United States Interwar Period, 1920–1941," *Western Economic Journal* (December 1972), pp. 474–476.
14. A complete consolidation requires that the goods and services supplied by the Federal Reserve minus the service charges collected be added to the deficit. However, this is a minor correction. It is noted only to emphasize that the Federal Reserve must be consolidated with the rest of the federal government in this analysis.
15. John Maynard Keynes, *The General Theory of Employment, Interest and Money* (New York: Harcourt Brace & World, Inc., 1964), pp. 98, 128–29, footnote 1.
16. Usually pure fiscal policy is associated with a constant level of some broader monetary aggregate, such as M1.
17. See the Federal Reserve Bank of Cleveland's "The Influence of Government Deposits on the Money Supply," *Economic Commentary* (June 28, 1971); and Richard W. Lang, "TTL Note Accounts and the Money Supply Process," *Review*, Federal Reserve Bank of St. Louis (October 1979), pp. 3 4.

STUDY QUESTIONS

1. What is the objective of Federal Reserve open-market operations?

2. Why does the Federal Reserve primarily use repurchase agreements in its open-market operations?

3. What are the advantages and disadvantages of Milton Friedman's plan to change Federal Reserve open-market operations?

4. Derive the monetary base identity and explain each of its components. Show how it differs from the sources and uses of reserves statements.

$$\Delta B = \Delta DEF + \Delta FLOAT + \Delta G + \Delta US + \Delta BONDS + \Delta DISC$$

24

Regulation

Introduction

This chapter begins with a discussion of the Securities and Exchange Commission. Its functions in regulating the issuance and sales of stock are described. The controversy over the value of the Securities and Exchange Commission's requirements for disclosure of financial data is discussed. Next, other government regulators of financial markets are described. The functions of the Commodity Futures Trading Commission are also discussed.

The considerable regulatory functions performed by private exchanges are not described. Some discussion of actions to remedy abuses in the New York Stock Exchange were discussed in Chapter 22. The NASDAQ over-the-counter computer system has a surveillance department in Washington, D.C.

The discussion in this chapter contains a report of regulators' worries about squeezes, corners, and unstable spot prices that might result from the introduction of futures contracts on financial assets. An assessment of their concerns and a discussion of efforts to curtail free markets follow. This discussion contains arguments for and against price change limitations in futures markets and the relation of limits to the size of cash margins on futures contracts.

The chapter ends with a description of experiments in interconnected stock markets.

The Securities and Exchange Commission

The Securities and Exchange Commission (SEC) was created by the Securities Exchange Act of 1934 to perform quasi-judicial functions to maintain "just and equitable principles of trade which would be conducive to an open, fair and orderly market."[1] The Act was also aimed at outlawing misrepresentation, manipulation, and other abusive practices in financial markets. The act contained the following six provisions.

1. Every company with securities listed on an exchange must file, with the SEC, annual and periodic financial reports. The Securities Act Amendments of 1964 extended this reporting requirement to companies with securities traded over the counter if the company has at least $1 million in assets and 500 or more shareholders. The SEC makes these reports public in *Form 10-K*. The cover of one of these is shown in Exhibit 24-1.
2. *Insider trading* in listed securities must be reported regularly to the SEC. Insiders are officers, directors, and 10 percent owners (owners who hold at least 10 percent of the stock).
3. The company's financial condition and other information must be contained in any solicitation for *proxies* (written authority to vote the shares of a stock owner).
4. Dealers and broker-dealers on exchanges and the over-the-counter market must register with the SEC and are subject to given rules. Most rules are applied by the exchanges themselves.
5. The SEC is empowered to police trading practices in the financial markets.
6. The SEC has the power to subpoena books and records, to take testimony, and to obtain court orders of injunctions to prevent practices that violate the Securities Act of 1934.

Summaries of five SEC investigations of cases of abusive trading practices illustrate some of the SEC cases and procedures.[2]

1 | CASE

Unsuitable Trading Activity by a Large Registered Broker-Dealer

In this early administrative proceeding, unsuitable transactions were entered into by a large registered broker-dealer for the account of a major public university. The broker-dealer also churned the account and failed to reflect the account's transactions properly on its books and records.

The subject transactions involved government securities, including forward commitments executed in 1974 to purchase GNMAs. The university had sought low risk investments for its investment account of approximately $1.5 million. Nevertheless, its account acquired commitments exceeding $3 million and sustained losses of nearly $1 million.

SECURITIES AND EXCHANGE COMMISSION
WASHINGTON, D. C. 20549

FORM 10-K

ANNUAL REPORT PURSUANT TO SECTION 13 OR 15(d) OF THE SECURITIES EXCHANGE ACT OF 1934

For the fiscal year ended December 31, 1981.   Commission file number 1-1861.

C. I. T. Financial Corporation
(Exact name of registrant as specified in its charter)

Delaware	13-2994534
(State or other jurisdiction of incorporation or organization)	(I. R. S. Employer Identification No.)
650 Madison Avenue, New York, New York	10022
(Address of principal executive offices)	(Zip Code)

Registrant's telephone number, including area code: 212 572-6500

Securities registered pursuant to Section 12(b) of the Act:

Title of each class	Name of each exchange on which registered
8.85% Debentures due December 1, 1982	New York Stock Exchange
7⅞% Debentures due April 1, 1986	New York Stock Exchange
Zero Coupon Debentures due December 1, 1988	None
9% Senior Subordinated Debentures due October 1, 1991	New York Stock Exchange
14¼% Debentures due December 1, 1991	None
8.80% Senior Subordinated Debentures due March 15, 1993	New York Stock Exchange
9½% Debentures due June 1, 1995	New York Stock Exchange
8⅜% Debentures due April 1, 2001	New York Stock Exchange
9.85% Senior Subordinated Debentures due August 15, 2004	New York Stock Exchange
11½% Debentures due June 15, 2005	New York Stock Exchange
8¾% Debentures due March 15, 2008	New York Stock Exchange
9⅝% Debentures due August 15, 2009	New York Stock Exchange

Indicate by check mark whether the Registrant (1) has filed all reports required to be filed by Section 13 or 15(d) of the Securities Exchange Act of 1934 during the preceding 12 months (or for such shorter period that the Registrant was required to file such reports), and (2) has been subject to such filing requirements for the past 90 days.   Yes ✓ No ___

State the aggregate market value of the voting stock held by non-affiliates of the Registrant.

None of the voting stock of the Registrant is held by non-affiliates of the Registrant. All of the voting stock of the Registrant is owned by RCA Corporation.

Indicate the number of shares outstanding of each of the Registrant's classes of common stock, as of the latest practicable date.

March 15, 1982 - Common Stock—1,000 Shares

List hereunder the following documents if incorporated by reference and the Part of the Form 10-K (e.g., Part I, Part II, etc.) into which the document is incorporated: (1) Any annual report to security holders; (2) Any proxy or information statement; and (3) Any prospectus filed pursuant to Rule 424(b) or (c) under the Securities Act of 1933.

None

The Registrant meets the conditions set forth in General Instruction I(1)(a) and (b) of Form 10-K and is therefore filing this Form with the reduced disclosure format.

Exhibit 24-1

These unsuitable trades had been handled by only one of the broker-dealer's registered representatives. The SEC brought an administrative proceeding against the broker-dealer and accepted a settlement which included findings of a failure to supervise the registered representative involved. In addition, the broker-dealer agreed to take remedial steps to prevent recurrence of these activities, including written approval of manager prior to execution of of GNMA forward commitments in excess of specified amount and the institution of procedures for the early detection of excessive trading activity by account executives. The registered broker-dealer reached a settlement with the university in which it agreed to share the losses that had been sustained and pay approximately $400,000 to the university, resulting in a net loss to the university of approximately $600,000.[3]

2 | CASE

Scheme to Interpose Corporation Between Registered Broker-Dealer and Outside Broker-Dealers

I was formerly an office manager for a large registered broker-dealer. J and K were registered representatives in the same office. I, J and K also owned one corporation and one partnership that traded in government securities.

Using information obtained from the broker-dealer, I, J, and K schemed to interposition their corporation between the registered broker-dealer and outside broker-dealers to make profits in government securities trades. They concealed this from the broker-dealer by the use of the government bond trading department of a large national bank. Beginning in late 1973, J arranged for the corporation to open a bank account and bond trading account at the national bank. All contacts with the bank were made through one of its vice presidents, who worked in its government bond trading department. This vice president was a long-time friend of J. For $2\frac{1}{2}$ years thereafter, numerous trades of government bonds were carried out among the broker-dealer, the interpositioned corporation, the bank's bond department, and outside parties.

J, who did most of the government securities business in the broker-dealer's office, determined each morning at what prices the broker-dealer's government traders in New York would sell certain bonds and related this information to I, K, and the bank's vice president. With this information and the aid of the bank's vice president, purchase prices were obtained from outside dealers. The bank's vice president, with I, J, and K, would then cause the bank to place orders through the broker-dealer to buy bonds at prices at which the broker-dealer was willing to sell. Once the trade was made, the vice president would execute another trade with the corporation buying the government securities back at a higher price. He would then sell the bonds out to the outside dealers.

Thus, profits which, but for the interpositioning, would have gone to the broker-dealer or to outside purchasers were diverted through the bank's bond department to companies owned by I, J, and K. These three men also made commissions from the broker-dealer on the orders of bonds the bank placed through them. In a two and one-half year period, I, J, and K made over 180 interpositioned trades and over $268,000 in profits.

When the scheme was discovered in mid-1976, I and the vice president were fired. J and K also left the broker-dealer in mid-1976.[4]

3 | CASE

Speculative Arbitrage

(See Chapter 10 for discussion of this term in relation to the term structure of interest rates.)

P Government Securities, Inc., is an unregistered affiliate of Q, a large registered broker-dealer. P was organized in 1973 to deal exclusively in government securities, and it is, accordingly, exempt from registration with the SEC. Nevertheless, all of P's accounts outside of New York City are serviced by registered representatives of Q. P and Q have established specialized securities transactions for their customers.

In late 1976, R, an account executive specializing in government securities employed by Q, opened and began servicing accounts at P for two medium-sized mid-western cities and a police and fire pension fund of one of the cities. The purpose of the new accounts was to engage in "arbitrage" transactions in United States Treasury securities. R's arbitrage strategy involved borrowing a Treasury Note through P and selling it on the market (the short position). Simultaneously, the proceeds from this sale were used to purchase another Treasury Note of the same denomination with a different maturity date and interest rate (the long position). The only funds that changed hands between P and the customer were wire transfers representing the differences in prices between the two notes.

The arbitrage position was established by selecting securities whose yield to maturity appeared to be out of line with their "normal" historical relationship. A security whose yield appeared to be low was sold short while a security with a current yield higher than its historical yield was purchased for the long position. R expected that the yield of the securities would return the arbitrage—i.e., selling the long position and buying in the short position. Securities with similar maturity dates were usually paired on opposite sides of the arbitrage, creating a partially hedged position. With this arrangement, market factors that caused one security to increase in value would also have an off-setting effect on the other security, resulting in little over-all effect on the account.

On R's recommendation, the cities and the pension fund engaged in arbitrage trading throughout the first half of 1977. None of them had engaged in arbitrage before, however, and they were not fully aware of the risks involved in an arbitrage strategy. The primary risk is that the yield of the securities involved may not move back to their historical relationship. In this event, the customer may recognize a loss on closing out the position. R apparently did not fully disclose this market risk to the cities. In addition, he failed to explain the borrowing charges assessed by P in connection with the arbitrage transactions.

At first, the transactions engaged by the cities and the fund were successful, and they recognized aggregate gains of nearly $170,000 in the first several months. Gradually, however, R began recommending transactions which resulted in larger and larger open positions and wider disparities between the maturity dates involved in the arbitrages. This strategy increased the possibility that a large loss could be realized if the market did not move as predicted. In addition, the transactions were not arbitrages in the same sense the earlier activities were because the partially hedged position which resulted from choosing securities with similar maturities was gone. R also failed to disclose the special risks inherent in this new strategy.

By mid-1977, the two small cities and the pension fund taken together had open positions of well over $300 million. (Between January and September, 1977, R effected 20 arbitrages for the account of each of the cities. He also earned $90,0000 in commissions during this period.) Beginning about that time, the market for Treasury securities failed to move as predicted, and losses resulted in a number of the arbitrages. Since the three entities each had large arbitrage positions, even small market movements caused large paper losses. By June 30, 1977, the three had sustained paper losses of over $670,000.

The cities' fiscal years ended on June 30, 1977, and they wished to close their accounts to recognize any gains. To avoid having to close the account and report losses to the cities, R devised a scheme whereby Q wired funds to each of the cities and the cities wired back approximately equal amounts the next day. R also prepared and mailed fictitious confirmation slips for P showing closing and reopening of the cities' open positions in the arbitrages. The prices shown on the confirmations were not market prices, but prices that would show no gain or loss to the cities. In fact, no transactions had occurred and the accounts remained open. (An investment manager for one of the cities knew it had a potential loss in its open positions and knew the June 30 "trades" were done away from the market. He approved the deal to give R time to remedy the situation.) The actual losses were not discovered until August 1977, during one of P's audits. By this time, further losses had occurred in the accounts.

As a result of R's arbitrage strategy, the accounts of the cities and the pension fund showed net losses of $1,300,000. Q assumed these losses. As a result of the SEC enforcement proceedings against R and Q and judicial settlement of these proceedings, Q instituted new procedures to (1) prevent use of false confirmations, (2) require additional approvals for fund transfers to avoid occurrences such as the June 30 sham transaction, (3) provide for disclosure of borrowing charges, (4) require approval of all arbitrage accounts, and (5) implement a periodic review procedure for P's accounts. R was barred from association with a broker or dealer for five years, and one of Q's supervisors agreed to undergo restraining.[5]

4 | CASE

Excessive Markup and Commissions

From 1976 until late 1977, the portfolio manager of a state university, who was charged with the responsibility of investing university funds in short-term highly liquid government securities, used the university's account to accrue financial benefits totaling approximately $1.3 million for himself and a group of friends and business associates through trading fees generated by transactions in government-guaranteed securities. Despite the university's conservative investment objectives, and without disclosure to the university, the portfolio manager engaged in a highly speculative, leveraged trading program. This program involved the GNMAs on a forward basis as well as when-issued trading of sponsored agency securities. After becoming overextended on these forward commitments the portfolio manager engaged in reverse repurchase agreements to fund delivery of the securities purchased. Through the use of reverse repos, the portfolio manager was able to "pyramid" the university's investments, i.e., borrow money against securities owned to purchase additional securities. This strategy resulted in university commitments exceeding

$250 million at a time when its assets available for investment were only about $60 million. Published accounts have estimated losses to the university of about $17 million.

While the portfolio manager often dealt directly with New York government securities dealers, he placed many of these transactions through broker-dealers owned by friends and associates, or that employed friends and associates. The portfolio manager himself was a part-owner of one such broker-dealer. One of those broker-dealers was registered with the SEC, while two others were not. In such instance the university was the sole, or at least the primary, customer of the broker-dealer or the salesman. These broker-dealers charged the university excessive markups and commissions, and failed to disclose that they were also being compensated, at market rates, by the other party to the trade.

The university has not honored some of its outstanding commitments, resulting in suits for damages totaling approximately $1 million by two broker-dealers. One of the broker-dealers involved in the scheme is currently in receivership.[6]

The assessment of the value of SEC regulation as it applies to disclosure requirements and supervision is controversial. On the negative side, two of the points raised are the following. First, it is very expensive, relative to the amount of capital to be raised, for small firms to comply with SEC disclosure. This relatively high cost may discourage otherwise profitable small firms from existing or raising small amounts of capital for expansion.[7] Second, George Stigler, who compared the five-year performance of new issues before (1923–1928) and after (1949–1955) SEC regulation, found no significant effect on information obtained by investors on new issues.[8] The test was made on the comparison of the issue price (which could be influenced by misinformation about new issues) with the later market price, where it was held that a wide range of investors are less likely to value it incorrectly. Using the same methods, others interpret the results differently; they consider the results favorable to the SEC.[9] George Benston tested the impact of SEC disclosure on stock prices to see if the information was useful and to see if it improved the overall flow of information.[10] Benston concluded from his tests that the evidence

> is not consistent with the assumption that financial data made public are timely or relevant, on the average.[11]

In general, many experts in economics and finance believe that nearly free financial markets will reflect nearly all available information and that the principle of caveat emptor (buyer beware) will cause more accurate information to be revealed than can a government commission on a Form 10-K. Others—economists and those in finance who disagree with the interpretation given by Stigler and Benston; accountants, who have prepared different interpretations of a firm's finances for different purposes; lawyers, who have followed SEC regulatory cases; and lay people, who do not trust the unfamiliar, and that certainly includes corporations and financial markets—all often take a more jaundiced view of voluntary disclosure. The internal pressures in the SEC staff and the policies of the SEC are therefore probably strongly determined by whether or not their chief economist and his or her staff have little or substantial influence and whether or not the members of the commission are trained in economics and finance.

The SEC had approximately 2141 full-time permanent employees in fiscal 1982 and a fiscal 1982 budget authority for $88.56 million.

Other Government Regulators

The *Commodity Futures Trading Commission* (CFTC), established in 1975, is composed of a chairman and four other commissioners. It administers the Commodity Exchange Act of 1936, as amended. The purpose of the CFTC "is to further the economic utility of the futures markets by encouraging their efficiency, assuring their integrity, and protecting their participants against abusive trade practices, fraud, and deceit. The object of commodity futures trading regulation is to enable the markets to serve better their designated functions of providing a price discovery mechanism and a means of offsetting price risk."[12] This language seems to go in the direction of free markets, but its generality leaves the interpretation to the eye of the beholder.

Some of its market surveillance activities, such as approving the specifications of new futures contracts and monitoring of exchange limits on speculative positions, is directed at limiting certain types of market activity. In addition, it conducts research activity, approves applications from individuals and firms, and carries on an enforcement program. The enforcement program is responsible for detecting "market manipulations, cheating and defrauding customers, and abusive trading practices such as fictitious trading, wash trading and pre-arranged trading."[13] It may obtain injunctions in federal courts and it handles investigations and litigation on a referral basis from federal and state agencies.

Commodity options have been illegal since 1978 because of fraud used in selling them. Options on financial assets or futures contracts for them, such as Treasury bonds and bills, are expected to be approved by the CFTC in 1982.

The CFTC had authorization for 550 full-time permanent employees and a $21 million budget in fiscal 1982.

The CFTC and the Federal Reserve Board competed to see which would set margin requirements on some new assets, such as the index funds sold at the Kansas City Exchange. The Federal Reserve sets margin requirements on stocks. The CFTC may win a temporary victory with the index funds, but its jurisdiction is threatened by the growing presence of banks and other financial intermediaries in the futures markets. Many of these financial intermediaries are controlled by the depository intermediaries' regulators discussed in Chapter 17 and by the SEC. The Federal Reserve, with net operating expenses estimated to be

$790.2 million in 1980 and land and equipment worth over $853 million, is much larger and has a much larger staff (approximately 22,000 employees, including 500 economists), is a much larger entity than any of the other regulators.[14] It is doubtful that the CFTC could handle a larger regulatory responsibility without being substantially larger.

As noted in Chapter 17, the Federal Reserve sets margin requirements on stock purchases. It also supervises *transfer agents*, together with the Federal Deposit Insurance Corporation and the Comptroller of the Currency, for the banks they regulate. So does the SEC. A transfer agent is an individual who formally transfers stock between buyers and sellers. These regulators require that transfer agents provide information to them on forms, which were somewhat simplified in 1982.

Squeezes, Corners, Unstable Spot Prices, and Controls

During the Carter administration there was concern about trouble in the futures market. W. Michael Blumenthal, secretary of the Treasury, and G. William Miller, chairman of the Board of Governors, sent the letter shown in Exhibit 24-2 to James M. Stone, chairman of the Commodity Futures Trading Commission. It is important to note the concerns in the attached staff report since they are frequently cited.

In order to corner or squeeze the market in a Treasury security futures contract, a buyer would have to drive up the price of that contract. The Treasury or the Federal Reserve could always step in and supply more of the underlying securities, an action that is unlikely to have much effect on economic activity, especially if the term structure of Treasury debt outstanding is readjusted (by adding and subtracting longer and shorter maturities) to leave the average maturity of the Treasury securities in private hands unaffected. It would be as profitable for a speculator to undertake such a corner as would be an effort to buy up all $10 bills with the intention of selling them later at a premium.

As far as the alleged unstable effects on spot prices, Blumenthal and Miller's concern appeared to be misplaced. They, together with Arthur Burns and Jimmy Carter, were in an administration with a very rapid and erratic money policy amid rising interest rates and falling bond prices. The temporary turnaround in money growth in November 1978, announced by President Carter with Chairman Miller of the not-so-independent Federal Reserve at his side, introduced a period of roller coaster, erratic money growth that continued under the chairmanship of Paul Volcker at the Federal Reserve, at least into 1982 in the Reagan administration. The financial markets were erratic partly in response to this type of erratic monetary policy. Financial futures contracts, which would allow nonfinancial firms, and especially financial institutions, to hedge against the effects of the administration's policies, should not have been stopped on the faulty grounds that the hedges would cause spot prices of financial assets to be erratic. Had these futures contracts

THE SECRETARY OF THE TREASURY
WASHINGTON 20220

May 14, 1979

Dear Commissioner Stone:

In our separate letters dated October 19 and 25, 1978, we expressed concerns over the possible consequences of further rapid expansion in trading of Treasury futures contracts and requested a moratorium on new authorizations of such contracts until our staffs could conduct a thorough study of the markets for Treasury futures. That joint study has now been completed. The Treasury/Federal Reserve recommendations stemming from it are enclosed for your consideration, together with a summary of the study. The full study itself will be separately provided to you.

We appreciate the assistance which you gave us in this effort and your understanding of the important public interest issues involved in futures markets based on U. S. Government securities. We look forward to working with you to assure the appropriate development of these markets.

Sincerely,

W. Michael Blumenthal
Secretary of the Treasury

G. William Miller
Chairman
Board of Governors of the
Federal Reserve System

The Honorable
James M. Stone
Chairman
Commodity Futures Trading
    Commission
2033 K Street, N. W.
Washington, D. C. 20581

Enclosure

Exhibit 24-2

Source: Treasury/Federal Reserve Study of Treasury Futures Market, Summary and Recommendations, Vol. I (May 1979), pp. 11–15.

TREASURY/FEDERAL RESERVE RECOMMENDATIONS

1. *The Impact on Spot Markets*

A basic concern has been that futures trading in Government securities will have a destabilizing effect on prices in the spot market for these securities and that investors on whom the Treasury normally relies to finance its debt may be dissuaded from bidding in Treasury auctions if prices become less stable, thus leading to higher yields or costs to the Treasury. It is important from a policy perspective to distinguish the case in which destabilizing effects might arise even if futures markets are perfectly competitive from the case in which a small group of investors looms large enough in the markets to have a significant impact on prices.

In the perfectly competitive case, the usual argument for a destabilizing influence from futures goes as follows: (1) futures trading encourages speculation by reducing the costs involved; (2) speculators are likely to drive futures prices to levels not justified by market fundamentals; (3) wide price swings in futures markets will be transmitted to spot markets via arbitrage. Whatever the intuitive appeal of such reasoning, empirical studies of both agricultural and financial markets have not been able to prove that there is greater price variability in spot markets during periods in which the good or security in question was traded on a futures market.

A supplementary argument (again, in the competitive case) stresses the danger that, should investors be unable to close out futures positions because prices have already moved the daily limit, they may try to cover their positions with offsetting spot market transactions, thereby imparting additional price variability to the spot market. So far, Treasury bill futures prices have never moved their daily limit. Treasury bond futures have done so on a number of occasions, but market participants indicated in interviews that this appeared to be essentially a response to abruptly changed expectations about cash market prices. They did not believe there was any substantial spillover to the spot market from events originating in the futures market.

Still, a third possible avenue for futures to have a destabilizing effect on spot prices is by drawing funds into the futures market which would otherwise be used in the spot market. The resulting thinness of the spot market could then make spot prices prone to wider swings. However, since securities dealers generally use the futures markets in conjunction with the spot markets, e.g., for hedging or for arbitrage, their activities should not contribute to any such diversion of funds. Moreover, many of the speculative positions taken by individuals in futures markets would probably have never been taken at all in the cash markets, given the costs of carrying the actual securities.

There is a related concern sometimes expressed that financial futures will divert funds from third markets, particularly the stock market. But buying a futures contract, for which securities in one's portfolio may be pledged as initial margin, does not reduce the volume of funds available to underwrite real investments. In sum, under the assumption of perfectly competitive futures markets, fears that futures trading in financial instruments will disrupt the spot markets have not been documented.

These fears cannot be so lightly dismissed once the competitive assumption is relaxed, however. In speaking of possible ways in which prices (futures or spot) could be distorted, no distinction will be made between a "squeeze" and a "corner." According to the CFTC Glossary, a "corner" means controlling enough of a commodity so that its price can be manipulated, while a "squeeze" refers to a situation in which those who are short cannot repurchase their contracts except at a price substantially higher than the value of the contract in relation to the rest of the market. These definitions are inexact and do not necessarily have any legal significance.

The possibility of either a corner or a squeeze in the case of the 3-month bill, for example, arises from the fact that the futures contract can be satisfied only with a single maturity, over which command of the available supply is not beyond the resource of a large securities dealer. The "available" supply may be considerably smaller than the total supply to the extent that a substantial portion of each auction goes to the Federal Reserve and to foreign central banks and other noncompetitive bidders who are not likely to be sensitive to price changes in deciding whether to resell. In some auctions during the last year, the Fed and foreign official accounts absorbed all but about $1 billion of the new 3-month issue.

On, say, a $3 billion issue, an individual dealer could take $750 million and still stay within the Treasury guideline of not allocating more than 25 percent to a single bidder. If, in addition, a dealer also took a sizable long position in the futures market, bought the new 3-month issue on a "when-issued" basis from others bidding or planning to bid in the auction, and had previously acquired a long position in the outstanding deliverable bill (auctioned originally as a 6-month issue), he might well be able to build a long position in the new bill that actually exceeded total auction awards to investors other than the Federal Reserve and foreign official accounts.

Interviews with market participants suggested that dealer positioning strategies of this kind may have succeeded in squeezing the secondary market price on one or two new bill issues during 1978. While market estimates of the resulting distortion in yield in those operations range from 10 to 40 basis points, such judgments cannot be effectively tested, due to the many other special factors that were influencing supply-demand relationships in the cash bill market at the same time. It should be noted, though, that observed spreads among immediately adjacent bill maturities did not widen to these proportions.

The Treasury bond contract differs from the bill contract in that an entire "market-basket" of securities is eligible for delivery. Although the basic trading unit is a bond with a $100,000 face value at maturity and an 8 percent coupon, any Treasury coupon issue can be delivered if it has at least 15 years to maturity (or to first call). The contract's settlement price is adjusted if other than 8 percent coupons are delivered.

Possibilities for the manipulation of Treasury bond prices, through joint action in the cash and bond-futures market, appear to be minimal, given the sizable number of issues deliverable under the current contract. While the market-basket approach thus reduces one major potential problem of financial futures, it also reduces one of the major benefits—that is, the uncertainty created as to which issue will ultimately be delivered makes the contract less useful for hedging. In the case of long-term bonds, this problem may be more hypothetical than real, given the flatness of the yield curve at the long end. However, it may pose a problem for the use of the market-basket approach in the intermediate portion of the maturity spectrum, where some of the proposed new contracts fall.

2. Constraints of Treasury

The central point to emerge from the above section is that, in the face of a relatively small deliverable supply of the security specified in a futures contract, the possibility of corners or squeezes leading to disruptive price movements in the spot market is a real one. The Treasury, in turn, could be hurt in the longer run if investors began to shun the market for its debt because of such factors. While the Treasury has the ability to prevent a squeeze by issuing more of the deliverable security, the Treasury should not be so constrained in its debt management decisions by problems in markets for financial futures.[15]

been more rapidly introduced, depository intermediaries and other lenders would have been able to begin to hedge their new loans against unfavorable interest rate movements. This would have induced greater loan activity and benefited the economy. This type of risk management for liabilities, during a period of rising rates, would have helped lenders make new, relatively capital risk-free loans. However, once rates are perceived to be at a peak, this kind of a hedge is less desirable. Lenders would not want to buy a hedge in the futures market to remove the risk of unfavorable interest rate movements unless they thought rates might go even higher. They would be reducing part of the expected profit from any decline in interest rates.

The public's view of all the esoteric jargon and complications of financial markets is a ready audience for trade books of both the gloom, doom, and collapse variety and the conspiratorial type discussed in Chapter 1. It is also a ready audience for posturing politicians and government officials who want a favorable and flashy headline or television spot. The public's view brings out in politicians and government officials a desire for control of market prices and the allocation of loanable funds.

The desire to control market prices and allocate loanable funds is familiar to anyone who has spent much time in congressional oversight hearings for federal regulators in any financial area. "Let's bring down interest rates by allocating credit to where it is really needed. Let's control prices and interest rates." It is frequently thought that the Federal Reserve could, by lowering its discount rate, directly change domestic interest rates. The Federal Reserve need only pull the handle on its interest rate machine. There is, of course, a relationship between Federal Reserve policy and interest rates, but it is not that simple or direct.

Politicians and regulators often act as if they can change, to a desired value, variables such as interest rates and change the allocation of funds to a vaguely defined alternative, more effectively, more fairly, and more efficiently than in freely functioning markets. There is always some truth to these claims. Beneficiaries of such policies can always be found. The costs are harder to identify and that often makes the policies difficult to assess.

For an example of an argument *in favor* of limits on price movements, consider limits imposed on the price fluctuations of futures contracts on formal exchanges. There have been virtually no major defaults on futures contracts in recent years despite the relatively low cash margin required to buy a contract and the huge volume of contracts. When the margin drops below the specified amount, due to a fall in the price of the contract, the dealer makes a margin call to the contract buyer by the following morning. If the additional margin is not paid, the contract is sold to prevent a default. The existence of limits on price movements gives dealers a safety net, it is argued, by providing time to make a call before the price drops further. Without limits, it is argued, a much larger margin would be needed.

The counterargument for eliminating limits is, first, that if the market does not clear because of a limit, a precipitous price decline may cause there to be no buyers for the dealer to sell the contract to at disequilibrium prices. Second, disequilibrium prices due to limits may give some traders an advantage when trading starts following the hitting of a limit the previous day, since the direction of the price change at the opening may be predicted with some certainty. Third, the market is not efficient if it does not reach equilibrium prices. Therefore, the savings in lower margin requirements may be more than offset by the cost of impairing market efficiency. The benefits from market efficiency are reviewed in Chapter 3. Most individuals who are dealers and those operating private futures exchanges and clearing companies are probably in favor of limits, and so are government regulators (the CFTC), who have approved the specifications of existing futures contracts with limits.

In 1971, the Nixon administration introduced wage and price controls. Arthur Burns, who was then chairman of the Board of Governors, fully supported these wage and price controls and chaired a committee on interest and dividends which was assigned the responsibility (but not specific powers) for holding down interest rates. Monetary policy was allowed to become expansionary, with the notion that the wage and price controls would prevent inflation. Chairman Burns was an active proponent of wage and price controls. The following excerpts are from the official minutes of the Federal Open-Market Committee meetings, which were kept secret for five years. (The minutes are in paraphrased form.)

> Chairman Burns added that he would take second place to no one in the fight against inflation. As the members would recall, he had argued for a wage and price policy long before the Administration had decided to adopt one, and recently he had advocated a reduction in the wage guidelines, provoking displeasure in some quarters. [August 15, 1972, p. 83]
>
> Chairman Burns said he had not planned to comment further until the remaining members had expressed their views on policy. In light of MacLaury's concluding remarks, however, he might say a word at this point about the Committee on Interest and Dividends, which as the members knew was a Government-wide Committee including only one representative from the Federal Reserve Board. A rather strong body of sentiment was developing within that Committee in favor of a public statement admonishing lenders in all categories to act prudently in setting interest rates, and suggesting gently—but still suggesting—that if they failed to do so the Committee would establish guidelines for interest rates. The proposal for such a statement was facing some opposition, but it might be approved. If guidelines were established the result would be a confrontation between the Federal Reserve and the Executive establishment—a prospect that was extremely disturbing. [September 19, 1971, p. 914] [Mr. Bruce K. Maclaury was president of the Minneapolis Federal Reserve Bank.]
>
> Chairman Burns remarked that at present no one could be certain about the future of price and wage controls. In his judgment, however, it was likely that the Administration would request extension of the legislative authority for controls and that the Congress would respond favorably. And while he believed that changes would be made in the specific provisions of the program, they were not likely to be made as early as November 15; such a date would not allow sufficient time for deliberation, since active discussions probably would not get under way until after the elections. Although the character of the changes could not be predicted at present, he expected the program to remain relatively effective. [October 17, 1972, p. 969]

Chairman Burns' advocacy of wage–price guidelines as a way to fight inflation was right on target with the Nixon administration's policies.

Price controls may, at times, be very popular. The support for rent controls in New York City and Washington, D.C., and the favorable treatment by many people in the public sector and in the press to calls for price and credit controls are some evidence of this point. When Ronald Reagan became president in 1981, he said he was committed to deregulation and free markets. But the cries for price controls, credit controls, and other forms of restricting free markets were strong.

Despite the pressures to restrict free financial markets, many new financial market instruments were being approved by the regulators. Part of the impetus may have come from the threat of competition from outside the United States, such as from the offshore exchange scheduled to open in Bermuda in June 1982. Its owners were rumored to be considering options on financial assets. It would be preferable to have new financial assets available in the United States, where remedies for abuses are available through the judicial system and the present regulatory apparatus.

An Experiment in Interconnected Markets

Congress passed the Securities Acts Amendment of 1975, directing the SEC to "facilitate the establishment of a national market system for securities."[15] The Philadelphia Stock Exchange became the first regional exchange to link up with the New York Stock Exchange in 1978 via the *Intermarket Trading System* (ITS).

The Philadelphia Exchange is a regional exchange that, although 192 years old, has been very innovative. It trades options contracts including currency options, and in addition to its multilisted stocks, it has approximately 100 stock listings that do not appear on other exchanges. To be listed a company must have at least $1 million in assets compared to $16 million for the New York Stock Exchange.

By looking up at the ITS monitor, a trader on the floor of the New York Stock Exchange can see the last trade and the local bid and offer prices on other markets. If, for example, the price on the Philadelphia exchange looks better, he or she can communicate with the regional exchange and make an order, a "commitment to trade" to the Philadelphia market, in a matter of seconds. Each commitment is validated by a central computer and assigned an identification number. If a commitment to trade is accepted by a broker or specialist at the Philadelphia Exchange, the system quickly reports an execution back to the New York Exchange.

The Los Angeles floor of the Pacific Stock Exchange was linked to ITS in June 1978. During the summer of 1978, the Boston Stock Exchange, the Midwest Stock Exchange, and the American Stock Exchange were linked to ITS. On February 11, 1981, the Cincinnati Stock Exchange was linked into the system. The SEC proposed that the National Association of Securities Dealers (NASD) also link into the system.

As of November 1980, 750 ITS stocks were listed on the New York Stock Exchange and 124 were listed on the American Stock Exchange. The overall average response time for a commitment to be accepted or canceled at the end of 1980 was 40.8 seconds.

The SEC also adopted Rule 19C-3, which allowed all stocks not traded on an exchange on April 26, 1979, to be listed off the board. This meant that the prohibition against off-board trading by members of the New York Stock Exchange was eliminated for any new listings after April 26, 1979. They could be simultaneously listed on NASDAQ, the computerized over-the-counter market described in Chapter 22. Thus began a consolidated quotation system for some stock on NASDAQ and the New York Stock Exchange.

In addition, NASDAQ began an experiment in executing orders through its computer system for approximately thirty stocks. For other stocks on NASDAQ, execution is by phone. Also, the Chicago Board of Trade and the New York Futures Exchange (a unit of the New York Stock Exchange) agreed in 1981 to an electronic linkage that can be used to integrate the trading of planned stock index futures contracts.

The SEC and the private exchanges are conducting studies to see if these experiments improved the efficiency of the markets.

NOTES

1. Securities Exchange Act of 1934, June 6, 1934 (48 Stat. 881; 15 U.S.C. 78a to 78jj).
2. These cases are taken from *Report of the Joint Treasury-SEC Federal Reserve Study of the Government-Related Securities Markets*, printed for the use of the Committee on Banking, Housing, and Urban Affairs, U.S. Senate (Washington, D.C.: U.S. Government Printing Office, December 1980).
3. Ibid., p. 141.
4. Ibid., pp. 147–148.
5. Ibid., pp. 149–151.
6. Ibid., pp. 151–152.
7. See James R. Barth, Joseph J. Cordes, and Gregory Tassey, *Evaluating the Impact of Securities Regulation on Venture Capital Markets*, U.S. Department of Commerce and National Bureau of Standards (Washington, D.C.: U.S. Government Printing Office, 1980).
8. George Stigler, "Public Regulation of the Securities Market," *Journal of Business* (1964), pp. 117–142.
9. I. Friend and E. Herman, "The SEC Through a Glass Darkly," *Journal of Business* (1964), pp. 382–405.
10. George Benston, "An Appraisal of the Costs and Benefits of Government Required Disclosure: SEC and FTC Requirements," *Law and Contemporary Problems* (Summer 1977), pp. 30–62.
11. Benston, "An Appraisal," p. 130.
12. *Budget of the United States Government, Fiscal Year 1982, Appendix*, Executive Office of the President, Office of Management and Budget, p. I-V 13. The personnel and budget estimates for the SEC and the CFTC are taken from this document and may differ from actual amounts.
13. *Budget of the United States*, p. I-V 14.
14. The cost and asset figures are estimates from the General Accounting Office that went into the Federal Reserve under a relatively new audit authority

(The Federal Banking Agency Audit Act—Public Law 95-320) in one of the first audits, published with the title *Report to the Honorable Henry S. Reuss, House of Representatives of the United States, Response to Questions Bearing on the Feasibility of Closing the Federal Reserve Banks*, U.S. General Accounting Office, The Controller General (May 21, 1981). The estimate was on the cover and p. 9.
15. *A Monitoring Report on the Operations of the Intermarket Trading System*, U.S. Securities and Exchange Commission (February 1981), p. 26.

STUDY QUESTIONS

1. Describe and assess the functions of the SEC and the CFTC.

2. What is a corner or a squeeze in a futures market?

3. What types of regulations of financial markets would be most beneficial to the society?

4. How would you measure in statistical tests the success or failure of the experiments in interconnected stock markets?

5. Are price fluctuation limits necessary in futures markets? Are they necessary in other markets? Explain your answers and why they are different, if they are.

Part VIII

Forecasting

25

State of the Art

Introduction

Forecasting is big business. Many firms specialize in making forecasts. How good are these forecasts? That is difficult to assess. Often they are close to the mark, as measured by the difference between the actual and predicted value of a variable in their forecast. Often, however, *turning points* such as the start of a recession are missed. These turning points may be the most important type of forecast to obtain since they involve major changes in investment plans and the rearrangement of portfolios. Thus, an attempt to look at quarter-to-quarter or year-to-year forecasting records may be a seriously incomplete guide to the reliability and usefulness of forecasts. First, the investor must decide which events would most affect the profitability of his or her investments. Then the forecasting technique or the forecaster who has the best track record for predicting those events should be chosen.

In this and the following chapter, techniques and associated analyses behind statistical forecasting are reviewed. *Judgmental forecasts*, based on the forecaster's general views, are not discussed. No attempt is made to cover all the statistical techniques used in forecasting; only some highlights are discussed.

First, a discussion of predictable and unpredictable events is presented. The first rule of assessing forecasts should be to ignore forecasts that exceed the limits of existing knowledge, unless the forecast itself induces a reaction.

453

Then conditional and unconditional forecasts are discussed. The point is made that all forecasts are based on a number of conditions. A consumption forecast example is presented showing that the forecast depends on both the hypothesis about consumption and the forecast of variables on which consumption depends.

A discussion of confused criticism of forecasting economic and financial variables is presented. The discussion then reviews the dramatic claims that were made and the widespread use of regression analysis as statistical capabilities developed after World War II. This is followed by a description of the forecasting ability of big models. Finally, a short section on new time-series methods is presented. The following chapter on money and its relation to stock prices develops the material introduced in this section.

Predictable and Unpredictable Events

If an individual knew the future for certain, he or she could rapidly become a billionaire. The financial markets offer a vehicle for rapidly rewarding such knowledge. If all individuals knew the future, there would be no need for financial markets. As indicated in Chapter 2, a central computer could clear the balances in the current period for all future transactions. The primary function performed by financial markets would not be needed. That function is to allocate claims to wealth to the place where individuals and firms can earn the highest rate of return (or, in view of the analysis in Chapter 13, to the place where the maximum present value can be achieved at market rates of interest).

Such perfect knowledge of the future is, of course, unattainable. Financial markets adjust to what is known about the future. New information is information that cannot be predicted on the basis of what was previously known. The prices of financial assets in efficient markets immediately discount new information. Thus prices are a forecasting summary based on what market participants (potential and active traders) believe is most likely. For example, insofar as the assumption of efficient markets holds, the forecasts of long and short interest rates, wholesale prices, and stock averages are recorded in the futures markets discussed in Chapter 22.

Many economic and financial events cannot be predicted with available knowledge. This inability to predict is not necessarily a failure of statistical testing procedure or of theoretical developments in economics or finance. For example, the onset of many general business contractions is a random event. Many recessions depend on random or nearly random events such as bad weather or a war that induces oil boycotts. Both of these events occurred prior to the 1975 business cycle contraction in the United States. The inability to forecast these events could be said to reflect on meteorology and political science (including the theories of government response studied in economics) at least as much as economic and financial analysis.

The failure to forecast the events that precipitate recessions is an important failure because knowledge of future turning points (the troughs and peaks of business activity) would be very profitable for firms and individuals. Because a string of lucky guesses will make a forecaster famous, many individuals attempt such forecasts. The kind of information needed for some of these forecasts is not yet known. If it were known, many business cycle contractions would be altered or ameliorated because the information would be rapidly discounted into market prices; investment decisions would be rapidly adjusted, inventories would be adjusted; and governments would respond, for better or worse, with policies.

If, for example, widespread bad weather affecting world food output is likely to occur one year from now, future market prices would immediately rise. It would be profitable to store food and purchase a futures contract to sell it at a higher price during the forthcoming period of reduced output. This kind of meteorological forecast—with the requisite concentrated probability distribution—is not normally available. This failure to forecast bad weather and a reduction in output one year in advance does not mean that finance and economics has little useful analysis.

Few critics would judge medical science to be useless because medical doctors cannot predict the date of an illness, or an epidemic, a year, a week, or a day in advance of its diagnosis. Medical science may have a remedy that produces predictable results once the illness strikes. This type of predictable outcome as a response to a random event is also often true for economic or financial analysis. Once the initial conditions of a business recession are known, the fields of finance and economics have a great deal to say about policies for producing a recovery. These fields of knowledge can also, like medical science, prescribe policies that will reduce the frequency and severity of disturbances caused by unpredictable events.

Conditional and Unconditional Forecasts

Economic and financial forecasting can be considered to be dependent on given *conditions*. For example, *new* favorable information about a stock will rapidly be discounted into its price, given efficient markets. The usefulness of the efficient market hypothesis—its robustness—depends on the likelihood of this price response under many institutional settings. This event and reaction—new favorable information and a stock price increase—should occur in 1912 just as it will in the future year 2002, under entirely different institutional conditions. The forecast of a rapid price rise following such new information must be made conditional on the existence of an efficient market (which assumes that the stock price is initially in equilibrium and the other conditions listed in Chapter 3 apply); and that the information is truly favorable (indicating an increase in the future net income of the firm) and new (it was not previously known to insiders in a position to take effective action). In addition, the subjective rate of discount cannot be rising so fast as to offset the present value of the good news. If the stock market is rising, the good news would take the form of an increase in the rate of rise of the price of the stock. If those conditions are likely to hold in many time periods, the efficient market hypothesis is said to be robust in the face of many institutional settings.

Thus a forecast based on a hypothesis from economics or finance is dependent on given *conditions*. A *conditional forecast* is defined to be a forecast subject to *specified* conditions. In an *unconditional forecast*, no explicit conditions are stated. Nevertheless, an unconditional forecast does rely on a number of unspecified, important, closely related conditions.

An unconditional forecast may simply state that the price level will continue to grow at its trend rate of growth. This forecast of the price level is an example of a *naive model*.

$$X_{t+1} = X_t \tag{1}$$

where X can be a level or, in the example of the price level, a rate of change, and t and $t + 1$ are successive time periods. This forecast attempts to capture the secular (long-run) forces, if any, that have affected the variable in the same way over a long period. The forecast assumes that a large number of plausible events that are known to change the trend rate of growth of the price level—such as prolonged bad weather that will ruin the food crop, a war, and revised data that show the trend rate of growth had previously changed—will not occur.

The real meaning of *unconditional* forecasts is that the conditions on which the forecast relies are not explicitly quantified and taken into account in computing the forecast.

A conditional forecast in economics and finance usually has a number of explicitly specified conditions stated in mathematical form. Some of the conditions are depicted as values for *parameters* in an economic model. For example, the following equation is a simple *hypothesis* about consumption behavior:

$$C_{T+1}^D = C_0 + bY_{D,T} \tag{2}$$

where C_{T+1}^D is real consumption demanded in the following period and $Y_{D,T}$ is real disposable income in the current period. The parameters of this hypothesis about private consumption behavior are C_0 and b (sometimes called the *marginal propensity to consume*). The variable C_{T+1}^D is called a *dependent variable* because it depends on $Y_{D,T}$, the *independent variable* in this equation.

Suppose that C_0 is \$10 million and b_0 is .9. Then, if real disposable income is \$2 trillion, the hypothesis alleges that real consumption in the next period will be \$1.81 trillion. Tests of Equation (1) made to estimate the parameters from historical data may indicate that confidence intervals of 95 percent can be placed on the probability of this hypothesis coming within a given tolerance range of the *point estimate* (a single value) given by Equation (2). In other words, in repeated trials, 95 percent of the time real consumption is expected to be within a band of plus or minus a given percent of the point estimate given by the hypothesis depicted in Equation (1).

So what is the nature of conditional forecasting in economics and finance? In addition to the parameters, the value of the dependent variables depends on the independent variables. A forecast of real consumption more than one period in advance, using Equation (2), depends on the estimates of the independent variables as well as the parameters of the hypothesis.

Since the values of these independent variables usually are not known far in advance, the validity of forecasts *deteriorates* the further in the future the forecasts are calculated, even if the parameters do not change from their estimated values.[1] This deterioration does not mean that the underlying economic and financial hypotheses are wrong. A vast amount of research using rigorous statistical testing procedures has supported a great variety of useful robust hypotheses. It does mean that a general model of the universe, with distant predictions of such variables as the dates and details of future rainfall and wars, is not yet available. Such a model is needed to predict accurately, far in advance, such economic variables as consumption and unemployment.

Confused Criticism

Newspaper and television journalists have tended to heap scorn on financial and economic analysis for not being able to predict the future. Unlike medical science, which is not berated for its inability to predict the onset of a disease in advance, the inability to forecast future government policy, bad weather, or an oil boycott is taken as evidence that economic and financial analysis is wrong. However, in response, it could be said that once these events do occur, economics and finance have many hypotheses that can render useful predictions of events that will ensue and government policies that can ameliorate problems caused by the new conditions.

Of course, the willingness to make unconditional forecasts far beyond the realm of what is known is likely to generate media attention and a very prosperous consulting business. This kind of forecasting can debase the more serious hypothesis testing, with its rigorously stated conditions.

Poorly specified forecasts often follow the rule of perfect forecasting.

> Describe a future event or a date, but never both. For example, specify that the Dow Jones industrial stock index will double in value. Or specify that something will happen in June of 1990. Never combine both statements into a refutable hypothesis.

Criticism sometimes takes the form that forecasting is faulty because of the poor state of the world that could have been altered by previous government policies if forecasts had been accurate. These criticisms can be an especially confused assessment because they mix in many different issues beyond the realm of forecasting. Consider, for example, the following assessment:

> Because of past failures to foresee or acknowledge trends, many of the problems now facing the United States seem worse than they might otherwise have been. The energy crises emerged as a result of unanticipated shortages of fuels and inadequate recognition of the implications of the continually growing demand for energy. City streets are clogged with too many cars. Colleges that suffered from overcrowding in the late 1960s, and expanded reactively, face bankruptcy in the present era of dwindling enrollments and economic downturn. Air and water pollution persist because of the failure to take remedial and preventative action years ago. Some of the anticipated "solutions" to these problems—electric cars, unlimited and clean nuclear energy, automated teaching machines—have failed to materialize, and indeed may have hindered problem-solving by holding out false hopes of easy solutions. All the technological sophistication of our public and private sectors has not produced an enviable record of forecasting future problems and events.[2]

So begins William Ascher in his recent book, *Forecasting, An Appraisal for Policy-Makers and Planners.*

First, it must be pointed out that the state of the world may have little to do with forecasting accuracy. One may accurately predict the effect of a hydrogen bomb attack without preventing such an attack.

Second, many of the present world conditions Ascher described may well be the result of, or have been intensified by, government actions, such as price controls on oil and gas. This point is well established in conventional price theory.

Third, the advice to U.S. policymakers has often been widely different from views generally held by professionals in economics and finance. Advisers in the federal government sometimes adapt their advice to fit the ideas of members of Congress or the administration. The public can be led for considerable time by these newsmakers, even if their ideas are not consistent with what is known. Paid advisers are sometimes retained for their ability to support these ideas and sympathetic witnesses at congressional hearings are sought as a "balance" for any other views.[3]

Fourth, in many of the areas Ascher cites, the private sector and private markets responded well with accurate forecasts. They responded to price controls and government subsidies exactly as conventional theory would predict. The failure of many early forecasts to foresee future shortages of energy may well have been due in large part to incorrectly specifying (or ignoring) the effects of price controls on the demand and supply of energy sources.

Ascher stresses the importance and slow implementation of "core assumptions" in forecasting.[4] However, in most currently used forecasting models, assumptions are rapidly updated. There is little "assumption drag" here.[5] Nor can it be said that most of the work in finance and economics in the period since World War II has been devoted to developing new forecasting techniques rather than developing better hypotheses. Much of the work has been devoted to building testable hypotheses that are essential parts of conditional forecasting.

Just as one can point to the confused criticism that is often directed at forecasting, one can also find fault in the exaggerated claims of some economists caught in the dramatic increase in statistical testing capabilities that followed World War II. This subject is discussed next.

Post-World War II Euphoria

Two developments occurred in the 1940s and 1950s that dramatically changed the capabilities for statistical testing from the horse-and-buggy era into the nuclear age. First, beginning in the 1950s, large high-speed computers were widely introduced. They were capable of performing the immense amount of calculations needed for many statistical procedures at the speed of electricity. Large high-speed computer facilities were introduced in businesses, colleges, universities, and government agencies. Second, beginning in 1940 with the U.S. labor market survey, economic data began to be collected in government surveys, at regular, uniform intervals of times.

These two developments led the way to a growth industry in statistical testing that produced an avalanche of academic and private statistical studies. The economic and finance journals became filled with descriptions of methods and the results of statistical tests of hypotheses. The training for an advanced degree in finance or economics contained large amounts of statistics (or econometrics, which is economic statistics) as well as the mathematics necessary to put a hypothesis in rigorous form. The old complaint that "It might be all right in theory, but it's no good in practice" appeared to be a nonsequitur for the methodology being used. If it did not test well—if it was not supported in practice—the theory was no good.

One of the most widely used statistical techniques was regression fitting. Equations of the following type were fitted to data:

$$y = b_0 + b_1 x_1 + b_2 x_2 + e \tag{3}$$

where y is the dependent variable, b_0 is a constant that is estimated from the data, and the x's are independent variables, each with its own coefficient to be estimated from the data. The variable e is the error term.

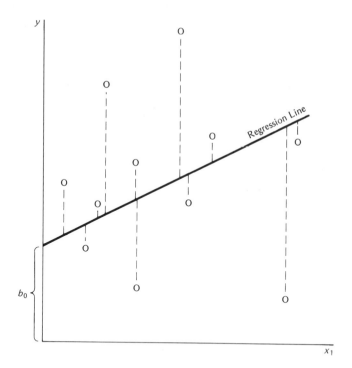

Figure 25-1

Regression line fitted to observations.

A simple regression line with only one dependent variable is shown in Figure 25-1. The O's are observations. The regression line is drawn so as to minimize the squared deviations of the observations, shown by the dashed lines, from the regression line. The variance of the dependent variable explained by the independent variable (or variables) compared to the total variance of the dependent variable is called the multiple correlation coefficient, R^2.

$$R^2 = \frac{\text{variance explained by regression equation}}{\text{total variance of dependent variable}} = \frac{\Sigma\,(Y - \bar{Y})^2 - \Sigma e^2}{\Sigma\,(Y - \bar{Y})^2}$$

(4)

where $\Sigma\,(Y - \bar{Y})^2$ is the variation in the dependent variable and $\Sigma\,e^2$ is the variation in the error term. An R^2 of .05 means that 5 percent of the variance in the dependent variable is explained by the independent variables.

Like a fairy tale come true, regression programs on all manner of economic and financial relationships produced high (more precisely, nearly perfect) multiple correlation coefficients. Some of the studies cited in the next chapter found that stock prices could almost perfectly be predicted with the prior values of one or two variables. If an R^2 was less than about .6, it was an embarrassment.[6] New independent variables would be added to turn out a "respectable" R^2.

The euphoric mood of this "age of certainty" was elegantly stated by George Stigler in his presidential address to the American Economic Association on December 29, 1964:

> The age of Quantification is now full upon us. We are now armed with a bulging arsenal of techniques of quantitative analysis, and of a power—as compared to untrained common sense—comparable to the displacement of archers by cannon. . . . It is a scientific revolution of the very first magnitude—indeed I consider the so-called theoretical revolutions of a Ricardo, a Jevons, or a Keynes to have been minor revisions comparable to the vast implications of the growing insistence upon quantification. I am convinced that economics is finally at the threshold of its golden age—nay, we already have one foot through the door.[7]

Something was wrong. The relationships in the world are not as simple or as obvious as to be so precisely explained. Several important developments changed the methodology and the assessment of statistical methods. First, new statistical techniques provided a more efficient and statistically superior way to solve large models. Large forecasting models became widely used. Second, beginning with the testing of stock prices, a new (for economics and finance) statistical methodology was introduced to test time series. This methodology highlighted the serious flaws in the earlier regression analysis. These developments are discussed in the next two sections.

Big Models

Although a large 24-equation model was developed in 1936 by Jan Tinbergen, the major development came in the post-World War II period. The early large model builders and the date of publication of their model in this period included Nobel Laureate Lawrence Klein (1950), Klein and Arthur Goldberger (1955), and the Brookings Institution model published in a monograph edited by James Duesenberry, Gary Fromm, Klein, and Edwin Kuh (1965).[8] From this beginning, large models became major vehicles for forecasting financial and economic variables. They were developed by private businesses, often closely associated with banks or universities. They sold their services throughout the United States to many businesses and government agencies. These firms grew rapidly until they became valued at many million of dollars. Almost daily coverage of their forecasts are provided in newspapers, national magazines, and television news programs.

An example of their usefulness is their applicability to estimating the costs of federal legislation. Under the new U.S. congressional budgetary process, all proposed laws of the U.S. Congress must be contain an estimate of their future cost. The estimated costs of all laws passed should not exceed the previously agreed spending resolution. This can be a complicated matter for proposed laws that are not direct spending authorizations. Consider the Monetary Control Act of 1980, which authorized lower reserve requirements on member banks of the Federal Reserve and, for the first time, imposed reserve requirements on all other depository institutions. The cost to the government included such items as future changes in corporate and personal income taxes that would be a result of these reserve requirement changes. Computer terminals at the Congressional Budget Office (CBO) plugged into one of the large models owned by private firms can rapidly obtain estimates of various variables in the years ahead that would facilitate such cost estimates. One problem that Congress has not addressed in its attempt to make the budget process precise is the precision of the forecasts on which these estimates are based.

When the problem of previous large forecasting errors was raised at a briefing by a large model company at CBO in 1980, the response from both CBO officials and personnel from the firm was not edifying. It must be concluded that the *convenience* of readily available forecasts was a major criterion. This is not completely unjustified if, for example, forecasts in the form of point estimates on macroeconomic variables up to 1993 (when the reserve requirements are to be fully phased in) are required immediately.

What is the economic rationale for large models? The answer to this question requires some general discussion of the techniques of statistical estimations used for large models. First, a brief description of large models is presented.

Large models combine many behavioral equations, such as Equation (2), and equilibrium relations, such as the equality between saving and investment. The large models contain relations in the form of equations. There are two kinds of variables. *Exogenous variables* take their value from information outside the model. [The size of the work force, F, specified subsequently in Equation (6), is an exogenous variable.] *Variables*, such as consumption and disposable income, are *endogenous* variables in a large model, if they are determined inside the model. The coefficients C_0 and b in Equation (2) are called *parameters*.

The major rationale for large models is that because the economy contains many important interconnected relationships, it is thought that consideration of these relationships jointly will yield superior forecasts of endogenous variables. The models will forecast the effects of changes in the exogenous variables on the endogenous variables. The more variables it can forecast in advance, the fewer exogenous variables are needed in the future. More weight is put on the model and less on other means of forecasting these variables. The initial values of the exogenous variables, from which future forecasts of endogenous variables are cranked out, are called *initial conditions*.

The principle of joint estimation of endogenous variables is only part of the rationale for forecasts that are jointly derived from a number of relations. The parameters, such as b in Equation (2), also need to be estimated jointly. If each equation in a model is independently estimated to obtain values for the parameters, as previously shown for Equation (3), the large models would merely be collections of single-equation estimates. They would lose their property of being a simultaneously estimated system that attempts to incorporate the major interactions of the variables in the economy in the estimation process. The estimates of the parameters could then be seriously flawed.

To understand this possible flaw in statistical estimates of one equation at a time, sometimes called *simultaneous-equation bias*, again consider Equation (2).[9] Real consumption demand is depicted as the dependent variable that depends on the value of disposable income, the independent variable, in the previous period. Suppose that the supply of consumption goods, C_{T+1}^S, is thought to depend on the size of the work force, F_T, and on disposable income, $Y_{D,T}$:

$$C_{T+1}^S = d_0 + d_1 F_T + d_2 Y_{D,T} \tag{5}$$

where d_0, d_1, and d_2 are parameters to be estimated. In equilibrium, the demand and supply of consumption are equal. Therefore, Equation (5) can be combined with Equation (2) to obtain what is called *reduced-form equations*. One reduced-form equation for the consumption equations takes the following general form after $Y_{D,T}$ is eliminated by substitution:

$$C_{T+1} = \pi_1 + \pi_2 F \tag{6}$$

where π_1 and π_2 are coefficients (parameters of the model) that are to be estimated.[10] The messy substitutions are left for Note 10, because the essential point to be shown is a simple, uncluttered one. Knowing the value of π_1 or π_2 will not allow the marginal propensity to consume, b in Equation (2), to be uniquely determined. There are multiple values of b that will be consistent with these estimated values of π_1 and π_2. This is a problem in many large models that try to estimate a simultaneous system of equations where the independent variables of single-equation estimation, such as $Y_{D,T}$, are endogenous, depending in part on the equilibrium values of the exogenous variables. The invention of two-stage least-squares estimation in the 1950s provided a way to obtain unique estimates of the parameters in an overdetermined model.[11] In the first stage the relations between the independent variables of each equation [such as $Y_{D,T}$ in Equations (2) and (5), and F] are estimated. That part of the independent variables that are unrelated (the independent variables purged of their dependent relationships) is reinserted into each equation for the second stage of the estimation process. All parameters in all equations are estimated in the second stage. There is the possibility that single-equation estimation would produce better results if sufficiently serious simultaneous-equation bias is not present. In that case, two-stage least-squares estimation can impair the estimates of the dependent variables.

The two-stage least-squares invention allowed models to grow to immense size. If the results produced did not seem sensible, or if a new relationship—say one more explanation of housing prices—looked informative, another relationship could be added. As new kinds of data became available, new initial conditions could be added.

The resulting large models could not be completely solved mathematically. That is, there was no direct way of asking how a 2 percent increase in the money supply would affect stock prices, holding other effects constant. (In mathematical terms, this deficiency could be said to be the inability to calculate a partial derivative.) Yet most hypotheses in economics and finance are couched in terms of these more simplistic relationships. Putting them all together in an overdetermined model with 100 factorial interrelations of variables, for example, makes a stew in which the effects of changes in a particular ingredient are difficult to determine.

The reader may wish to review Stephen K. McNees' assessment of the performance of a number of large models of the U.S. economy during the recession of 1975.[12] A major problem in judging these models' forecasting ability is that they continually update all initial conditions and parameter estimates. They justifiably try to base their forecasting on all available information. Thus the conditions for the forecasts continually change. There is the danger that they only forecast points along a trend and can not be used to predict turning points in the business cycle with any more precision than can be obtained from merely basing an estimate on the past history (its prior values) of a variable.

This is the point made by Charles Nelson.[13] An estimate procedure for fourteen variables by new time-series methods (called ARIMA) was used by Nelson to make forecasts. These forecasts were compared with those of the Federal Reserve Board–MIT–Pennsylvania (FMP) 171-equation model. Nelson finds:

> The results described suggest that the simple ARIMA models are relatively more robust with respect to postsample predictions then the complex FMP model is. . . . Thus, if mean square error (the average of squared differences between the forecast and actual values of variables) were an appropriate measure of loss, an unweighted assessment clearly indicates that a decision maker would have been best off relying simply on ARIMA predictions in the postsample period.[14]

Despite this finding, all would agree that a large model that correctly specified all relationships would be optimum. The controversy is not over the desirability of finding such a model. It is whether or not large models (1) replicate generally accepted economic hypotheses, and (2) produce better forecasts than either smaller models including single-equation models or other forecasting techniques. Alternative forecasting techniques are more efficient since they require data on fewer variables. For example, some monetarists predict inflation two years in the future primarily with a single variable, M, and a trend rate of change of the velocity of money. They claim that their predictions of inflation are at least as good as those of the large models, most of which underestimated inflation in 1980 despite previous rapid increases in the money supply. However, there are many other important variables in large models for which no small-model forecasts are available.

New Time-Series Methods

Work on the testing of stock prices in the 1960s and 1970s introduced new statistical techniques. (The techniques were new to economics and finance, but not to other fields, such as engineering.) An explanation of the reason for these techniques and tests of money and stock prices that use these techniques in a simplified form are discussed in the next chapter. These techniques were developed because it was found that trends and cycles, also called *periodicities*, in the data flawed much of the simple regression analysis that characterized the bulk of statistical testing through much of the post-World War II period. As explained in the next chapter, rising trends in many economic and financial data, as well as their similar movement (periodicities) over business cycles, has tended to bias regression tests of time series to show more and stronger relationships between these variables than actually exists. To remove these trends and periodicities, the new statistical techniques require many observations; that is, they need large samples. In view of these problems, one researcher assessed regression tests that show a rough relationship between money growth and rates of change of the U.S. price level in the following two years by noting that these test results may be the best information available. He went on to say:

> Shorter observations periods—going to quarterly data or weekly data—or larger models—adding a hundred more equations—will probably fail to eliminate the underlying problem. The underlying problem is that we only have a short period of data, which is marked by strong trends and periodicities. Furthermore, it is unreasonable to assume that individuals can make complete adjustments to economic changes in short periods of time. As the data intervals are reduced to periods smaller than a year, all kinds of inexplicable noise is picked up. Sophisticated filtering techniques may yet produce substantial results from these entrails; but they are more likely to turn up mostly precise information about economically insignificant phenomena.
>
> George Stigler was right in only one respect when he said that he was "convinced that economics is finally at the threshold of its golden age—nay, we already have one foot through the door." He was right in recognizing that we have sophisticated statistical techniques. He was wrong in assuming that we have enough observations available to obtain a wide enough view of the processes we are describing to be able to say that they are not time dependent. In less than one hundred more annual observations, we should be able to lift the other foot across the threshold, unless, of course, the trends and periodicities are longer than can be seen from the data point on which we now stand.[15]

This assessment and the promise of new times-series methods must be weighed against the claims of large modelers, who believe that they can produce reliable forecasts.

Modern time-series methods attempt to remove or take into account the past history of a variable in a time series. Correlations of changes in a variable with previous changes in the same variable are called *auto-*

correlations. These can be estimated by fitting a regression where the dependent variable is the value of a variable in time T and the independent variables are the values of the variable in $T - i$, where i equals 1 to as much as 60. (Normally, the variables are transformed into natural log form, as this produces better results.) The regression is called an *autoregression*. The error term in this regression, if all goes well, is equal to the changes in the variable free of autocorrelations.

The errors can be tested for this property. One way to make such a test is to run an *autospectrum*, which results in a line chart showing high points for cycles and trends. It is based on underlying autocorrelations. If none is found, the variable is said to be cleansed of its past history and is called the *innovation* of the variable.

The coefficients in the autoregression, called a *filter*, can be applied to data on the variable to take out its cycles and trends. The filter can also be used to estimate the future trend and cycle part of the variable. The values of the coefficients measure, on average, the size of periodic movement and trends in a series from its past history.

The innovations in two variables can be searched for a statistical relationship by running them through a *cross-spectrum* test. This test results in a line chart that shows if any of the cycles in the two variables are related. The measure of a relationship here is called a *coherence*.

Cross spectrums and autospectrums are extremely sensative devices for picking up relationships. They can search back and forth through time looking for minute associations of the cycles in two variables or, in the case of an autosprectrum, the autocorrelations in one variable. Unlike a single regression equation that tests for a single direction of causality from the independent to the dependent variable and only tests one relationship in time (the time domain), spectral analysis searches both directions of causation for any relationships between cycles (also expressed as frequencies) of all different lengths (the frequency domain).

The term ARIMA stands for *autoregressive integrated moving average*. The ARIMA process uses the coefficients in an autoregression to form a more compact filter that is a simplified (moving average) representation of the coefficients. The ARIMA representation of the cycles and trends in a variable can be used to estimate the expected future values of that variable.

NOTES

1. The common trait of rapid deterioration of forecasts with more distant horizons is shown by Stephen K. McNees, "An Evaluation of Economic Forecasts," *New England Economic Review*, Federal Reserve Bank of Boston (November–December 1975), pp. 3–39.
2. William Ascher, *Forecasting, An Appraisal for Policy-Makers and Planners* (Baltimore: The John Hopkins University Press, 1978), p. XI.
3. See Robert D. Auerbach, "A Convergence of Views," *The Federal Reserve Authorities and Their Public Responsibility, A Symposium* (Rochester, N.Y.: Center for Research in Government Policy and Business, Graduate School of Management, University of Rochester, 1980), pp. 5–33.

4. Ascher, *Forecasting*, pp. 201–202.

5. Ibid., pp. 202–203.

6. See Auerbach, "A Convergence," for examples of regressions with .99 R_2's

7. George Stigler, Presidential Address of December 29, 1964, *The American Economic Review* (May 1965), pp. 16–17.

8. The 1936 Tinbergen model of the Dutch economy was translated into English and published in J. Tinbergen, *Selected Papers*, L. H. Klaassen, L. M. Koyck, and J. H. Witteveen, eds. (Amsterdam: North-Holland Publishing Company, 1959), pp. 37–84. Other large models mentioned are found in L. Klein, *Economic Fluctuations in the United States 1921–1941* (New York: John Wiley & Sons, Inc., 1950); Klein and A. Goldberger, *An Econometric Model of the United States 1929–1952* (Amsterdam: North-Holland Publishing Company, 1955); and the *Brookings Quarterly Model of the United States*, J. Duesenberry, G. Fromm, L. Klein, and E. Kuh, eds. (Chicago: Rand McNally and Company/ Amsterdam: North-Holland Publishing Company, 1965).

9. Simultaneous-equation bias causes the independent variable to be correlated with the error term. When disposable income in Equation (2) takes a high value, the estimate of consumption may have a corresponding large error, for example. This impairs the validity of the estimate.

10. The disposable income variable $Y_{D,T}$ is an endogenous variable that is considered to be affected by future estimates of consumption and, in a wider model, by a number of interconnecting relationships. This assumption is made only to show the effect of simultaneous-equation bias with the equations in this chapter. No economic principle is being expounded. Solving Equations (2) and (5) for $Y_{D,T}$, the following equations are obtained in terms of equilibrium consumption:

$$Y_{D,T} = \frac{C_{T+1} - C_0}{b} \tag{7}$$

and

$$Y_{D,T} = \frac{C_{T+1} - (d_0 + d_1 F)}{d_2} \tag{8}$$

Setting Equation (7) equal to Equation (8) and solving for C_{T+1} produces

$$C_{T+1} = \frac{bd_0 + d_2 C_0}{b - d_2} + \frac{b}{b - d_2} F \tag{9}$$

Then

$$\pi_1 = \frac{bd_0 + d_2 C_0}{b - d_2} \quad \text{and} \quad \pi_2 = \frac{b}{b - d_2}$$

11. A two-stage least-squares estimation was developed by Henri Theil, "Repeated Least Squares Applied to Complete Equation Systems" and "Estimation and Simultaneous Correlations in Complete Equation Systems," both mimeographed papers produced in 1953 at the Central Planning Bureau in The Hague; and independently by R. L. Basmann, "A Generalized Classical Method of Linear Estimation of Coefficients in a Structural Equation," *Econometrica* (1957), pp. 77–83. Theil and Arnold Zellner developed a related methodology called *three-stage least squares*, which also takes into account the relationships between the error terms: "Three-Stage Least Squares: Simultaneous Estimation of Simultaneous Relations," *Econometrica* (1962), pp. 54–78.

12. McNees, "An Evaluation," pp. 3–39.
13. Charles R. Nelson, *Applied Time Series Analysis* (San Francisco: Holden-Day, Inc., 1973), p. 219.
14. Ibid.
15. Auerbach, "A Convergence," p. 28. An excellent discussion of much of the controversy surrounding the new time-series methods is found in *New Methods in Business Cycle Research: Proceedings from a Conference*, November 13–14, 1975, Federal Reserve Bank of Minneapolis Conference, Christopher Sims, ed. (October 1977).

STUDY QUESTIONS

1. What is the difference between a conditional forecast and an unconditional forecast?

2. Discuss the contention that statistics is in its golden age.

3. How should forecasting be judged?

4. What is the rationale for large models?

5. What can be wrong with single-equation estimation?

6. What is a parameter?

7. What is an exogenous variable?

8. What are dependent and independent variables?

9. Why do forecasts deteriorate?

26

Money and Stock Prices

Introduction

It is frequently argued that movements in aggregate indices of common stock prices can be predicted from prior changes in the money supply.[1] This belief has been supported by a number of statistical studies that appeared during the 1960s and early 1970s. Those studies purported to show that changes in the quantity of money have a strong influence on movements in future stock prices. More recent evidence, as well as the work done on the efficient market hypothesis, raises doubts regarding the accuracy of this simplistic linkage between money and future stock prices.

This chapter explores the relationship between money and stock prices. The next section briefly reviews and comments on some of the earlier studies that have dealt with this relationship. The following section offers evidence on the relationship in an attempt to correct some of the deficiencies of earlier studies. The results presented there indicate that, although money is statistically related to stock prices, the relationship is much weaker than claimed in some earlier studies. Also, and perhaps more important, changes in stock prices are found to be statistically related to both current and future changes in the money supply but not to past changes in money. Thus the common belief that stock prices can be simply predicted by prior changes in the money supply would appear to be unfounded.

Problems in Relating Money to Stock Prices

Early studies and much commonsense wisdom on and off Wall Street viewed an increase in the money supply as a stimulant to future stock price changes. After all, an increase in the money supply can be expected to stimulate spending and, eventually, the demand for stocks. This will drive up the prices of stocks at some point in the future.

In an influential book, *Money and Stock Prices*, Beryl Sprinkel compared the level of an "index of stock prices" with a moving average of "rates of changes in the money supply."[2] He then compared selected turning points in each of these two series with turning points in the business cycle. By visual examination of the data, he observed that changes in both money and stock prices led business cycle turning points. He also observed that changes in money had a longer lead time before business cycle turning points than before stock price changes. Hence money supply changes appeared to lead stock price changes. From these observations, Sprinkel concluded:

> the average lead of changes in monetary growth prior to the business cycle peak is about 19 months compared to a 4-month average lead of stock prices. Changes in monetary growth lead cyclical upturns by an average period of about 7 months, whereas stock price upturns occur about 5 months prior to business upturns on average. Therefore, changes in monetary growth lead changes in stock prices by an average of about 15 months prior to a bear market and by about 2 months prior to bull markets.[3]

There are three fundamental problems with Sprinkel's technique for relating money to stock prices and the business cycle. First, there is the problem of determining which movements in the time series of data on money and stock prices are significant turning points. Visual inspection of the data, as Sprinkel has used, is less exact than other statistical techniques. Some idea of this problem can be seen in the series of stock yields presented in Figure 26-2.

The second problem concerns the determination of whether it is money or stock prices that change first. It is not clear, as evidence presented here shows, that money supply changes always precede related stock price changes.

The third problem pertains to the use of averages, which raises the following question: Are the average time lags found between the change in one variable and the change in the second variable stable time lags? Stability means that over repeated episodes these lags will approach the same average time period.

As a matter of arithmetic, it is always possible to compute an average time lag between turning points in two series that do not have synchronous turning points. This is displayed in Figure 26-1, where, by judicious labeling of turning points in two hypothetical series, one can show that running faster in Idaho can make it rain in Brazil. However, it is not the existence of such a lag between turning points in two series, but

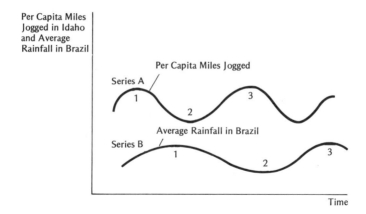

Per Capita Miles Jogged in Idaho and Average Rainfall in Brazil

Per Capita Miles Jogged

Series A

1   2   3

Average Rainfall in Brazil

Series B

1   2   3

Time

Figure 26-1

Hypothetical series on per capita miles jogged in Idaho and average rainfall in Brazil with turning points labeled to show association.

rather the stability of the lag, that supports the view that the two series are related.

In view of these problems, subsequent researchers have sought to employ other statistical techniques to examine the relation between money and stock prices. These studies used the standard present value approach presented previously for theoretically explaining stock prices. This formulation holds that the price of a share of common stock is equal to the present discounted value of the expected profits of the corporation.

Variations of the equation relating stock prices to the present value of earnings were examined in statistical tests with surprisingly good results. The results were suspect, however, because of the statistical methods that were used. The tests suffered from a common problem in the statistical analysis of variables. This problem arises when an attempt is made to find a relationship between variables from a time series (a series of observations from successive periods) showing common trends and/or common movements during business cycles. Adequate procedures must be employed to take account carefully of these common trends and cycles in the variables; otherwise, statistical tests may tend to support a close relationship between the variables even though they are basically unrelated.

Most economic series have tended to rise during the post-World War II period and would, in most cases, show a fairly strong association with each other if they were tested without adequately accounting for their common rising trend.[4] There are numerous examples of such faulty tests being conducted. It is necessary both for conventional statistical testing and for validating underlying economic relationships to account fully for the trend.

To state the matter more emphatically, no causal relation is implied by a finding that the quantity of grain harvested in one country is highly correlated with the application of fertilizer in another country on the basis of data that show both series increasing along a common trend.

Removing the trend is not enough! Cycles or periodicities in each variable must be accounted for or removed. *Periodicity* (or in the statistician's jargon, "autocorrelation") in a variable is the association between the values taken by the variable in different periods. The presence of such periodicities allows some of the future values of a variable to be predicted from the variable's own past history. Tests for causality can produce spurious results if these periodicities are left in the data. This problem is illuminated with three examples.

1. Every morning before the sun rises, roosters crow. This periodicity indicates a strong statistical relationship but does not prove that a rooster's brain makes the sun shine. Only the "irregular" event—say, when the roosters are sick and do not crow—tends to support or contradict the relationship. The variables, sun rises and rooster crows, follow each other, so that there is no meaning to the concept of causality. (This is similar to the question of which came first, the chicken or the egg.) Each variable, sun rises and rooster crows, has a precise repeating periodicity over time. Only that part of the change in either variable that is "not" part of this periodicity—the irregular event—can be used to test for an underlying causal relationship.

2. Many variables go up and down during business cycles. This does not necessarily mean that they are related. For example, during most inflationary expansions, income taxes rise, whereas miles jogged may decline (because of higher employment and more overtime). This association does not support the notion that higher taxes take your breath away, impeding jogging.

3. Suppose that in a coin-tossing experiment, two heads are always followed by two tails, which are again followed by two heads. Larger samples from this experiment indicate that, on the average, heads comes up almost exactly half the time, with the precision improving as the number of tosses increases. This last test result, taken by itself, is evidence that it is a fair coin with no bias toward heads or tails. However, the periodicity in the outcomes of the tosses, with the sequence of two heads followed by two tails, and so on, invalidates this conclusion. It shows that each toss has a perfect bias toward heads or tails, depending on the outcome of the previous toss. This is not a fair coin, and conventional statistics has nothing to say about future tosses. Again, only with the irregular events—where a head or tail deviates from this periodicity— can use be made of conventional statistics. For example, if the irregular event is random, the chance of heads might be predicted from the data using conventional statistics.

To illustrate the problems that can arise when no attention is paid to trends and periodicities, an artificial series having no economic significance was constructed by adding a trend onto a series of random numbers. This artificial series was then used in the same tests that were used in some studies to explain the quarterly levels of stock prices (measured by the Standard and Poor's index) from 1959 through 1974. The results show that this single artificial variable was able to explain 86 percent of the change in stock prices.[5] The finding that such an artificial variable can explain nearly as much of the variation in stock prices as reported in the previous studies underscores the possibility of producing results that are statistical illusions when trends in the data are ignored. A further problem with the earlier studies is that they tested one-way statistical association with money related to future changes in stock prices. They did not consider that changes in stock prices could be related to future changes in the money supply. If, for example, the stock market is as efficient as the efficient market hypothesis holds, stock prices are determined by market participants on the basis of all available information. If the public "expected" a change in the money supply to occur that would ultimately affect price levels, corporate profits, and so on, the public would immediately buy and sell stocks at prices that would take account of the expected effects. That is, expected changes in the money supply would immediately be discounted into the prices of stocks. "Consequently, if subsequent changes in the money supply were to occur as expected, stock prices would change before and not after observed changed in money supply."

Another aspect of the efficient market hypothesis involves an "unexpected" change in the money supply. In this case, the efficient market hypothesis would hold that "when the public observes an unexpected monetary change, they would immediately discount this information into stock prices." Hence an unexpected money supply change would produce a synchronous statistical relationship.[6]

Richard Cooper examined the leads and lags between rates of change of the money supply and the stock "yield" described previously.[7] Cooper related the stock yield to the current percentage change in money, to past percentage changes in money for up to twelve months, and to future percentage changes in money for up to six months. He used monthly data for the period 1947–1970, depicted in Figure 26-2. On the basis of his tests, Cooper concluded that it was difficult, with the type of statistical tests used in earlier studies, to assess the significant lead and lag relationships between rates of change of the money supply and stock yields. A new statistical test by Cooper produced results that were consistent with the hypothesis that the market was efficient. In addition, there was some support for a statistical association between stock yields and future changes in his money variable.[8]

Further Tests

Results of additional tests on the relation between money and stock prices are presented in this section.[9] As in Cooper's study, the tests examine the lead–lag relation between the stock yield and the rate of change of the money supply.

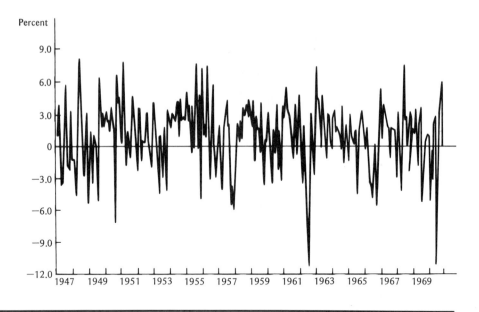

Figure 26-2

Stock yields monthly, 1947–1970 (Standard and Poor's common stock indexes).
Source: Robert Auerbach, "Money and Stock Prices," *Monthly Review,* Federal
Reserve Bank of Kansas City (September–October 1976), p. 9.

Two modifications were made in the approach used by Cooper. First,
the data for the variables were examined for evidence of trends and cycles. The examination revealed that both variables contained trend and
cycle elements that could bias the tests. The trend and cycle components
of each variable were removed and the cleansed series was tested to
make sure they were free of trends and cycles. Second, the degree of
association between the rates of change of the money supply and the
stock yield was measured by a statistic called a *correlation statistic,* a
measure of the degree to which two variables are related. It can vary
from +1 to −1. If two variables display little or no association, the correlation would approach zero. If there is perfect positive association, the
correlation would be +1. With perfect negative association, the correlation would be −1.

The correlation was computed between the current stock yield and
the current money variable. Next, correlations were calculated between
the current stock yield and the money variable in each of sixty prior
monthly periods. Finally, to test whether stock yields lead money, the
variables were reversed and correlations were computed between the
current money variable and the stock yield in each of six prior monthly
periods. These tests also were conducted using monthly data for the period 1947–1970.

As shown in Table 26-1, the correlations between the current stock
yield and sixty prior values of the money variable were not statistically
significant. Only the synchronous correlation was statistically signifi-

TABLE 26-1

Correlations Between the Money Supply and the Stock Yield After Both Series Are Cleansed of Trends and Cycles, 1947–1970

Period	Current Stock Yield with Percentage Change in M1	Current Percentage Change in M1 with Stock Yield
Synchronous	.18*	.18*
1 month prior	−.03	.12*
2 months prior	.07	.20*
3 through 60 months prior	None significantly different from zero	None significantly different from zero

*Significantly different from zero.
Source· Robert Auerbach, "Money and Stock Prices," *Monthly Review,* Federal Reserve Bank of Kansas City (September–October 1976), p. 9.

cant, at a value of .18. When the variables were reversed to test whether stock yields lead money, the synchronous correlation was equal to .18, as expected. Correlations between the current money variable and stock yields in each of the previous two months also were found to be statistically significant. Stock yields one and two months in the past had significant correlations with the current percentage change in money of .12 and .20, respectively. Taken together, the current stock yield and the two prior stock yields serve to "explain" about 8.7 percent of the variation in the current percentage change in money.[10]

These findings could be explained by the efficient market hypothesis and the belief that the public is knowledgeable about a relationship between money and other variables—such as the price level—as Cooper suggested.[11] If the public is able to predict some money supply changes, they would discount this information into stock prices one or two months before the money supply changes. Unanticipated money supply changes are discounted into stock prices in the same months that the monetary change occurs.

One reservation about this explanation of the results concerns the public's ability to forecast the monetary variable in advance. Since trends and periodicities have been removed from the money series in these tests, the public would be required to predict deviations from the trend and past periodicities. Prior values of the money supply series would provide no useful information for this forecast. It is questionable that anyone has the ability to predict more than a very minor component of these monetary changes. Thus other explanations might underlie these results.

An alternative explanation is that the relationship between prior and synchronous stock yield changes and current rates of change in money is the result of actions taken by the Federal Reserve. Suppose, first, that stock yields, or some variable related to stock yields, are used by the Federal Reserve as an indicator of business cycle fluctuations. Suppose further that the Federal Reserve acts to accommodate partially increased business activity by providing an increase in the money supply. Under these conditions, stock yields would increase slightly earlier and synchronously with monetary expansion, and one would observe the findings reported in these tests.[12]

NOTES

1. See Robert D. Auerbach's "Money and Stock Prices," *Monthly Review*, Federal Reserve Bank of Kansas City (September–October 1976), pp. 3–11.
2. Beryl W. Sprinkel, *Money and Stock Prices* (Homewood, Ill.: Richard D. Irwin, Inc., 1964). He used M1 as the concept of money. Also, his "Monetary Growth as a Cyclical Indicator," *Journal of Finance* (September 1956), pp. 333–346, presents similar methodology.
3. Sprinkel, *Money and Stock Prices*, p. 119.
4. This section is based on Robert Auerbach's "The Process of Inflation," a speech delivered at a seminar in monetary theory and policy in Belgrade, Yugoslavia, and published in *The Florida State University Proceedings and Reports*, Vol. 9 (Tallahassee, Fla.: The Center for Yugoslav-American Studies, Research, and Exchanges, Florida State University, 1975), p. 45.
5. The artificial series is denoted by X. It contains a trend at an annual rate of 2.5 percent. The equation estimated was

$$SP = -49647.3 + 0.11X$$

   with a correlation coefficient (squared)—a measure of association where 1 is perfect association—equal to .86. See Auerbach, "Money and Stock Prices," p. 6, footnote 8.
6. Transactions and decision-making costs may produce lags between monetary changes and changes in stock prices. Except for momentous events, these lags should be short.
7. Richard V. L. Cooper, "Efficient Capital Markets and the Quantity Theory of Money," *Journal of Finance* (June 1974), pp. 887–908.
8. Cooper used sophisticated spectral techniques to examine the relation of money and stock prices. These results showed that stock returns led money changes but did not lag money changes. On this basis he felt that his results offered support for the concept of market efficiency. See ibid., p. 898.
9. These tests were conducted by Auerbach and reported in "Money and Stock Prices."
10. Squaring and adding these correlations produce a statistical equal to .0868, which in concept is roughly equivalent to a squared multiple correlation coefficient in regression analysis explained in Equation (4) in Chapter 25.
11. It cannot be emphasized too strongly that the statistical tests presented in this section only look at the irregular movements in money and stock yields. That is, movements in money and stock yields are cleansed of trends and periodicities. This is not a serious problem for stock yields or rates of change of stock prices, since these variables have little trend or periodicity (see Figure 26-2). What about the trend in the money supply or the trend in the rate of change of the money supply? These trends may be and probably are used by the public to forecast future stock prices and the prices of goods and services. The problem is that conventional statistical tests are biased when the level of a series depends on time (it is time dependent) as occurs with a trend or periodicity. This does not mean that the trends and periodicities

should be discarded. On the contrary, they convey valuable information. See the last part of Robert Auerbach, "A Convergence of Views," *The Federal Reserve Authorities and Their Public Responsibility* (Rochester, N.Y.: Center for Research in Government Policy and Business, Graduate School of Management, University of Rochester, 1980).

12. If the public also uses stock yields or a related variable to signal business cycle fluctuations in the same way that the Federal Reserve does, the public would be able to forecast monetary changes, and this alternative explanation would not differ from the first explanation. The public would be discounting this information into stock prices.

STUDY QUESTIONS

1. Discuss the validity of a statistical test that matches turning points in a money series with future turning points in a stock price series.

2. How do trends and periodicities bias statistical tests of correlation between two variables?

3. Can money supply changes cause future stock price changes in an efficient stock market? Explain.

4. Under what conditions can future stock prices be predicted from changes in the money supply?

Part IX

International Financial Markets

27

Exchange Rates and the Balance of Payments

Introduction

The discussion begins with a description of international financial markets for foreign exchange. This institutional decription is followed by an explanation of currency prices in international markets and the summary statement of a country's international transactions called the *balance of payments*. The chapter ends with an explanation of some of the determinants of equilibrium in the balance of payments.

The Foreign Exchange Market

Payments that arise from international transactions usually involve parties that use different currencies (or monies). Each country has its own domestic currency, and other currencies are foreign currencies that are not a medium of exchange in the country. Arrangements must be made in foreign transactions to exchange the currency of the buyer or investor into the domestic currency of the seller. An *exchange rate*, the price of a unit of the foreign money relative to a unit of the domestic money, must be determined.

Foreign currencies and internationally accepted monies (the SDR, gold, and U.S. dollar) are sometimes referred to as *foreign exchange*.

Foreign exchange must be obtained by buyers or investors involved in international transactions. Foreign exchange is held by central banks and is traded in foreign exchange markets. The banks in financial centers that serve as the brokers and dealers for foreign exchange comprise the center of the foreign exchange market. Large foreign exchange markets are found in London, New York, Frankfurt, and Tokyo. The center for mark–dollar transactions is Frankfurt; Tokyo for yen–dollar transactions; London for sterling–dollar transactions; and New York is a secondary center for all foreign exchange. Banks communicate with each other by telephone and Telex (that records messages on word processors). Firms and banks that conduct international transactions generally have their phone number and their Telex number on their stationery. Funds and transactions can be rapidly transferred between foreign exchange markets with this instant communication technology.

The dealers at the foreign exchange markets list buy and sell quotes of various foreign exchange rates for their customers, the difference being called the bid–ask spread. Trading in foreign exchange occurs continuously since the markets are located around the world in different time zones.

The U.S. foreign exchange market has been described by Patricia Revey as follows:

> The United States foreign exchange market consists of a network of commercial banks—located principally in New York and, to a lesser extent, in other major cities—which buy and sell bank deposits ("exchange") in another currency, and of several organized exchanges, which trade foreign exchange futures contracts. Except for the currency futures market, there is no central marketplace where participants meet to trade. Instead trading is over the counter, with dealers communicating directly by telephone and telex or indirectly through foreign exchange brokers who serve as agents, bringing together buyers and sellers for a fee.
>
> While most banking institutions are prepared to offer their customers a service in foreign exchange, there are only about 80–100 banks that actively trade foreign exchange for their own account. Of these, relatively few act as market makers by standing ready to quote fresh prices and execute business up to recognized amounts. At the same time, foreign exchange brokers in the United States number less than a dozen. Thus, the heart of the market is comparatively small.
>
> The overwhelming bulk of all transactions occurs in the interbank market, where banks seek to hedge or manage their exchange risk and to anticipate exchange and interest rate movements. Their operations give the market liquidity and make possible the smooth transaction of customer business. The customer or retail market, which accounts directly for as little as 10 percent but indirectly for perhaps as much as 50–60 percent of all exchange deals, consists of multinational corporations, nondealing banks, other nonbank financial institutions, and individuals.
>
> Roughly two thirds of all foreign exchange transactions are conducted spot, that is, at current exchange rates. . . . Another 30 percent of all transactions are swaps involving the simultaneous purchase and sale of a specified amount of foreign currency for two different maturities. Swaps are most commonly used to fund exchange positions, to take a view on interest rate differentials between two currencies, and in borrowing and lending operations. Only 6 percent of total exchange transactions are outright for-

wards involving a single purchase or sale of foreign currency for a value date more than two days in the future.

Foreign exchange trading in the United States is highly competitive. No one bank or single group of banks commands a dominant share of turnover in such major currencies as the German mark, Japanese yen, Canadian dollar, or pound sterling. However, in other currencies such as the Belgian franc and Italian lira where the strength of commercial, financial, and speculative demand does not support an active market, trading is relatively more concentrated among a few banks.

In the United States, foreign exchange trading is not regulated, though bank examiners review exchange transactions as a normal part of routine bank supervision. Commercial banks operate under self-imposed internal controls that cover most aspects of their involvement in the market. Issues related to foreign exchange trading, operations, and technical practices are discussed on the institutional level in the forum of the Foreign Exchange Committee, established in 1978 under the sponsorship of the New York Federal Reserve Bank. The Foreign Exchange Committee consists of representatives from east coast, regional and foreign banks, brokerage firms, and as observers members of the FOREX Association of North America. The FOREX brings together as individuals a large number of traders and brokers from 220 banking and 19 brokerage offices around the country.[1]

Futures markets were described in Chapter 22. The forward price for currency is described in the next chapter.

Foreign Exchange

Many things of value are exchanged in international trade, such as goods, services, equities, bonds (used here as a general name for debt instruments), and domestic and international currencies. How are arrangements for the exchange of these assets made?

If, for example, Sarah Martin from South Bend, Indiana, wants to buy a hat in London, she needs British currency. The basic unit of account is the British pound, with the symbol £ (just as the symbol $ indicates dollars). The pound's price was $2.24 on January 2, 1980, when Sarah Martin was in London (see Table 27-1). On that day, suppose that £10 billion cleared the market at a price of $2.24 per pound, as shown in Figure 27-1. Suppose that Sarah Martin had come two weeks later, when a jump in income in the United States had caused an increased demand for British imports (foreign goods shipped into the United States) at every price along *DD* in Figure 27-1. Then *DD* would shift to *D'D'* and the market price of pounds would be $2.27. This price actually prevailed on January 16, 1980, as shown in Table 27-1. There would be an increase in demand for British pounds and an increase in the quantity of British pounds supplied, so that the market would settle down at an exchange of £12 billion.

Notice that two equivalent things have happened. The price of pounds went up by $0.03 and the price of U.S. dollars fell (from £0.446 to £0.441).

TABLE 27-1

Monetary Unit and Exchange Rates for U.S. Currency on January 2 and 16, 1980, for Selected Countries*

Country	Monetary Unit	Jan. 2	Jan. 16	Direction of Change
Australia	Dollar	110.8000	111.0500	+
Austria	Schilling	8.09061	8.07428	−
Belgium	Franc	3.58809	3.57782	−
Canada	Dollar	85.7781	85.8812	+
Denmark	Krone	18 7459	10.5529	−
Finland	Markka	27.0709	27.0856	+
France	Franc	24.9066	24.8016	−
Germany	D. Mark	58.3601	58.0889	−
India	Rupee	12.5000	12.6600	+
Ireland	Pound	215.1000	214.3000	−
Italy	Lira	0.12487	0.12419	−
Japan	Yen	0.41938	0.41990	+
Malaysia	Dollar	45.9348	45.9770	+
Mexico	Peso	4.3764	4.3802	+
Netherlands	Guilder	52.8485	52.6732	−
New Zealand	Dollar	98.5000	98.6800	+
Norway	Krone	20.3624	20.3459	−
Portugal	Escudo	2.0121	2.0060	−
South Africa	Rand	120.9000	121.3000	+
Spain	Peseta	1.5138	1.5142	+
Sri Lanka	Rupee	6.4300	6.9300	+
Sweden	Krona	24.1663	24.1196	−
Switzerland	Franc	63.3915	63.0915	−
United Kingdom	Pound	224.2700	227.1000	+

*Prices are in U.S. cents per unit of foreign currency.

Figure 27-1

Hypothetical demand and supply curves for British pounds. U.S. dollar prices for January 2 and 16, 1980, per pound, are used.

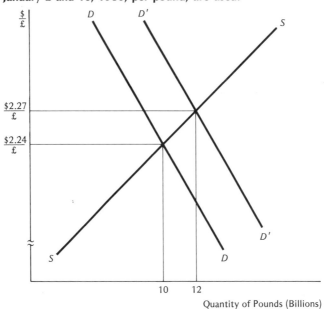

Quantity of Pounds (Billions)

The Balance of Payments

One way to arrange international transactions in analyzing their relationship with a number of variables is in a balance-of-payments accounting statement, shown in Table 27-2.

The two major accounts are the current account and the capital account. The current account records transactions in goods, services, and transfer payments. Gifts and grants are called *transfer payments*. The capital accounts record the transfer of assets such as bonds, stocks, and land.

In these two accounts, any transaction that gives rise to a payment to a foreigner is entered as a debit, whereas a transaction giving rise to a receipt from a foreigner is entered as a credit. Double-entry bookkeeping is followed, so that every transaction must be recorded twice. If $100 is recorded as the expenditure on an imported cup of crude oil, there must be another entry showing either an offsetting transaction or the form of payment.

The *trade balance* or *merchandise balance* is part of the current account. It equals exports (goods sold to foreigners outside the country)

TABLE 27-2

The Balance of Payments

I. Current account
  A. Private
    1. Trade balance or merchandise balance (exports minus imports)
    2. Tourism
    3. Transportation (e.g., shipping services)
    4. Interest, dividends, and other income from foreign investments
    5. Private gifts
    6. Other services
  B. Government
    1. Foreign military expenditures
    2. Aid programs, military aid, and so on
II. Capital account
  A. Investment (investment in the United States by foreigners minus U.S. investment abroad)
  B. Lending (sales of debt instruments to foreigners minus purchase of debt instruments from foreigners)
    1. Private long-term
    2. Short-term
      a. Private nonliquid — Liquidity Balance*
      b. Private liquid — Official Settlements Balance†
      c. Official liquid
  C. Official reserve transactions

*Under a Liquidity Balance, the last three entries are the means of payment.
†Under an Official Settlements Balance, the last two entries are a means of payment.

minus imports (goods purchased from foreigners outside the country). It is shown from 1975 to 1981 in Figure 27-2. A broader *goods and services balance* is sometimes referred to. It adds to the trade balance services, such as military expenditures and tourist spending.

The *capital account balance* is said to be in surplus if there is a *net capital inflow*. This would occur if receipts from foreigners from the sale of assets exceed the domestic country's payments for assets purchased from foreigners. If payments exceed receipts, there is a deficit on the capital accounts, which is called a *net capital outflow*. Foreign direct investment in the United States is shown in Figure 27-3.

Errors and omissions are simply goofs that are recorded in one spot, the last item in Table 27-3. It arises because the balance of payments is an accounting identity where total payments must equal total receipts. When the records do not reflect this equality, the remainder is put in errors and omissions. The balance of payments can be changed by putting errors and omissions in different places.

The sum of the current account and the capital account is the overall balance of payments. A negative value is a deficit and a positive value is a surplus. The *official reserve transactions*, item IIC in Table 27-2, is one measure of the overall balance of payments. It shows the amount of payments and the means of financing the deficit or collecting the funds from a surplus in the balance of payments.

Figure 27-2

U.S. export–import trade (1975–1981). *Source: International Letter,* **Federal Reserve Bank of Chicago (November 6, 1981), p. 2.**

*The trade balance for 1981 is based on January–September at an annual rate.

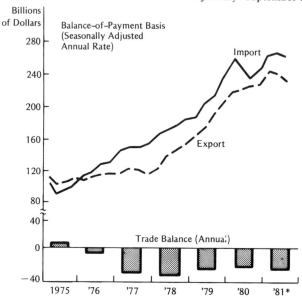

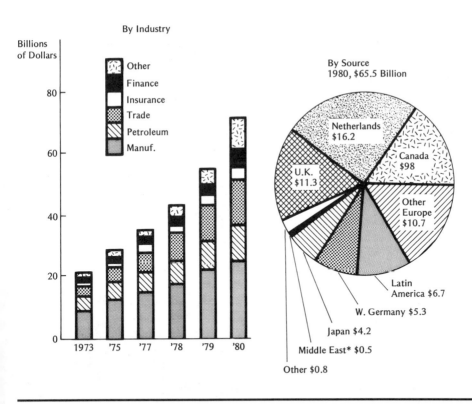

Figure 27-3

Foreign direct investment position in the United States. *Source: International Letter,* **Federal Reserve Bank of Chicago (November 6, 1981), p. 3.**

*Middle East excepting Israel.

Sometimes a broader class of transactions is defined to be payments. The *liquidity balance* shown in Table 27-3 separates transactions involving liquid from those involving nonliquid, private short-term debt instruments. A sale of a Treasury bill by a private U.S. resident to a foreigner is then considered a means of payment.

The *official settlement balance* can be described by the following classifications: (1) current account, (2) private capital flows, (3) transfers to and from official government holdings of liquid assets. The net of (1) and (2) is the balance of payments and (3) is the financing of the official settlement balance.

The official settlement balance excluded transactions in the private sector of short-term liquid debt instruments from the definition of the means of payment. Changes in SDRs and errors and omissions can be added into the balance of payments; in that case, they are not considered financing transactions. This is shown on lines 36 and 37 in Table 27-3. Special drawing rights (SDRs—international money discussed in the next chapter) and errors and omissions (on the grounds that many payments are unrecorded) can be included in the official means of payment.

TABLE 27-3

U.S. International Transactions (Millions of Dollars; Quarterly Data Are Seasonally Adjusted Except as Noted)*

Item Credits or Debits	1978	1979	1980	1981[†]
1 Balance on current account	−14,075	1,414	3,723	1,073
2 Not seasonally adjusted				2,369
3 Merchandise trade balance[‡]	−33,759	−27,346	−25,342	−6,914
4 Merchandise exports	142,054	184,473	223,966	60,477
5 Merchandise imports	−175,813	−211,819	−249,308	−67,391
6 Military transactions, net	738	−1,947	−2,515	−586
7 Investment income, net[§]	21,400	33,462	32,762	8,647
8 Other service transactions, net	2,613	2,839	5,874	1,456
9 Remittances, pensions, and other transfers	−1,884	−2,057	−2,397	−536
10 U.S. government grants (excluding military)	−3,183	−3,536	−4,659	−994
11 Change in U.S. government assets, other than official re-serve assets, net (increase, −)	−4,644	−3,767	−5,165	−1,475
12 Change in U.S. official reserve assets (increase, −)	732	−1,132	−8,155	−905
13 Gold	−65	−65	0	0
14 Special drawing rights (SDRs)	1,249	−1,136	−16	−23
15 Reserve position in International Monetary Fund	4,231	−189	−1,667	−780
16 Foreign currencies	−4,683	257	−6,472	−102
17 Change in U.S. private assets abroad (increase, −)[§]	−57,158	−57,739	−71,456	−19,141
18 Bank-reported claims	−33,667	−26,213	−46,947	−14,063
19 Nonbank-reported claims	−3,853	−3,026	−2,653	n.a.
20 U.S. purchase of foreign securities, net	−3,582	−4,552	−3,310	1,451
21 U.S. direct investments abroad, net[§]	−16,056	−23,948	−18,546	−3,627
22 Change in foreign official assets in the United States (increase, +)	33,561	−13,757	15,492	−3,009
23 U.S. Treasury securities	23,555	−22,435	9.683	−2,069
24 Other U.S. government obligations	666	463	2,187	536
25 Other U.S. government liabilities[¶]	2,359	−133	636	180
26 'Other U.S. liabilities reported by U.S. banks	5,551	7,213	−159	−2,286
27 Other foreign official assets[ǁ]	1,4530	1,135	3,145	630
28 Change in foreign private assets in the United States (increase, +)[§]	30,187	52,703	34,769	15,819
29 U.S. bank-reported liabilities	16,141	32,607	10,743	8,791
30 U.S. nonbank-reported liabilities	1,717	2,065	5,109	n.a.
31 Foreign private purchases of U.S. Treasury securities, net	2,178	4,820	2,679	701
32 Foreign purchases of other U.S. securities, net	2,254	1,334	5,384	3,450
33 Foreign direct investments in the United States, net[§]	7,896	11,877	10,853	2,878
34 Allocation of SDRs	0	1,139	1,152	0
35 Discrepancy	11,398	21,140	29,640	7,637
36 Owing to seasonal adjustments				1,221
37 Statistical discrepancy in recorded data before seasonal adjustment	11,398	21,140	29,640	6,416

*Seasonal factors are no longer calculated for lines 12 through 41.
[†]1981 figures are for April–June.
[‡]Data are on an international accounts (IA) basis. Differs from the Census basis data for reasons of coverage and timing; military exports are excluded from merchandise data and are included in line 6.
[§]Includes reinvested earnings of incorporated affiliates.
[¶]Primarily associated with military sales contracts and other transactions arranged with or through foreign official agencies.
[ǁ]Consists of investments in U.S. corporate stocks and in debt securities of private corporations and state and local governments.
Source: Data are from Bureau of Economic Analysis, *Survey of Current Business,* U.S. Department of Commerce. Table from *Federal Reserve Bulletin* (December 1981), p. A54.

The balance of payments for 1978, 1979, 1980, and the second quarter of 1981 is shown in Table 27-3. From one perspective it could be said that the deficit in the merchandise trade balance was primarily the result of the increased value of imports of foreign cars and of oil. Imported oil prices rose substantially in 1979. From another perspective, many would argue that a fall in the price of the international value of the U.S. dollar would have caused more exports to be sold and fewer imports to be bought. So an overvalued dollar was the cause. This subject is discussed subsequently. First, the meaning of balance-of-payments equilibrium is discussed.

The Balance-of-Payments Relationships

The components of the balance of payments may be classified into groups that show some important relationships between internal and external expenditure flows.[2] These relationships are useful in organizing some of the macroeconomic variables in an economy that is assumed to engage in international transactions (an *open economy*).

In an open economy, the demand for a country's output is increased by the foreign demand for exports and decreased by the domestic demand for imports. The components of the demand for a country's domestic output are as follows:

$$\begin{aligned} \text{total domestic output} = \ & \text{domestic consumption} \\ & + \text{ domestic investment} \\ & + \text{ exports} \\ & - \text{ imports} \end{aligned} \tag{1}$$

Equation (1) may be understood by noting that some of the domestic consumption and the domestic investment and even some of the exports consist of goods imported from abroad. Therefore, if one wants to examine domestic output, one must subtract imports from the sum of domestic consumption and investment and from exports.

Rearranging the terms, Equation (1) can also be written as follows:

$$\begin{aligned} \text{total domestic output} \ & - \text{ domestic consumption} \\ & - \text{ domestic investment} \\ & = \text{ exports} - \text{ imports} \end{aligned} \tag{2}$$

Saving is defined in Chapter 4 as output (= income) minus domestic consumption. Therefore, the equality between savings and investment for a closed economy must be amended by substituting saving in Equation (2):

$$\text{domestic saving} - \text{domestic investment} = \text{exports} - \text{imports} \tag{3}$$

Equation (3) is an equilibrium statement for the domestic economy if it is written in terms of "desired levels" of each variable except exports, which depend on foreigners. If desired domestic saving exceeds desired domestic investment, a country need not have a deflation. Foreign demand for products (exports) may exceed domestic demand for foreign products (imports), to bring about equilibrium.

Not all the increase in domestic wealth caused by domestic investment will be owned by residents. Foreigners may demand some of the new securities. This will cause a *capital inflow*, a foreign purchase of new domestic securities. Some domestic savers may buy foreign securities, reducing the demand for new domestic securities. This will cause a *capital outflow*, domestic purchase of foreign securities. The *net capital outflow* is the difference between capital outflows and capital inflows. Domestic saving can exceed domestic investment by the net capital outflow:[3]

$$\begin{aligned} \text{domestic saving} &- \text{domestic investment} \\ &= \text{net capital outflow} \end{aligned} \tag{4}$$

In other words, domestic saving can exceed domestic investment by the value of the purchase of foreign securities minus the purchase of new domestic securities. Equation (4) is the equilibrium condition in the capital market if domestic saving and investment are written in terms of desired levels.

Since the right-hand sides of Equations (3) and (4) both equal the same quantity, they may be set equal to each other, to form a third relationship, the overall equilibrium condition for the balance of payments:

$$\text{exports} - \text{imports} = \text{net capital outflow} \tag{5}$$

This is the identity for equilibrium in the balance-of-payments statement in Table 27-2.

Suppose that desired imports exceed exports and that the net capital outflow is zero. The conditions in Equation (5) are not met. Something must change. The country may lose reserves, paying for the imports until the reserves run so short that the country must borrow from abroad. At some point, if the deficit in the merchandise balance is chronic, the exchange rate of the currency must fall.

How is the rest of the world paid for this deficit in the balance of payments? The deficit country may use its international reserves (say, U.S. dollars and gold) until they are exhausted. It may raise the price of imports to domestic residents by imposing *tariffs*—taxes on imports (although there is still the question of how the government spends the proceeds from the tariffs). The country may contract its money supply and/or run a fiscal surplus to induce a lower domestic income and a consequent lower domestic demand for foreign imports. Part, and sometimes most, of the adjustment may come through a devaluation of the country's currency. This can occur through market forces under floating exchange rates, described in the next chapter.

The United States was able to sustain a persistent deficit in its balance of payments under fixed exchange rates in the 1960s because central bankers of many countries agreed to hold U.S. dollar assets. Most countries are not so fortunate. They cannot buy more from the rest of the world than the rest of the world sells them and have capital outflows for prolonged periods. They run short of reserves and credit, and they must eventually have some underlying adjustment, such as a change in the international price of their currency. (The U.S. *was* able to do this since U.S. dollars served as international reserves.) Similarly, a country with a chronic balance-of-payment surplus may not wish to sell the rest of the world more than it receives for an indefinite period. It may wish to revalue its currency at a higher level, a process that many economists believe would be automatic under floating exchange rates.

Income Changes and the Trade Balance

Economic models of international trade are frequently formulated so that (1) the trade balance (exports minus imports) depends primarily on changes in income, and (2) capital flows depend primarily on differences in real interest rates between the domestic economy and foreign economies.

Consider first the balance of trade; assume that there are no capital flows. Let B be the trade balance, X be exports, M be imports, and P be the price of imports, all in terms of domestic currency.[4] Then

$$B = X - PM \tag{6}$$

Suppose that huge imports (say, of oil) cause imports to exceed exports, so that B is negative. This trade balance is shown along QQ in Figure 27-4, drawn on the assumption that expenditues depend only on real income. The hypothetical size of different trade balances at each level of income before huge imports of foreign oil were demanded is given along QQ. Since the demand at a given "real" income is for a real amount of goods, line QQ is drawn on the basis of a given set of prices in Equation (6). After huge imports of oil are demanded, the trade balance is shown along $Q'Q'$. The higher real income is, the greater the demand for goods and services, including imports. Therefore, both QQ and $Q'Q'$ slope upward. At a real income of OA the trade balance is zero before huge oil imports are demanded. After they are demanded, the trade deficit is AF at that level of income.

The assumption underlying the shift in the curves in Figure 27-4 is that the increased demand for imported oil is not dependent on real income. Instead, it depends on a reduction in oil production in the United States, causing a switch to imported oil. At each level of real income there is a greater demand for imports. Also, a rise in the price of imports [changed in Equation (6) to units of domestic currency] means that the same quantity of imports demanded will cost more.[5]

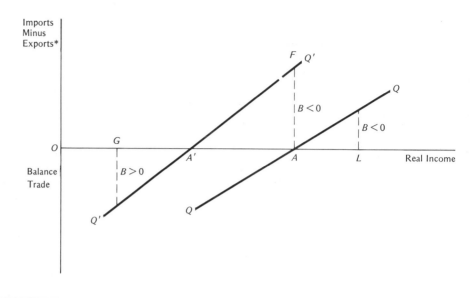

Figure 27-4

The trade deficit and surplus as a function of income.

*B is exports minus imports for equation (6), where both are measured in domestic prices.

One way to achieve equilibrium in the trade balance is to reduce real income. An engineered recession will reduce the demand for imports. In Figure 27-4 a real-income level of OG would produce a positive balance in the trade account and a level of real income of OA will reduce the trade balance to zero. This approach can be costly in terms of unemployment and substantially reduced real incomes.

Taxes on imports (tariffs) and subsidies on exports are direct ways to improve the trade balance. They can also be costly, since they change the allocation of goods available in the economy from that which is desired for efficient production. In addition, these steps invite retaliatory measures from other countries, resulting in a reduction in world trade; consequently, world income and, in many cases, the income of the domestic country may fall.

Devaluation

Devaluation, a decline in the foreign exchange value of the domestic currency, is another approach to achieving equilibrium in the trade balance. It can be achieved by market forces or government actions.

In Figure 27-5, the demand and supply for imports are depicted. The demand curve $D_{Y_0}D_{Y_0}$ slopes downward, on the usual assumption that a greater quantity is demanded at a lower price. An increase in income

Figure 27-5

The demand and supply of imports.

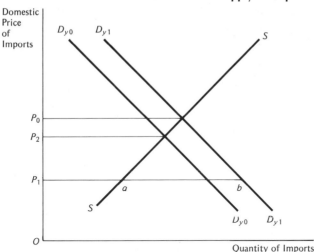

would shift the demand curve to the right. The supply curve *SS* is upward sloping, on the assumption that more will be supplied at a higher price.[6]

Suppose that the trade deficit is the excess demand for imports, depicted as *ab* in Figure 27-5. Then the price of imports is OP_1. Market forces would then cause the international exchange price of the domestic currency to fall, making imports more expensive. Remember, the import price is the foreign price times the exchange rate for foreign currency. That exchange rate rises. The import price—measured in domestic currency—rises to P_0.

The higher price of imports means that a \$1 bill buys less goods and services. Its purchasing power or real value has declined. If real expenditures depend on the level of real-money balances, *M/P*, in individuals' portfolios, real income will decline because of the rise in the price of imports. This decline in the value of *M/P* is called a negative "real balance effect." It will cause the demand for imports to shift to $D_{Y_0}D_{Y_0}$ in Figure 27-5. The price of imports will then rise by less than before, to P_2. The real balance effect will therefore cause a more rapid adjustment and require a smaller price change.

Does Devaluation Make Things Worse?

There are two views that hold that devaluation of a currency will not caus equilibrium in the trade balance to be achieved. Instead, devaluation will either have no effect on the trade balance or make things worse.

They are both opposite views about the nature of goods traded. One view holds that goods traded have very imperfect substitutes, and the other holds that goods traded have perfect substitutes.

Suppose that there are few substitutes for the goods that are imported.[7] Also, there is a trade balance deficit. This causes an excess supply of the domestic currency, which falls in value on international markets. Imports then become more expensive for residents. Because of the lack of substitutes for imports, the demand curve would be nearly vertical. This means that a rise in the price of imports is associated with a smaller percentage fall in the quantity of imports demanded. Since the price rises without substantially reducing the quantity demanded, domestic residents end up spending more, not less, on imports. The trade balance is then in greater deficit.

This worsening effect on the trade balance could be offset if foreigners began spending more for exports after the devaluation made the exports cheaper to them. Suppose, however, that the quantity of exports demanded is not very responsive to changes in the price of these exports on international markets. Rather than offsetting the preceding effects, this condition reinforces them.

The responsiveness to price changes of the quantity of imports demanded and the quantity of exports demanded from the domestic country can, therefore, be so sluggish that devaluation of the currency worsens the trade balance.

The devaluation may still work to improve the trade balance. If the devaluation sufficiently reduces either domestic income (by making imports more expensive) or the purchasing power of the domestic money supply (including its power to buy imported goods), or both, the demand for imports will be reduced. These two effects of devaluation are called the *income effect* and the *real balance effect*.

Fortunately, the preceding conditions that cause a devaluation to worsen the trade balance probably do not apply in general. They may apply to limited price ranges for the demand for imports by residents and for the demand for the country's exports by foreigners.

The second view holds that devaluation will have little or no effect on the trade balance; it will result in an offsetting upward movement in internal prices. Devaluation will only lead to internal inflation. It is in one respect opposite to the first view. It holds that traded goods have many nearly perfect substitutes. Arthur Laffer has pointed out that raw materials are the same everywhere.[8]

This view holds, under the *law of one price*, that identical goods tend not to differ in price from one place to another except by transportation costs. If devaluation raises the price of imports relative to domestic goods, domestic goods rise in price just enough to make their price relative to that of imports the same as before the devaluation. There is no incentive to switch away from imports and the trade balance is unaffected.

To see this, suppose that the exchange value of the U.S. dollar falls by

10 percent relative to British pounds. Imported silver rises in price in the United States. U.S. residents would immediately switch from the more expensive imported silver to the cheaper domestic silver, which is a perfect substitute. This would drive up the price of domestic silver. The result of devaluation would thus be an offsetting internal rise in prices.

The problem in going from this observation to a statement about the effect of devaluation is that not all individual goods and services are everywhere identical, available, and internationally traded.[9] Many economists would refute this second view of exchange rate changes by pointing out that international trade can be explained in part in terms of these differences. Because of differences between goods, differences in their availability in different places, and differences in the goods that are traded, international trade does improve world real income. That is, there are real effects, not just price-level changes from shifts in trade, and these shifts in trade can result from changes in the international prices of currencies. A devaluation can cause an increase in the price of imports for which there are no perfect domestic substitutes. This price increase is similar to a tax on a group of products, a tax that is not returned to the public. The tax changes the internal allocation of goods and services and lowers real income. This income effect acts to improve the trade balance.

Capital Flows

Sometimes, as in the preceding discussion, it is easier to limit analysis to the trade balance. However, one should always keep in mind that it is only part of the story. A large deficit in the trade balance can be more than offset by capital inflows.[10]

It is more difficult to predict the direction of capital inflows.[11] Capital is attracted by higher real interest rates—the nominal yield minus the expected change in value of the currency used for interest and repayment. The exact relationship between the expected change in the value of the currency and the rate of interest on assets is discussed in the next chapter. Real interest rate differentials can be closed very rapidly in international trade with modern communications, although whether or not they are is still being debated. The problem is that many other factors that are difficult to measure affect capital flows. These factors include various forms of risk premiums (for the stability of the government and the safety of funds) as well as preferences for places of investment.

Even more difficult to predict are portfolio changes where investors in international companies rearrange their foreign stocks and bonds. If the capital markets are functioning well, small real interest rate changes caused by these portfolio shifts will be rapidly arbitraged out, causing small interest rate and exchange rate disturbances. In crises, however, interest rates and exchange rates fluctuate widely and governments, for better or worse, step in to attempt to bring about more "orderly" movements.

NOTES

1. Patricia Revey, "Evolution and Growth of the United States Foreign Exchange Market," *Quarterly Review*, Federal Reserve Bank of New York (Autumn 1981), pp. 34–35.

2. For an excellent analysis of these relationships and a model of international adjustment, see Lloyd A. Metzler, "The Process of International Adjustment Under Conditions of Full Employment: A Keynesian View," in his *Collected Papers* (Cambridge, Mass.: Harvard University Press, 1973), pp. 209–233. This section is based on that article.

3. This relationship is defined for the demand for new domestic securities and the demand for foreign securities to saving and investment, which are "flows" in the current period. Changes in the ownership of existing financial wealth—portfolio changes—are not considered.

4. Domestic prices of imports are foreign prices times the exchange rate of the currencies.

5. The expenditures on oil and even on all imports may be greater at each level of real income if the price of oil rises. The elasticity of demand for imported oil and imports in general is then said to be *inelastic*. This means that the percentage change in quantity demanded is less than the percentage change in price at each level of real income. Conversely, the demand for oil and for imports may be *elastic*. The schedule QQ in Figure 27-4 would then shift (to the left if demand is inelastic and right if it is elastic) from a change in the price of oil alone. This change is in addition to a movement along the curve from a decline in real income caused by a rise in the price of imported oil.

6. The position of the supply curve is uncertain. As the quantity of exports demanded from the exporting country rises, the price level in the exporting country might be driven up, causing the supply curve SS in Figure 27-5 to shift to the left.

7. This argument can be put in mathematical form. With the price of exports fixed at unity, the change in the trade balance B with a change in the price of imports becomes, through differentiation of Equation (6),

$$M\left(\frac{X}{PM}\eta_X + \eta_M - 1\right)$$

where η_X and η_M are *elasticities of demand for imports* (by residents) and *demand for the country's exports* (by foreigners), respectively. The elasticity of import demand is the percentage change in imports divided by the percentage change in price. The elasticity of exports is the percentage change in exports divided by the percentage change in price. If the preceding expression for the change in the trade balance is positive, devaluation will improve the balance of trade. That is, the value of B will approach equilibrium—which is zero—on the assumption that there are no net capital flows. The condition that $\eta_X + \eta_M$ must exceed unity for the preceding expression to be positive and for the devaluation to improve the equilibrium balance of trade is known as the *Marshall-Lerner condition*.

8. Arthur B. Laffer, "The Phenomenon of Worldwide Inflation," in *The Phenomenon of Worldwide Inflation*, David T. Meiselman and Arthur B. Laffer, eds. (Washington, D.C.: American Enterprise Institute, 1975), pp. 27–57.

9. See Thomas D. Willet, *Floating Exchange Rates and International Reform* (Washington, D.C.: American Enterprise Institute, 1977), p. 50.

10. For a description of application of the *IS-LM* model to international trade, see Thomas F. Dernburg and Duncan M. McDougall, *Macroeconomics: The Measurement, Analysis and Control of Economic Activity* (New York: McGraw-Hill Book Company, 1980), pp. 207–229, 337–342.

11. Arnold C. Harberger in an insightful article, "Vignettes of the World Capital Market" (*The American Economic Review*, Papers and Proceedings of the 92nd Annual Meeting, Atlanta, Ga., December 28–30, 1979, pp. 331–339), eloquently describes the major problems in understanding international capital flows. He makes the following two important points: "We [the economics profession] seem to be genuinely schizophrenic in the ways we build models—many of them are closed-economy models in which the rest of the world does not even appear, yet others of them are models of the 'small, open economy' in which hardly any degree of freedom is left for economic policy to influence events. Lying behind the schizophrenia is, I believe, a genuine ignorance on our collective part of how the world capital market works" (p. 331). And, referring to the evidence he has assembled: "The evidence presented above tends to bolster the 'capital market' as against the 'quasi-closed economy' interpretation, but I must confess that I am not particularly at ease with all the implications of a really well-functioning world capital market. In particular, my own intuition does not want to accept the notion that increments of investment activity are in all or nearly all countries effectively 100 percent 'financed' by funds flowing in from abroad and that increments in saving simply spill out into the world capital markets" (p. 336).

STUDY QUESTIONS

1. What is foreign exchange, and where is it traded?

2. What is the balance of payments? Explain the difference between the balance of payments, the balance of trade, the current account, the capital account, and three different concepts of financing the balance of payments.

3. What is devaluation?

4. How are the values of different currencies determined in international trade? What are the effects on the international value of the U.S. dollar of a deficit and a surplus in the balance of payments? What is the effect of a deficit in the balance of trade?

5. How are real income and real-money balances related to the trade balance?

6. Under what conditions will a devaluation fail to improve the trade balance?

7. Assume that from an equilibrium position, Italian tourism in the United States increases. What effect does this have on the international value of U.S. currency and the U.S. balance of payments?

8. How is the savings-equals-investment identity changed for an open economy?

9. If foreign investments in the U.S. economy increased, causing a net capital inflow, what would happen to U.S. exports and imports? Explain.

10. If there is a large deficit as a result of oil imports, does a low level of domestic saving necessarily indicate a change of saving habits? Could it be said that the oil exporters are doing part of the saving if they buy Treasury bills with the dollars they earn?

28

Exchange Rate Systems, Forward and Spot Markets, and Optimum Currency Areas

Introduction

In this chapter the institutional characteristics of international arrangements for payments and the relative value of different currencies are discussed. A good question to start with is: What are the institutional arrangements for making payments between parties when each party uses money issued by different countries? The second question is: What arrangements are made for determining the relative value of these two kinds of money? The discussion explains the relation between the current or *spot* price of a currency and its future or *forward* price and how these prices are related to interest rates. Traders in international exchange markets who speculate or perform arbitrage are central to this discussion. Finally, it is useful to ask: What costs and benefits would follow from the use of a single form of money, not just to the participants in international transactions, but also to the economies of both countries?

Exchange Rate Systems

If a U.S. citizen buys a hat in London, the proprietor of the London hat store may insist on payment in the form of British money (£, pounds). The U.S. citizen has only U.S. money ($, U.S. dollars). What can be done

TABLE 28-1

Exchange Rate Policies, December 31, 1979

The 140 members of the IMF are grouped in the figures below according to the exchange rate policies they followed as of December 31, 1979. On that date, 94 members reported that their exchange rates were pegged and 45 reported that their exchange rates were governed by other policies (floating).[*]

The pegged group includes all currencies whose exchange rates were maintained within a well-defined range relative to a single foreign currency or a basket of foreign currencies. Sixty of the pegged currencies were tied to a single currency. Forty-two nations pegged to the U.S. dollar, 14 to the French franc, and one to the pound sterling.

The currencies of Lesotho and Swaziland were pegged to the South African rand and the currency of Equatorial Guinea was pegged to the Spanish peseta. Fourteen of the members that pegged maintained the value of their currencies in terms of a basket defined by the SDR, and twenty adopted other basket definitions.

Thirty-four of the 45 members that did not peg intervened at their own discretion to limit fluctuations in their otherwise floating exchange rates. Three members used economic indicators to determine the target levels of their exchange rates. And eight participated in a cooperative exchange arrangement (the European monetary system).

Pegs
Currency Pegged to

Single Currency						Basket	
U.S. Dollar		**£ Sterling**	**French Franc**	**Other**		**SDR**	**Other Composite**
Bahamas	Liberia	Gambia	Benin	Equatorial		Burma	Algeria
Barbados	Libya		Cameroon	Guinea		Guinea	Austria
Botswana	Nepal		Central African	Lesotho		Guinea-Bissau	Bangladesh
Burundi	Nicaragua		Republic	Swaziland		Jordan	Cape Verde
Chile	Oman		Chad			Kenya	Cyprus
Costa Rica	Pakistan		Comoros			Malawi	Fiji
Dijbouti	Panama		Congo			Mauritius	Finland
Dominica	Paraguay		Gabon			Sao Tome	Kuwait
Dominican	Romania		Ivory Coast			& Principe	Malaysia
Republic	Rwanda		Madagascar			Seychelles	Malta
Ecuador	St. Lucia		Mali			Sierra Leone	Mauritania
Egypt	St. Vincent		Niger			Uganda	Morocco
El Salvador	Somalia		Senegal			Viet Nam	Norway
Ethiopia	Sudan		Togo			Zaire	Papua New
Grenada	Surinam		Upper Volta			Zambia	Guinea
Guatemala	Syrian Arab						Singapore
Guyana	Republic						Solomon Is.
Haiti	Trinidad						Sweden
Honduras	& Tobago						Tanzania
Iraq	Venezuela						Thailand
Jamaica	Yemen Arab						Tunisia
Korea	Republic						
Lao People's	Yemen People's						
Dem. Rep.	Dem. Rep.						

[*] As reported by the IMF Treasurer's and Exchange and Trade Relations Departments. Information concerning the exchange arrangements of Democratic Kampuchea (Cambodia) is not available.
Source: Nicholas Carlozzi, "Pegs and Floats—The Changing Face of the Foreign Exchange Market," *Business Review,* Federal Reserve Bank of Philadelphia (May–June 1980), pp. 22–23.

TABLE 28-1 (*Continued*)

Exchange Rate Policies, December 31, 1979

| Indicators | Floats Float Governed by | | | |
	Cooperative Exchange Arrangements	Other		
Brazil	Belgium	Afghanistan	Iran	Saudi Arabia
Colombia	Denmark	Argentina	Israel	South Africa
Portugal	Federal Republic	Australia	Japan	Spain
	of Germany	Bahrain	Lebanon	Sri Lanka
	France	Bolivia	Maldives	Turkey
	Ireland	Canada	Mexico	United Arab Emirates
	Italy	China (Taiwan)	New Zealand	United Kingdom
	Luxembourg	Ghana	Nigeria	United States
	Netherlands	Greece	Peru	Uruguay
		Iceland	Philippines	Western Samoa
		India	Qatar	Yugoslavia
		Indonesia		

to bring about the transaction? There are numerous arrangements made for obtaining the foreign currency needed in international trade, which are summarized here and described in the following sections (refer to Table 28-1 for exchange rate policies at the end of 1979).

1. Fixed rates of exchange between domestic currencies.
   a. There may be a *fixed* or *pegged rate* of exchange between each country's money, arranged by the central banks of each country. The central banks must maintain a supply of foreign exchange to buy their own currency if it falls in price. The fixed rates may be changed according to some prearranged system.
   b. A special variant of the fixed exchange rate arrangement is the *gold standard*, whereby each government agrees to exchange a fixed nominal quantity of its money for a fixed quantity of gold.
   c. Commodities other than gold, such as silver, have been used as a means of international payment. Any group of commodities could theoretically be used, such as bricks or a large collection of different commodities.
   d. *Currency unions* are formed where a group of countries pegs the exchange rate between their currencies but is flexible with other currencies.
2. Flexible or floating rates of exchange between domestic currencies.
   a. *Flexible or floating exchange rates* are determined by market conditions. This is sometimes called a *clean float*. Currencies

are traded by foreign exchange dealers for themselves and for customers.
  b. *Limited flexible exchange rates*, where the central banks step in and buy or sell currencies to prevent them from falling or rising in value beyond predetermined limits, have also been used. These differ from a pegged rate by the specification of a range, although the distinction is arbitrary.
  c. Intermittent intervention by a central bank that attempts to control the value of its currency is sometimes a *dirty float* or a *managed float*. This method of influencing exchange rates is not always easy to detect. The central bank may have parties in the private sector intervene for them.

Countries may directly buy or trade their currencies in international exchanges to obtain the means of payment. They may also trade key currencies or international money.

  1. *International money* produced by an international organization has been used in international trade.
  2. Under a *key currency* arrangement, all participating countries agree to settle their foreign transactions with the currency of a particular country, the *key currency nation.* U.S. dollars have been a key currency in the free world.
  3. Gold has been used, together with U.S. dollars, since World War II in an international payment system called a *dollar-gold* or *gold-exchange* standard.

These arrangements for making payments in international trade involve both the exchange of reserves (commodities used in international payments) and a change in the relative prices of the currencies utilized. The relative price or value of a unit of domestic currency may be stated with respect to:

  1. A market basket of domestic goods and services.
  2. A unit of a foreign currency.
  3. A fixed amount of a particular commodity (or group of commodities) such as gold.

Relative prices 1, 2, and 3 are sometimes confused. The dollar price of gold can rise at the same time that the international domestic U.S. price level falls and the dollar price of another foreign currency, say, British pounds, also falls. There cannot be a worldwide inflation of all relative prices of type 2, the relative prices between currencies. If the relative price of U.S. dollars to British pounds (U.S. $/£) rises, the relative price of British pounds to U.S. dollars (£/U.S. $) falls by the same proportion.

It also follows that if there are N countries with N currencies and $N - 1$ exchange rates are given, all N rates are determined. For example, if there are only two countries, with two currencies, dollars and pounds, and the dollar price of pounds is given, then the pound price of dollars is also determined.

The government may directly affect the balance of payments not only by directly intervening in the markets for foreign exchange but also by directly intervening in the markets for foreign trade of commodities, services, and financial assets. Direct forms of intervention include import taxes (tariffs) or subsidies, export taxes or subsidies, taxes on foreign investment by domestic residents or on domestic investment by foreigners, and taxes on transfer payments such as repatriated (funds brought back into the country) dividends or interest earned abroad. Indirect effects of monetary and fiscal policy affect the balance of payments by changing domestic income levels, interest rates, and price levels.

Forward and Spot Markets

Besides a *current* or *spot relative price* for currencies (or monies) and spot markets, there are future markets, where future (or forward) prices are determined by buying and selling future contracts, as described in Chapter 22. Also, a large volume of forward contracts are made directly between participants in the foreign exchange markets. *Spot transactions* require the exchange of deposits by two days after the date of the contract. *Forward transactions* require an exchange of deposits at specified longer maturities on the forward contract. There are standardized maturities of three months, six months, and one year, and on major currencies, longer contracts are sometimes available. Banks, acting as financial intermediaries, make available forward contracts tailored exactly to their customers needs, such as a forty-six-day maturity.

If the spot price is below the forward price, the currency is said to be at a *forward premium*. If the spot price is above the forward price, the currency is said to be at a *forward discount*.

Both spot and forward markets for currencies are subject to control and intervention by governments. The governments may step in to support their domestic currency by buying it. They may impose exchange controls on the repatriation of profits or interest payments. The risk of loss in forward contracts because of these latter controls can be called *sovereign risk*. Thus spot and forward markets can suffer from imperfections.

The evidence, however, generally tends to support the hypothesis that these markets are approximately efficient, especially the offshore foreign exchange markets (such as is found on Caribbean Island nations) that are free of government controls.[1] Robert Aliber has pointed out that there is the political risk of governments imposing controls in the onshore markets exchange.[2] Increases in these risks do not necessarily make the foreign markets less efficient. These risks may be reflected in the prices and yields in the manner discussed in Part IV. However, such risks may make the market thin with incomplete information on current prices if banks refuse to supply forward contracts. The terms of all privately negotiated contracts may not be rapidly (if ever) known by other market transactors. Bid–ask spreads may become out of date with actual trades. Government intervention intentions may not be public information (they may leak out to only a few). Governments may discourage buying their currency forward when it is at a discount by telling traders to buy at spot prices or suffer some costs. These costs can include the informal prohibition from dealing with the nationalized banking system. Such arrangements have not been documented, but to assume that they do not exist appears implausible. Government, especially central bankers, have not always been apostles of free trade and free markets. Instead, there is the strong temptation to intervene directly or indirectly to keep the exchange rate of the domestic currency from falling or to produce a surplus in the trade balance or the balance of payments, two frequently inconsistent objectives. To some in government positions the forward market may seem to be a way to circumvent controls or intervention to maintain the spot rate. It is a slap in the face to some officials, seeking to preserve the spot rate, to be given a vote of no confidence in the forward markets as their currency goes to a forward discount.

Nevertheless, experts tend to agree that the foreign exchange markets are generally extremely competitive.

Speculation, Covered Arbitrage, and Interest Rate Parity

The foreign exchange markets offer a vehicle for spectators to take innumerable positions for expected profitable opportunities. They can buy a currency at spot and invest in foreign securities, hoping to convert back in a future period at a profitable exchange rate, more profitable than investing in domestic securities. They can hold a forward contract to buy or sell, and keep their funds invested domestically. If they hold a forward contract to sell a currency, they hope for a decline in the spot rate so that they can exercise the forward contract at a higher price and buy the foreign exchange back at a profit. They are in a short position. If they hold a buy contract, they hope for a rise in the spot rate so that they can exercise their forward contracts and sell the foreign exchange rate back at a profit. They are in a long position.

A more general definition of long and short positions relative to the spot exchange rate of a particular country can be defined as follows:

Short position:
Value of foreign assets < value of foreign liabilities

Long position:
Value of foreign assets > value of foreign liabilities

When the spot rate of the foreign currency rises, those holding a long position will have a net increase in the value of their assets. Those holding a short position will have a net decrease.

Traders and investors can change the composition of their portfolio by changing the denomination in which the assets are valued. Dollar-denominated assets can be changed for deutsche mark-denominated assets, a readjustment noted in Chapter 29 for those holding Eurobonds. This readjustment changes their speculative position.

Speculators take risks in order to gain from price changes. There is in the foreign exchange markets a basic kind of arbitrage, *covered arbitrage*, which involves little or no risk. Understanding covered arbitrage allows an understanding of one of the basic relationships hypothesized for international finance. That relationship is that the percentage difference between the forward and spot rates between two currencies equals the difference between the interest rates on default-free assets of the same maturity in each country.

The principle of covered arbitrage is shown in the following example using:

1. The U.S. one-year rate on T-bills, r_{US}.
2. The one-year rate on a British government security, r_B.
3. $, the U.S. dollar.
4. £, British currency, called the *pound sterling*, or the *pound*.

Henry, an interest arbitrageur, observes that the interest rate is sufficiently higher in Britain ($r_B > r_{US}$) to warrant covered arbitrage. Henry takes $1 million and converts it into sterling at the spot rate, SR. The SR is equal to (hypothetically) $2 per pound; that is, $2 US will be exchanged for 1 pound sterling. This conversion will change $1 million into £0.5 million ($\frac{1}{2}$ million pounds).

Next, the proceeds from this purchase are invested in a one-year British government security, which yields $(1 + r_B)$ of the purchase in one year. Suppose that $r_B = .10$. Henry will, therefore, receive $1 million/SR $(1 + r_B)$ in one year, or £0.5m(1.1) = £0.55m (here "m" means "million").

Simultaneously, Henry sells sterling one year forward in the full amount (£0.55m) that he expects to receive when the British government security matures. The forward rate, FR, of the sterling one year forward is $2.3 per pound; that is, $2.30 will be exchanged for 1 pound in one year. The value of Henry's return in dollars in one year is

$$\$1m(1 + r_B)FR/SR = R \tag{1}$$

or

$$\$1m(1.1)\ \$2.3/£/\$2/£ = \$1.265 \text{ million}$$

This series of transactions illustrates covered arbitrage. There is no capital risk since the purchase and sale of Henry's position at specified prices is contracted in advance.

To verify that each dollar invested in this covered arbitrage is more profitable than an investment in a U.S. T-bill, the following inequality must hold:

$$1 + r_{US} \neq (1 + r_B)\frac{FR}{SR}a \tag{2}$$

where a is used to convert the exchange rates into an annual rate. It is unity for one-year contracts and one-year government securities, 2 for a six-month contract and six-month assets, and 4 for a three-month (one-fourth of a year) contract and three-month assets. In other words, $12/a$ months is the maturity on the assets.

If covered arbitrage of the foregoing type—with forward sterling sold short—is profitable, the arbitrageur can (primarily) reduce the forward rate on sterling until there is no more profit to be made. (Reverse-type transactions, where forward U.S. dollars are sold short, would raise the forward price of sterling.) This will occur until Equation (2) is an equality, ignoring the costs of arbitrage:

$$1 + r_{US} = (1 + r_B)\frac{FR}{SR}a \tag{3}$$

This equality can be put in the form in which the relation is usually stated with some easy rearrangements and simplifications of terms. Rearranging the terms in Equation (3) produces:

$$1 + r_{US} - (1 + r_B) = (FR/SR - SR/SR)(1 + r_B)a \tag{4}$$

Simplify the terms in Equation (4) and divide by $(1 + r_B)$:

$$\frac{r_{US} - r_B}{1 + r_B} = \frac{FR - SR}{SR}a \tag{5}$$

or, if r_B is omitted because it is a small proportion of 1—that is, $1 + r_B$ is roughly equal to 1—

$$r_D - r_F = \frac{FR - SR}{SR}a \tag{6}$$

where the US and B subscripts are replaced by the more general D, for domestic, and F, for foreign.

Equation (6) is an equilibrium statement for covered arbitrage and also for short-term capital flows, under conditions of certainty. Where there is risk of the type described previously, investors may not wish to exploit fully the profit opportunities of covered arbitrage or speculation. Equation (6) as a statement under certainty is called the *interest rate parity theorem*. There would be no incentive to shift funds for investment in assets of a given maturity between two countries once the difference between the forward and the spot rate (expressed in annualized percentage form) is equal to the difference in yields on risk-free assets of the same maturity in each country. The difference between the forward rate and the spot rate is the expected change in the value of the currency. Thus the relation could also be interpreted as describing a relationship between the expected rate of change of the exchange value of the currency and the difference between domestic and foreign interest rates.

The interest rate parity line is shown in Figure 28-1. At point G, the difference in interest rates, say, on ninety-day government securities, between the foreign and domestic countries is −2 percent. It is shown as the negative of that difference in Figure 28-1. The annualized percentage difference between the rate forward rate (FR) and spot rate (SR) is also equal to 2 percent. At point H the difference between the forward and spot rates in annualized percentage form is 4 percent, which equals the difference between r_F and r_D, their respective government securities' interest rates.

The allowance for costs of covered arbitrage and speculation requires that a band be drawn for the interest rate parity line; that is, equilibrium need not be confined to the interest rate parity line in Figure 28-1. Instead, it may differ from that line by the cost involved in covered arbitrage operations and by speculation and risk premiums where risk-free

Figure 28–1

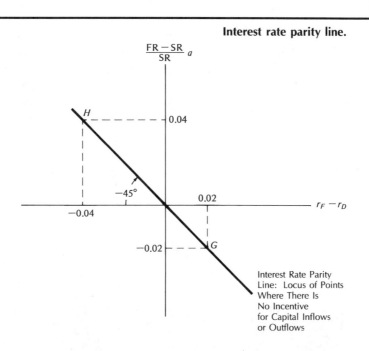

Interest rate parity line.

covered arbitrage is not available. Government intervention, preferences for a particular currency (say, by Canadians planning trips to the United States), and the unavailability of government securities in two countries that are perfect substitutes are three factors that could alter the relationship. Under crisis conditions, when the previously mentioned political risks intensify, the spot and forward exchange rates may swing widely away from the relation shown in Figure 28-1. However, tests tend to show that the forward rates' percentage differences from the spot rates are usually less than 1 percent—and often much less—than the interest rate differential shown in Equation (6) and Figure 28-1.

The Gold Standard

A country may adopt a gold standard for its money by either of the following equivalent policies:

1. The central government agrees to buy and sell an unlimited amount of gold at a fixed price, such as $800 per ounce of gold.
2. The central government intervenes in the world market for gold by buying and selling gold in exchange for its domestic currency, in order to maintain a fixed price, such as $800 per ounce of gold.

The official government price of $35 per ounce of gold was in effect in the United States from 1934 until 1971. Before that, the official government price of $20.67 per ounce was in effect from 1879 until 1933 (with the exception of World War I). Both prices seem like ancient fossils, with the price of gold reaching $835 per ounce in January 1980 (see Figure 28-2) or even after it fell from that height, reaching $340 per ounce on March 5, 1982.

If two or more countries adopt a system in which a fixed nominal quantity of their domestic currency is pegged to a given weight of gold, the relative prices between all their currencies are also fixed. The countries are then said to be on the *gold standard*. Suppose that the United States and Great Britain are on a gold standard. One U.S. dollar is pegged at 1 ounce of gold, and 1 British pound is pegged at 2 ounces of gold. Then 2 ounces of gold can be traded for £1 or $2. It follows that £1 is fixed at $2 in international exchange at current spot prices, ignoring transactions costs. The relative pound price of dollars is $2/£1 and the dollar price of pounds is £1/$2.

Suppose that a U.S. citizen buys a hat in London for £5. Most U.S. banks will sell him or her £5 for $10, ignoring transactions costs. Alternatively, the U.S. citizen in the hypothetical example could buy 10 ounces of gold from the U.S. Treasury and ship the gold to Great Britain, where the central bank would exchange it for £5. The £5 could then be sent to the London hat store.

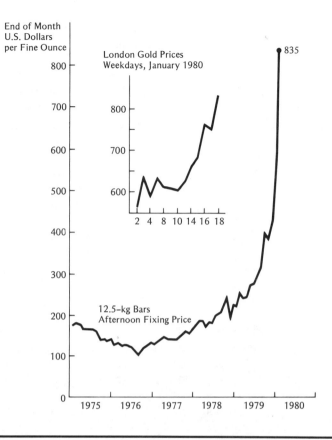

End of Month
U.S. Dollars
per Fine Ounce

London Gold Prices
Weekdays, January 1980

12.5–kg Bars
Afternoon Fixing Price

Figure 28-2

The price of gold in London. *Source:* **"The Surge in Gold Prices,"** *Economic Commentary,* **Federal Reserve Bank of Cleveland (January 28, 1980), Chart 1 [p. 2].**

The costs of transporting the gold back and forth across the Atlantic Ocean cause an increase in the price of the hat or, equivalently, a decrease in the value of dollars traded for pounds. These costs are reduced by keeping much of the free world's supply of gold deep underground in New York City, in the gold vault under the Federal Reserve Bank, where it can be inexpensively moved from one country's compartment to another.

Suppose that under a gold standard, the United States has a negative balance of payments with Great Britain. U.S. dollars are given to the inhabitants of Great Britain, who turn them into the U.S. Treasury in exchange for gold. Gold flows out of the United States to Great Britain, where it is turned in to the British central bank for pounds. The monetary base in the United States declines, whereas the monetary base in Great Britain rises. Through fractional reserve banking, the money supplies in the two countries change by multiples of the changes in their respective monetary bases. In the United States prices and real income fall, while in Great Britain prices and real incomes rise. (There is a time lag, which may be a number of years, for all those effects.) The demand for British goods by U.S. residents, who have declining real incomes and must pay higher prices for British goods, declines. The reverse occurs in Great Britain, so that the foreign demand for U.S. goods rises. The deficit in the U.S. balance of payments is eventually automatically corrected. The example illustrates the kind of adjustment that can occur under a gold standard to bring about a balance of payments automatically, without the "feeble hands and vacillating minds of men" who may take improper action.

Unfortunately, the adjustment period may be too long to be tolerated. No country is likely to completely give up control of its domestic money supply for very long if a severe depression or inflation occurs. The government is likely to change the proportion of the monetary base that is *fiduciary issue* (fiat money—see Chapter 2) or to completely abandon the gold standard. Perverse adjustments can also occur under a gold standard, where the world supply of gold for monetary uses changes or where the proportion of the money supply created by private banks or other financial intermediaries, through fractional reserve banking, is altered.

In the 1870s, many countries adopted a gold standard. The gold standard era lasted until the great depressions of the 1930s, with time out for World War I. Great Britain in 1931 and the United States in 1933 both went off the gold standard. During the heyday of the gold standard, there was a decline in many domestic price levels. Depressions and bank panics occurred during the 1890s in the United States. Output was increasing faster than gold production, and the monetary base was tied to gold. Then with the invention of the cyanide process (a less expensive method of extracting gold from gold ore) and with new discoveries of gold in the Yukon and South Africa, gold flowed into the treasuries of countries such as the United States. Internal inflation followed. The value of money fell in terms of the goods and services it could buy, as more and more gold was buried in the vaults of central banks. In the age where humankind has placed a man on the moon, we persist in digging deep into the earth to find gold, which we will bury again 76 feet under the Federal Reserve in New York City or underground at Fort Knox, from one hole to another. Why not bury bricks, as is suggested in the next section?

When there is a loss of confidence in fiat money, investments in commodities such as gold look attractive. Gold is a shiny, durable commodity that is limited in supply, as long as the big gold mining countries—South Africa and Russia—do not dig too much up and the United States does not precipitously run down its hoard.

World gold output in 1980 was estimated to be 42.5 million ounces by the Gold Institute, a trade association representing more than 200 companies that mine or refine gold.[3] South Africa, the largest producer, was estimated to have produced 48 percent of world gold output and the Soviet Union, the second largest producer, produced roughly 23 percent. The U.S. government had approximately 265 million ounces of gold in 1980, which, valued at $350 per ounce, would be worth $92,750 million.

It was an appealing way to store wealth, especially as world tensions flared after November 1979 when U.S. hostages were taken in Iran. There was a rapid rise in the price of gold, as shown in Figure 28-2.

The proponents of the gold standard argue that, however wasteful it may be to bury valuable resources in holes in the ground, people perceive utility from such activity, especially when the resources are shiny objects like gold. Therefore, they would say: "Set an appropriate price for gold so that there will be enough for purposes of world trade and let people do what they will do anyway!" The proponents of the gold standard also hold that the automatic adjustments of the gold standard are preferable to some of the manipulations of the money supply of governments that have poor monetary policies. In many countries where the currency has poor medium of exchange characteristics in the domestic country and/or is pegged at official rates at which it cannot be exchanged in international trade, the public may have confidence only in a commodity money such as that which exists under a gold standard.

There is even an *automatic countercyclical mechanism* under a gold standard. Assume that prices and real income fall, as the economy is thrown into a depression. One nominal price is fixed, the price of an ounce of gold. Assume that this price is $800 per ounce of gold. Suppose that there are domestic gold mines, and the cost of gold mining declines during the depression, so that there is an incentive to increase gold production. The gold is sold to the Treasury for $800 per ounce. The equilibrium (marginal) cost of producing $800 of currency is equal to $800. When the (marginal) cost of producing gold falls below $800 an ounce, gold output will be expanded until equilibrium is restored. Also, some gold that was stored for other uses (such as gold jewelry and gold dental inlays) is now worth less for industrial purposes and will be diverted to the monetary authority. The (marginal) return on the nonmonetary uses of gold will be smaller relative to the (marginal) return from selling it to the Treasury. All this will cause the money supply to increase, which will induce increases in real income and prices.

A similar explanation can be formulated to show how an inflation would be automatically stopped. The effectiveness of the response depends on the responsiveness of the supply of gold (i.e., how much gold is diverted from—or returned to—other uses and how rapidly gold production is changed with a change in the price of mining an ounce of gold, compared to the monetary value of gold). The more responsive the supply of gold is to changes in the price level, the more effective is the automatic mechanism for restoring equilibrium. Unfortunately, the supply of gold appeared to be rather unresponsive in some of the periods (especially around 1890) when falling prices failed to induce a rapidly increasing supply of gold for monetary purposes.

The most important argument in favor of such an automatic countercyclical mechanism is that it prevents government authorities from having a worse monetary policy. However, if a government is confronted with a five-year adjustment period and the possibilities of other conditions changing the outcome, the government may choose to go off the gold standard. Many factors can significantly alter the period of adjustment, such as new discoveries of gold and less expensive methods for mining gold. These are the kinds of things that a member of Congress would have trouble explaining to the folks back home, and for good reasons. "Don't worry, unemployed workers; you will get a job within five years, when gold mining picks up—barring unforeseen problems in the adjustment process." The historical record of the gold standard in the United States indicates that it was abandoned whenever major events, such as wars or depressions, occurred.

If one country suffers a depression, other countries may also be thrown into a depression, as the demand for their exports declines. Each country may prefer an independent monetary policy, in order to maintain internal price stability and to insulate itself partially from conditions in foreign countries, rather than being tied to an international gold standard.

Gold-standard countries sometimes *sterilize* the effect of gold inflows or outflows by arbitrarily adjusting the internal money supply in an offsetting direction. This practice bypasses the automatic adjustment process of the gold standard, and from the perspective of a pure gold standard, it violates the "rules."

President Reagan appointed a Gold Commission in 1981 to study the possibility of returning to a gold standard. It was composed of members of the U.S. Congress, a governor of the Federal Reserve, a member of the Council of Economic Advisers, the secretary of the Treasury (who served as chairman), and individuals from the private sector. The staff director was Anna Schwartz, an esteemed economist whose books, coauthored with Milton Friedman, are widely read. In 1982, the Commission voted against suggesting a gold standard. Instead, a weakly worded suggestion (the strongly worded suggestion resulted in a tie vote) for a monetary rule limiting the rate of money growth was suggested. It was also suggested that a gold coin, which would not be legal tender, be minted and sold to the public.

Commodity Standards

Gold is only one of the commodities that have been used or suggested for *commodity standards*, sometimes called *commodity reserve standards* (since warehouse receipts rather than the actual commodities would be traded).[4] Gold and silver have been used together in monetary standards, each bought and sold by the government at a different fixed nominal price. This is called a *bimetallic standard*. Under *symmetalism*, on the other hand, the government would agree to buy and sell a combined unit of gold and silver, in a specific proportion, at a fixed nominal price.

Charles Hardy is credited with the suggestion that bricks be used in a commodity standard.

> Bricks possess the minor virtues required of a commodity to be used as a currency—they can be reasonably well defined and checked for quality, they can be stored, etc. And they have the major virtue of an exceedingly elastic supply.[5]

As foolish as the brick standard may seem to those who cannot conceive of bricks as money or of tearing down brick houses and selling the bricks to the Treasury to halt a deflation, the example is very useful. It illuminates the operation of a commodity standard, such as a gold standard, with a substance that is in many ways superior to gold for monetary uses. At the same time, it illustrates the bizarre aspects of a commodity standard. The most important of these bizarre characteristics is the burying of valuable commodities.

One type of commodity standard would extend symmetallism much further than merely using gold and silver.[6] The government would agree to buy a specified bundle of goods at a fixed nominal price. The selling price could be slightly higher, to pay the costs and to earn a profit for printing money. This additional fee is called *seignorage*. The physical amount of each commodity in the bundle would be fixed, as would the total nominal price of the entire bundle. Many goods could be included in this bundle, such as nonperishable agricultural products and standardized manufactured goods. Agricultural goods might be ruled out because their short-run supply is relatively unresponsive to price changes.

The government must store large quantities of these bundles. This may be especially undesirable if some commodity in the bundle (say, a basic foodstuff) is in short supply. Benjamin Graham suggested that future contracts on the commodity be used to replace the actual commodity under these conditions.[7] This appears to be a poor suggestion because a higher future price may induce more private storage, worsening the current supply problems.

Notice that the commodities in the bundle can each fluctuate in price, as long as the total price of the bundle does not fluctuate from the price set by the government and the government does not exhaust its supply of the commodities in the bundle. This plan would stabilize the price level more rapidly than a brick or gold standard. Still, changes in the costs of producing the commodities in the bundle, caused by changes in technology, changes in tastes and preferences for these commodities in nonmonetary uses, and many other factors could cause substantial oscillations in the price level and real income. The chance of many countries adopting the same commodity bundle for an international commodity standard would be small. If the same bundle were not adopted, countries would be on different standards, and there would not be fixed rates of exchange between their currencies. The automatic countercyclical feature of the plan would still be operable in each country. Compared to the single-commodity gold standard, this commodity standard could produce more rapid countercycical adjustments. However, the alternative cost of the resources that might have to be stored by the government and the costs of storage are probably too large to make the idea more than an example to indicate the waste involved in commodity standards.

International Currency and the International Monetary Fund

The Bretton Woods Agreement of 1944 led to the establishment of the International Monetary Fund (IMF), an organization affiliated with the United Nations. The IMF began with 35 national government members and had 140 in 1979. Most noncommunist nations are members. Switzerland is a notable exception.

The IMF was created December 18, 1946, by the Articles of Agreement formulated at the United Nations Monetary and Financial Conference held in Bretton Woods, New Hampshire, in July 1944. The International Bank for Reconstruction and Development, known as the World Bank, was also concurrently created. All IMF members must also be members of this bank. The World Bank makes long-term loans for economic development.

The IMF originally negotiated the relative prices of all members' currencies in terms of gold or U.S. dollars, and members attempted to maintain their currency prices within 1 percent of these fixed exchange prices. Countries could vary the price between 90 and 110 percent of the fixed price after consultation, but such limited changes did not require permission from the IMF.

Each country was required to place funds at the IMF consisting of one-fourth gold or U.S. dollars and three-fourth of its own currency. The IMF loaned these funds, under certain conditions, to member countries that ran short of foreign exchange. The IMF was unable to provide sufficient credit to cover chronic balance-of-payments deficits or, in some cases, to restrain government policies to the maintenance within limits of the fixed exchange prices.

The exchange rate system, but not the IMF, fell apart when the United States closed its gold window in 1971 and generalized floating began in 1973. To supplement or replace this system, plans have been suggested to create an international money, managed by the IMF. Robert Triffin suggested a comprehensive plan that would require member countries to hold a fraction of their reserves with the IMF.[8] The IMF could engage in open-market operations to acquire dollars in exchange for IMF deposits. The deposits would be "guaranteed" by the reserves from members. The IMF would then be creating international bank money that all member countries would agree to exchange for their goods and services.

A plan was adopted by the IMF for issuing *special drawing rights* (SDRs). SDRs were created on July 28, 1969, to be used as reserve assets that could be used by member central banks to settle accounts among themselves. The value of the SDR was at first tied to gold and then on July 1, 1976, to a basket of sixteen currencies (see Table 28-2). On January 1, 1981, the basket was reduced to five currencies. The U.S. dollar was given a 42 percent weight; the German mark a 19 percent weight; and the French franc, Japanese yen, and British pound were each given a 13 percent weight. The SDR is an official international currency.

Since 1975 there have been some international transactions in SDR units. That is, transactors agree to pay in terms of the currency composi-

TABLE 28-2

Units of Currencies in the Special Drawing Rights Basket (Percentage Weight in Basket at Base Period in Parentheses)

Currency	Effective January 1, 1981		Effective July 1, 1978		Effective July 1, 1974	
United States dollar	0.54	(42.0)	0.40	(33.0)	0.40	(33.0)
German mark	0.46	(19.0)	0.32	(12.5)	0.38	(12.5)
Japanese yen	34.00	(13.0)	21.00	(7.5)	26.00	(7.5)
French franc	0.74	(13.0)	0.42	(7.5)	0.44	(7.5)
British pound sterling	0.071	(13.0)	0.05	(7.5)	0.045	(9.0)
Italian lira	—		52.00	(5.0)	47.00	(6.0)
Dutch guilder	—		0.14	(5.0)	0.14	(4.5)
Canadian dollar	—		0.07	(5.0)	0.071	(6.0)
Belgian franc	—		1.60	(4.0)	1.60	(3.5)
Saudi Arabian riyal	—		0.13	(3.0)	—	
Swedish krona	—		0.11	(2.0)	0.13	(2.5)
Iranian rial	—		1.70	(2.0)	—	
Australian dollar	—		0.017	(1.5)	0.012	(1.5)
Danish krone	—		—		0.11	(1.5)
Spanish peseta	—		1.50	(1.5)	1.10	(1.5)
Norwegian krone	—		0.10	(1.5)	0.099	(1.5)
Austrian schilling	—		0.28	(1.5)	0.22	(1.0)
South African rand	—		—		0.0082	(1.0)

Calculation of the SDR Value

The IMF, which publishes the official value or exchange rate for the SDR daily, and the commercial banks use the same method to calculate the value of the SDR in United States dollar terms. But the result varies depending on the spot exchange rates used. For example, on November 2, 1981, the IMF reported that the exchange value for the official SDR was $1.1596. This was based on the noon middle market rates in London provided by the Bank of England. (If the London markets are closed, the IMF obtains its exchange rates from the Federal Reserve Bank of New York; if the New York markets are closed, the Deutsche Bundesbank in Frankfurt provides the rates.) If the commercial banks had used the 10 a.m. middle market interbank rates in New York for the same date, the dollar value of the SDR would have been $1.1613.

Source: Dorothy Meadow Sobol, "The SDR in Private International Finance," *Quarterly Review*, Federal Reserve Bank of New York (Winter 1981–1982), p. 32.

tion of the official value of the SDR. This practice accelerated in 1981. Loans are said to be SDR-denominated if they are recorded on the basis of SDR units. Chemical Bank issued SDR-denominated CDs in 1980 through its London branch. The market in private SDRs was estimated to be roughly SDR3 billion at the beginning of 1981 and SDR5 to 7 billion by the end of 1981.[9]

There are three important stumbling blocks to the wide implementation by an international organization of an international money. First, it is difficult to work out a plan for the initial distribution of the international money between countries. Second, governments will be hesitant to allow international organizations to issue significant quantities of money that can be exchanged for goods and services in the country. Third, most countries can offer more substantial guarantees for their currencies. These guarantees are in the form of their total marketable stock of wealth and their current output of goods and services, for which their currency can be exchanged. An international organization with relatively small reserves of convertible currencies and precious metals and with virtually no power to force its large members to maintain their agreements may offer a less appealing guarantee than most larger countries provide.

Flexible Exchange Rates

If the internal price level of a country were perfectly flexible, the most important arguments for a flexible exchange rate would collapse. Assume that the balance of payments is initially in equilibrium at a full-employment level of output. There then occurs an increased demand for imports and a decreased demand for domestic goods and services by residents. This causes a balance-of-payments deficit. If the domestic price level rapidly falls, the internal demand for domestic output and the foreign demand for exports will normally increase to restore balance-of-payments equilibrium at a full-employment level. An important condition for unemployment equilibrium, downward rigidity in wages and prices, is removed.

Balance-of-payments equilibrium can be attained under fixed exchange rates if the internal price level adjusts to the new equilibrium level. However, if a fall in prices is necessary to attain equilibrium, and if prices are slow to fall, the adjustment period may be exceedingly long. In the meantime, the demand for domestic output will decline and domestic unemployment will rise.

This situation is somewhat analogous to that of a shoe store owner who demands $10 a pair for shoes that are currently thought by most customers to be worth $5. He sells very few shoes at $10 a pair and is driven into a depressed state, in which he must dramatically reduce his standard of living to a starvation level. "By gosh," he can assert, "no one can say my shoes are worth a cent less than $10." But if the volume of shoes he sells is small relative to the total market (as is true of the international trade of a small country), he may have to change his "fixed" rate of exchange for shoes. If the volume of shoes he sells is large, or his shoes have few substitutes, he may take much longer to adjust to the underlying equilibrium price.

The proponents of flexible exchange rates argue that a large part of the internal price-level adjustments and real income adjustments could be avoided by a small change in the exchange rates.[10] An increased demand by U.S. citizens for British goods could be partially absorbed by a change in the relative price of the two currencies. Instead of a prolonged adjustment in the United States, that may include a substantial income adjustment—a recession; the relative international exchange price of U.S. dollars would fall to a lower equilibrium level.

Proponents of flexible exchange rates argue that fixed exchange rates only camouflage the underlying adjustments in real variables. Fixed rates obscure the adjustment process by indicating that the relative prices of currency have not changed. Instead of uncertainties about future spot exchange rates, fixed rates produce increased uncertainties about future real income, other internal economic variables, and the supply of foreign reserves and credit that will be available to support the currency. Although a system of flexible rates does make future exchange rates uncertain, a forward market in currencies removes much of this uncertainty. The uncertainty about future exchange rates is borne by traders who stand willing to sell a contract for the delivery of foreign currency in the future at a fixed price.

Many economists (at least in the United States) are probably in favor of flexible exchange rates between some areas of the world. Many, perhaps the majority, advocate flexible exchange rates between all countries with different currencies. There are influential economists who disagree with the majority view. Jacques Rueff, for example, argued for a return to the gold standard because it alone has commanded confidence through the centuries.[11] Arthur Laffer and others, called *supply siders*, advocated the gold standard during the Reagan administration. They advocated tax cuts and a gold standard. Their views were widely publicized in the popular press in the early 1980s.

Optimum Currency Areas

If flexible exchange rates eliminate much of the costly changes in internal variables, such as domestic real income and internal prices, why not have different currencies for Indiana and Illinois, adjacent states in the United States? An increased demand by Illinois residents for goods in Indiana would not cause much unemployment in Illinois or inflation in Indiana. The relative value of Illinois currency would simply fall. This benefit from a single currency brings up the analysis developed by Robert Mundell on the optimum size of a currency area.[12] The more flexible wages and prices are and the more mobile labor is (between Indiana and Illinois), the less need for separate currencies. The adjustment to an increased demand for Indiana goods could be rapidly resolved without a recession in Illinois or an exchange adjustment in the relative price of their separate currencies. Workers would move to Indiana and the prices of goods and labor would temporarily rise in Indiana and fall in Illinois.

Suppose that wages and prices are fairly rigid in each state and that mobility of labor between the states is negligible. The increased demand for Indiana goods may cause a prolonged recession in Illinois if the two states have the same currency (as at present) and therefore have a fixed rate of exchange between their currencies.

On the other hand, separate currencies with flexible exchange rates reduce the services of money. The separate state currencies can be used only in a limited area. Costly arrangements must be made to maintain reserves of "foreign" currency continually and to trade the currency continually. If many of the goods consumed in each state are imported, frequent and large changes in exchange rates can cause frequent and large changes in the internal cost of goods. The increased variation in the internal cost of goods from flexible exchange rates may pose larger real costs than would be imposed by changes in real output under fixed exchange rates.

The balance of payments may be affected by *capital flows*. These are likely to be more rapid and more mobile than the migration of labor. The optimum currency area may be larger than would be indicated from a study of labor migration, once capital flows are considered.

Very few people would argue for a different currency in Illinois than in Indiana. The loss in the services performed by money and the mobility of capital and labor between these states are the basis of strong arguments for a single currency, a fixed exchange rate. The analogy leads to the more relevant question: What is the optimum size of a currency area; or, equivalently, what is the size of an area (or group of countries in different geographical areas) that should have fixed exchange rates? The difficulty in solving this question led Harry Johnson to make the following observation, given the present state of knowledge: "Specifically, it seems to me that the optimum currency area problem has proved to be something of a dead-end problem."[13] It may parallel problems such as determining the optimum size of firms or countries. Often these problems tend to be answered in an ad hoc way, according to the size of firms and countries that survive for a long enough period in a given (equilibrium) healthy condition. The world is split into national divisions that are taken as given in the immediate future. Each major country wishes to have control over its internal money supply. However, the attempt to form optimum currency areas, such as the European Monetary System, does transcend national boundaries. Mundell's insightful analysis provides a useful vehicle for evaluating the optimum size of a currency area and is not for this purpose a dead end.

A European monetary system went into operation in 1980. It followed many other attempts. In 1972, Belgium, West Germany, Luxembourg,

Denmark, the Netherlands, and France confined the relative price fluctuations of their currencies to narrow bands, called the "snake." France floated in 1976 and the snake broke apart.

The plan was an extension of the "joint float" or "snake." A monetary unit, the European Currency Unit, was created. It did not exist in a physical sense, but served as a reserve asset for the participating countries' central banks. Its value is a benchmark against which the values of the individual currencies are pegged. The currencies to be tied together in the agreement were the Belgian-Luxembourg franc, German mark, Dutch guilder, Danish kroner, French franc, Italian lira, and Irish pound.

Key Currency and the Gold Exchange Standard

The U.S. dollar has been a key currency in the post-World War II period, just as was the British currency prior to the 1930s. A *key currency* is a form of international currency that is created by a single country. Most of the free-world countries have agreed (in meetings of their central bankers) to use either U.S. dollars or gold in international transactions. This is called a *gold-exchange standard* or, more specifically in its post-World War II form, a *dollar-gold standard.*

The key currency country has certain advantages. For a negligible cost, it can print money and trade it for the output of foreign countries. A U.S. grant-in-aid of $100 to an underdeveloped country does not necessarily cost the U.S. $100 in goods and services. Suppose that the donee (recipient) country uses $50 to buy U.S. goods and $50 to buy Volkswagens in Germany. The German government keeps the $50 to use in world trade and, in effect, pays approximately half of the cost of the U.S. grant-in-aid, as long as the $50 is not exchanged for U.S. goods and services. For this reason, countries that use the key currency usually desire the key currency country to run a surplus, or at least to achieve a balance in its balance of payments. At the same time, there is sometimes the inconsistent desire to have an expanding international currency to accommodate the needs of world trade. The United States has run deficits almost constantly since 1959. By August 1971, the U.S. gold stock, valued at $35 per ounce, had been reduced through exchanges for U.S. dollars to $10.5 billion from its 1949 peak of $24 billion. The United States had over $60 billion in dollar liabilities held by foreigners which was convertible into gold at $35 an ounce at the U.S. Treasury.

Leland Yaeger described the drama leading to President Nixon's announcement that the United States was "going off gold." The final spark that put the plan in motion was provided by John Connally, secretary of the Treasury, in a meeting of high officials with the president at Camp David on Friday, August 13, 1971. "What is our immediate problem? We are meeting here because we are in trouble overseas. The British came in today to ask us to cover $3 billion of their dollar reserves [against loss].

Anybody can topple us—anytime they want—we have left ourselves completely exposed."[14]

When President Nixon closed the gold window in August 1971 (eliminating all transactions in gold by the U.S. Treasury except for an occasional sale of gold), U.S. dollars continued to be used, together with gold, as international money. U.S. dollars were then on a flexible rate with respect to gold and other currencies, with some intervention by the U.S. government to control the price of dollars.[15] U.S. dollars held by foreigners could still be exchanged for goods and services produced in the United States, even though they could not be traded for gold owned by the U.S. Treasury.

Proponents of flexible exchange rates praised the U.S. action. Some were concerned about U.S. intervention in the foreign exchange market to manipulate the exchange rate of dollars (a dirty float) at levels that were inconsistent with long-run equilibrium in the balance of payments.

The United States terminated the practice of giving what was, in effect, substantial foreign aid to the Soviet Union and South Africa (the two major gold-mining countries) by buying and burying the gold they dug up at a guaranteed price.

The U.S. monetary authorities (the Federal Reserve and the U.S. Treasury) were (according to proponents of flexible exchange rates) relieved of the task of maintaining a monetary policy with the often inconsistent external targets such as balance-of-payments equilibrium and internal targets such as price stability. The flexible exchange rate could be left alone. However, some observers believed that under a system of flexible exchange rates, devaluations and increases in the exchange value of the domestic currency sufficiently affect the internal price level to warrant a dirty float or even a return to fixed exchange rates.

Although some observers predicted dire consequences from floating, including the elimination of the U.S. dollar as a key currency, such consequences did not come to pass. However, it is not clear that the flexible exchange rate achieved all the objectives that its proponents envisioned. One of the reasons for this is that the period since 1973 has been marked by a number of problems and crises, which produced gyrations in many economic variables, including the exchange rate of the U.S. dollar. Those crises included, in 1973, the self-destruction of wage-price controls in the United States; an oil boycott against the United States by the OPEC countries; and rapid inflation, reaching double digits in 1973 and from 1978 through at least 1981. Partially because of the rising price of oil, the United States ran a persistently large deficit, with the U.S. dollar taking a precipitous plunge in value from April 1978 until November 1978. Was this a fall to a new equilibrium level for the U.S. dollar, or a short-run fluctuation that should be offset by government action?

On November 1, 1978, President Carter unveiled a series of measures to bolster the dollar, including his plan for massive intervention to buy U.S. dollars. There seemed to be general support in the United States for this intervention among government officials and members of the U.S. Congress. Some economists pointed out that this intervention would entail a high cost for a temporary lull in the fall of the dollar to its equilibrium level. From October 1977 to October 31, 1978, the dollar had depreciated by more than 12 percent (on a bilateral trade-weighted basis and by about 19 percent using multilateral trade weights). For a year after Carter's November speech, the dollar remained fairly stable. The value of the dollar may have been helped by other countries' policies of more rapid money growth, which tended to reduce the international value of their currencies; but more important, the intervention appeared to have been successful.

Opponents of a freely floating exchange rate can point to 1978 as a period in which the dollar fell so rapidly that it produced extreme uncertainty in domestic and foreign financial markets, not only about the future value of the dollar, but also about the general health of the U.S. economy. Those who favor flexible exchange rates would not, in many cases, disagree with this statement. They would add, however, that the basic cause of the problem was not falling exchange rates; it was merely a symptom of other problems, such as surging monetary growth and the resulting inflation.

It is very likely that a system of fixed exchange rates could not have been held in place in the period since 1973. If this is the case, the argument for or against flexible exchange rates should really be posed in terms of those who believe in freely fluctuating exchange rates and those who believe that exchange rates should be controlled for short periods.

Despite all these problems, the U.S. dollar continued to serve as the key currency.[16] However, in periodic meetings central bankers sometimes produced proposals for changes in the international payments system. Although it was becoming apparent that a return to a fixed rate system was impossible, some meetings of central bankers and heads of state emphasized close cooperation and even outlined the steps necessary to return to a fixed rate system. However, at the meetings of the heads of state at Rambouillet, France, in 1975 and the Interim Committee of Governors of the International Monetary Fund in Jamaica in 1976, there was a realization of the need for a flexible exchange system. There was disagreement over how much flexibility should be allowed. As Table 28-1 shows, intervention and pegging are prevalent.

In the spring of 1981, the new Undersecretary for Monetary Affairs of the U.S. Treasury, Beryl Sprinkel, strongly urged a policy of minimum intervention. He expressed this view and its rationale before the Joint Economic Committee of the Congress on May 4, 1981.

Intervention had occurred on March 30, 1981, following the attempted assassination of President Reagan, who was severely wounded. A total of $74.4 million in German marks was sold to support the dollar. After that, the minimal intervention policy remained in effect, at least into 1982. The dollar appreciated during the beginning of the Reagan administration in 1981 and early 1982 as inflation persisted, interest rates remained above 10 percent, and the economy fell into a serious recession.

Intervention in the United States has been carried out primarily by

TABLE 28-3

Federal Reserve Reciprocal Currency Arrangements (Millions of Dollars)	
Institution	Amount of Facility, July 31, 1981
Austrian National Bank	250
National Bank of Belgium	1,000
Bank of Canada	2,000
National Bank of Denmark	250
Bank of England	3,000
Bank of France	2,000
German Federal Bank	6,000
Bank of Italy	3,000
Bank of Japan	5,000
Bank of Mexico	700
Netherlands Bank	500
Bank of Norway	250
Bank of Sweden	300
Swiss National Bank	4,000
Bank for International Settlements	
Swiss francs–dollars	600
Other authorized European currencies–dollars	1,250
Total	30,100

Source: Quarterly Review, Federal Reserve Bank of New York (Autumn 1981), p. 47.

the Federal Reserve in consultation with the Treasury. Money used for intervention is often split between Federal Reserve and Treasury balances.

The Federal Reserve, without clear authority—as evidenced by the Federal Open-Market Committee Meeting minutes for 1961—supervises a huge reciprocal currency arrangement program. These so-called SWAP arrangements allow countries to swap currencies (such as dollars for pesos), ostensibly to support various currencies. By July 31, 1981, the Federal Reserve authorized $30.1 billion for SWAP lines of exchange (see Table 28-3). Neither the Congress nor the president of the United States nor the secretary of the Treasury officially apparently authorized the huge reciprocal currency facility. Since 1962, the Federal Reserve provided this facility. Attempts to have this authorization questioned in the Congress did not meet with interest, in part because it was felt to be very desirable to have intervention policies and to trust the Federal Reserve in this somewhat esoteric area.

NOTES

1. An excellent review of the extensive tests on the efficiency of the foreign exchange markets was presented by Richard M. Levich, "On the Efficiency of Markets for Foreign Exchange," in *International Economic Policy: Theory and Evidence,* Rudiger Dornbusch and Jacob A. Frankel, eds. (Balti-

more: The Johns Hopkins University Press, 1979), pp. 246–267. Whether one views the evidence of some inconsistencies with the efficient market hypothesis as strongly refuting evidence or slight inconsistencies can be judged in terms of the robustness of the underlying test. John F. O. Bilson believes in "a greater degree of optimism on the ability to test market efficiency [in the foreign exchange markets] than is present in Richard Levich's paper" ("Comment" on Richard M. Levich's papers, in *International Economic Policy*, p. 269).

2. Robert Z. Aliber, "The Interest Rate Parity Theorem: A Reinterpretation," *Journal of Political Economy* (December 1973), pp. 1451–1459.

3. *International Letter*, Federal Reserve Bank of Chicago (February 12, 1982), p. 3.

4. See Milton Friedman, "Commodity-Reserve Currency," reprinted in Friedman's *Essays in Positive Economics* (Chicago: University of Chicago Press, 1953), pp. 204–250.

5. Ibid., p. 212.

6. This was advocated by Benjamin Graham in *Storage and Stability* (New York: McGraw-Hill Book Company, 1937) and *World Commodities and World Currency* (New York: McGraw-Hill Book Company, 1944); and by Frank Graham (not related), *Social Goals and Economic Institutions* (Princeton, N.J.: Princeton University Press, 1942).

7. See Friedman's discussion, "Commodity-Reserve Currency," p. 225, footnote 15, and F. A. Hayek's support of this idea in "A Commodity Reserve Currency," *Economic Journal* (June–September 1943), pp. 176–184.

8. Robert Triffin, *Gold and the Dollar Crisis* (New Haven, Conn.: Yale University Press, 1960).

9. Dorothy Meadow Sobol, "The SDR in Private International Finance," *Quarterly Review*, Federal Reserve Bank of New York (Winter 1981–1982), p. 35.

10. The classic statement in support of flexible exchange rates is Milton Friedman's "The Case for Flexible Exchange Rates," in Friedman, *Essays in Positive Economics*, pp. 157–203. Henry C. Wallich presents an opposing view in a widely reprinted statement, "A Defense of Fixed Exchange Rates," from United States Balance of Payments, hearings before the Joint Economic Committee, 88th Cong., 1st Sess., Pt. 3. For a defense of the pure gold standard (and fixed exchange rates), see Jacques Rueff, *The Monetary Sin of the West* (New York: Macmillan Publishing Co., Inc., 1972).

11. Rueff, *The Monetary Sin of the West*. See also Robert Mundell, "The Monetary Consequences of Jacques Rueff—Review Article," *Journal of Business* (July 1973), pp. 384–395.

12. For an excellent discussion of optimum currency areas and many other aspects of the argument for and against flexible exchange rates, see Robert A. Mundell and Alexander K. Swoboda, eds., *Monetary Problems of the International Economy* (Chicago: The University of Chicago Press, 1969).

13. Harry Johnson believed that once the domain of capital mobility is introduced, the determinant of the optimum currency area "becomes too complex for its statement to be very illuminating." For his comments, see Mundell and Swoboda, *Monetary Problems of the International Economy*, p. 396.

14. Leland B. Yaeger, *The Night We Floated*, International Institute for Economic Research (Ottawa, Ill.: Green-Hill Publishers, Inc., 1977), p. 6.

15. Prior to August 1971, the U.S. Treasury bought and sold gold at $35 per ounce, whereas the gold traded in free markets was sold at a higher price. This *two-tier system* of separate official and market prices for gold was followed by many governments. After 1971, the U.S. government raised its official price of gold to $42.22 per ounce but still did not buy or sell any gold. On November 13, 1973, the United States, together with six European countries, agreed to recognize the "true price" of gold at $100 an ounce. Gold was to be officially valued at its market price. The purpose of this agreement appeared

to be to end the two-tier system and to enable governments to sell gold at the market price. The dollar-exchange price was generally pegged by foreign central bankers until March 1973, when there was generalized floating of exchange rates.

16. Rueff had argued in *The Monetary Sin of the West* that the gold-exchange standard in the post-World War II period would collapse after 1971, as it did in 1931. Mundell attempted to analyze why he was wrong in his elegant review, "The Monetary Consequences of Jacques Rueff."

STUDY QUESTIONS

1. How are international payments made? Describe the various types of arrangements.

2. What type of arrangement can be made for determining the international price of a currency?

3. How does the gold standard work, and what automatic mechanisms does it provide?

4. What are official and private SDRs and the European Currency Unit?

5. From the standpoint of optimum currency areas, should every country adopt flexible exchange rates? Under what conditions would it be desirable for a small country to peg the value of its currency to the value of the currency of a large country?

6. Why do countries still use U.S. dollars as a key currency? What circumstances would cause a shift to another key currency? Is it likely that an international currency such as SDRs will take the place of U.S. dollars as international money?

7. Describe covered arbitrage.

8. Describe the interest rate parity relationship. Is it achieved? Does it imply that internal inflation affects the expected change in the external exchange rate of the currency?

9. What are SDR-denominated CDs?

10. Describe the Federal Reserve SWAP facilities.

29

The Eurodollar Market

Introduction

A huge market for bank deposits, including U.S. dollars, has grown up in many parts of the world. The market is called the *Eurocurrency market* when reference is made to all currency and the *Eurodollar market* when reference is made only to the U.S. dollar part of the market. In December 1980, the estimated (gross) size of the Eurocurrency market was $1470 billion, of which 76 percent, or $1117.2 billion was Eurodollars (Table 29-1). The Eurocurrency market is not confined to Europe, which had 70 percent of the deposits (based on rough estimates) in 1978. The emergence of this huge market suggests a number of questions.

1. What is it?
2. Why did it happen?
3. What does it do?
4. Is it unstable?
5. Is it inflationary?
6. Does it interfere with control of the U.S. money supply?

The answers to those questions will be discussed, followed by a short discussion of the Eurobond market, where the trend since the late 1960s has been toward a smaller share of U.S. dollar-denominated assets.[1] Finally, the domestic deregulated international banking facilities established in the United States at the end of 1981 are discussed.

TABLE 29-1

Eurocurrency Market

Eurocurrency Market Size

Based on foreign liabilities of banks in major European countries, the Bahamas, Bahrain, Cayman Islands, Panama, Canada, Japan, Hong Kong, and Singapore.

Billions of dollars (rounded to the nearest $5 billion) at end of period

									1980	
	1972	1973	1974	1975	1976	1977	1978	1979	Sept.	Dec.
Gross liabilities to:										
Nonbanks	$ 35	$ 55	$ 75	$ 80	$100	$125	$170	$ 230	$ 270	$ 270
Central banks	25	40	60	70	85	110	120	155	170	180
Other banks	145	215	255	330	405	490	640	805	925	1020
Total	205	310	390	480	590	725	930	1190	1365	1470
Eurodollars as percent of total gross liabilities in all Eurocurrencies	78	73	77	78	79	76	74	72	73	76
Dollar liabilities of foreign branches of U.S. banks as percent of total gross liabilities in all Eurocurrencies	27	26	28	28	29	27	25	23	21	20

Eurodollar Deposit Rates

Eurodollar deposits are deposits denominated and payable in U.S. dollars held by banks located outside the United States. Rates (percent) are those bid in London at or near end of month.

	1977	1978	1979	1980		1981	
				Sept.	Dec.	Mar.	June
Overnight	6.62	10.73	9.03	10.95	21.11	13.37	19.17
Seven-day	7.39	12.88	9.45	11.04	19.88	13.45	18.95
One-month	6.98	11.48	9.23	11.42	19.33	13.84	18.59
Three-month	7.33	11.95	9.31	12.04	17.79	14.31	18.00
Six-month	7.66	12.48	9.30	12.56	16.69	14.38	17.20
Twelve-month	7.67	12.06	9.26	12.59	14.98	14.34	16.20

Source: International Economic Conditions, Federal Reserve Bank of St. Louis (August 15, 1981), p. 8, as adapted from Morgan Guaranty Trust Company, *World Financial Markets, Federal Reserve Bulletin,* and Board of Governors of the Federal Reserve System, *Selected Interest and Exchange Rates.*

What Is It?

What is the Eurocurrency market? Any bank deposit in any country that is denominated in another country's currency is a Eurocurrency deposit. A deposit in a French bank denominated in Dutch guilders qualifies as such a deposit. Most of these foreign deposits are denominated in U.S. dollars, so that the Eurodollar market is a substantial portion of the Euro-currency market. These deposits are not subject to the same stringent regulations as they would be if they were in their domestic country. Together with U.S. dollar-denominated securities, they are the financial assets of the Eurodollar market.

One of the first participants was the Soviet-controlled Banque Commerciale pour l'Europe, which had the code name Eurobank, from which the market took its name. In the 1950s, the bank began holding U.S. dollar-denominated deposits. The U.S. dollar was the key currency and therefore useful in international trade, but there was a preference for holding the funds outside the United States. This preference can be based on many factors, such as privacy and freedom from U.S. govern-ment regulations. An important factor is the avoidance of a freeze or an expropriation such as the U.S. freeze on Iranian government bank depos-its in 1979. (Although Eurodollar deposits in foreign branches of U.S. banks were ordered frozen by the U.S. government, the legality of this order under foreign laws is probably very questionable.)

Eurodollars are found in Europe, Canada, Hong Kong, Panama, Singa-pore, and Japan. Roughly 80 percent of gross (total liabilities without any offsetting adjustments) Eurodollar deposits were interbank deposits and 20 percent were nonbank deposits, according to estimates in mid-1980. Of the 20 percent nonbank deposits, approximately 5 percent were held by U.S. nonbank residents.

Overnight Eurodollar deposits of nonbank U.S. residents are included in the M2 definition of money. In 1981, they amounted to $5.9 billion, or .3 percent of M2 and of M1, Eurodollar deposits with maturities greater than one day, term deposits, of nonbank U.S. residents amounted to $61.6 billion, or 2.9 percent of M3 and 3.4 percent of M2. (See Chapter 2 for a description of these monetary aggregates.) These data are Federal Reserve estimates[2] and the overnight estimates are from the Caribbean branches of U.S. banks. The overnight Eurodollar deposits are officially added into M2, although an argument could be made to include them in M1. The term Eurodeposits are added in an aggregate called L (which is M3 plus other liquid assets), although an argument could be made to add them into M2 or M3. One thing is clear from these figures: The Eurodollar market contains little M1-type money and only a small amount of M2-type money compared to the respective size of these aggregates.

Eurodollar certificates of deposit (CDs), first introduced in 1966, amounted to roughly $50 billion at the beginning of 1980. There is an active secondary market in these CDs. Eurodollar floating-rate CDs and Eurodollar floating-rate notes have recently been used in the variable interest rate period in the early 1980s. The coupon rate is typically reset every three or six months between $\frac{1}{8}$ and $\frac{1}{4}$ percentage point over the interbank lending rate, the London Interbank borrowing rate, or LIBOR.[3]

Why Did It Happen?

The Eurodollar market is in part an extension of the services provided by U.S. dollars, which serve as the key currency in international trade. What caused the rapid growth of the Eurocurrency market beginning in the 1960s? The answer is stringent regulations placed on banking and currencies by domestic countries that are generally absent in the Eurocurrency market. For example, in the United States, reserve requirements on large banks were, until 1981, as high as $16\frac{1}{4}$ percent of any additions to demand deposits. Reserve requirements are generally not applicable to deposits of banks in the Eurodollar market. In addition, ceilings on interest payments on savings deposits and the prohibition against the payment of interest on domestic demand deposits were not applicable in the Eurodollar market. Domestic banks in the United States have kept only a portion of their deposits within the United States. Thus a large part of their deposits are free of reserve requirements or requirements affecting the maximum amount of interest that can be paid on deposits.

The Eurodollar market was greatly stimulated by the restraints on capital movements imposed by President Kennedy in 1963. A tax was placed on the sales of foreign bonds and equities in the United States. Guidelines were placed on American banks in 1965 that limited their acquisition of foreign assets. In 1968, a reinvestment requirement was placed on American multinational corporations, requiring them to raise funds for new direct foreign investments outside the Untied States.

Primarily because of the competition from the Eurodollar market, in 1970 the Federal Reserve allowed the sale by banks of certificates of deposit with no ceiling rates (in a minimum size of $100,000). Those CDs are very similar to most Eurocurrency deposits, which resemble short-term time deposits rather than demand deposits. However, until 1980, U.S. member banks could not write domestic CDs with maturities of thirty days or less. The Eurodollar market captured the short-term CD business. In 1980, the Federal Reserve announced that it would consider allowing CDs to be written for fifteen days or more.

The Depository Institution Deregulation and Monetary Control Act of 1980 removed many of the regulations that induced the export of the U.S. banking business to the Eurodollar market. Reserve requirements were substantially lowered, and the slow removal of interest rate ceilings was authorized. The phase-in for the provision of this law will not be complete until 1988 (1993 in Hawaii).

One way to view the controls placed on domestic U.S. banks is that they were the stimulus for exporting a large portion of American banking activity into the Eurocurrency market, where the regulations are more lax. The reader may ask: Why not impose the same requirements on branches of domestic banks operating offshore? One answer is that if such regulations were imposed only on U.S. banks, they would be at a competitive disadvantage in international markets. Regulations would have to be applied on the entire Eurocurrency market, and that appears to be unlikely. The reason is that some countries—from small Caribbean islands to England, with London being the center of the Eurocurrency market—where regulations are lax will probably refrain from participating in group action that would impede their profitable banking activities. In addition, capital is fungible, and new ways will be found to avoid the regulations. The regulations will therefore impose costs and inefficiencies without being equitable. Alternative solutions include the removal of onerous regulations that apply to domestic banks or to set aside an area in the domestic country that would be free of such regulations—a "free-trade area."

It is interesting to note that cities in Germany have not become major Eurocurrency centers because Germany does apply the same reserve requirements and interest ceilings to foreign deposits in Germany as it does to its domestic deposits, Deutsche mark deposits.

What Does It Do?

What does the Eurocurrency market do? First, it is a convenient and profitable way to conduct international trade-financing transactions. Under flexible exchange rates, transactors in international markets often desire to buy forward contracts on currencies so that they can avoid the risk of unexpected currency fluctuations, which would raise the price of the commodities they have ordered for future delivery. The Eurocurrency market is used to cover these forward contracts, that is, to hold currency for a future delivery. Since there are no regulations on the payment of interest, this currency can earn market rates of interest. Second, the Eurocurrency market provides a convenient place for U.S. banks to transfer deposits in order for these deposits to earn market rates of interest. Third, profits from foreign branches of U.S. banks often enjoy local tax rates that are lower than those of the state where their main office is located.

The Eurocurrency market can be looked upon as a group of depository intermediaries with few regulatory constraints. Borrowers and lenders, primarily commercial banks, can use the services of those financial intermediaries to exchange financial assets more efficiently and profitably.

Is It Unstable?

Is the Eurocurrency market unstable? Will such instability cause a wave of bank failures? There is controversy surrounding the answers to these questions. Perhaps the Eurocurrency market reaches some kind of an equilibrium level of growth, depending on the cost of restrictive regulations for domestic financial assets relative to those in the Eurocurrency market. If there is some change in this differential, funds would flow rapidly in or out of the Eurocurrency market. Thus, in 1969, when interest rates on Eurodollar deposits rose much higher than the ceiling rates on domestic U.S. bank deposits, there was a large shift of deposits from U.S. banks into the Eurocurrency market, deposits that could be "borrowed back" by domestic U.S. banks. In 1970, when ceiling rate limitations on CDs were lifted, the Eurodollar deposits were reduced. During such adjustment periods, the size of the Eurocurrency market may be unstable, that is, unpredictable.

However, since about 80 percent of the deposits are interbank deposits, they can be thought of as representing no liquidity additional to the amounts already included in the money supply of the domestic country. Remember that, to avoid double counting, interbank deposits are deducted from a bank's deposits in calculating the money supply held by the nonbank public.

Perhaps the greatest misapprehensions are that the Eurodollars represents either a claim on U.S. dollars that the U.S. government must satisfy or deposits of U.S. residents, and that both would suffer a huge loss of wealth in case of default. First, it must be understood that banks operating outside the United States can denominate their deposits in U.S. dollars, whether or not they have U.S. dollar reserves. If the depositor demands U.S. dollars as promised by a bank, the bank must borrow or buy U.S. dollars. This action, taken by itself, can increase the demand for U.S. dollars. The analysis is incomplete without considering what the depositor does with the U.S. dollar. If a bill is paid or a loan payment is made, the dollars are ordinarily redeposited in a bank. The U.S. dollar reserves are then reinvested and the supply of dollars can increase to offset the effect of the increased demand.

Second, the Eurocurrency liabilities of twelve European countries shown in Figure 29-1 (approximately 70 percent are Eurodollars) should be examined. Only 7.5 percent are owned by depositors with U.S. residence.

The question of extreme instability resulting in the collapse of many banks is broader than the question of instability in the Eurocurrency market. It is a question of whether or not a collapse of one or more large banks will severely injure other banks and other financial institutions, causing a major international banking collapse. It is presumed that governments would rapidly supply needed reserves to their own banks and thereby maintain their solvency. This may allow for a more orderly adjustment.

Instability can be caused by a number of sources. For example, economic sanctions were imposed by Britain and some other European countries against Argentina on April 3, 1982, following Argentina's seizure of the Falkland/Malvina Islands, a British possession. The freeze immobilized $1.4 billion of Argentine deposits in London banks, making it difficult for Argentina to service its $34 billion external debt. Although this did not seem to be a serious problem at that time, the solvency of particular banks could be affected by unexpected problems such as

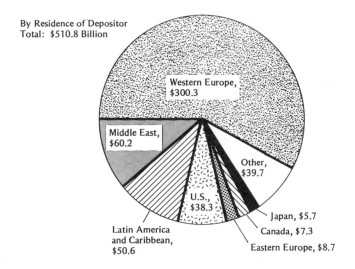

By Residence of Depositor
Total: $510.8 Billion

Western Europe, $300.3

Middle East, $60.2

Other, $39.7

U.S., $38.3

Japan, $5.7

Latin America and Caribbean, $50.6

Canada, $7.3

Eastern Europe, $8.7

Figure 29-1

Eurocurrency liabilities of banks in twelve European countries at the end of December 1978. *Source: International Letter,* **Federal Reserve Bank of Chicago, No. 400 (July 20, 1979), p. 1.**

these, where the banks have a significant part of their portfolio invested in loans that are in or subject to default. While the problems for banks with Argentine debts persisted, the banking industry was also burdened by the problems of the Mexican government in paying its debts, beginning in the summer of 1982, when world oil prices reduced Mexican oil revenues and caused a significant decline in the international value of the peso. These problems and the safety of interbank deposits in the face of such international events would be much the same under a number of plausible alternative relationships other than those in the Eurodollar market.

Is It Inflationary?

In a speech at the American Economic Association's annual meeting (1977), Robert Mundell, a leading international trade theorist, took exception to the argument that the Eurocurrency market is not inflationary. He held that even these interbank deposits could be conceived of as additions to the world's money supply. He presented rough statistical test results showing that world commodity prices had risen at about the same rate as the growth in the Eurocurrency market. He acknowledged that many of the deposits in the Eurocurrency market would be netted out under the conventional accounting procedures of deducting interbank deposits from gross deposits; however, he found no persuasive argument for following this conventional practice.

Many other experts view the Eurodollar market in the way financial intermediaries are viewed in the United States. They make the velocity of money higher than it otherwise would be.

With either view, there is an inflationary impact from a rapid increase in the Eurocurrency market. However, this inflationary impact may be negligible, since the existence of an interbank deposit may draw down the reserves of the bank in domestic country, creating little additional liquidity.

There is also rough evidence that the Eurodollar market is not very inflationary. If it were inflationary, it would be expected that the domestic counterpart to Eurodollars in the United States, old M2, would have had a rising income velocity that could not be explained by U.S. interest rates. Recall that M2 velocity is defined as real income Y times the price level P divided by M2:

$$V = YP/M2$$

The velocity of old M2 remained fairly constant during the 1960s and 1970s, indicating that Eurodollars probably did not drive up domestic prices.

Does It Interfere with the Control of the U.S. Money Supply?

The argument about the effect of the Eurocurrency market often settles on the issue of whether or not it interferes with the control of the domestic money supply. Insofar as the Eurocurrency market is fairly stable, it appears to have minimal impact on control of the U.S. money supply. The problem of monetary control arises if there is a technical problem, such as estimating the float between domestic banks and their foreign branches. In addition, transfer of money in and out of the Eurodollar market has been found to produce "minimal" changes in the U.S. money supply.[4] An example of one of these changes is depicted and described in Table 29-2.

Eurobonds

Eurobonds are the counterpart of Eurocurrency, with long maturities. International bonds, also known as Eurobonds, are underwritten by an international syndicate and sold principally in countries other than the country of the currency in which the bond is denominated.[5] Borrowing in international capital markets by businesses, governments, and international organizations rose to $115.7 billion in 1979. Medium-maturity

TABLE 29-2

T Accounts Showing a Conversion of Demand Deposits into Eurodollars

Public		U.S. Banks		Eurobanks	
Assets	Liabilities	Assets	Liabilities	Assets	Liabilities
DDP − $100 ED + $100			DDE + $100 DDP − $100	DDE + $100	ED + $100

In this transaction, a holder of demand deposits at a U.S. bank transfers $100 million into Eurodollar deposits at a Eurobank.* On the public's balance sheet, demand deposits (DDP) decline and Eurodollar deposits (ED) rise by the same amount. At the Eurobank, the individual's account is credited and the bank's Eurodollar liabilities rise by $100 million. When the check clears, the U.S. bank's demand deposit liability to the public (DDP) declines and the demand deposit liability to the Eurobank (DDE) increases. The Eurobank's balance sheet will record this transaction as an increase in assets.

The impact of this transaction on the U.S. money stock depends on how money is measured. Using the old definition of money (M1), which includes foreign commercial bank demand deposits at U.S. banks, the money supply is unaffected since DDP declined and DDE rose by the same amount. Because DDP and DDE have the same reserve requirements, excess reserves are not affected and no further contraction or expansion of loans and deposits in the United States is possible.

On the other hand, if money is measured either by M1A or M1B (which *exclude* foreign bank demand deposits at U.S. banks), then the money supply decreases by the amount of the transaction since DDP declines while the increase in DDE is not counted. Because excess reserves are still unaffected, there will be no further change in the money stock. Thus, the initial effect of deposit outflows into the Eurodollar market lowers the money stock, as currently measured, by an amount equivalent to the size of the transaction.

It is important to note that in this transaction Eurobanks collectively are assumed to hold total reserves (in the form of demand deposit balances at U.S. banks) equal to the initial dollar outflow from U.S. banks. If, in the extreme, Eurobanks hold *no* reserves at all, the U.S. money stock, however defined, will be *unaffected.*† However, to the extent that Eurobanks hold some precautionary reserves in the form of demand deposits at U.S. banks, the qualitative effect of the Eurodollar transactions is the same as outlined above.

*This Eurobank may be a foreign branch of some U.S. bank or an unaffiliated foreign bank.
† The Eurobank would create a new loan equal to the full amount of DDE, thereby drawing down such balances. The borrower would have to acquire a U.S. demand deposit before he could spend the proceeds of this loan. This transaction then restores the balance sheet of the U.S. bank to its original position. Note that this intermediation through the Eurodollar market generates a greater extension of credit than would have occurred if generated through the U.S. banking system only. *Source:* Anatol B. Balbach and David H. Resler, "Eurodollars and the U.S. Money Supply," *Review,* Federal Reserve Bank of St. Louis (June–July 1980), pp. 6–7.

lending, called *Eurocredits*, comprised two-thirds of those borrowings. The other one-third of the borrowing was Eurobonds (15.9 percent) and foreign bonds (16.8 percent). Foreign bonds are underwritten by a syndicate from one country; they are denominated in the currency of that country, and they are sold in that country—typically to nonresidents.

There was a gradual decline since the late 1960s in the percentage of U.S. dollar-denominated Eurobonds. From close to 90 percent in the late 1960s, the percentage fell to 59 percent at the end of 1979, although 1978 and 1979 were periods of an increase in that percentage. Borrowers have been diversifying their holdings. The diversification was caused by the weakness of the U.S. dollar relative to other Eurocurrency liabilities. The diversification does not necessarily reflect preference for a particular issuer. For example, a U.S. issuer can denominate its bonds in German marks. In November 1979 and January 1980, the U.S. government announced that it would sell $2.25 billion in German mark-denominated U.S. government securities. (This was part of a dollar-defense package begun at the end of 1978.) The U.S. dollar remained the most widely used denomination for debt instruments sold in international markets.

A novel "Euro-Swiss franc-dollar" bond was offered by the World Bank in 1982. Investors will pay for the bond in U.S. dollars. The interest and return of principal payments were calculated in terms of the Swiss franc/U.S. dollar exchange rate on April 19, 1982. Thus the bonds have a constant Swiss franc value. If the Swiss franc falls in value relative to the dollar, the World Bank guarantees the stated dollar value. The World Bank set a $6\frac{5}{8}$ percent coupon rate that was far below the 14 percent rate on dollar-denominated bonds. The World Bank was hoping that the dollar/franc rate will not change significantly. However, the lower market yield on these bonds may accurately reflect the cost of this risk, so that little benefit, except the appearance of low financing costs, will result.

Domestic Deregulated International Banking Facilities

The Board of Governors authorized the establishment of *domestic international banking facilities*, IBFs, by U.S. banks, effective December 3, 1981. The IBFs are, like Eurodollar banks, largely exempt from regulatory constraints. There are no reserve requirements or interest rate ceilings. However, deposits may generally be accepted only from non-U.S. residents and other IBFs and must have a minimum maturity of two days. In addition, all deposit transactions must be in minimum amounts of $100,000.

The IBFs had assets of $47.2 billion on December 23, 1981, only twenty days after they began operations.[6] This popularity attests to the inducement to evade reserve requirements and ceiling interest rates.

To avoid the use of IBFs for domestic business, the Board of Governors required customers of IBFs to sign a statement of intent. If a U.S.-controlled business makes an IBF deposit or negotiates a loan, a statement must be signed to assure that IBFs are not used via their foreign subsidiaries for domestic business. It is doubtful—more precisely, impossible—to earmark and monitor funds so that they do not return to the domestic economy after being borrowed from an IBF. Therefore, IBFs should be beneficial to firms with access to them in much the same way as Eurodollar banks. However, they are not perfect substitutes for Eurodollar banks. They still have regulatory constraints of the type mentioned, and state taxes. Nevertheless, they are a haven from the costs of much regulation for businesses with foreign business.

The exclusiveness of this haven should change by 1988. By 1988, depository institutions will have their federal reserve requirements on regular consumer savings accounts reduced to zero; business time accounts will be at a 3 percent reserve requirement, with authority to reduce to zero; and the ceiling rate on interest payments on consumer NOW accounts is scheduled to be removed by 1986. Logical steps at that time would be to remove ceiling rates on business demand and savings deposits and to allow businesses to hold more than $150,000 in a savings account at one depository intermediary, the present limit. The Eurodollar market has forcibly taught the partial ineffectiveness of onerous restrictions on financial institutions and on income from financial assets. Innovations to circumvent these regulations stimulated giant financial markets abroad.

NOTES

1. For a general description of the Eurocurrency market, see Ronald I. McKinnon, "The Eurocurrency Market," in *Essays in International Finance*, December 1977, International Finance Section, Department of Economics, Princeton University (Princeton, N.J.: Princeton University Press, 1977, pp. 1–40). Basic, but incomplete, data on the Eurocurrency market are calculated by the Bank for International Settlements, BIS. The estimates in the text were taken from *World Financial Markets*, Morgan Guaranty Trust Company of New York (February 1979), p. 15. A summary of some of the issues is found in Ann-Marie Meulendyke, "Causes and Consequences of the Eurodollar Expansion," Research Paper No. 7503, New York Federal Reserve Bank (March 1975). The development of the view that the Eurodollar market is analogous to credit creation in the U.S. fractional reserve banking system was presented by Milton Friedman, "The Eurodollar Market: Some First Principles," *The Morgan Guaranty Survey* (October 1969), pp. 4–15. See also Robert James Sweeney and Thomas D. Willett, "Eurodollars, Petrodollars, and World Liquidity and Inflation," in *Stabilization of the Domestic and International Economy*, a supplement to the *Journal of Monetary Economics*, Carnegie-Rochester Conference Series on Public Policy, Karl Brunner and Allan Meltzer, eds., Vol. 5 (1977), pp. 277–310.
2. *Federal Reserve Statistical Release*, Board of Governors of the Federal Reserve System (February 19, 1982), pp. 4, 8.
3. Marvin Goodfriend, "Eurodollars," *Economic Review*, Federal Reserve Bank of Richmond (May–June 1981), p. 14.
4. Anatol B. Balbach and David H. Resler, "Eurodollars and the U.S. Money Supply," *Review*, Federal Reserve Bank of St. Louis (June–July 1980), pp. 2–12.
5. Federal Reserve Bank of Chicago, "International Letter," No. 422 (May 23, 1980), p. 1.
6. Federal Reserve Bank of Chicago, "International Letter," No. 464 (January 1, 1982), p. 1.

STUDY QUESTIONS

1. What is the Eurodollar market?

2. Why did it happen?

3. What functions does it perform?

4. Is it a source of instability?

5. Does it cause inflation?

6. Does it interfere with the control of the U.S. money supply? Using T accounts, show the effect on M1, if any, of a transfer of funds from a domestic demand deposit in a U.S. bank to a foreign Eurodollar bank deposit. How is the effect on M1 changed by the level of reserves held in the Eurodollar bank?

7. What is an IBF? How can the Federal Reserve ensure that domestic deposits will not be rerouted through foreign banks into IBFs?

Glossary

Accrual deficit. The difference between expenditures and income when these items are recorded at the time they become due rather than when payment is actually made or received.

Active Assets Account. A checkable account plan by Dean Witter Reynolds. *See* Cash Management Accounts.

Adjustable rate mortgages. Mortgages whose interest rates are tied to the movements of market interest rates within specified limits.

Advanced refunding technique. A technique that allows maturing debt instruments to be traded for new debt instruments in advance of the maturity date.

Amortization. The reduction in debt (or payment due) by equal payments that exactly cover interest and principal, over a given number of periods.

Announcement effects. Short-run effects on economic variables such as interest rates and stock market prices resulting from the announcement of policies by the Federal Reserve or other parts of the government.

Annuity. A contract in which a given amount of funds, paid each period, accumulates with compound interest until they are repaid at maturity, either in a lump sum or by a specified schedule.

Arbitrageur (or *arbitrager*). One who simultaneously buys an asset in one market and sells it in another for profit.

ARIMA (Autoregressive Integrated Moving Average). A statistical procedure for separating a time series of values for a variable into two parts. One part contains that part of the series in which the numbers of the series are unrelated (the white noise portion). The other part of the series contains the related numbers (the trend and periodicities).

Autocorrelations. Correlations between the current observations of a variable and its past values.

Automatic countercyclical mechanism. A mechanism under a gold standard characterized by automatic changes in variables, such as the money supply, that tend to offset and correct business cycle fluctuations.

Autoregression. A regression in which the current values of a variable are regressed on its own past values.

Autospectrum. A statistical procedure resulting in a line chart showing high points for cycles and trends in a variable.

Balance of payments. An account listing all transactions that give rise to either a payment to a foreigner or a receipt from a foreigner. The balance of payments is in surplus when the country is receiving net payments from foreigners, and it is in deficit when a country is making net payments to foreigners. Different definitions of payments give rise to different values of the balance of payments for the same time period.

Banker's acceptance. A short-term, liquid debt instrument that has been guaranteed by a bank as signified by a notation, such as "Accepted by XYZ Bank," on the debt instrument.

Bank float. An increase in deposits recorded on bank records in the banking system that arises when funds deposited to a depository institution account are uncollected (not deducted) from the account they are drawn against.

Basis point. One hundredth of a percentage point variation in the yield on a bond. A change from 8.62 percent to 8.70 percent is 8 basis points.

Bear. An individual who believes that the average price of financial assets in a market will fall.

Best effort agreement. An underwriting arrangement in which any unsold issues are returned to the original issuer.

Beta coefficient. A summary statistic of a stock's systematic risk.

Bid and asked. As used in a quote, the highest price from buyers and lowest price from sellers, respectively.

Bill of exchange (or *draft*). A negotiable instrument with three parties to the agreement: the drawer of the order, the drawee, who is ordered to make payment, and the payee. For instance, a commercial bank check is a draft on the bank by the depositor payable to a designated payee.

Bills. Marketable debt instruments with an original term to maturity of one year or less. Usually, they provide for a single lump-sum final payment of their face value and are sold at a discount from that value. The most common example is the U.S. Treasury bill.

Bimetallism (or bimetallic standard). A commodity standard in which the prices of two precious metals (such as gold and silver) are pegged at separate levels.

Blind trust. A trust that provides the owner no specific information on the composition of its portfolio, used by some government officials to avoid conflicts of interest between the public interest and their private interests.

Block transactions. Purchase and sale of stock in very large quantities, usually by institutional investors.

Bond. An interest-bearing debt instrument, usually with a maturity of five years or more, formally offered for sale by a business or government. Sometimes it is used in economic analysis to refer to all debt instruments.

Bond brokers. Those who arrange bond sales and purchases, such as New York Stock Exchange bond traders, operating in the exchange's bond room.

Book-entry form. A nonphysical form of a debt instrument: the instrument merely exists in record keeping and is exchanged through the appropriate debits and credits to the accounts of the transacting parties.

Book value. The net present value per share of a firm.

Borrowed deficit. That part of the government deficit which is covered through sales of government securities rather than through, for example, an increase in the monetary base.

Bull. An individual who believes the average price of financial assets in a market will rise.

Buy contract. A futures purchase contract.

Buying on margin. *See* Margin.

Call date. On tax and loan accounts it is the date that the private bank must transfer the funds in tax and loan accounts to the Treasury.

Call loan. Short-term (overnight) loans by banks to finance the purchase of stock.

Call option. An option that gives the holder the right to buy (stock) at a fixed price.

Call provisions. Provisions of some bonds allowing for their redemption (recovery of face value) prior to maturity. Such a bond is termed callable.

Capital account. An accounting record that includes international investments and lending flows.

Capital gains and losses. Increases or decreases in the valuation of assets. National income estimates exclude capital gains and losses.

Capital market. Any of the various markets for relatively longer-maturity financial assets such as corporate bonds, stocks, and mortgages.

Capital market line. The straight-line relationship between risk and return on alternative efficient portfolios of risky and riskless assets in the capital asset pricing model.

Capital risk. The risk that a bond will unexpectedly fall in price prior to maturity.

Cardinal ranking. A ranking of alternatives in which preferences are quantified. For example, A is preferred three times as much as B.

Cash Management Accounts. Merrill Lynch accounts which allow checks to be written on Bank One of Ohio against the value of the cash assets (such as money market fund shares) and the unused margin on securities.

Centrals. Nonprofit cooperatives of credit unions within a state which lend to member credit unions as well as providing clearing house facilities for interlending among member credit unions.

Certificate of deposit. A deposit at a depository institution that may not be withdrawn without penalty before maturity.

Certificates of participation. Evidence of participation in a fixed trust investment company, constituting ownership of a pro rata part of a relatively fixed portfolio.

Chattel mortgages. Loans secured by movable property such as an automobile or appliance.

Churning. Unnecessary buying and selling of assets that drive up transaction costs. Some critics of the Federal Reserve have accused it of churning in the market for government securities.

Class of option. Options of the same type (put or call) on the same underlying security.

Closed-end investment companies. Investment companies that issue a limited number of shares of common stock which are traded in financial markets.

Closing date transaction. The liquidation of his or her position by a holder of an option through the sale of an option of the same series previously purchased.

Closing purchase transactions. A transaction in which an investor who is obligated as a writer of an option intends to terminate his or her obligation by "purchasing" an option of the same series.

Coherence. The measure of a relationship between the cycles in the time series of two variables. It is exhibited on a line chart called the cross spectrum of the two variables.

Collateral trust bonds. Bonds secured by other bonds and stocks.

Commercial bank deposits. Depositors' accounts in commercial banks.

Commercial brokers. Those who arrange buy and sell orders, such as stock exchange traders who act on orders from the public relayed through brokers.

Commercial paper. Short-term, marketable, low-risk debt instruments issued by corporate and institutional borrowers.

Commodity reserve standard. The use of any commodity or commodities as the monetary standard whose rate of exchange with a unit of the country's nominal money is pegged by the government.

Common stock. Basic equity form of ownership in a corporation that usually allows the holder to vote for the board of directors according to his or her pro rata number of shares.

Compensating balance requirement. The practice by commercial banks of requiring their borrowers to maintain at least a specified average bank deposit balance during the period of their loan.

Compound interest. An interest yield calculated on a balance increased by each interest payment.

Conditional forecast. A forecast made subject to specified conditions.

Consol. A name for a perpetuity originating from those sold by the British government in 1814. *See also* Perpetuity.

Consol equivalent. A perpetuity with the same interest rate and present value as a debt instrument with a maturity date.

Consolidated system wide bond. A short-term debt instrument issued by the Federal Farm Credit Banks, with maturities of six and nine months.

Consumer Price Index. The most commonly cited price index in the United States. It measures the average price change from a base period of a market basket of goods and services that is intended to represent items purchased by the "average" consumer. It is an example of a base-weighted, or Laspeyres, price index. *See also* GNP deflator.

Consumption (real). That part of current real output that is used up during the year.

Continuous (or instantaneous) compounding or discounting. Compounding or discounting where the number of compounding periods per year is allowed to approach infinity, so that the interest stream or the rate of discount is continuous rather than a series of discrete applications.

Contractual intermediaries. Financial intermediaries that create relatively long-term contractual claims on themselves, such as insurance policies, annuities, and pensions.

Conversion price. The price of common stock for holders of convertible preferred stock or convertible bonds who exercise the conversion privilege.

Convertible preferred stock and *convertible bonds.* Preferred stock and bonds that carry the privilege of conversion into specific common stocks at a specific price.

Corner. The purchase of enough of a stock or commodity so that those who sold the item short or have a future contract that requires them to purchase the item to liquidate their position cannot do so except at substantially higher prices than would have prevailed in a market with widespread ownership of the item. In the quote from the Treasury Report in Chapter 24, a corner is defined as the control of enough of a commodity or financial asset that its price can be manipulated. The above more standard definition of a corner is also called a *squeeze. See also* Squeeze.

Coupon rate. The yearly interest payment on a debt instrument, such as a bond, divided by its face value.

Correlation coefficient. A measure of the degree to which two variables are related, ranging between -1, for a perfect negative relation, and $+1$, for a perfect positive relation.

Correspondent banks. Commercial banks that supply services to other commercial banks.

Cost of intermediation. The spread between the rate of return financial intermediaries pay for their funds and the rate of return they earn on their assets.

Covered arbitrage. A method of hedging a forward purchase of foreign currency that exploits differences in internal interest rates and differences between the forward rates of the domestic and foreign country.

Covered call writer (or *covered options*). A call writer who owns the shares of the stock he or she may be required to sell under the option (which is thus a *covered option*) or who holds a call of the same class with an exercise price less than or equal to the one written.

Cross-section data. Data collected from the different values of a variable (such as consumer credit in each state) at one point in time. *See also* Time-series data.

Cross-spectrum test. A statistical procedure to discover the extent to which time series of two variables exhibit related cycles. The summary measure produced is a line chart showing the degrees of coherence between the series.

Crowding out. The phenomenon of crowding out private investment through government policies such as government borrowing.

Currency ratio. The ratio of the amount of currency outside depository institutions to the amount of checkable accounts at depository institutions.

Currency union. An arrangement between a group of countries to peg the exchange rate between their currencies while maintaining flexible exchange rates with other countries.

Current account. A part of the balance-of-payments accounting record that includes the goods and services balance and government and private transfer payments.

Dead weight loss. The loss in welfare to individuals from an economic change, such as a higher price due to a tax, which is not offset by a transfer to other individuals.

Debt instruments (bonds). Evidences of a loan issued by the debtor to the creditor. They may be marketable (or negotiable) prior to maturity.

Debt management. The issuing, refinancing, and management of the debt of an individual, business, or government. (For the U.S. Treasury, debt management also involves the regulation of the term structure of the national debt.)

Deep discount bonds. Bonds sold at a price significantly below face value.

Default risk. The risk that the issuer of a debt instrument will fail to pay an interest payment and/or the principal. Moody's and Standard & Poor's ratings rank bonds with respect to default risk.

Defensive open-market operations. The name applied by the Federal Reserve to an open-market operation directed toward offsetting disturbances to monetary policy. *See also* Dynamic open-market operations.

Deferred availability cash items. Deposits that have not yet been credited by the Federal Reserve to the bank that received the deposit. This amount is subtracted from cash items in the process of collection to obtain Federal Reserve float.

Deferreds. Futures contracts for delivery during a relatively distant month. *See also* Nearbys.

Deficit unit. A unit that invests more than it saves and is, therefore, a net demander of funds and a net supplier of financial assets.

Demand for money. The quantity of money demanded at each interest rate, for a given level of income.

De novo. Anew (Latin). De novo branches or subsidiaries of banks are new branches or subsidiaries.

Dependant variable. A variable that depends for its value on one or more other variables.

Depository intermediaries. Financial intermediaries that create deposit liabilities. Their checkable deposit liabilities constitute a medium of exchange.

Depreciation. The decline in the value of an asset over time because it is worn out, used up, or considered less valuable.

Devaluation. A decline in the exchange value of the domestic relative to foreign currency or, if specified, to a commodity such as gold.

Dirty (or *managed*) *float.* A flexible exchange rate regime with intermittent intervention by the central banks.

Discount. For a debt instrument, such as a Treasury bill, the difference between the amount due at maturity and the current market price of the T-bill. *See also* Discounts and advances.

Discounting. A computation for finding the present value of a future stream of payments; a loan in an amount that is less, by a discount, than the value of the loan paper used as collateral. *See also* Discounts and advances.

Discount rate. At the Federal Reserve, the basic interest rate charged to depository institutions that borrow from the Federal Reserve.

Discounts and advances. The names of loans to depository institutions borrowing from the Federal Reserve.

Discount window. The parts of the regional Federal Reserve banks and their branches that make loans to depository institutions. They are bank teller-type windows.

Disintermediation. Withdrawal of funds from financial intermediaries.

Diversification. A strategy to avoid widespread portfolio losses by holding a variety of assets that have prices that are not tied to each other and that can, therefore, be expected as a matter of random chance to have some offsetting movements. Risks of widespread default can also be reduced by diversification.

Domestic international banking facilities (IBFs). Domestic banking facilities exempt from domestic regulatory requirements, authorized in 1981 by the Federal Reserve. They are authorized to accept deposits (only from non-U.S. residents) with a minimum maturity of two days in minimum amounts of $100,000.

Dollar-gold standard. *See* Gold-exchange standard.

Double coincidence. A condition in a transaction in which each party wants to trade exactly what the other party offers in exchange.

Drift. For the money supply targets of the Federal Reserve, it is the phenomenon of building in errors from their attempts to hit previous targets in formulating new target ranges. It is not necessarily an improper procedure for the Federal Reserve to ignore past errors.

Dual banking system. The concept of the dual regulation of the banking system, whereby banks can operate under either state or federal charters and either state or federal supervision.

Dutch auction. An auction in which all accepted bids or offers are executed at a uniform price.

Dynamic open-market operations. Open-market operations designed to change the level of reserves in the banking system.

Economic efficiency. The use of inputs in a productive process so that for a given value of output the least expensive inputs are used.

Efficient market hypothesis. A hypothesis that applies to a market where all available information is immediately discounted into the price of the goods that are traded.

Efficient portfolio. A portfolio is efficient if no other portfolio exists providing either the same expected return but lower risk or the same or less risk with a higher expected return.

Elasticity of demand for imports. The percentage change in the quantity of imports relative to the percentage change in their price.

Endogenous variables. With respect to an economic model, those variables whose values are determined within the model, not outside it.

Equipment trust certificates. Loans secured by movable property of considerable value, such as airplanes or railroad rolling stock.

Equities. Evidence of ownership rights in a business. In the case of a corporation, they are called stocks.

Error-learning hypothesis. With respect to the term structure of interest rates, the hypothesis, by David Meiselman, that the term structure is changed by a proportion of the mistake in forecasting one-year rates, as revealed each period by difference between the actual and expected one-year rates. More of the correction is made on the shorter rates.

Euler's e. The limit of $(1 + 1/M)^M$ as M goes to infinity. (To 10 decimal places it is 2.7182818284.) The larger the number assigned to M, the closer the approximation.

Eurobonds. Bonds that are sold principally in countries other than that in whose currency they are denominated. They are the long-maturity counterpart of Eurocurrency deposits.

Eurocurrency market. The market for bank deposits and debt instruments denominated in currency units other than that of the country where the bank is located or the debt instrument is issued.

Eurodollar market. The dollar part of the Eurocurrency market.

Ex ante variables. *Ex ante* means before the fact. Planned values of variables, such as expected saving and investment. For an example of ex post and ex ante variables, *see* Price/earnings ratio.

Excess reserves. The total reserves minus required reserves of depository institutions.

Exchange rate. The price of a unit of one country's currency relative to the price of a unit of another country's currency.

Ex dividend date. The date on which a stock no longer carries the right to receive a dividend.

Exercise price. The price, specified in an options contract, at which the option holder is entitled to sell or buy the underlying asset. Also termed the striking price or strike price.

Exogenous variables. With respect to an economic model, the exogenous variables are those whose values are determined outside the model.

Expected income. The income payment stream expected in the future.

Expiration time. *See* Stock option.

Ex post. *Ex post* means after the fact. For an example of ex post and ex ante variables, *see* Price/earnings ratio.

Externalities or *neighborhood effects.* Costs or benefits that are not reflected in market prices.

Face value, par value, or *par.* The amount (not including any coupon payment) that the maker of a debt instrument is obligated to pay at the maturity date.

Factoring company. A finance company that buys the accounts receivable of the borrowing firm, then sends the firm its income minus a fraction for the loan payment.

Federal deficit. The cash value of expenditures for goods and services and transfer payments of the government minus its receipts from taxes.

Federal funds. Immediately available funds transferred through the Fedwire. Chiefly commercial banks are involved, although not exclusively. Commercial banks can obtain funds at the market interest rate to meet their reserve requirements through federal funds borrowing.

Federal funds rate (or *funds rate*). The rate prevailing in the federal funds market.

Federal Open-Market Committee (FOMC). A committee of the Federal Reserve that has primary responsibility for open-market operations.

Federal Reserve float. The difference between uncollected cash items and deferred availability cash items resulting from the inability to synchronously change the books of the banks where a check is deposited and where it is drawn. *See also* Bank float.

Fiat money. *See* Fiduciary issue.

Fiduciary issue. The proportion of the monetary base that is fiat money. Fiat money is money that cannot be converted to an alternative valuable substance such as gold by taking it to the issuer.

Filter. An arithmetic procedure that is developed to remove the cycles and trend in the time series of a variable. The simplest (and often unsuccessful) filter is to simply take first differences.

Finance companies. Financial intermediaries that hold a portfolio of consumer and business loans financed by both debt instruments and stock issues.

Financial assets. Claims against present and future income, such as stocks, bonds, and money.

Financial intermediary. A firm that earns its income on the spread between the financial assets it creates and the financial assets it buys. Unlike holding companies, financial intermediaries do not buy equities for the purpose of controlling other firms.

First differences. The differences between successive numbers in a time series.

Fixed exchange rate. A given price of a currency relative to one or more other currencies that a country effectively maintains within narrow limits through policy actions such as buying and selling its own currency.

Fixed (or fixed trust) investment company. An investment company selling units against its portfolio, which remains virtually intact.

Flexible exchange rates. A system for determining the international price of currency that relies on market conditions.

Float. *See* Bank float, Mail float, *and* Federal Reserve float.

Floating exchange rates. *See* Flexible exchange rates.

Floor brokers. With respect to members of the New York Stock Exchange, it is those who trade for other members on a commission basis.

Flow-of-funds. A method of analyzing asset prices and interest rates which involves constructing a matrix listing sources and uses of funds, sector by sector, for the entire economy.

Foreign exchange. A medium of international exchange. It can take the form of foreign currencies, gold, or the key currency.

Form 10-K. A publicly available annual and periodic financial report filed with the SEC, by law, by every company whose stock is listed on an exchange or, since 1964, traded over the counter, if the company has 500 or more shareholders and $1 million or more of assets.

Forward contract. A contract for the future delivery of an asset in which the future delivery price is negotiated by market participants so that the current price of the forward contract is zero (plus transactions costs). *See also* Futures contract.

Forward discount. The excess of the spot price of a currency over the forward price.

Forward markets. Markets where forward contracts are negotiated.

Forward premium. The excess of the forward price of a currency over the spot price.

Forward rates. Future one-year rates implied from the observed term structure of interest rates; or, in international trade, the expected rates of exchange of international currencies for given future dates.

Fourth market. Trades in stock between large institutional investors that take place outside a stock exchange and without stockbrokers.

Fractional reserve banking. The practice of keeping only a fraction of the deposits of depository institutions as cash reserves.

Free reserves. Excess reserves minus reserves borrowed from the Federal Reserve by depository institutions.

Funds rate. The rate of interest on federal funds borrowing.

Fungibility. The property financial assets possess of being easily altered in form. For example, a bond with the same present value and yield can be marketed in any number of different time patterns of payment.

Futures contract. A contract to buy or sell a commodity such as wheat or a Treasury bill at a specific future date at a fixed price, traded on formal exchanges. That fixed price remains constant while the present price of the futures contract fluctuates in the futures market. *See also* Forward contract.

Futures markets. Markets where contracts for the future delivery of assets are traded.

General obligation bonds. State or municipal bonds secured by the general credit of the issuer instead of by a specific source of revenue.

Global master custodianship. An arrangement providing for satisfaction of the provisions in U.S. regulations regarding pension plans requiring that indicia (evidence) of foreign investments be held in specified locations abroad if not in the United States.

GNP deflator. A price index of all goods and services in the gross national product.

Gold-exchange (or *dollar-gold*) *standard.* The international payment used since World War II whereby gold and U.S. dollars are international media of exchange.

Gold standard. A monetary system under which a central bank agrees to buy and sell gold for a fixed amount of the domestic currency. Under a pure gold standard the monetary base is changed only by this method.

Goods and services balance. A part of the balance of payments record that includes the trade balance, military expenditures, interest, royalty, and dividend payments.

Government budget constraint. *See* Monetary base identity.

Grandfathering-in existing structures. A law outlawing a practice, such as ownership by a bank holding company of banks in more than one state, that leaves intact arrangements existing at some date prior to enactment (such as the date when the law was proposed).

Hedgers. Participants in financial markets who purchase an asset because its price movements are expected to offset those of another asset because of a *nonrandom* relationship between the two prices. For contrast, *see* Diversification.

Hedging pressure hypothesis. The contention that individuals and institutions seek to match the maturity structure of their assets and their liabilities, which can cause the term structure of interest rates to diverge from the form indicated by the pure expectation hypothesis or the liquidity premium hypothesis if speculators do not fully exploit profit opportunities.

Hoarding money. The act of increasing one's money balances. When it is negative, it is called dishoarding.

Income. The flow of services from wealth. Real income is money income deflated by a suitable price index.

Income effect of a devaluation. The effect of a devaluation in reducing imports through its effect on the real income of residents.

Income velocity of money. The ratio of nominal income to the stock of nominal money balances.

Independent variable. A variable that depends for its value on factors outside the relationship being considered.

Indifference curve. A curve showing the various combinations of two goods between which an individual is indifferent. A higher indifference curve shows combinations providing a higher level of satisfaction.

Individual Retirement Accounts (IRAs). Retirement accounts allowing tax-free contributions and tax-free earnings on reinvested funds.

Initial conditions. The initial exogenous value of the variables in a model, from which future forecasts of the endogenous variables are generated.

Inside bonds, inside wealth. Financial assets that are exactly offset by the liability they represent to some other agent inside the economy.

Inside trading. Trading in a company's stock by its own directors, officers, and owners of 10 percent or more of its equity. Inside trading of listed securities must be reported to the SEC.

Instinet. The computerized network linking approximately 150 institutional traders in the fourth market.

Interest rate parity theorem. The postulate that, in equilibrium, the percentage difference between the forward and spot rates for two currencies equals the difference between the interest rates on default-free assets of the same maturity in the two countries involved.

Intermediation services. The services provided by financial intermediaries, including the provision of liquidity, the reduction of risk, alteration of the timing of income, and changes in the denomination in which financial assets are offered.

Internal rate of return. That discount rate that makes the discounted value of future net income from a project exactly equal to the cost of current investment.

International money. Money produced by an international organization.

Investment intermediaries. Financial intermediaries that issue shares against a portfolio of assets. They include investment and finance companies.

Investment, real net. That part of current output that is not used up in the year. Gross, as opposed to net real, investment includes real depreciation as well. Real net investment is equal to the change in real nonfinancial wealth.

Investors. Participants in financial markets whose primary interest is in the stability of income from an asset, rather than the possibility of capital gains. Those interested in capital gains are called *speculators*. *See* Speculators.

Involuntary investment. Unplanned accumulation of inventories.

Judgmental forecasts. Forecasts based on the forecaster's general views and knowledge, without a formal model.

Key currency. An arrangement in international trade whereby many countries agree to settle foreign transactions with the currency of a particular country.

Key currency nation. The country issuing the key currency.

Kiting. A scheme of deliberately planned float by which an individual can increase his or her bank accounts.

Lagged reserve requirements. The Federal Reserve regulation which stipulates that required reserves for the current week be calculated on the basis of deposits two weeks earlier. This regulation was put into effect in 1968.

Land trust. A trust formed for real estate assets.

Law of one price. The law that identical goods cannot differ in price from one place to another by more than the costs of transporting the good from one place to the other.

Lead manager. The manager of a purchase group underwriting a debt or equity offering.

Leverage factor. The ratio of debt (including preferred stock) to total assets.

Limit orders (and *stop loss orders*). Orders to buy or sell a stock when a given price has been reached.

Liquidity balance. A definition of the balance of payments which broadens the concept of payment, relative to the official reserve transactions balance, to include sales of liquid short-term debt instruments by both private transactors and the government.

Liquidity preference hypothesis. Hypothesis regarding the term structure of interest rates holding that there is a liquidity premium on implied future rates, which increases as the maturity is more distant.

Living trust. A trust made during its maker's lifetime, with stipulations about the chain of succession to income in the trust.

Load funds. Mutual funds that charge a separate commission cost instead of deriving all management fees from their portfolio income.

Long position. The ownership of an asset, such as a common stock, the value of which is increased by a rise in its price.

Mail float. An increase in the money supply due to the delay between the receipt of a check payment and its deposit in the banking system. *See also* Bank float.

Managed float. *See* Dirty float.

Managed liabilities. Marketable liabilities of depository institutions: negotiable certificates of deposit, Eurodollar borrowings, federal funds borrowings, and short-term repurchase agreements.

Margin. For securities, buying them partly on credit, called buying on margin.

Marginal propensity to consume with respect to real income. The change in real consumption divided by the change in real income with which it is associated.

Marketable. Salable in the market.

Market portfolio. The unique proportional combination of risky assets that will be held in each individual's efficient portfolio when it is in equilibrium in the capital asset pricing model.

Market segmentation. A condition of incomplete arbitrage among debt instruments in different markets and with different maturities.

Markov chain (or *process*). In the form sometimes used for stock prices, a series of numbers where each successive number is a multiple v of the previous numbers plus a random error term. For random first differences with no trend, v equals unity.

Matched sales agreements. See Reverse repurchase agreements.

Maturity. Generally, the time remaining from the present to the final payment on a bond. This is not to be confused with the original term to maturity, which refers to the time between the date of issuance and the final payment. These two concepts coincide only at the time of issuance.

Monetarist. An economist in a school of thought that emphasizes the relation of money to other variables, especially the long-run level of prices.

Monetary aggregate. The value of a group of items in a specific definition of money, such as M1 and M2.

Monetary base. Currency and coin outside depository institutions plus the cash reserves of the depository institutions. These cash reserves consist of vault cash plus deposits at the Federal Reserve or deposits at other depository institutions, which pass them through, dollar for dollar, to the Federal Reserve.

Monetary base identity (or *government budget constraint*). The accounting identity between the change in the monetary base and the different ways it is changed, classified by commonly used concepts, such as the deficit and government bond purchases.

Money. Any good used as a medium of exchange. Often the definition is extended to other goods that can be inexpensively changed into the medium of exchange. The concept of money that best predicts other variables in economic analysis is often selected.

Money expansion multiplier (or *monetary base multiplier*). The relation between the monetary base and the stock of money.

Money illusion. Economic behavior that disregards changes in the real value of a variable and instead is based on the variable's nominal value.

Money market. A market with traders who buy and sell short-term, liquid financial assets, such as prime commercial paper and certificates of deposit. Also a part of some economic models.

Money market certificate. A consumer time deposit that has a specific maturity and is nonnegotiable. It must be redeemed at the issuing depository intermediary. *See also* Certificate of deposit.

Money market fund. A mutual fund that invests in liquid, relatively risk free short-term money market instruments such as CDs and U.S. Treasury bills.

Moneyness. The characteristic of goods that are similar to those of money.

Mortgage. Loans to finance a real estate purchase, usually of long duration. (Thirty years is a common initial maturity for a loan on a single-family residence.)

Mortgage bonds. Bonds secured by fixed property such as a house.

Mutual fund. *See* Open-end fund.

Naive forecast. A forecast that a variable will continue growing at the same rate.

National banks. Federally chartered private banks.

Nearbys. Futures contracts for delivery during a relatively earlier month. *See also* Deferreds.

Negotiable instrument. Legally contracted debts calling for the payment of money and transferable from one party to another before maturity. Promissory notes and bills of exchange are the two broad classes of negotiable instruments.

Negotiable order of withdrawal (or *NOW*) *account.* Interest-paying consumer accounts, authorized for depository institutions, that may be drawn against with a check-type instrument called a negotiable order of withdrawal.

Net capital inflow (or outflow). The net flow of investment and lending funds into a country from abroad, minus the flow of these funds out of the country. A positive amount is an inflow and a negative amount is an outflow.

Net present value rule. A method of ranking mutually exclusive investment projects by their net present value. NPV is equal to the present value of future returns minus costs of investment, where the appropriate market or subjective interest rate is used for discounting.

Nominal rate of interest or *nominal yield.* The rate of return observed in the market for a debt instrument with a fixed payment stream.

Nominal wage. The money value of the wage payment per period.

Nonborrowed base. The monetary base minus borrowing by depository institutions from the Federal Reserve.

Nonborrowed reserve path. The sequence of desired target levels of total nonborrowed reserves planned by the Federal Reserve over time.

Nonborrowed reserves. Total reserves minus borrowings from the Federal Reserve by the depository institutions.

Noncompetitive offer. An offer to buy a U.S. Treasury bill at a price determined by the competitive bids in the auction.

Nonfinancial wealth or assets. Physical wealth—such as buildings, machines, and inventories of commodities—and human capital.

Note option. Under the terms of a 1977 law, one of two choices a commercial bank must make with respect to its holdings of tax and loan accounts, which requires that interest be paid to the Treasury on these accounts. The other option is immediate remittance of these funds to the Treasury, called the remittance option.

NOW account. *See* Negotiable order of withdrawal account.

Odd-lot dealer. A dealer who combines small orders of stock into 100-share multiples for sale.

Offering circular. An announcement of a new offering of tax-exempt municipal or state bonds giving the details of the offering. A prospectus, giving detailed financial statements, is not required for a tax-exempt bond as it is for a private bond.

Offering price. The price at which a financial asset is sold to the public.

Official reserve transaction. A transaction by the government, including the central bank, that adds to or depletes its own holdings of foreign currencies, international money, or gold.

Official settlements balance. The balance in the balance-of-payments statement where official short-term liquid debt instruments and official reserve transactions are considered the means of payment.

Open economy. An economy that is viewed together with its international trade and other economic international relationships.

Open-end (or mutual) fund. An investment fund that issues (or buys back) shares representing partial ownership of a portfolio of actively managed securities.

Opening purchase transaction. For stock options, the transaction from the side of the intended holder.

Opening sale transactions. For stock options, the transaction from the side of the writer of the option.

Open-market operations. The purchase and sale of securities. (In the case of Federal Reserve open-market operations, the objective is to carry out monetary policy.)

Operating instruments. The immediate and proximate variables changed by policy, such as the federal funds rate and nonborrowed reserves in Federal Reserve open-market operations.

Opportunity cost. The value of a good or service in its next best use (or some combination of optimum alternative uses).

Optimum currency areas. An area where economic criteria indicate that a single currency is optimum.

Option. A contract giving the holder the right to buy or sell an item at a fixed price before an expiration date.

Ordinal ranking. An ordering of alternative goods and services where each successive alternative is preferred to the previous alternative, but the magnitude of relative preferences (a cardinal measurement) is not specified.

Original term to maturity. The time from the date of issuance to the maturity date of a debt instrument.

Overnight repurchase agreements. A form of a short-term loan agreement in which one party sells a security to another party, agreeing to repurchase it the following day at the same price.

Paasche index. A price index that uses current period weights.

Parameter. In an equation, a given constant as opposed to one of the variables derived in the equation. The relationships between the variables are conditional on the values of the parameters.

Participating bonds. Bonds that carry the privilege of a share in the earnings as well as a specified interest return, under specified conditions.

Pecuniary. Consisting of money.

Pegged exchange rate. *See* Fixed exchange rate.

Pegged interest rates. Market interest rates held closely to a given target level by government open-market policies.

Perfect competition. A condition in a market for a good or service where each of the many competitors believes that his or her sales have no effect on the price of the good or service. (In price theory, the demand curve is perfectly elastic under perfect competition.)

Periodicities. Values of a series of numbers that can be predicted from the previous numbers in the series.

Permanent charters. Charters for financial institutions with no expiration date.

Perpetuity. A bond with no maturity date. (It has a constant payment stream, such as $5 a year, forever.)

Personal trust funds. Assets placed in the care of administrators, who are often employed by financial intermediaries in a trust department.

Point estimate. An estimate that is single valued as opposed to having a range of values.

Points. In the negotiation of mortgages, increases in the price of houses, sometimes to circumvent ceilings on mortgage interest rates. Each point is 1 percent of the house price and is paid to the lender.

Posterior probability. See Prior probability.

Precautionary demand for money. The demand for money as a contingency fund for emergencies.

Preferred habitat theory. See Hedging pressure hypothesis.

Preferred stock. Stock paying a fixed income stream, which has the economic characteristic of a perpetuity.

Present value. The discounted value of future income.

Price discrimination. The practice by a seller of charging lower prices to some buyers of the same service or good even though there are no economies of scale. The practice may require that buyers be separated so that those with more inelastic demands can be charged higher prices.

Price/earnings (or P/E) ratio. The ratio of the price of stock to its earnings. For predicting stock prices the ex ante or expected P/E is more important than the actual or ex post P/E. For perfectly efficient markets all such information is already discounted into the price of the stock.

Price index. A measure of the "average" price level of a specified group of goods and services compared to a base period. If 100 is the base period index, 110 represents a 10 percent increase in the price level.

Price of consumer expenditures (or PCE). A price index of all U.S. consumer goods.

Primary market. Markets where new assets are sold.

Principal. The amount borrowed in a debt contract. There is an ambiguity in the term's usage with respect to debt instruments, where it sometimes refers to the original market price of the bond but sometimes denotes the bond's face value.

Prior probability. In Bayesian statistics, the subjective probability attached to an outcome. The actual frequency of the event's occurrence is then used to revise the probability, producing a joint probability and a posterior probability, which in turn becomes a new prior.

Private placements. The direct sale of bonds to lenders by the debtor company, bypassing an underwriter for the offering.

Probability collapse. The phenomenon in Bayesian statistics resulting from radical differences between prior probabilities and relative frequencies of actual trials. The sum of the joint probabilities approaches zero and the posterior probabilities become unreasonably sensitive to small changes in trial outcomes.

Profits. The difference between revenues and costs. Different concepts of profit arise from different classifications of costs.

Proxy. An absentee ballot for voting shares of common stock. Economists also use the term to denote a substitute variable in analysis.

Purchase group. A syndicate of investment banks and brokerage houses formed to underwrite a large new offering of debt or equity by a corporation.

Purchasing power bond. A bond in which the face value and/or the coupon payments move up and down with the price level. Alternatively, such a bond is said to be indexed or to contain an escalator.

Purchasing power of money. The amount of goods and services that can be bought with a unit of money.

Pure expectations hypothesis. The hypothesis that explains long rates as geometric averages of expected short rates.

Pure fiscal policy actions. Changes in fiscal policy that do not simultaneously involve changes in the money supply, sometimes defined for this purpose as the monetary base.

Pure monetary policy. Monetary policy actions that do not simultaneously involve fiscal policy. A government deficit financed by money creation constitutes both monetary and fiscal policy.

Put. A stock option to sell.

Quote. *See* Bid and asked.

Random walk (or *Brownian motion*). A series with random first differences.

Real balance effect of devaluation. The effect of devaluation in reducing imports through its effect of lowering the purchasing power of the money balances of residents.

Real rate of interest. The rate (in equilibrium) at which wealth produces output and the rate used by individuals to discount future income from wealth.

Reduced-form equations. Solutions for simultaneous equations where each endogenous variable is derived separately as a function of the exogenous variables.

Registered trader. On the New York Stock Exchange, a member trading primarily on his or her own account.

Remittance option. *See* Note option.

Repurchase agreement. Agreement to repurchase a financial asset, such as a Treasury bill, at the same price. It is a vehicle for a short-term loan in which ownership of a security is temporarily switched to the lender.

Reserve ratio. The ratio of the amount of reserves at depository institutions to the amount of their deposits.

Reserve requirement ratio. The proportion of deposits required to be held as reserves by depository institutions.

Reverse repurchase agreement. A term for a repurchase agreement looked at from the side of the lender, who buys a security with the understanding that he or she may resell it.

Right. A short-term option to buy stock usually given by a company to existing stockholders for additional stock that the company is issuing. The right may be sold or exercised.

Risk averter. An individual who prefers a portfolio with lower risk to one with higher risk and the same expected return.

Risk lover. An individual who prefers a portfolio with higher risk to one with lower risk and the same expected return.

Rollover. The renewal of a loan; or the paying off of one loan by taking out another.

Sales finance company. A type of consumer finance company specializing in automobile loans and other installment credit.

Saving. That part of income that is not consumed.

Savings deposits. Claims on commercial banks or thrifts which can be withdrawn in the form of currency or coin or as a cashier's check of the bank. In the case of NOW accounts and ATS accounts, they can be transferred by check. Although technically subject to the depository institutions' right to refuse payment for 30 days, they are, in practice, withdrawable on demand.

Secondary market. A market for financial assets that have been previously issued.

Securities. General term for both debt instruments and equities.

Securities Investor Protection Corporation (SIPC). A nonprofit corporation created by the federal government to protect investors' cash and securities in the event a member brokerage fails.

Security market line. The equilibrium relationship between each risky asset's yield and its risk in the capital asset pricing model.

Seignorage charge. The charge for issuing currency when a precious metal such as gold is sold to a government. Originally, it was the charge for minting bullion into coins. When no profit is made and only costs are covered, it is called brassage.

Sell contract. A future sales contract.

Selling group. A group of investment banking or brokerage firms that purchases a large new offering of corporate debt or equity from a smaller group, called the purchase group, for resale.

Serial charters. Charters for thrifts used after 1854 (until permanent charters were adopted) that allowed new members to enter, but only under separate loan plans.

Series of options. Options of the same class, with the same exercise price, expiration date, and unit of trading.

Short position. A trading position that profits from a fall in price of an item. The short sale of a stock or the purchase of a futures contract to sell an item are examples of short position.

Short (long) position in foreign currency. A position involving holdings in foreign assets of a lower (higher) value than holdings in foreign liabilities. If the spot rate of the foreign currency rises relative to the price of domestic currency, there will be a net loss (gain).

Short sale. The sale of a stock that the seller does not own in anticipation of its price decline, which will allow replacement of the stock at a lower price. The short seller usually borrows the stock from a stockbroker.

Short-term investment pool (STIP). An investment intermediary that sells shares against a portfolio of liquid short-term assets. (The largest group of STIPs are the money market funds.)

Simultaneous-equation bias. The bias in statistical estimates that can occur in using ordinary least squares to estimate a single equation in a simultaneous system where the dependent variable partially determines one or more independent variables.

Sovereign risk. The risk of losses on forward contracts in foreign currencies due to the imposition of exchange controls on the repatriation of profits or interest.

Special drawing rights. An international money created by the International Monetary Fund in 1969. It is used by central banks.

Specialist. A trader in stock markets who takes a position in a stock (owns an inventory), matches buyers' and sellers' orders, holds limit and stop loss orders in the stock, and executes trades in his or her own account if the market price of the stock varies from the expected "normal" price. Specialists on the New York Stock Exchange are responsible for attempting to maintain an orderly market in a stock and to acting as a broker's broker by handling orders for traders. One specialist may handle several stocks.

Speculative arbitrage. Buying and selling an asset to profit from expected price differentials, where the purchase and sale cannot be simultaneously executed, so that speculative risk is involved. The term *speculative arbitrage* has been used for transactions involving the term structure of interest rates.

Speculators. Participants in financial markets who seek to profit from buying assets for resale that are expected to appreciate in price (a long position); or if prices are expected to fall, speculators may take a short position.

Spot markets. Markets for the sale and purchase of commodities or financial assets for present delivery as opposed to futures markets.

Spot price. Price for present delivery.

Spread. In underwriting, the difference between the price the underwriter pays for new debt or equity and the price for which he or she sells it.

Spreading. The simultaneous purchase and sale of different but related futures contracts.

Squeeze. A situation in a commodity or financial asset market where transactors who have gone short (expecting the price to fall) cannot repurchase except at a price substantially higher than the value of the contract in relation to the rest of the market. This is usually called a *corner.* The best way out of this definitional swamp may be to use *squeeze* and *corner* for the same type of phenomenon, with *corner* being the more extreme monopolistic condition. *See also* Corner.

Stability. Said to characterize the price of a variable, such as a stock price, if the price tends to settle down to a new value after a disturbance such as the announcement of a split or a new profit on a stock.

Standby agreement. An underwriting arrangement in which the responsibility for unsold issues is borne by the purchase group. *See also* Purchase group.

State banks. State-chartered private banks.

Static analysis. Economic analysis of equilibrium and changes in equilibrium without attention to the question of what time path the market will follow in moving to a new equilibrium.

Stationary state. A state of the economy in which gross investment equals depreciation, so net investment is zero and the entire income is consumed, leaving the capital stock at a stationary level.

Sterilization. For a country on a gold standard, the practice of offsetting the effect of an inflow or outflow of gold on the domestic money supply by an opposite discretionary change in the domestic money supply. Sterilization policies violate the rules for a strict gold standard.

Stock. *See* Equities.

Straddle. Taking both a long and a short position on an asset to take advantage of any large changes in its price: for example, the purchase of both a put and a call on the same asset.

Straight agreement. An underwriting arrangement in which the selling group takes full responsibility for any unsold issues. *See* Selling group.

Striking price. *See* Exercise price.

Strip bonds. Bonds in which the coupons have been stripped off and sold separately. The bond itself is then sold at a discount, and the holder receives "interest" through the capital gain over the term to maturity.

Stock option. A financial asset giving the owner the right to buy or sell a stock at a particular price before a specified date, the expiration time.

Stock split. The division of existing shares into a number of new shares that does not change the capitalization of the company.

Stop loss orders. *See* Limit orders.

Subjective rate of discount. *See* Time preference.

Surplus unit. A unit which, saving more than it invests, is a net supplier of funds and a net demander of financial assets.

Sweep service. Automatic transfer by a bank of depositors' funds above some minimum balance into money market funds. If the account goes below the minimum, funds are transferred back from the money market funds until the minimum is met.

Switch point. The interest rate at which two projects will have their ranking reversed according to the net present value rule.

Symmetallism. A commodity standard under which the government pegs the price of a combined unit containing specified proportions of two precious metals, such as gold and silver.

Synchronous (or *coincident*) *reserve requirements.* Reserve requirements calculated on the current week's level of deposits. *See* Lagged reserve requirements.

Systematic risk. That part of the variation in an asset's return that is related to the variation in the market portfolio. Systematic risk cannot be diversified away.

Tariffs. Taxes on imports.

Tax and *loan accounts.* Accounts of the U.S. Treasury with the private banking system. These accounts are authorized to receive taxes for the government.

Terminating charters. Charters for mutual savings banks or savings and loan associations with membership limited to the original members.

Term structure of interest rates. The relationship between yields on bonds that differ only by maturity.

Testamentary trust. A trust established in a will to be effectuated at the time of death of the maker.

Third market. A market for stocks that are listed on a stock exchange but are not traded through a stock exchange.

Thrifts. In the United States, savings and loan associations, credit unions, and mutual savings banks.

Time deposits. Interest-bearing accounts with commercial banks that carry specified maturities and are generally subject to penalties for early withdrawal.

Time preference. A measure of individuals' preference for present over future consumption. The rate of time preference is sometimes defined by the individual's subjective rate of discount.

Time-series data. Data for the values a variable takes over time (such as consumer credit in successive months). *See also* Cross-section data.

Tontine plan. A type of insurance plan originating in seventeenth-century France. In its purest form funds go only to the survivors.

Trade balance. Exports minus imports.

Transfer agent. An individual who formally transfers stock between buyers and sellers.

Transfer payments. Payments that are not associated with the production of goods and services.

Treasury stock. Stock purchased by the issuing firm.

Turning points. In a time series, the observations at which a variable reaches a maximum or minimum, beginning to fall when it had been rising or to rise when it had been falling.

Two-stage least squares. A method of jointly estimating equations in simultaneous-equation models.

Ultimate targets of policy. The variables that policy is ultimately intended to affect, such as the price level and employment.

Uncollected cash items. The value of checks deposited in the banking system that have not been cleared to the banks they are drawn against.

Unconditional forecast. A forecast made without any explicit conditions.

Uncovered call writer. *See* Covered call writer.

Underwriters. Brokerage firms or investment banks that purchase and resell new debt and equity issues of corporations. *See also* Purchase group *and* Selling group.

Underwriting syndicate. *See* Purchase group.

Unsystematic risk. That part of the variation in the return on an asset that is independent of the variation in the market portfolio and therefore can be offset through diversification.

Warrants. Options or rights to buy stock issued by the corporation that issues the underlying stock.

Wealth. The stock of items of value at a given instant of time.

Wednesday scramble. The scrambling in and out of reserves by depository institutions that must come up with their Federal Reserve reserve requirements on Wednesday of each week.

Years' purchase. The reciprocal of the interest rate. This is the number of years until repayment for lending at simple interest.

Yield (or *return*). The rate of return on an investment.

Zero-coupon bonds. Bonds with no coupons that are sold at a discount from their final redemption value. *See also* Strip bonds.

Index

577